Psychology

An Introduction

Third Edition

Nicky Hayes and Sue Orrell

Pearson Education Limited
Edinburgh Gate, Harlow,
Essex CM20 2JE, England
and Associated Companies throughout the world.

First published 1987
Third edition 1998
Fifth impression 2003

ISBN 0 582 31893 9

Set in 10 pt Palatino (DTP Linotron)

Printed in Singapore (MPM)

It is the publisher's policy to use paper manufactured from sustainable forests.

We are grateful to the following for permission to reproduce photographs: Ace Photo Agency, pages 119 (photo Alexis Sofianopoulos), 283 (photo Pat Shirreff-Thomas), 291 (photo Mauritius), 299 (photo Marting Riedl), 319 (photo Gabe Palmer), 328 left and right (photos Mauritius), 427 (photo Mauritius) Adil Bradlow/Impact, page 169; Bubbles Photo Library, pages 31 (photo J. Woodcock), 169 right (photo J. Farrow), 282 (photo Ian West), 336 (photo J. Woodcock), 408 (photo L.J. Thurston), 423 right (photo Ian West) and 435 (photo L.J. Thurston); Collections, page 41 (photo Anthea Sieveking); Hutchison Library, page 383 Left; Image Bank, page 413; Oxford Scientific Films, page 8 (photo David Thompson); Science Photo Library, pages 3 (photo Addenbrookes Hospital), 134 (photo UCLA School of Medicine); Colin Smith, page 20; John Walmsley Photo Library, page 38.

The photograph on page 349 was taken by John Birdsall; photographs from the old edition were taken by Gordon Nicholson.

The cartoon on page 226 was drawn by Edward McLachlan; artwork on pages 246 and 256 by Allan Lamb.

Contents

Introduction

What is psychology?

Psychology is all around us. It is all about understanding human beings: what makes us tick, and why we do what we do. Human beings shape most of the experiences in our lives; whether that is at home, at school, at work or during our leisure time. And in some ways everyone is a kind of psychologist. We are all applying psychology all the time: when we have a conversation with someone else; when we decide that a particular way of dressing is 'right' for us; or when we make a decision which we know will affect the other people around us.

The problem, though, is that this type of psychology is unconscious. We are not fully aware of what we are doing and can often think that we are doing one thing when, really, we are doing something quite different. Although we do use a sort of psychology in our everyday life, we do it as amateurs, learning from experience and from imitating other people, and without really being aware of what it is all about. Our everyday knowledge is intuitive and often very self-centred. There are reasons for that: it's a survival technique which helps us to cope with the world. However, it does also mean that we can often be mistaken, or simply wrong.

Studying psychology

The study of psychology is rather different. Psychologists are interested in learning about the human mind but they know how easy it is to be misled into being certain about things which are not really true. So psychology involves a lot of very careful investigation and a lot of checking and looking at things in different ways, to make certain we are sure of what we are saying. That investigation has to happen very systematically and in a scientific manner.

Psychologists investigate psychological processes, such as how we acquire language, or how we remember things. They investigate human experiences, such as play or obedience to other people. They also develop psychological models – explanations for why things happen or how a psychological process occurs – which can help us to understand what is going on. Psychologists investigate many different aspects of human experience and psychological studies can range from exploring the factors that will help someone to survive in a disaster, to investigating how we learn to read.

Psychologists are very careful about the research methods they use, in order to make sure that they are gathering information which is as accurate as it can possibly be. Some psychologists use experiments, either in the laboratory in or in real life; some conduct observational studies; some work with animals, both to understand more about how animal psychology works, and to understand more about our own evolutionary history; and some psychologists conduct case studies to examine individuals in depth. Whichever methods they use, though, all psychologists are concerned to ensure that they are systematic and scientific because unless we do that it is much too easy for us to be misled by our own beliefs or ideas.

When we are studying psychology, we don't just look at the research which psychologists have conducted. We also look at psychological issues, such as the way that psychology has been applied in real life, or the ethical implications of a particular bit of research or a particular discovery. Psychology can be applied in many ways, and in many contexts – and not all of those contexts are ethically acceptable. Professional psychologists operate under strict ethical constraints: there are many things which they are simply not permitted to do, and many others which can only be undertaken if they have been discussed and evaluated fully by ethics committees. It is equally important that psychology students should become familiar with psychological ethics: it is possible to do a lot of damage by applying psychology in the wrong way or without really knowing what you are doing.

Studying psychology, then, involves learning about psychological research and also about how psychology has been applied. Like any other science, studying psychology also means learning some new words. Scientists almost always have to develop new words because their work involves exploring phenomena in a very precise and exact way. Everyday language is often very vague or a bit woolly. It is important for a scientist to be able to say things in a way that makes certain they can't be misunderstood. So studying psychology inevitably involves learning some of the specialist vocabulary which psychologists have developed during the past 100 years or so.

Approaches to psychology

Psychology is a huge subject. After all, human beings are extremely complex and there is a great deal that we still don't know about how human beings function. So individual psychologists have to specialise: they conduct research into particular areas and they have their own special interests. Psychologists also adopt different approaches to the study of human beings, and hold different beliefs about what is important. Studying psychology means becoming aware of some of these approaches, and how they can all contribute to our understanding of human beings.

Someone who is beginning to study psychology is likely to encounter six main approaches. These are partly concerned with different ways of doing psychology and partly with different areas of interest. Each different area of psychology has its own research methods and its own ways of going about research, in the same way that physicists or chemists use different research tools when they are looking at different types of problem. However, all of them contribute to our awareness of human behaviour. The various approaches give us different ways of looking at things, and each of those ways can tell us something useful.

The six main approaches in psychology are:

- The **behaviourist approach** which looks at the way that our environment affects our behaviour. Behaviourists are interested in learning and habits, and they often believe that psychologists should study only behaviour, not thoughts and experiences, as behaviour is the only thing that other people can really see.
- The **cognitive approach** which is all about the study of our mental processes. Cognitive psychologists believe that if we want to understand why people act as they do, we need to understand how they think, remember and reason. They are interested in how we interpret and make sense of the world around us.
- The **biological approach** which is all about how our internal physiological processes and our genetic make-up influence our behaviour. However, human beings are not biological robots: our biology is designed to enable us to act more effectively in the real world. So biological psychologists are interested in the interactions between our environment and our internal physiology, and how those interactions influence our experience.
- The **social approach** which is to do with how we interact with other people. Some social psychologists emphasise the individual factors that are involved in social behaviour; some are interested in social beliefs and attitudes; others are interested in groups and shared social experiences.
- The **developmental approach** which is to do with how human beings (and sometimes animals) change over time. Developmental psychologists tend to be particularly interested in three areas of human development: emotional development, social

development, and cognitive development. However, as the person who is developing is a young human being, it isn't always easy to separate the three areas: each can influence the others.

- The **humanistic approach** which focuses on individual experience, rather than on people in general. Humanistic psychologists are particularly concerned with personal growth and with what people's subjective experience is like. They regard every individual as unique and are interested in helping people to uncover and use their own special potential.

We can see, then, that the different approaches each have their own areas of interest and their own views on what is important about human beings. It may seem a bit odd when you first begin to study psychology, but when we are looking at human beings it is perfectly possible for a problem to have several different right answers. People really are that complicated! All of us are affected by different levels in our experience: we are affected by our biology, our habits, our knowledge, our social lives, our past experiences and our cultures. Knowing something about different approaches in psychology helps us to see how those different levels may work together, and that helps us to understand people in a much better way than simply relying on intuition or our own personal beliefs.

People follow many different courses and syllabuses when they begin to study psychology. In this book we have tried to provide a basic introduction to most of the main areas of psychology, which will be suitable for most courses. We have described psychological research, discussed how psychological knowledge has developed and explored some of the issues and ideas which have helped to form modern psychology. The chapters also include some other material which we hope will help to make psychology more relevant to everyday living. Psychology is a very real and living subject. People are not simple but they are extremely interesting and studying them in a systematic, scientific way can be great fun. It can also tell us a great deal about ourselves. We hope you will enjoy it.

Nicky Hayes and Sue Orrell

Section 1 - Nature and nurture

In this section, we will look at the question of how we come to be as we are. It is clear just from our everyday experience that all the people we meet are individuals with their own ways of going about things, but at the same time we can see many ways in which people are similar or resemble each other. As part of studying human beings, we need to be able to explain both how the similarities have come about and also how the differences happen.

Broadly speaking, in psychology we consider that people have come to be who they are as a result of two sources of influence: firstly, their biological make-up; and secondly, the experiences which they encounter throughout life. Our biological make-up is largely something that we inherit, through the action of **genes** and **chromosomes**; but from the moment that we are conceived, we develop in an **environment** which can affect how we turn out. Changes in the environment provided in the mother's womb may, for instance, affect us before we are born, as in the case of children affected by their mother's contraction of rubella (German measles). And after we are born, our environment can affect us even more. Throughout this section, we will be looking at the many ways that genetics and the environment interact to produce the individual.

Chapter 1 - The process of maturation

Two theories of child development

Traditionally, psychologists were divided into two main schools of thought: the **empiricists**, who considered that our development mostly arises as a result of the influence of our environment; and the **nativists**, who attributed development mainly to the action of our genes and chromosomes. Nowadays, few psychologists would be prepared to say unequivocally that development was caused by one or the other of these - it seems clear that both of them contribute to who we are - but in the past people were not so reticent.

Behaviourism

In 1913, J. B. Watson produced a paper entitled 'Psychology as the behaviourist views it', which was an attempt to produce a new, scientific psychology based on the principles of learning, as they were understood at the time. Watson was a total empiricist and if we look at his theory of child development we can see how extreme his viewpoint was.

Watson considered that the child was born as a **tabularasa** - a blank slate which experience would 'write on' to produce a person. He argued that if he were given *'a dozen healthy infants ... and my own specified world to bring them up in, and I'll guarantee to take any one at random and train him to become any type of specialist I might select - doctor, lawyer ... and yes, even beggarman and thief, regardless of his talents, penchants, tendencies, abilities, vocations, and race of his ancestors'* (Watson 1924). We can see from this that he thought the environment was really the only thing that was important in an individual's development.

Nativism

By contrast, in 1943 Gesell argued that children develop almost entirely as a result of genetic influences, with their environment having little effect. The role of the mother is to provide an environment in which the child's natural development could take place with as little disturbance as possible. A handbook from Gesell's Institute for the Study of the Child, giving advice to mothers, said: *'First of all, recognise your child's individuality for what it is and give up the notion that you either produce (except through inheritance) or that you can basically change it.'*

You can see that these represent two extreme ways of looking at child development. As we said, nowadays few psychologists would be prepared to be so extreme, but the overall tendency to consider one side more important than the other still remains. When we are looking at the two ways that people can come to be how they are (the processes of inheritance and of learning) we need to know how these processes work. Otherwise we would sometimes end up making claims for one side or another that were quite 'magical', and didn't really explain anything at all. Accordingly, in this chapter we look at the way that we come to inherit characteristics, and in the next chapter, we will look at some of the ways that we learn, and acquire our environmental experience.

Genetic transmission

This is the name given to the way that we acquire characteristics through inheritance. Each of the cells in the body contains a nucleus, which contains a particular substance known as DNA. This DNA is organised into long strands which we call chromosomes, and each chromosome is made up of thousands of smaller units of DNA known as genes. The genes carry information about the biological development of the body. All living creatures have genes, and it is these which direct the way that growth and development happen within the animal or plant.

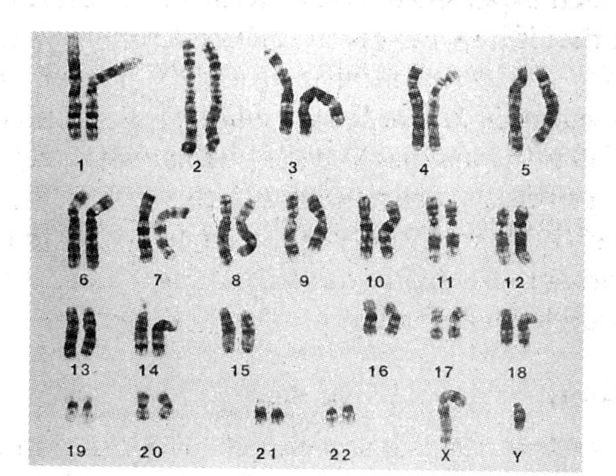

A full set of human chromosomes

Just after an animal is conceived, it consists of a tiny group of just a few cells. These grow and divide, so that the emerging embryo becomes much larger very quickly. If there were no direction for this growth, all that would develop would be a larger mass of cells, similar to the original one but much bigger. This isn't what happens, though. Instead, some cells take on specialised roles, and become adapted for particular purposes, like bone cells accumulating calcium and becoming strong, or cells lining the stomach becoming able to absorb nutrients. The living body consists of millions of cells performing all sorts of specialised roles - all working together to make a complete human being or animal. It is the genes and chromosomes which direct the way that the cells develop, and which in the end produce this highly co-ordinated living creature.

There is a set number of chromosomes for each species - human beings have 23 pairs of chromosomes, 46 altogether. We talk of chromosomes being in pairs, because when we are first conceived, we inherit half of our chromosomes from the mother and a matching half from the father. When they combine together a full set is produced and the new embryo has all the information needed to develop biologically, assuming that its environment is all right.

Sometimes an individual acquires an extra chromosome when she or he is conceived, and this produces special characteristics such as in **Down's syndrome**. How much the extra chromosome affects the person varies, and we don't yet fully understand all the implications, but many Down's syndrome individuals are able to live happy, normal lives given the right kind of training and care when they are younger.

Psychology in Action

Down's syndrome results from the presence of an extra chromosome. Although the degree of physical and mental handicap varies between individuals, recent research suggests that around 60 per cent of Down's syndrome children suffer only mild learning difficulties. With special exercises and training, begun in the first year of life, many learning difficulties can be overcome.

It is now recognised that many Down's syndrome children under-achieve due to low expectations and a lack of physical and mental stimulation. As far back as 1971, Bayley et al. recorded that the IQ of a Down's syndrome child could be increased, given the right environmental conditions, and, increasingly such children are able to attend ordinary schools and receive a normal education.

Because we inherit two different sets of chromosomes from our parents, we have a mechanism for 'sorting out' the two messages when they contradict each other. Some genes tend to be 'dominant' over other genes, while some tend to be 'recessive'.

Genes for brown eyes are dominant over genes for blue eyes, for example. If someone inherits one gene for each, from their parents, then they will end up with brown eyes. But they will still carry the blue-eyed gene and may pass it on to their children. If their partner also passes on a blue-eyed gene, then the child may have blue eyes even though both its parents have brown eyes.

There are many other 'recessive' characteristics like this, such as red hair, or disorders like sickle-cell anaemia; and you can see that with this sorting mechanism it is possible for a characteristic to 'skip' a few generations, and then reappear when two partners have the same 'recessive' genes. So two parents with one set of characteristics may produce children who are different from either of them. Different combinations produced by the same parents can also vary quite a lot: some brothers and sisters don't resemble one another much, while others are very similar. On average, a child will inherit half of its chromosomes from one parent and half from the other, but this is only an average - some children may resemble one parent more than the other.

We can see from all this that genetic mechanisms don't necessarily produce identical results. The shuffling of the genes which takes place when someone is conceived produces a range of individual variation. It is this variation, of course, that makes **evolution** possible: gradually, changes which give an animal a survival advantage become more common, as that animal is more likely to survive and to pass its genes on to the next generation.

Cloning

Recently, geneticists have become able to produce organisms from just one parent, by growing cells in a special environment and drawing on the genetic message contained in the cell's DNA. The animals that they produce in this way are known as **clones** and are totally identical to the parent animal, with no individual variation. Many plants which we encounter are produced like that: all the kiwi fruit sold commercially, for instance, comes originally from one plant which produced the right kind of fruit, and has now been cloned (by normal plant propagation) many thousands of times. This has also been done with sheep, and some agriculturists hope it may be done with other farm animals. The big disadvantage of cloning, though, is that a clone is just as likely to contract a disease as its parent, so one infection can cause immense damage if it spreads. Normally, individual differences mean that some animals are less susceptible to disease and so resistance can build up.

Ethical discussion

The idea that it may one day become possible to clone a human being is a recurrent theme in science fiction. In Aldous Huxley's *Brave New World*, society consists of just a few different types of people, all cloned, with different levels of responsibility. Some are cloned to be factory workers, some to do clerical work, some to be scientists, etc.

At present, scientists are not able to simulate the full conditions of the womb that are involved in nurturing a foetus, so although the technical capacity to clone human cells exists, it is unlikely that they could be grown into a human baby. However, it may become possible for scientists to do this in the future.

Do you think they should?

Genetic engineering

Another important aspect of genetics is the range of possibilities offered by **genetic engineering**. Scientists are developing techniques whereby they can adjust the genetic message carried on the chromosome, so as to produce a particular effect in an animal. One way that they do that is to cut out a particular section of a chromosome, containing just a few genes, and to splice in a new section that has been specially grown for the purpose. After that, whenever the cell reproduces it continues to produce the new genes as part of the whole chromosome. Once these techniques have been perfected, scientists hope that we will become able to sort out many of the genetic disorders which trouble people, such as sickle-cell anaemia or thalassaemia. Until now, such disorders couldn't be cured, because they were genetic in origin, and only the symptoms could be treated. However, there is still a long way to go yet, and it is open to question whether the new techniques could actually be used on adults, rather than on developing embryos.

Genetic transmission and genetic engineering may seem a bit far removed from what people do, but there are many theories in psychology which talk in terms of genetic influence, so it is important to be clear exactly what it means. Briefly: a gene has its effect by triggering the body to produce a particular protein at a particular time. This protein then influences some form of development, such as growth in a particular direction or a chemical change which makes a particular form of learning more likely to happen.

By and large, our genetic make-up is fixed at the moment we are conceived, although recent findings have suggested that in fact there may be some very minor adjustments which occur naturally in the body throughout life.

1.1 Investigating genetic differences

As you have learned, some genetic characteristics are dominant, while others are recessive. In this activity, we will look at a fairly common dominant genetic trait - that of tongue-rolling.

All you will need is several sheets of paper and a pencil.

First, ask each member of the class, or other people that you know, to have a guess at the number of people in the population at large who can roll their tongues along the middle. Did everyone say the same number?

When you have collected this information, go around the same group and ask them to have a go at rolling their tongues. How many people were able to do this? Is there any relationship between whether they could roll their tongues, and the estimate that they made?

How does the number of tongue-rollers compare with the average estimated number that you obtained?

Does this tell you anything about the assumptions we constantly make about other people? What other examples of this sort of thing can you think of?

Now ask each member of your group to find ten people during the next week, and do the same with each of them.

Compare the results from the large sample to your original group results. Does the size of the sample make any difference? Geneticists tell us that about three-quarters of the general population can roll their tongues. Which of your samples came nearest to this result?

Maturation

The process of **maturation** is important to our understanding of genetic influences on behaviour. As you know, things that we inherit don't necessarily show up all at once. The physiological changes which take place during puberty, for example, arise because of genes which are present at conception, but they only happen when the body is mature enough for them to take place. In the same way, certain forms of behaviour may only emerge once the individual is mature enough.

Whenever we try to divide influences into genetic or environmental, though, we hit the problem that really it is meaningless to try to talk about one without the other. Maturational changes, for instance, can be held back if the body is deprived of what it needs: one theory about **anorexia nervosa** (the 'slimming disease') is that teenage girls who develop it are subconsciously trying to retard their development into mature women, by keeping their bodies as child-like and small as possible. In this case, the body's *environment* is having an effect on its genetic changes, through lack of food.

Really, there is an inseparable link between genetic influences and the environment, and to talk about one as if it were independent of the other doesn't actually make sense. Hebb (1949) gave an example of this in terms of a developing egg. Without the genetic component, there is no egg at all, but take away the supporting environment and let the egg get cold, and it dies. So is it genetics or the environment which causes the egg to develop? The answer, of course, is that it has to be both, and we need to remember this when we study genetic influences.

Inherited behaviour

When we look at inherited behaviour, the interaction between the environment and inherited characteristics becomes even more apparent. Studies of sticklebacks in 1953 by Tinbergen showed how their attack behaviour was triggered off by a **sign stimulus** in the environment, which acted as a kind of releasing mechanism for the attack ritual. Although the attack behaviour was inherited (as could be seen from the way that it was performed in exactly the same way each time) it was an *environmental* stimulus - the flash of red on another male stickleback's belly - which triggered it off. And other red objects which moved in the right kind of way would also set the attack response going.

Species-specific behaviour in sticklebacks

Tinbergen also showed that an environmental stimulus which had an extreme amount of the right kind of characteristic would act as a kind of **super-releaser** and cause a heightened reaction on the part of the animal. It is thought that the reason why small birds feed adopted cuckoo chicks so frantically is because the cuckoo's large gaping mouth acts as a kind of super-releaser for their feeding behaviour. These forms of inherited behaviour, though, are very different from the kind of behaviour which is shown by human beings.

Characteristics of inherited behaviour

In 1938 Lorenz and Tinbergen put forward a set of characteristics to identify behaviour that is directly inherited (such as is found in many animals). These are:

1. That the behaviour is **stereotyped** - in other words, that it always occurs in the same way. Because we cannot change our genes, behaviour which is directly caused by genetic influence can't be changed by different experiences.
2. That the behaviour is **species-specific**. Since each species carries its own genetic make-up, the behaviour shown by members of one species should be different from that shown by those of other species.
3. That it should appear in animals which have been raised in **isolation** from others of their species. Because the behaviour is inherited, there is no need for the animal to learn it from others, and so it should still show the behaviour even if it hasn't had any chance to learn it.
4. That the behaviour should appear as a complete unit even if the animal has had no chance to **practise** it, since practising is a form of learning.

Although the last of these has been questioned, in general these principles seem to hold true for behaviour which is directly inherited. When we are talking about human behaviour, though, and whether it is influenced by genetic factors, we are rarely talking about fixed patterns of action like this. Instead, we are talking about a much more general tendency to act in certain ways.

1.2 Observing animal behaviour

Several psychological theories have been developed on the basis of observations of animal and human behaviour. In this exercise your task is to observe an animal, or a group of animals, for a set period of time and to collect an exact record of its, or their, behaviour.

To do this exercise, you will need to work with a partner, preferably one who is also studying psychology. You will also need to find an animal that you can observe without being interrupted for ten minutes or so. A household pet is usually OK, although make sure that it is a mammal (budgies and goldfish won't do!), and that it is active (elderly pet cats who sleep all day won't do either - the animal must be showing some behaviour for you to observe!).

Decide in advance how long you will observe the animal: ten minutes is probably long enough. You and your partner should work entirely separately for that time. Make sure that you have arranged yourselves so that you cannot see what the other person is writing.

During the ten minutes, make a note of everything that the animal does, as accurately as you can. When you have finished, before speaking to your partner make a quick note of any difficulties that you found in doing this.

Now, compare your report with that of your partner, and see just how they are different. What explanations can you find for these differences?

Try classifying each of the observations that you have made, and then comparing the reports to see if there are noticeable differences in the number of each type of statement that you have made. You will probably find that you have each made different kinds of reports. Two of the most interesting ways to classify them are:

1. **Molar/molecular behaviour**. Molar behaviour is when the animal has moved its whole body; molecular movements are movements of just one part, e.g. twitching of ears, tails, or whiskers.

2. **Behavioural/intentional/anthropomorphic observations**. Behavioural descriptions are those which are simple descriptions of actions that the animal has performed (e.g. 'turns round and sits down'). Intentional descriptions are descriptions of what the animal was meaning or wanting to do (e.g. 'tries to get out of box'). Anthropomorphic statements are those which imply that the animal has thoughts or feelings like a human being (e.g. 'gets annoyed'). You will probably need to discuss these as you count them.

Remember that a truly scientific observation should only include descriptions of behaviour, and not any anthropomorphic or intentional observations at all. How well did you do?

Human adaptability

One thing that characterises human behaviour all over the world is its **adaptability**. We are able to live in a variety of different climates and in many different types of community. In this respect, it wouldn't really make much sense for us to inherit rigid patterns of behaviour, because behaviour that is suitable for a tropical island environment would be entirely inappropriate for an Eskimo society! There are more general ways, though, in which our genes can influence how we learn things and the ways in which we behave, and in the next few chapters we will look at some of these.

Critical periods

An important feature of genetic influence is that it can operate hand-in-hand with the environment through critical or sensitive periods. A **critical period** is a time in an animal's life when it will learn a particular behaviour very rapidly indeed if it is exposed to the appropriate environmental stimulus. One of the clearest examples of how this happens is shown by studies of the process known as imprinting.

Imprinting

Lorenz, in 1937, demonstrated that young greylag geese would develop an attachment to a human being or any other moving object, and would follow it around until they were almost adult. This happened if they were exposed to the moving object at an appropriate time after their hatching, and were able to follow it continuously for about 10 minutes. Lorenz called this process **imprinting**, because it seemed that the young geese had formed a powerful imprint, or impression, of the object, as if it were their new 'mother'. One clutch followed Lorenz around all the time so devotedly that in order to get them to go in the water he had to swim with them, because they wouldn't go without him!

Lorenz performed several studies of imprinting, investigating the way in which these attachments were formed, and seeing when they took place. He found that there seemed to be a critical period after hatching, during which the attachment had to be made, or it wouldn't happen at all. This critical period, Lorenz thought, was 'switched on' by the action of particular genes. Although the gosling learned to follow its parent rather than inheriting that behaviour, it did so at a special time, when its genes had made it very ready to learn.

Instead of the young goose inheriting a direct picture of its mother – which would be a very complex thing to inherit, and would produce problems if the mother was different in some way - the gosling inherits a double tendency: firstly, to follow any moving object that it sees during the critical period; and secondly, to develop an attachment to that object if it manages to follow the object for ten minutes or so. Once the attachment has been formed, the gosling will go to great lengths to stay with its mother and will avoid other large moving objects. A study by Hess, in 1958, showed that rather than being put off by obstacles, a duckling would develop an even stronger attachment if it had to struggle to keep up with its imprinted parent.

Precocial animals

The same process happens with goslings, foals, and, it seems, with any animals which can move around freely soon after birth. We call these **precocial**, or early developing animals. Having a very rapid form of attachment like imprinting can represent a survival trait, because it makes sure the young animal doesn't wander off and get into danger. Animals whose young are helpless for a period of time after birth can afford to take longer to form attachments, but a mobile youngster has to develop one very quickly.

The important thing about imprinting, though, is that it is a form of learning. Although the genes still exert an influence, it isn't so much a direct pattern of behaviour that is inherited, but a **state of readiness** to react to something in the environment in a special way. The genes produce general tendencies for certain kinds of reaction, rather than producing behaviour directly.

Studies of the way in which imprinted ducklings and goslings behave have shown this. Bateson (1966) performed a series of studies, which showed that the young birds always attempt to keep at a certain kind of distance from their 'parent'. If the adoptive parent is large, they will follow from a greater distance than if it is a small one. It seems that they may inherit a sensitivity to a certain size of image on their retinas (perhaps those cells will fire more readily than the other ones), and their 'following distance' is the one which keeps the retinal image that they receive to this size.

It seems, also, that the young birds become highly anxious if this retinal image becomes too small, or if they lose contact with their 'parent' altogether. If they received tranquillisers, the effort which they put into following the parent decreased noticeably. It seems possible that they inherit some kind of **stress reaction** to separation, which is signalled by visual contact with the parent, and which triggers off the effort that they will henceforth put into following.

Sensitive periods

There are many other studies which have been done on imprinting, but here we want to concentrate on the ways in which genetic influences can work together with environmental ones. Some of the research, for instance, has shown that the period of time during which imprinting can take place isn't quite as critical as Lorenz had thought. Lorenz had thought that once the period of time (the critical period) was over, the genetic influence would 'switch off' so that imprinting couldn't take place at all. Instead, it seems as though it is a **sensitive period** rather than a critical one, which can be adjusted but is still the best time for this learning to take place. A study by Sluckin, in 1961, showed that if ducklings are kept in isolation, the period in which they can imprint can be as much as four or five times as long as normal.

1.1 Imprinted goslings following Konrad Lorenz

In Chapter 21, we will be looking at how human attachments seem to develop through a process of interaction between parents and infants. There, too, it may be more helpful to use the idea of critical and sensitive periods to explain how genetics can influence our behaviour, than to try to talk directly about inherited behaviour patterns. Genetic influences, as we have seen, can take many different forms, and the way that our environment can affect us can also take different forms. Human beings have several different kinds of ways that they learn and in the next chapter we will look at some of these.

Summary

1. There used to be a distinction in psychology between those who believe that development is mainly inherited and those who believe that it is mainly learned.
2. Through the process of genetic transmission we inherit half of our genes and chromosomes from each of our parents.
3. Each gene is responsible for a particular item of development, which will occur when the organism is at the right stage of maturity.
4. Knowledge of genes and how they work has enabled cloning and genetic engineering.
5. Inherited behaviour takes the form of fixed action sequences, which are triggered off by specific stimuli.
6. The process of imprinting shows one method by which genetic mechanisms and environmental stimuli interact.
7. Imprinting and many other aspects of development occur during a sensitive period when the organism is particularly ready for the right environmental stimuli.

Chapter 2 - Forms of learning

Psychologists have been studying how learning takes place throughout the whole history of psychology. There are a number of different ways that we learn, and these vary in their complexity from simple forms of **association**, which involve the linking of a particular stimulus with a particular response, to the complex building of new information into knowledge that we have been using for some time. In this chapter we will look at some of these forms of learning, ranging from the most basic types to some of the more complicated ones.

Classical conditioning

A basic form of learning is the way in which we come to associate a particular **response** with a particular **stimulus**, just because they have been linked together several times. This is known as **classical conditioning**, and it was studied in great detail by the Russian physiologist Ivan Pavlov, in 1911.

Conditioned reflexes

Classical conditioning involves what are known as **conditioned reflexes.** All animals have reflexive behaviour, which is not under conscious control but is produced in response to specific stimuli. An example of this is the 'knee-jerk' reflex - no matter how much you may try not to, you will still jerk your knee if it is tapped in the right place (just below the kneecap) while your lower leg is swinging freely. This reflex isn't controlled by the brain, but by the spinal cord, and it is a straightforward response to the stimulus, which happens whether we want it to or not. Another example of a reflex is the production of saliva in response to food when you are hungry, and it was this response which Pavlov first investigated when he discovered classical conditioning.

Pavlov had been studying the digestive process in dogs. In order to do this, he had the dogs in harness, with a tube set into the cheek so that he could measure the rate and production of their saliva. He noticed that the dogs would start salivating, not just when they were given their food, but also when they first caught sight of the assistant with the food pail. Pavlov realised that they must have learned to associate the sight of the pail with the food. So, he set up various studies to investigate whether dogs could learn to associate salivation with other responses such as a bell ringing. He found that after associating the bell with the presentation of food on several occasions, the dogs would salivate when they heard the bell. The reflex of salivation had become conditioned, even though it was such a basic form of behaviour.

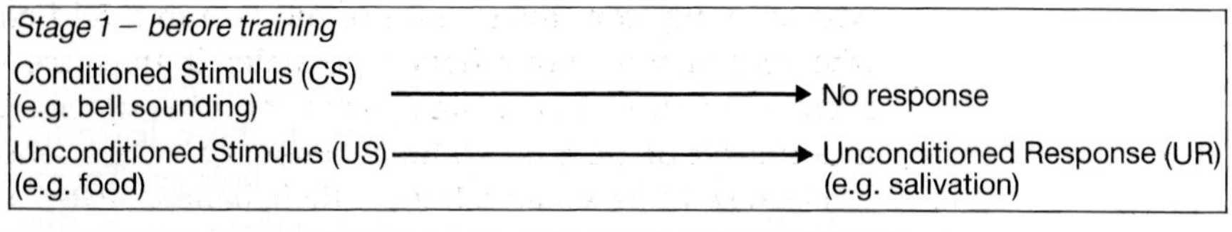

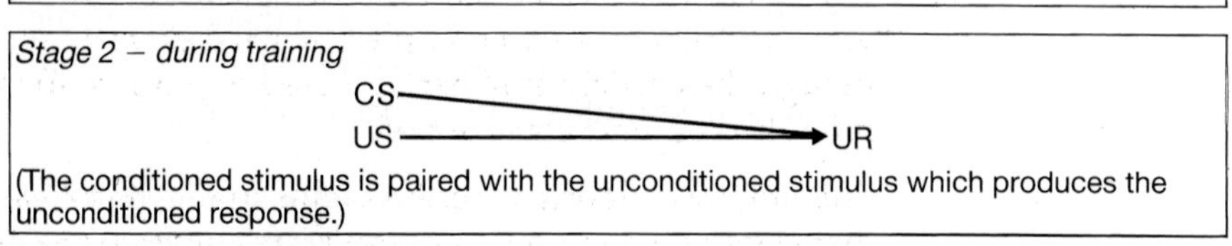

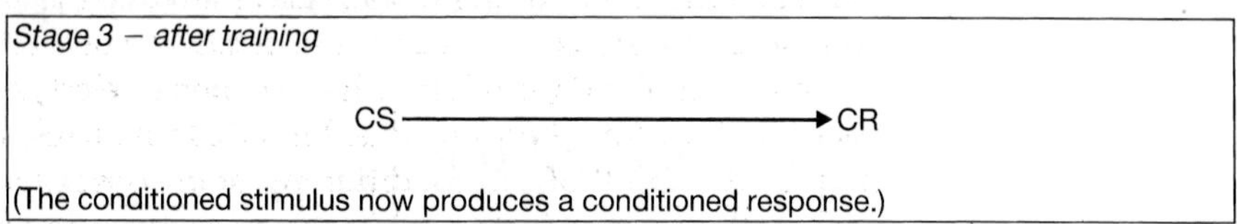

2.1 Classical conditioning

Generalising conditioned responses

Pavlov found that there seemed to be a tendency to **generalise** the learning to other stimuli. If a different bell sounded, the dogs would still salivate, and the more similar the tone of the bell was to the original one, the stronger the response would be. This became known as the **generalisation gradient**. In addition, it was possible to train dogs to **discriminate** between stimuli. In one study, Pavlov trained his dogs to discriminate between different shapes, like a circle and a square. He would do this by **reinforcing** the response to one but not the other (the response was reinforced - strengthened - by pairing it with the original, unconditioned stimulus).

When he gradually made the two stimuli more similar, eventually showing the dogs shapes which were halfway in between the original two, the dogs produced an interesting reaction. At the point where they were no longer able to distinguish between those that they should react to and those which had not been reinforced, they became highly agitated, and would whine and bark. It seemed that this blurring of the distinctions produced considerable anxiety.

Human conditioning

Although Pavlov's experiments took place with dogs, many studies showed that it was also a form of human learning. One study which demonstrated it was by Menzies in 1937. Menzies showed how a completely unconscious response could be conditioned in response to the sound of a buzzer. The response was **vasoconstriction**, which is the process of blood vessels withdrawing from the surface of the skin in a cold environment (the reason why your hands go paler if they are very cold). Menzies got human research participants to immerse their hands in a bucket of ice-cold water whenever a buzzer was sounded. This caused vasoconstriction in their hands. After a while, the vasoconstriction would take place when the buzzer sounded even though the participants' hands were not put into the water - the reflex had become conditioned.

This study is important because it illustrates very clearly the way that classical conditioning doesn't have anything to do with our conscious decisions. We can't just *decide* to contract the blood vessels in our hands, but it may happen nonetheless, as a result of conditioning. And there are other kinds of human response which may be the result of the conditioning of unconscious responses, such as the anxious feeling which exam rooms bring up in many people, even if they are not taking the exam themselves.

Other studies have shown how we may generalise conditioned responses which have been acquired through classical conditioning. A well-known study by Volkova (1953) involved presenting children with cranberry jelly - delivered directly to the child's mouth - paired with the stimulus word 'good'. When the children were shown other words or sentences which had an *implied* meaning of good, such as 'Leningrad is a beautiful city' (they were Russian children), they also salivated. This seemed to show that even though classical conditioning itself doesn't depend on cognition (thinking and understanding), the meaning of a stimulus may still be important.

The effects of presenting the **conditioned stimulus** - the one that is being learned, such as the bell in Pavlov's experiments - with the **unconditioned stimulus** - the one that originally produces the reflex - have also been studied. Broadly speaking, there are three different ways in which the two stimuli can be paired. These are simultaneous conditioning, delayed conditioning, and trace conditioning.

Simultaneous conditioning is when the conditioned and the unconditioned stimuli are presented at exactly the same time. **Delayed conditioning** is when the conditioned stimulus commences first, and is then followed by the unconditioned stimulus; but they both end at the same time. The third one, **trace conditioning**, is when the conditioned stimulus has been presented and is over before the unconditioned stimulus takes place.

Although these differences may be a matter of seconds, or even milliseconds, they do cause varying results in the effectiveness of the conditioning. Of the three, delayed conditioning is the one which is most effective, followed by simultaneous conditioning and, lastly, trace conditioning. The longer the time interval between the first presentation of the conditioned stimulus and the unconditioned stimulus, the less effective the conditioning becomes.

Psychology in Action

Classical conditioning can be used to reduce fear and anxiety and alleviate some medical conditions. For example, many ante-natal classes stress the importance of using relaxation techniques during labour. Partners are encouraged to work together to develop an effective system of relaxation. The mother-to-be is encouraged to adopt a variety of positions and breathing techniques that will ultimately help her during labour while her partner holds her and gives her verbal reassurance. The idea is that her partner's behaviour will become a conditioned stimulus and, during labour, will help to elicit the breathing and relaxation patterns built up in previous sessions.

Current research is also looking at the use of classical conditioning in alleviating allergies such as asthma and hayfever. Instead of relying on drugs which may have adverse side effects, the drugs are administered at the same time as another stimulus such as a very specific sound or smell, in the hope that, eventually, the symptoms will be alleviated by the sound or smell alone.

One-trial learning

One very fundamental form of learning which seems to be shared by even the most primitive animals, is known as **one-trial learning**. It is a rapid process of association, whereby we learn to react in some way to a particularly strong stimulus. For instance, a flatworm might learn to avoid a particular stimulus if it has been associated with an electric shock; or a human being may be permanently 'turned off' from eating a specific food by one experience of food poisoning.

The interesting thing about one-trial learning is that it only requires the event to happen once for the learning to take place; and once it is learned it is very resistant to **extinction**. If you have developed food poisoning after eating, say fish and chips, you may find that for many years - even the rest of your life in some cases

- just the thought of eating fish cooked in batter makes you feel slightly ill, and you cannot bring yourself to eat it, even though you know perfectly well that this time the fish is all right.

Seligman (1970) argued that it is forms of learning like this which make us realise how we are influenced by our evolutionary background. One-trial learning is a highly valuable survival trait for all animals - something which makes you sick is very likely to be poisonous, and if you have survived eating it once, then making sure you don't eat it again is likely to help you survive! The fact that we have the aversion so strongly even when we *know* that the food is alright this time, shows that it isn't really a form of learning which has much to do with thinking about things. Instead, it's to do with very basic emotional responses. The fact that even fairly primitive creatures like flatworms have it too shows that it is a form of learning which probably evolved very early on in the history of animals.

Some kinds of **phobias**, too, can be induced by a single frightening event. While Pavlov was studying classical conditioning there was a flood in his laboratory. Some of the dogs were trapped in the experimental apparatus and had to experience the water coming higher and higher with no means of escape. From that time on, they showed fear of water, although previously they had not shown any such reaction, and even though it was just one single event. We will be looking at phobias a bit more deeply in Chapter 6.

Operant conditioning

In 1911, E. L. Thorndike argued that some responses were learned, not simply because they were associated with an existing stimulus-response connection, but because they produced pleasant consequences. This was known as the **Law of Effect**, and formed the basis for investigations of a different type of learning. This became known as instrumental, or **operant conditioning**, and the psychologist who was most responsible for developing it was B. F. Skinner.

Although it is more complex than classical conditioning, operant conditioning is still a relatively simple form of learning. It deals with more complicated behaviour - with **voluntary** actions rather than purely with reflexes - and can allow for completely new kinds of behaviour to be learned. But it still involves learning on a purely behavioural level, where one kind of behaviour comes to be linked with a stimulus of some kind, and it still doesn't have very much to do with the **cognitive** aspects of learning.

Reductionism

Like Pavlov, Skinner investigated learning mainly with animals. The reason for this was because he wanted to study the simple forms of learning first, and human learning is usually quite complicated. By using animals he hoped that the basic units of learning could be discovered, and also the ways that they might combine to form complex behaviour patterns. This is an example of an approach known as **reductionism** - trying to understand things by reducing them down to their basic parts.

By using a **Skinner box** - a device which contained the simple elements needed for learning a response - Skinner could study this form of learning. He would place a hungry animal, usually a pigeon or a rat, into the Skinner box and observe their behaviour. The box would only contain three things: a lever, a food delivery chute, and a light. As the animal moved around the box it would eventually press the lever. When this happened a pellet of food would be delivered. This meant that the behaviour of pressing the lever was being rewarded, and it would have the effect of **reinforcing** (strengthening) that behaviour - making it more likely to happen again. Alternatively, a rat might learn to press the lever to escape from, or avoid, something unpleasant like an electric shock. Although it wasn't actually rewarded with anything, its action still had pleasant consequences (the Law of Effect), and resulted in the behaviour of lever-pressing being reinforced, so it would be more likely to happen again.

A skinner box. Notice the lever, the food delivery chute and the light which acts as a discriminatory stimulus.

Aspects of operant conditioning

Skinner used the Skinner box to investigate several different aspects of operant conditioning. One thing that he discovered was that it was very important that the behaviour should be reinforced *immediately* after it had taken place. The reinforcement would tend to strengthen the last behaviour that the animal had emitted, and so if there was a time lag it could reinforce the wrong behaviour. He even found instances of 'superstitious' behaviour happening as a result of this: an animal might scratch its ear or turn around just before looking in the food box, as this had been associated with the reward in the past.

Animals could also learn to recognise when a particular response was appropriate and when it wasn't. By using some kind of signal, such as a light or a sound, Skinner showed that animals could be trained to press a lever when the signal was on, but not when it was off, or the other way round. The signal formed a **discriminatory stimulus**, which indicated when the learned response was to be emitted.

Skinner also found that animals could be trained to produce complicated behaviours by a process known as **behaviour shaping**. This was done by gradually changing what the animal had to do to obtain the reinforcement (known as altering the **reinforcement contingencies**), so that a new response was 'built on' to a response that had already been learned. He might, for instance, train a pigeon to walk in a figure-of-eight by first rewarding it when it walked to the left, and then, once it was doing that and walking in a circle, changing its reinforcement contingencies so that now it would only be reinforced if it changed direction at the end of the circle and walked to the right. Other, more complicated forms of behaviour could be trained by this technique of behaviour shaping.

The ideas of operant conditioning have often been positively applied to human behaviour. Skinner himself considered that operant conditioning could explain pretty well everything that human beings did, including language and thinking, but not many psychologists would agree with him to that extent. There are many cases, though, where it is sometimes a useful way of understanding why we might react in certain ways. We might, for instance, have come to like a particular person because their company is rewarding for us - they might make us feel special or wanted in some way - and we might not be aware that that is the basis of our liking for them.

Ethical discussion

The behaviourist B. F. Skinner argued that all human behaviour is produced through conditioning, but that because society operates its reinforcement contingencies in an unplanned and haphazard way, we often end up reinforcing socially undesirable behaviour. Skinner argued that society should take a deliberate role in manipulating the reinforcement contingencies acting on its members, so as to produce socially responsible behaviour.

In response to this view, others argue that Skinner's approach is offensive towards human dignity, because it sees people as simply there to be manipulated and ignores their right to self-determination and to make their own decisions and choices in life.

What do you think?

Reinforcement in learning

Both classical and operant conditioning use the idea of the link between stimulus and response being reinforced, or strengthened. But in each of them, what counts as reinforcement is different. Reinforcement in classical conditioning consists of repeating the association between the conditioned and the unconditioned stimulus - in other words, presenting the two of them together repeatedly. If this doesn't happen and the conditioned stimulus is just presented on its own, the behaviour becomes **extinguished**, in other words the conditioned response dies out.

In operant conditioning, on the other hand, behaviour is strengthened, or reinforced, through the **Law of Effect**. This means that it is the consequence of the behaviour which will determine whether it is reinforced (and therefore more likely to happen again) or not. This type of reinforcement, as mentioned before, may be organised in two ways: by directly providing something that the animal likes, wants, or needs, known as **positive reinforcement**; or by allowing the animal to escape from, or to avoid, unpleasant stimuli, known as **negative reinforcement**.

Reinforcement schedules

Positive reinforcement has a different effect on the **extinction rate** (how rapidly a particular behaviour dies out) than negative reinforcement. Behaviour which has been learned through negative reinforcement is extremely **resistant to extinction** - it does not die out quickly, even when it is no longer being reinforced. Behaviour which has been learned through positive reinforcement, though, is not so resistant to extinction. How rapidly it dies out will depend on the kind of **reinforcement schedule** which has been used when it was being learned.

In general, there are four main kinds of reinforcement schedule, although a psychologist may use a combination of them when studying a particular form of learning. **Fixed-ratio reinforcement** is when the animal (or human) receives reinforcement according to the number of correct responses that they have made, and this number stays the same throughout the learning period. Because this means that the animal will be rewarded more if it makes more responses, fixed-ratio reinforcement produces a very fast rate of responding; but when reinforcement stops, it dies out quite quickly. In other words, it is not very resistant to extinction.

Sometimes a schedule may be used where the animal is reinforced according to the number of responses which have been made, but the required number changes each time. **Variable-ratio reinforcement,** as this is called, still results in a high response rate, but is more resistant to extinction than fixed-ratio - the response doesn't die out as quickly.

The time interval between reinforcements may also be used to produce a reinforcement schedule. **Fixed-interval reinforcement** is when a certain, set amount of time needs to pass since the last reinforcement was given, but once the time is up the animal is reinforced as soon as it makes the response. When an animal has been trained to press a lever according to this schedule, it produces a very low rate of response, pressing the lever at regular intervals, and also shows a low resistance to extinction: the response dies out quickly once it is no longer being reinforced.

Variable-interval reinforcement is when the time which has to pass before the behaviour is reinforced again changes each time. An animal trained according to this kind of schedule produces a steady, regular response rate, which is highly resistant to extinction - not unlike the kind of response rate that we see in people playing fruit machines!

Electrical Stimulation of the Brain

There is another kind of reinforcement which seems to produce rather different kinds of effects than that produced by food rewards. **Electrical Stimulation of the Brain (ESB)** is a term given to a special kind of reinforcement, in which an electrode is implanted directly into an area of the brain near to the hypothalamus. Olds and Milner (1954) discovered that if this area was stimulated, it seemed to serve as a powerful reinforcement: rats faced with the choice between ESB or food would choose ESB rewards even to the extent of starvation. A study by Campbell (1973) on human research participants receiving ESB reported that they felt 'wonderful', 'happy', or 'drunk', and they would continue to receive the stimulation for anything up to six hours at a time quite happily.

At first it was thought that the stimulation was contacting some kind of **pleasure centre** in the brain, but more recent work has suggested that there are several different areas for ESB, and also that they are linked in some way with the more conventional forms of reinforcement. Olds and Forbes (1981) found that hungry rats would press for ESB delivered to the 'feeding centres' of the brain more rapidly than for ESB to other areas. It still isn't clear exactly what this form of reinforcement represents, but in many ways it is rather different from giving food or drink directly.

Secondary Reinforcement

Reinforcement which directly satisfies some kind of basic need is known as a **primary reinforcement**. However, other things can also become reinforcing, if they are frequently linked with some kind of primary reinforcement. For instance, a credit mark in school or college may be something which reinforces behaviour, because it has been associated with approval in the past, and approval seems to be a very basic need in human beings. Another **secondary reinforcement** would be money: because it has been associated with things which satisfy basic needs, it has acquired reinforcing properties, so that receiving money is in itself a reward for most people. Almost anything can come to be a secondary reinforcer: rats will learn to press a lever in a Skinner box just to hear a 'click', if the clicking noise was previously associated with food rewards.

In both classical and operant conditioning, a response which has been extinguished may suddenly reappear. This is known as **spontaneous recovery**, and can happen even after several months have gone past. If this happens, and the response is reinforced again, the learning will show just as strongly as when it was originally learned.

We can see from this that reinforcement in learning may take several different forms. In general, anything which strengthens a particular form of behaviour is a reinforcer. Punishment is never a reinforcer, because all it ever does is to suppress, or attempt to suppress, a particular response but it doesn't strengthen one. Skinner and many other learning theorists who use his model of human behaviour have been very opposed to the use of punishment as a method of training for children, on the grounds that simply punishing children for doing things wrong doesn't stop them from going off and doing something else that is equally wrong. Instead, the child should be rewarded or encouraged when it is doing things that are right - this means that it will be more likely to keep on doing right things rather than wrong ones.

2.1 Investigating reinforcement

Reinforcement plays a very important part in our every day learning. According to learning theory, it is the things that we are praised or rewarded for that we are most likely to do again.

This is a test you can try out with a friend, or with other members of your class.

First of all, produce a list of about 30 ordinary words. Write each word down on a separate piece of paper using four or five different coloured pens.

Choose a certain colour which you will reinforce, but don't let your partner know what it is. Ask your partner to read out the list of words you have produced. Each time they read out one of the words written in the colour that you have chosen, say 'good', or make an encouraging sort of noise - but make sure that you do it as naturally as possible.

When they have finished reading through the words ask them to write down as many of the words as they can remember.

How many words written in each colour did they remember?

Did they remember more words of the reinforced colour?

If you were going to do this as a serious experiment, how would you need to change it?

Cognitive forms of learning

We mentioned before that some learning theorists, in particular Skinner, thought that classical and operant conditioning were enough to explain all human learning. This has been the source of a considerable amount of debate in psychology, because it ignores the fact that there are **cognitive** forms of learning as well. That is, forms of learning which are much more to do with thinking and understanding than with the reinforcement of behavioural responses.

Insight learning

Köhler, in 1925, investigated **insight learning** in chimpanzees. He was interested in the way that some problems seem to be solved, not because of trial and error, as in operant conditioning, but because of some kind of understanding or insight into what the problem consists of. He set his chimpanzees a series of problems which involved them trying to get hold of pieces of fruit which he had placed out of their reach. Somewhere nearby there would be the materials that they needed to solve the problem; if the fruit was hung up out of their reach, there would be some boxes that they could move to climb on; or if it was outside of the bars of the cage, there might be a stick which could be used to pull it in.

Köhler found that, typically, the chimpanzees would try at first to reach the fruit by stretching or jumping, and after this was unsuccessful they would seem to give up. But then, quite suddenly, they would begin to try a new form of behaviour, such as piling up the boxes underneath the fruit, or pulling the fruit in with the stick. The important thing was that this behaviour wasn't piecemeal, as if it was happening through trial and error, but would happen as an organised sequence of actions, as if the chimpanzee knew exactly what it was trying to do and why.

Köhler argued that this really was the case and that they had an insight into the nature of the problem, which meant that they could solve it. As further evidence, he showed how they could also solve different problems in the same kinds of ways, by using other things to climb on (on one occasion, one of the chimps even pulled Köhler himself to a position underneath the fruit and climbed on him!), or by joining two sticks to make one long enough to reach the fruit. Because they had used different things, he argued, this showed that it wasn't just a simple, stimulus-response form of learning, but that they really did have an insight into the problem.

Learning sets

Other psychologists, though, still thought that these results could have happened as a result of trial and error learning. They pointed out that Köhler's chimpanzees had spent their first few years in the wild, and could have engaged in similar kinds of trial and error learning then. This could have given them a **learning set**, which would mean that they would solve this kind of problem much more quickly.

Harlow (1949) demonstrated how these learning sets could develop. He trained monkeys to be able to solve 'odd-one-out' problems by trial and error: the monkey would be shown three shapes, such as two triangles and a square. Underneath the odd one would be a raisin or a peanut, and if the monkey chose the odd one this would be its reward. Harlow gave his monkeys many of these problems, all different, and he found that very quickly they developed a general ability to solve them. They would even be able to choose a different 'odd one' depending on other factors, so that if they were, for instance, shown a blue triangle, a red triangle, and a red square, they would look at the colour of the tray that they were on for the clue (again acquired through trial and error learning) as to whether they should go for the odd colour or the odd shape.

The point that Harlow was making was that people who saw these monkeys showing their quite sophisticated abilities might think that they had learned the answer to the problem through insight, but really it was just a generalisation - a learning set - from their experience with trial and error learning. However, many people think that there is still a place for Köhler's ideas on insight learning and that learning sets are really cognitive, too.

Latent learning

A different form of cognitive learning was demonstrated in rats by Tolman, in 1932. This is known as **latent learning**, and it challenged the idea put forward by the behaviourists, that learning simply involved a change in behaviour. Tolman showed that something could be learned without any apparent change in behaviour: that it could remain latent, and not show until it was needed. Tolman's studies are important because he showed that even rats could develop a **cognitive map**, or a kind of mental image which they could use when it was needed, and this implied that cognition (mental activity, or thinking) was important even in animal learning.

Tolman had been investigating the learning showed by rats running mazes. He set up a very complicated maze which involved several different sets of T-junctions. The experimental rats were placed at the start of the maze, and had to find their way to the goal box at the end, being timed as they did it. When a rat could go straight from the start box to the goal box without taking any wrong turnings, it was considered that it had learned the maze.

Tolman had three groups of rats in his study. One group were given a food reward when they reached the goal box. The second group were not given any food reward at all, but were placed in the maze and allowed to explore it freely just as often as the first group; and the third group were not given any food reward for the first 10 days, but then were rewarded from the eleventh day of the study.

Tolman found that the average number of errors made by each group was as follows: the first group made consistently fewer and fewer errors with each occasion that they were placed in the maze. By the 17th day of the study they were completing the maze very rapidly indeed, with an average of only 2 mistakes per trial. The second group did not show any particular improvement, and by the 17th day they were still making an average of about 6 errors per trial. The third group showed no noticeable improvement until the point where Tolman began to reward them, but then their performance improved dramatically, and within a couple of days they were performing as well as the rats which had been rewarded from the beginning. By the 17th day, their average number of errors was only just above one per trial. (See Fig. 2.2).

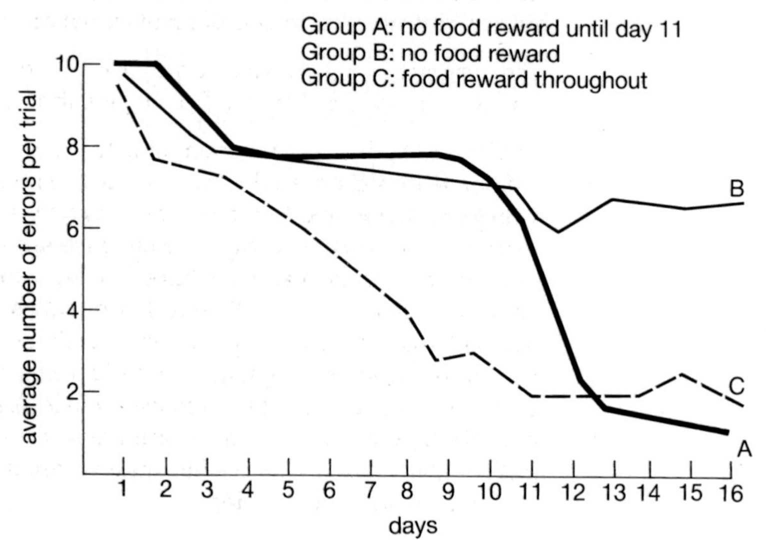

2.2 Tolman's findings

Tolman explained this by arguing that the rats were showing latent learning: they had been learning about the maze while they were exploring it, but this learning had remained unused, or latent, until such time as it was needed. Through their experience, the rats in the third group had been able to build up a 'mental image' of the maze - what Tolman called a cognitive map.

2.2 Investigating cognitive maps

It is often interesting to look at the different ways that we form cognitive maps of places. You can do this study on your own, but, as with most of the activities in this book, it's better if you do it with other people, and then compare the results that you have got.

Decide on a town that you go to sometimes or a part of your town or city which you know quite well, but not as well as the area that you live in. Now, each person should try drawing a complete map of the area, based on what they can remember, and including all the places that they would normally go to when visiting the area.

Compare your map with that of other people's. How do they differ? Which parts of the area do you know best? Do other people know of routes that you didn't know about?

Now, compare these maps with a street map of the same area. What are the main differences? Did you have the scale mostly correct, or did some roads seem longer/shorter to you than they really were? Can you think of explanations for this?

Finally, try to write down in a couple of sentences just how cognitive maps are different from conventional maps.

In Chapter 9, we will look more closely at some other aspects of human learning, especially the work that has been done on problem-solving and thinking. It seems clear that humans can learn in many different ways: we have the same basic forms of learning that simpler animals have, but we also have more complicated ones which allow us to understand and to learn abstract ideas, or to use sophisticated methods of communication like language. In understanding our day-to-day behaviour, it is often useful to look at things from both the behaviourist and the cognitive points of view; because both of them can be very useful when we are trying to understand why we do things.

Summary

1 Pavlov investigated the process of classical conditioning, in which involuntary responses can be produced to a learned stimulus.

2 Presentation of the stimulus in classical conditioning may vary. The three main methods are: trace conditioning, simultaneous conditioning, and delayed conditioning.

3 One-trial learning is a very basic form of learning. It involves a rapidly-formed association between a stimulus and a response.

4 Operant conditioning is the conditioning of voluntary behaviour through positive or negative reinforcement.

5 Operant conditioning can be used to create novel forms of behaviour, through the process of behaviour-shaping.

6 Reinforcement schedules may produce very strong forms of learning; and different kinds of reinforcements may have different effects.

7 Insight learning and latent learning are both cognitive forms of learning, which cannot be explained purely in behaviourist terms.

Chapter 3 - Intelligence and other controversies

Intelligence testing

At the beginning of this book, we mentioned that there were two basic schools of thought concerning where our behaviour comes from. The **nativists** are those who consider that our behaviour is mostly inherited, while the **empiricists** are those who consider that what we do happens as a result of the experiences which we have throughout life. But most psychologists consider that our behaviour is a mixture of both. There are some areas of psychology, though, where extreme views are found. One of those areas is the **nature - nurture debate on intelligence**.

The main supporters of the nativist side of this debate come from the field of **psychometrics**, and they are usually involved in developing and applying intelligence tests. We will be looking at psychometrics in more detail in Chapter 15. Intelligence testing began at the very end of the last century, mainly through the work of two important psychologists: Binet in France, and Galton in England.

Binet's intelligence test

Binet (1911) was the first psychologist to develop a systematic way of measuring intelligence. He was concerned about the way in which children who were not particularly academic were educated, and tried to develop a method whereby those children could be identified. The purpose of this was to enable them to go to special schools, where they would receive extra help in order to bring them up to the level of normal children.

Binet was very concerned that his method for identifying such children should not be misused. He had shown how it was possible to develop an idea of a child's **mental age** by developing a whole range of questions and establishing how old an ordinary child would normally be when it could first answer them. For instance, we would expect a child of just a few years old to be able to say the days of the week, and if we came across an eight-year-old who didn't know them, then we might use that as one indicator (out of many) that the child needed extra educational help.

Binet made three important points concerning his test. The first one, was that the tests were purely practical measures, which simply looked at what a child would normally know by a certain age, so they shouldn't be seen as some kind of measure of general intelligence. His second point, was that the scale was only really useful for identifying children who were retarded in some way, and should not be applied to normal children. And his third point was that the tests were not a strict measure of how much children could learn - they simply identified which children needed more help than others, but that didn't mean that those children were incapable.

Student receiving encouragement from teacher

Nowadays, people are starting to use intelligence tests in very much the sort of way that Binet intended. That is, simply as guides for identifying certain kinds of difficulties so that proper additional help can be given. But this is many years after Binet first developed his method, and in the meantime almost all of the points he made have been ignored or disregarded by psychologists and educators. The main reason for this has been the influence of several other psychologists, who argued from the 'nature' side of the nature - nurture debate.

Eugenics

One of the first of these was Galton, in 1884. At about the same time as Binet was just starting his researches, Galton wrote a paper on 'Hereditary genius', in which he showed that eminent people in society tended to be related, and that genius seemed to run in families. He argued that this showed that intelligence must be inherited. Galton went on from this to the idea of eugenics - that people of inferior abilities should be prevented from having families, because this in some way would result in a feebler society. As the ideas on intelligence testing developed, Galton welcomed them as a means for classifying people, and as developments which made eugenic ideas more practical.

The eugenic ideas held by Galton, and many of his contemporaries, resulted from their belief that genetics was far more important than the environment. People who lived in poverty or squalor, it was argued, did so because of a 'natural depravity' which was inborn in them. These ideas eventually led directly to the concentration camps of Nazi Germany, in which people who were considered to be inferior, such as Jewish people, gypsies, or Poles, were killed by the millions. The idea was that this would promote the development of the ideal human being, by preventing cross-breeding with those of 'inferior' origin.

Ethical discussion

The dramatic, and often tragic, applications of the hereditarian theories of intelligence and schizophrenia raise the question of the social responsibility of science.

Traditional views of science see it as an objective source of 'pure' knowledge or truth. They take the view that scientists have a duty to search after this truth, regardless of the consequences, and that they are not responsible for the social misuse of their knowledge.

A more modern view, associated with the social responsibility of science movement, argues that all people must take responsibility for their actions, including scientists. Science takes place within a social context, and scientists are members of society. As members of society they have a duty to act in a socially responsible manner. This doesn't just mean making sure that their research does not contravene ethical standards; it also means that they need to be fully aware of, and take some responsibility for, how their ideas may be misused.

What do you think?

Issues of nature and nurture

We can see from this that these ideas are not just academic theories. Throughout this century, ideas on inherited or learned intelligence have had widespread influence in one way or another, and this is one reason why the nature - nurture debate on intelligence tends to be quite hotly disputed. In many ways the problems arise from a belief that development is an 'either - or' process – but as we saw in the first chapter, genetics and environment often work together to produce a result. Binet argued that his tests simply diagnosed those who needed more help, but nativists argued later that this would be wasted, because limited genetic capacity meant that people couldn't learn enough to make any real difference.

In this respect, there has often been a misunderstanding of what genetic influence implies. Biologists make a distinction between the **genotype**, which is the set of genetic characteristics that we inherit; and the **phenotype**, which is the overall physiological and behavioural characteristics that the person develops. The genotype, as we have seen, is fixed from conception; but the phenotype is developing and changing all the time. This means that, throughout life, there is an *interaction* between our genes and our environment, so that both work together and are equally important. It is misleading to think that because someone inherits particular characteristics that means that their abilities are fixed, because we are continually developing.

Cyril Burt

One of the people most influenced by Galton's ideas was Cyril Burt. He specialised in intelligence testing, and was firmly committed to the idea that intelligence was inherited, and that it was pointless to educate people beyond the limits of their capacity. Burt, in conjunction with two research assistants, 'Miss Conway' and 'Miss Howard', produced a large number of research papers which seemed to provide unquestionable proof that intelligence was inherited. His statistics were often quoted as indisputable evidence for the heritability of IQ, and also influenced English educational policy, in the form of the introduction of the 11+ test, which determined what type of school a child should go to. This test, which included an IQ test, was said to have the power to select whether a child would benefit from academic education in a 'grammar school', or whether it should be sent to a less academic, 'secondary modern' school. Again, this was an outcome of these theories which influenced millions of people's lives.

In 1974, Kamin questioned Burt's statistics. He had found that many of them were self-contradictory, and concluded that as evidence they were not scientifically respectable. Later, it emerged also that Burt's two research assistants, Miss Conway and Miss Howard, didn't exist, and that he had made up almost all, if not all, of his evidence. Burt's case was one of the most influential scientific frauds ever known, and was a major scandal in the early 1980s. It seemed that his conviction that intelligence was inherited was so strong that he fitted the evidence into his ideas - but many other theorists drew their ideas about intelligence from his evidence.

Other evidence that intelligence was inherited was also questioned. There have traditionally been three main sources of evidence for inherited intelligence. One of them has been the observation that intelligence seems to run in families, as Galton proposed, but nowadays we would not jump to the conclusion that something that runs in families automatically happens because it is genetic. Families also provide environments for their members, and this can influence the way that people grow up to a high degree.

Twin studies

Another major source of evidence has been the study of twins. There are two kinds of twins: **monozygotic (MZ) twins**, which come from the same egg and are identical genetically; and **dizygotic (DZ) twins**, which come from different eggs, and are related in the same way as ordinary brothers and sisters are. Psychologists thought that by studying twins who had been brought up together and comparing them with identical twins who had been brought up separately, they would be able to tell how much their environment was important.

Unfortunately, the main twin study was the one which was reported by Burt and which turned out to have been almost totally invented, so we can't take much notice of its findings. Other twin studies have also suffered from problems. A well-known study by Shields (1962) involved looking at twins who had been reared apart and comparing them with those who had been brought up together. But in many cases, the 'separated' were living simply with other members of the same family, such as one being raised by a mother and the other by an aunt. Often the twins knew each other and attended the same school, and in one case it was reported that they were 'always together'. Even in cases where the separated twins were brought up by different families they were usually of the same background and social class and the most usual pattern, it seems, was that the mother would raise one of the twins while the other would be brought up by close friends of the family. So although these studies often seem to support the idea that intelligence is inherited, they don't really provide very valuable evidence for it – and, of course, none of them have provided such strong evidence as Burt's studies!

Adoption studies

The third main source of evidence for hereditary effects in intelligence has been **adoption studies**. Skodak and Skeels, in 1945, reported finding a significant correlation between adopted children's IQs, and those of their biological mothers. This seemed to show that there was a strong genetic influence in intelligence, as the children hadn't lived with their biological mothers. But this study, too, shows problems. One of them is that they didn't actually test the IQ of the adoptive mothers – they only made an assessment of their 'educational level' – so we don't know how that correlation would have turned out. Another problem was that there were sampling errors: in many cases the data were incomplete, because people dropped out of the study. And the third problem was that, overall, the children's IQs were much higher than their biological mothers and seemed to be closer to that of their adoptive parents, but the kind of statistical test chosen to analyse the data didn't take account of that.

There were other problems with this study, as there have been for most studies of this kind. It seems that almost all of the well-known studies in IQ and inheritance have had difficulties, both with the ways that the samples were obtained and with the ways that the findings have been interpreted. So we cannot really use their findings as convincing evidence.

Individual differences in intelligence

On the other hand, we also wouldn't argue that everyone was exactly the same. It seems clear that there are individual differences, and that people have different **cognitive styles** which mean that they take to some kinds of learning more readily than others. But it is a long step from there to argue that our whole capacity for education depends on some single thing called intelligence. Many adult students find that they can easily learn things that they found difficult in school, and we are constantly changing throughout life. When we look at cognition, we will be seeing some of the things which influence how human beings learn, and how they remember what they have learned, which may account for many of these differences.

One of the arguments which psychologists have about intelligence, is whether the single thing called intelligence exists at all. Many modern critics of IQ testing argue that there is a difference between saying that someone acts intelligently, and saying that someone has got a high intelligence. In the first case, it is looking at what someone actually does, but in the second case it is assuming that there is some general ability. There are many cases where a person can be quite brilliant in one area and quite stupid when it comes to dealing with other things, and to think of intelligence as some general capacity may be very misleading.

3.1 Practising intelligence tests

Many psychologists are doubtful about just how useful intelligence tests are; especially when they are being used to measure an ability which people think might have been inherited. One of the reasons why they are doubtful, is because people can learn to improve their scores on IQ tests, simply by practising them - but presumably, the intelligence that they have inherited doesn't change.

You can try this out, by using two of the intelligence tests available in small paperbacks (e.g. *Check your own IQ* by H. Eysenck). Do one of the tests one week, and then go through and mark it, keeping a record of your score. A week later, do another of the tests. Did you do any better?

A good way to do this is with several people, as a class exercise. When you have the scores from several of you, you can look at them to see more clearly how many people improved; whether anyone got a lower score than before, and what the average difference was.

If you were doing this as a formal experiment, what controls would you need to include?

Schizophrenia

A similar controversy occurs about the genetics of **schizophrenia**. This is a problem in which an individual becomes withdrawn from reality, and often has hallucinations or hears voices. Many people think that schizophrenia means 'split personality', but in fact that's another thing altogether. When psychiatrists or psychologists use the term they are referring to a condition in which the 'split' is between the individual and the outside world so that they don't seem to be in contact with the real world at all.

Kallman's twin study

For most of this century, it was assumed that this happened because of some kind of physical cause which hadn't yet been discovered. When drugs were developed which could subdue people so that they acted more normally, it was thought that this 'proved' that schizophrenia must have a biological cause. A famous twin study by Kallman, in 1946, showed that if one twin suffered from schizophrenia often the other twin would do too and that this was much more common in MZ twins than in DZ twins. This has often been used to show that schizophrenia can be inherited but a careful re-evaluation of it by Marshall (1984) showed that the study suffered from many of the same sorts of problems as the twin studies of intelligence.

Kallman believed very strongly that schizophrenia was inherited and because of that his research findings seem to have been influenced. He did not take many of the precautions that we would consider to be necessary nowadays, such as making sure that the assessments were performed by independent, unbiased observers; and his diagnoses of whether people were either schizophrenic or had schizophrenic tendencies were very open to question.

Problems of diagnosis

One of the problems with this sort of study is that the ways in which schizophrenia, or a tendency towards schizophrenia, is diagnosed are not always very precise. Ideas and forms of behaviour which are quite common in ordinary people can sometimes be included as evidence of a tendency to schizophrenia. Because everyone sometimes has thoughts or moods which are not quite 'normal', we find that it is quite possible for psychiatrists to diagnose wrongly.

Rosenhan's study

A study by Rosenhan (1973) involved people who were established professionals (nurses, doctors etc.), going to see psychiatrists and reporting simply that they heard voices. Although in every other respect they acted quite normally, they were diagnosed as schizophrenic and spent some time in psychiatric hospitals. Once they were there, they said that their symptoms had ceased and continued to act normally but often very ordinary things, like keeping a diary, were taken as evidence of how disturbed they were. It seems that in some cases the difference between 'normal' and 'disturbed' behaviour has more to do with the expectations we have of that person than with what they are actually doing. It was interesting also that once their findings were made known, the hospitals in the area showed a significant drop in admissions for schizophrenia, as if the psychiatrists were being much more careful about who they diagnosed in that way than they had been before.

Modern society, seems to take a much more rigid approach to 'normal' behaviour than many previous societies have done, and some of the criticisms of psychiatric diagnosis of schizophrenia arise because of this. It has been pointed out that many of the great social reformers of previous times, such as George Fox who founded the Quakers, would nowadays have been simply diagnosed as 'schizophrenic' and what they were saying would have been ignored.

Laing's view of schizophrenia

The belief that schizophrenia is inherited is one side of the nature - nurture debate. The other side was stated in quite an extreme form by R. D. Laing. Laing began in 1959 by arguing that schizophrenia wasn't something that just happened to individuals without any apparent cause, but that their personal lives were often intolerable, and that a 'retreat into madness' was often the only way that they could deal with the conflicting demands that were put on them. He argued that psychiatry failed to recognise the very real stresses which schizophrenics were often under and which, in many cases, made their disorders make sense.

One example which he gave was of a girl who imagined that she was constantly caught up in a game of tennis. When the family was looked at, it turned out that she was stuck in the middle of two hostile and opposing sides: her father and his mother against her mother and grandmother. Often, the only way that they would communicate was through the girl herself, and this situation distressed her greatly. Eventually, she was unable to cope any longer, but even though she appeared to be completely out of touch with reality the delusion that she had of the tennis game reflected in a disguised form the real problem that she had with her family.

Laing's early writings influenced many people, and showed that there might be an important environmental aspect to schizophrenia, but in later years he went on to argue that schizophrenia was entirely the person's choice, and that in many ways people who were in a schizophrenic state should be regarded as 'hypersane' - more sane than most normal people. This extreme view, which he put forward in *The Politics of Experience* (1967) seemed, to many people, to ignore the fact that many schizophrenic people were deeply distressed at what was happening to them, and also didn't really deal with the question of why some people became schizophrenic while others seemed to have the same stresses but be able to cope.

Therapy groups can help people to learn social skills

It seems that taking an extreme view of the nature-nurture debate on schizophrenia, from either side, is open to criticism. As Rose, Kamin and Lewontin (1984) point out, we need to investigate the *interaction* between a person's physiology and their experience; and to consider that something is determined purely by either one or the other is bound to lead to an inadequate understanding of it.

Aggression

Aggression is another area where the theories which have been put forward form a kind of nature - nurture debate. Some theorists think that aggression is something which we all have, instinctively, and which we need to release; while others consider it as something which arises as a result of environmental circumstances. In this section, we will look at some of the different work that has been put forward on aggression, and see what general conclusions we can come to.

Aggression as an instinct

Freud (1920) argued that aggression was an instinctive **drive** in human beings. Initially, he had thought that the main motivating force in the human being was the **libido**, the life-force which was involved in all pleasurable sensations, but after the First World War he came to the conclusion that human beings also had a destructive instinct, which he called **thanatos**. This, like libido, was a strong motivating force for the human being and so it was necessary to find ways of expressing it safely.

Lorenz, too, considered aggression to be a basic drive. He saw it as a continual source of energy being produced by the organism, like a tank which is filling up constantly. And, like the tank, he considered that if it was not released from time to time then it would overflow into extremes of aggressive behaviour. Aggression, Lorenz thought, was expressed safely in most animal societies by means of **ritualised fighting gestures**, in which an animal's natural weapons, such as horns or teeth, were displayed to its opponent. These aggressive gestures had their counterparts with what Lorenz called **appeasement gestures** - when an animal would place itself in a highly vulnerable position, which would signal to the aggressor that the attack should stop. When a puppy roles over on its back on meeting a larger dog, it is making itself vulnerable, and Lorenz thought that this would act as a sort of automatic 'stop' signal which would prevent further attacks.

Lorenz considered that human beings and rats were distinctive among all of the animal kingdom, because neither was particularly well equipped with natural weaponry. This meant that they hadn't developed the ritual aggressive gestures and appeasement gestures that most animals had, which also meant that they didn't have an automatic signal to stop them from fighting, so they would continue to fight to the death. Because of this, it was essential that human beings found safe ways of releasing their aggression, for instance in competitive sports, or society would continue to experience large and destructive wars.

Since Lorenz first put forward his ideas, in 1966, many studies of animal behaviour have shown that his idea of appeasement gestures doesn't seem to be as common as he thought. Goodall (1978) observed one troop of chimpanzees in Tanzania attacking another group and killing many of them, and other ethologists (people who study behaviour in the natural environment) have seen aggressive behaviour continuing in gulls even though they were showing appeasement gestures.

3.2 Defining aggression

One of the main problems which psychologists encounter when they study, or make theories about, aggression is that everyone seems to have a different idea of just what aggression is.

This is a very simple test that you can do, which will allow you to investigate some of the different ideas that people have. All you need to do is ask as many different people as you can for one word which has the opposite meaning to the word 'aggressive'.

If you like, you can follow this up by asking them also to give you five different examples of aggression.

When you have done this, compare your results with those obtained by a friend, or by the other members of your class. Can you all agree on a definition of aggression?

Alternative explanations for aggression

Many psychologists also disagree with the whole idea that aggression is an inherited drive, or instinct. Rose et al. (1984) point to the way that we use the same word 'aggression' to describe all sorts of different behaviours, from mice killing one another in laboratory cages to human achievement or competition, and they argue that it is unlikely that these are in any way the same sorts of things.

Rose et al. also disagree with the idea that aggression is a set quantity which people have, and must express. To say that a particular kind of behaviour is aggressive, is not to say that it therefore arises from an amount of aggression. One is a description of what something is like, but the other implies that there is an independent something which people have more or less of.

The frustration-aggression hypothesis

One approach to aggression which has been more popular among many psychologists is the **frustration-aggression hypothesis**. This is the idea that aggressive behaviour happens, not because of an instinctive drive, but as a result of frustrating circumstances. If people are unable to achieve the goal that they are aiming for, they respond angrily or aggressively. So, someone who feels unhappy and frustrated as a result of high unemployment or impoverished social conditions is more likely to respond to situations in an aggressive way than someone who has a comfortable lifestyle.

Several studies of animals have shown that overcrowding can lead to much higher levels of aggression than are found normally. Calhoun (1962) set up a study in which a colony of 32 rats were established in an area, with enough food and water for their needs. Over time, the number of rats increased, through breeding, but the amount of food and water which each received remained the same. At first, the rat colony showed little aggression, but as they became more and more overcrowded they became more and more aggressive, a process which eventually resulted in fighting to the death. Some people think that a similar process is responsible for our inner-city violence - overcrowding, frustration and competition for limited opportunities.

Learning by imitation

Even though the frustration - aggression hypothesis can explain quite a lot of human aggression, it still doesn't explain why some people react aggressively in certain circumstances, while other people in the same situation don't. One reason for this is the idea that we also learn by **imitation**, and we are most likely to turn to the kind of behaviour which we have seen before. So individuals who have been exposed to aggressive behaviour in the past will be more likely to react aggressively in a frustrating situation. We will be looking at this more closely in Chapter 21.

Another set of reasons why some people react aggressively while others don't, seems to be to do with our levels of **arousal**. Arousal is a physiological term which is used to describe what happens to the body when we are in an excited state or when we are under stress. In Chapter 6 we will be looking at the way that high levels of arousal may make us more inclined to react angrily in situations where we might not react that way if our arousal levels were lower.

Psychology in Action

If a country is at war, it is necessary to build up and maintain a sustainable level of aggression in its people. In many instances a certain sense of anger will already be present, while in other cases, such as where the country itself is under no direct hostile threat, aggression has to be more carefully manipulated.

British involvement in the Second World War and the Gulf War illustrates these cases. Both made careful use of propaganda, although there are important differences to note. In the Second World War, the whole economy and population were geared to the war effort, so it was important not only that the non-military population agreed with the objectives, but that its aggression was sustained at a high enough level to accept and support the great social and economic changes that were necessary.

By contrast, Iraq posed no direct threat to Britain (other than to Britain's oil supplies). The Iraqi leader, Sadam Hussein, pictured less than a year earlier as a trading partner and ally, was now portrayed as a mad butcher and likened to Hitler. Only negative aspects of Iraqi culture and positive aspects of Kuwaiti culture were shown. Soldiers and civilians alike were treated to stories of Iraqis taking Kuwaiti babies out of their incubators before transporting the incubators home. That this story subsequently turned out to be false is of little relevance to its effect at the time.

Implications of nature - nurture theories

When we look at the nature - nurture debates on intelligence, schizophrenia and aggression, we can see that these theories can have a lot of influence on the way that society organises itself. If we believe that intelligence is a fixed quantity which is inherited, then 'streaming' children into appropriate forms of education becomes an efficient way of using a country's educational resources. If, on the other hand, we see intelligence as something which can change and develop as the individual develops, then streaming children becomes something which is likely only to be damaging, by stereotyping them and preventing them from getting full benefit from their studies.

Similarly, if we see schizophrenia as happening because of inherited weaknesses in the individual, then it makes sense to try to suppress the disturbing symptoms with drugs, and to treat the individual alone. If, on the other hand, we see it as a reaction to intolerable social pressure, then individual treatment becomes inadequate and it becomes necessary to treat the whole family as well. Partly as a result of Laing's work, and that of later theorists, there has been a growth in approaches to clinical problems through family therapy - getting the whole family together for professional help, to try to sort out deeper disturbances which might be affecting individual members of the family in such a way that they appear to be psychiatrically disturbed. Although few modern family therapists would agree fully with Laing, his writing nonetheless started off an interest in that area which is now proving to be very useful in the treatment of many kinds of disturbance.

Ideas on aggression are perhaps the most politically sensitive of all. If we see aggression as resulting from an instinctive drive in human beings then it follows logically that we need to keep that drive under control. People will need to have external forces preventing them from showing that aggression and to have their aggression 'channelled' into safe outlets, like competition at work. If, on the other hand, we see aggression as arising from frustrating circumstances, then the way to prevent civil unrest or other kinds of aggression isn't by tighter control which only increases the amount of frustration, but is in improving social conditions and opportunities for people, so that the frustrating circumstances don't happen in the first place.

Although this chapter has only been able to skim over the surface of these debates, they are very real and continuing, and there is much more that could be said about each of them. In later chapters we will be looking at other nature - nurture debates, including sex-role socialisation, and the development of language. In the next chapter, we will examine a rather less contentious nature - nurture debate: that of the nature - nurture debate on perception.

Summary

1 Intelligence testing was first developed for identifying children who needed special help with schooling.

2 Ideas of inherited intelligence developed through the work of Galton and his followers. The most influential was Cyril Burt, but he committed fraud in obtaining his data.

3 Obtaining evidence for the nature-nurture debate on intelligence is extremely difficult. Most of the studies are inadequate as evidence.

4 Ideas that schizophrenia is inherited have been very popular, but the evidence rests on very wide definitions of 'schizophrenic'.

5 Laing suggested that schizophrenia could arise from family interactions. Rose et al, suggest that the interaction between physiology and experience is most important.

6 Freud and Lorenz saw aggression as an instinctive drive in human beings, and suggested that channelling aggression safely was necessary for society.

7 Other studies have emphasised the way that aggression seems to arise as a response to frustrating circumstances, rather than automatically.

Chapter 4 - The nature-nurture debate on perception

In this chapter we will be looking at the way that our perception develops and how it responds to different influences. Perception is the interpretation of information which we receive through our senses: whenever we receive sensory information, like smells, sounds or noises, we make sense out of them, both consciously and unconsciously, and this allows us to fit the new information in with other things that we already know. In Chapter 12, we will be looking more closely at other aspects of perception, but here we will look in particular at the way that it develops the nature - nurture debate on perception. As we do so, we will concentrate on visual perception - the way that we make sense out of what we see – because that's the form of perception that we know most about.

Can perception adjust?

When we are looking at whether perception has been learned or inherited, one way that we can do it is by seeing how fixed and unchanging it is. In the first chapter, we saw that one of Lorenz's criteria for inherited behaviour was whether it was fixed and unchanging, because if it was passed on through the genes, we wouldn't be able to change it because we can't alter our genes.

One of the first studies to look at this was by Stratton, in 1893. He spent a week wearing an inverting lens over one eye (the other eye was covered with an eyepatch). For the first couple of days, he had great difficulty in adjusting to an upside-down world, but after a while his perception adapted, and he didn't have any trouble. It was only when he saw something that was obviously wrong, like a candle flame pointing downwards, that he remembered that he was seeing upside down.

A study by Kohler, in 1962, investigated whether perception can adapt to different colours. He wore goggles which had tinted lenses so that the left half of each was green and the right half was red. After he had been wearing them for about half an hour he stopped noticing them but when he took them off he found that, for a while, he seemed to see the opposite colour! So to the left of his vision, everything seemed to be reddish, while to the right it all seemed green. This seemed to imply not only that our visual perception can adapt, but also that there is some kind of physiological mechanism which corrects our vision and takes some time to get back to normal.

Not all animals, though, seem to have this flexibility in visual perception. Hess, in 1956, placed prism lenses over the eyes of chickens. This had the effect of making everything seem about 10 degrees to the side of its real place. When the chickens tried to peck at corn that they could see, they would miss it, but even when they had been wearing the lenses for some time, they still continued to miss. It seemed that their perception couldn't adapt to the new situation.

We can explain this in terms of the ways that genetic influence seems to work. In Chapter 1, we saw how an increase in learning ability means that an animal would have fewer strictly inherited responses: birds in general inherit quite a lot of their behaviour and it is quite possible that more of their perception is inherited than a human's.

Physiological adaptation

Some other studies have looked at the way that the environment can affect the physiological arrangements for perception in the visual system. A study by Blakemore and Cooper, in 1966, involved kittens being reared in the dark, except for a period each day when they would be placed in a 'vertical world' - an apparatus which meant that they were surrounded only by 'vertical' lines. When eventually tested it was found that these kittens had adapted their perception so that they had very good perception of vertical things, such as chair legs, but would not seem to see horizontal things, such as a rope stretched out in front of them. Blakemore continued his investigations and in 1984 he reported on the ways that this had taken place in the kittens' visual systems.

In 1968, Hubel and Wiesel had discovered that there were special cells in the thalamus and the visual cortex which reacted to lines at different angles. So, if an animal was looking at a vertical line it would trigger off different nerve cells than if it was looking at a diagonal or a horizontal line. Blakemore found that about 90% of the cells seemed to be able to change their function, if the animal had restricted stimulation throughout the early period of its life. About 10% of the cells seemed to be fixed in their functions, but the others could change in response to environmental stimuli.

Activity and perception

Some other studies have shown the importance of being active when perception is developing. A study by Held and Hein involved a 'kitten carousel', which was an apparatus which made sure that two kittens could have exactly the same visual experience, although one was walking and the other was being carried. The kittens were brought up in the dark except for a period each day when they were put in the carousel. As one of the kittens walked around, the other one swung round with it so they ended up seeing exactly the same things. When their visual perception was tested it was found that, although the active kitten was normal, the passive kitten did not seem to be able to make sense of the visual stimulation it received: it acted as if it were blind even though physiologically, its visual system seemed to be working normally. So it seems that some kind of active experience is needed in order for perception to develop properly.

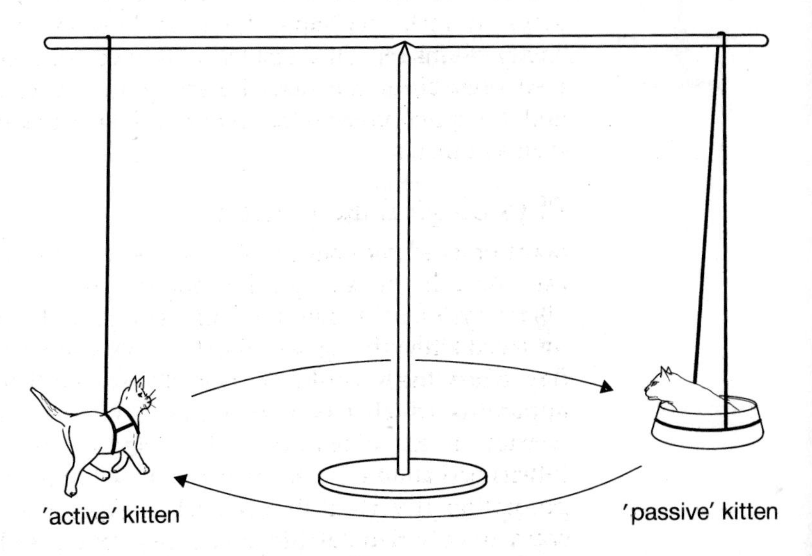

4.1 A kitten carousel

Environmental influences on perception

This may present an explanation for why human visual perception can often adapt to different kinds of environments. A study by Annis and Frost, in 1973, compared the visual perception of urban Cree Indians, in Canada, with those who lived a more traditional lifestyle. The urban people lived in the normal kind of Western environment: in houses, with straight walls, and walked through regular streets. This type of environment is known as a **carpentered environment,** because it is full of straight lines at right angles to one another. In a normal Western environment, most lines are either vertical or horizontal, and diagonal lines are fairly uncommon.

In the traditional Cree lifestyle, on the other hand, diagonal lines are much more common. They live in tepees made from straight birch poles and there are many other straight lines in their environment which are not necessarily vertical or horizontal. Annis and Frost found that the Cree Indians who lived the traditional lifestyle were much better than the urban ones at telling whether two lines were parallel or not. Those who lived the Western lifestyle were very good at the vertical or horizontal ones but not very good at the diagonal ones, whereas the traditional Cree Indians were good at judging lines at all angles. Perhaps our Western lifestyle has made us a bit like Blakemore's kittens and given us a restricted visual environment!

Ethical discussion

Deprivation studies, like Held and Hein's 'kitten carousel' study, were a traditional method of studying the influences of nature and nurture. Typically, deprivation studies involved depriving a young animal of some normal aspect of experience, and then observing whether this lack affected their normal development. It is sometimes argued that such studies are not cruel because no actual physical pain is inflicted on the animal.

Opponents of such studies argue that depriving the animal of normal experience is in itself cruel, as the animal does not have the opportunity to live an ordinary life. Consequently, scientists have no right to treat animals in this way.

What do you think?

Size constancy

When Colin Turnbull, an anthropologist, was studying pygmies in 1961 he took one of them, who had become a friend, out of the forest on a trip. The pygmies he was studying had spent their whole lives in the forest - they were known as 'the forest people' - so to go outside it and see for miles across the plains was a new experience. Normally, we use **size constancy** to interpret things that are a long way away but the pygmy had never experienced long-distance viewing before. When he saw a herd of buffalo in the distance he thought they were ants and refused to believe that they were buffalo because they looked so small. And when he saw a boat some distance away across a lake he thought that it was just a scrap of wood. As it got closer and he could see people on board, he became very agitated and thought that it must be magic. So it seems that humans, too, need the right kind of experience to develop perception.

The Muller-Lyer illusion

Another way that our perception may be affected by our experience, is in the way that we interpret drawings. A study by Segall, Campbell and Herskowitz in 1963, investigated a particular visual illusion, known as the 'Muller-Lyer Illusion'. They tested Europeans and also Zulus who were living in their traditional environment. What they found was that the Europeans were taken in by the illusion - they thought that the line with outward-pointing fins was longer - but the Zulus weren't. They saw it for what it really was: two lines with no significant difference in length.

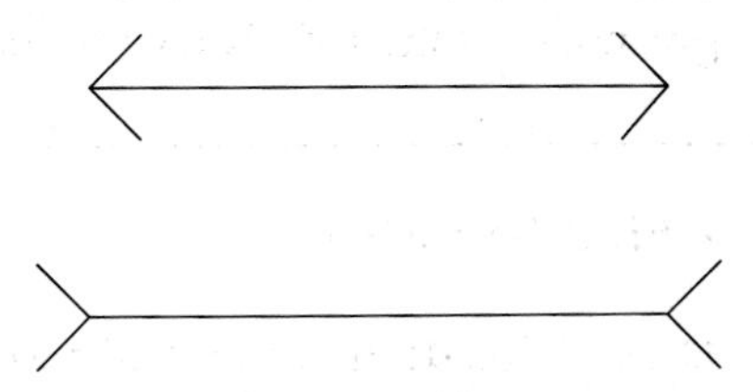

4.2 The Muller-Lyer illusion

Gregory (1963) argued that this was because the Muller-Lyer illusion works by bringing up unconscious size-constancy and perspective cues. For Europeans, who are accustomed to a carpentered environment, the illusion would remind them of edges of buildings and corners of rooms. Traditional Zulus, though, don't live in a carpentered environment, but have round houses and circular arrangements to the villages. So for them the illusion doesn't happen.

4.1 The Muller-Lyer illusion

One interesting study that you can do is to investigate the Muller-Lyer illusion. To do this, you will need some thin card, some glue, a felt-tip pen and a ruler to make an adjustable Muller-Lyer figure. First, cut out a rectangular piece of card, about 15 cm long and 5 cm wide. Score it in a straight lengthways line down the middle, fold it over, and glue it to itself. This will strengthen the card, and leave you with a strip 15 cm long and about 2.5 cm wide. This will form your centre strip.

Next, cut out another rectangular piece of card, this time about 12 cm long and 7 cm wide. Place the centre strip lengthways down the middle of this piece, and score along both edges. Fold it over the centre strip, so that it makes a kind of sheath for it. Remove the centre strip, and glue your outer case together along the long open edge.

When the glue has dried, fit the centre strip inside the outer case and make sure that it can slide in and out. Pull it almost completely out and, using the ruler, draw a thick line along the middle of the outer case and along the centre strip. Start the line about 2.5 cm from the end of the outer case and end it about 2.5 cm from the end of the centre strip.

Make sure that the line is continuous and also that it is parallel to the edges.

Now, when you slide the centre strip in and out, the line should stay continuous, but appear to get longer or shorter. Draw large outward-pointing arrow-heads at each end of the line on the outer case. Draw a large inward-pointing arrow-head at the end of the line on the centre strip.

Now try looking at the two halves of the figure, and moving the centre strip in and out until you think you have both lines exactly equal. Measure them with a ruler. Were you correct? (If you like, you can draw a measuring scale on the other side of your adjustable Muller-Lyer figure, so that you can quickly read how accurate or inaccurate people have been.

There are a variety of experiments you can try with a figure like this. Try seeing if presenting it vertically or horizontally makes any difference, or if different groups of research participants (e.g. children/adults) will give you different results.

Developing perception

Another investigation of size constancy was performed by Bower in 1966. Bower set up an arrangement whereby very young babies could be shown different shapes, and could indicate whether they recognised them, by moving their heads very slightly to the side, triggering off a switch set into the pillow at the side of their heads. The way that Bower trained the babies to react in this way was by rewarding them with a 'peek-a-boo' game from the experimenter if they moved their heads when they were shown a particular cube.

Once the babies were reacting to that particular cube, Bower tried varying what the babies were shown. He showed them the cube at different angles, at different distances, and also showed them differently sized cubes at various distances. The idea was that if the babies were born with size constancy, they would still recognise the cube even when it was further away and looked smaller. He could also find out if they had shape constancy, and could still recognise something when it was shown to them at a different angle.

Bower found that even very young babies had the basics of size and shape constancy, although it was nowhere near as highly developed as an adult's. So it seems that there is some inherited aspect to this type of perception but we still need to develop it with our experience.

Visual cliff studies

A study by Gibson and Walk investigated depth perception in new-born animals, such as goat kids and day-old chicks. They set up a 'visual cliff' which was a platform which seemed as though it had a sheer drop on one side of it. In fact, both sides of the platform (the 'shallow' side and the 'deep' side) were covered with thick glass, and so the drop was only a 'visual' one, but even new-born animals refused to go onto that side. Kittens whose eyes had just opened wouldn't go on it either and babies wouldn't crawl on it. Rats would go on it quite happily, but if their whiskers were removed, then they refused: it seems that vision is only the second most important sense for rats – touch is more important.

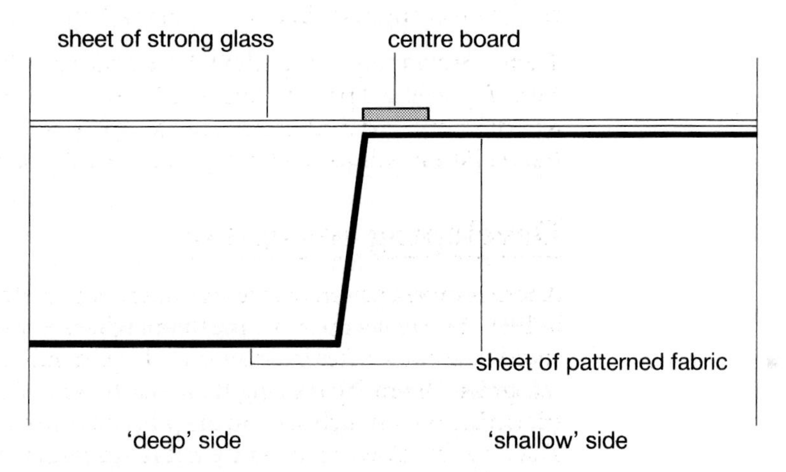

4.3 A 'visual cliff'

This study seemed to indicate that many animals have an inherited kind of depth perception, which would serve at least to prevent them from falling over cliffs! We cannot tell much about human perception from it, though, because the babies were old enough to be able to crawl on the apparatus, and so would have had quite a lot of experience of distance by that time. But even for an adult who knows it is safe, the experience of going on a 'visual cliff' is very disconcerting. At the time of writing, there is such a 'cliff' in the Human Biology Hall of the Natural History Museum in London, so perhaps if you are visiting there you could try it.

Blind people with restored vision

One problem with investigating babies is the fact that they can't really tell you anything about what is happening. However, there have been two studies of adults who suddenly obtained their sight after a lifetime of being blind. Von Senden, in 1960, studied a group of people who had gained their sight in this way and found that what they could actually perceive was very limited. They could detect figures against backgrounds but they couldn't recognise simple shapes like triangles, even after a few weeks, without counting the corners. They were also able to detect colours (although obviously they had to learn what they were called) from the very start but just about all the other kinds of perception had to be learned gradually later.

Cross-modal transfer

A different study was performed on a single adult, by Gregory (1963). This was a 47-year-old man, who had wanted to see all his life, and when he obtained his sight he had far more abilities than Von Senden's research participants. He could recognise familiar objects by sight, and could even read a little! The reason for this was that he was using **cross-modal transfer**: when he was younger, someone had given him a set of building blocks with raised letters on, and he had often handled these and tried to imagine what they must look like.

Because Gregory's research participant had such high motivation, and could use cross-modal transfer to interpret his new sense, it isn't really possible to use this study as evidence on the nature-nurture debate on perception. We perceive with our other senses too, and his previous experience meant that he was not learning to see just from scratch but was applying what he already knew. So in many ways it isn't the same as a new-born baby.

Pattern perception among infants

In some cases, though, it is possible to find out something of what new-born babies can see. We have already looked at one approach by Bower, but a different method was tried by Fantz in 1961. He set up an apparatus which allowed him to detect what very young infants were looking at and then tried showing them different shapes, two at a time. By measuring how long the infants looked at each shape, Fantz was able to tell which one they preferred and he deduced from this that they must be able to detect what was on it or they wouldn't prefer it.

Fantz found that babies tended to prefer patterns to plain shapes. This was important because it showed that the infant had basic figure-ground perception (the ability to distinguish figures against backgrounds). He also found that, given a choice, the stimulus which they liked most of all was a representation of a human face. So it seems that some kind of basic pattern perception is inherited and also a tendency to look at other people. As we will see in Chapter 21, a tendency towards sociability seems to be very basic in children and Fantz's study seems to support that.

Infants looked for longer at the patterned figures, and most of all at the face-like one. (The plain figure has exactly the same amount of light and dark areas.)

4.4 Fantz's figures

We can see that studies of the nature-nurture debate on perception have taken many different forms. There are distortion and readjustment studies, which have looked at how people can adjust their perception to new stimuli There are cross-cultural studies which have looked at people who have grown up in very different environments to see if their perception is different from that of Westerners. There are deprivation studies which have involved bringing animals up in restricted environments and seeing if that affects their perception. There are studies of blind people seeing for the first time, and there are studies of how much infants and new-born animals can perceive.

From all of these, we can end up drawing a general conclusion that the basic aspects of perception seem to be inherited, such as colour and figure-ground perception, or the basics of depth perception. However, other aspects of perception are learned, or at least developed more through experience. Again, as with so many nature-nurture debates, we find that the important thing is the *interaction* between what we have inherited and our experience as we grow up.

How perception happens

We mentioned before that perception is interpreting the information that we receive through our sensory organs. There is an important difference between **sensation**, which is the way in which our sense organs react to the outside world, and **perception**, which is the process by which we make sense of our sensations.

In this section we will look at some of the ways that our sensory equipment may influence our perception.

Processing visual information

When light enters the eye, it has two main characteristics: brightness (intensity), and colour (wavelength). The vast range of different things that we see are a result of combinations of these two kinds of information. The light triggers off sensitive cells at the back of the eye, known as rod and cone cells, which are arranged as a kind of screen called the **retina**. The light which has entered the eye through the pupil is focused onto the retina by a lens, which adjusts its shape to make the image as clear as possible. The cells which make up the retina respond when light hits them, by producing an **electrical impulse** which is passed along nerve fibres to the brain.

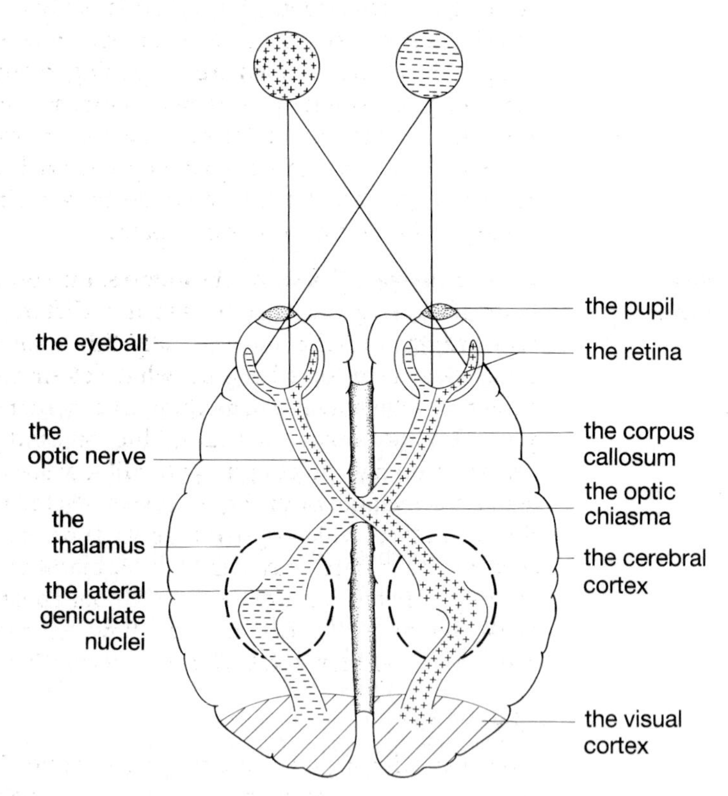

4.5 The visual system

Perceptual constancies

Shape constancy

When we are looking at something, it forms an image on the retina, and the brain receives information on the size and shape of the retinal image. However, if we just responded to the sensations that we receive, we would not be able to allow for the way that our retinal image of the same object can change. When we look at familiar things, like cups, the retinal images that we get of them may be totally different, depending on the angle that we are looking at them from. You can see this when you try to draw something: a drawing of a cup from the top is very different from a drawing of the same cup from the side. However in everyday life when we are looking at things, we do not think that they have changed their shape each time we see them from another angle. Instead, our perception allows for this: we have **shape constancy**, which means that we perceive the shape as staying the same, despite the changes which are happening to our sensations. **Size constancy** is a similar process that happens with sizes of objects. If we see someone down the street, walking towards us, we don't think that they are growing as they approach us! Although the retinal image becomes larger, we perceive their size as being the same, because we have size constancy.

Colour constancy

Colour constancy, too, works in the same sort of way. We have cells in the retina which respond differently to different wavelengths of light, and normally this is the main mechanism which we have for telling us what colour something is. But sometimes we may see something in different circumstances. If you know that a particular car is blue, say, and you see it at night under an orange street light, you will just see it as blue. But the actual wavelength of the light that is reflected from the car is not the normal one which signals blue, and someone else, who hasn't seen the car before, may easily think that it is a different colour entirely. This is because we have colour constancy: because we *know* the colour of the car we allow for the changes to our sensations and they don't affect our perception.

Depth cues

One interesting aspect of our visual perception is the way that we perceive distance or depth. We have two main sources of cues which let us know how far away things are: one set is known as the monocular cues to depth, while the other set is known as the binocular cues. **Monocular depth cues** are cues which work just as well if we are looking at something with just one eye as they do with two, while **binocular depth cues** are those which operate because we have two eyes which see almost the same things.

Relative size

One of the monocular depth cues is the **relative size** of objects. As we have already seen, things that are further away produce a smaller retinal image and the brain uses this as a cue to tell it how far away something is. A well-known visual illusion called the **Ames room** uses this cue to 'trick' our perception. The room is arranged and painted in such a way that, if it is seen from the front, it looks rectangular, but actually one of the far corners is much further away than the other one. This means that if someone is standing in one corner they will seem much smaller than someone standing in the other corner, or if they walk from one side to the other they will seem to grow or shrink dramatically.

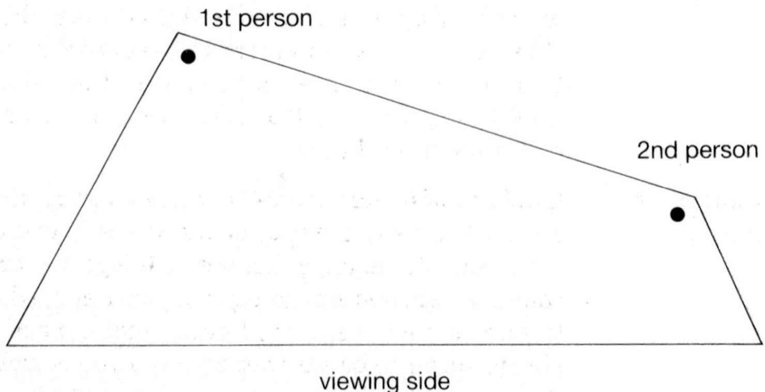

4.6 The Ames room

Height in plane

Another monocular depth cue is how high up something is in our visual field, known as **height in plane.** We tend to think that things that appear to us higher up are further away - so, for instance, if you were painting a picture and wanted to imply that something was in the background, you would tend to make it smaller and higher up. A visual illusion which is thought to use this cue is known as the **Ponzo illusion**. This illusion happens because we are using our unconscious knowledge of depth cues, and think that the top line is further away, because it is higher up. Because that would mean that the more distant line seemed smaller than it really was, we unconsciously enlarge it and it seems longer than the lower line. This is the process of **constancy scaling** – using perceptual constancies to adjust what we see.

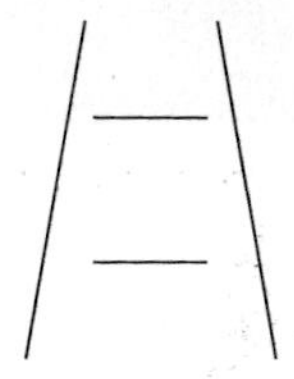

4.7 The Ponzo illusion

Superposition

A third monocular cue to depth is **superposition**. If something seems to be obscuring the view of something else then we tend to assume that it is in front, in other words that it is closer. The 'playing card illusion' works from this cue and can make the cards seem very different sizes purely because the cut-out corner is carefully positioned so that it looks as though the one that is further away is obscuring the nearer one.

Shadow

We often use **shadow** as a cue to depth. Light usually falls on things from above, so we will tend to use this as an indication of which way up something is, and shadows to the side often tell us about distance. Signwriters use shadows a lot when they are trying to give the impression that their painting is three-dimensional, so that their words or pictures seem to 'stand out' from the background.

Gradient of texture

Gradient of texture is another monocular depth cue. Things that are further away seem to be smoother, because we can see the detail and all the imperfections of things that are closer to us. A common experience is going on a picnic and, when you are trying to find somewhere to sit, finding that a bit of grass further on always seems to be a bit better - until you actually get to it. Then it's the next bit that seems smoother, and often you can end up walking quite a way before you finally give up, and settle for something that isn't quite perfect!

How many depth cues can you identify in this photograph?

Motion parallax

Another monocular depth cue is **motion parallax**. If we are moving, things which are closer to us seem to go past at a different rate than things which are further away, and things which are in the distance even seem to be moving along with us by comparison with nearby objects. The brain can often use that as an indication of how far away something is, in conjunction with the other depth cues that it has available.

Binocular disparity

The brain can also use binocular depth cues. Because our eyes see slightly different pictures of the world, the brain can use the **disparity** - the difference - between the two images to judge how far away things are. Try holding a pencil at arm's length and, with one eye closed, lining it up with an object in the distance. Then, without moving the pencil look at it with the other eye. You will find that the pencil image seems to have 'jumped' and isn't lined up properly any more. This is because your other eye receives a slightly different picture. If you try the same thing, but this time line the pencil up with something nearby, you will find that it seems to 'jump' even further. The brain compares the images from each eye and is able to tell how far away things are by the disparity between the two images.

Convergence

In addition to binocular disparity, the brain is able to judge distance by the **convergence** of the eye muscles. If we look at some particular thing, our eyes angle themselves so that both receive a full image of it. When we are looking at something a long way away, they don't have to angle towards each other much, but for close-up things the two eyes need to 'point' towards each other.

You can see this when you see children making their eyes go 'cross-eyed' (usually to their parents disapproval) by pointing a finger at their nose and bringing it in closer. The muscles of the eyes converge as the finger gets closer. This is another way that the brain can judge how far away something that we are looking at is.

We can see that there are several different mechanisms that we can use to judge distance. As we saw in the section on perceptual development, it may be that some of these mechanisms are inherited, but our depth perception certainly improves as we get older.

Visual illusions

Often, when we are studying how perception works, it is useful to look at the ways that it can go wrong, such as studying **visual illusions**. They can sometimes help us to understand just what sorts of cues the brain uses, to allow it to interpret the sensations that it receives through the visual system.

Psychology in Action

By now many of you will have seen films displayed on Cinema 2000 or Imax screens which give the onlooker the feeling of taking part in the action. Typically, such films might make you feel as though you are actually flying over open countryside or rafting over rapids, rather than merely watching a film of these activities. This effect is achieved by using very large, curved screens which extend beyond our normal visual field, so reducing other perceptual clues to our surroundings.

One of the most exciting recent developments in the computer industry has been the invention of virtual reality machines. These go one step further than large cinema screens. Participants receive little perceptual feedback from their environment other than what can be seen through the visor or heard through headphones. They enter a world of 3D computer graphics over which they have increasingly sophisticated control. Besides games, applications vary from the medical, where students can take a trip through the body and learn how it works, to the commercial, where an architect can show a potential buyer what a new office block will look like.

When we are trying to understand why visual illusions work, we find that they often involve the use of depth cues, but in an inappropriate way. Gregory, in 1963, argued that we interpret geometric illusions in the way that we do because of constancy scaling. By this, he means that we apply our perceptual constancies to the figures of the illusions, which results in an exaggerated view of what we are looking at. We have already mentioned his explanations of the Muller-Lyer illusion and the Ponzo illusion, and he considers that it is the inappropriate application of perceptual features, like size constancy (which uses all the depth cues), which produces these effects.

Moon illusion

Another visual illusion which is thought to work because of constancy scaling is known as the **moon illusion**. This is the way that the moon can seem very large when it is low down in the sky, but when it is higher up it seems to be its normal size. A study by Kaufman and Rock (1962) involved showing research participants artificial moons against different kinds of background. They found that the moon appeared to be its normal size when it was not close to any specific background - like when it is high up in the sky. But when there were other recognisable features (such as a horizon) near it, the moon seemed larger. It seemed that if the horizon looks to be a long way away, the perceived size of the moon is enlarged to allow for the extra distance. When the moon is high up in the sky, it doesn't seem to be as far away, and so is seen as its normal size. Next time you see an 'enlarged' moon, try looking at it through a small hole in a piece of paper, cutting out the background. This seems to make it 'shrink' back to its normal size.

Auditory information processing

Our possession of two frontally-mounted eyes allows us to judge depth by comparing the two visual images. In the same way, our two ears allow us to tell where particular sounds are coming from because our ears are located on different sides of the head. This means that a sound from a source over to the side will reach one ear a fraction of a second before the other. The brain detects these fractional differences and this allows us to tell the direction of the source of any particular sound.

4.2 Direction in hearing

To do this you will need at least two people, a blindfold, and something that will make a short, clear sound, preferably of the same volume each time. A bell would do.

Clear a space on the floor on which you can draw marks, and place a chair in the centre of it. Mark with chalk where someone's feet will be when they are sitting on the chair.

Draw straight lines out from there 2 m long in front, behind, and to the sides of that person. Do this so that the points make a circle.

One person should be blindfolded, and should sit on the chair with her feet on the chalk marks. Another person should, very quietly, move to one of the marks on the circle and make the signal sound, numbering that spot 1. Then the blindfolded person should point to the place where she thinks the sound is coming from.

Make another mark of 1 at the spot where the blindfolded person has pointed. Then try again from a different place, numbering it 2 this time. Make 10 test sounds in all, from all round the person in the chair.

When you have finished, note down the differences between the signal, and the person's answer. Then rub the numbers off the floor and test another person.

Which points seemed to be the most difficult? Did everyone find this?

What can we conclude from this about directionality in hearing?

N.B. Don't forget to clean the chalk off the floor when you've finished!

Some animals are extremely accurate in their abilities to judge direction of sounds. For instance, dogs can distinguish between sounds which are only 11 degrees apart, whereas human beings can usually only tell sounds which are about 45 degrees apart. The directions that we find easiest to identify are those which produce the greatest separation between the two ears: the hardest ones are those which reach both ears at exactly the same time, as they could be above or below the head, directly in front or directly behind, and still produce the same effect.

We can tell how far away a sound is mainly by how clearly we can distinguish the tones. Sounds which are coming from a source which is far away tend to sound muffled, because there is a phase shift in the sound waves as they travel long distances. Sounds from a source which is close to us tend to sound very much more crisp and clear.

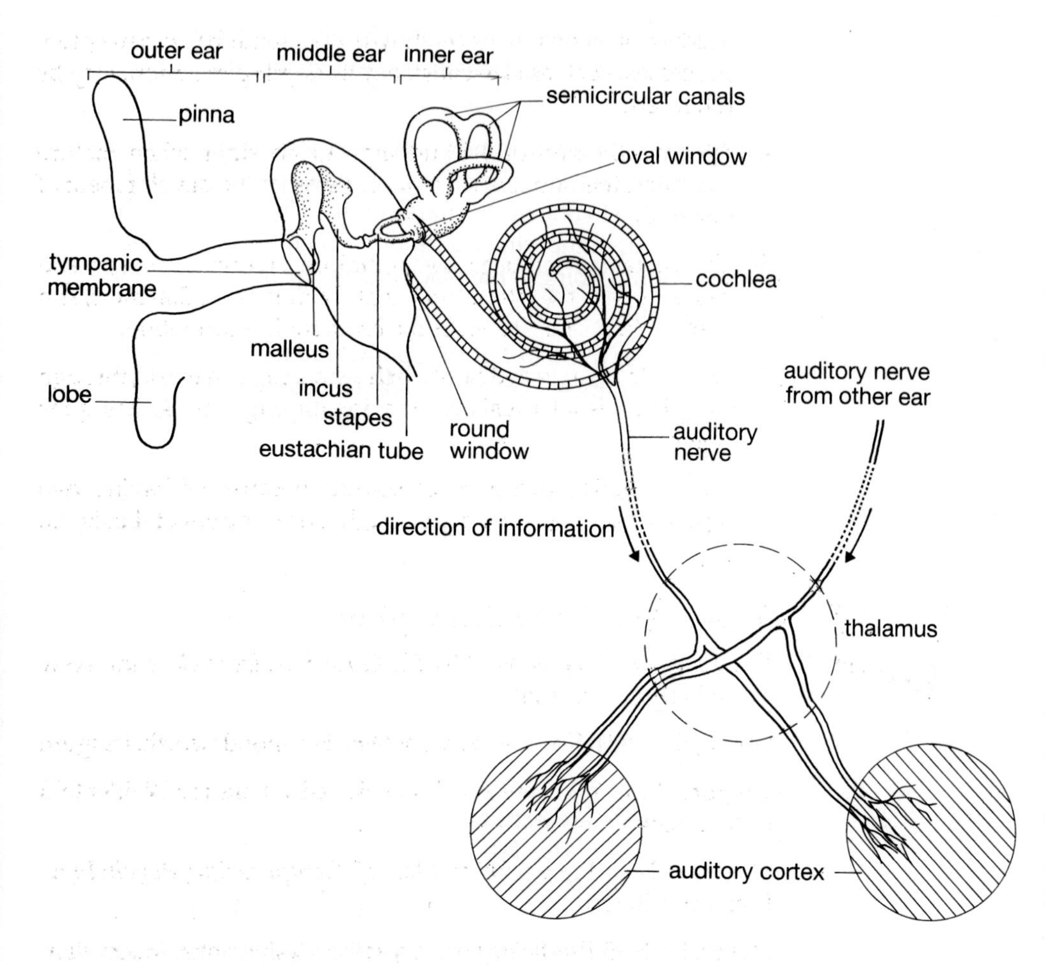

4.8 The auditory system

In Chapter 12, we will go on to look at some further aspects of perception, and in particular, how perception is an active process which can be influenced by our expectations and ideas. But first, in the next section of this book, we will look at how our physiology can influence our experience, starting with how the brain works. Then we will go on to look at some more specific examples of how what happens to us on a biological level can affect the experiences that we have.

Summary

1 Distortion and readjustment studies suggest that human perception is flexible, which suggests that it is probably not inherited.

2 Deprivation and cross-cultural studies emphasise the need for certain forms of experience in developing accurate perception.

3 Studies of neonates have shown that some basic perceptual processes, such as size constancy or depth perception, may be inherited.

4 An investigation of a blind man given sight when mature indicated the importance of motivation in the development of perception.

5 The visual system organises light information in the eye, and passes it on to the lateral geniculate bodies of the thalamus, and then to the visual cortex of the brain for interpretation.

6 We can learn a great deal about how perception works through studying visual illusions, and identifying why it has gone wrong.

7 We can judge direction of sounds because of having two separate ears, and distance through the fading out of the signal.

Suggestions for further reading

Gonick, L. & Wheelis, M. 1991 *The Cartoon Guide to Genetics.* New York: HarperPerennial.

Gould, S. J. 1981 *The Mismeasure of Man.* Harmondsworth: Penguin

Gregory, R. L. 1991 Eye and Brain. 4th edn. London: Weidenfeld & Nicholson

Hayes, N. 1993 *Principles of Comparative Psychology.* London:Erlbaum

Hayes, N. 1995 *Psychology in Perspective.* Basingstoke: Macmillan

Hayes, N. 1993 *A First Course in Psychology.* London: Nelson

Kamin, L. 1974 *The Science and Politics* of IQ. Harmondsworth: Penguin

Malim, T. 1994 *Cognitive Processes.* Basingstoke: Macmillan

Rose, S., Kamin, L. & Lewontin, R. C. 1984 *Not in our Genes.* Harmondsworth: Penguin

Walker, S. 1984 *Learning Theory and Behaviour Modification.* London: Methuen

?

Self Assessment Questions

1 **Empiricists:**

a) believe that our development is largely determined by the environment in which we live.

b) believe that our development is largely determined by the genes we inherit.

c) believe that our development is the result of an interaction between the genetic material we inherit and the environment in which we live.

d) are scientists involved in genetic engineering.

2 **Human beings possess:**

a) 23 pairs of chromosomes.

b) 2 pairs of chromosomes.

c) 21 pairs of chromosomes.

d) 23 pairs of genes.

3 **Each human egg or sperm cell contains:**

a) 12 chromosomes.

b) 23 chromosomes.

c) 23 pairs of chromosomes.

d) 23 pairs of genes.

4 **Down's syndrome babies possess:**

a) 2 extra chromosomes.

b) 1 extra chromosome.

c) 1 less chromosome.

d) the same number of chromosomes as non-Down's syndrome babies.

5 **Cloning occurs when:**

a) an organism is produced by two parents.

b) an organism loses one parent.

c) an organism is produced from one parent only.

d) a cell divides in two.

6 **One disadvantage with cloning is that:**

a) clones are very resistant to disease.

b) a clone is as likely to contract a disease as its parent.

c) clones have abnormal genes.

d) each organism can only be cloned once.

7 **In 1953 Tinbergen discovered that:**

a) the attack behaviour of sticklebacks was inherited.

b) the attack behaviour of sticklebacks had to be learned in early life.

c) the attack behaviour of sticklebacks was inherited but needed to be triggered off by a stimulus in the environment.

d) sticklebacks do not display attack behaviour.

8 **Species-specific behaviour is:**

a) behaviour peculiar to a specific species.

b) behaviour that is common to many species.

c) behaviour that is only demonstrated by mammals.

d) inherited behaviour.

9 A critical period refers to:

a) a period of time during which learning has to take place or it never will.

b) a special phase of language development.

c) a period of time during which an animal is most prepared for learning to take place but which may be extended so that the learning can take place later.

d) a period of stress.

10 Imprinting refers to:

a) the attachment of young animals to other animals or moving objects in their environment.

b) the learning of attack behaviour in young animals.

c) changing the message carried in our genes.

d) courtship behaviour among animals.

11 Classical conditioning was studied in depth by:

a) Ivan Pavlov in 1850.

b) Ivan Pavlov in 1911.

c) J. B. Watson in 1900.

d) Sigmund Freud.

12 Classical conditioning deals with:

a) involuntary responses.

b) involuntary responses and voluntary behaviour.

c) voluntary behaviour.

d) learning sets.

13 Generalisation occurs when:

a) an animal responds to a stimulus that is similar to the original conditioned stimulus.

b) an animal learns to discriminate between two stimuli.

c) an animal responds to stimuli that are very different from the original conditioned stimulus.

d) an animal develops a phobia.

14 Delayed conditioning occurs when:

a) the conditioned stimulus and unconditioned stimulus are presented at the same time.

b) the conditioned stimulus has been presented and stopped before the unconditioned stimulus is presented.

c) the conditioned stimulus commences first, is then followed by the unconditioned stimulus and they both end at the same time.

d) none of the above.

15 A reinforcer is:

a) something that strengthens behaviour or makes it more likely to occur again.

b) something that decreases the strength of a response or makes it less likely to occur again.

c) a punishment.

d) a positive response.

16 Which of the following is an example of a secondary reinforcer?

a) money.

b) food.

c) comfort.

d) all of the above.

17 Negative reinforcement occurs when:

a) something pleasant is given to an animal in order to get it to repeat an act.

b) something pleasant is taken away as a means of preventing an act from being repeated.

c) something unpleasant is removed in order to encourage an act to be repeated.

d) something unpleasant is given in order to stop an act being repeated.

18 Whilst working with chimps, Köhler found evidence of:

a) insight learning.

b) learning through reinforcement.

c) learning by trial and error.

d) cognitive maps.

19 'Latent learning' refers to:

a) learning that can be immediately observed in an animal's behaviour.

b) learning that has taken place but which lies dormant until a later period.

c) learning that only lasts for a very short period of time.

d) learning that takes a long time to instil.

20 'Spontaneous recovery' refers to:

a) a response that has died out.

b) the learning of a new response.

c) a response that has been extinguished but reappears at a later date.

d) insight learning in chimps.

21 Which of the following psychologists was among the first to develop a systematic way of measuring intelligence?

a) Arnold Gesell.

b) B. F. Skinner.

c) Alfred Binet.

d) J. B. Watson.

22 Genotype refers to:

a) all the genetic characteristics that we inherit.

b) only those genetic characteristics that can be seen to develop.

c) a person of inferior intelligence.

d) gifted children.

23 The statistics of Cyril Burt were used as evidence for:

a) intelligence being determined by the environment.

b) intelligence being due to an equal mixture of environmental factors and genetic inheritance.

c) intelligence being inherited.

d) identical twins being more intelligent than non-identical twins.

24 Monozygotic twins are more commonly known as:

a) identical twins.

b) non-identical twins.

c) fraternal twins.

d) none of the above.

25 Schizophrenic patients usually display:

a) a split personality.

b) several personalities.

c) a withdrawal from reality.

d) dyslexia.

26 According to Freud, "Thanatos" is:

a) a life force.

b) a destructive instinct.

c) a pleasure zone.

d) a stage of development.

27 Ethologists study:

a) animals in a laboratory.

b) groups of people.

c) behaviour in the natural habitat.

d) children.

28 The frustration-aggression hypothesis states that:

a) people are naturally aggressive.

b) frustration prevents aggression.

c) frustration serves to increase aggression.

d) people are naturally passive.

29 Appeasement gestures are:

a) signals to aggressors to stop their attack.

b) signals to continue fighting.

c) signals to attract a mate.

d) gestures of courtship.

30 While working with rats, Calhoun found that:

a) when overcrowded they co-operate with each other.

b) when overcrowded they become aroused.

c) when overcrowded they become more aggressive.

d) their behaviour does not alter when they become overcrowded.

31 A definition of perception would be:

a) a process that enables us to hear.

b) the interpretation of information that we receive through our senses.

c) the interpretation of visual information only.

d) communication by touch.

32 If people were unable to adapt to a different visual world we could conclude:

a) that human perception is largely inborn.

b) that human perception is largely learned.

c) that human perception involves an interaction between learning and innate abilities.

d) none of the above.

33 Von Senden found that on recovering their sight, his patients:

a) demonstrated excellent perception.

b) had very limited perceptual abilities.

c) possessed many basic perceptual abilities which needed further development.

d) could not see colours.

34 Fantz discovered that new-borns:

a) preferred plain figures to patterned ones.

b) were afraid of human faces.

c) preferred to look at patterned figures before plain.

d) preferred to look at lines rather than circles.

35 The cells in the retina:

a) reflect light.

b) change light energy into electrical impulses.

c) allow light to pass through them.

d) affect the colour of eyes.

36 Hubel and Wiesel discovered special cells in the brain which reacted to lines of different angles. These cells were in:

a) the hypothalamus.

b) the brain stem.

c) the thalamus and visual cortex.

d) the cerebellum.

37 Monocular cues to depth:

a) are cues that work just as well when we are looking at something with one eye as they do when we are looking with two eyes.

b) are cues that only work when looking at something with one eye.

c) are cues that only work when looking at something with two eyes.

d) are cues based on what we hear.

38 Retinal disparity refers to:

a) looking at the world through one eye only.

b) a detached retina.

c) the differences in the images produced by two eyes.

d) cross-cultural differences in perception.

39 In addition to monocular cues the brain is also able to judge depth and distance from:

a) pupil constriction.

b) the convergence of eye muscles.

c) texture and shadow.

d) auditory information.

40 Gregory argued that some visual illusions occur when:

a) we use depth cues that are inappropriate to a figure.

b) we fail to use depth cues.

c) we apply depth cues to a figure accurately.

d) none of the above.

Section 2 - Physiological psychology

In this section, we will be looking at the various ways in which our physiology can affect our behaviour and our experiences.

In order to do this, we will first look at the way that the human nervous system works, as this is the part of us which is responsible for co-ordinating and controlling what happens in the body. The human nervous system also includes the brain and we will be looking at this in detail: seeing which parts of the brain seem to influence different aspects of our behaviour and experience.

As we go through we will look at such aspects of our behaviour and experience as sleep, emotion, arousal and stress, motivation, memory, perception, sensory experiences, language and learning. With each of them we will look at some of the things that psychologists have discovered about the way that our physiology and our experience interrelate.

Chapter 5 - How the brain works

If we are to understand how our physiology can affect us, we need to look first at how the brain and the nervous system are organised.

We can divide the nervous system into roughly two main parts: the central nervous system and the peripheral nervous system. We will look at each of these in turn.

The nervous system

The central nervous system consists of the brain and the spinal cord. It is concerned with actions and reactions of the body to information which is received through the senses, and with co-ordinating other major functions of the body, such as eating, sleeping, waking, and so on. But it is also involved in more complex functions, such as memory, thinking and attention. Also, the brain makes important links with other systems of the body - in particular with the endocrine system, which releases hormones into the bloodstream and maintains different 'states' of the body, like pregnancy or anger. (Strictly speaking, pregnancy is a whole series of different 'states' of the body, rather than just one, but all of them involve the action of hormones in the bloodstream.)

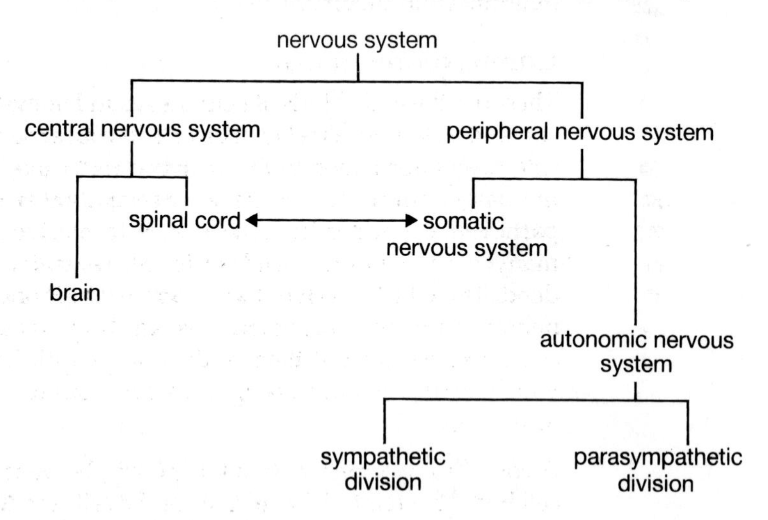

5.1 Divisions of the nervous system

The peripheral nervous system consists of two distinct parts: the somatic nervous system and the autonomic nervous system.

Somatic nervous system

The somatic nervous system is the network of fibres which the body has, bringing information to the central nervous system (CNS) from the senses of the body and passing information from the brain to the muscles. It consists of sensory neurones (carrying the information from the senses), and motor neurones (taking information to the muscles). So the fibres of the peripheral nervous system cover the entire body.

Autonomic nervous system

The autonomic nervous system, on the other hand, consists of fibres running from the lower part of the brain and the upper part of the spinal cord, to the internal organs of the body. It is particularly involved in the emotions, such as fear and stress. We can subdivide the autonomic nervous system (ANS) into two further parts: the sympathetic division, and the parasympathetic division. We will look at this more closely when we look at the emotions, in Chapter 6.

How nerve cells work

The nervous system is composed of millions of nerve cells, arranged into large structures in the brain, or in threadlike groups which form the nerves which run from the brain and spinal cord to all the parts of the body. In general, there are three main kinds of nerve cells **(neurones)**. These are: connector neurones, sensory neurones, and motor neurones.

Connector neurones

These are the main kinds of neurones found in the brain. They are sometimes known as relay neurones, because their main function is to relay information from one nerve cell to another - or, most of the time, from several neurones to several other neurones. Any particular connector neurone is able to receive messages from many other neurones, and so it has several branches, called dendrites, which reach out and form connections with the other neurones around. These dendrites can also pass messages to other cells, because each of them ends in a synaptic button, or knob, which is involved in passing messages from one neurone to the next.

A connector neurone looks a bit spidery, because it has a central cell body, containing the nucleus of the cell, and lots of dendrites branching out all around. (See Fig. 5.2)

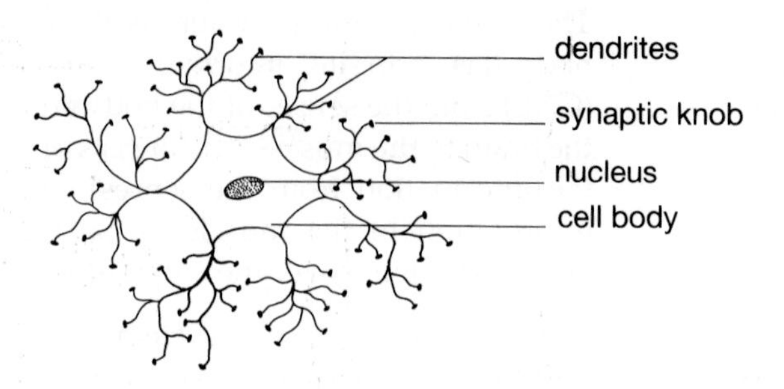

5.2 Connector neurone

Synapses

The way that all neurones (not just connector neurones) pass messages from one to the other is by *synaptic transmission*. This happens at the *synapse*, which is the gap in between the synaptic knob of the dendrite, and an area very close by on the dendrite of the next neurone, which is known as the *receptor site*. This site is particularly sensitive to chemical changes in the fluid between the neurones. When the synaptic knob is activated it releases a chemical, known as a neurotransmitter, into this gap, which is then picked up at the receptor site of the next neurone. The chemical causes a change to happen in the cell membrane which can work in two ways. Either it will make the cell membrane more receptive to sodium ions outside the cell, so they enter and cause the cell to fire, or it will make the cell membrane more receptive to sodium ions, so that it is much less likely to fire.

When we talk about a nerve cell 'firing', we mean that it is producing an electrical impulse. If a neurone's cell membrane allows sodium ions to pass into the cell, these act with the potassium ions inside the cell to produce a rapid burst of electricity. Until quite recently, it was thought that this electrical impulse was always the same strength, but some recent research seems to indicate that neurones can fire at different strengths in response to different strengths of stimulus. Producing and transmitting electrical impulses like this is the way that the nervous system works and there have been various methods developed, through electrical stimulation or recording the electrical activity of the brain, which allow us to study these workings.

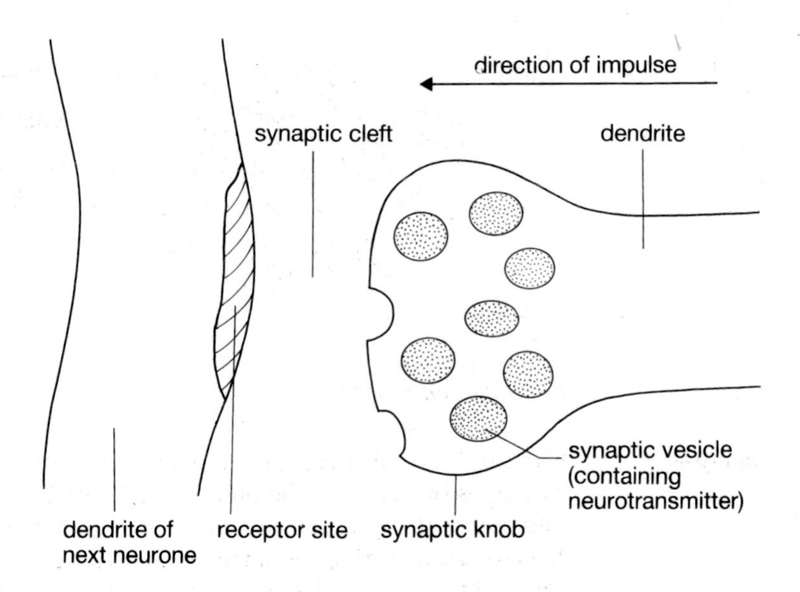

5.3 The synapse

Synapses which make a neurone more likely to fire are known as **excitatory synapses**, while those which make a neurone less likely to fire are known as **inhibitory synapses**. A neurone is not really very likely to fire, though, if it only receives an excitatory signal from one other nerve cell. It has what is called a **threshold of response**, which is a certain minimum amount of stimulation (by neurotransmitters at receptor sites) that it must have before it will fire. If enough neurones stimulate it, then the total amount of stimulation will exceed the threshold, and the neurone will fire. This process is known as **summation**.

After a nerve cell has just fired, there is a period of time when it will not fire again. This is very short - just a couple of milliseconds – but during this period no amount of stimulation will be enough. This period is known as the **absolute refractory period**. Once the absolute refractory period is over, there is another short time before it returns to normal. This is known as the **relative refractory period.** During this time, only a very strong stimulus, such that the cell is receiving impulses from a very large number of other neurones, will cause the cell to fire. In other words, the cell's threshold of response is very much higher than normal.

Sensory neurones

In addition to connector neurones, the nervous system has a network of **sensory neurones**, which pick up information from the sense organs of the body, and take it to the central nervous system – the brain and spinal cord. The sense organs of the body can pick up roughly five different kinds of information from the outside world - what we know as our five senses: touch, taste, smell, hearing, and sight. The sense receptors for each of these senses are very different, because the kind of information which is coming in is different: for the visual sense, information arrives in the form of light, and so we have special sense receptors in the eye for detecting light; for hearing, the information arrives in the form of sound waves; while for taste it is chemicals which are in contact with the tongue. Each of these need a different form of equipment to detect the information, but what they will all have in common is **transduction**. The role of all the sense receptors is to transduce (alter) the incoming information to a form that the brain can understand. Since the brain consists of a mass of nerve cells which work by passing electrical impulses from one to another, this means that the sense receptors must change the incoming information they receive into electrical impulses and code them in such a way that the brain can interpret the message which is being sent.

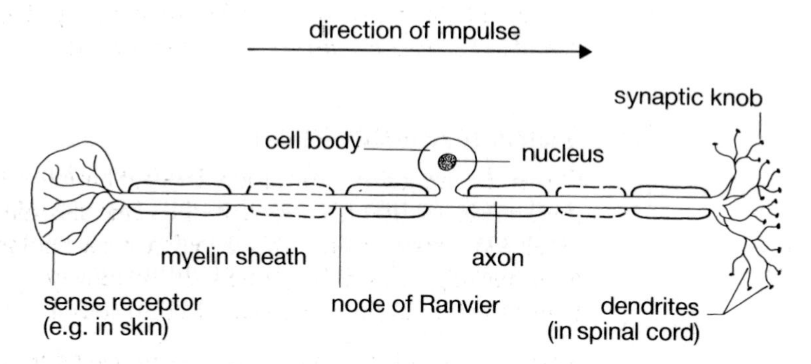

5.4 Sensory neurone

Coding sensory information

Not every message will be the same, so if the sense receptors and the sensory neurones sent exactly the same message whenever they received any stimulation, the brain would not be able to tell the difference between different bits of information. Imagine only being able to tell that there was a sound but not how loud it was, or what tone it was, or even how many different sounds were taking place at a time! Since the sensory neurones, by and large, do seem to work in the 'all-or-none' manner (that is, either they fire or they do not, the impulse does not vary in strength), this means that they need a kind of code, so that the brain can tell the difference. Rather than trying to took at all the senses, we will look at the way that the auditory neurones code information from sounds.

Sound waves carry two main kinds of information: loudness (or **intensity**), and pitch (or **frequency**). To indicate to the brain how loud a sound is, the sensory neurones use the number of neurones firing. Quite simply, loud sounds cause more neurones to fire, so the brain knows that the more neurones firing, the louder the sound. Even though the signal itself does not vary, the brain is informed about the intensity of the information being received by the sense receptor.

The way that the pitch of a sound is transmitted to the brain is different: and although it has parallels with the other senses, it is not exactly the same as them. The pitch, or frequency of a sound, is sometimes coded by which particular sensory cells are stimulated: different cells in the ear are sensitive to different pitches.

For lower frequencies all the cells are stimulated, and the brain has to use a different system. It does this by using the rate of response. Tones of, say, 500 kH will produce messages sent to the brain at the rate of 500 per second; while a tone of, say, 2,000 kH results in messages sent at the rate of 2,000 per second.

5.1 Visual after-effects

One interesting thing to explore is what happens to our visual perception when it is faced with the same stimulation for an extended period of time. If we look at a particular colour for a long period, we find that, when we look away and on to a blank sheet of paper, we see a different colour.

First, try exploring which colours produce which after-effects. Collect a number of brightly-coloured objects or pieces of coloured paper, and try them out. Each time, have the colour that you are going to look at (the stimulus colour) ready, and also a blank piece of white paper. Look at the stimulus colour for a period of two or three minutes, without taking your eyes off it. (You may find that you need to ask someone to time you on this, or you may be able to use a kitchen timer if you have one.) When the time is up, immediately transfer your gaze to the blank paper. The after-image will appear within a couple of seconds.

Note down what colour the after-image was, and also what you first saw on looking away from the stimulus material. When your eyes have rested, try it again with a different stimulus colour.

Make a chart of the colours you have looked at and their after-effects.

Now see what happens when you look at two contrasting colours together. Try, for instance, a strip of maroon against a turquoise background, or any other combination that you feel like looking at. When you have got some interesting ones, try them out on your friends, and see if they experience the same after-effects as you did.

What explanations can you offer for what you have found?

The volley principle

As mentioned before, though, there is a limit to how rapidly a neurone can fire, because after firing it has to go through the absolute and relative refractory periods. If each neurone is firing very rapidly indeed, then the brain 'knows' that the stimulus (the sound) must be a certain frequency, because it has overcome the high threshold of response of the relative refractory period. But during the absolute refractory period, the neurone will not fire at all, so, if that were all, we would not be able to tell when the frequency was any higher than that indicated by the maximum firing of one cell.

However, if the stimulus does need more rapid firing the brain is able to receive the signals even more rapidly, because the neurones fire in volleys, 'taking it in turns' to fire. While one set of neurones is going through the absolute refractory period, another set is firing and the brain is receiving the signals far more rapidly than any one cell could send them. It seems that this 'code' – the volley principle – operates for almost all sensory information, no matter what kind, but that the particular information which is transmitted will depend on which senses are involved.

Once the information has been transduced into a form that the brain can understand, it must be transmitted to the central nervous system. Sensory neurones have a particular structure that enables them to do this very efficiently (Fig. 5.4).

Sensory neurone structure

Each sensory neurone has a very long 'stem', which stretches from the sense receptor all the way to the brain or spinal cord. Somewhere along the 'stem' (it is different for different neurones), is the cell body, which contains the cell nucleus. The part of the 'stem' before the cell body is known as the dendron, but the part after the cell body is known as the **axon**. However, for convenience, we will refer to the stem as the axon throughout this text from now on.

A typical sensory neurone will pick up the message, say, from the skin, and transduce it into an electrical impulse. The message then passes along the axon to the other end where the axon branches out into several small dendrites. Each dendrite ends in a synaptic knob, which forms a synapse with another cell (usually a connector neurone) in the brain or spinal cord. The axons of sensory neurones are normally myelinated, which means that the message travels very rapidly along the axon. This allows the brain to respond to incoming information as quickly as possible.

Motor neurones

It is the job of the motor neurone to take messages from the brain or spinal cord to the muscles of the body. This results in movement, which is why they are called 'motor' neurones.

Each motor neurone has its cell body in the brain or spinal cord, and it is surrounded by dendrites which make connections with other cells (usually connector neurones). From there, a long myelinated axon leads to a muscle fibre. At that point, the axon fans out to become what is called the motor end-plate - the place where a chemical message is passed from the neurone to the muscle. Once the message has been passed on, that muscle fibre contracts. If this happens with enough motor neurones, the whole muscle will contract and that part of the body will move (Fig. 5.5).

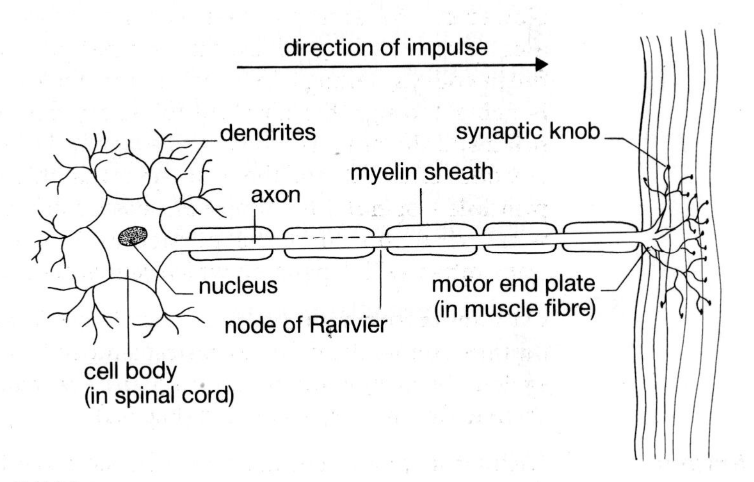

5.5 Motor neurone

Myelin sheaths

The axons of both motor neurones and sensory neurones are covered with a *myelin sheath* of Schwann cells. This is a coating which is formed from fatty cells which wrap themselves around the axon, forming an insulating cover. This in turn means that the chemical change of ionic transfer between sodium and potassium ions through the outer membrane, which produces the electrical impulse, cannot happen. Instead, it has to take place at the gaps between Schwann cells, which are called **Nodes of Ranvier**. Because the impulse is only generated at the Node of Ranvier, instead of continuing along the axon, it travels in large jumps, from one Node of Ranvier to another. This means that an electrical impulse can travel more quickly along a myelinated axon than along an unmyelinated one. In the case of motor neurones, we often find that we need to move very quickly, so a myelinated axon is a definite advantage. **Multiple sclerosis** is a brain disease which results in neurones being gradually stripped of their myelin sheaths. Nobody understands quite why this happens, but the result is a progressive degeneration in the individual's ability to control and co-ordinate their movements and actions.

The reflex arc

One of the simplest ways that neurones may link together is known as the reflex arc. It would happen, for instance, if you were to touch a hot surface: the message would be picked up by sense receptors in the skin and passed quickly along myelinated nerve fibres to the spinal cord by means of sensory neurones. In the spinal cord, the message would be passed to a connector neurone, which would do two things. It would pass the message straight on to the motor neurones, which would send the message to the motor endplate causing your muscle to contract and pull your hand away. But also, the connector neurone would send a message up the spinal cord to the brain, so that you knew what you had done. The reflex arc itself, though, is the sequence formed by the sensory neurone - connector neurone - motor neurone messages. You can see from this example why it is a good idea that motor and sensory neurones are myelinated and can pass the messages on fast. Otherwise, you might have been badly burned before you pulled your hand away.

5.2 Studying reaction time

For this investigation, you will need a reaction-time ruler. If you haven't got one, then you will need either a metre ruler, or a piece of very stiff card or smooth wood about 1m long and 5cm wide.

The purpose of this study is to investigate reaction time: how quickly someone can respond to a signal. There are lots of different aspects to reaction time that you can investigate once you know how. For instance, as you will find in Chapter 8, different sides of the brain control different sides of the body. The left side of the brain controls the right side of the body, and vice versa. You could investigate which side of your brain provides the quicker reaction, by comparing reaction time for your right and left hands.

Reaction time can be measured by dropping a ruler, without warning, so that it falls from above, down between someone's thumb and forefinger; and seeing how long it takes them to close their fingers and catch the ruler. Some schools and colleges are lucky enough to have electrical reaction timers, which involve an apparatus where you have to press a button when a light comes on, or a tone sounds. But a metre ruler will do as a substitute.

By measuring how far the ruler has dropped (by how far along it the person's thumb and forefinger are), you can see how quickly they have reacted. A fast reaction will mean that the ruler hasn't fallen very far and a slow one will mean that it has fallen almost to its whole length. A very slow one, of course, will miss the ruler altogether, but as long as you have a ruler which is at least 1m long, everyone should be able to catch it sometimes.

Try measuring your reaction time several times. (Remembering that someone else has to drop the ruler for you!) Is it the same or different each time? Does it improve with practice?

What other studies which use reaction time can you think of?

Neurotransmitters

We mentioned before that the way that a neurone passes its message to the next neurone along the chain is by releasing a chemical into the *synaptic cleft* - the gap between the synaptic button and the receptor site on the next neurone. Each receptor site is sensitive only to certain kinds of molecules, rather like a 'key and lock' system.

There are many different neurotransmitters, each of which are seen to have different roles within the nervous system. Some of the best known ones are: noradrenaline (called norepinephrine in the USA), dopamine, serotonin (which used to be called 5-hydroxytryptamine), acetylcholine and enkephalin. We will describe very briefly a little of what is known about each of these. It must be remembered, though, that there are at least twenty different substances which act as neurotransmitters in the brain, and that we are very far from understanding what all of them do. Even with these well-known ones, our understanding is relatively limited by comparison with the very complicated ways in which synapses work.

Acetylcholine

Acetylcholine is the neurotransmitter which is found at the motor end-plate. It is the chemical which is involved when the brain passes a message to the muscles to tell them to move. Some military nerve gases operate by destroying the enzyme which breaks down the acetylcholine after it has been released into the synaptic cleft. This means that the acetylcholine remains and builds up, ending in the muscles being over-stimulated, which causes people to lose control of the body.

Nicotine, on the other hand, works by getting picked up by the receptor site, which means that the acetylcholine message is partly blocked. This means that when the brain sends a message to the muscles to move, only part of the message gets through - which is why smoking too much can make you feel very 'sluggish'. People who give up smoking often find that they get very restless and fidgety. This is because the motor end-plate is no longer blocked by the nicotine and all the message is getting through to their muscles, so that they become far more active than they were before. If you are planning on giving up cigarettes, you should be aware of this and save up plenty of active things that you can do while you adjust to having this extra energy!

The poison curare can work in a similar kind of way, but with a very much more dramatic effect. This is a paralysing poison that some South American Indian tribes use in blowpipes for hunting. Curare is picked up by acetylcholine receptor sites, causing the animal or human to become paralysed, so that it dies from suffocation. If an individual is paralysed with curare, they can be kept alive until the effects wear off by artificial respiration. The paralysing effect, though, is caused by the curare 'filling up' the acetylcholine receptor sites, so that there is no 'room' left for the acetylcholine to pass the message from the brain to the muscles.

Dopamine

Another well-known neurotransmitter is called **dopamine**. People who suffer from Parkinson's Disease often find that their symptoms can be relieved by a substance known as L-dopa, which builds up dopamine levels in the brain. Many of the psychoactive drugs which are prescribed for psychiatric use also affect dopamine levels, which suggests that this particular neurotransmitter may be involved somehow in psychiatric disturbance. The tranquilliser chlorpromazine (Largactil) seems to work by blocking dopamine receptors, while amphetamines seem to increase the levels of dopamine and noradrenaline in the brain.

Noradrenaline

Noradrenaline seems to be very involved in certain 'moods'. It is one of the main neurotransmitters of the autonomic nervous system, which we will discuss more thoroughly when we look at emotion. In addition, the drugs cannabis and cocaine seem to have their effect by increasing the noradrenaline levels in the brain, while sedatives such as alcohol and barbiturates reduce the overall levels of noradrenaline.

Serotonin

The hallucinogenic drugs LSD and psilocybin appear to work by being picked up in the receptor sites which are normally used for the neurotransmitter **serotonin**. The opiates heroin and morphine seem to have their effect because they have a similar chemical structure to the naturally occurring painkillers known as

endorphins and **enkephalins** which the brain produces in response to injury or exercise, and so they can be picked up by the same receptor sites.

Psychology in Action

An imbalance of certain neurotransmitters can be the cause of behavioural dysfunction. A tragic example is that of Alzheimer's disease. This is a brain disorder resulting in loss of memory which manifests itself in a decreasing ability to perform everyday tasks and is often accompanied by a change in personality. This disorder has been linked to a loss of cholinergic neurones (neurones that use acetylcholine to transmit information) in the basal forebrain. There is an increasing amount of evidence that suggests that aluminium - from drinking water or other sources - is involved in Alzheimer's disease in some way.

The artificial stimulation of cholinergic neurones with drugs that simulate acetylcholine has been shown to aid memory processes and so slow down the rate of deterioration. However, there is currently no drug available that can reverse the effects of Alzheimer's disease.

Although this is only a brief look at the effects of some of the main neurotransmitters, you can see from this that they can have quite dramatic and interesting effects. We will look at some of these effects more closely in the section on drugs in Chapter 7. Different moods, feelings, and emotions may have their chemical correlates in the brain. However, we need to be very wary of concluding that this therefore shows that these moods are actually caused by the chemicals. It could just as well be the case, that the chemicals are produced in response to specific environmental causes, and if we just think in biological **reductionist** terms (trying to reduce feelings down to the action of neurones alone), we are likely to miss out on a whole host of other influencing factors, as we saw in Chapter 3. What people do is always complicated, and can be understood on many different levels: biological, social, cognitive, or economic, to name but a few. It would be foolish to try to explain everything just in terms of one level of explanation alone.

The structure of the brain

Within the brain itself, neurones are grouped together into many different structures, each of which seems to be involved in different functions of the organism. If we dissect a human brain, we can see that it is organised into different sections. If we examine people who have suffered brain injuries or strokes, it is possible to connect the behavioural changes with damage to particular sections. But we cannot really conclude from this that one particular structure *causes* one particular behaviour. The central nervous system works as a *system*, not as just a collection of different mechanisms.

For example, if you cut through the wire that leads from a door to the bell in the hallway, the doorbell will not work when you press the bell-push. But that does not mean the wire *causes* the bell to ring. What makes the bell ring is the whole system, of bell-push, wire, bell and battery working together. It is the same with the brain. Just finding that damage to one part causes problems with a certain form of behaviour does not tell us that that part *causes* that behaviour - it just tells us that it is involved, somehow, in that behaviour happening. It is very important that we do not make the mistake of thinking that the brain operates as a simple kind of machine, with one bit causing one effect, because it really seems to be much more complicated than that. Different parts of the brain work together, in systems and sub-systems, to produce certain effects - and often they are also influenced by what is happening in the rest of the body as well. Because of this, when we are talking about a part of the brain being strongly involved in a particular kind of behaviour, we prefer to say that the part *mediates* the behaviour, not that it causes it.

Ethical discussion

Studies of brain functioning have often involved the removal or destruction of part of the brain of a living animal. The animal is then observed and tested, to identify what the consequences of the operation have been. This type of research is an example of vivisection: operating on a living animal to discover how physiological mechanisms work.

Scientists who use vivisection argue that it is necessary to use animals in this way, in order to discover how physiological mechanisms work, and because it would be unethical to perform such studies using humans.

Those who oppose vivisection argue that this type of research is (a) cruel and (b) unnecessary, and that there are other ways of obtaining equivalent information. What do you think?

Brain evolution

If we look at the brain in detail, and at the kinds of functions which each part mediates, we can see that there is a kind of progression in how complex or highly-developed the functions are, as we move higher up and further away from the spinal cord. The earliest nervous systems that evolved in animals were simply fibres which spread out from a 'neural tube' in the centre, to the outer parts of the organism. These allowed the organism to become informed about different things in the environment: such as a painful stimulus, or an extreme temperature. Gradually, as organisms evolved and became more complicated, they became able to receive more complex forms of information and also to react to them in more complicated kinds of ways. Also the organisms became more physically sophisticated and it was necessary for them to develop systems for co-ordinating different bodily functions. For instance the digestion of different kinds of food needed different chemicals to break them down, and the substances being carried around the bloodstream needed regulating and balancing. As all this happened, the front part of the neural tube became enlarged and developed, and different parts of it developed different functions.

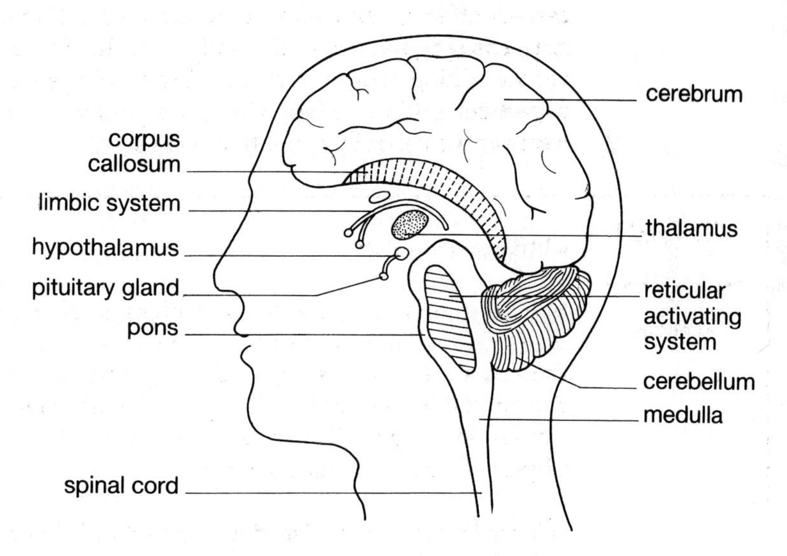

5.6 Structures of the brain

Progressing from the spinal cord upwards, the different parts of the brain and the functions which they mediate are roughly as follows:

The spinal cord

This passes nerve fibres up and down the body to and from the brain itself. Sensory and motor neurones leave the spinal cord at various places and pass to the skin and the muscles. The spinal cord also mediates the most basic of the organism's reactions which are reflexes, usually (although not always) concerned with the avoidance of pain. The kind of reaction we normally give to being pricked with a pin is a spinal reflex - it doesn't have to pass to the brain at all.

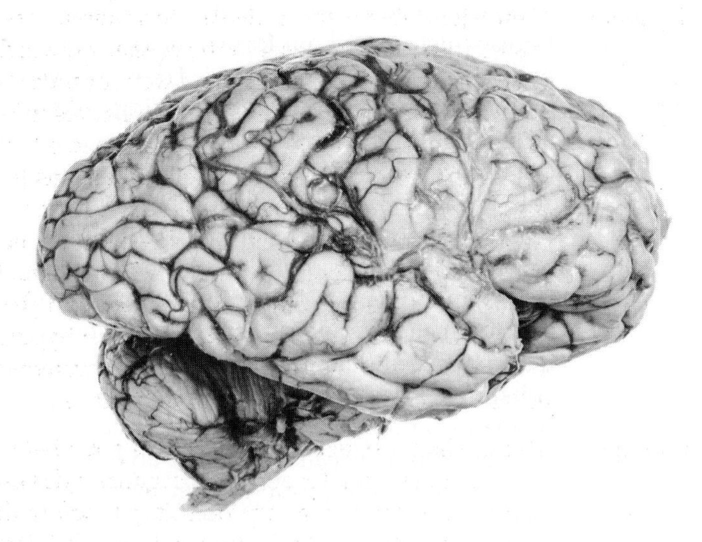

A human brain

The brain stem, or medulla

This receives neural impulses from the autonomic nervous system, such as from the stomach. It is the part of the brain which regulates the chemistry of digestion, heart rate, breathing and other such 'automatic' functions. Through the autonomic nervous system, it is also involved in basic arousal and emotional states of the body, although not the more complicated forms of emotions as far as we can tell.

The cerebellum

This is a largish structure which protrudes from the medulla and which is responsible for such functions as co-ordinating body balance and voluntary (deliberate) movements. It receives information from the kinaesthetic sense receptors about the position of limbs and muscles, and also from the balance organs in the inner ear.

The pons

This is a swelling just above the medulla, which consists of fibres which join the two halves of the cerebellum. It seems possible that the pons is involved in the functions of sleep and dreaming, but as these are also mediated by other areas of the brain, it is not very easy to identify exactly what its role is.

The reticular formation

The pons and reticular formation together form a part of the brain which is often known as the midbrain. The reticular formation is found above the pons, and is also involved in the functions of sleep, dreaming and attention. In fact, it seems to act as one of the main 'switching' mechanisms for the brain when we become more or less alert.

The hypothalamus

This is a relatively small but very important structure which is found just above the reticular formation. Its main role is in maintaining **homeostasis** in the organism, which means keeping the organism roughly in the same state, despite changes in external circumstances. The hypothalamus receives information from all over the body, and if one of the many states of the body is out of balance, it will set off correcting mechanisms to put it right. For instance, if the blood sugar level falls below a certain point, the hypothalamus will trigger off feelings of hunger in the organism, so that it will seek food to restore the blood-sugar level in the body; or if the body's temperature falls too low it will instigate shivering, as a way of warming the body up. The hypothalamus keeps a general check on the way that the body's systems are working, and acts to correct it if things get out of balance.

The thalamus

This is a larger structure, above the hypothalamus, which receives information from all the sensory organs, and is involved in sorting out that information and processing it, before the information is passed on to the cerebral cortex, where it is interpreted and acted upon. One area of the thalamus - the lateral geniculate nuclei - deals with visual information. Another area deals with auditory information, decoding it and sorting out the mass of information which has been received by those sense receptors. In this way, the thalamus acts as a kind of 'relay station' for sensory information on its way to the cerebrum.

The limbic system

This is not really a structure as such but a general name which is given to a whole set of small structures which are found around the thalamus and hypothalamus. Different parts of the limbic system seem to be involved in different things. One part, known as the hippocampus, seems to be involved in memory, while another part, the septum, may be involved in aggressive behaviour and emotion.

The pituitary gland

In addition to the major brain structures which are composed of neurones, the brain also contains two extremely important glands, which are part of the endocrine system of the body. These release hormones into the bloodstream, and are very important in mediating and maintaining 'states' of the body, like emotions, or pregnancy - anything which lasts for a while. Because the endocrine system works closely with the central nervous system, its main gland is found very close to the hypothalamus in the brain, and receives information directly from it.

The pituitary sends messages to the other glands in the body, and acts as a kind of 'main control' for the endocrine system.

The pineal gland

Another important gland which is situated in the middle of the brain is the pineal gland. We are only just beginning to learn about how this gland works and what its functions are. It seems, though, to be very actively involved in body rhythms, both circadian ones (24 hour rhythms) and seasonal ones.

The cerebrum

All of the parts of the brain that we have described so far are known as the **sub-cortical structures**, because they are found below the cerebral cortex. But it is the uppermost structure, the cerebrum, which is by far the largest and most important in the human brain, and it is this which makes human beings able to perform those feats which distinguish us from other species (such as our ability to learn and remember new information rapidly, or to discuss abstract features of the environment). In human beings, the cerebrum is a comparatively massive structure, which spreads over all the rest of the brain, and it is responsible for a whole host of functions: sense perception; memory and learning; directing bodily movement; language; emotions; and especially consciousness. Occasionally, babies are born who have no cerebrum - known as anecenphalic children. Although they can survive for the first couple of months of life, because they have the structures which are necessary for basic life, they do not learn new things, and they never really become aware of their surroundings at all. As they grow, and their needs become more complex, they become unable to survive, and so they rarely reach more than four months of age.

Many psychologists refer to the cerebrum simply as the 'brain', because it is such an essential part of the brain for the human being. And, although we are aware that the sub-cortical structures are important, it is the cerebrum which is most interesting for a psychologist.

The cerebral hemispheres

The cerebrum is split into two halves, which are joined in the middle by a band of fibres known as the corpus callosum. These two halves are sometimes called the **cerebral hemispheres**, because they are rounded in shape. For convenience, we divide each cerebral hemisphere into four lobes: the frontal lobe, the parietal lobe, the occipital lobe, and the temporal lobe. This allows us to describe more clearly just whereabouts on the cerebrum a particular part may be found. Because it is the outer 'skin', or cortex, which seems to do most of the work of the cerebrum (underneath the cortex is a mass of fibres carrying information from one part of the cortex to another), we sometimes refer to the whole of the cerebrum just as the **cortex**, or even the **neocortex**.

('Neo' means 'new', and this term is describing the way that the enlarged cerebral cortex is a recently evolved part of the brain.)

In the rest of this section, we will look at some of the aspects of our experience which link directly with our knowledge of how the brain works. However, it must be emphasised that we are a very long way indeed from understanding everything about the brain, or about exactly how our experience and our knowledge of brain processes link together. All that we have so far is a set of tantalising hints, which always seem to be telling us that it is very much more complicated than we thought!

Summary

1. The nervous system can be divided into the central and peripheral nervous systems. The central nervous system consists of the brain and the spinal cord; the peripheral nervous system consists of the somatic and autonomic nervous systems.
2. There are three main types of neurones: connector neurones, sensory neurones, and motor neurones. Together these form the *reflex arc*.
3. Neurones connect by means of synapses. Neurotransmitters are chemicals which pass messages from one neurone to another. Different neurotransmitters have different effects.
4. The brain works by electrical messages being passed from one neurone to another. Information is coded so that the brain can interpret the information which it receives from the sensory cells.
5. There are different structures in the brain itself, which mediate different functions. The oldest part of the brain consists of the medulla, cerebellum, pons, and the reticular formation.
6. The middle part of the brain consists of the thalamus, limbic system, and hypothalamus. It mediates slightly more sophisticated functions than the older part.
7. The most recent part of the brain is the cerebrum, which mediates cognitive processes.

Chapter 6 - Emotion and arousal

One of the important functions which is controlled, or mediated, by the medulla, is that of emotional states. In the same way as we can be alert or sleepy, we can be aroused or calm and these states represent different ways of dealing with situations. In a sense, they are 'states of preparedness' which the body has, so that it can deal more effectively with anything unusual which happens. If we are alert, for instance, we are ready to notice anything unusual and to think about what it might be. If we are anxious, we identify worrying things or problems which might arise more easily. If we are frightened, we are ready to run away if things get dangerous.

Arousal

The alarm reaction

In 1920, Walter Cannon investigated how the body changes when we are ready to react, that is when we are highly aroused, either by anger or by fear. In a series of imaginative investigations, which included asking his research participants to swallow a balloon which he could then inflate to measure their stomach contractions, he identified a whole range of physiological changes. These changes operated together to form what he called the **emergency reaction**, or the **alarm reaction**. They form a *syndrome*, or a whole collection of different symptoms which work together to produce a result. The result which is produced, Cannon called the **fight or flight response**, because its effect is to produce a great deal of energy at very short notice which allows the person either to run away from the alarming stimulus, or to attack it. In both these situations, the body will need a great deal of energy if it is to be successful and the alarm reaction provides that. Other animals show the alarm reaction too. In fact, it seems to be a very fundamental survival process which evolved in mammals quite early on.

If we look at the alarm reaction in detail, we can see that it involves quite a few complex changes in the body. To be able to use our energy effectively, we need to get a good blood supply to the muscles, and many of the changes are concerned with that. The heart beats faster, blood pressure increases, and more blood is directed to the muscles than usual, leaving less going to the visceral organs like the stomach and liver. We also need to have a high blood-sugar level, which gives us the 'fuel' for our energy, and many of the changes in the 'fight or flight' reaction provide that. Stored sugar is released into the bloodstream, and sugars are digested very rapidly while long-term digestion of other kinds of foods is delayed; our saliva changes, becoming very enzyme-rich (again so that sugars can be digested quickly), but also becoming quite thick which can make the mouth feel very dry. As well as sugar, we need plenty of oxygen in the blood for energy and so during the emergency reaction we breathe more deeply and more rapidly. There are many other changes which form the alarm reaction such as the blood changing so that it will form clots more quickly; or the pupils of the eye dilating; or the **pilomotor response** (hair standing on end) which in humans only shows up as 'goose-pimples', but which can produce quite a dramatic and alarming change in an animal's appearance as anyone who has seen a frightened cat will know. All of these small changes happen together to form a collection of responses to a dangerous situation, which increase our chances of emerging from that situation reasonably safely.

For most modern sorts of danger, though, we are not really expected to react physically by fighting or fleeing, and so the alarm reaction can be inappropriate. You will know this if you have been in a car which has just missed an accident. A couple of seconds after the danger has passed the reaction comes on, but there is no need for any physical movement at all, so you just sit and feel 'edgy' and anxious. The body has generated all that energy, but with many modern dangers the threat is over before any of it could be at all useful. One reason why people with stressful jobs are healthier if they take regular exercise may be because the exercise is enabling them to 'work off' some of the physical energy that the stresses of their job will have brought on in the form of the alarm reaction.

The General Adaptation Syndrome

In 1946, Selye investigated how the alarm response altered when animals experienced continuous stress, rather than just one or two sudden shocks. He found that there was a long-term adaptation which the body made to stress, which became known as the General Adaptation Syndrome, or GAS. In this, the body continues to produce very high levels of **adrenaline** (which is the hormone that keeps the emergency reaction going in the body) and is easily startled into an emergency reaction, but most of the time, the very active symptoms of the alarm reaction have died down. The person appears outwardly calm but isn't really. A later study, by Solomon (1963), showed that this long-term adaptation to stress seriously affected the body's immune system, so that individuals under long-term stress were far less resistant to disease and illness.

Measuring emotional responses

There are several different ways that we can measure emotional reactions in the body. As we have seen, emotional responses are collections of different responses, which happen together.

Although many of them are changes which we cannot observe directly, some of them can be measured. **GSR (Galvanic Skin Resistance)**, is one way of measuring emotional reaction. When we are alarmed or stressed, we sweat slightly more than usual. Sensitive electrodes on the skin can detect this, because the electrical resistance of the skin will go down if we sweat more. Also, changes in the amount of sweat in the skin happen more or less instantly, so we can tell when something is making us tense. Many **biofeedback** machines work like this, using a noise to signal to the individual when they are becoming tense so that they can see how effective their relaxation exercises are. Pulse meters and blood pressure meters can be used in the same way, and so can heart-rate monitors.

Some machines involve all of these, measuring GSR, heart and pulse rate, blood pressure, etc. at the same time. These are known as **polygraphs**, and are sometimes used as 'lie-detectors'. As we have seen, though, what is being detected is anxiety, or mild versions of the alarm reaction. Most people are anxious when they tell a lie, and so it will show on the 'lie-detector', but other, truthful answers may be just as stressful and someone who could be totally relaxed while lying would never be detected. **Voice Stress Analysers** work by detecting small tremors which have been suppressed in a person's voice when they are under stress. They too are sometimes used as 'lie-detectors', but are not very effective for the same reasons.

The autonomic nervous system

Despite their shortcomings for lie-detecting, though, these machines have been extremely useful in allowing psychologists to investigate emotional responses and how they happen. All these changes are caused by the part of the nervous system called the **Autonomic Nervous System (ANS)**, which has unmyelinated nerve fibres running from the brain stem and the top of the spinal cord, to the internal organs of the body. There are two sections to the ANS. One brings about the emergency reaction, and triggers off the production of adrenaline to keep it going. This is called the **sympathetic** division. Another division operates later to correct the balance and to restore body functions to normal operation, known as the **parasympathetic** division. The parasympathetic division of the ANS seems to be involved in the quiet emotions like depression, sadness or contentment, when we are not really active at all; whereas the sympathetic division seems to be involved in 'active' emotions like fear, anger, or excitement.

The effects of arousal

Many studies have investigated the effects of **arousal**, and some of them have produced quite surprising results. A study by Levine, in 1971, showed that arousal can actually accelerate development in young animals: Levine compared two matched groups of rats, one which had experienced five minutes of handling by humans once a day, and the other which had been left alone and reared normally. The group of rats which had been handled when they were pups developed at a faster rate than the control group: opening their eyes a couple of days earlier, leaving the nest earlier, and so on. It seemed that the extra stimulation which the pups were receiving was producing arousal, and this led to the accelerated development.

6.1 Reactions to stressful events

The activity of the autonomic nervous system is reflected in our pulse rate. This activity is designed to look at your pulse rate before and after a stressful situation.

For this activity you will need to obtain a large dot-to-dot problem (with about 100 dots). Sit down with a friend and ask the friend to join the dots but before they begin make sure that you have invisibly rubbed out one of the dots toward the end - say dot 83! (You may find it better to 'white-out' the dot, and then take a photocopy of the puzzle, so the white-out doesn't show.)

Before your friend begins to do the dot-to-dot, tell them that it is a study to measure levels of concentration and so you are going to take their pulse twice whilst they are completing the task. Take their pulse for the first ten seconds from when they begin the task and then again for ten seconds after say dot 87.

Why should it be taken after dot 87 and not dot 83?

Before you begin the exercise, practice taking a pulse reading. To find someone's pulse, take hold of their wrist and place your index and second finger on the wrist about one inch below the thumb. You should be able to feel a steady throbbing below your fingers. If you count the number of beats which occur in a period of ten seconds and then multiply this by six it will give you their pulse reading per minute.

Is there much difference between the pulse reading taken in the first 10 seconds and after dot 87?

What reasons can you give for your findings?

Why do you think it was best to tell your friend that you were investigating concentration and not stress?

Do you think that taking a person's pulse is an accurate way of measuring their level of stress? What other ways can you suggest?

Can you suggest an alternative method of investigating stress or arousal?

Stress-related illness

A famous study by Brady in 1958 showed that being placed in a stressful situation could lead to stomach ulcers. In a paper called 'Ulcers In Executive Monkeys', Brady described how he set up a study involving pairs of monkeys set up in different roles. One monkey was the active participant in the experiment or 'executive', and the other was a 'yoked control' who received exactly the same stimuli or experiences that the executive monkey did. Each monkey was restrained in an experimental chair, and each had a lever to press. The executive monkey had to press the lever at least once every twenty seconds; otherwise it would receive an electric shock (and so would the control monkey, of course). The control monkey could do nothing to avoid the shock, and so just received the shocks which happened if the executive monkey did not keep active.

Most of the executive monkeys which Brady used developed stomach ulcers, but the control ones did not. This was thought to be a direct consequence of the extra stress experienced by the executive monkey, because of the importance of its actions in avoiding the shocks. You could draw a parallel here with human beings in stressful jobs, as stomach ulcers are a fairly frequent cause of illness among people who experience long-term stress. It is thought that this is because of the digestive changes brought about by the sympathetic division of the ANS mentioned earlier.

A further investigation into this, by Weiss in 1972, showed that rats which were given a signal allowing them to predict when a shock was going to happen (though not to avoid it), developed stomach ulcers, although yoked controls which received the shock but not the signal did not. However, an interesting finding, which may, on the surface, seem to conflict with Brady's study, was that rats which could *do* something to avoid the shock, like jumping into a shuttle box, did not become ill. It seems that developing **coping behaviour** like this can allow us to avoid the ill-effects of stressful situations. Many humans who seem to deal with stress effectively have developed a range of coping behaviours, which they can use to help them deal with problems as they arise, without becoming too anxious and worried.

Coping with work-related stress

A study by Friedman and Rosenman in 1974 investigated why some people in highly stressful jobs seem to be more likely to suffer from stress-related coronary (heart) attacks. These are quite common among high-grade executives, who often have a high level of stress and have to engage in intensive and rapid decision making. Friedman and Rosenman found that reactions to situations seem to vary in two main ways, and that any particular individual would tend towards one of these two characteristic styles of reacting. Friedman and Rosenman called these styles 'Type A' and 'Type B' behaviour. Type A individuals tend to be highly competitive, tense people, who always expect the highest possible standards, and worry a lot about their work even when they are at home. Type B individuals may be just as energetic and work just as hard, but their attitude to their work is much more relaxed and practical. They do not worry so much about things that they cannot do anything about, and they are able to 'leave their worries behind' when they go home at the end of the day. In terms of physiological reactions to stress, Type A individuals often show Selye's GAS - adaptation to long-term stress - and Friedman and Rosenman showed that these people are very much likely to suffer from coronary attacks than Type B individuals are.

Psychology in Action

Most large companies run stress management courses for their executives, many of which are based on 'internal locus of control'. Participants are made to feel that they have a high degree of control over stressful events in both their work and personal life and are able to take realistic steps towards reducing stress. Time management is seen as one way of alleviating stress by encouraging people to make the most effective use of worktime and reduce the number of stressful events that arise out of poor planning.

On a personal level, many doctors and dentists are coming round to the idea that patients finding themselves in an unusual or unpredictable situation are likely to suffer higher degrees of stress, and therefore pain, than those who are well informed. Many now tell their patients what they are going to do, how long it will take and what kind of pain they can expect. Additionally, they may allow patients some degree of control over their situation. In these ways, the doctors and dentists hope to relieve stress caused by the unknown.

Biofeedback

The process of **biofeedback** is one way that people can be helped to overcome these stress-related illnesses. With biofeedback, some kind of mechanism is used which allows the individual to get information, or feedback, about their particular body processes, and so realise when they are tense. Most people find it very difficult to know when they are tense, and have to learn to relax by using special relaxation techniques. A machine which sounds a tone when you are tense and changes the tone as you start to relax can give you enough feedback to learn to bring your autonomic nervous system under control. GSR meters and blood pressure meters are particularly useful for biofeedback and using them for medical purposes like this is becoming more and more common. If an individual with high blood-pressure can learn to control it voluntarily through biofeedback, this is a much more desirable treatment than using drugs which can have undesirable side-effects and often cause the individual more problems.

Subliminal stress

Sometimes we can be totally unaware that we are becoming aroused or stressed by a stimulus. A study by Lazarus and McCleary in 1951, involved showing research participants particular words on a screen and then with some of the words giving them an electric shock. Other words were neutral and did not accompany a shock at all. Not surprisingly the participants in this study developed a reaction, through classical conditioning, to those words which had been accompanied by shock, and when they saw them again they produced a strong GSR response. But the interesting thing which Lazarus and McCleary discovered was that when they presented the words *subliminally* (in other words, so faintly that the participants were not aware of having seen anything at all) they still showed a strong GSR reaction. So we may be experiencing stress from something even though we do not realise it at the time. This kind of stress can be very subtle and we may only become aware of it when we have a change and it goes away - for instance, when we go away on holiday, or move to live in a different place.

The Yerkes-Dodson Law

When we are studying the way that stress or physiological arousal affects what we do, we find something very interesting. The word 'arousal' refers to the amount of excitation of the Autonomic Nervous System (ANS) which a person or animal is experiencing - so it can apply just as much to the excitement of a particularly happy or thrilling time as to the excitement of fear or anger. Studies which have measured how the amount of arousal that we are experiencing affects our performance, have found that up to a point, arousal can improve our performance on a task, but beyond that point performance will tend to decline. If we are too aroused, whether by fear, anger or happiness, we are unlikely to be able to do our best possible work; the optimal (best) level of arousal is not the same as the highest level.

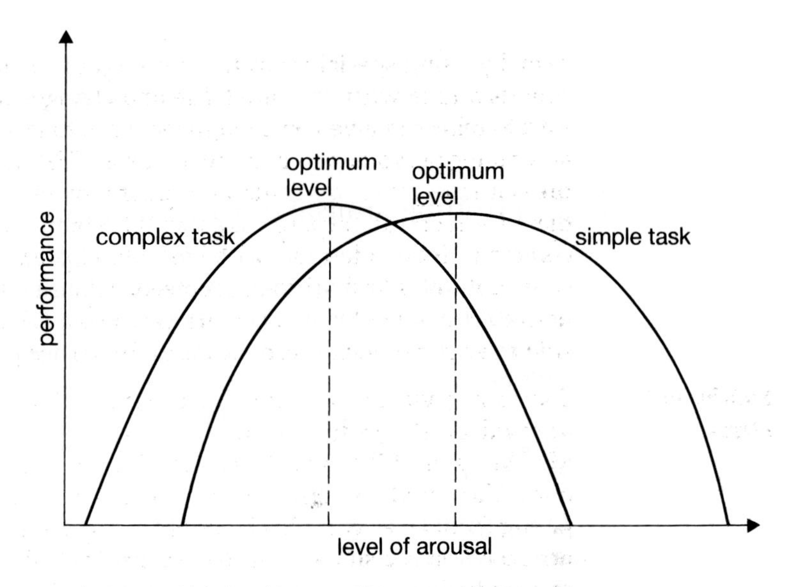

6.1 The Yerkes-Dodson Law of Arousal

This relationship between performance and arousal is known as the *Yerkes-Dodson Law*. It states that the relationship between performance and arousal forms an inverted U curve, and that the optimal level of performance will be obtained with a level of arousal that varies with the complexity of the task which we are doing. A complicated task, such as an exam, will suffer very readily from a level of arousal which is too high, as anyone who has had the experience of getting too 'worked-up' in an exam and then not doing the work that they knew they were capable of, knows. A simple task, such as sorting out sweets on a production line, will not suffer so rapidly if the person who is doing it is upset or aroused in other ways, but if the arousal level gets too high then that also will suffer. One way that many people find they can do much better in exams, is to develop simple strategies which will reduce arousal, such as doing deep-breathing relaxation exercises while revising, or walking to the exam so they do not have to worry that the bus might be late. Quite small strategies can keep the arousal level low enough so that it does not go 'over the top'- or beyond the optimal level, and so that the person is able to do their best in the exam, despite being worried about it.

Treatments for phobias

For many people, stressful situations such as entering a room that an exam was held in may bring about an emotional reaction. This has been acquired simply through classical conditioning - *associating* the room with the exam fear, so that later on the room itself is enough to bring back the fear. If we are aware of this, we can make allowances for it or try to deal with it in more practical ways, such as visiting the same room when we are not frightened or worried and allowing the fear to wear off.

6.2 Controlling arousal during exam times

One of the main reasons why so many people don't do as well as they should during examinations is because they get too worked up about them. The Yerkes-Dodson Law of Arousal shows us that too much arousal means that our performance falls off. For some people, this can mean that they get so nervous that they are almost unable to write, or have memory 'blackouts' when they just can't remember anything, even though they know that they have learned it.

Our overall level of arousal, though, is a cumulative thing: each new stressful event will add to the general level of arousal that we feel. Some parts of our examination stress come from things that we can't do anything about, like the exam being really important for our future careers. But there are a whole host of other, smaller things that you can control, like getting an earlier bus than the one you need to catch, so that even if it is late or breaks down you can still get to the exam on time.

Working in groups of three or four if possible, take a piece of paper and divide it down the middle. Head one side: 'Stressful things that have happened' and the other side: 'Stressful things that might happen'. Use these columns to make two lists - one of all the upsetting things that have happened to you or to people you know just before doing an exam (like, for instance, going to the wrong exam room); and the other of all the things that could easily happen just before the exam (like sleeping through the alarm clock ringing).

When you have finished your lists, go through them and work out a way that you could make absolutely certain that every item on them couldn't happen to you before any one particular exam.

Try putting these ideas into practice next time you do any exams. You'll be amazed at how much more confident it can make you feel! Even though the exam is still just as important, knowing that things are organised and can't add to your stress helps you to keep your stress level down, so that you can achieve your best performance.

Some kinds of fear, though, produce such an extreme amount of arousal that the individual is unable to deal constructively with it. Mostly, we call these kinds of fear **phobias** - a phobia being an irrational fear directed towards an object, which is so strong that it ends up dominating the person's life. **Agoraphobia** - the fear of being outdoors - is one phobia which is quite common in our society, and many people have mild phobias to spiders and snakes. The treatment of phobias, which has been developed by psychologists, tends to concentrate on bringing the client's arousal level down, so that they are able to face whatever it is that they are frightened of, easily. Broadly speaking, there are three main techniques which psychologists use for doing this.

Implosion therapy

Implosion therapy, or **flooding**, is a technique which involves facing the client with the thing that they are most frightened of for a long period of time. At first, this tends to bring about a fear reaction which may be quite strong. For instance, someone who has been in a road accident and developed a fear of cars might be put in a room with large wall screens showing films of cars coming towards them. Although this tends to bring about the 'fight or flight' reaction, there is very little that the client can do about it, and so they just have to stay there and see the fear through. As we have seen, the emergency reaction is a very demanding one for the body's resources, and it uses up a great deal of energy. After a while, it dies down even though the stimulus which triggers it off has not gone away and when this happens the person feels calmer. The fear that they felt has been extinguished and they are now in a better position to go ahead and come to terms with the thing which frightened them before. Implosion therapy is a very useful technique for treating phobias and has a very high success rate.

Systematic desensitisation

Systematic desensitisation is a different technique for treating phobias which still allows the fear to be extinguished, but much more gradually. In systematic desensitisation, the aim is to teach the client to have a totally different reaction to the thing which is frightening them. The new reaction should be so different from a fear reaction that the fear cannot happen at all. To provide a new reaction, most people are trained in relaxation techniques, as it isn't possible to feel relaxed and frightened at the same time! Arousal is almost the opposite of relaxation. What happens is this: the client and the therapist draw up a list of the situations that the client would feel frightened in. With any phobia, some situations are more frightening than others. If you were frightened of cats, having a cat jump on your lap suddenly would be much more frightening than seeing a cat walk past outside the window. So they put the list in a hierarchical order, from the least frightening to the most frightening of all. Then the client starts with the least frightening thing on the list, and practises relaxation techniques until it is easy to be perfectly relaxed while thinking about or watching the least frightening of the stimuli on the list. When that has been managed successfully, they move on to the next item up the list, and the client practises relaxation techniques again. In this way, the phobia is dealt with gradually, one step at a time with the client learning to relax at each step. Eventually, when they reach the top of the list and the most frightening of all, the client does not feel the fear as strongly, and it is much easier to learn to be relaxed in that situation too.

Modelling

Modelling is the third main technique for getting rid of phobias, and it is one that seems to happen quite often in everyday life as well as in therapy. With this method, the client learns to overcome the fear because they see someone else, or maybe several other people, in the frightening situation and showing no fear at all. Bandura et al. in 1977 showed how clients could learn to overcome phobias of snakes by watching other people handle them confidently. The other person provides a model for the client, showing them different ways of behaving. Imitating other people is an important way that human beings learn, not just when they are children, but right through their lives, and imitating someone who is confident in a situation which frightens you is a good way of learning to be more confident yourself. The best sort of models for this kind of treatment of phobias are models who are like the client. If the client can identify with the model, and see them as similar, then it will seem much more practical to copy that model's behaviour. One who is very different would not be very effective in encouraging the person to overcome their fear, as that person would just think, 'Well, it's all right for them, but I'm not like that...'.

Phobias are perhaps one of the most extreme ways that arousal can affect our behaviour, but there are many others. We may feel mild arousal in any situation where we have previously had tense experiences; or the arousal that we are feeling for one thing may affect our reactions to other things. If you have just missed a bus that you have been running for, your body will be very aroused, because of the exercise-producing adrenaline which will be affecting the ANS and activating the sympathetic nervous system, and quite often people find that they are far more irritable at times like that than they would normally be. It is often the same at times of high excitement too - just before an exciting event it is easy to get very irritable with a partner. But knowing how the ANS is affected in this way can help us to make allowances for how we are feeling.

Theories of emotion

If the physiological state that we are in can affect how we feel so much, it raises the question of what is happening when we do feel an emotion. Is it that we are feeling something which is purely psychological and which just happens to have physiological changes which correlate with it? Or is it that unconsciously we recognise the physiological state that our body is in and attribute feelings to it, depending on what is happening at the time?

The James-Lange theory

Many psychologists have investigated this question, and developed theories to explain what is happening. One of the first of these theories is known as the *James-Lange theory of emotion*, because it was developed independently by William James and Carl Lange, at the end of the last century. James (1890) argued that what is happening when we feel an emotion, like fear or anger or sadness, is that we are unconsciously perceiving the physiological changes which happen in the body. For instance, if you have a frightening experience (the example he gave was tripping up as you go down the stairs) you tend to react almost by reflex, such as rapidly grabbing the rail before you fall. But just after that you find that your heart starts beating faster, and the alarm reaction happens. James argued that the actual event is not the thing which makes us feel frightened, but that our fear comes from the physiological changes which happen as a result of that event. Without those physiological reactions we would not feel any emotion. In other words, the James-Lange theory of emotion states that the emotion we feel arises from our perception of the physiological state of the body. James's famous quote on this theory is: 'We do not weep because we feel sorrow; we feel sorrow because we weep'. The physiological changes happen first, and the emotion that we experience comes as a result of the brain interpreting the physiological changes.

6.2 The James-Lange theory of emotion

Cannon's theory of emotion

Not every psychologist has agreed with this idea. Interestingly enough, Walter Cannon, who discovered the 'fight or flight' reaction, had an entirely different theory of the way that we feel emotions. The *Cannon-Bard theory of emotion* states that the emotion that we experience - in other words, the psychological feelings that we have - and the physiological reaction that happens are entirely separate and independent of one another. Although Cannon had investigated these physiological changes, he thought that the mind and the body were entirely separate, and that the state of the body did not really affect the mind. That type of approach is known as **dualism**, because it is seeing the psychological and physiological aspects of emotion as two separate things.

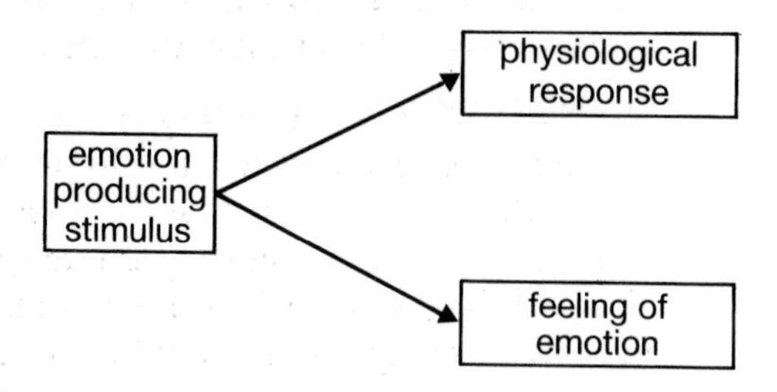

6.3 The Cannon-Bard theory of emotion

Interactionism

Both the James-Lange theory and the Cannon-Bard theory are rather extreme points of view: one saying that our feelings are completely caused by our physiology, and the other saying that our feelings have nothing to do with our physiology. Most modern psychologists see the answer as being somewhere in between the two - as an *interaction* between the psychological aspects of emotions and the physiological ones. They also see the social environment and previous experiences as contributing to emotion as well: the first time that the doorbell rings in the night you may feel curious, and perhaps a little anxious in case it is a serious emergency, but if it happens most nights for a couple of months you are likely to feel a very different emotion when you hear it again - either anger or irritation, or a much stronger fear! In that case, previous experience has brought about a very different reaction to what is in the end the same stimulus of a doorbell ringing. So there seem to be quite a few things that can affect our emotions, and most of the modern ideas involve an approach known as **interactionism**, which stresses the way that all these things can work together to produce an effect.

Studies of emotion and physiology

There are several studies which have attempted to find out just what sort of a connection there is between the feelings that we have, and the physiological changes which we experience.

Marañon's study

One of the first studies was performed by Marañon, in 1924. He injected 210 research participants with adrenaline, and simply asked them to report what they felt. From them, he obtained three kinds of replies: most of the participants, 71%, simply reported their physical symptoms: heart beating faster, etc. The other 29% reported how they felt in terms of emotions: most of them using words like 'as if '. For example, 'I feel as if I were awaiting a great happiness', or 'I feel as if I were afraid'. But a handful of the 29% seemed to experience 'real' emotional reactions. When Marañon reminded them of events which they could normally remember without emotion, under the influence of adrenaline their mood was affected and they experienced the emotion which had been associated with the event at the time.

Marañon's study is interesting, because it shows that many people do see a similarity between the physiological sensations produced by an adrenaline injection, and emotions which they feel. But it also shows that it is not as simple as the James-Lange theory would imply: if the physiological changes *caused* our emotions, then it should not really matter how they were brought about, and yet even for those research participants who felt a 'real' emotion, it was necessary to trigger it off with some kind of emotional memory. It seems that our understanding of events - the **cognitive** side of our experience - is just as important as the physiological side.

Ax's study

Another study, by Ax in 1953, investigated Cannon's 'fight or flight' response. Cannon had spoken of the emergency reaction as if it were just one type of response for all the aroused emotional states. Ax created laboratory conditions of fear and of anger, and showed that in fact research participants tended to produce different reactions to the two types of emotion. He measured their physiological reactions in many different ways: muscle tension, GSR, blood pressure, hand and face temperature, heart and respiration rate.

The research participants were asked to lie down and relax in the laboratory, while listening to their favourite music. They were told that it was a study of differences between people with and without hypertension, and that the relaxation was all they had to do. Ax used a related-measures design, with each participant experiencing both the fear and the anger conditions, and **counterbalanced** the order of the conditions, so that half of the participants had the fear experience first, and the other half had the anger experience first. With the fear condition, participants were given a very light repeated electrical shock to the little finger, after they had been connected up to a large number of wires and recording electrodes. When they told the experimenter about it, the experimenter seemed very surprised, checked the wiring, and pressed a button which made sparks jump from a piece of the apparatus near the participant. After exclaiming that it was a dangerous, high-voltage short-circuit, and seeming to be very worried about it, the experimenter made some alterations, and after about five minutes removed the shock wire which had given the shocks in the little finger, and told the participant that it was safe now. With the anger condition, participants were told that the experimenter had had to use a polygraph technician who had previously been sacked for incompetence and arrogance. This technician then proceeded to be very rude to both the experimenter and to the participant, making sarcastic remarks and criticising everything involved, when the experimenter was out of the room. After about five minutes, the experimenter returned and the technician left, and the experimenter apologised to the participant. There was a fifteen minute relaxation period between each of the conditions, so that the participant had time to recover from the arousal.

Ax identified the two types of reaction as being similar to those produced by the actions of two different hormones. The fear reaction was similar to that produced by an injection of adrenaline, but the anger reaction was like the response produced when research participants were injected with both adrenaline and noradrenaline simultaneously. The anger reaction seemed to produce lots of energy which was more highly co-ordinated than it was in the fear condition. Therefore Ax suggested that there was a difference between 'fight' and 'flight', with attack behaviour needing much more organisation than running away!

Schachter and Singer's study

The classic study of the relationship between emotion and arousal was performed by Schachter and Singer in 1962. This involved injecting research participants with adrenaline, and then putting them in situations where they were with someone who was acting either very happily ('euphorically'), or angrily. Schachter and Singer had seven conditions altogether in their experiment. When they arrived, each of the participants was given an injection which they were told was a vitamin compound named 'Suproxin', and then asked to wait for twenty minutes until it had taken effect. One other person, a 'stooge', was in the waiting room, as if also waiting for the experiment. The stooge then acted in a particular way, either happily playing paper basketball and making paper aeroplanes, or angrily. In the anger condition the research participants were asked to fill in a long and extremely personal questionnaire, and the stooge became increasingly angry about the insulting questions. Hidden observers noted how the participant reacted to the behaviour of the stooge, and after the 'waiting period' the participants were asked to report on how they felt.

With the euphoria condition, there were four different groups of research participants, who had had slightly different instructions. One group had been given the injection and been informed about the reactions that they should expect. The injection was, in fact, adrenaline. Another group was given an injection of adrenaline and told nothing about any side affects. A third group was given adrenaline and told a misleading collection of possible side-effects, such as their feet feeling numb, and a possible slight headache, while the fourth group was given a placebo injection (which had no effect at all) of saline solution, and told nothing.

With the anger condition, there were three groups of research participants which were the same as the euphoria condition, but missing out the 'misinformed' group. As this had only been intended as an extra control, and was not much different from the 'uninformed' group, Schachter and Singer did not see it necessary to include it.

Schachter and Singer found that in all the situations research participants tended to fall in with the mood of the stooge, but that the *amount* of emotion which they reported feeling was different. Participants who had been misinformed reacted more strongly than uninformed participants, who in turn reacted more strongly than those who had been told what to expect, or the 'placebo' group. So they suggested that the social situation which we are in is the most important factor in which emotions we feel, but that the arousal which we are experiencing will affect the degree to which we feel the emotion - how strongly we feel it.

Ethical discussion

In Schachter Singer's study of emotion, research participants were deliberately manipulated in a number of ways. One group of participants was given false information about the effects likely to be produced by the injection, and all participants were deceived about the nature of the injection they were receiving. In addition, the "stooge" who was used to influence mood was a confederate of the experimenters, although the participants were unaware of the fact.

Some people would argue that this degree of deception was necessary, and that the benefits which came from the study, in terms of our increased understanding of emotion, made it worth while.

Others would argue that it is ethically unacceptable to manipulate and deceive people in this way, especially when they are taking part in the experiment in good faith.

What do you think?

There are, however, problems with this study, which may affect how much we can go by its findings. One of them, and by far the most serious, is that nobody has been able to **replicate** it - in other words, to repeat what was done and get the same results. Perhaps one possible reason for this is that although Schachter and Singer checked on the moods of their research participants after the study was completed, they did not check them beforehand. Also, some research participants did not seem to produce the expected reactions from the adrenaline injections, and so they were dropped from the experiment and their results were not included. Another problem which Schachter and Singer identified was that since many of the participants were students who were obliged to participate in psychological studies as part of their course requirement, they were determined to be 'good' research participants, and so they would not express anger about the questionnaire when they were asked how they felt about it, in case it meant that they did not get a good grade from the experimenter.

Valins' study

A different study, which showed how research participants might react to autonomic feedback, was conducted by Valins in 1966. In this, the autonomic effects were artificial - participants heard a recording which they were told was a recording of their own heart-beat. Valins used male research participants, and showed them photographs of semi-nude women, taken from *Playboy* magazine. For some of the photographs, the sound of the heartbeat was speeded up or slowed down, but for others it remained unchanged. A control group of participants still heard the heartbeat sounds but were not told that it was anything to do with themselves. Those who thought that the increased heartbeat was their own, also reported that they liked that particular picture more than others. This preference lasted even a few weeks later, when they were asked to choose a set of preferred photographs as part of a supposedly different study. Although none of the participants realised that it was in fact the same study, they still tended to choose those photographs which they thought had produced a change in their heart-rate. Valins suggested that this study shows that we may **attribute** changes in our arousal state to emotion, so in some respects the physiological changes which we are experiencing do affect the emotion that we feel.

Hohmann's study

In another study, Hohmann (1966) observed and interviewed people who had suffered injuries to the spinal cord such that they did not experience autonomic arousal. He found that they still felt emotions, but that they said that the emotions which they experienced were not as extreme as they had been before the injury. This study also suggests that the autonomic nervous system does have an effect on our emotions, but that it is not as clear an effect as the James-Lange theory of emotion implies.

Schachter's theory of emotion

In 1964, Schacter put forward a theory of emotion, which seems to express the relationship between physiological and psychological factors in emotion very clearly. He suggested that the emotion which we experience comes from two main sources: the physiological changes which we are experiencing, and our interpretation of the events around us. So social and cognitive factors play a very large part in emotion but so also do arousal levels. It is the way that we *interpret* the physiological changes happening to us that matters. Schachter's theory provides a contrast to both the James-Lange theory and the Cannon-Bard theory, and is an example of the 'interactionist' approach in physiological psychology.

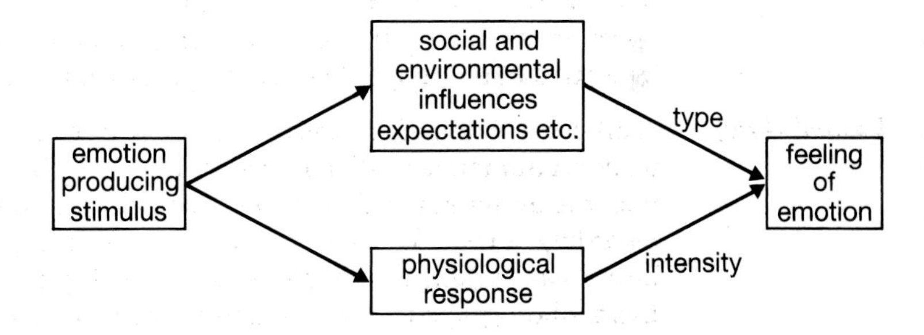

6.4 The Schachter and Singer theory of emotion

In the next chapter, we will look at some more of the 'states' of the body: the states of sleep, dreaming and consciousness.

Summary

1 Emotions like fear or anger produce an alarm reaction in the body, which is the activation of the sympathetic division of the autonomic nervous system.

2 Arousal may be measured by galvanic skin response (GSR) or other techniques. Polygraphs or lie-detectors measure arousal.

3 Long-term stress has been shown to lead to illnesses such as heart attacks or stomach ulcers. Biofeedback is one way of dealing with control of stress.

4 Phobias (extreme irrational fears) may be treated by therapies designed to reduce the levels of arousal, by conditioning.

5 Various theories have been put forward to explain how we feel emotion. The James-Lange theory stated that we feel the physiological change first, and interpret it as the emotion.

6 The Cannon-Bard theory stated that physiological reactions and our feelings of emotion happen totally separately.

7 Schachter and Singer's theory stated that the social situation affects the type of emotion that we feel, but the physiological changes affect how intensely we feel it.

Chapter 7 - Sleep, dreaming and consciousness

Sleep

All of us spend a considerable proportion of our lives sleeping, and we all know how necessary it is. But sleep is something which in many ways is quite hard to study, because we are not conscious while we are sleeping and cannot very easily be aware of what is happening. Accordingly, quite a lot of research on sleep has involved studying people who have volunteered to sleep in a special room so that they can be monitored by psychologists as they sleep through the night.

Physiological correlates of sleep

One thing that has been found is that there are quite distinct physiological changes which seem to happen to us as we sleep. These are known as the **physiological correlates** of sleep, because they correlate, or go together, with experiences of sleep that people have. For example, measuring the electrical activity of the brains of people who are sleeping with an EEG has shown that there seem to be distinct levels of sleep.

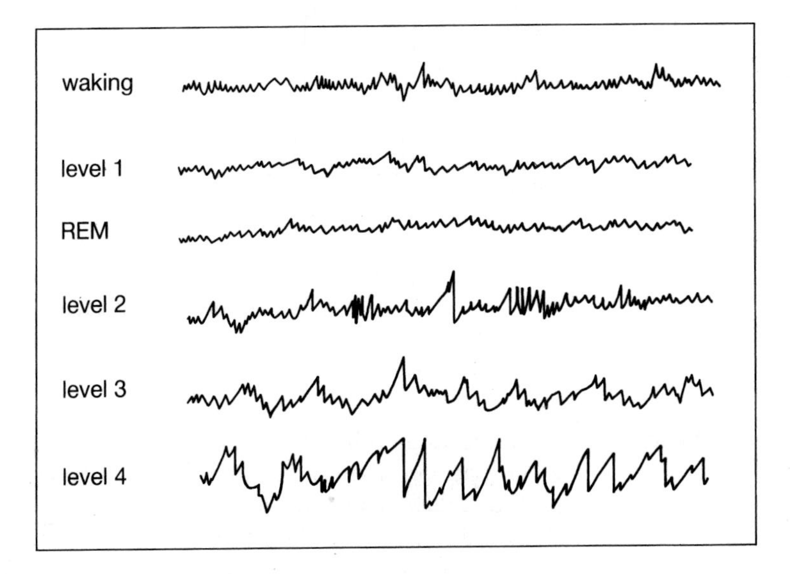

7.1 EEG changes during sleep

As a person sleeps, the pattern of the EEG changes and forms several different types. These EEG patterns correlate with the way that a person feels if they are woken up. For example, the pattern of level 4 sleep, which seems to be the most relaxed and has the most regular and deep waves in it, correlates with people reporting that they felt as though they were very deeply asleep and found it hard to wake up. On the other hand, people in level 2 sleep, which shows a rapid and variable wave pattern, reported that they had only felt lightly asleep and found it quite easy to wake up. There are four of these levels of brain activity, and we seem to pass from one to the next quite easily as we sleep through a night.

Sleep cycles

During the course of an average night, most people seem to go through five or six distinct cycles of sleep. For each of the first couple of cycles, they will pass gradually from level 1 to level 4 sleep, spending a period of time on each level (judging from their EEG record). When they reach level 4, they spend a period of time in that, and then change to level 3 sleep, then level 2, and then back up to level one. But in the later cycles of sleep, we rarely go as far as level 4, and in the very last couple of cycles during the night we often only go down to level 2.

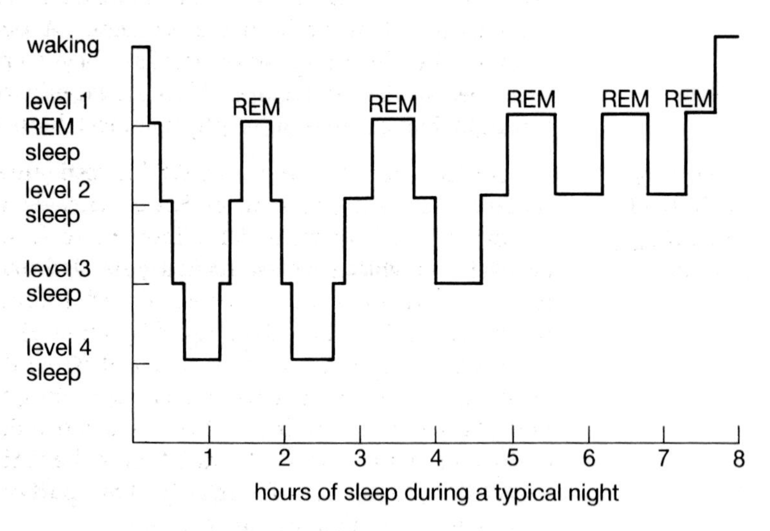

7.2 Sleep cycles

Paradoxical sleep

An interesting finding about these cycles of sleep is what happens when a person has been through a cycle and goes back to level one. A study by Dement and Kleitman, in 1957, found that this level 1 sleep did not fit with the general 'rule' that the deeper the EEG record the harder it was to wake up. Although research participants might appear to be sleeping very lightly, to judge from their brain activity, it appeared that they were very hard to wake up - sometimes just as hard as they had been in level 4. Because of this, sleep of this type is sometimes called 'paradoxical sleep', whereas the more conventional sleep on the other levels is called 'orthodox' sleep.

Rapid eye movement

Another characteristic of paradoxical sleep which Dement and Kleitman observed, was that when in it, people tended to make very rapid irregular eye movements, REMs for short; and also that if they woke people up from this kind of sleep they would report that they had been dreaming. It seems that it is during REM, or paradoxical sleep, that dreaming occurs.

Animal studies

Apart from observing and measuring changes in people as they sleep, there is some evidence from animal studies about which parts of the brain seem to be involved in sleep and dreaming. A study by Jouvet, in 1967, showed that lesions or damage to the pons in a particular area, tended to increase REM sleep. Animals with such lesions spent a much larger proportion of their time in REM sleep than they had done before, but a lesion lower down the pons seemed to decrease the amount of REM sleep which they engaged in. However, we do not know how true this would also be of humans. Although some evidence from accidental injuries seems to suggest that it would be true, we do not know what other changes might result from the accident. A person might, for instance, be dreaming more because they were frightened or disturbed by the accident itself as an experience to have lived through, than because of the physiological damage.

The role of the Reticular Activating System

An earlier study, by French in 1957 investigated the role of the reticular activating system, or RAS. This seems to be a very important mechanism, which allows us to focus attention and arousal, and which seems to act as a general switching mechanism for whole areas of cerebral cortex. French found that cats which had had their RAS ablated (removed by surgery), went into a coma from which they never recovered. He also found that if a cat had an electrode implanted in its reticular activating system, and then was allowed to sleep, it could be wakened quite naturally and easily by a slight electrical stimulation of the RAS. So this would seem to suggest that it is the activity of this part of the brain which allows us to be either awake or asleep.

Circadian rhythms

As infants, we tend to alternate time between periods of sleeping, quiet wakefulness, and active wakefulness. The average new-born baby spends about 14 hours of its day asleep, but this can seem to be much longer, because it will also tend to spend time being quietly awake, when often people will think that it is asleep. As new parents know to their cost, babies may be asleep or awake at any time during the 24 hours, but gradually they tend to extend the amount of time that they sleep at night, and spend more time awake during the day. For some years, though, they will retain the need for a 'nap' during the daytime, and many adults, too, take naps during the day. A study by Evans, in 1977, surveyed a large sample of college students - about 900 in all - and asked them if they ever took naps during the daytime. Twenty per cent of them replied that they did, as often as they felt like it, and another 40% answered that they took naps during the daytime if they had been short of sleep, or lost sleep recently. So it seems that we are far from losing the ability to sleep during the day, but nonetheless we do most of our sleeping at night.

In addition to spending time sleeping during the night and waking during the day, we have times when our waking periods seem to be more alert than others, and also times when we seem to become very quiet and subdued, and find it very easy to fall asleep. Many people, for instance, experience a quiet period in the early afternoon, and those who do take naps during the day often do so at this time. In some of the hotter countries, it is even established as a cultural practice, in the form of the 'siesta' during which everyone rests. The patterns which we show over a 24-hour period are known as **circadian rhythms**, or sometimes **diurnal rhythms**. ('Diurnal' means 'of the day', and 'nocturnal' means 'of the night'. Because we are habitually active during the day, humans are diurnal creatures, whereas animals that are habitually active at night, like bush babies, are nocturnal).

External cues and circadian rhythms

There have been several studies done to investigate diurnal rhythms, and how they occur. A study by Aschoff, in 1965, investigated how accurate the human being's internal 'body clock' was. By asking his research participants to live for a period of time in an environment that did not include any clues at all as to the time of day, he was able to see if they would maintain a precise 24-hour rhythm. In fact, the participants tended to average out on about 25-hour cycles, once they were away from time cues like daylight and temperature, but the overall pattern of quiescent periods and active periods remained very similar.

Aschoff's study showed how much we rely on external cues, like light and dark, to keep our bodies on the normal 24-hour rhythm. If we do not have these, our cycle can slip slightly and we can end up being completely out of phase with the rest of our world. A case study of a blind man who had a very strong circadian rhythm was performed by Miles, Raynal and Wilson in 1977. They found that because he did not experience the normal cues he was unable to maintain a 24-hour rhythm and his body's natural cycle of 24.9 hours was too strong to change, even by controlling his sleep in a sleep laboratory. As a result of his strong natural rhythm, he would find himself completely out of phase with the night-day cycle frequently, and had to use stimulants and tranquillisers to conduct his working life at the normal times.

Shift work

In the normal run of things, we are not often required to change our diurnal rhythms, but there are two frequent circumstances when we may end up having to adjust our 'body clock'. One of them is shift work. In our society many people, particularly industrial workers, find themselves doing shift work which involves changing shifts frequently. If the shift takes place at a quiescent time, we may find that we do not work very efficiently at all. Some people, who work permanently on one shift, find that they adapt to that time. Night shift workers sometimes find that their diurnal rhythms have reversed and that they are more awake during the times that other people are asleep. Other people, like nurses or care staff, who work a different shift each day, also find themselves able to adapt. The most difficult kinds of arrangements are those in which the individual spends, say, a fortnight on one shift, then the next fortnight on a different shift, and the next fortnight on a third. With those kinds of working arrangements, the body is just beginning to adjust itself to the new timetable when it has to change again, and this can make that form of shift working a considerable strain for the people doing it.

Jet lag

We can see just what sort of a strain it can be when we look at the other modern situation in which we have to change our 'body clocks'. That is when we move from one time zone to another so that everything around us is out of phase with the country that we have just left. 'Jet lag' is the process of trying to adapt to an unfamiliar 24-hour pattern, and can leave a person feeling tired, headachy and with all sorts of minor adjustment problems. Some people can take days adapting to the new time zones, and people who need to conduct serious business immediately after flying from one continent to another can experience difficulties as a result. A study by Webb, Agnew and Williams (1971) showed that the problem of jet lag does not really relate to how much sleep the person has had, but rather to their adjustment to the new time zones. Diplomats who have to do a lot of flying from one place to another often find that sticking rigidly to the schedule of meals and exercise which they had at home helps them to operate efficiently, even if others do find it odd that they are having breakfast at 10.00 p.m.!

In 1972, a study by Klein, Wegmann and Hunt investigated the effects of moving rapidly from one time zone to another. They tested a group of students who flew to Germany from the USA, and back again. To do this, they used tests of manual dexterity at different times of day. They found that the students did not do nearly as well as before, when they were required to adjust to new time zones; and that the adverse effects lasted as long as 12 days in some cases. On returning home, there were similar effects as the students readjusted, but they did not take as long to recover as before.

7.1 Investigating your own circadian rhythms

Many researchers have found that there is a definite relationship between changes in body temperature and times of day. You can investigate your diurnal rhythms, to find out whether there is a correlation between the times that your body temperature is at its highest and the times that you feel yourself to be at your most alert.

What you can do is to take a series of measurements, over a period of two or three days, at different times of day. One of the measurements will be your body temperature and the other will be of how alert you feel. When you have obtained a set of about fifteen such measurements, you can plot them on a scattergram, and see how well they correlate.

You will need: a small thermometer, a postcard or postcard-sized piece of paper, and a pen.

First, draw five columns lengthways on the postcard. Head the first one 'date'; the second 'time'; the third 'alertness'; and the fourth 'temperature'. The fifth column is for 'notes'.

Now, decide on the days when you are going to do your study (they should be days which are fairly typical of your usual routine). Decide on five or six equally-spaced times throughout those days; with the first one about an hour after you have got up and the last one just before you go to bed. Draw enough lines on your postcard to allow for a separate entry for each of those times, over the whole three days.

You will now need to work out a way of measuring your alertness. One way is simply to use a five-point scale, from 'A' to 'E', with 'A' representing the most alert that you usually get in a normal day; and 'E' representing the least alert. Remember that this is a personal scale - you are not comparing yourself with anyone else, only with what you are normally like. Remember too, that you should use all of the points on the scale in the course of a normal day.

At each of the times that you decided on (or as close to them as possible), first make your judgement of how alert you feel, and note it down. Then, take your temperature, and note that down. (The procedure takes about a minute and a half, so you can do it no matter where you are. This is why you need a small card - so that you can carry it round easily!) When you have finished, draw a scattergram of the results. (Ask your teacher to show you how.) Then answer these questions:

Do these results show a positive, a negative, or a zero correlation?

Why was it necessary to rate alertness before temperature each time?

What type of a study is this?

Try comparing your results with those of a friend or the others in your class. Did everyone obtain the same results, or are some people's circadian rhythms stronger than others?

Dreaming

The discovery of REM sleep meant that researchers were now able to investigate the phenomenon of dreaming. By asking for volunteers to come and sleep in the laboratory, being monitored by recording equipment while they slept, investigators were able to identify several different characteristics of dreaming.

A study by Goodenough et al. in 1959 established that, even though some of us do not remember it, we all dream for several periods during the night. Webb and Kersey (1967) investigated this further, and found that the difference between 'recallers' and 'non-recallers' (people who remembered their dreams and people who did not) is to do with what period of their sleep cycle the individual wakes up from. People who recall their dreams tend to wake up from a period of REM sleep, whereas those who don't remember their dreams tend to have woken up from level 2 or level 3 sleep. A study by Dement in 1969 showed that if people are deprived of the opportunity to dream (by being woken up each time their sleep entered a REM phase), when they are finally allowed to sleep normally they spend very much more time in REM sleep, as if to make up for the time that they have lost.

The nature of dreaming

Investigations were also undertaken into the nature of dreaming. An early study by Dement and Wolpert demonstrated how dreamers were not totally unconscious of external stimuli, even though they might seem to be. One of the tests that Dement and Wolpert performed was to spray their dreamers with cold water, lightly, and then to wake them up after a few minutes and ask them what they had been dreaming about. Typically, research participants would report having dreamt about washing, or a flood, or being out in the rain: the stimulus of the water had become incorporated into their dreams.

Dement and Wolpert also managed to investigate how long dreams last and found that, by and large, dreams seem to occupy 'real time' rather than to flash by rapidly. If a sequence had seemed to last a couple of minutes to the dreamer, then it was probably really the case. They argued that 'instantaneous' dreams - such as the kind where a whole long dream seems to happen in an instant before the ringing of an alarm clock - were most often 'memory flashbacks' of longer dreams that had taken place earlier in the night, and which had been brought back rapidly by the ringing of the bell.

Lucid dreams

A study of **lucid dreams** was performed by Hearne in 1981. Lucid dreams are the kind of dreams where you are aware that you are dreaming, but you carry on doing it nonetheless. Hearne had been performing laboratory investigations of sleeping and had been looking for a way that he could signal to his research participants when they were dreaming. Finally, they settled on a signal of a very light electric shock to the wrist, whenever the participant entered the REM sleep phase. This signal would not be strong enough to wake them, but enough to make them aware of it even in their sleep. When the participants felt this, they remembered that the signal meant that they were now dreaming, and Hearne found that many of them entered lucid dreams from then on.

Hearne and his research participants developed various kinds of signalling techniques using a code of eye movements such that, say, three rapid flicks to the left might mean the start of a flying sequence or four might mean the end of such a sequence. Research participants were able to 'explore' their dreaming to try out different things that they had discussed with the experimenter and see if they would work. Hearne's research participants found that they could control their dreams. By thinking of something that they wanted to happen in the dream, and thinking of practical ways that it could fit into the dream scenario, participants were able to make them take place.

The secret of controlling your dreams, apparently, is that the thing that you try to make happen should be realistic within the context of the dream. You are not likely to be able to make someone just appear out of the blue, for instance, but you might manage to make them step through a particular door. Hearne said the key is to look around the dream for a plausible way of doing this, and work out a realistic scene whereby the thing that you want can be introduced.

Functions of dreaming

There have been several different theories put forward as to the reasons why we dream. One of the most famous was put forward by Freud (1901), in which he suggested that it was in dreams that the unconscious part of the mind came to the fore. It would express the hidden desires and wishes which a person has so deeply buried in the mind that they are not aware of them consciously. Because the conscious mind does not recognise these preconscious desires, they need to appear in the dream in a disguised form. So Freud developed a theory of dream symbolism, which argued that the unusual or surreal images often produced in dreams symbolised things that the conscious mind was unaware of.

Dreams and dreamwork

Freud based much of his psychoanalytic theory around the interpretation of dreams. In his theory of personality (see Chapter 13) he portrayed the mind as being rather like an iceberg, with only one part - the ego - conscious, and the other two parts - the id and the superego - buried below the consciousness in the unconscious mind. Because these two were continually making demands and trying to break through to the ego, the ego had to protect itself. The demands of the id and the superego were seen as too threatening to be acknowledged consciously. Even in dreams, the demands had to be made in a disguised form. Dreamwork is the term used by Freud to describe how these wishes and impulses can be disguised.

One important feature of dreamwork is the use of symbols to represent hidden desires. So, for instance, a tall tower might be a phallic symbol, representing the male penis, and a cave or tunnel might represent the female vagina. (Freud considered sex to be the most important human motivation, and so his theory draws heavily on sexual imagery.) Houses might symbolise the womb, or vultures might symbolise death.

Other aspects of dreamwork which Freud described were the processes of condensation and changing into opposites. In condensation, the unconscious mind might cause several different images to be combined, so a person might suddenly turn into an animal, or be half-bird, half-human. The combination would have some hidden significance. Something which could not be faced up to consciously might be altered into its opposite to avoid detection.

Archetypes

Freud's ideas were taken up by one of his followers, Jung. Jung developed a far more elaborate system of dream symbolism than Freud. He considered that when we dream, the unconscious mind keys into the deepest levels of our unconscious - genetic memories shared by all human beings, and presented in the form of archetypes - original forms which human societies all seemed to recognise. The sorts of things that Jung was referring to were things like water to symbolise birth and rebirth, or images like the earth mother or the all powerful father. Because these seemed to be very common in European and Classical literature, Jung argued that they probably represented a very basic aspect of the human psyche, which was contacted in an individual's dreams.

Other researchers, though, have questioned these ideas. For one thing, if the role of dreaming is to play out unconscious wish-fulfilment's, and engage in elaborate symbolism, that makes it very hard to explain why infants and animals spend so much time in dreaming sleep. (Although we cannot know for certain that animals dream, they show all the physiological signs of it, including muscle twitching and EEG activity.) According to Freud, at least, very young infants have not yet established the hidden traumas and wishes that the ego has to keep buried well away from the conscious mind, and yet they still dream.

Dreams and organisation

A theory put forward by Evans, in 1984, expresses one of the alternative ways that psychologists see the functions of dreaming. Evans argued that dreaming allows the brain to sort out and to organise all the myriad sensory impressions that we receive during the course of a day so that we can work out what things can be forgotten, and what things can be sorted for retrieval later. This might explain the findings of Oswald in 1970, that individuals who were sleep-deprived often ended up with very paranoid thoughts, as if they could not keep things in perspective any more. And most of us have had the experience of sleeping on a problem and finding that it seems very much less difficult in the morning. It seems that having been able to organise our thoughts and to forget irrelevant things, we are in a stronger position to see things in perspective. As you can see, this is a very different way of looking at dreaming than that put forward by the psychoanalytic theorists Freud and Jung, but many modern psychologists prefer it as an approach.

Consciousness

The question of what consciousness is, is one that has intrigued psychologists since the beginning of psychology. The introspectionist psychologists investigated consciousness by trying to analyse their own mental experience. By monitoring experiences such as paying attention, daydreaming, or just being aware of surroundings, they hoped to become able to identify what the crucial aspects of consciousness are, and how they come to distinguish human psychology. William James (1890) saw consciousness as a continuous stream, like a kind of internal monologue, that is always present in our minds. He also identified the way that actions and routines can change, from being conscious activities to unconscious ones. For example; if you are learning to drive a car for the first time, you have to be very aware of each action that you are making, but as you become more expert, the acts become routine, and unconscious. So, part of skill learning, according to James, is the transfer of activities from consciousness to unconscious routine.

Another of the early psychologists, Wilhelm Wundt (1879) described consciousness as arising from two factors. The first of these is the sensory information that we receive from the outside world, through the sense receptors of vision, hearing, and so on. Being aware of this incoming information was, in Wundt's opinion, very much part of being conscious. In addition to this, our internal feelings and emotions contribute directly to what we are aware of. In later chapters we shall be looking at how cognitive processes are influenced by internal states, like motivation and emotion. It was the combination of these two sources of information, according to Wundt, that produced consciousness.

Sensory deprivation

This leads naturally to the question of what happens if at least one of these sources of information is removed. Lilly (1977) conducted a series of experiments on **sensory deprivation**. Research participants were enclosed in special tanks, where they floated in water wearing earpads and blindfolds, so that they didn't receive any sensory impressions at all. Several of the participants said that they felt this had enabled them to reach a deeper level of consciousness, like meditating. Others had hallucinations and became very distressed. Some researchers believed that this occurred because the brain couldn't operate without sensory input and so it produced these images to substitute for the external sensations, but other researchers argued that the hallucinations occurred as a result of the participants' own anxieties or expectations, and didn't show anything of the sort.

Consciousness and neural activity

EEG studies have shown that it is possible to distinguish between some general states of consciousness. Earlier on in this chapter, we saw how different levels of sleep show different EEG traces. The same thing applies to general states of awareness: we all know the subjective difference between being mentally alert, concentrating hard on something, or being relaxed and daydreaming. These seem to be general states of mind, which most people experience regularly. They are also reflected in electroencephalograms - measures of brain activity taken by attaching electrodes to the skull and 'listening in', as it were.

When we are awake and reasonably alert, the EEG trace is irregular and of a moderate amplitude - in other words, its 'peaks' and 'troughs' are not particularly extreme. However, if we are daydreaming, or in a relaxed mood, regular rhythms, known as *alpha rhythms*, appear in the EEG record. These are of a higher amplitude, showing higher peaks and troughs, but they also show a regular pattern. Stroh (1970) showed that, in some people, the appearance of alpha rhythms in the EEG pattern meant that they were likely to lapse in their concentration on a task requiring vigilance.

There are other distinctive patterns which appear in EEG traces as indicating states of consciousness. For example, when we are concentrating deeply on something, another kind of rhythm appears, known as a *delta rhythm.* A sudden change in an external stimulus, which catches our attention, also produces a sudden change in the EEG pattern, which is known as an *evoked potential.* So, some changes in consciousness do seem to be detectable, although these are very general ones.

Psychology in Action

Hypnosis is one example of an altered state of consciousness. Although the word "hypnosis" is derived from the Greek word *hypnos*, meaning to sleep, the person being hypnotised is seen to be awake but susceptible to suggestions made by the hypnotist.

Hypnosis is used for entertainment value, when a hypnotist will invite members of an audience on stage and lead them to act in an uncharacteristic manner. For example, they may be led to eat an onion while being made to believe that it is an apple.

The medical and dental professions sometimes use hypnosis as an alternative to more conventional forms of pain relief. A variety of work, ranging from minor dental treatment to major surgery, has been carried out under hypnosis. In a recent murder investigation, a policemen who remembered seeing a car at the scene of a crime, was able to remember the full number-plate under hypnosis, which he had not been able to do previously. However, memory is very unreliable under hypnosis, and sometimes people can invent false memories.

The implication, then, is that consciousness is somehow linked to brain activity, although it is very difficult to work out exactly how that comes about. In Chapter 8, we shall be looking at how some of the "higher" mental processes are linked with areas of the cerebral cortex; but there is no specific area of the brain which mediates consciousness, although, as we saw in the last chapter, some sub-cortical structures, like the reticular activating system, do seem to be able to act as switching mechanisms for sleep, consciousness and attention, turning them on or off. Most of our knowledge about brain physiology and consciousness, however, has come from the study of psychoactive drugs. It has long been known that introducing certain chemicals into the body can have a direct effect on consciousness, and it is worth looking at these in more detail.

The effects of drugs

Drugs that influence consciousness are known as psychoactive drugs, because they are active on the mind (the psyche). Some of these are freely available in Britain, while others are only available for medical use, or illegally. As they can have very different effects, it is worth looking at some of the more common drugs used in our society.

Ethical discussion

Psychological ethics committees consider it ethically unacceptable for a psychology student to conduct a study that involves administering drugs to participants. This applies even if the drugs are ones that the participants would be likely to take anyway, such as alcohol or caffeine.

Why do you think this is?

Socially accepted drugs

Nicotine

Some drugs acts on the peripheral nervous system to have their effect. As we saw in Chapter 5, the drug nicotine, for example (the active drug found in cigarettes and tobacco) blocks the nerve messages at the motor end plate, so that only part of the message from the brain to the muscles gets through. This produces a feeling of lethargy, which some people find relaxing, although others find it unpleasant. It also increases tiredness: people who smoke get tired more quickly than those who don't, and again some people interpret this as relaxation. As we saw earlier, this also helps us to understand why people who have given up nicotine often feel restless and fidgety: the brain has got used to getting only a partial response from the muscles, but now that the nicotine is no longer blocking those receptors, the full message from the brain gets through.

Alcohol

Alcohol, like nicotine and caffeine, is a powerful drug, although a legal one. It is a sedative, which has its effect by inhibiting noradrenaline receptors in the brain. This produces drowsiness and lower alertness to incoming sensory information. Because of its sedative effect, alcohol reduces tension, which may be why it sometimes appears to have an 'uplifting' effect, despite being a sedative. It is also an amnesiac drug - people forget things while under the influence of alcohol, and this, too, may contribute to making them feel more carefree and therefore more energetic. Long-term continual use of alcohol can eventually result in the destruction of the ability to store any new memories at all, a phenomenon known as Korsakoff's syndrome.

Socially acceptable drug taking

One of the most obvious effects that alcohol has on consciousness is to impair our ability to make judgements properly. When we have been drinking we may make decisions that we would not make while sober. The classic example of this, of course, is those people who believe that they drive perfectly well when they have been drinking. Their belief comes from alcohol's tendency to inhibit critical judgement: numerous studies have shown that even a very small amount of alcohol causes drivers to make far more mistakes and to have a slower reaction time. Drivers are also far more likely to shrug their mistakes off, or even not to notice them at all, which is why they sometimes believe that they can drive better when, actually, they are driving far more dangerously.

Caffeine

Caffeine, another common, everyday drug, is a powerful stimulant. It acts directly on the central nervous system, producing a heightened level of autonomic arousal (see Chapter 6). Like other stimulants, prolonged heavy use of caffeine can have a debilitating effect on the individual: it can produce disturbed sleep or insomnia, nervousness and irritability, and even anxiety attacks. In some women, it also seems to increase menstrual pain. Caffeine is found in tea, coffee and cola drinks, although its level is lower in tea than in coffee.

7.2 Everyday drugs

Many people are becoming much more aware of the everyday drugs which are in coffee, tea, cigarettes and alcoholic drinks. But how much do people actually know of the effects of these drugs? And how much of them do they actually consume? Try drawing up an interview schedule that will allow you to find out what people know about how these drugs work, and what the normal rate of consumption of these drugs is. Try it out among people that you know. When you are sure that you have got your questions right, interview half a dozen people, and find out which of these drugs they take, and in what quantity. You might also find it interesting to see if they recognise that these really are drugs.

An additional possibility is extend your questions, in order to see if their use of everyday drugs seems to be correlated with anything else about them - for example, their age, their lifestyle, or their occupations.

If you wanted to expand this into a full-scale formal survey, what steps would you have to take?

We can see, then, that psychoactive drugs have a variety of different effects on consciousness. While we may be no further on in understanding exactly what consciousness is, we can describe some of the factors that are involved in changing states of consciousness, and infer from these something of how consciousness might be formed. Even then, we cannot say directly that such-and-such a physiological process causes such-and-such a change in consciousness, because that seems to be so strongly linked with external circumstances too. Nor can we identify a localised area of the brain for consciousness: although consciousness does seem to be something to do with the cerebral cortex, it seems to be much more concerned with the action of the cerebrum as a whole, rather than being a localised function. This is true of a number of other mental processes, too, like learning. In the next chapter, we shall look at what is known about how some of the other mental processes are mediated by the cerebral cortex.

Nicotine, alcohol and caffeine are all legal drugs in our society, and available to anyone who wants to buy them, even though they are quite powerful in their effects. Other drugs, however, are only legally available for medical use, although they are sometimes used illegally as recreational drugs. We shall look at some of these.

Prescribed drugs

Stimulants

Amphetamines are powerful stimulants (stronger than caffeine) which have been used by medical and military personnel to prolong endurance and attention over long periods. In the short term, amphetamines increase concentration and appear also to produce feelings of social confidence. They can be addictive, however, and they also reduce appetite, which means that the prolonged use of amphetamines can often lead to serious physical debilitation through malnutrition, as well as to psychological disturbances, notably feelings of paranoia.

Cocaine

Cocaine is another type of stimulant drug, used in medicine for its anaesthetic qualities, and used illegally for the feeling of euphoria and increased energy which it produces. In the past, it was widely used, and believed to be completely safe, by many professional figures. Freud, for example, was a heavy user of cocaine. As with other drugs, prolonged use can lead to serious physical debilitation as well as distorting the individual's view of reality, partly because its energising effects mean that the person becomes insensitive to their body's need for rest or for proper nourishment. The long-term use of cocaine also produces a physical addiction, with unpleasant withdrawal effects.

Sedatives

Sedatives like diazepam (Valium) and chlorpromazine (Largactyl) have been used by the medical profession, particularly in the treatment of people who are psychiatrically disturbed. They act to damp down the activity of the autonomic nervous system (see Chapter 6) and so quieten people down. Diazepam is the milder of the two, and was widely prescribed for everyday anxieties during the 1960s and 1970s, before it was discovered to be physically addictive. Chlorpromazine is a powerful tranquilliser which can induce heavy sleep, or even unconsciousness, if administered in appropriate doses. Because of this, it is often used to subdue psychiatric patients whose excitability is judged to make them a danger to themselves or others.

Narcotics

Narcotic drugs, quite literally, are drugs which induce sleep or unconsciousness. Many narcotic drugs are used therapeutically, as pain-killers. The two most powerful of these, morphine and heroin, are opiates, synthesized from the naturally-occurring drug opium. They were both used extensively by the medical profession as analgesics (pain-killers) before it became apparent that they were highly addictive. Now, they are still used, but only in very extreme cases where milder drugs would be ineffective. They appear to simulate the action of the brain's own analgesics - the endorphins and enkephalins which are produced during strenuous exercise, and which inhibit feelings of pain and produce a sense of euphoria.

Opiates are widely used as illegal drugs, and are probably the most dangerous of all. When they are first taken, they seem to induce a feeling of happiness and well-being, which encourages the person to try them again. Relatively little contact with the drug is sufficient for someone to become addicted, and, as the addiction progresses, the drugged experience becomes seen as a necessity for living. A physical habituation occurs too: larger and larger doses become necessary in order to produce the same effect. All this, coupled with the unpleasant withdrawal symptoms which addicts experience when they stop taking it, mean that the person usually becomes increasingly desperate to maintain their habit, and may easily turn to crime if they cannot satisfy it any other way.

Hallucinogens

Some drugs produce direct changes in consciousness, producing hallucinations or enhancing perceptual awareness. These are rarely used therapeutically nowadays, although Aaronson and Osmond (1970) suggested that LSD could be effective in psychotherapy with mildly neurotic individuals. In general, however, these substances are used illegally as recreational drugs, as they are known to produce powerfully enhanced sensations and sometimes even hallucinations. Most hallucinogenic drugs come from natural sources, and were frequently used as a source of inspiration by writers and artists right up until the early part of this century. Mescaline, for example, is extracted from the peyote cactus, and psilocybin is obtained from psilocybin mushrooms. The most powerful hallucinogen, however, seems to be the drug LSD (lysergic acid diethylamide) and this is manufactured synthetically. Hallucinogens have a chemical structure which is similar to that of the naturally-occurring neurotransmitter serotonin, and they seem to have their effects by being picked up at the serotonin receptor sites.

Studies of LSD by psychologists during the 1960s, notably Timothy Leary, emphasised the importance of **set** and **setting** - that the effect of the drug depended on a combination of the mental set, or state of readiness, of the person, and the setting in which they were going to take the drug. If this was such as to produce anxiety or fear, an unpleasant experience would result. This interaction of the physiological effect of the drug with the environmental and social circumstances raises a number of questions about the relationship between consciousness and understanding, although since the 1960s psychologists have looked for rather less controversial ways of exploring this connection.

Summary

1. Sleep takes place in cycles - while sleeping, we alternate between different levels of sleep. We also show diurnal, or circadian rhythms in our pattern of sleep and wakefulness.
2. There are physiological correlates to sleep, which mean that we can see by EEG records when people are deeply asleep and when they are dreaming.
3. Studies of dreaming have shown that external stimuli can be included in dreams, and that people can learn to control lucid dreams.
4. Several different theories have been put forward to explain why we dream. Freud suggested that it was unconscious wish-fulfilment; but Evans suggested that it is our way of sorting out sensory information.
5. Early investigations of consciousness included the idea that consciousness comes from a combination of external sensations and internal states.
6. Investigations of consciousness have shown that different states of consciousness may connect with physiological indicators, like EEG patterns.
7. Psychoactive drugs such as stimulants, sedatives, narcotics and hallucinogens can produce powerful changes in states of consciousness.

Chapter 8 - Cognitive functions and the brain

As we look at the 'higher' mental processes of human beings, we will be concentrating mainly on the cerebral cortex, as this mediates most of these kinds of functioning. However, as with all the other parts of the brain, the cerebral cortex does not work alone but as a *system* with other parts of the brain such as the thalamus or the hippocampus, which we will also be looking at where relevant.

The study of the cerebral cortex is often concerned with the question of **localisation of function** - how far the functions of the cerebral cortex are located at one specific site, or how far they are non-localised and occur as a result of the general action of the whole of the cerebrum. As you read through this chapter, you will see that some of the cerebral functions are very clearly localised, such as the language or sensory functions, while others such as learning seem to be diffused throughout the cortex. In addition to this, we will be looking at the different roles taken by the two halves of the **cerebrum** - the cerebral hemispheres.

In this chapter we will look in turn at the functions of memory, sense perception, language and learning. Then we'll look at some of the work on hemisphere differences. It must be emphasised, though, that we are still a very long way from understanding completely how the cerebral cortex works. As with every other part of the brain, we know a little about its functioning, but by no means everything about it!

Memory

One of the human abilities which psychologists have studied in most detail is memory, but its relationship with the brain and how memories are stored and coded is not yet understood at all. We can get some ideas about it from some cases where brain damage has resulted in loss of memory (amnesia), but often different findings seem to contradict each other, and what one researcher finds is not the same as that found by another.

The role of the hippocampus

Although we are a long way from understanding just exactly which parts of the brain store memories (if any), we do know that there is a particular part of the limbic system, known as the **hippocampus**, which is very important in the process of storing new information. A study by Milner in 1966, of a patient who had undergone surgery which damaged the hippocampus, reported that this man was unable to store new information. He could remember well information which had been stored before the operation and he had what seemed to be a short-term memory so that his conversation, for instance, was normal. However, information which had to be stored and retained for a long period of time, like a new address, did not seem to 'sink in'. It seemed that the damage to the hippocampus had made him unable to learn new information, although he could still remember the old things.

However, Milner's conclusions were criticised by Warrington and Weiskrantz in 1973. They re-examined the same patient, and found that in particular situations he could recall new information and retrieve it when he needed it. Warrington and Weiskrantz suggested that the problem was coding the information - connecting it with other things so that it could be recalled easily.

Korsakoff's syndrome

Baddeley (1982) suggested that one reason why patients with **Korsakoff's Syndrome** were unable to remember new information might be because they were suffering from damage to the hippocampus and the temporal lobes of the brain. The syndrome is brought about by drinking excessively and eating too little over a long period of time which results in a thiamin deficiency. Many long term alcoholics end up with the syndrome, a serious form of amnesia, whereby they are unable to recall events from one day to the next, even when they are not drinking. It seems that this is an effect of long-term thiamine deprivation. Although, as said earlier, we do not really know very much about how memories work in the brain, it does seem that the hippocampus is involved in long-term memory in some kind of way.

Perception

Although most of perception – i.e. the interpretation of information that we receive through our senses - takes place in the cerebrum, the **thalamus** is also involved in the senses for sight and hearing. Information from the eyes and ears passes through the thalamus, and the neurones which are carrying it synapse there, passing the messages on to other neurones which will carry it to the visual cortex. In the process, the information is sorted out and organised, so that when it is transmitted to the visual or auditory cortex it arrives in a fairly coherent form.

Specialised cells for visual coding

In 1968, Hubel and Wiesel published a paper which was the result of several years of painstaking research using micro electrode recordings to study the action of single neurones in the thalamus. Using cats, they implanted electrodes into the **lateral geniculate nuclei** of the thalamus, and then presented very specific visual stimuli to the animal. The cat would be facing a blank screen, and then might be shown one single short line on that screen, or just a dot. By recording which neurones fired when a particular stimulus was presented, Hubel and Wiesel were gradually able to 'map out' a picture of the way that neurones in the thalamus organise visual information.

Simple, complex and hypercomplex cells

They found that there were three distinct types of cells in the thalamus which responded to specific visual stimuli, and that these seemed to be organised into a kind of hierarchy, with some cells receiving information from a large number of other cells. The basic 'receiving' cells were called **simple cells**. Simple cells would react to a dot or a line which was presented to a particular part of the visual field, say, to the upper left of your field of vision. Any stimulus which included visual cells being stimulated in that part of the visual field would cause those simple cells to fire. In addition, simple cells would fire in response to a line at a particular angle, or orientation. So there would be some cells which would respond, say, to a horizontal line presented in the centre of the visual field, other cells which would respond to a line 10 degrees off horizontal in the centre of the visual field, and some cells which would respond to a horizontal line in the lower left of the visual field. In the thalamus there were enough simple cells that all of the information which was being picked up by the retina could be coded in this way.

Blakemore (1983) showed that this range of simple cells was partly acquired through experience. Although some of the cells in the thalamus seemed to have 'pre-set' functions, in that they would respond to lines of particular orientation regardless of the animal's experience, this was only about 10% of the total. If cats were brought up with restricted visual experience, such as only seeing vertical lines, most of their simple cells would become attuned to vertical lines, and would fire in response to vertical visual stimuli.

Hubel and Wiesel showed that the simple cells would also set off other cells in the thalamus which they called **complex cells**. These cells would receive information from several different simple cells, so that they would fire in response say, to a line found in a particular part of the visual field but at any angle; or to a line at a particular orientation which occurred in any part of the visual field. So these complex cells were the first stage in organising and grouping the visual information which was being received.

In turn, the complex cells sent information to another set of cells in the thalamus. These would receive information from several different complex cells, such that the cell would receive information about lines of several different orientations. This meant that these cells, which Hubel and Wiesel called **hypercomplex cells**, would respond to simple patterns or shapes.

So, with these patterns, we have the beginnings of perception taking place in the thalamus. The visual information from the retina has been sorted out and organised into figures and groups ready for the visual cortex to interpret it.

Ethical discussion

The detailed investigations conducted by Hubel and Wiesel, and by Blakemore, have told us a great deal about how visual information is processed. We now know more about the visual cortex and how it works than about any other part of the cerebrum, and these studies have also enhanced our understanding of human sight problems, such as astigmatism.

Hubel and Wiesel shared a Nobel Prize for their work.

However, the only way to find out exactly which brain cells were involved in processing visual information was to kill the animals that were involved in the experiment, so that their brains could be dissected for microscopic analysis.

Was it worth it?

Sensory projection areas

When we look at other areas of the brain, we find that the cerebral cortex contains several different areas which are concerned with sensory perception, i.e. the interpretation of information coming through the senses. These are known as **sensory projection areas**.

The cerebral cortex is a large area of neurones on the outside of the cerebral hemispheres. (It seems to be the outer surface of the cerebrum that is important.) It is very highly folded, with a large number of ridges and grooves. A ridge is known as a gyrus and a groove or fissure is known as a sulcus. Each cerebral hemisphere is divided into four lobes: the frontal lobe, the parietal lobe, the occipital lobe, and the temporal lobe.

The motor cortex

Running from the top of each hemisphere roughly downwards, is a fissure known as the **central sulcus**. In 1950 a neurosurgeon called Penfield was performing a series of studies on patients who had to have brain surgery, by stimulating the surface areas of the cortex electrically. Penfield found that when he stimulated a strip of the frontal lobe which ran alongside the central sulcus, his patients would produce sudden movements of the body. Different parts of this strip would produce movements in different parts of the body, so that one part might be flexing of the leg muscles, while another might be movement in the tongue.

Penfield found that the more mobile a particular area of the body was, the larger the area of brain would be which seemed to stimulate it.

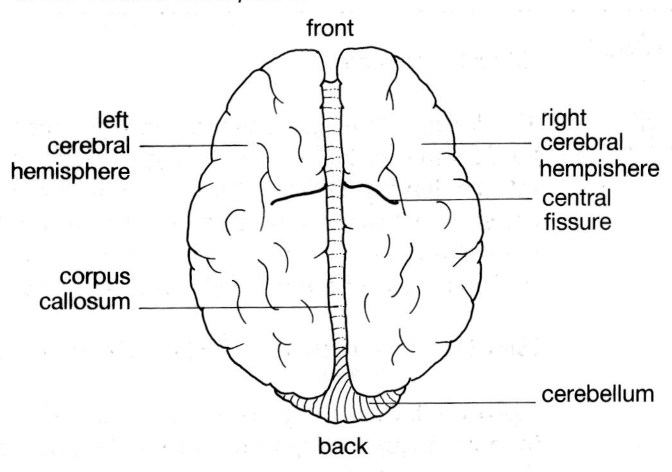

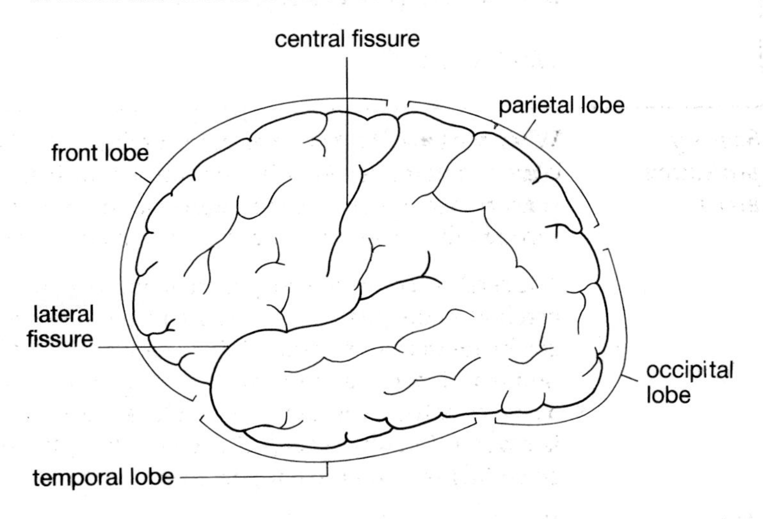

8.1 The main areas of the cerebrum

The sensory cortex

On the other side of the central sulcus, in the parietal lobe, Penfield found an area which seemed to mediate perception of touch. When this strip of cortex was stimulated, patients reported feeling as though they had been touched on a particular part of the body. Different parts of the body corresponded to different parts of the cortical area, and again the most sensitive areas seemed to have the largest area of cortex devoted to them.

The visual cortex

At the back of the brain, in the occipital lobe, is the area which mediates visual perception. Studies of servicemen who suffered shrapnel injuries during the First World War showed that those who had bits of shrapnel lodged in this particular region of the brain tended to suffer from partial blindness. Since most servicemen's sight is thoroughly tested, it was possible to know what damage had resulted from these injuries very clearly. Often when we are looking at the results of accidental injury to the brain, we are hampered by not knowing very well what the person was like beforehand, and our beliefs about injuries can create effects which seem to be the result of the injury but aren't really. Personality changes, for instance, may be more the result of people *expecting* the individual to behave differently, than of the damage itself. But visual faults such as partial blindness are much more clear cut.

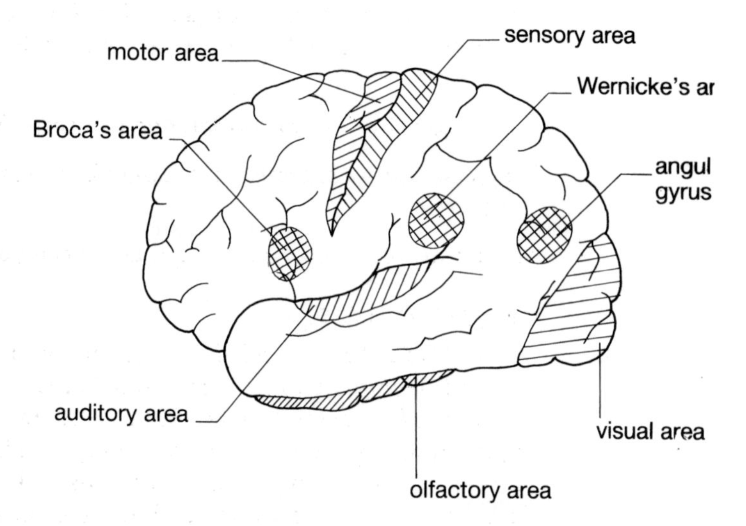

8.2 Localised functions of the cerebral cortex

Partly as a result of studies such as those by Penfield, and studies of accidental injury, we know of two other main sensory areas in the cortex. These are the olfactory cortex, which is a strip at the base of the temporal lobe, involved in interpreting the sense of smell, and the auditory cortex, mediating hearing, which is an area of the temporal lobe just below the lateral fissure.

8.1 Sensory habituation

Sensory habituation is the way that we become accustomed to certain continuous stimuli, so that we don't really even notice them any more.

One very simple way of investigating sensory habituation is by using the difference between the evening and the morning. In some situations we are more adjusted to an intensive amount of stimulation than we are at other times. But on each occasion we tend to think of each level as being quite adequate and we don't really notice the difference.

Try setting things up so that you will notice the difference. For instance: if you have a dimmer switch in your living room, try setting it to a comfortable level of brightness just before you go to bed. In the morning, go into the room again and notice how dark the room seems to be, even though it seemed fairly bright the night before!

Alternatively, use auditory stimuli. Set your record player or radio to a comfortable level the night before. As soon as you wake up, put it on again. Does it still feel like a comfortable level? For most people, it is far too loud for first thing in the morning.

What explanations can you provide for these effects?

Why do you think we need more light but less noise in the mornings?

What other forms of sensory habituation can you investigate?

Language areas

Broca's area

In 1865, Paul Broca published a report on a patient who had suffered damage to one specific, small area of the cortex, at the base of the frontal lobe on the left hemisphere. As a result of this injury, Broca's patient was unable to say certain words, and had problems with getting ideas into words. The area which was damaged came to be known as Broca's area, and as a result of many subsequent studies as well as Broca's own, we now know that this is the part of the brain which is responsible for formulating speech. It is usually situated on the left hemisphere, but in some people it is on the right.

Wernicke's area

Another specific area on the left hemisphere is found in the parietal lobe, and is known as Wernicke's area, after Wernicke who identified it in 1874. This area is also concerned with language functioning but seems to be the part that mediates comprehension of language – understanding what has been said to us, or what we have read. People with damage to this area may be able to speak perfectly well, but have difficulty in understanding what is being said to them.

The angular gyrus

A third area to do with language is found in the occipital lobe of the brain, again on the left hemisphere. This area is known as the angular gyrus, and its function seems to be receiving visual information from the visual cortex, and translating it into the equivalent of the spoken word, so that it can be understood. This area plays a large part in reading. Reading difficulties, or dyslexia, may sometimes be a result of damage to this area, although not always.

Psychology in Action

Although having a good grasp of spoken language, dyslexia sufferers find it difficult to interpret written words. Words and numbers may appear scrambled, sometimes resulting in confusion of memory and lack of physical co-ordination. Although many studies of dyslexia have been carried out, the cause is as yet unknown. One theory is that sensory memory for written words lasts for a longer period of time in dyslexics and interferes with their translation by the perceptual centres of the brain.

In a recent study carried out by the makers of the television programme *Public Eye*, learning difficulties were strongly linked to delinquent behaviour. They interviewed 115 offenders and found that 52 per cent displayed dyslexic tendencies, a rate ten times higher than in the general population. Although they had only studied a small sample, their findings are borne out by many similar studies in America. These concluded that learning difficulties can lead to frustration and low self-esteem and in some cases to a life of truancy and crime. Once learning difficulties have been overcome, many offenders do not re-offend.

Experts are now being called in to help dyslexia sufferers in court. Due to problems with short-term memory, sequencing and perception, dyslexics may incorrectly interpret a situation. For example, they may not understand police cautions or may be asked to sign statements which they cannot read.

Adapting to injury

If the left hemisphere is damaged in somebody under 12 years old, the language functions usually change hemispheres, switching across to the right. Children can usually recover well from specific forms of damage to the brain, as it seems that the neurological circuits are quite flexible and can change or adapt to new circumstances readily. In adults things are normally much more fixed, although people recovering from strokes have shown that, if they try hard, adults too can regain a surprisingly large amount of brain functioning after injury. Also, a study by Gooch, in 1980, showed that patients who had suffered severe damage to the left hemisphere, such that their language functions were seriously impaired, could sometimes recover their speech functioning almost completely if they then had a total left hemispherectomy, in which the whole of the left hemisphere is removed. However, this is a very drastic sort of operation, so it could only be done on patients whose brain functioning was very seriously impaired already, and we have no way of knowing how typical they are of most people. Still, it does seem as if, even in adult humans, the brain is very adaptable.

Learning

Although sense perception, movement and language are functions which seem to be highly localised in the cerebral cortex (that is, they are found in particular places), there are other functions which are not. No one, for example, has found a localised area for time perception, or for consciousness, and there are large parts of the cortex which, although active, seem to have a general part to play rather than one specific one. We call these parts 'association cortex', as they seem to be concerned with things like thinking, memory, and learning, and a large part of those activities consist of associating one thing with another.

The law of mass action

In 1929, Lashley investigated learning and the cerebral cortex. He trained rats to run particular mazes, until they could reach the goal box in as short a time as possible. Then he selectively destroyed parts of the cerebrum, 15% at a time, and measured how good they were at remembering the mazes they had learned, and at learning new ones. There were two main findings which arose from his work: the **Law of Mass Action**, stated that the whole cerebral cortex seemed to work together, as a mass, and the more of it that was destroyed the more impairment there was to functioning. Lashley also discovered the **equipotentiality** of the cortex - that it did not matter which particular parts of the association cortex were destroyed, as each part seemed to have an equal role in learning and no one part seemed to be more concerned with learning than any other part. So it seems that the functions of the cerebral cortex are only partly localised for language, sense perception and movement, and that the other functions are not localised at all.

In broad terms of preferred functioning, however, there do seem to be some large overall differences between the two hemispheres of the brain. We have already mentioned that language functions are usually located on the left hemisphere rather than on the right, and other functions seem to vary from one side of the brain to the other as well. For instance, in terms of which parts of the brain co-ordinate which parts of the body, the left hemisphere controls the right side of the body, and the right hemisphere controls the left side. So, for instance, if a person has had a stroke, we can tell what side of the brain it is on, because the effects will tend to happen on one side of the body only. Also if it is on the right side of the body then there is a good chance that they will have suffered some language damage as well. People who are right-handed are said to be left-hemisphere dominant, because it is the left hemisphere that controls the right hand. Although, interestingly, handedness does not go along with what side the language functions are on at all. Some people are right-handed but also have language in the right hemisphere.

Methods of studying the brain

By now you will probably have noticed that the way that the brain works has been studied in many different ways. Although none of these methods of study will give us all of the answers, by using a variety of different investigative techniques we can find out a great deal about how the brain is working.

Physical

One way to identify brain functions is by physical intervention, for example by surgical **lesions** - cutting through a part of the brain and seeing what changes occur as a result. **Ablation** is similar, but in this case a part of the brain is completely removed or destroyed. Studies of accidental injury can also sometimes provide us with useful information.

Chemical

Other studies have concentrated on the chemical functioning of the brain, by either chemical injection, in which small amounts of particular neurotransmitters are injected directly into the brain; or by chemical sampling, in which a small amount of the chemicals present in the brain are removed and analysed.

Electrical

A third set of investigations involve looking at the electrical activity of the brain. **EEGs** and **evoked potential** recordings take measurements of the overall activity going on in different parts of the brain, while microelectrode recordings simply involve the recording of single nerve cells, or small groups of nerve cells. Sometimes, too, electrical stimulation is used, to see what happens when a particular part of the brain is stimulated.

Scanning

The fourth kind of method which we have for studying how the brain functions has been developed more recently: scanning. There are two main kinds of brain scanning techniques. **X-ray tomography** involves taking a series of X-rays at different levels through the head, and building them up together to form a complete X-ray picture of the brain. **Radioactive labelling** involves giving the research participant a harmless substance to eat, which will pass around the bloodstream and show up on a scanner. Because nerve cells obtain their nutrients from the countless blood vessels which fill the brain, and because nerve cells which have been active require more nutrients to restore them, it is possible to detect the areas of the brain which are using most blood - in other words, which are most active - while the person is doing a particular task.

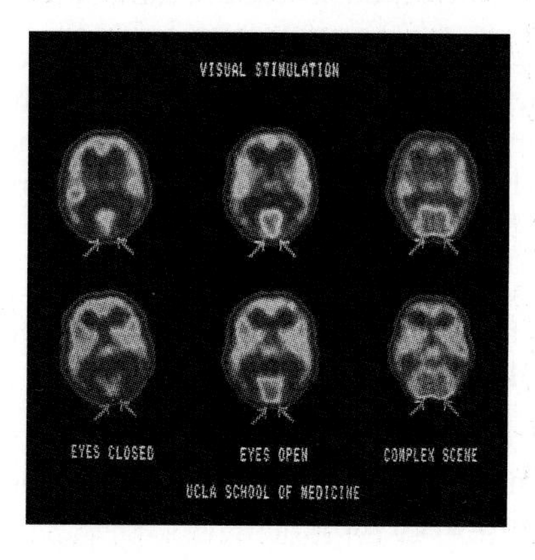

Scanned images of cerebral activity

Each of these techniques has its disadvantages as well as its advantages. Many of them have also been used in studies described in these chapters. You may find it interesting to look through and see how many different methods of study you can find examples of, and also to discuss each technique and try to identify the advantages and disadvantages of each one.

8.2 Cerebral dominance and mirror-drawing

The cerebrum is divided into two halves, known as right and left cerebral hemispheres. Each half controls the opposite side of the body: the right side of the cerebrum controls the left side of the body, and the left side of the cerebrum controls the right side of the body.

Most people have one hemisphere which is dominant, and they find it easier to learn physical skills with the parts of the body controlled by their dominant hemisphere. You can investigate this.

For this study, you will need a shoe box, some 'Blu-tak', some books, and a mirror-tile. You will also need some copies of a star-shape with a double line around the edges, or some similar type of pattern.

The task that you are going to do is to learn to draw round a shape, without being able to see your hand directly – only reflected in the mirror.

Set the mirror-tile up on a desk or table, using Blu-tak and some kind of support, such as a book. Cut off one end of the shoe-box, enough of the other end for you to be able to put your hand into it while it is standing upside-down on the table. Arrange the shoe-box in front of the mirror in such a way that, when you put your hand under the shoe-box, you can see it reflected in the mirror, but you can't look at it directly.

Now, try drawing round the shape between the two outlines, and without touching the sides or going over the lines. Do it first with your favourite hand, and the next time with your other hand. Then, do each hand again with a fresh copy of the puzzle.

For each of your trials, count up the number of times that you have touched the edge of the puzzle or gone over the lines. Did you improve the second time?

Subtract the score that you got the second time you tried each hand, from your score the first time that you tried each hand. Which hand improved most?

Can you think of any other things that you could investigate using this technique?

From looking at the brain and the different ways that it works, we can see that it is involved in many different aspects of our behaviour. In these chapters, we have only been able to select a few of those aspects, but researchers are continually discovering more and more about it. In the next section, we will go on to look more closely at the cognitive functioning of human beings.

Split-brain studies

In 1952, a study by Myers and Sperry showed that the two halves of the brain could act almost as two separate brains, if they were separated. By cutting through the **corpus callosum** and the **optic chiasma** in cats, they showed that the right side of the cat's brain might learn to solve a puzzle, say, but if the left eye had been covered when it was learned and the same puzzle was shown to the left eye (with the right eye covered), then the cat would behave as if it had never seen the problem before.

The optic chiasma is a part of the optic nerve where the fibres from each eye meet and join up. If it is severed, then the fibres from the right eye will only connect with the right side of the brain, and fibres from the left eye will only pass to the left side of the brain. So showing the cat a problem while it is wearing an eye-patch over the left eye, means that only the right side of the cat's brain is dealing with and learning the problem. The left side has not received any information at all. In a normal cat, the optic chiasma and the corpus callosum carry messages from one side of the brain of one eye, to the other side, so the messages received by one eye are dealt with by both halves of the brain.

Suppressing epilepsy

Human beings have the same arrangement of nerve fibres in the brain, so when it was discovered that in all other respects the cats seemed to be perfectly normal and unharmed, there was considerable interest in whether the severing of the two halves of the brain could be done with humans. The main reason for the interest was the medical case of severe epilepsy. In an epileptic fit, there is a sudden firing of the neurones in the cortex, which spreads uncontrollably to include large areas of the cerebrum. This results in a seizure, and in severe epileptic fits the person may become unable to control the body, so their muscles go into spasm. People recovering from an epileptic fit are often confused, and do not remember their immediate circumstances until they have had time to recover. Although this condition is not dangerous to other people, it is extremely disturbing to the epileptics themselves, and means that they are not able to do things like driving or operating other kinds of machinery. Drugs which suppress epilepsy have serious side-effects which also interfere with normal living. Normally, an epileptic fit will start in the temporal lobe of one side of the brain, and spread across, and so surgeons wondered whether severing the corpus callosum would help people who were very severely epileptic. At least, it was thought, it would mean that only one side of the brain would be affected, and so only one half of the body.

When the operation was performed on human beings, the results were very interesting. It seemed to reduce the number of epileptic fits far more than people had hoped; instead of only having seizures on one half of the body, patients did not seem to have them at all, or only very small outbreaks of neuronal firing in the temporal lobe. But, in addition, psychologists and neurosurgeons were now able to investigate the ways that the two halves of the cerebral cortex worked.

Hemisphere differences

In 1967, Gazzaniga and Sperry published a paper which reported some of the findings from these studies. It became clear that the left hemisphere was usually responsible for language, as mentioned before, but also that it seemed to be very much better at mathematical and logical tasks than the right hemisphere. On the other hand, the right hemisphere seemed to be better at tasks which involved drawing, or spatial tasks. If a picture was shown to the left eye, research participants could say what it was, but if it was shown to the right eye they could not. Initially, this was taken to mean that the right hemisphere was incapable of identifying objects, but then they found that although participants could not say what they had seen in a picture, they could identify it by pointing with the left hand, or by selecting the relevant object from some others.

Cross-cueing

It seemed that the right hemisphere was not totally without language. Research participants could perform simple language tasks, such as picking out a pencil from a group of unseen objects with the left hand, if the word 'pencil' was flashed to the right eye. But they could only manage simple nouns, and did not seem to be able to deal with verbs of more complicated phrases. Sperry and Gazzaniga also found that there was a certain amount of **cross-cueing** from one hemisphere to the next, by the brain using actions to inform the other half. For instance, in a typical experiment, research participants would be shown a red or green light to the right hemisphere, and asked to name the colour. Split brain participants could always get this right if they were allowed to say more than one word, for instance, to a red light they might guess 'green', then frown and shake the head, then say 'no, red'. The frowning or head-shaking would be the right hemisphere's way of informing the other hemisphere that it had guessed wrong, and the left hemisphere (being, of course, a human brain and therefore highly intelligent!) would quickly catch on and correct the guess. Gazzaniga and Sperry found that these cues could become very subtle, which is only to be expected since the human brain is extremely complex and capable of highly sophisticated learning.

Because the left hemisphere seemed to be more involved with the sorts of abilities valued by our society, such as logic, language and calculation, Sperry concluded that it was superior in functioning to the right hemisphere, and this supported the idea that it was the 'dominant' hemisphere. Gradually, however, researchers became more aware of the way that the right hemisphere functioned. Ornstein (1974) argued that the two hemispheres had very different functions, with the left hemisphere having verbal, analytical and sequential functions such as are needed for science and mathematics, while the right hemisphere had holistic, intuitive and artistic ability such as are found in the creative arts and humanities. Ornstein also considered that society had come to reflect the prevailing hemisphere dominance, while other societies in the past had valued the other kinds of abilities more. However, Ornstein's views are rather extreme and exaggerate the differences between the two too much. Each hemisphere can do the other's functions a little; it is just that each is slightly better at its own.

Recovery from hemispher-ectomy

Gooch's studies of hemispherectomies, which we mentioned before, showed that to think of certain abilities as possessed *only* by one hemisphere was misleading. One of the research participants studied was a 47-year-old man who had suffered very frequent seizures in the left hemisphere, resulting in partial paralysis of his left side, and continual serious speech disorders. This was brought on by a large tumour, and although surgeons are usually reluctant to perform left hemispherectomies (because they think it will leave the patient totally without language for the rest of their life), they were obliged to do it. At first, after the operation, the participant found it difficult to understand more than a few words. But as the weeks went by, his language abilities became better and better. Ten weeks after the operation he could communicate with simple questions and answers, which was a great improvement on before, when the seizures had greatly interfered with his speech. Five months after the operation, he suddenly became able to remember a whole range of familiar songs, hymns and other songs that he had known since his childhood, and six months after his operation he could use irony and repartee. This recovery was totally unexpected, and raises several interesting questions about how language functions are stored in the brain. Another three cases of left hemispherectomy in adults reported by Gooch showed similar results.

It seems that both hemispheres are capable of both sets of functions, but do not use their abilities if the other hemisphere is present. Gooch argued that if such recoveries were to happen as a general rule, then complete hemispherectomy might be a much better way of dealing with such serious disorders than partial removal of damaged areas of the cortex, because then the potential in the other hemisphere would emerge. As a general rule, he argued, one hemisphere being present inhibits the other one from taking over any of its functions, at least in adults; although as we have seen, functions can transfer from one hemisphere to the other in children if there is damage.

Summary

1 The cerebrum seems to be involved in a wide variety of cognitive functions. Some of these functions are localised in particular areas of the cortex.

2 Memory is usually a cerebral function, but the hippocampus of the limbic system may also be involved.

3 Sense perception appears to operate in the sensory projection areas of the cerebral cortex. Vision, touch, smell and hearing all have specific areas on the cerebrum.

4 There are three specific areas for language on the cerebrum. These are Broca's area, Wernicke's area, and the angular gyrus. Each area is concerned with a different aspect of language functioning.

5 Learning does not seem to be a localised cerebral function. The cerebrum seems to operate on the basis of equipotentiality - the whole of the cortex seems to be equally important in learning.

6 The main methods of studying the brain are by using physical, chemical, electrical or scanning techniques.

7 Sperry showed that the halves of the cerebrum can operate as separate 'brains' if they are divided surgically. The left side deals more with language and logic, while the right side seems to deal more with creative pursuits.

Suggestions for further reading

Beaumont, J. G. 1988 *Understanding Neuropsychology.* Oxford: Blackwell

Bloom, F. E. & Lazerson, A. 1988 *Brain, Mind and Behaviour* 2nd edn. New York: W. H. Freeman

Evans, P. 1989 *Motivation and Emotion.* London: Routledge

Gray, J. 1989 *The Psychology of Fear and Stress* 2nd edn. London: Weidenfeld

Green, S. 1993 *Principles of Bio-Psychology.* London: Erlbaum

Hayes, N. 1998 *Foundations of Psychology* 2nd edn. London: Nelson

Kalat, J. W. 1992 *Biological Psychology.* Pacific Grove: Brooks Cole

McIlveen, R. & Gross, R. 1996 *Biopsychology.* London: Hodder & Stoughton

Nathan, P. 1988 *The Nervous System.* Oxford: Oxford University Press

Sacks, O. 1986 *The Man Who Mistook His Wife for a Hat.* London: Picador

? Self Assessment Questions

1 **The central nervous system consists of:**

a) the brain and spinal cord.
b) the brain.
c) the spinal cord.
d) the somatic nervous system.

2 **Messages pass from one neurone to another across:**

a) a synapse.
b) a receptor site.
c) an axon.
d) a cell body.

3 **When a nerve cell produces an electrical impulse, we say it is:**

a) receptive.
b) firing.
c) transducing.
d) charged.

4 **Synapses that make a neurone more likely to fire are known as:**

a) inhibitory synapses.
b) refractory synapses.
c) excitatory synapses.
d) olfactory synapses.

5 **When a nerve cell has fired there is a short period of time during which it will not fire. This is known as:**

a) the relative refractory period.
b) summation.
c) the absolute refractory period.
d) the dormant period.

6 **A motor neurone takes messages from the brain or spinal cord to:**

a) the muscles of the body.
b) the feet.
c) the sense organs.
d) the heart.

7 **The corpus callosum is:**

a) a band of fibres which joins the two cerebral hemispheres.
b) a lobe found in the cerebrum.
c) responsible for language.
d) involved in creative thinking.

8 **Babies born with no cerebrum are known as:**

a) anencephalic babies.
b) epileptic babies.
c) anorexic babies.
d) dyslexic babies.

9 **The pituitary gland is part of the:**

a) autonomic nervous system.
b) somatic nervous system.
c) endocrine system.
d) lymphatic system.

10 **Homeostasis refers to:**

a) the body's normal state of functioning.
b) lowering one's heart rate.
c) increasing the number of hormones released into the bloodstream.
d) controlling the body's responses through meditation.

11 Sensory deprivation means:

a) loss of sight.

b) being over-stimulated.

c) being deprived of sensory stimulation.

d) suffering from hallucinations.

12 Biofeedback is connected with:

a) sight.

b) receiving information about the workings of the body.

c) hearing.

d) visual illusions.

13 The term "arousal" refers to:

a) stress.

b) excitement and fear.

c) the amount of excitation of the autonomic nervous system.

d) anxiety.

14 A phobia is:

a) a fear of water.

b) an irrational fear of anything.

c) a fear of being in open spaces.

d) a fear of being enclosed.

15 Agoraphobia is:

a) a fear of spiders.

b) an irrational fear.

c) a fear of being in open spaces.

d) a fear of animals.

16 Implosion therapy involves:

a) confronting the fear.

b) gradually introducing a client to the thing they fear most.

c) showing a 'model' person coping adequately.

d) using drugs.

17 Which theory of emotion states that 'We feel sorrow because we weep'?

a) the James-Lange theory.

b) the Cannon-Bard theory.

c) Schachter and Singer's theory.

d) Ax's theory.

18 Brain activity can be measured using:

a) EEG traces.

b) ECG traces.

c) biofeedback techniques.

d) radar.

19 Schachter and Singer misinformed some subjects about physiological changes they were about to experience. These research participants:

a) interpreted the physiological changes in terms of what was going on around them.

b) felt no emotion.

c) felt less emotion than others.

d) were totally confused about what they felt.

20 A placebo is:

a) a salt solution.

b) water.

c) a substance that has no effect on a person.

d) a drug.

21 REM stands for:

a) rare eye movement.
b) right eye movement.
c) rapid eye movement.
d) risky eye movement.

22 An important brain system which appears to play a part in attention and arousal is the:

a) limbic system.
b) endocrine system.
c) reticular activating system.
d) lymphatic system.

23 The average new-born baby tends to spend:

a) 24 hours sleeping.
b) 20 hours sleeping.
c) 14 hours sleeping.
d) 6 hours sleeping.

24 The bodily patterns that we show over a 24-hour period are called:

a) adrenal rhythms.
b) diurnal rhythms.
c) day rhythms.
d) body clock rhythms.

25 Another name for 24-hour cycles of bodily functioning is:

a) circadian rhythms.
b) circus rhythms.
c) circumference rhythms.
d) cyclic rhythms.

26 Which one of the following statements is true:

a) some people never dream.
b) we all dream for several periods during any one night.
c) we dream continuously through the night.
d) we have only one dream period per night.

27 Several studies have shown that people who are able to recall their dreams when woken are very often in a period of:

a) REM sleep.
b) non-REM sleep.
c) level three sleep.
d) level two sleep.

28 Freud suggested that we dream in order to:

a) develop the superego.
b) let our unconscious wishes and desires come to the force.
c) relax.
d) get rid of aggression.

29 Alcohol is a:

a) sedative.
b) stimulant.
c) placebo.
d) narcotic.

30 Hunger seems to be controlled by the:

a) hippocampus.
b) hypothalamus.
c) visual cortex.
d) the pons.

31 Amnesia means:

a) a good memory.
b) loss of memory.
c) improving memory.
d) not being able to understand spoken words.

32 Most of our perception takes place in the:

a) cerebellum.
b) cerebrum.
c) auditory cortex.
d) the hypothalamus.

33 Simple cells:

a) respond to a dot or line presented to a particular part of the visual field and at a particular angle.
b) respond to any dots or lines in the visual field.
c) respond to a dot or line presented to a particular part of the visual field but at any angle.
d) respond to sounds.

34 Hyper complex cells:

a) respond only to dots or lines.
b) respond to simple shapes or patterns.
c) respond only to squares.
d) respond to sounds.

35 Narcotics are drugs that induce:

a) fear.
b) excitement.
c) pleasure.
d) sleep.

36 The auditory cortex is a part of the brain concerned with:

a) taste.
b) sight.
c) hearing.
d) touch.

37 If we were to say that language is highly localised in the cerebral cortex we would mean that it is:

a) controlled entirely by the cerebral cortex.
b) is controlled by one area of the cerebral cortex.
c) is controlled by specific areas of the cerebral cortex.
d) is not controlled by the cerebral cortex.

38 It is a well-known fact that the left hemisphere controls:

a) the left-hand side of the body.
b) all of the body.
c) the right-hand side of the body.
d) thinking.

39 The optic chiasma is:

a) the blind spot in the eye.
b) the iris.
c) a part of the optic nerve where the fibres from each eye meet and join up.
d) a band of fibres joining the two halves of the brain.

40 An epileptic fit is:

a) a sudden firing of neurones in the cortex.
b) a disease of the nervous system.
c) a fit of uncontrollable anger.
d) a hearing disorder.

Section 3 - Cognitive psychology

In this section we will be looking at that part of psychology known as cognitive psychology. Cognition is the name that we give to 'mental' functions, such as thinking, remembering, perception, and language. Cognitive psychology involves studying the processes involved in how we carry out those functions, and looking at the ways in which they work.

We will begin this section with an examination of what psychologists have found through the study of thinking: different forms of thinking, strategies for solving problems, and the ways in which concepts are formed and used. From there, we will go on to look at the way in which the language that we use may affect thinking, and how language itself is acquired. After that, we will be looking at how memory works: the way that we store our memories, for instance, and how we can improve our ability to remember things. And from there we will go on to consider our perceptual processes and the ways in which they may be influenced by other factors in our lives.

Chapter 9 - Thinking and problem-solving

Defining thinking

When we use the word 'thinking', we can mean quite a number of different things. We might mean, for instance, the pondering or reflecting on an issue which we often associate with intellectual activities such as philosophy. Alternatively, we might mean thinking *about* a problem, like the best way to get to the hospital in time for a clinic appointment. Sometimes, we use it to mean daydreaming: 'I was just thinking how nice it would be to win lots of money.' Or we might mean the process of making a decision: 'I don't know whether I'll be going to that party. I'll think about it.' These are all very different kinds of mental activities, which we call by the same name: thinking.

But what is thinking? Many psychologists have tried to define just exactly what we mean when we use the term, but it is a task which turns out to be very hard. Osgood, in 1953, defined thinking as 'the internal representation of events', which is rather vague, but probably a definition which few psychologists would disagree with. This way of defining thinking though, means that there is an extremely broad range of mental activities which could be called thinking. A dog, for instance, going into a house where it used to live and walking straight to the place where it used to keep its bones, would be said to have some kind of internal representation of events – so we would have to include its mental activity as thought. Some psychologists would find this acceptable, and some would insist that what the dog is doing is not 'really' thinking at all. As we look through some of the work which has been done on the study of thinking, you will be able to judge for yourself how far you consider this definition to be adequate.

The origins of thinking

There have been different ideas put forward on the origins of thinking - how it starts in the first place. Freud (1900) thought that thinking originated from the need to find ways to satisfy biological urges. By association, images of objects which satisfied needs like hunger would arise when an infant was hungry, and the thinking would arise from the need to make the internal image into reality, in the form of mechanisms to control movement in order to achieve a goal.

Piaget (1952) on the other hand, saw thinking as arising from a biological process of adaptation to the environment. The infant would develop its understanding of the world about it by forming internal representations or **schemata**. These would not only enable the child to direct its current behaviour so that it could adapt successfully to its environment, but would also provide a basis for future actions in new circumstances. These schemata were being continually developed as the child's experience grew, through a twin process of assimilating, or absorbing, new information, and adjusting the schema to fit new kinds of experiences – a process known as **accommodation**.

Dewey (1933) saw thinking as something which arises when we have a mismatch or discrepancy between what we expect to happen and what really happens. Many of the things which we do are done quite automatically: if you see a pen in front of you and you want to write something, you would just reach out, take hold of the pen, and very probably think no more about it. The behaviour and the mental processes underlying it are habitual and don't involve thinking. But if there was a discrepancy - say you reached out for the pen but your fingers closed on nothing - then you would certainly be likely to think about it! In fact, if you couldn't find an explanation, you would be likely to think about it quite a lot – it would form a problem to be solved. Dewey's theory is known as the **trouble theory** of thought – the idea that thinking happens when there is a mismatch between what we expect, and what we actually find.

Creativity

For the most part, when psychologists have studied thinking, they have tended to concentrate on what we call **directed thinking**, that is, thinking which is directed towards particular goals, such as problem-solving. Other forms of thinking have not been studied as deeply, partly because they are very difficult to get at experimentally. However, there has been a certain amount of work which has involved looking at highly creative people and the way that their work develops. In descriptions of the work of eminent scholars, artists, and scientists, a common theme often seems to emerge: that creativity happens as a three-stage process (Ghiselin 1952). Firstly, there is a long period of exposure to the kind of work they are doing – like techniques of painting or of scientific or literary study – which seems to familiarise the person thoroughly with the 'tools of the trade'. This is followed by the process identified by Wallas (1926) as **incubation**, in which nothing much seems to happen on a conscious level, but in which the unconscious mind seems to be continuing to work on ideas. Koestler (1964) referred to this period as a kind of dialogue between an 'inner self' and some 'other'. Many people seem to experience this as if there was some inner self that they are not quite familiar with, driving them towards the goal. You often hear writers, for instance, saying that their characters do not seem to be acting in the ways that they wanted them to. Once the period of incubation is over, the third stage is a period of activity, often quite intense, in which the person attempts to describe or express the ideas, theories, or artistic works which have become quite clear to them, sometimes very suddenly.

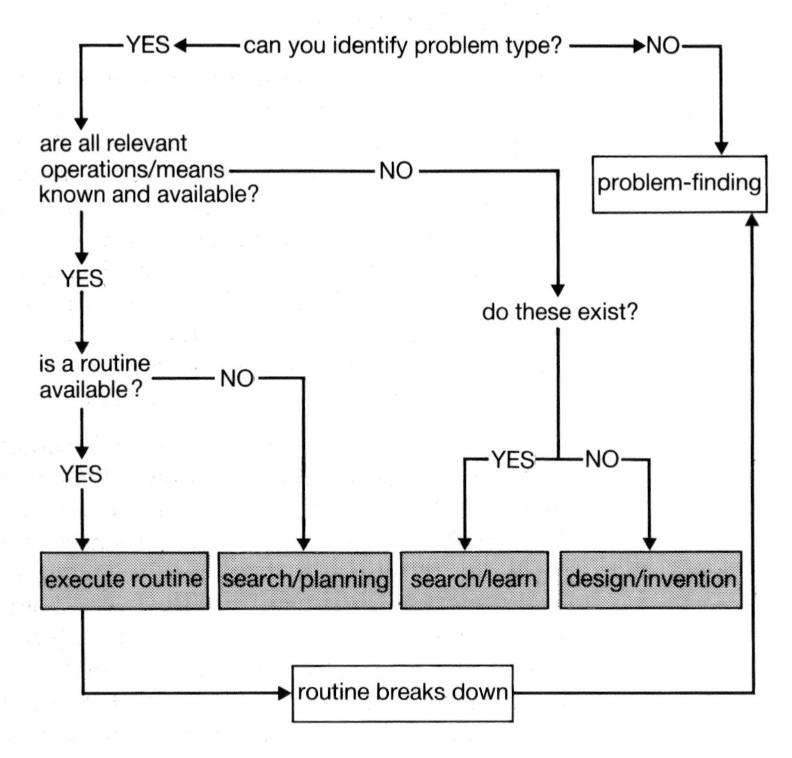

9.1 Howarth and Gillham's model of problem-solving

Creativity as problem-solving

Many people see this kind of creativity as a special kind of process, having very little in common with ordinary thinking. But Howarth and Gillham (1981) produced a model of problem-solving that could include the creativity process as a very extreme form. They consider that problem-solving as an activity may be broken down into a series of stages: (a) the identification of the problem type (familiarisation); (b) the acquisition of necessary skills (incubation); and (c) utilising aspects of design or invention to develop the solution (activity). Highly structured problems, with one 'right' answer, would have a greater emphasis on the identification of the problem type, but highly creative processes have a greater emphasis on the development of design and inventive aspects. Certainly, one thing which does seem to characterise highly creative people is the way that, once they have actually started to work on their creation, be it a theory or a work of art, they have a very clear sense of exactly what they need to do and a strong sense of whether it is 'right' or not. Often they won't stop until they feel that it is exactly right, and they can recognise this even though they were not clear about what they were doing when they started.

Problem-solving

Trial-and-error learning

An early study of problem-solving was performed by E. L Thorndike, in 1898. Thorndike set up a 'puzzle box', which was designed to examine how cats devise methods of escape. The cat would be shut in the box, and if it pulled a particular string which dangled down, the box would open. Thorndike found that the cats learned to escape from the box by a systematic process of trial and error - as they explored the box, eventually they would paw at the string and escape. Next time they were put in the box, they would paw at the string after a shorter time, and each further time they would get quicker and quicker, until eventually they would escape almost as soon as they were shut in.

Insight learning

This method of trial-and-error learning, Thorndike argued, was the basis for most forms of learning, both in animals and in humans. However, some studies performed on chimpanzees by Köhler (1925) suggested that there was another method of solving problems, which Köhler termed insight learning (see also Chapter 2). In Köhler's studies, the chimpanzee would be given a problem which involved reaching a piece of fruit which was outside its grasp, either suspended from the ceiling of the cage or just too far outside the bars of the cage to be reached. The chimpanzee would be provided with the material which would be needed to solve the problem: like sticks which could be used to pull the fruit in, or boxes which could be piled high for climbing on. In some experiments, the fruit would be outside the bars of the cage, and the chimpanzee would have a stick in the cage which was too small to reach the fruit. However, it could be used to reach another, longer stick which was also outside the bars of the cage. So the problem would have to be solved in two stages: first obtaining the right tools, and secondly using them to reach the desired goal.

Köhler described the typical process by which the chimpanzees would deal with these problems. At first, he said, they would make unsuccessful attempts to reach the fruit, either by jumping up for fruit which was out of reach or by reaching out through the bars. After a few attempts, they seemed to become dispirited, and would sit in the cage showing every sign of having 'given up', although typically they would keep looking at the fruit from time to time. But after a period, quite suddenly the chimpanzee would jump up and start to move the boxes around or seize the stick and start to poke it through the bars. It seemed, according to Köhler, that they had had some kind of 'insight' into the nature of the problem, and what would be required to solve it. Köhler considered that this was the same kind of process as many human beings use for problem-solving: suddenly appreciating the type of problem and its requirements. The flash of insight which this involves is often called an 'Aha!' experience, because it occurs to us so suddenly, and once it has happened we understand exactly what is needed.

Cognitive styles

Other researchers have looked at the kinds of styles of thinking which people adopt. Hudson (1966) performed a study on schoolboys, investigating the different ways that they were likely to go about solving problems. He identified two main types of thinking which the boys were using: **convergent thinking** and **divergent thinking**. Convergent thinking involved focusing tightly on a particular problem, and looking for the right answer - divergent thinking involved a much looser approach, with the possibility of a variety of answers to any given problem. Hudson argued that standard measures of intelligence only really measured convergent thought, since they used problems which tended to have only one right answer. Furthermore, answers which approached the problem in an unusual or unorthodox way were penalised because they would simply be marked wrong. This, he said, meant that the more creative people were less likely to be successful in education. He also found that there was a strong correlation between the kinds of subjects which a boy was good at in school and the tendency towards divergent or convergent thinking. Divergent thinkers were largely better at 'arts' subjects such as English Literature, or History, whereas convergent thinkers tended to do better on the science side.

One of the tests which Hudson used to measure divergent thinking was one which simply asked: 'How many uses can you think of for a brick?' He used the term convergent thinkers for people who tended to think of only a very few answers, which would mostly be concerned with the original function of the brick, such as building, propping things up, and so on. But divergent thinkers would be able to come up with a wide range of ideas, such as paperweight, anchor, door stop, and so on. Typically, a strongly convergent thinker would have about four or five items on their list, while a strongly divergent thinker would have fifteen to twenty. This kind of approach has formed the basis of many creativity tests which have been devised in order to measure those original forms of thinking that intelligence tests cannot handle.

Lateral thinking

Another form of cognitive style which in some ways is rather similar to divergent thinking was studied by de Bono (1977). He, too, was interested in how people went about solving problems, and in particular the use of strategies which would give a satisfactory right answer to a problem but which would be obtained in an unusual way. These strategies might involve very unusual approaches, or types of solution, whilst providing adequate answers to the problems. De Bono called this **lateral thinking**, and showed how, if an individual was able to escape from the habitual forms of strictly conventional thought, they could tackle a far wider range of problems in a satisfactory manner.

An example of lateral thinking might be shown in a problem like this: a man returns from a business trip abroad in the small hours of the morning, and finds that the locks of his car, which he left in the airport car park, have frozen up. What does he do? Typically, a conventional thinker will tend to look for ways that the man can unfreeze the locks, suggesting things like heating the key, etc. But a lateral thinker might ask how important it is to get home that night anyway - couldn't he spend the night in the airport and sort it out the next day, when he is more rested and refreshed, and the temperature is higher? A typical lateral thinker will be able to jump sideways, from the strict boundaries of the problem, to looking at it in a new way. (Of course, that doesn't always mean that the lateral approach is the best one, but having a range of ways of thinking means that you are more likely to be able to deal with novel and unexpected situations.) De Bono's techniques for developing lateral thinking are used in many business situations, for instance in marketing meetings, where ideas for promoting a new product need to be developed. Some therapists have also used it to encourage their clients to take a completely fresh approach to their situation and problems, in order that they may develop new coping strategies.

Brainstorming

Another approach to problem-solving which is used often in business and management circles, is known as **brainstorming**. In a situation where a new approach to something has to be developed, the members of a team will sit together, and, to generate ideas, will say any idea at all that comes into their heads - no matter how silly it might appear. Instead of having to produce complete ideas, they can come out with half-formed impressions, or ridiculous and impractical things if that is what happens to occur to them. In this way, the group obtains a rich fund of ideas, and at the end of the session, they can sift through them and see if any of them can be turned into a new approach. It is one way to encourage people to develop original ideas, rather than simply thinking along the established lines and practices which have been used before.

Psychology in Action

Many companies recognise the benefits of sending employees on outward-bound courses. Participants are usually divided into teams and given a variety of unusual tasks to perform. The tasks are generally designed to encourage participants to solve problems in ways that are different from their usual problem-solving strategies. For instance, they might be given the task of getting several objects across a river without any obvious method of transport. Not only does this encourage people to think about using everyday objects in unusual ways, it can also promote positive social relationships among the group.

Irrespective of a person's position within a company, all have a chance to participate in the decision-making. At the end of each session, teams get together and explore the variety of problem-solving strategies used. Most participants are surprised at the levels of co-operation fostered during the day and the fun to be had!

Learning sets

From looking at these techniques, we can see that the problem of originality in problem-solving is quite a big one. Individuals have a tendency to work in established patterns and often they will have a fixed approach to problems, which is fine as long as the problem is of the kind that they are used to. It can be a handicap if the problem would benefit from being tackled in a different way. **Learning sets** of this kind are another aspect of problem-solving which psychologists have studied.

Luchins (1942) devised a study which showed how learning sets could work to help or to hinder problem solving. Research participants were given a problem to solve which involved three water-jars of different capacities. By pouring water from one jar into another they were asked to measure out a specific amount. The solution could be obtained by following a particular sequence of steps. When the participants had solved the first problem by the appropriate steps, they were given several more problems. These had different amounts of water and different capacities of the jars, but could still be solved by the same series of steps. This was the training period, and the participants solved these problems easily. The first problem had given them a 'set' which was helpful. But then Luchins presented two more problems.

One of them could be solved in two ways: either by using the same sequence of steps, or by a much simpler method. Luchins' research participants all went about solving the problem in the long way, because they were 'set' in that way of thinking – they did not perceive that they could do it an easier way. For the second problem, there was one very easy solution, but it couldn't be solved following the method that the participants had previously learned. Luchins research participants were unable to solve this one – their learning set had made their thinking rigid, so that they couldn't find new solutions.

The Gestalt view

The **Gestalt** psychologists, who were the first to study problem-solving and insight learning systematically (Köhler was one of the Gestalt psychologists), called this kind of rigidity **Einstellung**. They argued that human beings have certain innate principles of thinking, and that they tend to look at problems in certain kinds of ways, which, unless the individual is careful, can lead to rigid ways of tackling things.

The principal of closure

One of these innate principles is known as the **principle of closure**, and it can be observed in work on perception as well as in work on thinking and problem-solving. The principle of closure is a tendency we have to see things as complete units with boundaries. We will tend to join up figures into complete ones rather than to see incomplete lines or shapes, or, say, given a series of dots we will tend to organise them into patterns and forms. While this is usually an advantage to our perception as it allows us to pick things out very quickly when we see incomplete parts of them, it can also be a disadvantage in problem-solving. One famous problem which the Gestalt psychologists used was the nine-dot problem. (See Fig. 9.2.) In this, research participants are asked to join together an array of dots with four straight lines, without taking the pencil off the paper or going over the same line twice.

● ● ●

● ● ●

● ● ●

Join up all the dots with four straight lines, without going over the same line twice or taking the pen off the paper.

9.2 The nine-dot problem

This can only be done by going outside the square of the dots themselves (see Fig. 9.4.), but many people don't think of doing that. The principle of closure means that they tend to look for solutions within the 'closed' square of the dots, even though they haven't been asked to do that.

Functional fixedness

Einstellung often means that we end up making assumptions about problems in this way, and then find ourselves unable to solve them. An example of this might be the problem of how to arrange six matches into four equilateral triangles. Try working this out for yourself! Another form of rigidity in thought which comes from this kind of process is known as **functional fixedness**. With this, research participants find themselves unable to solve a problem because they think of its components in terms of their usual functions, rather than in terms of their actual properties. The convergent thinkers identified by Hudson, for instance, were unable to think of alternative uses for a brick, because they were so used to the functions which bricks usually had - of being used for building. This meant that it didn't even occur to them that they would be able to use a brick for a variety of other purposes, because of its properties such as rectangularity, or heaviness, or having a dip in the middle which could be used for holding paper clips!

9.1 Studying decision-making

Quite often, decisions are made in committees rather than simply by individuals. It seems that sometimes committees can actually make riskier decisions than those individuals would make on their own. This is known as the 'risky-shift' effect.

You can investigate the risky-shift effect by developing a set of problems which outline decisions that have to be taken. Each decision should involve a certain amount of risk: for instance whether someone should decide to give up a secure job with very little prospects and go to University; or whether someone should invest some inherited money in a speculative venture which will give a highly profitable return if it comes off, or in a safe but not highly profitable investment.

Working with a friend or in groups of three or four, develop three different risky-decision problems. Each problem should end by asking the person to decide on the level of risk that they would consider to be acceptable, in order to make the risky decision. The level of risk should be measured on a scale which goes from 1/10 to 10/10, with 10/10 being 100% certain, and 1/10 being a one in ten chance that the risk will come off.

You will need to test at least four people at a time. First, ask each one to do the problems individually and make their own judgements on the table levels of risk. Make a note of the judgements that each person has made. Then ask them to discuss the problems, and come to a group decision that they all agree on.

Compare the score that the group obtains on each problem with each group member's individual result.

Which score was the more risky - the individual or the group?

What explanation can you give for these results?

Did the type of problem make a difference?

Human logic

In 1972, Wason and Johnson-Laird demonstrated that **human logic** is not always quite the same thing as formal logic, as people tend to adopt patterns of reasoning which include judgements of probability, as well as strictly logical sequences. Their most famous example of this involves a study using cards, where research participants were asked to check whether certain statements were true or not. For instance, participants might be presented with four cards: A, B, C, and D. These would have, on the side that was showing, a black circle, a white circle, a black triangle, and a white triangle. Participants would be asked which cards they would have to turn over, in order to verify the rule: 'If a card has a black triangle on one side, then it will have a white circle on the other'. Very few participants would solve the problem correctly, because they would tend to look for cases which would confirm the rule, rather than looking for cases which would overturn it. So in the example that we have just given, the necessary answers would be A and C, because if A turns out to have a black triangle on the other side, the rule is disconfirmed. But most participants tend to say either C, or B and C - which will only confirm the rule, not establish whether it always holds true.

Processing negative statements

Wason also argued that people tend to have a certain amount of difficulty in handling negative statements. Our tendency is to look for positive instances, rather than negative ones. An earlier study by Wason involved investigating the difficulty that research participants have in establishing whether a statement is true or false (Wason 1965). It seems that we find it harder to check a statement like, 'Seven is not an even number', than to check a statement like 'Sixteen is an odd number', even though the first one is true and the second is false. Wason argued that this was because it adds an extra step to the reasoning process: first, we have to convert the negative into a positive (if it's not an even number, then it must be an odd one), and then we can check on whether it is true or false.

In real life, Wason says, negative statements tend to mean that something is false, and so we find it harder to accept that a negative statement can be true. In addition, we tend to think of negatives as implied by positive statements. If we were to say something like, 'If it's a sunny day on Sunday, then I'll go for a walk', and you happen to hear that I have been for a walk on that day, then you would be likely to conclude that it was sunny on Sunday. But if we look at the strict logic involved, this doesn't have to follow at all. I didn't say that I would *not* go for a walk if it was cloudy, merely that *I would* if it was sunny. In strict formal logic, the statement 'Guitars are musical instruments' does not imply that the statement 'All musical instruments are guitars' is true. But in our everyday reasoning, we would consider it to be quite acceptable to deduce that my Sunday walk implied that the weather was fine. Wason argued that this showed how human reasoning was often not strictly logical, but took into account our knowledge of what people were likely to do, and what the probabilities were.

The Stroop Effect

A rather different aspect of the way that we process information is shown by a phenomenon known as the **Stroop Effect**. This involves looking at what happens when we need to deal with two conflicting signals. Specifically, the Stroop Effect is most clearly shown in the identification of colours, when they are used to spell out the names of other colours. If you show people nonsense syllables printed in different coloured inks, and ask them to name the colour of the ink each time they see the word, they will be able to do it with very little trouble. But if they are asked to do the same thing with a list of names of colours (such as orange, green, etc.), and those names are not the same as the actual coloured inks, people find it very much more difficult (Stroop 1935). This seems to happen because a set of more or less automatic processes is being triggered off. Once we have learned to read, we tend to do it automatically when we are faced with printed words. In the Stroop experiments, research participants are slowed down because their main tendency is to read the word which is printed, rather than to identify the ink. Reading forms a sort of automatic routine which we find very hard to stop.

9.2 The Stroop Effect

It seems that once we have learned to read, the brain automatically applies 'reading' to any printed words that we look at. This is fine if the material we are reading is very straightforward, but what happens when we are looking at two different messages at the same time?

In this activity we are going to investigate the Stroop effect.

First of all you will need two sheets of paper and some coloured pens or crayons.

On the first sheet you should write the names of six colours, writing each name in its correct colour. So for example, the word 'blue' should be written in blue ink. On the second sheet of paper you should write the same colour words, but this time write each word in a different colour to its name. For example: the word 'orange' could be written in blue ink.

You will also need to find a watch with a second hand or a stop watch.

Ask a friend or another member of your class group to act as 'research participant' for you.

Then, place the first list face down in front of the participant. When this participant is ready, look at the watch and then turn the paper over, asking the participant to read the list out loud through to the end. Then repeat the procedure with the second list of words.

Was there a difference in the time taken for list 1 compared to list 2?

What explanation can you give for these results?

Does it matter which list the participant reads first?

If this were being done as a formal experiment, what controls would you need to include?

Models of thinking

Association

From the work on problem-solving, we can see that the process of thinking is a complex one, which can involve all sorts of factors in addition to the actual problem itself. As we have seen, human beings don't often tend to work strictly logically, like computers, although there are many computer models of decision-making which can sometimes be usefully applied to some of the things that we do.

One of the first attempts to put forward a model of how thinking worked was by the philosopher Locke (1632-1704). He considered that thinking occurred as simple chains of ideas, with one idea leading on to the next. It worked, he thought, by association (the linking of one idea with the next one) and because there are many possible ways that one idea can associate itself with another, we can produce a wide range of different thoughts. However, we have already seen that our thinking may be influenced by many other things, such as set assumptions and habitual routines. Because of this, linear (straight line) models of human thinking such as Locke was proposing are not really acceptable nowadays.

Cognitive mapping

A theory by Tolman (1930) put forward a different approach to thinking. Tolman considered that much of our learning as human beings arises from the building of cognitive maps which we can then apply to situations when we need to act on them. We looked at the experimental work on learning which Tolman used to support his ideas in Chapter 2. Tolman considered that cognitive development mostly consisted of forming cognitive maps, which would be extended and developed through our experience with the environment, and that most of the learning that we do is not necessarily used immediately in our behaviour, but goes towards refining and applying these maps in more appropriate ways. This was an important theory, because Tolman was writing at a time when ideas about learning were beginning to be influenced by the behaviourists, such as Watson and Skinner, who we looked at in the early part of this book. Their argument was that learning, by definition, was something which produced a change in behaviour. Tolman showed experimentally that some kinds of learning could happen simply on a cognitive level, and that thinking – at least in the form of cognitive maps – was an important factor.

As you can see, Tolman's approach of cognitive maps was very different from Locke's idea of the straightforward association of one idea with another. A cognitive map is a much more wide-ranging and complex concept, which shows how we might store and integrate many different aspects of information, and use them later in dealing with problems.

Computer models of thinking

Work on the kinds of strategies that we use in problem-solving has led to attempts to program problem-solving strategies into computers. In its turn, this has led to models of the way that we think being developed to provide the kinds of steps needed to establish such programs.

Work on computer thinking has tended to fall into two kinds: **computer simulation** and **artificial intelligence** (**AI**). In AI the important thing is the final result, and the strategies that the computer uses don't have to replicate human thinking at all.

Artificial intelligence

Some of the work on AI has been very interesting. There are, for instance, some therapeutic programs in the USA which are used to identify emotional or simple psychiatric difficulties that people are having. When an individual is interacting with the program (by typing answers to questions into a computer), it seems as though there is a realistic conversation going on, and often it is difficult to tell that the computer is not a real person at all! Abelson (1973) simulated part of the belief system of a Conservative politician in this way, and the computer was able to draw inferences and conclusions from the new information it was given in a way that seemed to be consistent with the individual himself.

Some recent work on artificial intelligence has been on the development of 'self-programming' computers, which can 'learn' from their experience, modifying their programs and using different strategies to adapt to different information. It is unquestionably true to say that AI systems nowadays are far more complicated than many people thought was possible. Just how far their capacities can really be considered to be equivalent to those of human beings is the subject of considerable debate.

Ethical discussion

The relationship between human beings and machines has become an important issue in recent years. Effectively, there are two angles to this. The first concerns the way that research into computers has encouraged people to think of the human brain as being like a computer - a metaphor that some people see as intrinsically dangerous as it ignores important aspects of being human, like social conscience, morality, social responsibility, free will and voluntary action.

The second angle concerns the attempt to produce 'intelligent' computers. Is it a desirable goal to get computers to emulate humans anyway?

What do you think?

Computer simulation

Computer simulation processes attempt to go through the kinds of stages that a human being might use in problem-solving. One of the most famous of all of the computer simulation models is the General Problem Solver (GPS) suggested by Newell and Simon in 1972. Their model adopted an approach known as **means-end analysis**, which involved starting off by specifying two things: (a) what the situation was to begin with, and (b) what the ultimate goal of the problem was. Once these two things were known the 'problem distance' could be calculated. In other words, how far away the situation was from where it had to end up. From there, it was a matter of devising strategies which would reduce the problem distance. Sometimes this would mean identifying a series of sub-goals, and taking steps to reach those first rather than aiming directly for the overall goal.

Heuristics

One important aspect of this approach is the use of **heuristics** in deciding just which steps should be taken to reduce the problem distance. For instance, if the computer was trying to find out what the best strategy was likely to be, it might be impractical to try out all the possible alternatives. Instead, the computer would be programmed to make a best guess, and to try out first only those strategies which looked likely to reduce the problem space (another term for problem distance). Alternatively, it might tackle the problem by working backwards from the desired goal, instead of by trying to work towards it. Sometimes that can be a practical strategy for solving problems which have a number of different possible starting points.

Using protocols

Newell's approach to problem-solving involved formulating the steps which were undertaken as a problem was tackled. These steps are known as **protocols**. Often, they have been identified by asking people to state the ways in which they go about solving a particular problem. But the criticism has been raised that, since a large number of the strategies which we use in thinking are unconscious, people may not really know exactly how they go about doing such things and so the steps which they describe may not really be the right kind. Piaget, in his Centre for Genetic Epistemology in Switzerland, once invited visiting academics from different disciplines to describe the way that infants crawl along the floor. He found that mathematicians and philosophers tended to give very elegant but unworkable descriptions, whereas psychologists and physicists gave much more realistic but lengthy accounts. This would seem to indicate that even the types of explanations which we use to describe how we do things are influenced by our characteristic ways of thinking and by our experience.

Criticisms of computer models of thinking

Many criticisms have been put forward concerning this approach to thinking. Neisser (1963) argued that computer simulation was not really like human thinking at all, mainly because it tended to be very 'single-minded' and goal oriented, while human beings don't often operate in such a straightforward manner. Wilding (1978) argued that computer models only really deal with one class of thinking, and ignore those which aren't specifically goal oriented. He also argued that, in trying to replicate thinking, researchers have completely ignored work on human perception and memory coding. Instead of engaging in a large amount of research on exactly how human beings do think, people working on computer models of thought have tended to use simple, 'commonsense', or strictly logical approaches and, as we have seen with the work of Wason and Johnson-Laird, this often isn't really the way that individuals do think.

Another, more general criticism of the approach which sees the brain as being like a computer, is that computers work by digital coding, and recent research suggests that brains don't. Computers work by 'on-off' switching – either a connection is made, or it isn't. Until quite recently, it was thought that human brain cells, too, operated by digital coding: the 'all-or-none' rule meant that a neurone (a brain cell) would either fire, or it wouldn't, without any in-between steps. But Blakemore (1984) showed that in fact, cells in the brain can fire at several different strengths, according to how strong the stimulus which the cell is receiving, is. This seems to be quite typical of how the brain works generally, and so it seems that the estimates which were made of human potential were wildly underestimated. The brain operates in a far more complex manner than a computer can, even in its most basic units, and many people argue that this makes the idea of truly simulating thought, or of understanding it in any meaningful way with computer models, completely unrealistic.

Concept formation

One of the most important aspects of the study of thinking has been the way that we form and use concepts. We do not treat each new fact or item that we come across as if it were unique – if we did, we would soon become overwhelmed by the mass of information that we have to deal with all the time. Instead, we tend to group things together, recognising similarities which they have, or ways in which they might connect with something else. These groups are known as concepts, and, as our thinking develops with experience, the kinds and number of concepts that we use also develop.

Types of concept

In work on concept formation, some psychologists have found it useful to distinguish between two different types of concept: **classical concepts**, in which every aspect or property of the concept is shared by its members; and **probabilistic concepts**, in which the members of the concept are likely to have certain characteristics, but might not. To give an example: the concept of 'bowl' could be considered to be a classical concept, because we would expect all bowls (the members of the concept) to have a rounded inner shape, and to be concave. But if we tried to identify the properties implied, for instance, by the word 'bird', we would be likely to say things like 'has wings', 'flies', etc. This time it is a probabilistic concept, because we accept that things might not have those properties, and yet still be birds – ostriches and penguins, for example. Most of the formal studies which psychologists have performed on concept formation have dealt with classical concepts, but it would seem that in fact most of the concepts which we use in everyday life are probabilistic ones.

Strategies in concept formation

A study by Bruner, Goodnow and Austin investigated the strategies which people used to learn new concepts. They had a pack of 81 cards, which differed in four characteristics: (a) the symbols on the cards were either in green, red, or black; (b) they were either circles, squares, or crosses; (c) the cards showed one, two, or three symbols, and (d) they had either a single, a double, or a treble margin round the edge of the card. The cards were laid face upwards, and the experimenter would decide in advance on a concept, such as 'circles', or 'green crosses'. Research participants had to work out which rule applied by asking questions, and the ways that they went about doing this were studied.

Bruner *et al.* found that there were two main types of strategy which research participants used, which could be detected by the types of questions they asked the experimenters in investigating the rules. One was what they term a **wholist** strategy, which involved taking the first correct answer as being typical of the concept, and then amending it in the light of other correct answers. Bruner *et al.* also called this a **focusing** approach, as the participant gradually focused their ideas more precisely. The other type of strategy was a **partist** one, and participants who used this one would tend to concentrate on just one feature of the first correct instance, and see if this was also true of other correct instances. If it wasn't, they would go back and take the next single feature, and see if that one was correct. This was also known as a **scanning** approach.

There were some other interesting tendencies which Bruner *et al.* observed in their research participants' approaches to the problem, which in many ways are similar to some of the other issues on problem-solving which we have already looked at. One of them was the tendency that participants had to use particular features or cues which had worked for a previous problem, regardless of whether they applied this time. This is similar to the Gestalt idea of Einstellung. Also, they found it much more difficult to use negative information than to use positive instances – as in Wason's findings.

The important aspects of this work on concept formation really seem to come from the way in which it demonstrates that people may go about the business of solving problems, or forming and identifying concepts in their own individual ways. Not everybody is alike in their use of strategies, and their **cognitive style** will produce characteristic questions and approaches. This is a very long way from the early 'associationist' ideas of thinking put forward by the philosopher Locke, or by the early behaviourists in psychology.

Storing concepts

Some psychologists have investigated the ways in which we store our concepts, by looking at the time that it takes an individual to be able to agree or disagree with a certain statement. A study by Collins and Quillian involved asking research participants about particular concepts, with different questions involving different numbers of steps. For instance, the statement: 'a blue jay is a bird' involves fewer steps than the statement 'a blue jay is an animal', if we assume that the information is stored as a hierarchy with 'animal' as a main concept which can be sub-divided into 'birds', 'mammals', 'fish', and 'insects'. They found that the length of time that participants took to agree or disagree with such statements corresponded with this form of organisation, and suggested that this is how we do store our concepts.

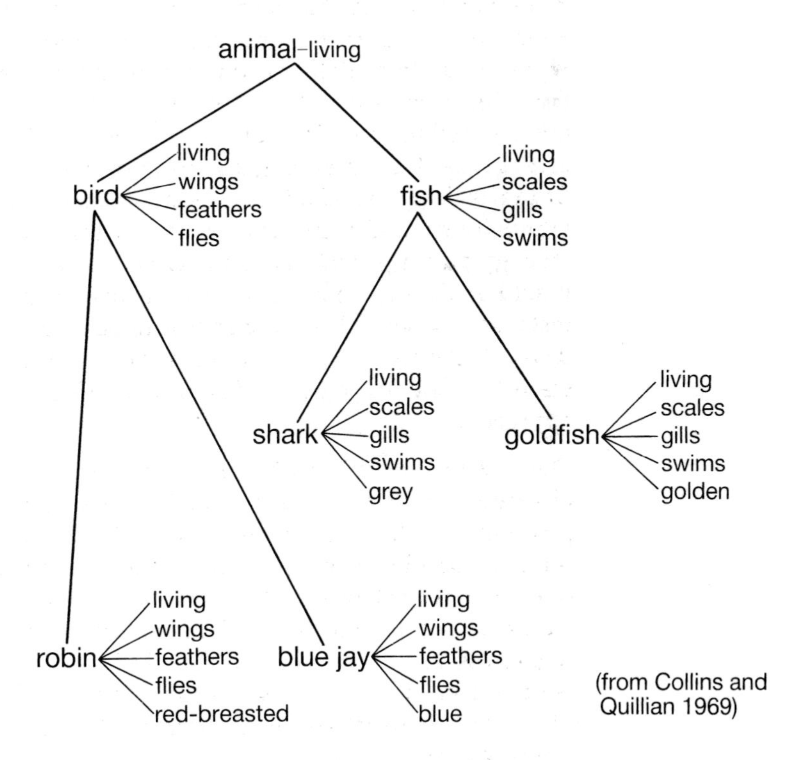

9.3 Possible hierarchical storage of concepts

One problem with seeing concepts as organised into hierarchies though, is the way that different concepts overlap. For instance, we may see the idea 'robin' as being a sub concept of 'bird' or of 'animal' but it is equally well a sub-concept of the category 'friendly animals', or, if you are interested in animal behaviour, 'extremely territorial animals'.

The way that concepts can overlap and the same things go to make up several different sets of concepts, or link in widely different ways, makes it very difficult to construct models of how we organise our concepts.

The formation of schemata

The theory of cognitive development put forward by Jean Piaget, in 1952, explains the way in which we acquire concepts as the formation of schemata. A schema is a hypothetical cognitive structure, which contains all the information, ideas and associations which we need to operate on our environment. So it is a possible way that we can group the information that we know into sets, which we can then use to guide our behaviour. For instance, we might develop a schema concerning catching buses. This would store all our experiences and all the things that we know about catching buses to get from one place to another. If we were in another country, and wanted to get somewhere, we would be able to use that schema to let us know what to do. Even though the circumstances might be different in many respects from the ones that we are used to, we still wouldn't be totally lost, because we would have a rough idea of how to go about getting a bus.

For Piaget, the importance of intellectual development by the formation and development of schemata was that it allowed individuals to adapt successfully to their environment. He considered that organising the information learned from experience into schemata, which would direct the individual's future behaviour, was the way that adaptation would take place most effectively. Because of this, he considered that it wasn't really possible to separate concepts from the way that individuals use them in interaction with their environment - we don't deal with concepts in the abstract in our day to day living, but instead we tend to us them for specific purposes. The idea of a schema includes this idea of action and interaction, and so it isn't quite the same as a concept, although in many ways it is quite similar. We will look at this more closely in Chapter 21.

Summary

1. Thinking can be defined as 'the internal representation of events'. Psychologists have seen the origins of thought in different ways: Freud saw it as goal-oriented; Piaget saw it as adaptation; and Dewey saw it as arising from discrepancies.
2. Very creative people seem to show a three-stage process to their work: familiarisation, incubation, and activity.
3. Two main mechanisms of learning to solve problems are trial and error learning, and insight learning.
4. Work on cognitive styles has shown that people may be either convergent or divergent thinkers, and that this may affect their success in school. Another aspect of cognitive style is lateral thinking, which is looking for unusual approaches to problems.
5. Work on human problem-solving has looked at learning sets, functional fixedness, and Einstellung. Wason showed that human logic could differ from formal logic, and the Stroop effect shows how we use automatic routines in our thinking.
6. Various models of thinking have been developed: associationist; cognitive maps; and computer models.
7. Work on concept-formation has shown that people use different strategies to identify concepts. Piaget argued that concept-formation occurred through the formation of schemata.

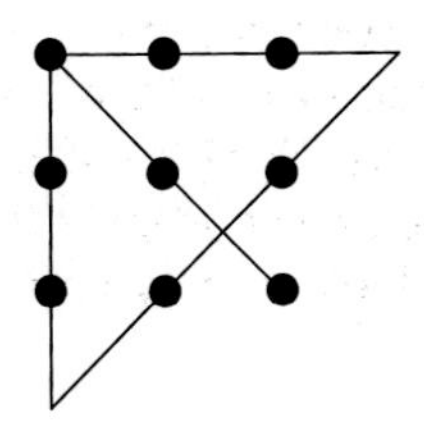

9.4 Solution to the nine-dot problem

Chapter 10 - Language

Language and thinking

Watson's theory

There have been several different theories put forward concerning the relationship between language and thinking. One of the first was put forward by the behaviourist psychologist J.B. Watson (1913), that thought was, in fact, nothing more than language. He argued that when we are thinking, we are making tiny unconscious movements of the throat and larynx - similar to the way in which people who are unfamiliar with reading move their lips as they pronounce the words to themselves.

A study by Smith, Brown, Toman and Goodman investigated this idea. If Watson was correct, they reasoned, then research participants who were in a position where such tiny movements were impossible should be unable to think. Accordingly, they used the paralysing poison curare to prevent such movements of the throat or larynx (keeping the participants alive through artificial respiration) and showed them problems and puzzles. They found that the participants were perfectly able to think even when paralysed, which discredited Watson's theory.

Wittgenstein's theory

Another version of this idea was put forward by the philosopher Wittgenstein, who argued that thought was purely linguistic (to do with language), and that the kinds of mental processes which animals or small children engaged in wasn't really thinking at all. In this part of his reasoning, he was putting forward a view very similar to that of a much earlier philosopher, Descartes, who saw human beings as totally different in every respect from animals, in that animals had mechanistic, instinctive ways of responding to events, whereas human beings could think about them. However, although these views have been important for philosophy and have had their influence on some psychologists, very few modern psychologists would be quite so prepared to disregard the work on animal problem-solving which has been done, or to regard very small children as unable to think. They regard the way that Wittgenstein defined 'thinking' as being extremely narrow. For instance, a study by Humphrey (1951) in a series of concept formation studies, showed that research participants were often able to use concepts quite correctly but unable to state in words what the rules they were following were. It seems that we do not necessarily have to be able to verbalise (put into words) concepts in order to use them, so we can have forms of thinking which are more than just language in use.

Linguistic relativity

Another view of the way that thinking relates to language, which is not quite as extreme as the one put forward by Watson or by Wittgenstein, is the idea that thinking is dependent on language in some way. This was first stated in an extreme form by the two anthropologists Sapir (1927) and Whorf (1952), who implied that in order to think about something, your language had to contain the words for it. So people who had, say, only three words for colours would be unable to think about, or distinguish, more than three grades of colours. This extreme version is known as the strong form of the theory, which is known as the **linguistic relativity hypothesis**. However, a considerable amount of cross-cultural work has shown that in fact thinking is not so dependent on language. A study by Rosch, in 1974, showed that a tribe with only two colour terms, the Dani, could still perceive colour variations; in fact they were just as good at it as people with 11 different words for colour in their language.

Although the strong form of the linguistic relativity hypothesis has been discredited, a weak form of it seems to be much more acceptable. Having the words available in the language encourages the individual to make sense of their experience in certain kinds of ways: having 27 different words for snow in one's language, like the Lapps, means that one is better equipped to notice and make sense of variations in snowfall than having only the three or so words that there are in English. If someone uses the same word for the colours orange, red, and purple, as the Shona do, then they may be more likely to notice similarities between these colours.

10.1 Investigating linguistic relativity

The linguistic relativity hypothesis suggests that our language affects the way that we see the world and that by looking at a language we can come to some kind of understanding of a particular culture.

Although it is probably rather difficult for you to perform a cross-cultural study at the moment, you can still investigate how this might apply to your own culture.

Working in pairs, or in small groups of not more than four people, firstly think of some fairly common items which you encounter in your everyday life: such as pens, cups, cars, dogs etc. Make a list of five of six of these.

Then, develop a second list of items which you don't come across very often in your everyday life: such as cages, volcanoes, camels, tractors etc..

Now, imagine that you are a visiting but friendly alien from the star-system of Betelgeuse. Using the 'brainstorming' technique (see Chapter 9), take each item on the first list in turn and think of as many other names for the same item as you can. (The reason why you need to pretend to be an alien is because an alien probably wouldn't notice the kinds of subtle differences in things that you have grown used to. For instance, it would probably think of a crayon, a biro and a pencil as being all the same, because they are all things that you use to make marks on a piece of paper.)

Do the same thing for your second list.

Add up the total number of words that you have been able to think of for each list. Which list had the most words in it?

What explanation can you put forward for the differences?

If you were doing this as a formal experiment, how would you need to change it?

Language as a tool of thought

A third way of looking at the relationship between language and thinking is the one put forward by Piaget, in 1952. Piaget regarded language, at least as adopted by the very young child, as being simply an external manifestation of the child's thought processes. So where Watson was saying that thought is language, Piaget was saying the opposite, that language is thought. When a child first starts to talk, Piaget says, its speech is largely **egocentric** - not being used for any social purposes, but coming from the child's need to organise and restructure the problems arising from its interaction with the environment. The child is simply saying its thoughts out loud. Only gradually does the child come to perceive that language can also be used for the purposes of communicating its thoughts, and even then this will only happen because the child sees language as an important tool for problem-solving. So, for Piaget, it is thinking which is most important, and the child only develops language because it is a useful tool of thought.

The social origins of language

Other psychologists disagreed with Piaget on this. The Russian psychologist Vygotsky (1962) saw the child's acquisition of language as having mainly social origins, arising from the need to communicate with other people. He saw language as developing directly from the early social interactions which infants have with their parents and in fact, much of the modern work on parent-infant interaction seems to support this idea. Children, Vygotsky argued, have a powerful need to interact with other people, and their language develops because it allows the child to engage in social interaction more effectively.

Vygotsky did not deny that the child might also use language as a tool of thought. He considered the behaviour that Piaget had observed and labelled 'egocentric speech' of children talking to themselves as they played, as being an example of what he termed the **expressive function** of language. Vygotsky saw this kind of language as being used to monitor and to direct the child's internal thought patterns, much as Piaget did. And, like Piaget, he saw this form of language-use as enabling the child to reorganise and restructure situations, on a cognitive level. But he considered this to be only one of two important ways that children used language, and the communicative social function was if anything the most important one.

Formal and informal language

Forms of language

Elaborated and restricted codes

Perhaps the most important and controversial theory which has been put forward about forms of language was suggested by Bernstein, in 1961. He argued that there were strong and definite class differences in the ways that people use language. Middle and upper-class individuals tended to use what he called an **elaborated code** of language, which was characterised by the use of a wide range of nouns, adjectives and verbs, and lots of explanations for things, for instance when parents were communicating with their children. Working-class individuals, on the other hand, tended to use what Bernstein termed a **restricted code** of language, which used fewer nouns but more pronouns, and much less explanation. Working-class parents, he argued, were more likely to give their children orders without explanations for them, such as just saying, 'Be quiet' rather than, 'I would like you to be quiet while I make this phone call'.

Bernstein argued that middle-class people could use both forms of language, but that working-class people only used restricted codes. Because Bernstein also held a view of language and thinking similar to that of Whorf, he thought that working-class children were unable to develop more abstract forms of thinking, and that their thought tended to be **context-bound** rather than independent of the context that it was said in. Accordingly, working-class children would do less well in education than their middle-class counterparts.

Bernstein's work was very widely criticised in several ways. The question of whether the use of restricted codes of language inhibited the development of abstract thought was taken up by Labov, in 1970. He showed that the usual method of testing the use of language was often inadequate for finding out just what individuals were capable of. In one study, he looked at the language of a young black child by the name of Leon. In the formal testing situation Leon said very little, and spent a considerable amount of the time in silence. If his results on this test had been taken as indicating his abilities, as they often are for many children, then it would have been easy to conclude that Bernstein was right and that Leon was incapable of abstract reasoning. But Labov showed that when Leon was in an informal atmosphere with a black experimenter and they were both chatting and sharing a packet of crisps, Leon's use of language extended considerably. He chatted away happily to the experimenter and in so doing showed that he could discuss both moral and abstract concepts in his own dialect very easily. It seemed that it was the demands of the social situation which Leon found intimidating in the first situation. (Incidentally, a previous formal interview with the same black experimenter had also produced very little response from him.)

Labo work demonstrated that working-class children could hold complicated concepts, even though their language was not considered to be an elaborated one. Other psychologists have argued that the use of restricted codes occurs not so much because the individual is incapable of other forms of language, but because the individuals concerned share common *assumptions* about things, so that they don't need to explain them as much. It has also been argued that looking simply at the words which are used in restricted codes gives an unrealistic picture of the **semantic** aspects of the language (the question of its meaning), because people who habitually use restricted codes often get a considerable range of shades of meaning into the non-verbal aspects of their speech, such as tones of voice, or the timing of a statement. So what is actually communicated may in fact be very subtle, even though it doesn't actually use many words.

10.2 Elaborated and restricted codes of language

Bernstein tells us that one difference in the ways that different social groups use language, is whether they use an elaborate or a restricted language code. An elaborated code involves using many more words to express things and also having several alternative ways of saying the same thing.

Decide on some everyday examples of simple requests or comments: such as a request to someone to look after someone's cats or house plants while they are away on holiday, or an invitation to dinner, or for help in solving a puzzle or crossword.

Ideally, you should do this in class, or in several small groups but you will probably also find it quite enjoyable with just a couple of friends. The task is that each group should write down as many different ways of saying the same thing as it can possibly think of. (You may find it fun to 'act out' different characters while you are doing this.)

Dialect

Nowadays, both linguists and psychologists tend to accept that the actual dialect which someone speaks is unlikely to restrict their cognitive abilities. But it is one thing for them to believe it, and another thing for members of society generally to believe it. Edwards (1979) performed a study in which tape recordings of children from different socio-economic backgrounds were made. Each child read the same passage but they each had very different accents. Research participants were asked to rate the children on a variety of scales, ranging from academic ones like 'intelligence', to personality ones like 'enthusiasm' and 'happiness'. The children who had working-class accents were rated lower on *all* of the scales, not just the ones which implied success in education.

Self-fulfilling prophecy

Findings of this kind show that, even though the actual dialect which someone uses may not affect their abilities it can still affect the expectations that people have about them. Several studies performed by Rosenthal (1966) showed that people's expectations can have a considerable effect on how much a child achieves. In one study, teachers in an American school were led to expect that certain (average) children would show dramatic improvements over the next year. When Rosenthal and his colleagues returned to the school the next year, they found that those children were all achieving far more because of the extra help and encouragement which the teachers had unconsciously given them. This kind of an effect is known as a **self-fulfilling prophecy**, and it can easily work in reverse as well. If children are judged to be less capable because of their accents or dialects, then they may receive far less help and encouragement than other children and come to under-achieve dramatically. Most unconscious racism in schools in Britain works in this way, as teachers are often unaware that they are neglecting those children whose dialect is most different from the ideal version of English which they think 'clever' children use.

How children acquire language

Stages of language acquisition

There have been several different studies of the ways that children acquire language. Fry (1977) identified the main sequence of changes that children go through as follows:

From 0-2 months, the only vocalisation that the child is making tends to be discomfort sounds, crying in particular. From the age of about 2 months, though, a new type of sound begins as the child also makes noises indicating pleasure, such as burbling or cooing. Between 4 and 9 months, this develops considerably, and the child begins **babbling** - practising repetitive sounds, such as saying 'dadadada' repeatedly. This process continues during the period 9-18 months, but the child is now exploring and developing specific **phonemes** (units of sound). At this time it also starts to produce similar-sounding noises, such as 'mamamama' and 'babababa' - experimenting with the different ways that sounds can be put together. During this time, the child is building up a phoneme system, which it will use later when it is making words. It is as if it were acquiring the necessary physical skills prior to using them for more complicated reasons. This is also the time when the first words start to appear.

From 18 months to two and a half years of age, the child is beginning to produce two-word phrases, like 'allgone milk', and then from two and a half to 4 years it is learning the rules of grammar, expanding its vocabulary, completing the development of the phoneme system, and putting together often quite complicated sentences. By 4 to 6 years old, it has acquired all the basic adult grammar and syntax needed for communication, and the main task from now on is extending and developing its vocabulary.

Pivot grammar

Several theorists have looked at the ways that children develop their speech. In 1963, Braine examined the ways in which children organised their two- and three-word utterances, and found that they seemed to develop two main classes of words, which he called **pivot words** and **open words**. Pivot words were ones which could be used for several different utterances: the meaning of the utterance would hinge on which particular pivot words were used. Words like 'mine', or 'allgone' were examples of pivot words – the child could use them in conjunction with several different open words. Open words would be things like 'ball', 'milk', 'walk', etc. – words which indicated specific things in the child's world. Braine argued that this 'pivot grammar' was one which all children developed, and which was the earliest kind of grammatical sequencing which the individual engaged in. Later, it became developed and extended into more adult-type grammar.

Semantic relations grammar

In 1970, Brown put forward a slightly different idea of infant grammar, which became known as **semantic relations grammar**. In this, he argued that the important thing for the child was the meaning (semantics) underlying what it was saying - the *intention* that was being indicated by the utterance. Brown emphasised the idea that the child was using speech in order to communicate. He regarded the shortened versions of children's utterances as being **telegraphic speech**, as speech was presented like a telegram with unimportant function words left out, but getting the main meaning across. So a phrase like 'want milk' would be adequate to convey the meaning 'I would like some more milk', in the same way that a telegram saying 'send money' would convey the meaning 'Please send me some more money'. By missing out function words like articles, prepositions, and conjunctions, the child developed a shortened version of speech, but one which nonetheless was adequate in semantic content.

Longitudinal studies of speech

Brown (1973) performed several longitudinal studies of children's speech. In a well-known study of three children: Adam, Eve, and Sarah, he highlighted the way that the child's acquisition of language seemed to follow distinct sequences, which could be organised into roughly five main stages:

In Stage 1, the child was uttering only simple two-word sentences: 'want teddy', or 'mummy gone'. As it went into Stage 2 it would start to include endings of words, and some articles. It might say, for instance, 'that a doggy', or 'I goed'. By stage 3, the child was beginning to ask the 'wh' questions, beginning with the relatively easy ones of 'what?', 'where?', and 'when?', and then later going on to 'how?' and 'why?'. Stage 4 was characterised by the introduction of simple sentences which had more than one clause, such as 'I had milk and teddy had milk'. While in stage 5, the child was able to join sentences together with conjunctions, and to use sub-clauses: 'Mary, who lives over there, goes to our school'. By this time, Brown said, the child could formulate most kinds of adult grammatical constructions, and would develop further mainly by extending its vocabulary.

These accounts of stages in the acquisition of speech, and of infant grammars, differ mainly in the ways that they look at what is happening as the child acquires language. Fry and Brown, for instance, do not really contradict one another in their views of stages in infant language, but each has a different emphasis: Fry identifies the development of vocalisations from the earliest months as being of interest, while Brown largely takes that for granted and is more concerned with the ways in which the child strings actual words together. Braine's pivot grammar emphasises the structure of the child's early language, while Brown's semantic relations emphasises the meaning of the child's utterances.

Theories of language acquisition

These differences in emphasis represent important distinctions, because there have been many theories of language acquisition put forward, each with a very different emphasis. We can divide these roughly into four main perspectives: behaviourist, nativist, cognitive, and social.

Behaviourist theories

The behaviourist approach to language was put forward by B.F. Skinner in his book *Verbal Behaviour* (1957). Skinner argued that the child acquired language as the result of a process of operant conditioning: that is, the principle that if you do something and it has pleasant consequences, then you are more likely to do that thing again. Skinner took infant babbling as his starting point. When an infant is babbling, it is producing lots of different phonemes. In all, human beings are capable of producing a very large number of different phonemes - far more than are used in any one particular language. (You will probably have found this out if you have learned another language, as there may be sounds which happen in that language which are completely different from those which happen in English, or some of the English sounds may not be used.) As an infant babbles, it produces the whole range of phonemes which human beings use anywhere in the world. This, Skinner argued, is the operant behaviour which is then conditioned by the child's interaction with its environment (i.e. its parents).

What happens is this: as the child babbles, it comes to string together some phonemes accidentally which its parents take as being the first word - such as 'mama'. When this happens they are very pleased, and the child is rewarded for this behaviour by lots of attention and encouragement. This makes it more likely to repeat the behaviour. Gradually, through a process of **trial and error learning** and **behaviour shaping** (in which the child is only rewarded for some sounds and not others), it comes to form more and more words and also comes to produce them in the 'appropriate' situations. As it becomes more proficient, it may also extend its vocabulary by imitation and will again be encouraged to do this by parental enthusiasm and encouragement.

Skinner's view of the way that the child acquired language has two main characteristics: (a) it is a **behaviourist** theory, seeing language as simply the production of a certain kind of behaviour – verbal behaviour – and arguing that sounds only develop meaning because they become associated with particular kinds of environmental stimuli; and (b) it is a **reductionist** theory, because it attempted to reduce the acquisition of language down to the simple elements of stimulus-response (S-R) links.

Nativist theories

A review of Skinner's book was written by the linguist Noam Chomsky. In this review, Chomsky put forward his own ideas about language acquisition, as well as criticising Skinner's theory. His main objections to Skinner were fourfold. Firstly, that if all children acquired language by this individualistic process of trial and error that Skinner outlined, they would tend to learn language very differently, and yet language and children's learning of it shows the same basic structures all over the world. Secondly, Chomsky argued that the time that it took the individual child to acquire language was far too short for this to be explained in terms of trial-and-error learning. To acquire such a complex system in about two years from the first word would be impossible if everything had to be learned by operant conditioning. A third objection that Chomsky put forward, was that infants seemed to be 'pre-programmed' to attend to the speech in their environment, as opposed to all the other sounds, and that this needed explanation. His fourth criticism was that what also needed explaining was the way that nobody actually teaches language to children, and yet they seem to be able to extract enough from the bits of incomplete and often ungrammatical language which they hear from others to develop linguistic rules and principles.

One of the fundamental differences between Skinner and Chomsky was that Skinner was analysing child language in terms of **performance** (the behaviour that the child actually emits) while Chomsky was analysing it in terms of **competence** (the skills that the child acquires), which can also be applied to new situations. What the child actually acquired, argued Chomsky wasn't so much the behaviour, as a rule-governed system, and this meant that the child was able to generate new utterances which it had not heard before, as well as ones which it had. When a child says 'I goed to the park', it isn't *imitating* the word 'goed', and it is very unlikely that its parents have actually *rewarded* it for saying 'goed'. Rather, it has learned the underlying rule and is applying that.

Chomsky argued that children inherit what he termed a **Language Acquisition Device**, which operated to extract the rules underlying language from the mass of spoken words which the child heard. The child didn't need to be taught language, because it could identify the rules of language simply from hearing the language others used. In order for the Language Acquisition Device (LAD) to operate the individual simply had to hear spoken language and that was enough. It was an automatic, innate system.

Obviously, it isn't the case that we inherit our language, nor could we inherit all the specific grammatical rules which any particular language has. But Chomsky argued that the grammatical rules which we are aware of, or which we learn when we learn a new language, are only the **surface structure** of that language. The surface structure differs from one language to another, but below all that is a **deep structure** of language which is the same for all human languages. The child is born with an innate awareness of the deep structure of languages, which makes it very readily able to pick out such things as nouns and verbs as long as it hears language spoken.

Chomsky's theory of language acquisition was also a **reductionist** approach in its own way, even though Chomsky was disagreeing with Skinner's S-R reductionism. However, Chomsky was arguing that language acquisition in the child was a genetic process. The child wasn't really active in learning as the learning happened more or less automatically as a result of genetic influence. So in this theory, language acquisition is reduced to the action of genes rather than to the action of S-R connections.

Lenneberg's theory

Other theorists, too, took up Chomsky's idea that language acquisition was inherited (known as the nativist approach). E. L. Lenneberg, a biologist, argued that language was a biological inherited capacity of the human being, which was demonstrated by the way that children acquired language without being taught. In addition, Lenneberg said, language had to be acquired during a **critical period** in the child's life, and if it wasn't learned then, then it would never happen. This critical period was before puberty, as Lenneberg believed that after that the areas of the brain which dealt with language became too rigid and inflexible for a new language to be learned. Adults who learned a new language, he argued, never learned it as well as they had learned their first one.

Part of the reason for Lenneberg's idea of the critical period for language development had come from studies of language areas in the brain. These are usually (though not always) located on the left hemisphere of the cerebrum, and if they are damaged in an adult, then permanent interference with language abilities can result. However, if such damage happens to children below the age of puberty, language functioning usually shifts across to the other side of the brain and so the child is able to recover fully from the damage.

Lenneberg's idea that language had to be acquired during a critical period was called into question by study of a child named 'Genie', who was discovered in Los Angeles in the 1970s. Genie had been kept tied to a chair in an attic since she was 20 months old. She had had no language contact with anyone, but had been beaten if she made a noise, and occasionally barked at, because her father said she was no more than a dog. When she was discovered she was over thirteen years old, and well past puberty.

Genie did not have any language when she was first found, but as she adjusted to the very different care she was receiving in her foster-home, she acquired language very rapidly. Interestingly enough, she passed through all of Brown's stages, but in some cases in an accelerated form, such as learning all the 'wh' questions together. Although she did learn to use language, there were some significant differences in the way that she did it which meant that she has not ended up, at this stage, with full grammatical fluency.

The nativist approach to language has been very useful to our understanding, as it has shown the way that children are prepared for language, and ready to pick it up very rapidly. But it does seem as though Chomsky and Lenneberg rather over-stated their case, as we will see when we look at the social theories. Nobody would really dispute that there is probably an inherited *tendency* to learn language, but we would not nowadays perceive it as operating in the automatic and independent way that Chomsky and Lenneberg suggested.

Cognitive theories

Other theories of language acquisition have stressed the **cognitive** side of why the child acquires language. To a large extent, we have already looked at these theories when we looked at the relationship between thinking and language. The linguistic relativity hypothesis, for instance, puts forward the idea that language serves to direct and to organise thought. Therefore, the reasons why the child acquires language are seen in terms of the increasing demands made by the environment, which the child needs to be able to come to terms with.

Piaget's approach to language acquisition, as we mentioned before, was that children acquire language as a tool. They are engaging in a considerable amount of problem-solving and learning about their environment, and their acquisition of language serves to direct and to organise their thinking. Piaget considered that the egocentric speech which children show, in which they talk to themselves while they play, does not originate from any need to communicate, but rather comes from a need to re-structure the child's cognition to deal with the world more effectively.

These cognitive theories approach the question of language acquisition from a rather different angle. Rather than trying to explain it in terms of *how* the child acquires language, and what exactly it is doing, they look more at *why* it does, and the purposes that language serves.

Social theories

Brown (1973) argued that the theories of language acquisition which had concentrated on the 'how' of the way that children develop their language, had often missed out on the purposes and meanings underlying the child's use of language. He developed what is now becoming a widely accepted theory which emphasised the **social** aspects of language development. This theory took the view that language arises from the child's need to communicate with others, above all else. We have already looked at Brown's idea of semantic relations grammar, which emphasises the meanings and the kinds of ideas which the child can deal with. Other researchers took up Brown's approach, and examined the interactions by which this social process took place.

Chomsky's idea that children could acquire language simply by hearing it spoken around them, without any need for being taught, had been called into question by a case study reported by Bard and Sachs in 1977. They studied a child called 'Jim', who had been born to deaf-and-dumb parents. Jim could hear and vocalise normally, and so his parents were concerned that he should learn ordinary spoken language rather than the sign language which they used between themselves. Accordingly, they did not teach Jim sign language, apart from a few simple commands, but instead encouraged him to watch TV and to listen to the radio. Jim grew up in an environment which was full of spoken language, but without anyone actually speaking it to him. According to Chomsky's theory, this should have been enough to allow his innate LAD to work.

By the age of three and a half years, Jim had still not acquired language. At this point, he was sent for speech therapy, and within three months had caught up with other children of his age. It was clear that he was ready to start speaking, or he would not have been able to learn so fast. But it was also clear that just hearing spoken language around him hadn't been enough. Jim needed the human contact of the sessions with the speech therapist in order to develop language.

Autism and language

It was becoming clear that it was not really possible to ignore the social influences on the way that the child acquires language.

Further evidence for this was put forward in a study by Brown (1973) on an autistic child called John. Autistic children are characterised by a withdrawal from social contact, and this avoidance of human interaction was reflected in John's speech. Although he did talk (some autistic children are mute and have to be trained to talk), John only imitated what he had heard other people say: he did not seem actually to use language for himself. So, for instance, he did not reverse the pronouns in his speech, as children normally do. When he spoke of himself he said 'you', because that was what other people said to him, and when he spoke of his mother he said 'I', because that was what he had heard. It seemed that this was because of his avoidance of human contact. Children seem to need it if they are to develop a true use of language, rather than simply imitating what they hear without being able to use the underlying rules and principles.

The role of parents in language development

Work by Jill and Peter de Villiers, in 1978, highlighted the way that social interaction between parents and children does in fact form a kind of teaching. They argued that simplifying words and eliminating the difficult phonemes, as in 'baby-talk', gives the child a simpler model of language which it can imitate more easily: 'din-din' is far more tailored to a child's abilities than 'dinner', for instance. The way that parents tend to use these forms with small babies, but to use 'proper' words once the child has mastered these, shows that there is a form of teaching going on, even though it is largely unconscious on the part of the parents.

Similarly, parents continue to develop their children's speech in a variety of ways. They use familiar sentence 'frames' to introduce new words which means that the child's attention is drawn to the new word, while at the same time its confidence grows because it is familiar with the sentence frame being used. So a semi-chant, like 'What's this? It's a cow. And what's this? It's a frog. And what's this? It's a duck...' allows the child to learn new words and to practice familiar ones, which is one of the best forms of teaching, and one which parents do more or less automatically. Also, parents tend to expand their children's utterances: a child that says 'want milk' might be answered with 'Do you want some milk? In this way the child is being encouraged by example, to include more words in its utterances.

There are many other ways that the interaction between parents and children can be shown to form a kind of teaching which allows the child to pick up language more easily. The de Villiers also showed, for instance, that parents tend to speak far more grammatically to their children than they do to other adults, as well as making their sentences simpler and easier to understand. So a child who is ready to pick up the rules and 'deep structure' of language will have its job made very much easier by the nature of the social interaction which it has with others.

Psychology in Action

At present there is no known cause or cure for stuttering. It appears that up to 5 per cent of children and 1 per cent of the adult population stammer or are disfluent in speed and many learn to avoid words and situations that increase their anxiety. Various speech therapy programmes are available and many seem to be based on the principles of operant conditioning rewarding the child for fluent speech. A particularly interesting programme, however, is based on Kelly's personal construct theory.

In the late 1960's, Fay Fransella hypothesized that the stutterer understands and to some extent feels comfortable with, the role of the stutterer. They have learned to anticipate how people will respond to them and how they, in turn, will react. She felt that learning to speak fluently was only one part of therapy. Stutterers must also learn to construe themselves as 'fluent persons'.

In 1983, Evesham and Huddleston developed a speech therapy programme that incorporated Kelly's personal construct theory. Stutterers used techniques such as learning to speak very slowly to develop fluent speech and, at the same time, learned to build new personal constructs for themselves as fluent speakers.

Part of the therapy involved trying out their fluency in everyday situations. Accompanied by other members of the group, they would go into shops and onto buses and enter conversations. Together, the members of the group would then evaluate the situation in terms of each participant's behaviour and feelings in an attempt to alter the stutterers' personal constructs.

Mother - infant interaction

Work on **mother-infant interaction** suggests that the background for this is established long before the child actually utters its first word. A study by Stern (1977) showed that interaction between mothers and quite small infants showed the same sort of patterns, timings, and turn-taking that you would find in adult conversations. Also a study by Snow (1977) showed that mothers tend to adopt a conversational approach when they are dealing with even very small babies - talking to them, asking them questions, and treating even quite small actions which the baby makes as if they were replies - so that the child is familiar with the conventions of using language long before it actually begins to talk.

We can see from this, that all of these different perspectives of language acquisition have helped us to understand how it develops to some degree. By taking some of the most valid ideas from each one, we can learn a great deal about the ways that children come to use and understand language.

Animals and language

Traditionally, one of the important distinctions between human beings and animals has been the fact that human beings are the only species which uses languages to communicate. This idea has stimulated a considerable amount of research into animal communication; both to see whether there are similarities between the methods of communication that other animals use and human language, and to investigate how far other species can be taught to communicate using human languages.

What can we learn by studying animals?

The reasons underpinning the teaching of human languages to animals are based on the concept of **evolution**. If we see humans as related, in evolutionary terms, to the other great apes, then we need to ask at what point did language evolve, and are there half-way stages? So a considerable amount of research has gone into investigating, not so much whether chimpanzees or other apes use language in the normal run of things, but whether they can, if taught, learn to use language. By studying the ways that they learn it, or at least learn something which comes close to it, we may eventually be able to develop a kind of model for how language might have evolved. In the same way that our ideas of children's acquisition of language comes as much from the mistakes that they make as the things which they do right (like saying 'foots' instead of 'feet'), we can learn about the possible basics of language by looking at what animals can learn, and what they cannot.

The phylogenetic scale

In order to study this, one important distinction that we have to make is that of the **phylogenetic scale**. In Chapter 2, we showed how some forms of learning seem to be very much more 'basic' than others; and how even very simple animals can show one-trial learning and classical conditioning. But language is a highly sophisticated ability mediated, as we saw in Chapter 8, by the most recently developed part of the brain: the cerebral cortex. So if we are to talk sensibly about animals learning language, we can't treat all animals as if they are the same.

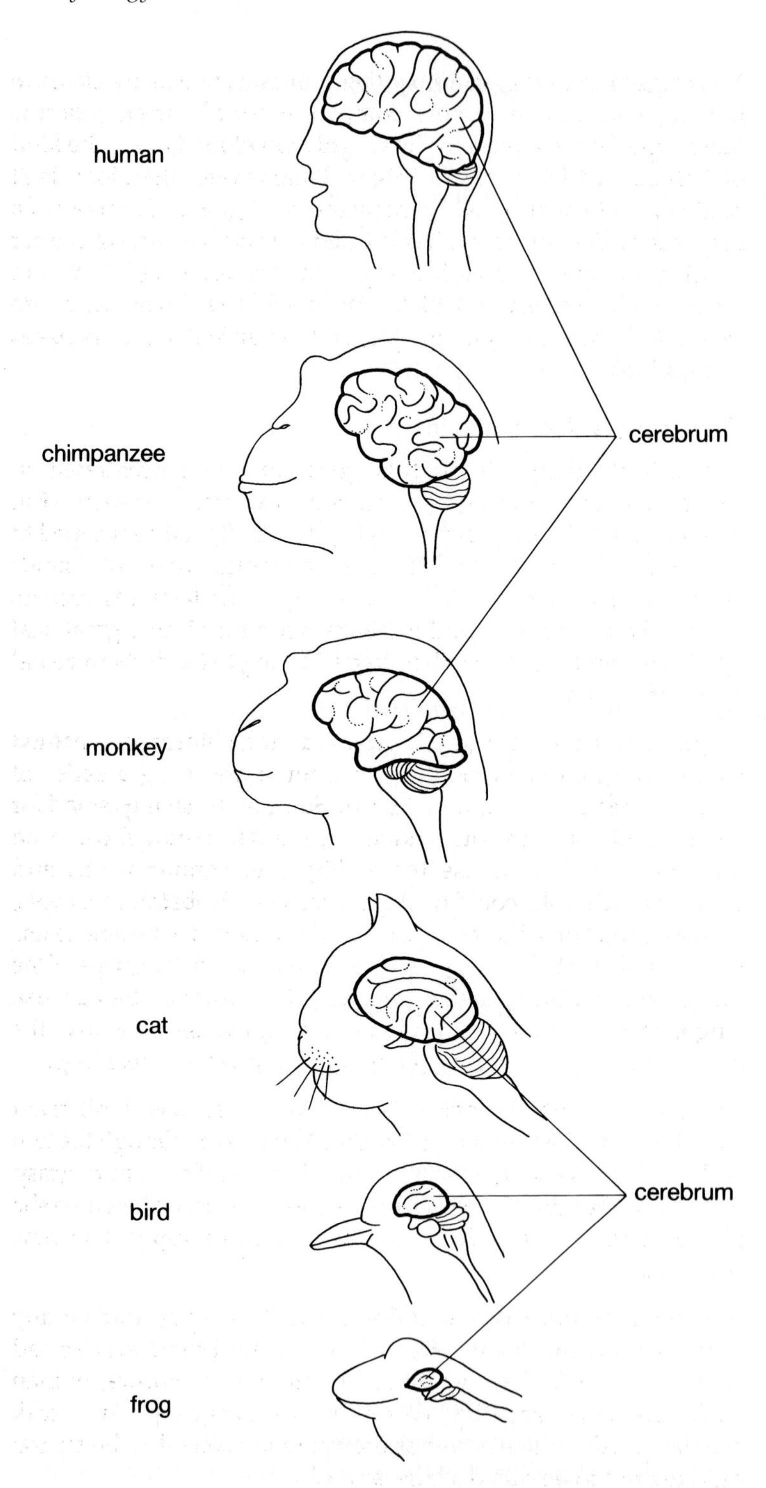

10.1 Phylogenetic differences in the cerebral cortex

You can see from Fig. 10.1 how those animals which are closer to human beings have a more complex cerebral cortex, whereas others, like birds, have a far less highly developed one. The kind of 'talking' which a parrot might demonstrate, therefore, isn't really likely to be truly what we mean by language - it's more of a response which the parrot has learned to produce, through either classical or operant conditioning. The research which we are interested in here is that which concerns those animals which are closest to human beings: the apes, and in particular chimpanzees and gorillas.

Primate studies

The earliest attempts to teach language to apes concentrated on trying to teach them to speak, and were extremely unsuccessful. It seems that the chimpanzee vocal system isn't really equipped to deal with producing the different phonemes (units of sound) which human beings can use so freely. But later researchers observed that, in the wild, chimpanzees communicate a great deal by visual symbols, and so they started trying to teach them visual forms of language.

Sarah

Premack and Premack (1983) reported on a chimpanzee named Sarah, who had been taught to communicate using a series of shapes, placed on a magnetic board. Some of the shapes stood for names, and some for other kinds of words. Sarah showed an impressive ability to use these shapes to communicate, and showed too that she could deal quite easily with abstract concepts, such as 'same' or 'different'. But she did not seem to be able to use the symbols that she was provided with as a true language. One thing which distinguishes the way that human beings use language is that they seem to have a natural sense of **syntax** - the correct ways that words can be ordered to produce meanings.

For instance, the sentence, 'Mary likes Joan' has a different meaning from the sentence 'Joan likes Mary', even though the two both contain the same words. Sarah didn't really seem to grasp this idea: although she would use the correct word order when she was trained to, she didn't seem to be able to apply it to new situations.

Another difference was that Sarah didn't actually initiate any conversations, but she would always wait until someone else had 'spoken' to her before replying. As any parent knows, human children very rapidly catch on to language and talk spontaneously. Sarah's use of the symbols seemed to be far too rigid overall to be called a true language.

Ethical discussion

Jane Goodall gives an account of a chimpanzee, named Lucy who was brought up in a human family and taught to use sign language. Inevitably, Lucy grew too big to be kept around the house, and so she was put in with a colony of wild chimpanzees. In other words, she went from being treated in all respects like a member of a human family, living in a house, with toys and so on, to being treated in exactly the same way as a wild chimpanzee. It was obvious that she was very unhappy. When a visitor whom she recognised came to visit the colony, Lucy signed desperately: 'Please help. Out.'

Was it ethically acceptable to bring Lucy up to use language?

Washoe

More convincing evidence that chimpanzees can get some way towards learning human-type language came when researchers began to teach American sign language (Ameslan) to chimpanzees and gorillas. The first of these studies was by Gardner and Gardner (1975), who trained a chimpanzee called Washoe. Washoe developed a rapid ability to use sign language, both through 'moulding', i.e. having her hands shaped into the correct pattern when being shown an object, and through imitation. Washoe also showed that she could combine words to express a meaning: when she first saw a duck, she made the sign for water and the sign for bird, calling it a 'water-bird'. And she frequently initiated 'conversations' with her trainers.

In order to make sure that she really was making the signs that they thought she was making, the Gardners used a 'double-blind' technique to test her. They showed Washoe objects which she had to name, and an observer was hidden in such a way that it was only possible to see Washoe, and not the objects that she was being shown. The observer wrote down the signs that she made, and then they were compared with the experimenter's list. In this way, the Gardners were able to show that Washoe's signs were realistic, and could compare with those that human Ameslan users would make.

It was clear that Washoe was able to go some way towards using language, but there is still considerable debate about whether it is truly the same as human language. Some critics, such as Terrace (1979) argued that all that she and the other chimps who had learned Ameslan were doing was producing responses through operant conditioning. While others, such as Van Cantfort (1982), argued that the chimpanzees were really using the language in a similar way to that of young children, and that although their grammar and syntax were not perfect, they were manipulating the symbols of language in a manner that should be accepted as language.

Characteristics of language

One of the problems with this debate is the fact that there are not really very clear criteria for just what is meant by language, which makes it easier to support any particular point of view. One approach which some researchers have taken, is to use a set of criteria for what constitutes a language which were laid down before this debate existed by Hackett in 1958. The most sophisticated of these criteria in terms of the abilities of the language user are: traditional transmission, displacement, the production of novel utterances, prevarication, and reflexiveness.

Traditional transmission is the passing of language from one generation to the next, and it was observed that when Washoe was older, she taught sign language to her infant. The Gardners later set up a colony of about half a dozen young chimpanzees, being brought up by people who were fluent Ameslan speakers (they thought that some of Washoe's early mistakes might have been a result of their not being very fluent in the sign language). Many of the young chimpanzees in this colony seemed to learn signs from each other.

Displacement is the ability to refer to objects or situations that are not immediately present. Fouts (1972) showed that chimpanzees could 'inform' each other where objects had been hidden, if one of them was taken away from the other and shown something, and then returned to the others later. As we have seen, Washoe showed an ability to combine the signs to produce new words, or **novel utterances** and the other chimpanzees sometimes seemed to do that as well.

Koko

Prevarication is the ability to tell lies, or to talk about things which are impossible. Although there doesn't seem to be much evidence for this from the chimpanzee colony, a study of two gorillas, Koko and Michael, who were taught Ameslan, indicated that they could prevaricate. Patterson (1981) described how Koko might reply to the request, 'Tell me something you think is funny' by signalling, 'That red', pointing to a green toy. And Koko also demonstrated **reflexiveness**, or the ability to use language to talk about language itself, in her 'conversation' with the younger gorilla, Michael. When he obtained something he particularly wanted from the trainer by using a sign which Koko had shown him, she signalled 'Good sign, Michael'.

Using these criteria, then, it seems as though some apes can use language, but it is very clear that the way that they are using it is not as sophisticated as human language use, and also that it takes them very much longer to learn it, as they are not prepared for it in the way that human infants seem to be. It does seem, though, that the readiness which these apes have to use symbols and simple language could show a route by which human language could have evolved. Certainly their learning of language signals and the way that they use them is far more flexible and adaptable than that of, say, parrots and mynah birds.

Summary

1. The relationship between language and thought has been seen in different ways: thought as sub-vocal behaviour; thought as dependent on language; and language as a tool of thought.
2. Bernstein identified elaborated and restricted codes of language, and argued that working-class people could only use restricted codes. Labov and others showed that this was not the case, but social expectation may have an influence on development.
3. Children go through identifiable stages as they acquire language, which have been studied by Brown and other psychologists.
4. The behaviourist view of language acquisition was put forward by Skinner, who said it happened through operant conditioning of the child's babbling.
5. Chomsky and Lenneberg put forward nativist theories of language acquisition. Chomsky proposed an innate Language Acquisition Device (LAD) and Lenneberg said there was a critical period.
6. Social theories of language acquisition have emphasised the need for human interaction which children have when they are learning language. Parents teach their children naturally, through 'baby talk', expansion of the child's utterances, and other devices.
7. Studies of animals learning language have shown that apes may be able to learn to use simple language, but not as easily as human children can.

Chapter 11 - Memory

Memory as an active process

The effects of language on memory

The use of language can also affect other cognitive processes, such as memory. A well-known study by Carmichael, Hogan and Walters (1932) demonstrated this very clearly. Research participants were shown pictures (known as stimulus figures), with verbal descriptions of them. A short while later, they were asked to draw the picture that they had seen. There were two groups of participants: each group was shown the same stimulus figures, but given different verbal descriptions of them - so, for instance, one group might have a stimulus figure described as 'curtains in a window', while the other might have the same figure described as 'a diamond in a rectangle'. When they were asked to remember the shapes that they had seen, Carmichael et al. found that the participants drawings were much more like the verbal description than the original stimulus figures had been. The research participants remembered the figures as being different, because of the verbal descriptions that they had had. This showed quite clearly that a person's memory can be changed by the kind of language which is involved.

Another study on the effect of language on memory was performed by Loftus and Loftus, in 1975. They showed research participants a film of a traffic accident, and then asked them questions about what they had seen. After a week, the participants were asked about the film again. Loftus found that the way in which the questions were asked had quite an effect on what the participants remembered. For instance: one group of participants was asked, immediately after seeing the film, 'How fast were the cars going when they hit each other?'. The other group of participants was asked, 'How fast were the cars going when they smashed into each other?'. When they were tested later, the participants were asked if they had seen any broken glass in the film. (There hadn't been any.) Those research participants who had heard the word 'smashed' remembered seeing broken glass scattered around after the accident. In fact, their memory of the accident was of a much more serious one than in the other participants' memories, even though they had both seen the same film. So it seems that, if we are asking someone to remember something, we have to be very careful that we do not accidentally say things which will distort their memories. It is for this reason that people are concerned about 'leading questions' in court, or in police questioning of witnesses.

Ethical discussion

When people are hypnotised, they enter a highly suggestible state, in which they are extremely willing to co-operate with the person who has hypnotised them. Gibson (1982) reported on the increased use of hypnosis in police investigations, performed in the belief that using hypnosis would enable witnesses to recall details more effectively.

Do you regard this as an ethically acceptable practice?

Constructive memory

In addition to the importance of language, what these studies show us is the way that memory is an *active* process, and not an automatic 'tape-recording' of past events. Psychologists have been studying memory for about a hundred years now, and this is one finding which has recurred time and time again. Although we all think that we are remembering things accurately, in fact it is very rare for us to do so. Because we are continually trying to make sense of what is around us, our memories tend to be fitted into that and if the information does not quite fit, then we will alter it until it does (without realising it, of course!). This process was called the **effort after meaning** by one of the first psychologists to investigate active memory: Bartlett (1932). We try to make the things that we remember meaningful, by fitting them into the existing ways that we remember things - our existing **schemata**.

Bartlett

Bartlett's most famous study involved a method known as **serial reproduction**. In order to study the way that memory works in everyday life, he reasoned that we usually tell others about something that we have heard or come across. So his technique of serial reproduction was for a research participant to listen to a story, or read one, and then to reproduce it by either writing it down or telling another person about it. The next person would then have to do the same thing, so Bartlett could see how the story would gradually change in the re-telling.

The war of the ghosts

One story which Bartlett used was called *The War of the Ghosts.* It was an account of a war between two North American Indian peoples, and was written in such a way that the tribes' ancestral spirits were in the story. But you could either consider them to be very important or you could see them just as part of someone's dream and not really important at all. Bartlett found that his European research participants tended to leave out the spirits when they were re-telling the story, because they did not really see them as important. Rather than remembering the whole thing that they had been told, they remembered only those bits which fitted with the styles of thinking which they already had.

In general, Bartlett found that people would alter information as they remembered it in such a way as to make it make more sense to them personally. Because details which did not fit with the research participant's own schemata would tend to get left out, the story would gradually become shorter, and also more conventional. By the fourth or fifth re-telling, Bartlett found that it often wasn't the same story at all. You can see the same sort of thing happening in the old party game 'Chinese Whispers', where a message is whispered to someone, who then whispers it to the next person in line, and so on until they reach the last person, who says what they have heard out loud. Almost always, the message is totally different when it reaches the end of the line!

In 1947, Allport and Postman published a study of the way in which this kind of effect had taken place during wartime. Because, generally, there wasn't very much known about what was going on, people had tended to try to make sense out of what they had heard, and to add bits on in order to achieve this. In addition, much of the information that *was* known tended to be ambiguous (having more than one possible meaning), and people would seize upon the meaning which seemed most likely to them. This resulted in all sorts of wild rumours flying around, throughout the war. You can often see the same sort of thing happening today, when alarming events take place - like the stories about the 'Yorkshire Ripper' which went around before he was caught, or about the 'M4 murderer'. Again, these illustrate the way that we are continually making an 'effort after meaning', as Bartlett said.

Effects of emotion on memory

Bower showed the way that our emotions may influence what we remember. In a study in 1981, he asked research participants to keep a diary for a week and to note down all the things which happened to them which were either pleasant or unpleasant. When the week was over, the participants were put into a light hypnotic trance and asked to remember their week. Before that, however, it was suggested to them that they were either in a good mood or a bad mood. The participants who were in a good mood remembered far more of the pleasant things that had happened to them that week, while the participants who were in a bad mood remembered far more of the bad things. It seems that the mood which they were in had given them a 'set', similar to the **learning sets** we have already looked at, which made them more likely to remember things which fitted with that mood.

All this shows us that memory, far from being the static, passive thing that many people think it is, is an *active process*, which is affected by the ways that we understand events and by our subjective feelings.

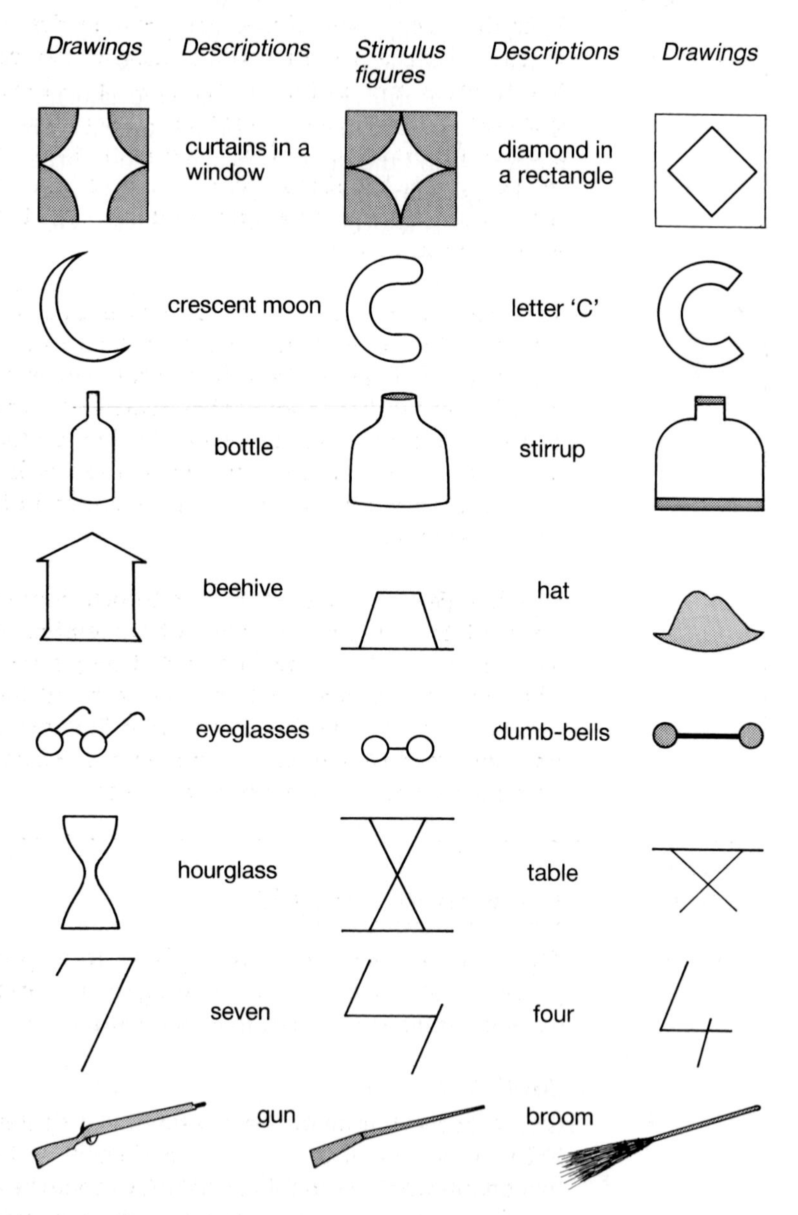

11.1 Symbols and descriptions used by Carmichael et al.

Psychology in Action

With the recent spate of miscarriages of justice coming to light in the UK, the accuracy of forensic evidence, eyewitness testimonies and police interviews have been called into question. There are many factors surrounding a case which can influence the outcome. Using their knowledge of the nature of memory, psychologists have been able to help police improve their interviewing techniques and increase the accuracy of eyewitness accounts.

The first basic premise is that memory is an active process and the eye-witnesses will reconstruct a sequence of events in a way that is unique to them. The job of the police interviewer is to help the witness recall the scene of the crime with as much accuracy and as little bias as possible. This involves understanding that memory is selective and that the witness will already have processed some information as important and discarded other details as trivial.

Psychologists have also been able to help improve the use of photofit techniques. Instead of remembering individual features of a face, it is now known that people store the memory of a face as a 'whole' and are able to recall the relationship between certain facial features. It may be much more difficult for a witness to assemble a picture of a face from hundreds of unrelated shapes of eyes, noses and so on.

Why do we forget?

There have been several explanations put forward by psychologists for why we forget things that we used to know. We will look at a few of these theories in turn.

Amnesia

One of the most dramatic reasons for forgetting things is as a result of brain damage or disease. Some kinds of accidents can mean that people don't recall things that they should be able to, and this loss of memory is known as amnesia. Broadly speaking, there are two kinds of amnesia: **retrograde amnesia** and **anterograde amnesia**.

Retrograde amnesia

Retrograde amnesia is when a person loses their memory of the events which have led up to their accident. In its most dramatic form, it can lead to an individual forgetting who they are and where they live, but this is very rare. Most commonly, people tend to forget just the events for the 10 minutes or so leading up to the accident. It seems as though memories have a 'settling' time, and the most recent ones are the ones which are most easily lost.

Anterograde amnesia

Anterograde amnesia is when the individual is not able to remember things after the accident has happened. In Chapter 8 we looked at a study of anterograde amnesia studied by Milner (1966), which showed that this could arise as a result of damage to the hippocampus.

This form of anterograde amnesia is also very rare, but a more common form is found in Korsakoff's syndrome, which is shown by long-term alcoholics (see Chapter 8). Although they may appear normal, they are often unable to retain information and may not, for instance, remember people whom they have met only that same day. They often learn to disguise this by making very general remarks about things but it is a serious problem nonetheless.

Amnesia through brain damage is an extreme form of forgetting, but in everyday life we forget things too. When psychologists have tried to explain just how forgetting happens, they have turned to several different explanations.

Motivated forgetting

One of the earliest theories of forgetting was put forward by Sigmund Freud in 1901. He argued that all forgetting results from **repression** - that we forget things because in some way we are motivated to forget them. If we didn't, they would remind us of things which were deeply emotional and traumatic. Because this would be threatening to the conscious mind it is repressed, and therefore the individual 'forgets' it and is unable to bring it to mind.

Although there has been a certain amount of support for the idea of motivated forgetting, such as Bower's study of pleasant or unpleasant memories which we dealt with in the last section, very few psychologists nowadays would agree with Freud that *all* forgetting can be explained in that way. Rather, they would regard it as one out of many ways that forgetting can happen.

Interference

Proactive interference

Another way that forgetting can take place is by **interference** from other information. This can take two forms: **retroactive interference** and **proactive interference**. Proactive interference is when one thing that we have learned interferes with the next one, such as learning a French term for something and then trying to learn the German term for it. If our learning of the German term was interfered with so that we weren't able to remember it, that would be proactive interference.

Retroactive interference

Retroactive interference is when something that we have learned interferes with something that we learned previously. So, for instance, your learning of French and then German might mean that you couldn't remember the French term which you had learned in the first place. That would be retroactive interference.

In the 1950s, many psychologists considered that interference could probably account for all cases of forgetting, but other theories have been put forward since which have challenged that idea. Interference is almost certainly an important factor in forgetting, but so are many other things.

State-dependent learning

One of the ideas which emerged to question the belief that interference could account for all forgetting, was that of **state-dependent learning.** A study by Overton in 1972 showed how individuals who were under the influence of alcohol could remember things that had happened to them on similar occasions much more readily than when they had not been drinking. It seems that being in the same physiological state meant that people could recall things that had happened previously, more easily. Other studies showed that this applied to other drugs too and it seems likely that it also happens when we are in particular emotional states.

State-dependent learning seems to work by providing a **context** for helping us to remember, and many studies have shown that the context in which we set our memories is important. Just think, for instance, of the way that hearing a particular record can bring back a whole set of memories because the record was part of the context that those events happened in. The record is part of the **external context**, and alcohol is part of the **internal context**. Some theories of forgetting state that the reasons why we forget is not because the information isn't there, but because we can't re-create the context to get to it.

Context and cues

A reason why context seems to be important in remembering is because it provides **cues** for us to link one part of memory with another. Tulving and Pearlstone (1966) showed how important cues could be. They gave their research participants lists of words to memorise, and the participants were divided into two groups. Both groups were given the same lists, which were arranged in sets with a category name above each set (e.g. 'animals' above a set of words consisting of animal names). When it came to remembering them, though, one group was just given a blank sheet of paper and asked to write down as many as they could remember, while the other group was given a piece of paper with the category names on it. (They hadn't been asked to memorise the category names, only the lists.) Not surprisingly, the group which had been given the cues (the category names) remembered far more than the group who were just given the blank piece of paper.

This kind of work suggests that having the right cues is crucial to being able to retrieve our memories, and some psychologists have suggested from this that the reason why we forget things, at least temporarily, is because we haven't got the right cues. Many **mnemonics** (memory aids) work by giving us sets of cues which will lead us to the things that we want to remember.

11.1 Imagery in memory

One of the good things about studying the psychology of memory, is that it gives you something that you can actually put into practice to help you in your revision!

When you are revising, there are times when you will be able to use the levels of processing approach to learning which we have suggested in the next activity box; but there are other times when you simply have to sit down and learn things.

You can use some of the ideas which have come from the work on imagery in memory to develop tactics for remembering things. One helpful way is to use a combination of the 'method of loci' and the 'key word' technique.

Your first step is to develop a 'key' for each of the words that you have to remember. Suppose, for instance, that you are trying to memorise a set of biological terms. Look for some everyday word which sounds like part of the word you are trying to learn: for instance, you might think that the word 'agglutinogen' sounds a bit like 'a glue tin'. Make sure that the thing that you think of is easy to visualise in your mind.

When you have done that, imagine a walk or journey which you take often, such as the journey to your school or college, or the route you usually take when you go shopping. Taking each of your items to be remembered in turn, imagine each one at a different place on that route, making sure that you form a vivid mental picture of the 'key' item in that particular place.

When you have been all through the list forming a mental picture and location for each item, test yourself by mentally running through the list again. You'll be surprised at how easily you remember it!

Remember, though that it must be your *own* images. Trying to learn ones which have been developed by other people only gives you even more to learn and you've got enough as it is!

Can you think of a way that you could investigate this technique by doing a formal experiment?

Forms of remembering

From the work on forgetting, we can see that there is more than one way to remember or to forget things. One of the first psychologists to study memory was Ebbinghaus, who produced a book about human memory in 1885. Ebbinghaus was very careful and systematic in his research, getting himself and his assistant to memorise long lists of nonsense syllables, and studying the ways in which they came to remember or forget them.

Recall

Ebbinghaus found that there were four distinct ways that we could remember information. One of the first was **recall**: the kind of process that we would generally call remembering. Recall involves bringing information out of memory without any external assistance, like the way that we remember things for exams.

Recognition

A second kind of memory was the kind that we call **recognition**: sometimes we can't recall things, but we can recognise them when we come across them. This is the kind of memory that is being tested by multiple-choice exams, when even though you may not be able to bring the correct answer to mind spontaneously, you may still be able to know which is the correct one once you see it and that is still remembering.

Reconstruction

Sometimes, Ebbinghaus found, he was unable to recall or to recognise a list that he had learned previously. However, if he had to rearrange it in some way, he found that he would have reconstructed the original order of the list. This **reconstruction**, too, seemed to be a kind of remembering, but not the conscious kind that we are normally used to.

Re-learning

The fourth kind of remembering that Ebbinghaus identified was also a long way from conscious remembering. Ebbinghaus found that a list which he had learned once, even if it was totally forgotten as far as he could tell, would show **re-learning savings**. In other words, it took him less time to learn that list again than a totally new list which he had never seen before in his life. So it seems that even if we think that we have forgotten the material entirely, the act of having learned it may mean that we have less trouble re-learning – a point to remember next time you're revising!

Modes of representation

We seem to code our memories in a variety of different ways. Bruner (1956) argued that we develop different **modes** for storing our memories as we grow older and need to store more complex kinds of things.

Enactive

The first kind of memory which we have, he said, is **enactive representation**. In this, the infant stores information as muscle memories: remembering the feel of actions as it does different things.

However, this means that the infant is only really able to remember things which it has been active in doing. While it is very small, this doesn't really matter but as it grows older and its experience grows, it may want to remember different kinds of things, such as different programmes seen on TV. With memories like these, our actions would be the same for all the different programmes and yet we would have different things to remember.

Iconic

Accordingly, Bruner says that we develop a second method for storing information, which he called **iconic representation**. In this, information is stored as sensory images usually visual ones, like pictures in the mind. Some children develop quite an extreme form of this, known as **eidetic imagery** (photographic memory) but they usually lose this as they grow older.

Symbolic

Iconic representation isn't always enough though, because as we grow older we learn about some things that are very difficult to picture, such as abstract concepts like 'peace' or 'justice'. So the third mode of representation which we develop, according to Bruner, is **symbolic representation** - the ability to store things in the form of symbols. In a sense, we are doing this from the minute that we learn about numbers, because they are symbols which stand for more complex things. But we extend this facility and develop considerably more symbolic representations as we grow up. Words, of course, are very powerful symbols, and we can store a lot of information as verbal memory, which provides an example of symbolic representation as Bruner means it.

Bruner's three modes of representation are all available to the older child or to the adult. Often, though, we find that we prefer to use one mode rather than another with certain kinds of material. There has been quite a lot of research into the way that the iconic mode, in particular, affects memorising; and several mnemonics have been developed which involve using imagery to enhance remembering.

Improving memory through imagery

Key word technique

A study by Raugh and Atkinson (1975) showed how using **imagery** could increase the amount that people could remember. They asked research participants to remember a list of 60 Spanish words, with their meanings. One group was just asked to learn the words, and the other group was asked to use a particular memory aid which Raugh and Atkinson had developed known as the **key word** system. With this, they were asked to look at each Spanish word and to imagine an English word that the Spanish word (or part of it) sounded like. For instance, they might have to remember the Spanish word for tent -'carpa'- so they might find a key word in English of 'carp'. Once they had done that, they were expected to form a mental image which would link the meaning of the Spanish word with the English key word, such as imagining a fish in a tent.

Raugh and Atkinson found that there were striking differences between the two groups. The ones who had not been asked to use any particular technique remembered an average of 28% of the words, while those using the 'key word' technique remembered an average of 88%. So it seemed that forming a mental image helped them to remember.

Method of loci

Another well-known technique for memorising things by using mental imagery is known as the **method of loci**. In this, an individual uses a well-known place, or regular walk as a memory aid. When trying to remember a list, such as a shopping list or list of things for an exam, they form a mental image which links each thing on the list with a particular location on the walk in sequence. In this way, they are able to use the walk and the mental image associated with it, to give themselves cues for the things that they are trying to remember. Because they are reminded of them in this way, they become much easier to recall.

How memory works

We can see from the work on imagery that cues are important in bringing things to mind, and that different information can be stored in different ways. It seems as though the various modes that we use in coding information may have an effect on how well we are likely to remember it.

Levels of processing

A study by Craik and Lockhart in 1972, illustrated this point very clearly. They gave research participants lists of words to look at, but the participants were not told that it was a memory experiment. The participants were divided into three groups, and were asked different kinds of questions about the words while they were looking at them. One group was asked about the way that the words were presented visually: whether, for instance, they were in capital or small letters. The second group was asked about the way that the words would sound: whether they would rhyme with certain words, for example. And the third group was asked about the meanings of the words: whether they could meaningfully be fitted into a particular sentence. Later on, the research participants were asked to remember the words that they had been looking at.

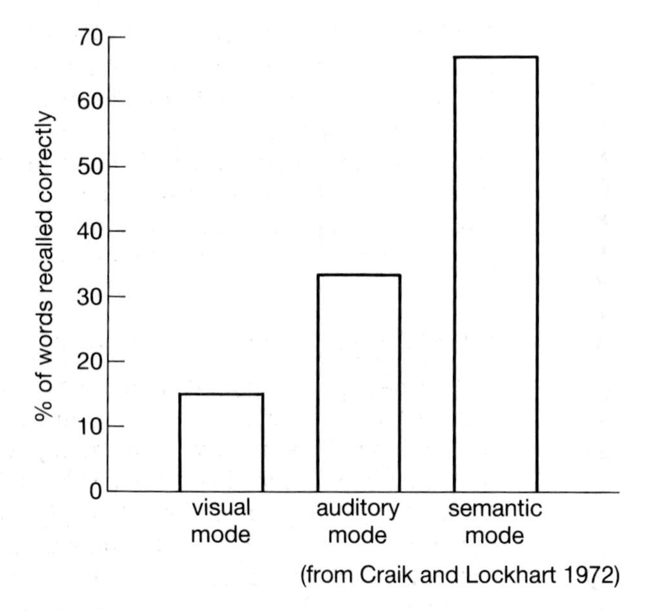

11.2 Levels of processing in memory

Craik and Lockhart found dramatic differences between the different conditions of the study. Those in the visual condition (who were asked what the words looked like) remembered an average of 15% of the words. Those in the auditory condition (who were asked what the words sounded like) remembered an average of 35%. And those in the semantic condition (who were asked what the words meant) remembered an average of 70% of the words that they had seen. See Fig. 11.2.

Craik and Lockhart explained their results in terms of **levels of coding**. They argued that it is possible to look at the differences between the three conditions of the study in terms of the amount of processing that was done with the information. To answer questions about what the words looked like didn't involve very much processing, as the words were being presented in a visual form anyway (the research participants had them in front of them and were reading them). But in order to answer questions about what the words sounded like, the participants had to convert the visual image into an auditory one, so that they could imagine what it sounded like and see if it would rhyme with another. This involved more processing of the information. And to answer questions about the semantic content of the words, the participants couldn't just look at the words: instead they had to think about the *meaning* of each word and see whether it would make sense in the sentence that was suggested to them. This meant that they had to process the information to quite a complicated level.

Craik and Lockhart argued that the levels of processing theory can explain why we remember some things and not others. We tend, for instance, to remember things that we pay attention to, because when we are paying attention to them we are thinking about them as well, and thinking about what else they might connect with. All this means that we are processing it quite deeply. Information that we are not paying attention to doesn't seem to 'sink in' in the same way, because we haven't processed it as deeply.

11.2 Levels of processing in revision

The levels of processing theory of memory tells us that if we process the information we are receiving in some way - in other words, if we actually do something with it, and change its form - then we are likely to remember it better. It also tells us that things are processed most deeply if we have to deal with their meaning, or semantic content, rather than if we just concentrate on more superficial aspects, such as how it looks on the page.

Either on your own, or working in small groups of not more than four people, think about the revision that you will have to do for your next set of exams. (It's a good idea to start by naming a couple of actual topics that you know you will have to learn.) Then, between you, work out six different revision strategies that you could use, which would force you to process the material in a different way.

For example, even a simple thing like making a tape of the information and playing it back to yourself at times when you are doing other things, means that you have processed the information in a different way than if you simply read through it. Drawing up flowcharts which summarise topics means that you have processed it semantically, as you can't draw up a flowchart of a topic unless you have thought about what the information actually means. Doing it forces you to process the information differently, so the drawing up of flowcharts becomes a strategy that you can use when you revise.

When you have developed your six strategies, think again about what you have to revise and decide which of the strategies are most suitable for which material.

Compare your list with those of the other groups, if you are working in class. Are any of them the same?

Which strategies involve processing the information most deeply?

Most important of all, try putting these into practice next time you have an exam, coming up. You won't regret it!

The two-process theory

Before the levels of processing theory was put forward, many psychologists had been concerned with the way that we seem to have more than one system of memory. One kind of memory seemed to be concerned with remembering things for very short periods of time, and this was known as short-term memory (STM). The kind of memory that we use for remembering things for longer periods of time seemed to be a bit different, involving different kinds of codings and having other different characteristics. This was known as long-term memory (LTM).

Atkinson and Shiffrin's model of memory

One example of the two-stage theory of memory, as this was known, was put forward by Atkinson and Shiffrin in 1968. They argued that we have two separate memory stores: a short-term one and a long-term one. The STM store, they said, acts as a kind of first stage for the storing of longer-term memories. Information that we don't particularly need or try to remember, they said, goes into the short-term store and the memory trace decays rapidly if we don't rehearse (practice) it. If we do practice it, though, by repetition, then the information is transferred to a long-term store. Material that we are interested in is often unconsciously rehearsed, and so we remember it better. See Fig 11.3.

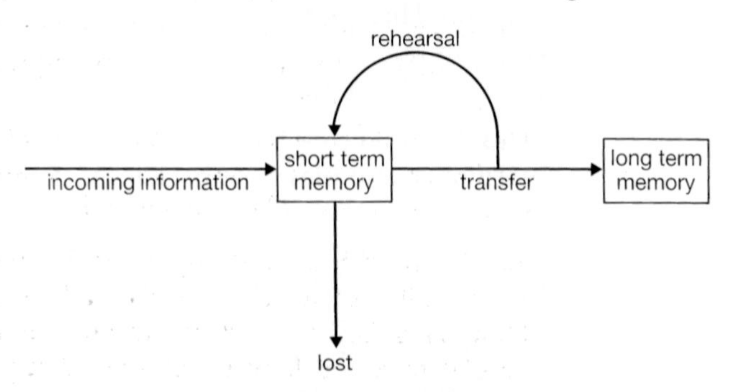

11.3 Atkinson and Shiffrin's model of memory

Does repetition work?

However, the idea that information goes into long-term storage through repetition has been seriously questioned, mainly because studies investigating different methods for remembering things have shown that repetition doesn't really seem to be a very good method at all. A study reported by Bekerian and Baddeley in 1980, investigated people's memories for the new radio frequencies that were introduced by the BBC in the 1970s. Despite the fact that the new frequencies had been broadcast repeatedly and that people had heard them literally hundreds of times, they still didn't seem to recall them, when asked to. In this case, as well as in several others that were studied, repetition didn't really seem to work as a technique for memorising.

Craik and Lockhart explain the structure of memory in a different way. Instead of saying that the differences between long and short-term memory arise because there are two different stores, they argue that they arise simply because the information in short-term memory hasn't been processed as deeply. Because it has only been coded superficially we forget it within a couple of seconds, whereas if we coded it more deeply we would remember it better. The reason why repetition works sometimes in helping us to remember is more because of the effort that we put into it leading to deeper coding - than because of the number of times we go over the material.

Studying for examinations

You can put this idea into practice when you are revising for exams. We have all found, at one time or another, that it is easy to remember things that we understand. That's because the process of understanding involves **semantic processing** - the highest level of all. So one way that you make sure that you are likely to remember things is by making sure that you really do understand everything that you have to remember.

Another way, if that isn't enough, is to develop mnemonics that will help you to recall, like the 'key-word' system, or the method of loci. The reason for this is that by converting the information into a different form we are processing it more thoroughly - so again we are more likely to remember it. Even developing diagrams and flow-charts of the main ideas in your work involves a higher level of processing than just reading it through, and so you are much more likely to remember it.

And finally, if it should happen to be too far away from your exams for it to seem hardly worthwhile revising, remember what Ebbinghaus found about re-learning savings! Having learned material once, he found that even though he thought he had completely forgotten it, it was easier to re-learn it than it would have been if he'd never seen it before.

So this means that time you spend learning things is never wasted – even if you seem to forget it, it will still save time for you when you start your serious revision later.

Summary

1. Memory is an active process which can be affected by factors like language and expectation.
2. Bartlett showed that we make an 'effort after meaning' in which we try to fit our memories into the existing schemata that we hold.
3. Many theories have been put forward to explain forgetting; ranging from brain damage or disease, through repression, interference, and state-dependent learning, to the lack of context and cues for recall.
4. Ebbinghaus identified four ways of remembering: recall, recognition, reconstruction, and re-learning savings.
5. Our use of imagery in memory may change as we grow older. Revision techniques involving imagery can be highly successful in improving memory.
6. Craik and Lockart developed the levels of processing approach to memory, which argued that apparent differences between long and short-term memory arose as a result of less thorough coding or processing of the information to be remembered.
7. The two-process theory of memory argues that short-term memory and long-term memory are separate processes. But it has been criticised by researchers.

Chapter 12 - Perception

Perception as an active process

By perception, we mean the act of interpreting the information which reaches us through our senses. For instance we saw in Chapter 4, when we look at something our eyes receive information in the form of light waves reaching the retina. The visual cells in the retina then convert the light waves into electrical signals, which are sent to the visual area of the brain. The information that is sent is coded in terms of patterns of light and dark and different colours, but when we actually look at something, we see very much more than that. What we actually perceive when we look at something, isn't patterns of light and dark and colour - we see objects. Not only that, but we also recognise them or know if we've never seen anything like them before. The brain doesn't just receive the information passively; it interprets what it has seen and tries to make sense out of it.

The Necker cube

We can see this process more clearly when we look at the way that the brain makes sense out of things when it doesn't really have enough information to go on. If we look at a figure like the Necker cube for any length of time, we find that what we are seeing changes. At first, we will tend to interpret it as a cube facing in one way. But if we keep looking at it, we find that it suddenly reverses itself, so that the face which seemed to be at the front is now at the back of the cube. Not only that, but this happens even if we are trying not to let it: it isn't a deliberate or conscious thing, but something which the brain does whether we want it to or not.

Hypotheses in perception

The Necker cube shows us a very important aspect of perception. When we look at something, we are unconsciously 'guessing' or forming hypotheses about what we can see. Most of the time, we don't realise that it's a hypothesis because there isn't any problem with the guess anyway - if we look at a table and hypothesise that it's a table then nothing is likely to make us realise that it was only an estimate. But with the Necker cube, there are two distinct but equally likely hypotheses which the brain can hold about what it is seeing and it has no way of deciding that one of them is more right than the other. So the brain alternates between the two hypotheses and what we see appears to 'flip' backwards and forwards.

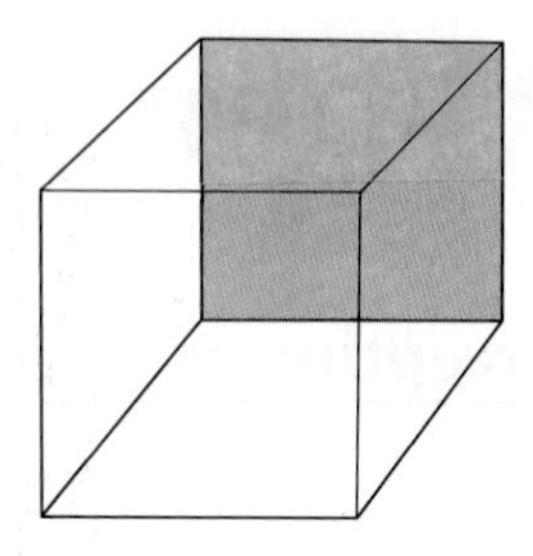

12.1 The Necker cube

Of course, if we were really just seeing what was there, all we would see is a set of lines on a piece of paper! The Necker cube also shows us how we don't necessarily see what is there, but that we interpret what is there instead. If we could just see the Necker cube as lines on paper, we wouldn't have any trouble with it at all, but instead the brain sees it as a representation of a three-dimensional object, and so it can't decide which way round the thing is supposed to be.

Perception, then, is interpreting and making sense out of the information that we receive through our senses. The study of perception involves looking at the ways that we do this, and the kinds of things that can affect our perception.

The Gestalt laws of perception

Some of the early investigators of perception were the Gestalt psychologists, who were mentioned in Chapter 9. They investigated the ways in which our visual perception comes to be organised, in other words, the way that we don't just see random patterns of light and dark but objects and people. The Gestalt psychologists identified several **principles of perception** which seemed to be very basic.

Figure/ground

One of the first of these is the principle of **figure/ground organisation**. When we look at things, we tend to see them as shapes or figures set against backgrounds, and this seems to be very basic in our perception. We can see this very clearly when we look at ambiguous figures, such as the Rubin's vase figure (Fig 12.2). When we are looking at this we see either the vase or the silhouettes. The point, though, is that when we are looking at the vase, the silhouettes disappear, they become background. And if we are looking at the silhouettes, the vase disappears. We can't look at them both at the same time, because our perception organises things into figures against backgrounds.

12.2 Rubin's vase

Figure/ground perception is important, because it forms the basis for almost all of the rest of the way that we see things. Pattern perception is based on the ability to distinguish figures against backgrounds and so is face recognition. Figure/ground perception seems to be one of the earliest of the perceptual abilities that we have. A study by Fantz in 1966, showed that infants preferred patterns to plain shapes, and human faces most of all, even when they were only a few days old. And a study of a man blind from birth who was given sight through an operation when he was 47, showed that he had figure/ground perception even though he seemed to have to learn most other things. It seems that this is one of the perceptual abilities which is innate in both human beings and other animals. (This topic was looked at in more detail in Chapter 4.)

Similarity and proximity

Apart from the figure/ground principle, the Gestalt psychologists identified some other ways in which we tend to organise our perception. Two of these were the principles of **similarity** and of **proximity**. By similarity they meant that, all other things being equal, we tend to group together things which look the same. So if we were looking at a line of figures, say, like this:

ooooooooxxxxxxxxxooooooooxxxxxxxxx

we tend to group the similar ones together because they are like each other.

The principle of proximity is that we tend to group things together if they are near each other. So if, for instance, you saw a line of figures like this:

xxxxxxoo   oooxxxooo   oooxxxxxx

you would tend to see it as three groups of mixed 'o's and 'x's rather than seeing the similar ones grouped together. There are several other principles like this that the Gestalt psychologists identified, and they referred to them as the laws of Pragnänz (or meaning), because that was the way, they thought, that we give meaning to what we are able to see.

Psychology in Action

The Ninja warriors of ancient Japan put their knowledge of perceptual processes to good use in combat. Their reputation for disappearing into thin air led many to believe that they possessed special powers. Now we know that they used psychological phenomena such as figure/ground to move around undetected and fool their opponents' perceptual systems into believing that they had become invisible.

Figure/ground perception refers to the way in which we try to make sense of our environment by distinguishing figures from their backgrounds. Knowing that figures stand out from their backgrounds when they are of a different colour, pattern or brightness, the Ninjas wore clothes of the same contrast and brightness as their surroundings and acted at dusk when contrast between objects is less obvious.

Other rules of perception helped them to avoid detection. They would remain on the edge of their enemies' field of vision. Knowing that the edge of the retina is more sensitive to rapid movement, they would stay still or use extremely slow movements to cover large distances. They also used the principles of similarity and proximity to assume non-human shapes and be "perceived" as part of a group of rocks or trees.

The principle of closure

One of the most important of the Gestalt principles, and one which has much wider implications than just the way that we interpret drawings or visual stimuli, is known as the **principle of closure**. If you very briefly show someone an incomplete figure and then ask them to say or draw what they have seen, they will tend to draw the whole thing, filling in the gaps. Often, in fact, they are not aware that there were actually any gaps at all. The principle of closure seems to be a very strong tendency in our perception.

The Gestalt psychologists identified another way that the principle of closure manifested itself, in an illusion known as the **phi phenomenon**. Briefly, this happens if, say, you flick two adjacent lights on and off in rapid succession. Instead of seeing the two lights, an observer will tend to see just one light moving backwards and forwards as we tend to join up the two distinct points. You have probably seen this happening often, in such things as advertisement lighting in streets, where illusions of movement are created by using the phi phenomenon.

Another example of the principle of closure is in the experience of **stroboscopic motion**. When we are shown a series of pictures in rapid succession we tend to link them up and just see one picture moving. This is the basis of films, and is one way that we can see the principle of closure in operation in our perception. Some psychologists also draw parallels between the way that the principle of closure works in visual perception and the way that we tend to link up information that makes sense to us in memory and thinking, through the formation of schemata. But not every psychologist would agree with that way of looking at things.

From the work of the Gestalt psychologists, though, we can see that perception is an active process, and that we organise our perception in certain definite ways which help us to make sense of the information that is around us.

Perceptual set

To a large extent, our everyday perception is influenced by our environment and the kinds of things which we are used to. For instance, a study by Annis and Frost in 1973 showed how visual perception in urban-living Canadian Cree Indians was different from the visual perception of traditional Cree Indians. When Annis and Frost tested their perception, they found that the traditional Indians were much better at visual tasks like judging whether two lines were parallel or not. They could do this with lines at any angle, while the urban Canadians could only do it well for vertical and horizontal lines. This seemed to be because the urban Canadians lived in a 'carpentered' environment, and they tended to be exposed to vertical and horizontal lines for the most part. Whereas the traditional Indians, who lived by hunting in the tundra, tended to encounter lines at all angles.

However, perception is also strongly influenced by other factors, such as our expectations and our motivation. What seems to happen is that we develop a state known as **perceptual set**, in which we become prepared, or ready, to take in certain kinds of information rather than other kinds.

Expectation

A famous study by Bruner and Minturn in 1955 demonstrated this. Research participants were first given a perceptual set, by being shown a series of either numbers or letters. Then they were shown an ambiguous figure, like the letter 'B', but with a gap between the vertical line and the curved parts. Those participants who had been looking at numbers reported this as a '13', whereas those participants who had been looking at letters reported it as a 'B'.

The Bruner and Minturn study is typical of many others which have demonstrated the power of expectation in perception. It seems that just having similar previous experiences is enough to allow us to develop a readiness to see more of that same type of thing. In many ways, perceptual set is very similar to the learning sets that we looked at in Chapter 9, and the study by Carmichael, Hogan and Walters that we looked at in Chapter 11 could just as well be taken as showing the way that language can generate perceptual sets, as well as its effect on memory.

12.1 Perceptual set

You can look at the way that our expectations can influence our perception, by using Bruner and Minturn's ambiguous 'B/13' figure.

You will need: two postcard-size pieces of card, one larger piece of card, a pen, a piece of paper and a watch with a second-hand (or a stop watch).

First, write out a list of about 12 numbers on a postcard-sized piece of card. Include the 'B/13' figure as one of them, near to the end of the list (but not at the very end). Then take another piece of card and write out a list of about 12 letters, again including the 'B/13' figure near the end.

Taking another, larger piece of card, make a small hole in it, just large enough to form a 'window' to read the numbers of letters through; but small enough that you would only be able to see one number at letter at a time.

When you have done this, ask a friend if they will help you in a test of speed in visual perception. Tell them that you are going to show them a set of numbers or letters very quickly and that they should note down on the paper what they see.

Taking the list of numbers, slide the 'window' over each of the numbers in turn, making sure that your research participant doesn't get more than one second to look at each one. Don't go too fast, though! Then, do the same for the list of letters. Make sure that you take exactly the same length of time to cover each item on the lists.

Finally, look at the way that your research participant has noted down the 'B/13' figure each time. Does it look more like a 'B' or a '13'?

What controls would you need to introduce if you were doing this as a formal experiment?

Can you develop any other ambiguous figures that you could use in a study of this kind?

Primacy effects

Other factors, too, can result in perceptual set. Jones, in 1968, demonstrated the way that primacy effects can happen. Research participants were asked to watch someone answering a set of 30 multiple-choice questions, and then asked to estimate how many the participant had answered correctly. In each condition, the problem-solver got 15 out of the 30 correct, but in one case the participants saw him get most of the ones at the beginning right, whereas in the other condition the correct answers were more towards the end. When they were asked to estimate the number of correct answers, those who had seen most correct answers at the beginning guessed an average of 18.6 correct; while those who had seen later answers given correctly guessed an average of 12.5 correct. It seems that getting the early ones right had set up a 'set' in the observers, so that they judged the participant to be more intelligent or successful.

Motivation

Motivation can also affect perception. A study by Gilchrist and Nesburg in 1952 involved research participants rating pictures according to how brightly-coloured they were. Participants who had gone without food for a period of four hours reported the pictures of food and drink which they came across as significantly more bright than the other pictures, and also as more bright than they had done when they were not hungry. It seems that their motivational state of hunger had influenced their perception.

Emotion

Some studies have shown that emotions, too, may affect perception: a study by Solley and Haigh in 1958, studied the anticipation of an exciting event - Christmas in children. Their child participants were asked to draw pictures of Santa Claus in the weeks leading up to Christmas and in the weeks afterwards. As Christmas approached, the pictures became larger and larger and the number of presents around Santa increased. After Christmas, the presents disappeared and the pictures of Santa became smaller.

Another study, by Erikson in 1951, showed that highly aggressive people were more likely to interpret ambiguous stimuli as being aggressive. They showed participants pictures which represented ambiguous scenes. Participants who were not particularly aggressive tend to give interpretations of what was happening which were not aggressive, but aggressive individuals tended to see violent things either happening or likely to happen in the scene. It seems that they had a stronger perceptual set towards violence than the others did.

Values

Our own values can also affect what we see. A series of studies by Postman, Bruner and McGuiness in 1946, investigated people's **word recognition thresholds**, that is, the minimum amount of time that it took a research participant to recognise a word. They found that participants had lower thresholds for pleasant or highly valued words (like, for example, 'peace'), than they had for unpleasant or 'taboo' words. In other words, they were likely to recognise the pleasant words more quickly. They interpreted this as being a kind of **perceptual defence**. The idea being that our perceptual system will tend to defend us against words which are disturbing or unpleasant.

12.2 Investigating perceptual defence

To do this, you will need a set of about 30 postcard-sized cards, three differently-coloured felt-tip pens, and a watch with a second hand.

Divide the cards into two sets of 15. Write a word, in colour, on each of the cards, making sure that each set has five cards written in each colour in it.

For the first set, the words should be the kinds of words which people are usually reluctant to use in everyday conversation - not swear words, necessarily (although you can include these if you want to), but words which have slightly seedy or immodest connotations, like 'crotch' or 'penis'.

The second set of words should consist of ordinary, everyday words. Make sure, though, that you have words which are of exactly the same length as the ones in your other set.

Now shuffle each set of cards separately, and then ask another person - your experimental research participant - to deal one set out as rapidly as possible into piles: one pile for each colour. Time how quickly they do it. Then time them while they sort out the other set.

According to Worthington and other psychologists, perceptual defence can operate subliminally, so even though the research participants aren't really reading the cards, it should take them longer to sort out the 'taboo' words than it does to sort out the neutral ones. Did you find this?

Why do you think it was important for the words to have the same number of letters in?

How many research participants should you use to investigate this?

Would it have made any difference if your research participants had been different (e.g. older)?

What controls would you need to include if you were doing this as a formal experiment?

Howe and Solomon, in 1950, disagreed with the idea of perceptual defence. They thought that it was much more likely that Postman et al. had simply encountered a **response bias** on the part of their research participants, i.e. that they had recognised the unpleasant or taboo words just as quickly as the other ones but had been unwilling to say so until they were absolutely sure that it really was that word. This meant that they seemed to take longer to recognise them.

Subliminal perception

The argument about whether these findings represented perceptual defence or response bias continued until a study was performed by Worthington in 1969. Worthington used **subliminal perception**: the phenomenon by which we can sometimes perceive something without realising that we have done so. For instance, a picture which is flashed to us very quickly may happen so fast that we cannot tell what it is, but it still may influence the way we respond to another task. This means that we have actually perceived it, but unconsciously.

Worthington's research participants were shown two dots of light on a screen, and they were asked to say which one of the two was brighter. In each of the spots of light, a word was placed, but so faintly that it could not be perceived consciously, only subliminally. The participants were totally unaware that there were any words in the spots of light, but nonetheless Worthington found that if the spot had an emotional word in it, it would be judged as being dimmer than a spot with a pleasant or neutral word. It seems that our perceptual system really does 'defend' us against unpleasant stimuli!

Ethical discussion

When subliminal perception was first discovered, a number of investigations showed that it might be effective in advertising. In one study, the word ice-cream was flashed up subliminally in a cinema. Sales of ice-cream in the interval were much higher but, on the other hand, about half of the customers complained that the cinema was too cold. Nowadays, the use of subliminal signals in advertising is illegal, as it is felt that this is taking unfair advantage of the consumer.

However, some advertisers argue that using subliminal advertising is effectively no different from what happens in existing advertisements, where highly sophisticated uses of colour, images and associations are deliberately combined for maximum effective. They claim that consumers are equally unconscious of the way they are being manipulated in both cases, so what's the difference?

What do you think?

Selective attention

If we are trying to understand the way that our cognitive processes work, we come up against the question of attention and the way that this can affect such things as memory, thinking, and the like. We find it very easy to direct our attention - to select some things which we will pay attention to, while ignoring others. But when people have actually tried to reproduce this ability in computers, they have found it a very difficult thing to do. If you have ever tried to make a tape-recording of a conversation in a crowded room, you'll probably understand why. When we are in a conversation with someone, it seems to 'stand out' from all the background noises, but when we are listening to a tape-recording, we become aware of all the other noise, and it is very difficult to pick out the conversation itself.

Attention was studied in detail by the early **introspectionist** psychologists, such as William James and Wilhelm Wundt. However, when the **behaviourists** started to argue that psychology should only concern itself with data that was objective and scientific, work on attention drew to a halt. It wasn't until the Second World War, with its great increase in communications technology (such as tape recorders) and the emerging need to know exactly how people do interact with machines, (just how does an aeroplane pilot direct attention to exactly the right dial out of all those in the cockpit?) that research into attention started again.

The cocktail party problem

One of the main topics of interest in work on attention was selective attention, and in particular the thing that came to be known as the **cocktail party problem**. This is the one that was outlined before: how is it that in a crowded room we can direct our attention just to one conversation and ignore all the rest?

Dichotic listening tasks

Cherry (1953) developed a laboratory method of studying this kind of attention. This was known as the **dichotic listening task**: research participants would wear headphones, and be presented with two different messages at the same time - a different one to each ear. They would be asked to pay attention to one message rather than the other one. In order to make sure that they were doing it a technique known as **shadowing** was used whereby the research participants had to repeat aloud what they were hearing. In this way, the psychologist was able to check that the thing that they were attending to was the message from the ear they had been asked to listen to.

Cherry found that, after a task like this, research participants didn't really know very much about the information that they had received in the other, unattended ear. They could identify some physical characteristics of the sound, like the fact that it was a human voice, or whether it was a male or female speaker but that was about all. They certainly didn't know anything about the semantic content (the meaning) of the unattended message.

Split span tasks

Some other studies on selective attention were performed by Broadbent in 1958. He gave research participants what he called **split span** tests in which they were played recordings of strings of digits simultaneously to each ear. When he asked participants to remember the numbers that they had heard, they would always give only the digits presented to one ear and would never mix up digits from the two messages, even though they hadn't had any instructions to do so.

Broadbent's model

Taking this finding and those of Cherry into account, Broadbent reasoned that we must have some kind of a mechanism for filtering out information that we are not attending to. He considered that such a filter would work on the basis of the physical characteristics of the message, such as which ear it was coming to. Information that had the wrong physical characteristics would be filtered out, and only that with the right characteristics would pass through the filter, to be stored in memory or to be acted upon.

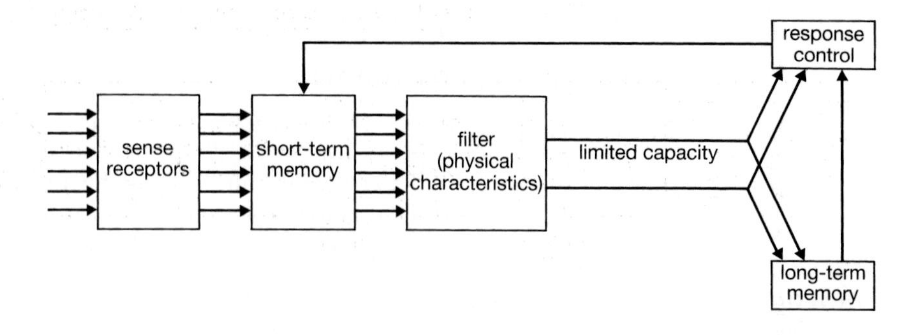

12.3 Broadbent's filter model of selective attention

Triesman's model

Another series of studies on the cocktail party problem, by Moray in 1959, challenged this model of attention. Moray was concentrating on a rather different aspect of the problem: not so much the way that we attend to one conversation among many, but the way that, if someone in another conversation nearby mentions our name, we tend to hear it even though we haven't heard anything else they have said.

Moray performed dichotic listening tasks in which he embedded the research participant's own name in the unattended message. He found that the participants noticed this in about one third of the trials. This seems to imply that the participants must have been monitoring the message unconsciously, because otherwise they wouldn't have known what was being said.

Triesman, in 1960, performed dichotic listening tasks in which the research participants were listening to a continuous message, which suddenly switched from the ear that they were supposed to be attending to, to the other ear. She found that the participants changed over automatically, following the sense of the message, but that they tended not to be aware that they had done this. Another series of studies by Triesman, in 1964, used bilingual research participants having dichotic listening tasks where one message was in one of their languages, and the other one in the other language. Both messages, though, had the same meaning, and the participants were aware of this, even though they had been 'shadowing' only one of the messages.

Triesman argued that this showed that there must be some kind of **semantic processing** of the message. Rather than Broadbent's idea that information was filtered out on the basis of physical characteristics, Triesman put forward a model of selective attention which suggested that the information was only weakened (attenuated) if it had the wrong physical characteristics.

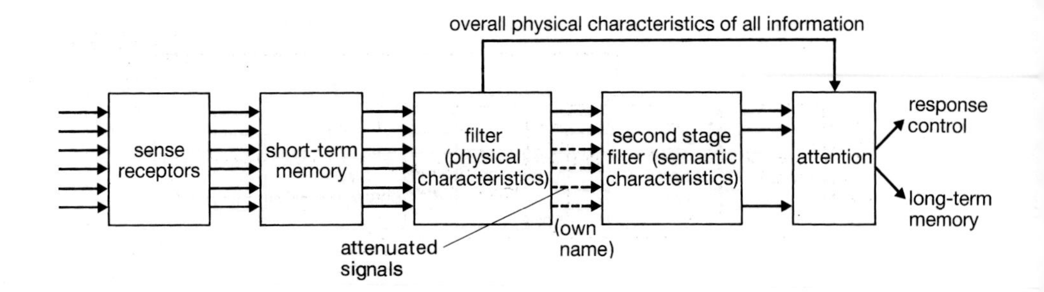

12.4 Triesman's attenuation model

Instead, it would still get through the filter but in a much weaker form than information which was being directly attended to. Information which was particularly strong in semantic content, such as the research participant's own name, would trigger off **dictionary units** which would strengthen the signal again so that the participant was aware of it; but information which wasn't particularly important would be filtered out again by a second-stage filter which worked on the basis of semantic content. So with Triesman's model there were two filters, not one. The first would work on the basis of physical characteristics, as Broadbent suggested, but would attenuate the 'wrong' information; and the second would work on semantic content.

Studies of semantic processing

Other experimental work continued to support the idea that there was semantic processing of information. A study by Moray (1969) showed that if research participants were given an electric shock when they heard certain words, they would show a stress response, (galvanic skin response or GSR), if those words were later embedded in the unattended message. Corteen and Wood (1972) took this further, and showed that research participants would even show the GSR reaction to synonyms (words which meant the same) of the words which had previously received shocks. So it seems that there was a definite amount of unconscious analysing of sensory information going on, even though participants might be unaware of it.

Deutschs' model

Deutsch and Deutsch in 1963, proposed a rather more elegant model of selective attention than Triesman's. They argued that information was analysed for semantic *and* physical content first, and was filtered afterwards. This meant that the filter could also be receiving other cognitive information, such as perceptual set, and would operate to 'screen out' the most irrelevant information on the basis of physical and semantic properties. So instead of two different filters, they proposed just one, but a high-level one.

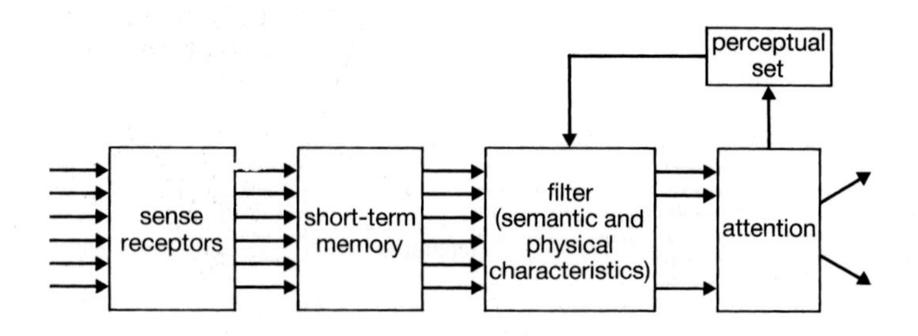

12.5 Deutsch's filter model of selective attention

Both of these filter models of attention would manage to explain the data which has emerged from the experimental work. However, a completely different theoretical approach was put forward by Neisser, in 1976. Neisser argued that we don't really filter out information that we don't want: rather, we tend to emphasise information that we *do* want, and enhance that.

Neisser considered the perceptual process to be the key to understanding the way that human cognition worked. He thought that perception worked as a cycle, which was continually being developed and modified in the light of new information which was perceived. Drawing from the kind of work that we have been looking at in this section, he argued that we have a continual cycle of operations, as follows.

Anticipatory schemata

On the basis of our previous experience we develop **anticipatory schemata**. These allow us to predict and anticipate the information that we are likely to receive through interacting with the environment, and so direct our exploratory behaviour, i.e. what we actually do. The exploratory behaviour that we show allows us to *sample* the environment – to select relevant information and to do things likely to confirm our ideas and schemata. The new information that we gain in this way from objects in the environment serves to build up and to modify our anticipatory schemata. This means that the anticipatory schemata are in turn developed on the basis of information received.

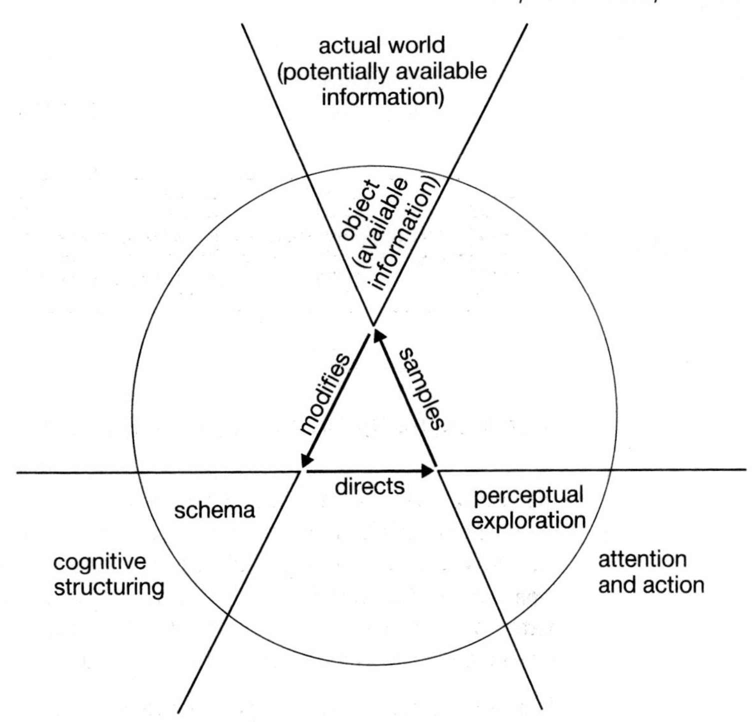

12.6 Neisser's model of the perceptual cycle

Neisser's model of cognition

Neisser's model can show us a way that we can understand such things as thinking, perception and memory as active processes; the way that language and thinking interrelate; the way that human interaction is so important for language acquisition; and how perceptual and learning sets can develop. As such, it seems to provide us with a way of making sense out of the work on cognition that psychologists have been undertaking over the last hundred years. It may be that new models which are more appropriate will be developed soon, but this one does seem to work very well for now.

We have looked now at the cognitive processes of thinking, language, memory, perception, and attention. Although we have only really been able to skim the surface of the work that psychologists have undertaken in investigating these processes, we can begin to detect some overall similarities between them. One of the most important of these general features is the message that our cognition is active, rather than passive. As people, we are actively involved in making sense out of what is around us, and we put our own 'stamp' on our interactions and interpretations of the world. In cognitive psychology, we find a picture of human mental activity which can help us to understand not only ourselves, but also other people, a bit better than we might do otherwise. That alone, we feel, makes it a worthwhile subject for study, and we hope that you have enjoyed this brief introduction to the area.

Summary

1 Perception is the brain actively interpreting the information which it receives through the senses.

2 The Gestalt psychologists identified some basic principles of perceptual organisation, which they called the Laws of Pragnänz. Some of these were: figure/ground organisation, similarity, proximity, and the principle of closure.

3 Perceptual set is a state of readiness to perceive certain things rather than others. Studies have shown how emotion, motivation, and other factors can affect perceptual set.

4 Perceptual defence was put forward by Postman et al. to explain why we are less ready to perceive unpleasant things.

5 Work on selective attention and in particular the 'cocktail party problem' resulted in the development of a series of filter theories, showing how information might be filtered out.

6 Neisser's model of the perceptual cycle shows a different approach - that information which is expected or anticipated is included more strongly, rather than anything being filtered out.

Suggestions for further reading

Banyard, P. et al. 1991 *Cognition: Open Learning Units*. Leicester: British Psychological Society

Bruce, V. & Green, P. 1985 *Visual Perception: Physiology, Psychology and Ecology*. London: Erlbaum

Eysenck, M. 1992 *Principles of Cognitive Psychology*. London: Erlbaum

Garnham, A. & Oakhill, J. 1994 *Thinking and Reasoning*. Oxford: Blackwell

Gregory, R. L. 1991 *Eye and Brain* 4th edn. London: Weidenfeld and Nicholson

Hayes, N. 1998 *Foundations of Psychology* 2nd edn. London: Nelson

Malim, T. 1994 *Cognitive Processes*. Basingstoke: Macmillan

Matlin, M. 1989 *Cognition* 2nd edn. London: Holt Rinehart & Winston

Mayer, R. E. 1992 *Thinking, Problem-solving, Cognition* 2nd edn. New York: W. H. Freeman,

Neisser, U. 1976 *Cognition and Reality.* San Francisco: W. H. Freeman & Co.

Smyth, M., Morris, P., Levy, P. & Ellis, A. 1987 *Cognition in Action.* London: Erlbaum

?

Self Assessment Questions

1 Dewey's idea that thinking occurs whenever there is a mismatch between what actually happens and what we expect to happen is called:

a) the turbulent theory of thought.

b) the creative theory of thought.

c) the trouble theory of thought.

d) the frustration theory of thought.

2 Divergent thinking occurs when a person:

a) looks for one right answer.

b) fails to find a suitable answer.

c) considers many possible answers.

d) thinks of two totally different answers.

3 Hudson argued that standard measures of intelligence only assess:

a) convergent thinking.

b) divergent thinking.

c) illogical thinking.

d) creative thinking.

4 In 1966, Hudson, found that schoolboys who performed well in arts subjects tended to be more:

a) divergent thinkers.

b) convergent thinkers.

c) illogical thinkers.

d) creative thinkers.

5 The principle of 'closure' as stated by the Gestalt psychologists, refers to the idea that:

a) we tend to see things as complete units.

b) we tend to have difficulty in seeing shapes.

c) we tend to see 'dots' more easily than we see lines.

d) we see the parts of an object rather than the whole.

6 Lateral thinking involves:

a) escaping from habitual forms of conventional thought.

b) looking for one correct answer.

c) learning which has taken place but which lies dormant until a later period.

d) using images.

7 One approach to problem solving is to use the technique of brainstorming. This is where:

a) all members of a group say any ideas that come into their heads, no matter how silly.

b) all members of a group sit and think for a long time in order to decide upon sensible solutions to a problem.

c) only the leaders of a group are allowed to offer solutions to a problem.

d) a computer is used to find alternative solutions.

8 An example of a probabilistic concept would be:

a) the concept of a bowl.

b) the concept of a saucer.

c) the concept of a bird.

d) none of the above.

9 Tolman believed that much of human learning involves:

a) simple association of one idea with another.

b) reinforcement.

c) building cognitive maps.

d) using schemata.

10 A schema is:

a) a neurone.

b) a computer model of thinking.

c) a hypothetical cognitive structure consisting of information that we need to operate on our environment in some way.

d) a group of similar objects.

11 The linguistic relativity hypothesis states that:

a) thought is independent from language.

b) thought is the same as language.

c) thought is dependent on language.

d) language is dependent on thought.

12 Elaborated codes of language are characterised by:

a) little explanation

b) no explanation

c) lots of explanation, a wide range of nouns, adjectives and verbs.

d) lots of explanation, few nouns, adjectives and verbs.

13 According to Bernstein, restricted codes of language are more likely to be used by:

a) upper-middle-class people.

b) middle-class people.

c) working-class people.

d) people in Western society.

14 Semantics is the study of:

a) words.

b) sentence construction.

c) the meanings of words.

d) speech abnormalities.

15 Brown argued that the most important aspect of speech for a child was:

a) the meaning that it was trying to get across.

b) the utterance of any words that it had learned.

c) hearing the sound of its own voice.

d) listening to its parents' speech.

16 Telegraphic speech is:

a) speech with the most important function words left out.

b) speech with all the verbs left out.

c) speech with all the unimportant function words left out.

d) words that are written rather than spoken.

17 Operant conditioning occurs when:

a) we repeat an action because it has pleasant consequences for us.

b) we repeat an action because it has unpleasant consequences for us.

c) we fail to repeat an action.

d) we repeat an action irrespective of its consequences.

18 Behaviour shaping refers to a process whereby:

a) all behaviours are rewarded.

b) some behaviours are rewarded but others are not.

c) the child is punished if it is naughty.

d) the child is taught to speak properly.

19 LAD stands for:

a) Language Ability Device.

b) Language Ability Difference.

c) Language Acquisition Device.

d) Language Aiding Device.

20 Chomsky believed that language was acquired through:

a) learning.

b) learning, but was also influenced to some extent by our genes.

c) our genetic inheritance.

d) classical conditioning.

21 Which of the following statements are true?

a) memory is an active process.

b) we always remember things accurately.

c) eye-witness accounts are rarely accurate.

d) a) and c) above

22 Which of the following would be an example of retrograde amnesia?

a) when a person loses their memory of events leading up to an accident.

b) when a person cannot remember any of the events that have occurred since their accident.

c) when a person loses their memory totally.

d) when a person loses their speech.

23 Which of the following would be an example of anterograde amnesia?

a) when a person loses their memory of events leading up to an accident.

b) when a person cannot remember any of the events that have occurred since their accident.

c) when a person loses their memory totally.

d) when a person loses their hearing.

24 Korsakoff's syndrome may be present in:

a) severe anorexics.

b) long-term alcoholics.

c) epileptic patients.

d) sufferers of dyslexia.

25 Repression refers to:

a) a showing of aggression.

b) a form of forgetting that occurs when we push unacceptable thoughts from our conscious mind.

c) being dominated.

d) the learning of unacceptable behaviour.

26 Proactive interference occurs when:

a) something that we have learned in the present interferes with something that we have learned in the past.

b) we are unable to learn new material.

c) something that we have learned in the past interferes with something that we are learning at present.

d) learning languages.

27 According to Bruner, the first type of memory that we possess is one of:

a) symbolic representation.

b) iconic representation.

c) enactive representation.

d) words.

28 If people concentrate on meaning rather than appearance, Craik and Lockhart found that they remember:

a) more words.

b) fewer words.

c) the same number of words.

d) only the first and last words of a list.

29 STM stands for:

a) Short Term Memory.

b) Semantically Trained Memory.

c) Short Timing Memory.

d) Standard Test of Memory.

30 Mnemonics are:

a) words with an "s" in them.

b) words that can have two possible meanings.

c) aids to help memory.

d) words that conjure up images.

31 A group of early investigators into perception were known as:

a) psychoanalysts.

b) ethologists.

c) Gestalt psychologists.

d) behaviourists.

32 Postman et al. (1946) suggested that perceptual defence was taking place when:

a) research participants took longer to recognise taboo words than neutral words.

b) research participants had a liking for certain words.

c) research participants recognised taboo words quicker than neutral words.

d) research participants recognised aggressive words quicker than passive words.

33 One of the criticisms of Postman's study, provided by Howe and Solomon in 1950 was that:

a) research participants may not have been willing to repeat taboo words

b) research participants liked taboo words more than neutral words but this fact did not emerge from the experiment.

c) research participants could only think of taboo words.

d) more aggressive words than passive words were used.

34 Subliminal perception occurs when:

a) we perceive something without being aware that we have perceived it.

b) we repress taboo words.

c) we are fooled by visual illusions.

d) we are aware of what we have perceived.

35 Research participants in Cherry's dichotic listening task were:

a) presented with the same message in both ears.

b) presented with two different messages, one in each ear.

c) presented with one message in one ear only.

d) presented with several messages in both ears.

36 "Shadowing" is a technique whereby research participants have to:

a) guess what the experimenter is looking for.

b) ignore the messages coming in through both ears.

c) repeat aloud what they are hearing.

d) ignore the messages coming in through one ear.

37 William James and Wilhelm Wundt are known as:

a) psychoanalysts.

b) introspectionists

c) behaviourists.

d) ethologists.

38 The early behaviourists wanted psychology to be:

a) objective and non-scientific.

b) concerned with inner feelings and emotions.

c) objective and scientific.

d) the study of how the mind works.

39 The 'cocktail party phenomenon' is concerned with:

a) how people communicate at parties.

b) what words capture our interest in any conversation.

c) how we are able to attend to specific conversations in a crowded room where there are many conversations taking place.

d) non-verbal communication.

40 In Cherry's dichotic listening tasks:

a) research participants knew everything about the information being presented to the unattended ear.

b) research participants did not know very much about the information that they had received in the unattended ear.

c) research participants did not listen to anything they were told to.

d) research participants were confused by the information presented in both ears.

Section 4 - The Individual

In this section, we will look at some of the things which make people distinctively different from one another. We are all different, and yet we all have some things in common. Sorting out which are the things which are shared by everyone, which are things which are shared by groups of people, and which are distinctively individual is a fascinating part of psychology, and all of the psychological theory which you could learn contributes to that.

We will begin this section by looking at how psychologists have studied the self-concept, and the factors which contribute to how we see ourselves, including gender identity. We will follow this by looking at some of the main theories of personality which have been put forward by psychologists as attempts to explain how people are different and why they are like they are. We will then go on to look at some of the ways that psychologists have attempted to measure psychological characteristics - at the process of psychometrics, particularly with respect to intelligence testing although we will look at some other forms of testing as well. We will go on to look at some of the different aspects of human motivation. The different factors which motivate us to do what we do are extremely diverse, and range from basic physiological drives to broadly shared social beliefs, with any number of different psychological mechanisms in between.

Chapter 13 - Self, gender and identity

How do you know who you are? You might think that's a silly question, but having a sense of self is an important basis for living our lives. In this chapter, we will look at some of the factors which contribute to our knowledge of ourselves. We will be looking at the self-concept and its various components, and also at the question of gender identity and how our biological sex can influence the way that we think about ourselves.

The self-concept

The self-concept is the idea that you have about yourself and who you are. If we didn't have a self-concept, we would find it very difficult to make decisions about what we were going to do (after all, who would do it?). And we would find it even more difficult to interact with someone else. Each time you say 'I', you are drawing on your self-concept: the knowledge and ideas that you have about yourself. Your self-concept includes everything you know or believe about yourself – your beliefs, wants, characteristics, feelings, even the image of yourself that you present to other people. In other words, your self-concept is your private way of summing up who you are, to yourself.

Psychology in Action

The existence of a self-concept is all bound up with our awareness of self and others. For most children, such an awareness is acquired automatically: it unfolds as the child interacts with family members and the other people that it meets, and as it develops an increasing competence in dealing with the world.

Although many psychologists see the self-concept as only emerging fully during childhood, even in infancy there are many signs that the young child is clearly able to distinguish itself from others. One of them is the emergence of reflexive speech. This involves being able to manipulate pronouns properly. For example, a child mostly hears itself referred to in conversation as 'you'. Yet, very quickly, children learn to refer to themselves as 'I'. If we try to break down this type of rule and express it in an abstract manner, we discover that the child is actually performing quite a complicated transformation. Yet it does so easily and naturally.

In special cases, though, children don't develop this ability. Autism is an emotional disorder which focuses the child inwards, and seems to affect the child's ability to perceive others as actual people. Many autistic children don't learn to speak at all, but some do. When they do speak, though, autistic children tend to produce sentences which have been directly learned from other people. As a result, they often refer to themselves as 'you', and to their mothers (or main caretakers) as 'I'. It seems that their inability to perceive and interact with other people also links with a lack of reflexive speech.

Some psychologists have even suggested that it is having a self-concept that makes us different to most other animals. Only those animals which are very close to us indeed – such as chimpanzees and gorillas – seem to have a self-concept like our own. For instance, if they see themselves in a mirror, most animals react as if they were seeing another animal. However, Gallup (1979) experimented by putting a spot of brightly coloured dye on the foreheads of chimpanzees while they were anaesthetised, and then allowed them to look in mirrors when they awoke. The chimpanzees were fascinated by the coloured spot and touched the same spot on their own foreheads as they examined their images in the mirror. They realised it was their own self that was being reflected, and not some other animal.

We can't really know what an animal's self-concept is like, of course, but we believe that human self-concepts are much more complicated. There are several different aspects to a human being's sense of identity, and in this chapter we will be looking at some of them.

To begin with, the human self-concept has many parts. There is the factual part which we call the self-image; the evaluative part, which we call the self-esteem; the part which describes you as you would like to be, which we call the ideal-self; the part which knows about your competencies and abilities, which we call your self-efficacy beliefs; the part which is to do with how you identify with groups in society, which we call your social identifications, and the way in which your sense of self has been shaped by the cultural context that you grew up in.

Self-image

The **self-image** is essentially a set of descriptions of what you are like. It includes factual information about your physical self, such as your height, your hair or skin colour and your sex. It includes personal information, for example about your knowledge and abilities, your likes and dislikes, and your attitudes. It also includes social information about you, such as your relationships with other people; whether you are a daughter or a son; whether you are a mother or an aunt; and who your closest friend is.

The self-image also includes factual information about you in relation to the wider society to which you belong: for example, it includes information about where you live, and how; what clubs or societies you belong to; and which school or college you attend. All of these go to make up your self-image, and they form an important basis for your self-concept.

The self-image partly develops from our own experience but it also arises partly as a result of the way other people behave towards us. Cooley (1902) argued that we develop a kind of 'looking-glass self' a self-image based on the way we think other people see us. This means that our self-image is strongly shaped by other people's reactions, as well as by our own personal knowledge. Several other researchers, such as Mead (1934), also emphasised how our self-image is very powerfully influenced by the social context in which we live and how other people react to us. Part of the reason why other people's reactions are so influential for us is because the self-image is so closely connected with another part of the self-concept – self-esteem.

Self-esteem

Your self-concept isn't just factual. It also includes an evaluative part which we call the **self-esteem**. The process of 'evaluation' means weighing up, or judging, how valuable something is. You may, for example, be proud of being good at maths. There is a factual description there – you are able to solve maths problems without difficulty and that belongs to the self-image. However, there is also an evaluation: that being good at maths is something to be valued and proud of. So it is also part of your self-esteem.

Coopersmith (1968) studied self-esteem in a number of American boys aged between 10 and 12. He found that boys with a high level of self-esteem tended to be active, expressive and, when followed up over time, were more likely to be successful. The boys set higher targets for themselves and they also tended to have supportive parents with high expectations and high levels of self-esteem themselves. Other researchers have found that high levels of self-esteem contribute to positive mental health in many ways, encouraging people to achieve more and to be happier with what they do achieve.

It is realistic to be aware of what you can do well, and for that to contribute positively to your self-esteem. It is also realistic to be aware of your weaknesses and the things that you don't do well, as long as you don't exaggerate them. All human beings have both strengths and weaknesses and our self-esteem is a mixture of both. We all have things that we like about ourselves and things that we don't. Overall, though, psychologists have found that most of us have a reasonably positive self-esteem: we would like to improve some things about ourselves but, for the most part, we are reasonably content with how we are.

Ideal-self

Some people, though, have particularly low self-esteem. They concentrate only on areas where they feel incompetent or inadequate, and don't value the things about themselves which are positive or which other people value. All of us feel like that sometimes, of course – it is hard to feel positive about yourself if you are very tired, disappointed or upset. However, feeling like that all the time is not psychologically healthy. People with chronically low self-esteem are vulnerable to a great many other problems, including physical illnesses. In extreme conditions, chronically low self-esteem can even contribute to mental illness.

People who have a chronically low self-esteem are generally those whose **ideal-self** has been set at an unrealistically high level. Your ideal-self is how you would like to be if everything was perfect. Butler and Haigh (1954) looked at the match between self-concept and ideal-self-concept in ordinary people and found that the average correlation between the two was +.58. So most people felt that some parts of themselves did match up to their ideal selves, while other parts didn't. Severely neurotic people, on the other hand, showed a correlation of -.01, which meant that their self-concept was completely different from their ideal-self-concept in all respects.

Butler and Haigh used these findings to measure the effectiveness of a particular kind of therapy on several neurotic clients. The therapy was **client-centred therapy** which was developed by the humanistic psychologist Carl Rogers. We will be looking at Rogers's theory of personality in the next chapter, but client-centred therapy concentrates on developing a positive, unconditional relationship between the therapist and the client, so that the client can be secure in their therapist's approval while exploring personal choices and possibilities. When they tested these people again after six weeks of therapy, Butler and Haigh found that the correlation between their self-concepts and their ideal-self-concepts was now +.31, which was a great improvement.

Self-efficacy beliefs

Self-efficacy beliefs are all about how effective or competent we feel ourselves to be. They can contribute quite a lot to our self-esteem but they are not really the same thing: self-esteem is widespread and general, whereas self-efficacy beliefs are very specific. They are about particular skills, abilities or competencies. So you can have high self-efficacy beliefs in some areas but not others: you may know, for instance, that you are good at learning physical skills or at picking up new ideas. However, your self-esteem will depend on how widespread those areas are and how much you value those competencies.

Having positive self-efficacy beliefs does make a lot of difference to our motivation. People with high self-efficacy beliefs learn more effectively than people with low ones, even if their actual ability is the same. If you believe that you are capable of doing something, you try harder, and so you are more likely to be successful. Bandura (1989) described a study which compared children with low and high self-efficacy beliefs in respect to school maths. The ones with high self-efficacy beliefs did better than those with low self-efficacy beliefs – even when their ability was actually lower. Because they believed they could be successful if they tried, those children worked harder and eventually learned more than children who had higher maths ability, but low self-efficacy beliefs. So knowing that you are capable of achieving something if you make the effort, is very important. Your self-efficacy beliefs are another significant part of your self-concept.

Social identifications

Your **social identifications** are another important part of your self-concept. None of us lives in a vacuum: we grow up in a particular society and we are surrounded by other people. Those people generally belong to identifiable groups, and so do we. We will be looking at social identity theory and its psychological mechanisms in Chapter 20, so we won't go into too many details here. However, the social groups that we belong to form an important part of our self-concept.

For example, the first group you may be aware of belonging to is your family, so one of your first social identifications is likely to be of yourself as a family member. As you grow older, there will be others: going to one particular school, as opposed to some other school; sharing a particular hobby with some friends and not with other people; working for a particular organisation, or in a particular profession, and so on. Sometimes, these group memberships have always been there but you simply become more aware of them, such as your gender group, being of a particular nationality, or coming from a particular ethnic background.

Identifying with a social group gives you a feeling of belonging and that is another important part of your self-concept. It becomes part of the way that we define who we are. Feeling that we belong is important to people. It gives us a sense of 'us' and 'them' which doesn't have to be about competition or rivalry, but does help us to structure and understand your social world. It's a very fundamental part of human thinking: we organise our social world by classifying people into groups in the same way that we organise our perceptual world by classifying what we see into categories, such as furniture, animals, buildings and so on.

Our tendency for social identification has everything to do with having evolved as social animals throughout our evolutionary history some people have been very important while others were less so, and classifying them into 'them' and 'us' is the way that we acknowledge that. This can backfire, of course, and in Chapter 17 we shall be looking at the problem of prejudice. For all of us, however, our social identities are an important part of our self-concept.

Cultural contexts and the self

Another important influence on self-concept is the **cultural context** that we belong to. Although everyone is aware of themselves as a human being, the idea of the person as a separate 'individual', which is common in industrialised European and North American societies, isn't really all that common across the whole world. In most of the world, and also in some subcultures in industrialised Western communities, people are seen as part of their cultures and family groups, not as separate, isolated individuals. Separating the individual from their family and culture is seen as unrealistic and impractical. That doesn't mean that people are not recognised as different to one another, but it does mean that the social influences on people are seen as part of who they are.

Different cultures have different ways of thinking about the self. For example, Mbiti (1970) discussed how, in traditional African societies, the individual self is seen as firmly embedded in the collective self of the tribe or people. Someone's personal life forms part of the ongoing life of their people, and is also seen as closely linked to the rhythms of the natural world. That person's actions, decisions and beliefs are not separate from those of others: they will all have their effect on the community in general, and the community, in turn, will have its influence on the person.

Many other cultures hold similar views. For example, in traditional Asian families the person is seen as part of the family as a whole, rather than as an independent individual. When the children of those families grow up in industrialised cultures which emphasise individuality, they can sometimes experience some difficulty in reconciling the different concepts of self maintained by their family and the culture in which they are growing up. So it is important to bear in mind that the way that British and American psychologists have regarded the self may not actually reflect the way that the self is experienced by many other people throughout the world. This is particularly relevant as we look at what psychologists have said about how the self-concept develops.

13.1 A sense of self

Having a sense of who we are is very important in our conversation, but if you were an alien from the planet Zarggh, things would be very different. Aliens from Zarggh are able to speak English, by a remarkable intergalactic coincidence which also seems to happen quite often in science fiction films. However, they have no sense of self. This means that they are unable to use the words 'I' and 'we', and also other words which depend on them, like 'mine' or 'us'. They can't even think them.

Imagine you are an alien from Zarggh, who has just landed on Earth. You want to open up some trade links between Earth and Zarggh.

Zargghians are particularly interested in buying Mars Bars (although they want to rename them Bhlynx bars, after Bhlynx which is a small planet in their own solar system). They are also interested in buying roofing tiles, garden gnomes and felt-tip pens. Nobody knows why they want the garden gnomes and Earth people are quite curious about this. The Zargghians are quite happy to explain and also to describe what Zarggh can offer as trading goods of its own.

Have a conversation to discuss trade possibilities with a friend who will act as the Earth representative. Remember not to include 'I' or anything which might imply that you have a self-concept in your conversation.

Were there some things that were easy to say in Zargghian?

Were there some things that were difficult to say in Zargghian?

Are trade discussions easier or harder if you have a self-concept?

How would you explain the concept of self to a Zargghian?

The development of the self-concept

Lewis and Brooks-Gunn (1979) distinguished between three different parts of the self-concept: the existential self, the categorical self, and the private self. The **existential self** is all about our sense of being different from other people, so it contains information on the things about us which help to make us unique and special. The existential self is also the first part of the self-concept to develop. Being separate from others, and different, it is much more important to a young child than the other part, the categorical self.

The **categorical self** contains information such as our height, sex, age and so on – information which describes how we may be similar to other people or how we fit into certain categories or types. The **private self**, in this model, is all to do with evaluation and self-esteem as the child develops a sense of how different aspects of itself measure up to the expectations and demands of society.

Age	Sense of self	Description
0-1	None	The child mainly reacts to events and learns how to do things. It is developing a body-schema, but doesn't have a self-concept yet.
1-2	Existential	The child is developing a sense that it is separate from other people and has its own ideas, abilities, and preferences.
2-3	Existential and categorical	The child begins to compare itself with other people, through language and noticing what counts as important in its social world.
3-5	Existential, categorical and private	The child begins to develop a private self with personal value-judgements, including elements of self-esteem such as pride or guilt.

Adapted from: Lewis and Brooks-Gunn, 1979

13.1 Typical ages for the development of the self-concept

Lewis and Brooks-Gunn went on to look at how children develop their self-concept. They used a number of different approaches, including the same type of mirror study that Gallup had used with the chimpanzees – a child would be encouraged to look at itself in a mirror, then its attention would be distracted and a blob of lipstick put on its nose. If it showed surprise, or touched its own nose when it turned back to the mirror, the researchers concluded that the child knew that the image in the mirror was itself. From this, and other studies, the researchers were able to describe typical ages for the development of the self-concept (at least in Western industrialised cultures), which are given in Table 13.1

Sex and gender identity

We have already mentioned how belonging to a particular gender group can influence the self-concept. Just about every human society makes distinctions between men and women, and expects different types of behaviour from them. However, not all human societies make those distinctions in the same way; and not all are equally rigid in how they maintain them.

Sex and gender identity

Our **sex** is a biological matter. It depends on the genes that we inherit from our parents. As we saw in Chapter 1, human beings have 23 pairs of chromosomes, each of which carries millions of genes, and these genes carry information about heredity. When a gene is activated, it causes the body to produce a particular protein which affects how the body functions. Biological sex is the outcome of lots of genes working together.

One particular pair of chromosomes determines biological sex. These are known as X and Y chromosomes because, under a microscope, they sometimes look a bit like those letters. A baby inherits one of these chromosomes from each parent. If it inherits XX, with two X chromosomes, the baby develops as female, but XYs, with one X and one Y chromosome, usually develop to be male. That development, however, is a biological process and can be interrupted. If it is, the person reverts to being female.

Sex identity, then is determined by the genes that we inherit from our parents. Most people are either male or female with no question about it, but just about everything in nature shows variation, and sex identity is no exception. A few people, for example, are **hermaphrodite** which means that they develop both male and female characteristics. There is also a very rare genetic condition in which the child seems female but male genitalia appear at puberty. Or, sometimes, a child is born who is genetically male but does not develop male genitalia, or not fully. Then his parents must choose whether the child should be brought up as a male or a female, and whether surgery is needed.

Gender identity is not the same as sex identity. Sex identity, as we have seen, is a biological matter. But gender identity is social: it is about how children of different sexes are shaped to conform to society's expectations about what they should be like. Sometimes, these expectations are so strong that girls and boys have different experiences almost from the moment they are born. Those experiences affect how the child develops. Gender identity is the part of our self-concept which comes from our experiences of being male or female in society. It is a combination of biological condition and social experience.

Ethical discussion

Some psychologists are becoming increasingly concerned about research into gender differences. They point out that a lot of research of this kind appears to be trying to prove that people of different sexes are totally different to one another and act in opposite ways. Looking for differences between men and women, they argue, makes you blind to what men and women have in common because nobody conducts any research into gender similarities to even up the balance. They also point out that, for many of these studies, if the same research was proposed for studying racial differences, it would be seen as totally unacceptable.

What do you think?

Theories of gender identity development

Over the years, psychologists have suggested several different explanations for how gender identity develops. Five main theories have been put forward:

- the biological approach
- psychoanalytic theory
- social learning theory
- cognitive-developmental theory
- gender-schema theory.

Each of them looks at different psychological or physiological mechanisms involved in producing gender identity.

The biological approach

The biological approach assumes that it is biological sex which leads, automatically, to gender identity. The idea is that a combination of genetic factors, and influences from sex-related hormones, will produce the personality and behavioural characteristics which society associates with being male or female.

People who adopt this view, such as Hutt (1972) often draw on studies of differences in infant behaviour and play between boys and girls.

The trouble is that the studies often produce conflicting evidence. In 1974, Maccoby and Jacklin reviewed over 1500 studies of sex differences in children's behaviour, and found that, overall, they showed little evidence of consistent sex differences. There were some general tendencies: girls tended to be slightly better at language-based activities and tests of verbal reasoning, while boys tended to be more aggressive, both physically and verbally, and also to be slightly better at tests of spatial ability and (in adolescence, though not as children) at arithmetic.

Maccoby and Jacklin found that comparisons of IQ scores were ambivalent, but there are problems with these as girls have to get more items correct in the same test than boys if they are to achieve the same IQ. So it isn't really appropriate to compare IQ scores when we are looking for sex differences as they have already been adjusted to make sure that girls don't appear to be cleverer than boys. In general, though, Maccoby and Jacklin concluded that there wasn't really all that much evidence for the idea that behavioural sex differences come from biology

Sex typing

An alternative is to look at people whose biological sex is different from their gender identity. When an infant is born, the first question people usually ask is what sex it is. They decide by looking at the baby. This process is known as **sex typing** – allocating a sex to the child on the basis of its appearance at birth. Sometimes, however, sex typing doesn't reflect the child's biological sex. Goldwyn (1979) described a married woman, Daphne Went, who had sought medical treatment for infertility. The examination showed that genetically, she was actually male – she had XY chromosomes instead of XX. But she also had a condition known as **testicular feminising syndrome** (TFS) which meant that her body was immune to the effects of the hormone testosterone. This hormone causes male characteristics, such as the penis, to develop: without it, an infant will develop as female.

Although Daphne was genetically male, she had been brought up as female and had developed a very strong female gender identity. Although the discovery that she was male was, understandably, rather a shock, she adjusted to it, continued to live happily as a woman, and eventually adopted two children. Her case history implies that gender identity is a result of how people are brought up, rather than a straightforward result of their biology. It isn't complete evidence as the biology of sex involves both genetics and hormones, not just genetics alone. However, the importance of hormones has been challenged, as well.

Money and Ehrhardt (1972) studied 25 girls, aged between 4 and 16, who all had what is known as **androgenital syndrome**. Their mothers had been given male hormones while they were pregnant, so the girls had been exposed to this in the womb. The girls remained female internally, but the hormones caused them to develop male genitalia which were removed by surgery at birth. Money and Ehrhardt compared these girls with a matched control group, using interviews and preference tests. They found that gender identity wasn't affected – none of the girls felt that they would like to change sex and they were no more aggressive than the control group. They were a little more tomboyish, however, and didn't play with dolls or dress up as much as the others. So there was a hint that the hormones might have affected them.

We have to be careful in drawing that conclusion, though, as there are so many individual differences in how little girls behave, and 25 is not a large enough sample to take account of them all. Also, the parents, teachers and the girls themselves all knew about the androgenital syndrome, and this could easily have meant that the girls were living up to different expectations.

Overall, then, the evidence suggests that genetic sex and gender identity can be quite different, and that social learning as a result of sex typing plays a very strong role in the gender identity that the child develops. That doesn't rule out all biological influences: hormones may have an influence on childhood behaviours such as rough and tumble play, or language play, for instance; but it certainly implies that it would be much too simplistic to say that gender identity is purely a result of biology.

The psychoanalytic approach

Psychoanalytic theory, as we shall see in the next chapter and in Chapter 22, works on the idea that much of the human mind is buried below the surface, and that what we are aware of is really only a small part of what is going on. Unconscious memories, emotions and impulses are part of what makes human beings act as they do. Psychoanalysts believe that gender identity, like other aspects of personality, arises as a result of early experiences which are so deeply buried that we are unaware of them.

We shall be looking into this in greater detail in Chapter 22, but, in essence, the idea is that boys come to identify with their fathers in order to resolve what Freud called the Oedipus conflict. This is a young boy's unconscious wish to possess his mother entirely, which leads him to see his father as a more powerful and dangerous rival. The conflict is resolved by identifying with his father. In young girls, an equivalent conflict, called the **Electra** conflict, which derives from unconscious penis envy, also has to be resolved and results (eventually) in the girl coming to identify with her mother. According to Freud and other psychoanalytic theorists, both of these conflicts are quite traumatic for the young child and occur while the child is very young – only two or three years of age. This is why, psychoanalysts claim, adults have no memory of them.

Problems with the psychoanalytic approach

There are, of course, a number of criticisms of psychoanalytic explanations for gender role. Many of them have centred around the idea of penis envy which is regarded as a rather questionable concept, particularly in view of the fact that Freud was writing about middle-class children brought up in a culture of extreme sexual prudery. At that time, children were even bathed in their shifts to avoid them catching sight of their own naked bodies, and were made to sleep with their hands on the pillow so that they did not touch their private parts at night. So it is hard to see how a small girl-child could become aware that she was missing a penis or how she could even know that penises existed.

Another criticism is that the theory reflects the patriarchal view of Freud's own times, assuming that what was male was superior so the girl would inevitably feel envious of it. These assumptions reflected Freud's own acceptance of Victorian values and prejudices. But difference does not necessarily imply superiority: in many non-technological cultures, for instance, women are envied because of their ability to bear children, and it is men who are considered to be deprived.

A further criticism of the Freudian idea of gender role development comes from observation of other societies. Freud believed that it was vital that the father should be the most powerful figure in the child's life because that was what provided the motivation (and fear) which led to identification with the father. Yet Malinowski (1927) observed that the Trobriand islanders, who had perfectly conventional gender identities, grew up without their fathers being important in their lives. Instead, it was the mother's brother who was the child's guardian. According to orthodox Freudian theory, this implied that male children should grow up identifying with the mother, but the social organisation of the Trobriand islanders didn't show any such effect.

Social learning

For many years, social learning theory (e.g. Bandura, 1977) provided the main alternative to psychoanalytic explanations of gender. This approach suggests that children learn to adopt appropriate gender roles through a number of learning processes, such as classical and operant conditioning which we looked at in Chapter 2, and the social-learning mechanisms of imitation and identification which we will be looking at in Chapter 21.

Conditioning

A number of researchers have observed direct conditioning of gender-role behaviour in children. **Operant conditioning** seems to be the most common, where children are rewarded for behaving in gender-appropriate ways. For example, a little girl who likes wearing pretty clothes will often receive smiles and social approval for her preference, while a little boy with the same interest would receive a very different reaction.

Although approval and reward are the common mechanisms in modern society, there are times when children are actively punished for behaving in ways which are thought inappropriate. For example, Newson and Newson (1968) showed that aggression from young girls is punished much more severely by parents than the same behaviour from young boys. While young boys who want to play with clothes or make-up usually receive severe disapproval from other family members.

Smith and Lloyd (1978) showed that conditioning the child into sex-appropriate behaviour begins while the child is still an infant. They asked new mothers, with babies of five to ten months, to play with another baby for ten minutes. The researchers told some mothers that the child was female when it was male; others that it was male when it was really female; and some the correct sex of the infant. They found that the mothers acted differently with the babies depending on what sex they believed the child to be.

The mothers encouraged the baby to be physically active if they thought it was a boy, but if they thought it was a girl they would 'shush' it if it seemed active. They were much more inclined to give what the researchers called 'whole-body stimulation' to what they believed to be boy babies – bouncing them up and down and moving them around a lot. Girl babies (or, at least, babies that they thought were girls) were soothed and petted and given soft, cuddly toys to play with.

Other researchers have found that people interpret babies' reactions differently, depending on their perceived sex. Condry and Condry (1976) asked adults to judge reactions from nine-month infants. When the children were startled by a jack-in-the-box, Condry and Condry found that if the adult believed that the child was a girl, 'she' was likely to be described as showing 'fear', but if it was believed to be a boy, the same reaction would be described as showing 'anger'. The researchers also showed how parents have very strong expectations about gender-role behaviour, and discourage their children from acting in 'inappropriate' ways.

Imitation and identification

Imitation and **identification** are also important social-learning processes for gender-role learning. We will be looking into them in more detail in Chapter 21. The important thing is that they allow a child to learn through imitating other people. The child obtains models of behaviour to copy by observing people in its own family and in books or on television. As the child copies people who are 'like itself', the behaviour becomes internalised until it forms part of the child's self-image.

Cross-cultural evidence for social learning

Social learning can explain a lot of the variation in gender roles in different cultures. For example, the anthropologist Margaret Mead studied a number of tribes in what was then New Guinea (Mead, 1962). Each of these tribes had very different cultural practices and social expectations and each socialised its children accordingly, rewarding 'appropriate' behaviour and providing role-models of adult behaviour for the children to imitate. Mead studied many tribes, but three in particular showed huge differences in gender role.

The Arapesh people emphasised co-operation and tended to interact in very gentle sorts of ways. The men, as well as the women, were affectionate and emotional, and social life was seen as all about sharing and supporting one another. The Mundugumor, by contrast, were a warlike tribe who valued aggression and assertiveness. Their young people, both girls and boys, were encouraged to be independent and stoical at an early age and to grow up to be competitive and fierce. Among a third tribe, the Tchambuli, the women were responsible for the family welfare and well-being. They also did all of the hard work (although that, in fact, is quite common in rural communities: something like 80% of the world's work is done by women). The men, on the other hand, engaged in artistic pursuits and were seen as being too irresponsible to do much towards contributing to the family's well-being.

Each of these tribes showed a very different approach to gender identity. Among the Arapesh, traits which in the West would be seen as 'feminine' were shared by both men and women; while among the Mundugumor it was the traits which Westerners see as 'masculine' which were shared by both. The Tchambuli showed sex roles which were almost, though not quite, the reverse of Western cultural expectations. What these studies also tell us is something of the flexibility of human social behaviour and how influential social learning processes can be.

Criticisms of social learning theory

There have been a number of objections to this explanation for gender identity, although not all of them are equally powerful. One criticism, for example, is that reinforcements for the conditioning are not consistent enough to explain differences, yet, as we saw in Chapter 2, intermittent reinforcement schedules are generally much more powerful than consistent ones. So that isn't really a very convincing criticism. Another is that it does not account for the way that children in homosexual or one-parent families tend to have normal gender identity; but that assumes that the child has no contacts outside of the family – while, at the very least, television provides a rich store of role-models, as does contact with other adults. It also assumes that imitation is the only learning mechanism available, which isn't true either.

A more useful criticism is that the social learning approach doesn't take account of biological factors. As we have seen, hormones may have some influence and that needs to be taken into account. Nor does the theory take account of the child's personal understanding of sex roles, and its own ideas about what is appropriate and what isn't. These criticisms do suggest that social learning isn't everything, but it is still likely to be an important part of how gender identity develops, even if it doesn't provide all of the answers.

The cognitive-developmental approach

The **cognitive-developmental approach** to gender identity was proposed by Kohlberg in 1966. Kohlberg suggested that the child acquires gender identity by stages and that these stages are linked with other stages in cognitive development (see Chapter 23). The stages which Kohlberg identified are set out in Fig 13.2. They suggest that the process of acquiring gender identity begins with the child first classifying itself as a boy or a girl, and then paying attention to what boys do or girls do and constructing its own ideas about gender and what is appropriate. The child then acts in ways which fit those ideas and learns to value behaviour which is appropriate to its own sex.

Kohlberg combined biological and social learning approaches in this theory. The idea was that the stages were largely to do with biological maturation, but what the child learned during those stages was largely a matter of social learning and the way that the child (and its family) had classified itself.

Age (Years)	Stage	Description
2/3-5	Basic gender identity	The child knows its gender, but lacks gender consistency, e.g. believing that it could change its gender by dressing differently or playing different games.
4/5-6	Gender stability	The child begins to develop an understanding that gender does not change in later life.
6-7	Gender constancy	The child now sees gender as consistent over time, and also over situations. It becomes aware of its own gender as helping to define its sense of self, and pays more attention to same-sex role models than to those of the other sex.

Adapted from: Kohlberg, 1966

13.2 Kohlberg's stages of gender identity

But there are some problems with this approach to understanding gender identity. One of them is the idea that cognitive development has stages at all, which is challenged by many modern researchers. Kohlberg developed his theory at a time when developmental psychology was heavily influenced by Piaget's stage theory (see Chapter 23), and at that time stages were taken for granted. Nowadays, we are less sure about them.

Another problem is presented by sex-typing. Parents, and other people, don't wait for a child to be six or seven years old before they encourage it to act according to its own sex. As we have seen, even in infancy babies are treated differently according to the sex that people think they are; and children learn gender-role stereotypes very quickly from other people. Maccoby (1980) showed that even three year olds had learned about sex stereotypes and showed a preference for friends of their own sex far earlier than Kohlberg's model predicts.

Gender-schema theory

Bem (1984) put forward a theory which is like a combination of social learning and cognitive-developmental theory. According to Bem, once children know their own sex, they begin to learn about 'appropriate' types of behaviour for it. In the process, they develop complex and sophisticated **gender-schemas**. These, like all schemas, direct their actions and choices of activity. Effectively, the gender-schema helps the child to make sense of its world, by organising the information about gender that it is picking up. New information is evaluated against the schema, and the schema also directs the child's awareness and interpretation of its own actions, and its plans.

What gender-schema theory also implies is that the child's gender-identity will reflect the information, values and behaviours that it is exposed to – by its family, by its playgroup, by the television it watches, and by books and pictures. Much of the research into gender identity has assumed that it is largely homogenous – that children of the same sex will all act in much the same way. Yet there is much more individual variation than that. There may be general tendencies, but there are also individual differences. For example, most boys enjoy physical play more than most girls. Yet some girls enjoy physical play more than other girls, and some of them enjoy it more than some boys do. A theory of gender identity development which can't account for individual differences between children of the same sex isn't going to be very helpful to us in understanding what is really going on.

Androgeny

Bem (1974) argued that part of the problem in understanding gender identity is that researchers have focused too much on differences between the sexes, and not enough on similarities. The problem, Bem argued, is that the research methods which have been used to study gender identity assume that masculine traits and feminine ones are entirely opposite to one another. Yet the same person can often possess traits which fit with both masculine and feminine stereotypes. Moreover, Bem argued, to possess both masculine and feminine traits is psychologically healthier than having just one set or the other. People who have some of both are mentally more balanced, and more likely to lead a fulfilling and rewarding lifestyle.

Bem devised the BSRI (the Bem Sex Role Inventory) which is different from other measures of sex roles because it allows people to respond positively to questions about both masculine and feminine traits, instead of assuming that the two are always opposite, so that answering positively to one means scoring negatively on the other. Bem, and other researchers using the BSRI, found that **androgynous** people – whose scores showed that they had both masculine and feminine traits – were flexible and adaptable in different situations, had higher self-esteem and also a greater sense of emotional well-being. It is psychologically healthier to be androgynous than to be stereotypically 'masculine' or 'feminine'.

The implication from Bem's research is that it is good for both children and adults to be able to draw on both masculine and feminine traits, and this finding has been supported by several researchers. One reason why androgynous people are more mentally healthy, Bem suggested, is because they are able to respond to situations freely, without feeling the need to act in a way that corresponds with their gender stereotype. People fitting into traditional gender stereotypes often have very powerful gender-schema which they use for guidance even in situations which don't require it, but androgynous people use other, often more appropriate, cognitive styles.

Some psychologists suggest, however, that androgynous traits might be healthier because they allow people of both sexes to be able to behave in 'masculine' ways and it is these which are the psychologically healthy traits. Taylor and Hall (1982) argued that many traditionally 'feminine' traits, such as being eager to soothe hurt feelings, shy, gullible, or yielding, are actually behaviours related to having inferior social status, and are not particularly healthy for anyone. These traits also appear in men who are placed in consistently powerless positions. But 'masculine' traits, such as independence, making decisions easily, defending one's own beliefs and being self-sufficient, are psychologically healthy for all people. It is only because of social biases that they have traditionally been considered to be 'masculine' qualities.

Cultural and media influences

As we've seen, the exact form that gender identity takes depends on many different influences. One of them is the culture that the person grows up in. Some cultures have more rigid ideas about what is appropriate for men and women than others, and cultures also change over time. For example, Britain in the 1960s had much more restrictive ideas about gender behaviour than it does now. Socio-economic factors, such as social class or geographical district, also matter. A third and very important set of influences is to do with the beliefs and ideas of the particular family to which the person belongs. There is often much more variation between families than people realise.

The family is the first source of gender socialisation but, as the child grows older, it also develops ideas from other sources, such as television. In one study, Williams (1986) looked at the effect of introducing television into a remote Canadian community. There were noticeable differences between the children's attitudes at the beginning of the study and their attitudes at the end of the study two years later. Their sex-role beliefs had become noticeably more stereotyped and the themes of their play (and also their behaviour) had become significantly more aggressive.

Williams investigated the introduction of television into a town which didn't have it before. But other psychologists have found that the amount of television that we watch also makes a difference. For example, Rothschild (1984) found that children who watch a lot of television have more stereotyped attitudes and values than those who don't watch television very often. The nature of these stereotypes has an effect too. Kubey and Csikszentmihalyi (1990) found that heavy TV watching was associated with negative feelings about themselves for girls but not for boys, and they linked this finding with the way that men, not women, are usually shown in the more exciting and active roles.

Kubey and Csikszentmihalyi also found that boys tended to become more involved in their TV watching than girls, and to get more emotional about it, which seemed surprising at first as 'emotionality' is usually considered to be a 'feminine' trait. When they looked more closely, however, the researchers found that it was closely related to content. The boys tended to watch more sport than girls, and also to watch music videos and films which were clearly targeted for male audiences and designed to be emotionally arousing for them.

13.2 Gender stereotypes in advertising

Condrey (1989) suggests that the gender stereotypes in advertisements are gradually changing, and that women are being portrayed in much more active roles than they used to be. For example, in the 1960s women usually appeared in advertisements about cleaning and cooking, but there were also men who were the 'experts', telling the women what to do. Most domestic advertisements still feature women but nowadays they are portrayed as making their own decisions much more often.

You can look at this for yourself. While you are watching television, take notes about the gender roles portrayed in advertisements. Do women feature in the ads? Do men feature in them? Who is the main character, or are they both equal? Who makes the decisions? Is somebody 'scoring a point' against another person and, if so, is it a man or a woman who scores?

Sort out your notes into advertisement categories: domestic ads, car ads, beer ads, food ads, and so on. Then look at your findings in each category. Use the following questions to guide your investigation.

Do some types of ads feature more women than men? Do some feature more men than women? Are there any ads where women are simply background or 'decoration'? Are there any ads where men are used in the same way? Are decisions made in the ad? If so, is it a man or a women who makes the decisions? Is somebody 'scoring a point' against another person and, if so, is it a man or a woman who scores?

Do you personally think that the ad portrays men and women reasonably equally?

When you have answered these questions, compare your results with those of a friend and see what they have found.

If you wanted to conduct a systematic psychological investigation of this, how would you go about it?

In general, television tends to portray women as housewives and mothers, with men as active, adventurous leaders. As we have already seen, this can affect how children develop their understanding of sex roles. But Condrey (1989) suggests that this stereotype is gradually changing. Although women are still much more likely to be portrayed in domestic roles than men, the range of roles for women is becoming wider. For example, Signorielli (1987) showed that recent TV dramas had more female characters in major roles than those of the 1960s and 1970s, and Scheibe (1983) showed that TV advertisements are also drawing on a wider range of roles and role-behaviour for women.

Overall, then, the psychological evidence is that television is an important factor in sex-role learning. After all, it is usually the young child's first introduction to the wider world and also a main source of information about the world as the child grows older. However, the messages of television are also offset by the values and attitudes that the child learns from direct experience with family members and other people.

Gender identity, then, seems to result from a combination of many influences. Biological, cognitive, social and cultural factors all contribute to the final outcome. Overall, though, the evidence seems to suggest that social learning and gender-schema mechanisms are more influential than purely biological ones in determining someone's gender identity.

Summary

1 The self-concept is our awareness of ourselves as individual people. It forms the basis for our personal decisions and for our interactions with other people.

2 The self-concept incorporates many elements, including the self-image, the self-esteem, the ideal-self, our self-efficacy beliefs, social identifications and cultural influences.

3. Gender identity is an important part of the self-concept. Sex identity refers to our biological sex, while gender identity is psychological in nature.

4. The biological explanation for gender identity is that it arises purely because of genetic and hormonal influences. The psychoanalytic approach attributes it to the resolution of early conflicts.

5. The social learning approach sees gender identity as acquired through socialisation. Kohlberg's cognitive-developmental approach tried to link social learning mechanisms with biological development.

6. The gender-schema approach to gender identity emphasises the child's developing understanding of gender role. It also introduces the concept of androgeny as psychologically healthier than sex-stereotypical roles.

7. In conjunction with family and personal influences, the media can exert a considerable influence on the child's developing understanding of gender role.

Chapter 14 - Theories of personality

When we are looking at theories of personality, we find that psychologists have often used the term to mean slightly different things. In 1937, Allport undertook a review of all the work on personality performed by psychologists, and found some fifty different definitions of the term. Although each psychologist seemed to have a slightly different idea of what is meant by personality, Allport found that their ideas did seem to have three concepts in common: firstly, that each one of us has a unique personality, secondly, that our personalities are made up of lots of different characteristics, and thirdly that these characteristics remain stable over a long period of time - in other words, they are reasonably consistent.

The idiographic Vs nomothetic approach

Allport saw theories of personality as being of two main kinds. Some psychologists have adopted an approach which involves studying each person in their own right, and looking at the individual ways that people's personalities operate. This is known as an **idiographic** approach to personality. Other psychologists have looked at the ways that people's personalities can be ordered into some kind of pattern, so that they can be compared with others, which is known as a **nomothetic** approach. In this chapter, we will be looking at examples of each kind of theory.

Personality theories in general have tended to arise as a result of psychologists being involved in clinical work, dealing with people who have psychological problems of one kind or another. There are roughly three main schools of psychological thought which have contributed to psychological theories of personality. These are the **psychoanalytic school** of Sigmund Freud and his followers; the **psychometric school**, of whom perhaps the most well-known is Hans Eysenck; and the **humanistic school**, involving the theories put forward by Carl Rogers and other psychologists with a similar approach. We will look at each of these groups of theories in turn.

The psychoanalytic approach to personality

Freud's theory of personality

Freud developed his theory during the second half of the nineteenth century. He was dealing with the problem of **hysteria** - a clinical problem in which people can suffer extreme pain, and even be crippled by it, but which doesn't seem to have any physical origins. Freud observed the work of Charcot, a French physician who used hypnosis to demonstrate that a psychological 'cure' of hysteria could happen by suggestion; and he also worked with Breuer, who had found that allowing his patients to talk over their problems would often relieve their pain.

Freud found that his hysterical patients often seemed to have deeply-buried and highly emotional memories and associations. Bringing these to the surface seemed to help their problems. He developed a technique of free-association and of analysis of 'slips of the tongue' and dreams, which allowed him to probe into these buried memories.

Gradually, Freud developed what became known as the **psychoanalytic** technique. The purpose of this was the process of **catharsis**, in which all the buried emotional traumas would come to the surface, allowing the individual to relive them, and to find constructive ways of dealing with them.

Conscious and unconscious

Freud developed a model of the human mind as being like an iceberg, with most of it hidden beneath the surface. The part of the mind which we are aware of he called the **conscious** mind. We also have memories and thoughts which are temporarily forgotten, but which can be brought to consciousness if necessary: the **preconscious** mind. Buried below those, Freud thought, was a deeper layer of the mind, which never came to consciousness: the **unconscious**. It was this part of the human psyche which kept those buried conflicts and traumas which had been laid down in earlier life. Although we were not aware of it, Freud believed that the unconscious would influence our behaviour and our emotions, often causing severe disturbance, such as hysteria.

The id

Freud considered that there were three parts to the human personality: the **id**, the **ego**, and the **superego**. The id was the first part of the personality to develop, and contained all the basic drives, impulses and instincts. It was totally selfish, operating entirely on the **pleasure principle** of immediate satisfaction of any wish. The id was also very extreme in its reactions: frustration would result in total aggression, or hunger might result in instantly grabbing the first possible thing to eat.

The ego

As the child developed from infancy, though, it was clear that such behaviour would not be socially acceptable, and so a more realistic offshoot of the id began to emerge. This worked according to the **reality principle**, trying to satisfy the id's demands but in such a way that it also fitted in with reality and didn't just produce more difficulties later on. This part of personality was called the ego, and rapidly became entirely separated from the id.

The superego

A third part of the personality also developed as the child grew older. This formed a kind of 'internalised parent', issuing commands about what the individual 'ought' or 'ought not' to do and containing all the ideas, duties and responsibilities which the individual had to develop as part of growing up in society. In many ways this part of the personality was as unrealistic as the id, since it would make such high demands on the person that they would be impossible to fulfil. It was up to the ego again, operating on the reality principle, to keep a balance between reality and the demands of the superego.

14.1

Defence mechanisms

This kind of approach to personality is often referred to as **psychodynamic**, because it portrays the ego as keeping a dynamic (constantly changing) balance between the three sets of demands which are on it: those from the id, from the superego, and from reality. The id and the superego, though, were in the unconscious mind and it was important that the ego prevented them from breaking through to consciousness, because that would be far too threatening for the individual to face up to. Accordingly, the ego developed a series of **defence mechanisms** which allowed it to protect itself against the pressures from the id and the superego.

There are several of these defence mechanisms, including:

- **projection** - e.g. attributing a 'bad' feeling or idea to another person.
- **repression** - burying a memory so thoroughly that it is not recalled at all.
- **reaction-formation** - suppressing something so strongly that it comes out as its opposite.
- **rationalisation** - finding a reasonable excuse for a particular action, when really the action was just made on the spur of the moment.

Many people consider that it was the identification of these defence mechanisms which was the main contribution of Freud's work: often, psychologists who disagree with the overall Freudian approach acknowledge that these are very useful concepts.

Libido

One central idea which Freud used to explain the origins of personality was the idea of **libido**, which he saw as a general, motivating life-energy. Freud considered the libido to be basically sexual in nature, although many of his followers, like Jung or Adler, considered it to be less specifically sexual and simply referred to it as to do with life itself. Freud believed that the libido focused itself on different parts of the body during infancy, and that the way that the individual experienced pleasure through libido influenced the development of personality. We will be looking at this in more detail in Chapter 22, when we look at Freud's theory of child development.

Criticisms

There have been many criticisms of the Freudian approach to personality. One of them has been the way that it is impossible either to prove or disprove his theories. Freudian theory can be used to explain almost anything after the event, but it is difficult to use it to *predict* what is likely to happen and many people consider that a properly scientific theory must be able to provide predictions.

Another criticism has been of Freud's idea of 'psychological truth'. The idea is that if something seems true to a person, (such as a highly emotional fantasy, or a subconscious wish that someone would die) then it doesn't matter whether it is really true: the psychological effect on the individual would be just as important. Although this idea makes the theory very interesting, many people consider that it also makes it very unscientific, as one important characteristic of a scientific theory is that it should be possible to test it against reality.

Sampling

Another set of criticisms aimed at Freud refer to his sample of research participants, which was limited to Victorian middle-class women, and also the methods that he used, in which only people who were already familiar with his theory were considered competent to interpret findings. This seemed to rule out the possibility of other people looking at the same information and interpreting it differently. And some researchers, e.g. Eysenck (1966) have argued that there isn't actually any evidence that people are helped by the process of psychoanalysis: that there seems to be about the same proportion of people recovering from their problems under psychoanalysis as would have recovered naturally.

So we can see that the psychoanalytic approach to personality is not considered to be acceptable by all psychologists. We will now go on to look at some of the alternative approaches which have been put forward by psychologists during this century.

Ethical discussion

In 1966, Eysenck reported on a study of patients undergoing psychoanalysis, in which only a third showed a noticeable improvement. As a third of all patients usually recover from psychiatric problems spontaneously, he claimed that this showed that psychoanalysis was completely useless. Effectively, Eysenck was claiming that psychoanalysts were charlatans, rooking a gullible public with a highly expensive and worthless treatment.

Other psychologists argued that what was important wasn't whether the therapy actually cured the patient or not, but what went on during the psychoanalytic process. If a patient was prepared to spend money that way, it was up to them.

What do you think?

The psychometric approach to personality

Eysenck's theory of personality

Freud, at the beginning of the century, was concerned with the preconscious and the unconscious mind, but a different set of approaches to personality developed throughout the 1940s and 1950s. Freud's approach was an **idiographic** one, which means that he was concerned with understanding how the different aspects of personality were balanced within each individual. But some other psychologists began to focus their interests on how people could be grouped and compared with one another. This is an approach known as the **nomothetic** approach to personality. These psychologists were very involved in the development of **psychometric tests**, which are tests used to measure psychological characteristics like intelligence, creativity, or personality. We will be looking at psychometric testing more closely in the next chapter. One of the most famous of these psychologists was H. J. Eysenck.

Eysenck was very influenced by the behaviourist tradition. Behaviourists argued that the only way that a truly scientific approach to understanding people could be obtained was to look at objective evidence. In the case of humans and animals this meant looking only at their behaviour and not at things like thinking or intentions which observers could never really see for themselves.

When we are studying personality, however, we can't go round watching people's behaviour all day in order to find out about them! (Even if we could, the fact that someone was being followed around would mean that they would act differently from their normal behaviour.) So Eysenck adopted the approach of *sampling* different bits of a person's behaviour, by asking them questions about the way that they normally behaved. His tests were developed as questionnaires, and by analysing the results of these questionnaires, he was eventually able to develop a theory of personality which was very different from that of Freud.

Personality dimensions

Eysenck used a technique known as factor analysis to try to identify basic aspects of personality. He investigated 700 servicemen, who were being treated for neurotic disorders at the Maudsley hospital, while he was developing his model of personality. Eysenck eventually concluded that there seemed to be two major dimensions of personality which accounted for the many different types of people which we encounter. The two main personality dimensions were **Extroversion** and **Neuroticism**. Later on, in 1976, he added a third dimension of 'Psychoticism' because he felt that this aspect of personality wasn't really accounted for by the other two factors.

You can see from this diagram that Eysenck considers the four personality types outlined by the ancient Greeks – phlegmatic, choleric, sanguine and melancholic – to be an astute assessment of types of personality to be found today. An unstable extrovert would be characteristically touchy and restless, an unstable introvert would be moody and anxious. A stable extrovert would be lively and carefree and a stable introvert would be calm and reliable.

EXTRAVERT

sociable
outgoing
talkative
responsive
easygoing
lively
carefree
leadership
(SANGUINE)

active
optimistic
impulsive
changeable
exciteable
aggressive
restless
touchy
(CHOLERIC)

STABLE — NEUROTIC

(PHLEGMATIC)
calm
even-tempered
reliable
controlled
peaceful
thoughtful
careful
passive

(MELANCHOLIC)
moody
anxious
rigid
sober
pessimistic
reserved
unsociable
quiet

INTROVERT

14.2 Eysenck's model of personality

Personality traits

Each of these main factors was made up of several different second-order factors. By looking at these second-order factors we can see more clearly just what Eysenck meant by his two main factors. The second-order factors for Extroversion are: activity, sociability, risk-taking, impulsiveness, expressiveness, reflectiveness, and responsibility. A questionnaire measuring how extrovert or introvert someone was would ask lots of questions which would sample behaviour typical of each of these second order factors, such as, 'Do you like plenty of excitement around you?', 'Can you mostly put your thoughts into words quickly?', or, 'Would you generally call yourself happy-go-lucky?'. From these, Eysenck would obtain an overall score of the general trait of extroversion.

The second-order factors for Eysenck's trait of 'Neuroticism' are: self-esteem, happiness, anxiety, obsessiveness, autonomy, hypochondriasis, and guilt. He would sample them with different questions, like, 'Do you get nervous in places like lifts and tunnels?', 'Do you sometimes feel self-conscious when you are with your superiors?' or, 'Do you get bad headaches?'. From the answers to questions like this, which would sample the seven second-order factors above, he would obtain an overall score for the general trait of Neuroticism.

The second-order factors which are involved in the trait of 'Psychoticism' include items like being solitary, insensitive, not caring about others, being unconventional, being opposed to social custom, and lacking in conscience. This dimension of personality isn't quite the same as the other two, because Eysenck reported that most people will obtain low scores on it (he thought that the other two factors would be balanced in their numbers of extreme scorers, with most people coming in the middle of the scale).

Eysenck considered that extroversion and neuroticism were totally independent of one another, and didn't really connect at all. There could be neurotic introverts or neurotic extroverts, or there could be stable introverts or stable extroverts. But, between them, he considered that they accounted for most of the main personality types that we encounter in society. A neurotic extrovert, for instance, would be an excitable and possibly an aggressive type of person, while a stable extrovert would be easygoing and lively. Someone who was of only average extroversion but very stable would probably be very good at leadership.

The biological basis of personality

Extroversion

Eysenck (1963) argued that these basic factors of personality were probably inherited, and that this meant that they must have a biological basis. He considered that the trait of extroversion was due to the general state of excitation of the cerebral cortex, in other words, how much the neurones in the cortex were likely to fire in response to a particular set of stimuli. The main mechanism which the cortex seems to use for general excitation of this kind seems to be the **Reticular Activating System (RAS)** of the brain (see Chapter 7). The RAS can either 'switch on' areas of the cortex, by 'boosting' the signals coming in from different sets of stimuli, or it can lower the general state of neural excitement by inhibiting, or 'damping down', the incoming messages.

Eysenck thought that extroverts had inherited a 'strong' nervous system, which meant that the RAS would tend to inhibit incoming messages. This meant that the person would quickly become bored by one set of stimuli, and would look for variation and novelty, which would usually be provided by socialising with other people. Introverts, on the other hand, had a 'weak' nervous system, which meant that the RAS would tend to amplify incoming information, so that they were less likely to become bored by one set of stimuli. Because an introvert was able to maintain cortical activity with comparatively little stimulation, they would be happy with solitary pursuits and with their own company or the company of just a few other people.

Neuroticism

The biological basis of neuroticism, according to Eysenck, shows itself in differences in the **limbic system** which produce different ways that the **autonomic nervous system (ANS)** operates (see Chapter 6). The ANS is the part of the nervous system which responds to stress, and some people react much more strongly to stressful events than others. Those who score highly on neuroticism, Eysenck argued, are people who have highly labile autonomic nervous systems. In other words, those who have an ANS which responds rapidly and strongly to stressful events. This implies that they are more likely to react emotionally to things that happen, and this shows up in their personality as a tendency towards neuroticism. Eysenck argued that people with autonomic reactions which are slower and less strong, will tend to score as 'stable' on the personality questionnaire.

Eysenck was very much more vague about the biological basis for psychoticism. He thought that it might be something to do with the amounts of the hormone androgen which the body produces but he didn't really go into very much detail. In general, though, his descriptions of the possible biological basis for the personality traits which he describes mean that this is a complete theory to explain how those particular traits of human personality come about.

Criticisms of Eysenck's approach

There have been several criticisms of Eysenck's approach. One of them is the very limited sample which he used to develop his original ideas. Many psychologists feel that he didn't really obtain a good range of personality characteristics from normal individuals to work on, and that this may have resulted in his theory being biased towards certain kinds of personality. Heim (1970) argued that personality is very much more complex than Eysenck's ideas seem to suggest, and that his use of **factor analysis** to draw out just a couple of major factors meant that the theory had been much too over-simplified.

Another criticism is that his use of questionnaires means that the results are easily influenced by the moods of those responding. A question like, 'Would you rather stay at home on your own or go to a boring party?' may be answered in different ways by the same person, depending on how they feel at the time (and possibly, how long it has been since they were last at a party!).

14.1 Investigating Eysenck's theory of personality

Eysenck's theory predicts that introverts will have higher levels of cortical arousal than extroverts, which is why they don't get bored as quickly. You can try testing this, by using a measure of cortical arousal and seeing if it will correlate with a person's introversion/extroversion score.

To do this you will need one of Eysenck's extroversion questionnaires - perhaps from his *Know your own Personality* book - and something that will measure cortical activity. One measure that people often use is the diagram of the Necker cube. (You will find a copy of it in Chapter 12.) The Necker cube changes its orientation even when you are trying to stop it and it changes more quickly for some people than for others.

Firstly, you should obtain a measure of the fluctuations of the Necker cube. (Can you work out why this should come first?) To do this, you need to work in pairs; one person (E) having a watch and a pen and paper, the other person (S) having a diagram of the Necker cube. S should stare at the Necker cube, without moving his or her gaze off it, for a set period of time (perhaps three minutes). During that time, it is important that S should try not to let the cube change but each time it does, S should tap the table clearly, so that E can hear. E records the number of taps that S makes and keeps track of the length of time, telling S when the time is up. Then E and S can change places.

After that, E and S should complete the extroversion questionnaire. If you do this with enough people, you can compare the results and see if those people who obtained high scores on the Necker cube have low scores on the extroversion scale and vice versa.

How many research participants would you need for a good comparison?

What kind of a correlation is this?

Can you think of any criticisms of the two measures being investigated?

Cattell's theory of personality

The type of theory put forward by Eysenck is often known as a **trait theory** of personality, because it involves trying to compare people by using different traits or aspects of personality, and seeing how they match up. There have been several trait theories of personality: perhaps the second most famous one is the one that was put forward by Raymond Cattell, in 1965.

Source and surface traits

Cattell developed his theory in a similar manner to Eysenck, using factor analysis to group together information which he obtained about individuals. He considered that personality traits could be divided into two kinds: **surface traits** and **source traits**. Surface traits are the overt personality - those traits which other people see. But underlying these are a set of source traits, which are the basis of the personality. Although surface traits do reflect the underlying source traits, they may vary from person to person. Cattell considered that there were sixteen major source traits which everyone possessed to a greater or lesser degree.

Cattell's traits were identified by using factor analysis on three different kinds of data which he called L-data, Q-data, and T-data. The L stands for 'life-record', which included such information as school grades, absences from work, and other such observations of a person's behaviour. The Q scores were obtained from questionnaires which the research participants answered about their personal habits and feelings, similar to the Eysenck ones, although rather more detailed. Lastly, the T-data came from the research participant's results on objective tests, such as intelligence tests.

The 16PF test

Cattell concluded that there were 16 major personality factors, which could be used to provide a personality profile of any given person. He developed a personality test known as the **16PF**, which has been used to provide such profiles, and which is used quite extensively in many fields of applied psychology.

Criticisms of Cattell's theory

However, many psychologists have criticised Cattell's ideas, on the grounds that the data which he used, both in formulating his theory and in drawing up his personality tests, were rather superficial. They consider that he may have overstated his case, and produced a model which is too simplistic.

The dimensions of Cattell's Sixteen Factor Theory of personality are as follows:

Factor	Low	High
A	reserved	outgoing
B	less intelligent	more intelligent
C	affected by feelings	emotionally stable
E	submissive	dominant
F	serious	happy-go-lucky
G	expedient	conscientious
H	timid	venturesome
I	tough-minded	sensitive
L	trusting	suspicious
M	practical	imaginative
N	forthright	shrewd
O	self-assured	apprehensive
Q1	conservative	experimenting
Q2	group-dependent	self-sufficient
Q3	uncontrolled	controlled
Q4	relaxed	tense

14.3 Cattell's 16 personality factors

Another criticism of Cattell's approach is that his personality factors form a set of categories which are too rigid for everyone to fit into them easily. Some of the factors may be totally irrelevant to understanding certain people, and there may be other kinds of attributes or traits which would be more valuable in those cases. By trying to classify everyone in the same way, we can blind ourselves to the ways that people are different. We will be looking at this more clearly when we look at Kelly's personal construct theory, later in this chapter.

Criticisms of the psychometric approach

An important general criticism of trait theories, put forward by Mischel (1968), is that trait theories of personality don't really take adequate account of the ways that people's behaviour varies in different situations. Different social situations can produce very different types of behaviour in people, and so it can often be a serious mistake to attribute their behaviour to a personality trait rather than to the situation that they are in.

Another criticism which has been made of the psychometric approach to personality is that it treats personality as if it were far too static. Classifying people doesn't really take account of how a person can grow, psychologically. The next approach to personality which we will look at is the **humanistic approach**, which concentrates on different aspects of personality to those examined by either the psychoanalytic theorists or the psychometricians.

Humanistic theories of personality

Carl Rogers

The theory of personality put forward by Carl Rogers in 1959 formed one of the first real challenges to the psychoanalytic and psychometric approaches to personality. Rogers considers that those views of personality are very limited ones, which present very narrow ideas about human potential. For the psychoanalytic theorist, a healthy personality is simply one who has managed to reduce the tensions of the different parts of the personality down to a manageable level; and for the psychometric theorists the simple absence of symptoms of disturbance implies that the individual is mentally healthy.

Human needs

Rogers considers that there is a more positive side to human personality, that there is a continuous striving to grow and to develop, which people engage in all the time (unless they are disturbed or under pressure). He argues that human beings have a basic need to develop their potential as fully as possible and, from his clinical work, he sees neurotic or psychotic problems as developing when this aspect of a person's personality is consistently denied. He refers to this as the **need for self-actualisation** - the need to actualise, or make real, one's potential.

Because this is such an important need, Rogers argues that we use it to evaluate all of our life experiences. Those which encourage our development are experiences which we see as positive, or valuable, whereas those which inhibit or suppress our self-actualisation are ones which we see as negative or unpleasant. Because each individual has different potentials and tendencies, we all develop our own special set of values, but these are often generally similar to those of others, even though not exactly the same.

Self concept

Another difference which Rogers has with the psychoanalytic and psychometric approaches to personality is that he sees personality as a coherent unit, not broken up into separate sections or parts. He centres his theory around the idea of the 'self' because, when he was working with his clients, he found that they had very clear ideas about their 'inner selves', which he referred to as the **self-concept**, and that often they were troubled by behaviour which didn't seem to fit with those ideas. 'I don't understand it, it isn't like me to do that', would be a typical remark indicating this kind of worry.

Psychology in Action

The concept of the "self" is central to Rogers' theory of personality. He discovered that many of his patients had a strong image of how they wanted to be (the ideal self) which was very different from how they thought they really were. The further apart the ideal self was from the real self, the more anxiety and unhappiness the patient felt. This discrepancy between the ideal and real self is often apparent in people suffering from eating disorders.

In her book *Fat is a Feminist Issue*, Susie Orbach argued that eating disorders such as bulimia and anorexia nervosa are the result of the importance placed on beauty and slimness in Western society. Women are continually subjected to images of how they should look and self esteem is related to their success in providing for and feeding others. Preparing food also becomes a way of expressing personality.

Sufferers of anorexia often have abnormal body images, seeing themselves as fat when they are exceedingly thin. Part of Orbach's therapy is to work on the sufferers' self image, bringing the image of the ideal self closer to the real self.

Positive regard

The other basic need of the human personality which Rogers outlined is the **need for positive regard**. He argued that every human being needs to have some kind of positive regard - whether that be love, affection, or even simply respect - from other people. Because it is truly a need, and not something which we can do without, it becomes very important to the person that they secure that regard, and in some cases it can become so important that it interferes with the need for self-actualisation. It is then, according to Rogers, that problems develop for the individual.

Conditions of worth

For the most part, other people tend to make positive regard conditional upon 'good' behaviour. That is, they will like someone if he or she behaves in certain ways, but not if he or she behaves in other ways. This means that each person develops ideas about which kinds of behaviour are likely to earn positive regard, and which kinds will not. These ideas are known as **conditions of worth**, and they are very important in directing the individual's behaviour, since they direct the person towards the kinds of behaviour which will gain social approval.

When these conditions of worth cause the individual to act in ways which directly oppose the self-actualising behaviour which is valued by that person, then **threat** results, because the individual's need for self-actualisation is being threatened. This produces anxiety, because the person becomes aware, (at least dimly) that there is a lack of congruity between his or her actions, and his or her values.

Defence mechanisms

Because of the threat produced by this incongruity, the person develops **defences** which protect the self from facing up to what is happening. These defences are of two kinds: **denial** (i.e. refusing to admit that there is any incongruity); and **distortion** (i.e. falsifying or changing the memory of the experience so that it becomes less threatening). This can sometimes lead to serious psychiatric problems, although most people use these defence mechanisms a little during their everyday lives.

Rogers' view of personality

Rogers saw personality as being a kind of 'mask' that we use to deal with other people in day to day living. It was important, he thought, that this 'mask' should be similar to the real 'inner self' because otherwise they would feel all the time that they were acting out a sham. But even if the personality is congruent with the inner self, it still isn't quite the same, and we are the only people who can truly know what we are like inside.

Unconditional positive regard

Healthy personality development, according to Rogers, does not have conflicts between the 'conditions of worth' and the drive towards self-actualisation, because most individuals have at least one or two people during the course of their lives who offer them **unconditional positive regard**. That is, the individual knows that there is someone, or has been someone in the past, who is fond of her regardless of how she chooses to act.

Unconditional positive regard is particularly valuable because it frees the person from the need to seek social approval all the time, and instead leaves her free to explore talents, inclinations and capacities. In other words, they can express their need for self-actualisation without having to worry that it may cause social disapproval.

Rogers insists that most, if not all, of his neurotic clients had parents who did not give their children a strong sense of being loved and approved of unconditionally, but instead always made their love conditional upon 'good behaviour'. This, he said, was conveying to the child the message that it (the child) wasn't really loved at all - instead, the parents would really have liked some other, ideal child who never misbehaved. Accordingly, these children grew up striving for approval from others, and neglecting their own self-actualisation in the process. People like this tend to have very unrealistically high standards for their own behaviour, that is, their ideal self-concept doesn't correlate with their own self-concept much at all.

Assessment and therapy

One technique which Rogers developed for assessing personality and seeing if his form of therapy had helped people was known as the **Q-sort**. It consisted of a series of statements which the person had to sort into piles. The piles would range from 'very like me' to 'very unlike me', and clients would have to sort the cards out twice, once into a set of piles which described themselves as they were, and the second time into piles which described their ideal self, or 'myself as I would like to be'. By comparing the two sets of piles, it was possible to tell how close the person's self-concept and their ideal self-concept were.

Rogers believed that people were able to sort out their own problems, if they were just freed from the need to seek approval and given a situation in which they had unconditional positive regard from someone else. The job of the therapist was to provide that relationship, and in order to do that the therapist had to be very accepting of other people, and very genuine. Rogers also emphasised that it was important that the therapist should be **non-directive** - should avoid telling the other person what to do - as this would mean that the outcome of therapy wasn't the person's own needs being expressed.

Encounter groups

Rogers didn't necessarily believe that this unconditional positive regard had to come from a psychologist. It could be provided by a new relationship which the individual developed, or from other people which that person met. Rogers developed the idea of **encounter groups**, which were ways that people could come together and really get to know one another without pretences. Although it often took some time to break down the defence mechanisms and barriers which people had, he found that once personal contact had been established, people were able to provide positive regard and support for one another. Furthermore, this kind of group experience could often make a lasting difference to someone's life.

Incidentally, this potential for change in later life is another way that humanistic theories are different from those of either the psychoanalysts or the psychometricians. Both of the other two tend to see human personality as fixed once the individual has reached adulthood, the psychoanalysts seeing it as mainly established in the first five years of life, and the psychometricians (or at least Eysenck) seeing it as basically inherited. But humanistic theorists recognise that people may change at any age, and that it is possible even in adulthood to undergo quite extensive personality changes if your expectations and circumstances alter.

Kelly's personal construct theory

A different theory of personality was put forward by George Kelly in 1955. Kelly also disagreed with the psychometric approaches to personality, as he felt that they didn't really say very much about how people themselves interpreted what was going on around them. He considered that it is the way that we *understand* what is happening to us that is most important, and so a personality theory needs to provide a way in which a therapist can see how someone makes sense of their world. This is known as a **phenomenological** approach.

The human being as scientist

Kelly said that people were like scientists in their everyday experiences and activities. We don't just passively recall the things which happen to us, we think about them, and we develop theories about what's really happening. For example, if a friend who you normally chat to, didn't answer you one morning when you said 'hello', you wouldn't just think 'Oh, so-and-so didn't answer me' and leave it at that. You'd think about it, and try to work out why. You might ask yourself if you'd done something to annoy that person, and mentally 're-run' all the recent occasions when you'd met. When you did this, you would be behaving like a scientist in the sense that Kelly meant it. You would have developed a theory, which provided a possible explanation - that your friend might be annoyed with you because of something you did or said - and then you would test that theory by 'running over' recent memories in the same way that a scientist tests a theory by devising experiments.

Kelly argued that social cognition consists of continually developing these small theories, and then testing them out against the facts that we gather in our everyday experience. If the theory doesn't fit, then we look for another one: if you couldn't work out anything that you'd done, you might also review what you knew about other things going on in your friend's life, to look for another explanation. All the time, we are developing and adjusting our ideas about what is happening around us.

Kelly's model of 'Man-as-Scientist' applies to all of our cognition, but he considered that the most important things in our individual worlds are other people. He argued that we are continually developing ideas about the way that other people are, and using these ideas as the basis of our reactions when we meet new people.

Personal constructs

Kelly stated that we each develop a set of **personal constructs** which we use to make sense of the world and the people around us. These constructs are **bipolar**, which means that they have two opposite ends. For instance, one of my constructs might be 'sensitive/unfeeling'. This would mean that I would use this to assess the people that I met, and I would look at people in terms of how sensitive or unfeeling they were. Although the construct itself is bipolar, any one person can be judged as somewhere in between the two ends, if they don't seem to be extremely one thing or the other.

The important thing, though, is that these constructs are personal. Someone else might not use the sensitive/unfeeling construct at all, but instead may use quite different ones. Typically, we have a set of about eight or nine main constructs, but we may also have several minor ones. We can also have some constructs which are **superordinate**, like good/bad, and others which are **subordinate**, or less generally applicable like 'makes good coffee/makes bad coffee'.

14.2 Looking at personal constructs

This is an exercise which you can do to find out what the main personal constructs that you use are. When you have completed it, try comparing what you have said with other people's results. If you feel self-conscious about it, you can use codes to stand for the people that you are talking about, so that only you will understand who they are;

1 Name eight people who are important in your life:

A . . . . E . . . .

B . . . . F . . . .

C . . . . G . . . .

D . . . . H . . . .

Think about these people in groups of three at a time. From the following groups, work out a way in which any two of the three are similar, and different from the third. Once you have done this, describe it in the appropriate sentence:

(A,B,C) . . . . . . and . . . . are . . . . , but . . . . is . . . .

(D,E,F,) . . . . . . and . . . . are . . . . , but . . . . is . . . .

(A,F,G) . . . . . . and . . . . are . . . . , but . . . . is . . . .

(B,D,H) . . . . . . and . . . . . . are . . . . , but . . . . is
. . . .

(C,E,G) . . . . . . and . . . . . . are . . . . , but . . . . is
. . . .

(H,B,F) . . . . . . and . . . . . . are . . . . , but . . . . is
. . . .

(A,E,H) . . . . . . and . . . . . . are . . . . , but . . . . is
. . . .

(D,G,C) . . . . . . and . . . . . . are . . . . , but . . . . is
. . . .

Investigating personal constructs

Kelly developed a technique which a therapist could use to find out how a client's personal construct system worked. The first part consisted of finding out what the main constructs were. This involved eliciting the constructs by asking clients to think about the people that they knew and to find words to describe them. After that, the main constructs would be arranged in a grid form (known as a **repertory grid**) and the client's reactions to other important people would be noted down on the grid. In this way, the therapist would be able to see if certain constructs were likely to cluster together, or if the person had used distinctive ways of understanding the world that might help the therapist to understand the problem.

For example: if a highly neurotic client consistently used personal constructs such as 'safe/frightening' about other people, and the repertory grid showed that they found most of the important people in their life frightening, then they would be likely to spend their days being continually under stress, and this could be an important factor in their neurotic disorder. Of course, not everyone who used a safe/frightening construct would automatically be diagnosed as neurotic, because that would depend on all sorts of other things too, but it could still be an important factor for the therapist to understand.

We can see from this that Kelly's theory is more concerned with how we make sense out of what is happening to us, than with describing personality. So it doesn't really contradict other theories, but can be fitted in with them; for example, it could go quite well with Rogers' theory. With his development of the repertory grid, Kelly provided the first kind of personality test which could really give an insight into the way that someone understands their world, and there are many therapists who find both his theory and the test very helpful in their work.

The eclectic approach

From looking at these theories of personality, we can see that the psychoanalytic, psychometric and humanistic approaches to personality are very different, and lead both to very different practices and to different goals for successful treatment of people with personal problems. Many psychologists use a mixture of different theories - known as an **eclectic approach** - taking what they consider to be the most valuable parts from each one. In the next chapter, we will look at some of the everyday ideas about personality which people hold, and how they may affect the ways that people interact.

Summary

1 Personality theories may be divided into two main kinds: idiographic theories, which study the individual in depth; and nomothetic theories which look for characteristics which people have in common.

2 Freud considered that personality consisted of three parts: the id, ego and superego. A dynamic balance between them was maintained by the ego.

3 The ego develops defence mechanisms which protect it from threat, which can mean that hidden traumas affect the person without their knowledge.

4 H. J. Eysenck developed a 'trait' theory of personality, in which he identified two major traits: extroversion and neuroticism. He suggested that these arose from underlying inherited biological factors.

5 Cattell's theory of personality suggested that there were 16 major personality traits which affected the individual's behaviour.

6 Carl Rogers put forward a humanistic theory of personality, suggesting that we have two basic needs: the need for positive regard and the need for self-actualisation. Each of these needs must be expressed or the individual will develop problems.

7 Kelly developed a theory of personal constructs, which explained how the individual makes sense out of the world.

Chapter 15 - Psychometrics

In the last chapter, we looked at some theories of personality and also at some of the personality tests that have developed from them. In one way, personality tests, are attempts to measure the mind, and there are other kinds of tests which also do this. Tests which measure mental characteristics are known as **psychometric tests.** In this chapter, we will look at how a number of different types of psychometric tests have developed. In particular, we will look at intelligence tests, and some of the specialised tests used in occupational psychology.

Issues in psychometric testing

Before we do that, however, it is worth looking at some of the major issues in psychometric testing, which explain why psychometric tests are like they are. There are a number of aspects of psychometric testing which are generally true for all types of tests. These include, for example, the distinction between **nomothetic** and **idiographic** tests; and questions of reliability, validity and standardisation.

Nomothetic and idiographic tests

The issue of nomothetic and idiographic tests is closely associated with the purpose for which the test will be used. Nomothetic tests are tests that are used to describe general laws or principles about people in general. So, nomothetic tests are those that are used to compare different individuals along the same scale. Idiographic tests, on the other hand, are concerned only with looking at the distinctive characteristics of just one person - they are not really concerned with comparing several people in any systematic way. Instead, they aim to provide a close insight into that one person's abilities or character.

Perhaps the best way to understand this is to consider the theories of personality that we looked at in the last chapter. The theories that were developed by Eysenck and Cattell are both nomothetic theories. Eysenck and Cattell both identified general principles of personality (personality traits) and then developed tests which measure how people score on each of those traits. So, both Eysenck's Personality Inventory (the test which forms the basis of Eysenck's theory) and Cattell's 16PF personality test are nomothetic tests.

However, if you look at the personality tests that developed from the personality theories of the humanistic psychologists Rogers and Kelly, you will see that they are quite different. These are idiographic tests, concerned only with giving a therapist an insight into the mental workings of the individual person doing the test, and not concerned with seeing how several other people compare with them, or with how they compare with the majority of the population. Rogers' **Q-Sort technique** is concerned with the difference between how someone sees themself and how they would like to be. This test allows therapist and client to note areas where the self-concept and the ideal-self-concept are very different, and to use these as the basis for therapy. Although the test can be used to make general comparisons with other people, that is not its main purpose.

Similarly, Kelly's **personal construct test**, which you may have attempted when you read the last chapter, allows therapist and client, jointly, to look at how the client understands his or her world. It isn't about seeing how the client measures up against a more general set of standards - in fact, quite the opposite. The theory emphasises the fact that each person sees their world in an individual and unique way, and the method for testing personality reflects that individuality.

Idiographic tests, then, are concerned with exploring uniqueness – the special attributes of the individual person. Because of that, they can penetrate quite deeply into the inner workings of the person's mind. Nomothetic tests, however, work on the principles that there are general laws or traits governing human behaviour, and these tests assess how a given individual measures up against these general traits. So, although they are often quite complex, they tend to be less intensive than idiographic tests, and also more superficial - concentrating mostly on identifying general trends of behaviour rather than on inner motivations or perceptions.

The normal distribution curve

The essence of nomothetic testing is the **normal distribution curve**. The normal distribution curve was first identified by Francis Galton in 1885. Galton had set up an anthropometric centre as a tourist attraction in London, and people paid to come and have their physical characteristics measured - things like height, weight, width of upper arm, lung capacity, strength of grip, and so on. By doing this, Galton had collected data about different physical characteristics, from thousands of people When he plotted the scores from each characteristic on a graph, he obtained a normal distribution curve. From this Galton went on to argue that, as mental characteristics were presumably dependent on physical ones, mental characteristics would also show a normal distribution curve. Although the initial assumption here (that mental characteristics depend on physical ones) seems a little questionable, the normal distribution curve has been the basis of psychometric testing ever since.

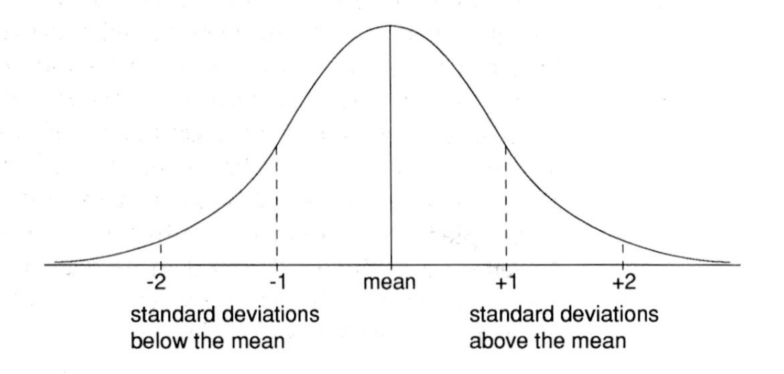

15.1 The normal distribution curve

The normal distribution curve (also known as the Gaussian distribution) is a bell-shaped curve that has special mathematical properties. As you can see from the diagram, a normal distribution curve is symmetrical, and tails off at each end. The line at the central point on the diagram is the **mean**, or average score. In a normal distribution, this point is also the **mode**, or most common score, which is why it is the highest point on the curve. It is also the **median**, or middlemost score, because the rest of the scores are scattered equally to either side.

The lines on either side of the mean represent the **standard deviations**, which are a measure of how much the scores are spread around the mean. As you can see from the second diagram, a normal distribution curve can be tall and thin, if the standard deviation is small, or it can be broad and spread out. No matter what the standard deviation is, however, the curve is still bell-shaped and it still has the same special properties. These are that, in a normal distribution curve, there is always the same proportion of scores between the standard deviations. Roughly 68 per cent of the scores fall in the area between one standard deviation above the mean and one standard deviation below it; and this is the same whether the curve is tall and thin, or broad and flattened. About 95 per cent of the scores fall between two standard deviations above the mean and two standard deviations below it; and about 99.7 per cent of the scores fall in the area between three standard deviations below the mean and three above it.

This is not just a mathematical curiosity, it is crucial to understanding nomothetic tests. What it means is that if we know the mean and standard deviation of the general population on a given trait, then we can tell instantly whether one particular person whom we have tested is typical or not. Suppose, for example, that the mean score for Eysenck's extroversion/introversion scale is 12.5, and that the standard deviation is 3. If we test someone, and they come out with an extroversion score of 14, we can see that this is within one standard deviation of the mean. So, we would conclude that this person is only averagely extroverted and not at all exceptional. However if we tested someone who scored 20, that would be different. Their score is more than two standard deviations above the mean, so less than 2.5 people in every hundred – or five in every two hundred, since it seems a bit silly to talk about half a person – would score that way. This tells us that the person is extremely extroverted, and not at all typical of most people.

Validity

Of course, that assumes that the test is really measuring what it is supposed to be measuring. If it is, we would be likely to find that the person is always very lively, inclined to play practical jokes on other people, hates being on their own, is easily bored, and so on. For this reason we wouldn't ask them to take on a job that required long periods of solitary concentration - like manning a radar screen, for example. It might be, however, that the test only actually measured how someone answered those kinds of questions in a personality test, and that, really, they were quite different, in which case, we shouldn't use it as a basis for our judgement at all. The question of whether a test really measures what it is supposed to be measuring is the question of **validity.**

There are four types of validity: face validity, criterion validity, construct validity, and ecological validity. **Face validity** is sometimes also called surface validity, and it is the simplest of them all. Essentially, it is just whether a given test looks as though it measures what it is supposed to. **Criterion validity** is a little more rigorous than that. In this, the test's validity is assessed by comparing its results with some other criterion - like comparing the outcome of an intelligence test with how well people usually do at school. There are two types of criterion validity: **concurrent validity** and **predictive validity**. Concurrent validity is when the test is compared with some other measure that is immediately available - like giving an intelligence test and comparing it with exam results that the student has already achieved. Predictive validity is when the test results are compared with something that is to happen in the future, after the person has taken the test - like giving someone a test for selecting managers and then, later, seeing how their actual performance in a management job compares with their test results.

Construct validity is to do with whether a psychometric test measures the theory that it is based on. So, for example, Guilford (1982) developed a theory of intelligence in which he argued that intelligence consisted of 150 different factors. So, an intelligence test based on Guilford's model, if it had construct validity, would need to contain a variety of different types of test items designed to test a good range, if not all, of these different factors of intelligence. **Ecological validity** is concerned with whether the test measures the real phenomenon in the everyday world that it is meant to represent; whether, for example, a paper-and-pencil test of extroversion really does identify people who are sociable and outgoing in their day-to-day lives.

Reliability

Then there is the question of reliability. A psychometric test is no use to anyone if its results are affected by things that are temporary or transient. If an extroversion test reflected the mood that you were in, it wouldn't be much use in identifying your underlying personality. If you were in a bad mood at the time, you might readily say you didn't like to be with other people or to go to parties, whereas if you were in a good mood you might give quite different answers. So a test needs to produce consistent, reliable results if we are to believe that it is measuring consistent aspects of personality or mental functioning.

There are three ways in which psychologists assess the reliability of a psychometric test. The simplest of these is known as the **test-retest** method. In this, the test is given to a group of people, and then later on the same test is given to them again. If the test is reliable, the results should be pretty well the same each time. However, as I'm sure you will have realised, the problem with that is that people can remember what they said the first time. Another technique is to develop two different versions of the same test and see if it produces the same outcome if you test the same people on different occasions. This is known as the **alternate-forms** method. The third technique used for testing reliability is known as the **split-half method**. In this, a test is divided in two, usually by taking each alternate test item. Half of the questions are given to a group of people on one occasion, and the other half to the same people later. If the test is reliable, the two halves should give similar results.

Reliability is expressed in the form of a correlation coefficient. This is a figure, between -1 and +1, which states how accurately the two tests, or the two halves of the test, match up. As a general rule, tests of ability are required to have a correlation of +.8 or higher to be regarded as reliable, and personality tests are expected to show a correlation of +.6 or more. If the figure is any lower than this, the test would be considered to be too unreliable to be useful. Of course, the higher the figure is (the closer it gets to 1), the better.

Standard-isation

Psychometric tests also need to be standardised. There are three parts to this process. The first involves making sure that everyone who takes the test gets the same experience, so that it really is the contents of the test that produce the result, and not the fact that some testers explained what needed to be done more clearly, or any other such random factor. So, the exact conditions for administering the test need to be clearly worked out and specified in the tester's manual, and the exact words of the instructions that the testers will give to the people doing the test have to be fully written out.

Another aspect of standardisation is developing **population norms** - general tables which allow the tester to see how one person's score compares with other members of the population. Standardising a test involves giving it to a very large number of people in order to find out what the typical results are and what the mean and standard deviations of a given population are. If it is a general test, then of course this will need to include large number of different people, representing the general population. However, some tests are designed for a much more limited range of people. The Occupational Personality Questionnaire (OPQ), for instance, is a personality test that is designed for job selection, particularly for management or executive jobs. For that test, there would be no point in developing population norms for schoolchildren, housewives, or retired people, as they wouldn't be taking that test. Instead the populations norms are developed from large samples of the working population at professional and managerial levels, instead.

The other aspect of standardisation is a little more controversial. It involves making sure that the outcome of the test conforms to established standards. New intelligence tests, for example, have to give results that are similar to the Stanford-Binet tests, and the test has to produce a normal distribution if it is tested on enough people. As we saw earlier, however, the principle of the normal distribution curve in psychometrics was originally based on Galton's assumption that mental characteristics were dependent on physical ones, so it is all rather circular! We couldn't use a new intelligence test to find out if previous intelligence tests were wrong, because they are not considered accurate unless they give similar results to the ones previous to them, and we couldn't know if there were aspects of mental functioning that don't conform to a normal distribution, because a new test wouldn't be accepted if it didn't give normally distributed results.

Intelligence testing

As we saw in Chapter 3, intelligence testing is one of the most politically controversial areas of psychology. Many of these political issues centre around the nature-nurture debate on intelligence. In this section, we will look at some of the more specific ways in which intelligence tests have developed. Inevitably, given the nature of the subject, political issues are involved here too, but as the emphasis in this chapter is on psychometric testing, we shall look mainly at the practical aspects of intelligence tests.

Ways of testing intelligence

Binet's test

One place to begin is to look at the type of content usually found in traditional intelligence tests. As we saw in Chapter 3, the very first intelligence tests were developed by Binet, at the end of the last century, and were used to identify children who would be likely to benefit from special schooling. Binet did not see his tests as a measure of what the child was capable of, but rather as a guide to what the child had achieved at the time. He believed that even very slow children could improve if given special training.

Binet's tests consisted partly of simple, familiar tasks, which children of different ages could be expected to achieve - like being able to name the months of the year in order, or naming objects in pictures. A child who could do the appropriate tasks for its own age-group was considered to be normal; one who could do tasks typical of older children was scored as above average in intelligence; and a child who could only do things that younger children could do scored as below average. The test also included some novel tasks, however, so that it was possible to see how the children would respond to new types of problems.

In 1916, Terman developed a version of Binet's intelligence test suitable for North American populations, which became known as the Standford-Binet test. It is still in existence today, although it has been revised since then, of course. In the new version of the test, Terman adopted a system of calculating an intelligence quotient, by comparing mental age with real, or chronological, age. The formula for this was:

$$\text{IQ} = \frac{\text{mental age}}{\text{chronological age}} \times 100$$

So, if a child was ahead of other children in its age group, having, for example a mental age of 12 but a chronological age of 10, then dividing 10 into 12 gives 1.2, and multiplying it by 100 gives 120, so we would say that the child's IQ was 120. If a child was behind its age group , things would be different. If, say, it was really 10 years old but had a mental age of 8 (in other words, it could solve problems typical for eight-year-olds but not those for older children), then its IQ would come out as 80 (try working it out yourself). While a child who was exactly typical of its age-group would come out with a score of 100.

Psychology in Action

Assessment tests are currently being carried out on 7-, 11-, 14- and 16-year-olds as part of the national curriculum in the UK. The original idea behind the testing was to assess the standards being achieved by each of the age groups in reading, writing and arithmetic.

A battery of tests designed to measure achievement in core subjects such as maths, English and science are given either throughout the year or towards the end of the academic year in the hope of raising overall standards and identifying children with special needs.

There has been a great deal of controversy surrounding the testing procedure in general and also the specific tests for seven year olds. The tests for seven year olds have recently been revised to make them less practical and based more on written assessments.

Many educationalists opposed the tests on the grounds that children may be streamed too early. They also argued that administering and marking the tests takes up time which could be better spent in teaching. But the government are interested in a child's overall performance, whereas schools are involved in the pastoral process of reviewing a child's levels of attainment.

We expect you can imagine how this type of IQ formula would tend to give a normal distribution curve. Most people, by definition, would tend to have scores that were typical of their age-group, and so the highest point of the curve would be at 100. Some would be ahead of their age group, some behind, but there would be only a few who were very far ahead and only a few who were very far behind. We would find fewer and fewer people who had scores that were extremely different from the average.

As you might imagine, though, one problem with using age to calculate IQ scores is that adult mental development is very much more variable. Although some adults continue to increase their

IQs throughout their lives, others show a decline as they get older. (It seems to have everything to do with practice - people who continue to learn and are open-minded in seeking out new information increase their IQs, others seem to let their 'mental muscles' atrophy through disuse.) However, this means that we cannot say anything definite about mental growth in adults, so a formula based on age is really only suitable for children.

15.1 Developmental tasks

Binet developed his very first test by identifying different tasks which children could do at different ages. However, that was a hundred years ago, in France. Society and culture are very different now.

Why not devise your own list of developmental tasks. Here's one to begin with: being able to name the days of the week, without any help. Think of some more, until you get a list of 20 or so different things that children learn to do as they get older.

Then find some children of different ages (you could ask your friends if they have any younger brothers or sisters) and see how many of the things on the list they can do.

Which tasks do they seem to learn first?

Do there seem to be clear ages for achieving each task? Or were the children all different from each other?

How could you develop this into a more systematic test?

The Wechsler scales

In 1939, Wechsler proposed a modification of Terman's formula, moving the emphasis away from chronological age and towards the idea of an average score for that person's group. In this system, IQ was calculated according to the formula:

$$IQ = \frac{\text{actual test score}}{\text{average score for norm group}} \times 100$$

This is known as deviation IQ, because the score is a measure of how different someone is from other people in their group. Of course, one of its implications is that if there are general changes in the population, for example, if intelligence in general becomes higher in the population as a result of social factors such as improved nutrition or better education systems, then it is possible to bring the test up to date simply by developing new population norms, without having to revise each item in the test.

The Wechsler intelligence scales are now probably the most widely used individual intelligence tests of all. They consist of 11 subtests, six of which are designed to measure 'verbal intelligence', and five 'performance intelligence'. The verbal intelligence subtests are tests of vocabulary, general comprehension, general knowledge, mental arithmetic, identifying similarities between pairs, and digit memory span - how many digits you can repeat accurately if a list is read out to you. As you can imagine, someone who is good with words and who reads a lot will be more likely to do well in most of these subtests.

However, some people are not so good with words but may still be intelligent. So the performance subtests consist of tasks that people can do which involve things like spatial relationships. One, for example, is block design, where the person is shown a pattern and asked to recreate it using a set of small, red-and-white blocks. Another is picture arrangement, where three or more cards have to be arranged in order so that they make a consistent sequence. The other performance subtests are object assembly (like a jigsaw), picture completion, where the person has to say what is missing from a picture, and digit symbol, in which symbols are used as a kind of 'code' to stand for other digits, and the person has to translate as many of these as they can in one and a half minutes.

Some clinical psychologists have found that some of the subtests of the Wechsler scales may be helpful in identifying brain disorders. Morow and Mark (1955) studied 44 psychiatric patients and found that half of them scored very low on five subtests: similarities, arithmetic, block design, digit symbol, and digit span. When these particular patients later died, autopsies revealed that the patients had serious organic brain damage, and it was this which seemed to have been detected by the WAIS tests.

The Army Alpha and Beta tests

The Stanford-Binet and the Wechsler intelligence tests are both individual tests, which have to be administered to just one person at a time by a single, highly trained tester. Following the development of the Stanford-Binet test by Terman, however, some psychologists began to develop intelligence tests that could be used to test many people at the same time. These were developed mainly as screening tests for the United States Army, but very rapidly they also came to be used as a means of selection for refugees from Europe who wanted to enter the United States.

The first of these tests was the Army Alpha test, which consisted of a number of different types of questions, including asking people to unscramble a mixed-up sentence and then say whether it was true of false; asking for the next number in a sequence; identifying words with the same or opposite meanings, and so on. As the Army Alpha test involved quite a good knowledge of English, a pictorial version of the intelligence test was also developed, known as the Army Beta Test. This involved tasks like tracing the outcome of a maze; picture completion, where the research participant had to say what was missing from each of a set of pictures; counting the number of cubes in a stack; and combining shapes to make others.

The developers of these tests, and other psychologists who were involved in applying them, were quite convinced that intelligence was inherited. As we saw in Chapter 3, this view was firmly linked with **eugenics** - the belief that people of low intelligence should be prevented from breeding, whereas those of high intelligence should be encouraged to breed more. These political views very quickly led to the new tests being used to discriminate between people of different racial groups in American immigration policy, as well as in the US Army and other areas. The tests, however, fell far short of providing an objective measure of intelligence, if such a thing can actually be achieved. Gould (1981) pointed out, for example, that the pictures used in the Army Beta test were extremely culturally biased, assuming that the person taking it was familiar enough with American culture to be able, for instance, to locate a missing ball in a picture of a bowling alley, or make sure a spoon was placed in the correct i.e. (right) hand of an infant with a feeding bowl.

Modern group intelligence tests

Throughout the twentieth century, a number of different group tests of intelligence were developed, each of which was standardised to give comparable results to the Stanford-Binet. In Britain, some of the best known of these group tests are the AH tests, developed by Alice Heim. There are three of these in popular use: AH4 is used for the general population, and consists of a number of different types of mental problem covering a mixture of intellectual skills; AH3 is more visual and spatial, for those whose language skills are not particularly good for one reason or another; and AH5 is a demanding test for those in the higher ability ranges.

As a general rule, although modern intelligence tests are less culturally biased than the early US Army tests, they have still been criticised as giving an unfair advantage to those sharing the same white, middle-class values and background as the people who write the tests. As a result, groups of people with different values or cultural assumptions often perform less well in them. In 1969, Jensen pointed out that black Americans scored an average of 15 points lower than white Americans, and argued that this showed that there was a genetic difference between the two groups. However, Tyler (1965) showed that these differences were far more closely linked to culture and background than to ethnic group: black Americans from the northern states scored higher than either black or poor white Americans from the south. Tyler argued that this was a direct result of the extreme differences in environment and expectations between the two parts of America, and had nothing to do with genetic differences.

Theory and testing

If we look at how intelligence testing has developed, we can see that different people have held very different ideas about what intelligence is. Binet, for example, saw it very differently from Terman (at least in the early years - Terman later changed his mind and argued that intelligence could be influenced by environmental factors after all). A number of different theories of intelligence have been put forward by psychologists, and it is worth looking at some of the main ones.

The 'g' factor

In 1904, Spearman proposed that applying the statistical technique to the scores from the different tasks involved in intelligence tests could identify a single, common factor underlying intelligence. This single factor became known as general intelligence, or 'g' for short, and many psychologists, including Spearman, believed that this was the manifestation of a biological capacity of the brain, producing 'mental energy'. In addition to the general intelligence factor, there were also specific skills, like verbal fluency or numerical ability, which also contributed to intelligence. According to some psychologists, a measure of IQ was partly a result of these specific mental skills, but mostly a measure of 'g'.

Other psychologists, however, see intelligence as being much more diverse. Guilford (1967) argued that whenever we perform an 'intelligent' mental task, we are combining three components: mental operations, like cognition, memory, or evaluation; content, such as visual, auditory or symbolic representation; and products, such as units, systems or implications. Combining all the possible mixtures of these three types of component produced a model of intelligence made up of 120 different factors. Guilford later extended this figure to 150 (Guilford, 1982).

Multiple intelligences

Gardner (1985) proposed that the reason why there was so much debate between whether intelligence was a single 'g' factor or a diversity of different abilities, was because there were actually several different kinds of intelligence, acting independently but side-by-side. Gardner identified seven of these intelligences: linguistic intelligence, to do with language; musical intelligence; mathematical-logical intelligence, used in calculation and logic; spatial intelligence; bodily-kinaesthetic intelligence, used in sport and everyday movement; interpersonal intelligence, used in relating to others; and intrapersonal intelligence, used to understand and predict one's own behaviour.

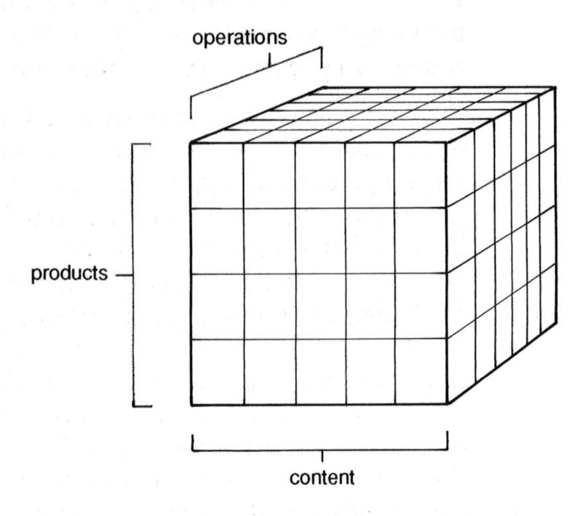

15.2 Guilford's multi-factor model of intelligence

According to Gardner, seeing intelligence as consisting of seven entirely different abilities meant that we were better placed to understand how some people could be extremely good at some types of intelligent activity, but hopeless at others. It can also explain how idiots-savants can know so much about one narrow area and yet be seriously challenged in just about every other kind of mental activity. From studies of brain damage, Gardner argued that there are physical parts of the brain which are responsible for each of these types of intelligence. In many respects, however, this is going beyond the evidence - although some types of brain injury do seem to affect certain specific skills, like verbal abilities, there do not seem to be specific brain locations for many of the others. Gardner's theory also tends to ignore the social role played by other people in helping different kinds of intelligence to develop - having positive and friendly maths teachers, for instance, can make all the difference to whether someone later develops a talent for mathematics.

Triarchic intelligence

Sternberg (1985) proposed that there are three distinct aspects of intelligence, and that each works with the other two to produce what we would recognise as intelligent behaviour. Sternberg referred to these aspects as subtheories. The first is the subtheory of **contextual intelligence**, which is to do with the cultural context within which intelligent behaviour happens. A decision or act may be considered intelligent behaviour in one culture, but not in another. Renouncing all of your possessions and going off to live a holy life dependent on other people's charity would be regarded as a perfectly valid and intelligent thing to do by some traditional Asian societies, but as an extremely unintelligent thing to do in

Western culture. Sternberg points out that in real life (as opposed to intelligence tests) we always do things for a reason, and what counts as a good reason can differ from one culture to the next.

The second subtheory is **experiential intelligence**, and this is to do with how our own past experiences have affected how we act. As you probably found if you tried the exercise in Chapter 3, you can improve how well you do in intelligence tests by practising them. We all learn skills and build up our experience as we grow older, and this manifests itself in the way we go about things. In particular, Sternberg argued, having prior experience has two effects. Firstly, it affects how we see and respond to different situations - we often become quicker at grasping the actions that a situation demands. We also become more skilled at processing information. Because we have learned to cope with similar situations in the past, we process the information involved more automatically, and so can act quicker. For example, if you have only just learned to drive a car, each situation is new to you and you will take longer to respond if another driver does something unexpected. As you gain in experience, however, you process information more quickly and automatically, and so you can respond more quickly.

The third subtheory is **componential intelligence**, and this is to do with the basic cognitive mechanisms that are involved in intelligent behaviour. Sternberg (1977) identified three types of cognitive mechanisms involved in intelligence: metacomponents, to do with general things like planning or decision-making; performance components, which are the specific skills needed for each particular task; and knowledge-acquisition components, which are the skills involved in learning or grasping new information. Most intelligence tests, Sternberg argued, are actually testing componential intelligence rather than giving a complete picture of intelligence as a whole; and he argued that identifying these three types of components shows how items in intelligence tests could be chosen to make sure that they give the best picture of the person's intelligence. He said that it was important to bear in mind that test items would be unlikely to tap into contextual intelligence, and would only give a limited picture of experiential intelligence.

Problems of defining intelligence

We can see, then, that what researchers consider intelligence to be directly affects the ways in which they try to test it. Many researchers consider that it will never be possible to define exactly what intelligence is, because it encompasses so many different types of activities. Heim (1970) defined intelligence as 'grasping the essentials in a situation and responding appropriately to them'. While this is probably a pretty accurate summary, it is far too general and wide-ranging to allow us to use it specifically.

Other researchers, however, argue that the reason why psychologists have never been able to agree on exactly what intelligence is because it doesn't really exist. While it is very clear that there are lots of individual differences between people, and that some people are very good at certain kinds of activities while others are not, that doesn't mean that there is a 'thing' called intelligence, which people have more or less of. Rose *et al.* (1984) argued that we should really think of intelligence as an adjective, not a noun, because intelligence is always manifest in a descriptive context - we perform an intelligent act, or say something that is intelligent. Referring to intelligence as if it is an independent 'thing', is, they argue, extremely misleading.

Occupational testing

As we have seen, psychometric tests are not perfect but they can often be fairly useful in providing background information to help people to make decisions, as long as those people don't take the results of the test as being the only important information! Occupational psychologists (that is, psychologists who are interested in psychological aspects of work) use psychometric tests quite frequently in a variety of contexts.

Vocational guidance

Sometimes, psychometric tests are used in vocational guidance - to help people to identify the kinds of jobs or careers in which they might be happy, if they are currently unemployed or if they are thinking of making a change of direction. The person completes a series of questionnaire-style tests, which gives the psychologist or the person who is doing the career counselling a range of possible options that look, on the surface, as though they might be suitable for that person.

Vocational guidance tests can take a number of forms. One form involves asking people to make choices between pairs of possible career alternatives: 'Which would you rather be, a train driver or an artist?' Although this might sound a bit silly, when you take just one example out of context, it does force the person to think about which they would prefer if they had to pick one or the other. By the time they have dealt with a large number of these pairs, the test can identify a group of different types of occupations which the person might like. These tests have been carefully standardised by administering them to groups of people in a wide range of different jobs. The way that scores are interpreted draws on this - people involved in, say, insurance sales tend to give different kinds of answers than, say, people involved in teaching. So the vocational guidance test will be able to identify which occupational groups an individual person's answers seem to fit.

Job selection

Occupational tests are also used to select people for promotion or training, but they are most commonly used in selecting people for jobs. Although no psychometric test can really predict exactly what someone is like, or how well they will do in a particular job, the outcome of a psychometric test can add to the amount of useful information that needs to be taken into account by the person making the decision. The important thing that they must do is to identify whether someone seems to have the right kinds of qualities for a particular job.

Some tests are used in this way as a preliminary stage to an interview. A candidate for a job might be asked to take a test, and the results from this will be used, along with information from references and the application form, when the person is being interviewed. As a general rule, most people would just be asked to take a single test, possibly related to the work they would be expected to do if they got the job; but for important jobs, like high-level management posts, a candidate might have to take a range of different tests so as to give the fullest information possible.

Selecting for promotion

Another approach to using psychometric tests in occupational contexts is often applied when people in middle-to-high management or equivalent levels are being chosen for promotion. At such times, the decisions that need to be made are rather different from a decision about whether to employ someone or not, because the organisation is already familiar with how that person is doing their current job, and doesn't have to rely on references or other information which might not be true. Here, the question is very much more specific: will the person be able to respond to the demands and requirements of the new job, or not?

As this is a much more 'known' situation, the types of psychometric tests that are involved are very much more carefully tailored to the job and its demands. This type of testing is often undertaken in a specialised assessment centre, where occupational psychologists apply a range of different types of tests over a few days. The potential candidates for promotion often stay on a residential basis, usually for the working week. A whole battery of tests is used in these situations, ranging from paper-and-pencil (or, more likely, computer-administered) questionnaires to simulations or work-sample of the real kinds of tasks they would need to do in the job, to team exercises and games designed to identify leadership and executive abilities. At the end of that time, they, as well as their employers, receive a detailed report on how they have performed in the test.

The importance of feedback

Providing feedback to the candidate from any type of job selection or promotional selection, including interviews, is very important. One reason is so that they can judge for themselves whether they have been able to show their best side or not, and, if they haven't, to make sure that they bring it out better in future. Another reason is so that they can see which skills or abilities they need to work on if they aim to get on in the future. If someone was applying for a higher management position, for example, and their test results showed that they always felt that they, personally, had to attend to details to make sure that things went right, they would be unlikely to be successful. Receiving feedback about why they failed would show them what they needed to learn for the future. In this case, it would show that they needed to train themselves to delegate responsibility and to allow other people to do things in their own way, even if it wasn't exactly the way they themselves would have done it.

Occupational tests, then can be useful in indicating what seem to be suitable options, in providing information about how people typically approach tasks, and in providing background information about that person's general aptitudes and abilities. All of this is useful information when personnel managers or company directors are making decisions about who they should employ. Of course, they are not enough on their own. They can assist in decision-making, but to base a decision only on test results would be very unwise. Nowadays, psychologists involved in psychometric testing insist that any type of psychometric test is just an indicator of personality or potential, not an absolute measure.

Types of occupational tests

Three main types of tests are used in occupational contexts. These are:

1 general mental ability tests - in other words, intelligence tests of one sort or another.

2 personality tests.

3 job aptitude and ability tests.

General mental ability tests

General tests of intelligence are quite often used when trying to select people for jobs. For instance, an intelligence test forms a routine part of the selection process to join the civil service, and for many managerial jobs. The idea is that these tests will be able to say something about the general level of intellectual functioning that someone has; to indicate whether they are likely to have a general level of competence. Usually, this type of test will be used in conjunction with a personality or aptitude test, not just on its own. As we looked at intelligence tests in quite a lot of detail earlier on in this chapter, there isn't much point in describing them again here.

Ethical discussion

Some studies have shown that IQ tests systematically disadvantage people who come from anything other than a white, middle-class background. This means that using IQ tests, for example, in selecting for jobs, might be construed as discriminating against some groups of people in favour of others. Other psychologists argue that the groups overlap quite a lot, so a mental ability test will still identify the brighter people from any cultural group, and most people won't be disadvantaged at all.

What do you think?

Personality tests

Personality tests are often used in occupational selection, as employers often want to know whether someone is likely to 'fit in' or not. Of course, no test can really say that for certain, as all sorts of other factors will apply when somebody is actually in place. None the less, it is often the case that a trait that shows up as particularly strong or particularly weak may be one that is important to the job in some way, and this will provide guidance to an interviewer as to the sort of further information that is needed before making the decision.

Cattell's 16PF test, based on the theory that we looked at in the last chapter, is a questionnaire-style personality test which is often used for occupational purposes. It gives information about how the person scores on the 16 personality traits of Cattell's theory. The final test outcome is a profile of 16 different measures, displayed on a chart, rather than just a single score.

There are other types of personality tests which are specifically designed for occupational purposes. The **Myers-Briggs Type Indicator**, for instance, identifies basic personality types, and the scoring norms which are provided with the test, indicate which sorts of jobs seem best to fit the personality types that the test identifies. The **Occupational Personality Questionnaire**, or OPQ, identifies three aspects of personality that are specifically relevant to aspects of work: how we relate to other people; thinking styles; and how we deal with feelings and emotions. Properly speaking, of course, these are questionnaires rather than tests, in the sense that tests tend to be more rigid, done under time pressure, and have definite right and wrong answers. You can't give the wrong answer on a personality test, as all it is trying to do is to describe your personality, and it can only reflect what you tell it!

Aptitude and specific ability tests

These are tests that have been explicitly designed to see whether someone is able to do a particular task or not. Effectively, these tests fall into two types. Some tests find out whether someone has the particular skills that they need already - these are the specific ability tests. Other tests try to see whether the person has an aptitude for the job - whether they would be likely to learn it quickly and do it well, if they had the training and opportunities.

Specific ability tests have often developed as a result of sampling different bits of the work that is actually involved. So, for example, clerical aptitude tests have been developed by taking a sample of several different types of clerical work, standardising them so that each person who does the sample gets exactly the same experience, and then applying them to large numbers of people already doing that type of work, to see how the test results match up to doing these tasks successfully in real life. There are several different types of ability test, each of which is appropriate for people going into a particular type of job.

Some ability tests, particularly the ones used in assessment centres, involve simulating the work for which the person is being selected as closely as possible. A good example of this is the Manager's In-Tray exercise, in which a person is told to imagine that they have just come back from a week's holiday, and have found a number of different items on their desk. They are given all of the different items, and have to plan how they would deal with these problems during the course of the next week. Some of the items have timings that clash, so the person needs to decide which problems have priority; and some are more serious than others. Looking at the way that someone deals with the problems can provide a good indicator of how someone would cope with managerial responsibility at that level - especially if this test is accompanied by other assessments.

15.2 Work-sampling

Many occupational tests involve work-samples. For example, people who apply for typing jobs are generally given a typing test - a sample of the kind of work they would be expected to do. Why not develop your own work-sample test? For example, you might take a sample of the kind of work involved in being a student, say, taking notes from books.

To create a proper test, you need to standardise all of the conditions involved. Which aspects of the task need to be the same each time?

You would also need to standardise it by developing population norms. How might you go about that?

How could you assess the test's reliability?

Do you think this test might be useful in selecting students for some courses? How might you find out if it was?

Aptitude tests don't measure how good someone is at doing the job, because they are for selecting people for trainee positions or other jobs where learning the new skill will be part of what they are expected to do. Instead, these tests assess whether someone has the mental abilities and inclinations to help them in coming to grips with the new job. So, for example, there is a series of programmer aptitude tests, which have been designed to assess whether someone has the type of thinking style, reasoning skills, and numerical ability which a good computer programmer needs. Some aptitude tests, like this one, are highly specific. Others are more general - the Isihara Colour test, for instance, indicates how accurate a person's colour perception is. Even though it is not tailored to any particular job, it is often used as an aptitude test because being able to distinguish colours accurately is an important prerequisite for many jobs. For example, a telephone engineer has to be able to deal with a myriad of wires, each of which is colour-coded differently. Accurate colour vision is essential for a job like that, as a mix-up could take a long time to sort out.

We can see, then, that occupational tests can be quite diverse, but all of them need to have gone through the rigorous processes of reliability, validity and standardisation that we looked at the beginning of this chapter. They all need to be administered by people who are trained in them and understand how to use them.

That doesn't mean that only psychologists can use them, but it does mean that the people who administer them have to be trained to do it properly. Some test publishers run their own training courses for this, and the British Psychological Society runs a qualification of competence in occupational testing which can be taken by personnel officers, career guidance officers, or anyone else involved in occupational testing. The qualification makes sure that they understand the importance of standardising tests, and of administering them properly, as well as making sure that they understand the advantages and limitations of the tests. No psychometric test can probe the hidden depths of anyone's mind, but they can be useful in providing additional information to people who need to make decisions.

Summary

1. Nomothetic tests attempt to generalise about populations, whereas idiographic tests attempt to present a detailed picture of one individual.
2. Nomothetic psychometric tests are based around the idea of the normal distribution curve, which has mathematical properties enabling us to say how typical a single score is of the population as a whole.
3. All reputable psychometric tests need to go through rigorous validity, reliability and standardisation procedures.
4. Early tests of intelligence used age to establish IQ scores, whereas later tests used the norms for that person's group instead. Some intelligence tests have to be individually administered; others can be applied to large groups.
5. There has been much debate as to whether there is a general 'g' factor in intelligence, or whether it is a collection of diverse skills or intelligence. The triarchic model presents intelligence as a combination of context, experience and mental skills.
6. Occupational tests are used for vocational guidance, job selection and in choosing people for promotion. Feedback to the candidate, as well as to the employer is important.
7. Occupational tests can be divided into three kinds: general mental ability tests, personality tests, and tests of job aptitude and ability. People administering these tests should have been specially trained.

Chapter 16 - Motivation

Why do we do what we do? The study of motivation is concerned with exploring what underlies our actions: how we come to be active, and what sort of factors influence us when we are being active. Motivation is a complex phenomenon: most of us will usually have several different reasons for our actions. If you've decided that you are going to study today, rather than go swimming with your friends, there will normally be several factors involved: perhaps you're not feeling energetic, perhaps you have exams coming up, perhaps it will be easier than justifying your behaviour to your parents. What is likely, is that all of these factors will have had some say in what you eventually decide to do.

Domains of the psyche

The model of human motivation held by the early Greeks was part of their triple-sided theory of human nature: the cognitive, conative, and affective domains of experience. The analogy which they used to explain this was of a chariot being pulled by two horses: the cognitive domain was the charioteer, who made the decisions and steered the course; but the motive power (the horses pulling the chariot) came from the combination of intentions (the conative domain) and emotions or feelings (the affective domain). For the Greeks, it was these two domains of experience which provided the motive power for human behaviour.

Instincts

In the early days of psychology, instinct theories were often used to explain human motivation. James (1990) and McDougall (1908) suggested that most of what people did happened because they had an instinct which drove them to do it. McDougall (1932) produced a list of 18 different instincts, which, together, he saw as being sufficient to account for all human motives.

There are two main problems with the concept of instinct. One of them is that it tends to be very retrospective: once we know what someone has done, we could probably come up with an 'instinct' to explain why they had done it, but that doesn't mean that we could predict what they would be likely to do beforehand. This comes partly from the second problem, which is that instinct is a sort of 'magical' concept: it sounds like an explanation, but it isn't really. All it does is raise more questions: if it's an instinct, how did it come about, and what is it that happens as a result?

When it really comes down to it, saying that something comes from an 'instinct' hasn't really told you very much, and it certainly doesn't tell you anything about people's actual behaviour. For example, it's one thing to assert that people have a basic instinct for security, and it may sound plausible, but security means different things to different people. To some, it may mean having savings to fall back on; to others, it can mean a close and supportive family; to others still, having a comfortable and paid-for house to live in. When you really try to pin down what it means, the concept of instinct is not very valuable.

16.1 Instinct as motivation

Many of the early psychologists believed that the reasons why human beings acted as they did was because of instincts - inherited tendencies that would push people to act in certain ways. A problem with instinct theory, though, was that it ended up proposing longer and longer lists of instincts that human beings had, in order to explain what they actually do.

Why not try developing your own list of instincts? Think of all of the different things that you do in the course of an ordinary day, and work out how each of them might be seen as the outcome of some possible instinct which you might possess.

Try comparing your list with that of a friend. Did you suggest the same instincts to explain the same things?

Are there ways that you could group some of your instincts together, because they work in similar types of ways?

Are there simpler ways of explaining why you have done these things?

Drive theories

As a result of these and other criticisms, psychologists began to concentrate more and more on the concept of 'drive', as something that provides the underlying motive for action. Drive theories evolved from instinct theories, but they were more concerned with starting with the behaviour shown by a human or animal, and then inferring what the underlying state was that had produced that behaviour.

Drive theories rely heavily on the concept of homeostasis. Homeostasis, literally means 'same state', and the concept of homeostasis is the idea that we have internal mechanisms that serve to compensate for external influences or circumstances, in order to keep things much the same as usual. Physiological homeostatic mechanisms tend to be closely associated with the region of the brain known as the hypothalamus. For example: if the body temperature becomes too low as a result of external factors, like cold winds or chilly atmospheres, the hypothalamus triggers off 'warming' mechanisms, such as shivering, which help to raise body heat slightly. Alternatively, if we get too hot, sensory messages are relayed to the hypothalamus and it initiates sweating, which helps the body to cool down. Drive theories of motivation rest on the assumption that similar types of mechanism underlie other kinds of behaviour, too. If the system becomes unbalanced in some way, the individual is motivated to take action that will put it right.

Types of motivation

Human beings are complex creatures who act on a number of levels. While some of what we do is undoubtedly strongly influenced by physiological factors - sleeping, for instance - other actions seem to be less obvious. In the rest of this chapter, we shall look at five different types of human motivation. First, we will look at physiological motivation - at what psychologists have discovered about basic motives concerned with keeping the body alive, like hunger and thirst. In this research, the motivations are assumed to be similar for all animals, human beings included. We shall then go on to look at some of the uniquely human aspects of motivation. This involves looking at the psychological mechanisms involved in motivating the four human areas of cognition, personal action, affiliation and social interaction.

Physiological motivation

Morgan (1943) classified types of motivation into two broad categories: *primary drives*, by which he meant physiological drives such as hunger, thirst, sex, sleep and more general drives such as activity and exploration, affection and fear; and *secondary drives*, such as social motives for doing things, or learned fears and worries.

Primary and secondary drives

The kind of motivation which has been most thoroughly researched by psychologists is the first type, and more particularly the physiological drives, such as hunger, thirst and sex. In this discussion, we will concentrate on one specific drive and look at some of the main findings.

Hunger

Control of hunger seems to be centred about the hypothalamus in that stimulating or damaging the hypothalamus seems to produce some quite clear-cut effects. But the hypothalamus is not the only brain structure involved in hunger. As we said before, the brain works as a complex set of systems and sub-systems, and just interfering with one part and producing an effect does not show that that part *causes* that effect. Bearing that in mind, we will look at what has been found about hunger.

Researchers have concentrated on two main aspects of the hypothalamus when looking into hunger: the neuroanatomical aspects, which look at which parts of the brain are involved; and the neurochemical aspects, which look at the particular neurotransmitters and the effects which they may have. The particular parts of the hypothalamus which seem to be concerned with hunger and feeding behaviour are the **Ventro-Medial Nucleus (VMH)**, and the **Lateral Hypothalamus (LH)**. These seem to have different and opposing functions: if the VMH is stimulated electrically, it seems to suppress eating behaviour in animals, whereas if the LH is stimulated by the same method, eating behaviour increases, and the animals will also learn entirely new forms of behaviour to obtain food, which suggests that their motivation is very high. When researchers caused lesions (cuts) in the VMH, rats would start to over-eat dramatically, and so it was suggested that this part of the hypothalamus was mediating **satiation** - the stopping of eating when enough food has been consumed. On the other hand, lesions to the LH produced a lack of eating behaviour - rats with such lesions would starve themselves to death if they were not force-fed and so it seems that the LH is involved in the motivation to obtain food.

Neuro-transmitters

On the neurochemical side, Grossman (1960) found that different neurotransmitters seemed to have different effects on hunger. When he injected chemicals directly into a particular part of the hypothalamus, he found that **noradrenaline** would produce eating behaviour in rats, but **acetylcholine** would produce drinking behaviour. Another neurotransmitter, **serotonin**, seems to be involved in motivation as well, and so it seems that this is another mechanism which the brain can use to organise different forms of behaviour.

When we are learning about these mechanisms from studies of laboratory rats, though, we need to be very careful in generalising the findings to other species, especially humans. A study by Fisher (1964) showed that acetylcholine injected into exactly the same part of the hypothalamus in both rats and cats could produce entirely different effects. In rats it produced eating behaviour, whereas in cats it produced aggressive and rage responses.

Obesity

Despite this, work on feeding and hunger in rats has produced some findings which may be useful in understanding humans. **Obesity** is a major problem in Western society, and many obese people show striking parallels in their behaviour with rats that have become obese by VMH lesions or similar. The ventro-medial hypothalamus, as said before, seems to be involved with satiation - stopping eating when the animal has had enough. Rats with VMH lesions become obese because they eat large amounts at a time but they do not work hard to obtain food. Also, they respond very strongly to different tastes in food. Schachter (1971) performed a series of studies in which he showed that obese human beings behaved differently from normal weight people in their eating behaviour. In one study people were asked to perform a task which required concentration, and were provided with bags of either shelled or unshelled peanuts. Obese people ate more of the shelled peanuts, but far less of the unshelled ones, which required the 'work' of unshelling them first. Also, obese people seemed to be far more sensitive to different tastes, especially sweet ones.

The hypothalamus seems to have a kind of 'set-weight' for the body. Rats will tend to eat as much as is necessary to maintain that weight, and then stop. Lesions to the VMH seem to alter the set-weight, which in turn leads to obesity, whereas lesions to the lateral hypothalamus seem to lower it. Reeves and Plum (1969) reported on a single case study of a young woman who developed a tumour in the VMH. In the two years before her death, she ate far more than she had done previously, and doubled her body weight. Although this is just a single case study, it does seem to show parallels with the experimental findings with animals.

Other forms of motivation may also be mediated by the hypothalamus, and there is some evidence that thirst has a similar set of mechanisms. However, much of what motivates human behaviour is far more complicated than just a physiological drive - we are also influenced strongly by social and cultural factors.

16.2 Motivation and perception

In Chapter 12, we looked at the study by Gilchrist and Nesburg, which showed how motivation can affect people's perception. You may like to try doing something similar yourself.

Collect a number of colour photographs from magazines, making sure that they include a number of pictures of food, as well as of other subjects. Then draw up an answer sheet, giving a rating scale from 1-5 for a few different factors, like 'appropriateness of colours for the topic', 'aesthetic appeal of colours' and, of course, 'vividness of colours'. Then ask people to look at the photos and rate each one.

If you ask people just before lunch, do you get different answers for the food pictures than if you ask them just afterwards?

What controls would you need to include if you were doing this as a formal practical assignment?

Electrical stimulation of the brain

Hunger is one form of motivation which occurs when there is a **need** in the organism, which has to be satisfied. For a long time, psychologists thought that all motivation involved satisfying needs. The need would produce a **drive** in the animals or people, which would lead them to act in ways that would reduce the drive. Gradually, however, it became clear that many forms of behaviour are not necessarily concerned with reducing drives at all: sometimes an animal or human will work *for* something, which they do not necessarily need, but which they find pleasant.

One of the most striking examples of this kind of motivation is shown in studies of **electrical stimulation of the brain** (ESB for short). In this, electrodes are implanted directly into the septum and a small electrical impulse, similar to that produced by the neurones themselves, is delivered directly to the brain. A famous study by Olds and Milner (1954) showed that rats who received this sort of brain stimulation as a result of pressing a lever in a Skinner Box would continue pressing the lever repeatedly at an extremely rapid rate. In addition, given a choice between obtaining food or ESB they would continue with the ESB to starvation point. Obviously, it is not possible to perform this kind of experiment on human beings, but with some terminally ill cancer patients or severe epileptics it was tried, as a possible relief from pain. Campbell (1973) reported that the patients said they experienced relief from anxiety, and felt 'wonderful' and 'happy'.

At first it was thought that this area of the brain represented a 'pleasure centre' which was involved in all pleasurable sensations but the kind of experience that it provides does not seem to be the same type as other pleasurable events. Rats which have been receiving ESB for one hour may ignore the lever completely the next time they are put in that situation, showing that extinction is much more rapid for this kind of learning than it is for food-reinforced learning. However, it does show that not all forms of motivation involve reducing drives: ESB seems to be something which animals work for, rather than something which simply reduces an unpleasant need.

Cognitive motivation

Understanding physiological motivation is important, but there is much more to why human beings do things than just satisfying basic drives. Human beings have other sources of motivation too, and some of these are directly concerned with the way that we think and understand ideas. For example, sometimes we change our ideas or opinions and come to the conclusion that our previous ideas were not quite right. At other times, we stick to our beliefs like glue, even when it is clear that the evidence is against us. History is full of examples of people being persecuted because they brought in new ideas at times when other people were not ready to receive them. In everyday life, we may not react so dramatically towards people who try to make us rethink, but we can be just as stubborn.

Cognitive dissonance

An interesting study on this was performed by Festinger, Riecken and Schachter in 1956. They were interested in how beliefs influence human motivation and, in particular, what happens to our motives when a belief that we hold very strongly is very obviously contradicted by events. They studied a quasi-religious cult in Los Angeles, which believed very firmly that the world was going to come to an end on a particular date. Using participant observation, Festinger *et al.* joined the group and talked to the members to find out what they believed. On the appointed day, the cult members sold all their possessions and all congregated on a hilltop outside of the city, to spend the night in prayer while they waited for the end of the world. When the world didn't end on schedule, Festinger and his colleagues talked to the group members to find out whether this had affected their beliefs.

Interestingly, despite the obvious contradiction between what they had been expecting and what had actually happened, the group members did not change their beliefs substantially - they certainly didn't admit that they had been wrong! Instead, they modified their beliefs a little, claiming that it had been their actions which had saved the world. Festinger attributed this to **cognitive dissonance**, a concept that we shall meet again in Chapter 17.

Ethical discussion

In order to observe the process of cognitive dissonance at work in the religious cult, Festinger and his colleagues posed as members of the cult and joined them on their religious vigil. In other words, they were deliberately deceiving the research participants in their investigation, who were interacting with them in good faith, not realising that they were actually psychologists.

Was this an ethically acceptable thing to do?

Cognitive dissonance motivates human action or beliefs, partly because we feel uncomfortable if our beliefs contradict one another. The idea that the world was going to end on that date directly contradicted what actually happened, and Festinger argued that this resulted in dissonance - a lack of balance between the two cognitions. Somehow, the people concerned had to find a way of balancing them so that they didn't contradict one another. Admitting that they had been wrong would have produced even more uncomfortable cognitions - these people had sold their possessions in preparation for this event, so admitting that they had been wrong would also have meant admitting that they had been stupid or gullible neither of which is a particularly comfortable thing to think about yourself. However, by modifying their beliefs so as to attribute the continuation of the world to their own efforts, they could retain their self-respect. At the same time, they could balance their knowledge of what had actually happened with their beliefs about the end of the world.

Avoiding cognitive dissonance, then, is a major source of motivation for people. Most everyday examples of cognitive dissonance are nowhere near as dramatic as that, but the next time you become frustrated with someone because they just don't seem to be facing up to reality, it's worth asking yourself whether to do so would cause them a cognitive dissonance.

Defence mechanisms

Saying that cognitive dissonance is an important aspect of human motivation isn't the same as saying that we are aware that we are using it. Many of our cognitive motivations operate unconsciously and in such a way that we are almost entirely unaware of them. Freud (1901) was perhaps the first person to identify the way that unconscious defence mechanisms can provide powerful motivators for human behaviour, but many other researchers and clinical psychologists, even if they don't accept the rest of Freud's ideas, have found that defence mechanisms are a useful way of understanding why people do some of the things that they do.

Freud talked of defence mechanisms as strategies that the ego adopts in order to protect itself against threat. Sometimes, that threat comes from an internal source, so, for example, people who are unconsciously frightened of their own homosexual urges can sometimes defend against them by adopting a strongly anti-homosexual attitude. The threat is internal, but it serves to energise and motivate their actions. That defence mechanism is known as reaction formation, where the mind represses something so strongly that it can turn into its opposite. Repression itself is another defence mechanism. As we saw in Chapter 11, Freud considered that forgetting was the unconscious mind protecting the ego from remembering something that would be deeply disturbing or traumatic, like an early childhood experience. Although not all psychologists see forgetting in this way, it does seem clear that people will sometimes repress memories which are deeply disturbing for them, and that the anxiety produced when these memories threaten to pop up - perhaps because there has been some recent reminder - can motivate their behaviour.

There are other kinds of unconscious motivators, too. We often seek to protect things that are closely linked with our own self-esteem. Someone may be able to cope with criticisms of a number of personal attributes, but if something represents an important source of pride, they may become very defensive, and even hostile, if it is criticised.

Personal constructs

In Chapter 14, we looked at personal construct theory – the idea put forward by Kelly, that we each develop our own personal set of theories which we use in making sense of the world. These theories don't just help us to make sense out of what is going on. They also direct our actions and affect how we are prepared to interact with other people. In other words, they have a direct effect on our motivation. For example, imagine dealing with someone who comes across, interpersonally, as very abrupt and sharply spoken. If you have a set of personal constructs that means that you construe their behaviour as intolerant and frightening, you will interact with them quite differently than someone with a set of personal constructs which means that they construe this behaviour as decisive and positive. The person is the same, and their behaviour is the same, but the way that it is construed affects how you will behave towards that person. It also affects whether you will tend to seek that person's advice or ask for their help: if you find them frightening or intimidating, you will not be motivated to approach them, or have much to do with them. In fact, your motivation is likely to be entirely the reverse – you will be motivated to avoid them wherever possible. If you construe them as decisive and positive, however, you would be motivated to approach them when you need advice about a particular decision or situation.

Approach-avoidance

Another aspect of motivation is known as the approach-avoidance conflict, which happens when you are confronted with some goal that is both attractive and also negative in some way. For many people, leaving home and going away to college is simultaneously attractive and aversive. They feel that it will be good to go away and explore a new life, but at the same time it is anxiety-provoking to think of leaving home and all your family and friends. If you were in that situation, and particularly if you were leaving someone or something that you were very fond of, you might feel ambivalent about going – part of you would want to go, but another part wouldn't. This is the approach-avoidance conflict.

Early studies of approach-avoidance tended to be entirely behavioural. For example, Miller (1959) set up an experiment in which hungry rats were taught to run through a bright alley to reach food. When they had learned this, they were given a brief electric shock while they were eating the food. Naturally, when the next occasion came, the rats were very hesitant about approaching the food. As they went down the alley, they would become more hesitant, and stop, making a couple of false starts before they finally went to eat. Miller found that increasing either the shock or the hunger would change the point in the alley where the rat would stop: if the rat was very hungry, it would get closer to the food before it stopped (because the goal seemed more attractive). If the electric shock was lower, the rat would also get closer to the food – the aversive stimulus was less powerful. The point of vacillation – where the rat would stop – was the point where the attractiveness of the goal exactly balanced out the aversiveness of the punishment.

These studies with animals tended to adopt a behavioural approach, seeing approach-avoidance as a product of stimulus and response associations. More recently, however, we have tended to see approach-avoidance (at least in humans) as a cognitive motivation. Approach-avoidance, in cognitive terms, is all to do with how attractive a major action or decision appears to be. The principle can be stated as follows: the more distant a major challenge or event is, the more attractive it will seem; but the closer it is, the more we will feel inclined to avoid it. For example, when you were first thinking of going away to study, it was a distant prospect, and the idea of leaving and going away seemed very attractive. You would be likely to think about all of the positive aspects, like the new experiences you would have. As the date gets closer, however, the negative sides of the experience become more important: you think more about what you will be missing and about the friends you will be leaving behind.

Each new experience presents some kind of approach-avoidance conflict, because even the very smallest change involves something that is new and unfamiliar, and leaving things that are familiar behind. It is not uncommon for people to come very close to making changes in their lives, which they genuinely want to make, but then to back off because they become frightened of the unknowns that the change actually involves.

Motivating personal action

Have you ever noticed how differently people react to setbacks? Some people will have something unpleasant happen, like failing an exam, but will pick themselves up and try again. Others seem to give up, and appear to take it as a message that it just isn't worth trying any more.

Locus of control

In 1966, Rotter proposed that these differences come about as a result of people's sense of locus of control. Locus of control refers to where you think control for events is located, in particular, whether you think it is located inside yourself or whether it is located in external events. If you have an internal locus of control, you tend to see what happens to you as largely the result of your own efforts. If you have an external locus of control, you tend to see what happens to you as a result of the situation you are in, or luck, or factors that have nothing to do with you.

Feeling in control is important to people

Rotter showed that, over all, it is psychologically healthier to have an internal locus of control than an external one. There are a number of reasons for this. One is that people with an internal locus of control generally experience less stress than those with an external locus of control. A number of researchers have shown that simply being out of control is stressful for human beings – we like to feel that our actions make a difference. Indeed, many of the old superstitions that people in agricultural cultures developed can be interpreted as attempts to feel that they could exert some control over the things that happened. Also, if you tend to see yourself as being able to exert some control over what happens to you, then you will also tend to look for ways of coping with unpleasant events, instead of just receiving them passively, and, more often than not, you will find that there are things that you can do. Even if you can't stop the event itself, there are often things that can be done that will mean that its effects aren't quite as serious as they might otherwise have been. Such people cope better with stressful events than people with an external locus of control, who just accept what happens to them and don't try to change it.

Self-efficacy

A lot of this has to do with what Bandura (1989) called self-efficacy beliefs. Self-efficacy beliefs are to do with your sense of personal competence - how good you think you are at doing things. This is not just what you have already done, because some people can achieve a great deal yet still not believe that they are really any good at it. Rather, it's to do with how good you believe yourself to be. If you have a high self-efficacy in one area, like, say, your ability to do school-work, then you will make more effort and take more pains than if your self-efficacy beliefs are low and you don't feel that it is worth making an effort because you wouldn't get anywhere anyway.

Collins (1982) performed a study of how self-efficacy beliefs affected children's schoolwork. He sorted children into three groups according to how good they were at maths. In each group there were some who had high self-efficacy beliefs and some who did not. Collins found that the children with high self-efficacy beliefs did better than those with low self-efficacy, even when they were just the same in mathematical ability. Since they believed that they could be effective, they bothered to make sure that they learned, going back over problems and correcting them, and rejecting faulty solutions more quickly. Their beliefs affected how much effort they put in, and their efforts affected how well they did.

Weinberg, Gould and Jackson (1979) manipulated self-efficacy beliefs about stamina in sport, and found that people with high self-efficacy beliefs were likely to persist longer and make more effort. They also found that when they manipulated female self-efficacy beliefs to be high, and male self-efficacy beliefs to be low (by giving them false feedback about how well they had done on endurance tasks), the normal sex differences disappeared – suggesting that what we expect of ourselves, and believe we are capable of, may have a much more powerful influence than we think.

Attribution

You can see from this that the question of attribution (the reasons we give for why things happen) is closely linked with this area. Locus of control and self-efficacy are really all to do with the causes you attribute to things - why you believe things happen. We will be looking at attribution more closely in Chapter 17, but it is important to recognise that the types of attributions we make can be important in motivating what we do.

Stratton and Swaffer (1988) analysed the attributions which mothers made about their young children as they watched them play and talked about them. They had several different groups of mothers, including a group of mothers whose children had been physically abused ('battered' children). They found that when the attributions were analysed, those mothers made attributions which indicated that they saw their children's behaviour as far less controllable than other mothers did. When their children were naughty or badly behaved, as all children are sometimes, they felt frustrated and unable to cope. This meant that stress built up and they resorted to hitting their children. On the other hand, mothers who made more controllable attributions, saw their children's behaviour as something that they could influence, and so, although they got annoyed, they didn't feel as helpless and frustrated, and didn't take it out on the children.

Learned helplessness and depression

Other kinds of attributional styles can motivate personal action. Seligman (1975) identified a depressive attributional style, in which the individual always opts for the most negative way of looking at things, and tends to see events as always bad, wide-ranging in their implications, and uncontrollable. Perhaps not surprisingly, this depressive attributional style leads them to feel that they are powerless to influence events, and it is particularly common in people who are seriously depressed. Seligman considered this to be similar to the learned helplessness that can develop in animals put in a situation where they are powerless to prevent unpleasant consequences. Even when the situation changes, and they could now prevent the unpleasantness, the animals do not learn the new response - they have learned to be helpless.

The attributions that we make, however, can change. Cognitive therapy is all about changing the ways that people interpret events, so that their personal motivation changes and they take a more active and controlling approach to the things that happen to them. Beck *et al.* (1985) argued that adopting this type of approach to therapy meant that people could learn to live their lives entirely differently, and that this would allow them to be active agents in their own lives. Nowadays, many clinical psychologists are adopting the techniques of cognitive therapy. Indeed, many people argue that the old behavioural therapy techniques, like behaviour shaping or systematic desensitisation, really worked because they showed people how they could take control over their own feelings and circumstances. Although the behaviour therapists believed that they worked because of the new stimulus-response connections that were being forged, the realisation that they could do something and didn't have to suffer passively may have been just as important, if not more so.

Psychology in Action

Victims of long-term physical and mental abuse sometimes learn to adopt a set of behaviours which approach learned helplessness. A lack of control over situations is seen to be a very important factor in making people passive rather than active participants in events. Sometimes one single traumatic event, such as rape or the death of a spouse, may be sufficient to make someone feel out of control and induce a sense of isolation. A culmination of several minor events, such as burglaries or arguments with neighbours, may lead to the same problems.

Assertiveness training programmes have been set up to teach people to be more assertive in everyday social situations. The programme may be specifically tailored to the social problems of the individual. For example, rape victims can be encouraged to hold themselves better and walk with confidence, so communicating more positive non-verbal signals to potential attackers. They may also learn self-defence techniques to increase their confidence and, therefore, sense of control. Role modelling is used to help those who find it difficult to be assertive in other social situations, such as those who find it difficult to say "no" or those who find it difficult to make demands.

Affiliation motives

Another important aspect to human motivation is our affiliative needs, the needs that we all have for relationships, positive regard from others, and to mix with other people. As we saw in Chapter 14, Rogers (1961) argued that one of our most basic psychological needs to is have positive regard from other people. This may take the form of love, friendship, or even just respect, but in Rogers' view it is a need that must be satisfied if we are to function in a healthy way psychologically.

Aggression

It has often been argued that human beings are inherently aggressive, and certainly there are many examples of aggression that have been perpetrated by members of the human species. As we saw in Chapter 3, however, it is open to question how far these can be explained by looking for sources of aggression in individual human beings, rather than in their social situations or social settings. While it's unquestionably true that putting people under stress makes them very much more likely to act aggressively, it isn't at all obvious that that is the same type of aggression that is involved in wars between nations, where a large propaganda machine is needed to keep people feeling hostile. The fact that, during wartime, public information is so tightly controlled (even comedy shows that criticise war are censored from the mass media) suggests that that kind of aggression may not actually be as basic to human motivation as all that - if it were, why would we need to go to so much trouble to keep it going? Towards the end of this chapter, we shall be looking at how the shared beliefs known as social representations are involved in human motivation, and it may be that these have something to say here.

In Chapter 6, we looked at some of the features of arousal, fear and anger in human beings; and at how stress may produce interpersonal aggression. When we look at individual human beings, however, we find that there are many other characteristics of human psychology which seem to be more important for understanding human motivation.

Social respect

The motivation to avoid looking foolish is closely tied in with this last example. Harré (1979) argued that social respect is a very fundamental motive in human behaviour - none of us like to look stupid in front of others. We internalise that, too - we don't like to seem foolish to ourselves either. We prefer to maintain an image of ourselves as reasonable and sensible. If admitting that we were wrong, or changing our minds in the face of new evidence, would also be associated in our own minds with looking stupid or ridiculous, that provides another source of cognitive dissonance, and we seek to avoid facing up to it. In this way, people can end up refusing to acknowledge things that are apparently very clear to others, because they are not able to cope with the cognitive dissonance of accepting them and appearing to look foolish. However, if they can find a way of 'saving face' and still accepting the information, they will often accept it readily.

Rom Harré saw the need for social respect as being a powerful motivator of human behaviour. He argued that people want to be respected for who they are and will go to great lengths to avoid looking ridiculous or foolish. Harré identified this as a very basic need in social behaviour, which manifests itself from early childhood. Small children in a playground are generally far more concerned with showing off and showing what they can do, than they are with playing competitive games or expressing aggression or hostility. Harré argued that social theorists have not paid nearly enough attention to this basic source of human motivation, and that more detailed psychological research into it is badly needed.

Co-operation and reconciliation

Similarly, many psychologists are coming to believe that there has been too little psychological research into co-operation and reconciliation. In a survey of research into ape and human behaviour, de Waal (1989) argued that what was important about primate social behaviour wasn't so much aggression (which has been extensively studied), but reconciliation: how social animals resolve their differences, in such a way as to make sure that the group still functions socially. De Waal identified a number of different reconciliation strategies used by chimpanzees, gorillas and other apes, and showed that these often have direct parallels with how human beings behave.

Even a relatively superficial observation of human behaviour shows that, TV scriptwriters notwithstanding, most people seem actively to avoid any sort of aggressive confrontation, even to the point of not asserting themselves when they know that they should. The Asch work on conformity, and Milgram's work on obedience, which we shall be looking at more closely in Chapter 18, show that there seems to be a powerful tendency for people to try to go along with the majority, or to obey someone who is in authority, rather than to challenge them. This seems to represent a strong social need to be accepted by other people rather than rejected, and this, in turn, may link in with Harré's idea of the need for social respect as a fundamental human motivator.

Empathy

Empathy is another human attribute that has been studied relatively little by social researchers, even though it is clear from looking at society that empathy can represent a powerful social motive.

There are many instances of people devoting their spare time, and even their lives, to worthwhile causes that they believe in; and many other acts of everyday kindness that go almost entirely unnoticed by psychological research. Psychological research into helping behaviour, as we shall see in Chapter 19, shows that, in most circumstances, people will tend to help others unless they have developed some reason to do otherwise, like defining the situation as a non-emergency, or trying to avoid looking silly in front of other people. The main outcome of this research is to show that if people are sure that their help would really be useful or wanted, they are almost always ready to help out when they can.

Social and group motives

We have broader social motives, too. In Chapter 20, we shall be looking at the theory of social identification, which discusses how the social groups to which people belong affect how they see themselves. An important part of social identification is social comparison - we compare our own group with other social groups in terms of their respective status, prestige and power. If this comparison means that our own self-esteem is threatened, it can often lead to intergroup rivalry.

Social identity theory was first developed in an attempt to explain social prejudice, like racism, in which members of one group are hostile to another without there necessarily being any direct personal contact between them. Indeed, people who are racist can sometimes even have personal friends in the group to which they are hostile - personal contacts seem to have very little to do with it. Tajfel (1969) argued that it isn't really to do with how one sees oneself as an individual, but to do with the way people identify with their social groups. By trying to enhance the status of their own group by denigrating the other, racists protect their own social identification.

Research into social identification has shown that intergroup conflict isn't an inevitable consequence of group identification; it can also result in group co-operation if people see themselves as having common goals. In Chapter 17, we shall be looking at how Sherif *et al.* (1961) produced intergroup rivalry among boys at a summer camp, which became quite intense, but were eventually able to produce group co-operation when all of the boys had to help out in an emergency.

Scapegoating

There are other aspects to social motivation, as well. As we shall be seeing in Chapter 17, one of the mechanisms that seems to underlie social prejudice is that of scapegoating. If we are frustrated and upset, we often look around for someone else to blame - it's easier to deal with the emotion by becoming angry with someone else. (An even better way is to work it off in vigorous exercise, but that's not usually the kind of thing you think of at the time!). This type of process seems to happen with wider social groups as well. It is noticeable that there is almost an increase in expressed racism at times of economic recession, when unemployment is high and living standards are threatened. It seems that instead of putting the blame on the economic factors that cause such recessions, many groups in society look around for more visible targets, and express their own frustration as racial prejudice.

Social representations

Part of this is also to do with the existence of shared explanations and beliefs that are held by society in general, or by groups of people in society. These beliefs are often not true, but in many ways they might as well be as large numbers of people accept them as true and act as if they were. Also, they often have a germ of truth in them, which has been changed into something quite different. For example, Moscovici and Hewstone (1984) showed how the scientific split-brain studies which we looked at in Chapter 8 had become transformed into social representations. In the process, they had changed: where the scientists concerned were talking only about a tendency for one half of the brain to be more concerned with mathematical functions and the other with artistic, more mystical things, people had seized on the idea and changed it into a whole set of theories about how one side of the brain was more intuitive, caring and gentle, while the other half was authoritarian and tightly focused. Moreover, it was argued that this could explain what is wrong with modern society - that it favours the left brain over the right one. You can see how very different these ideas are from the basic scientific research that you learned about in Chapter 8!

Part of the reason for this is the way that these ideas are negotiated. Social representations are spread through conversation, and in the same way that we fit other ideas into our existing schemata (see Chapter 11), we also modify the social explanations that we hear so that we can fit them with what we already believe. So, through conversation and negotiation, social explanations change in nature. They can be very powerful indeed in motivating human action. It was the shared racist beliefs that so many people held that legitimised what happened in Nazi Germany; and it is the shared social representations about intelligence as inherited and 'fixed' that have made such a deep impact on British schooling, so that attempts to develop educational systems which really give people equal opportunities have almost always failed. If people simply don't believe that some children can be taught, then they won't address the issues of how to teach them seriously enough to overcome difficulties. In other countries, however, which don't share the same social representations about intelligence, the picture is very different.

We can see, then, that human motivation is complex, and operates on many different levels. In fact, almost any part of the psychology that you read about in this book contributes to motivation in some way or other. Coming to understand why people act as they do is a fascinating study, and one that is never really likely to end! In the next section, we shall look more closely at some of the social aspects of human behaviour that we have touched on here.

Summary

1. Early psychological theories of motivation argued that motivation came from 'instincts' - inherited forces that compelled certain kinds of behaviour.
2. Drive theories of motivation assume that an organism (person or animal) is trying to maintain homeostasis, and that motivated behaviour aims to restore homeostatic balance.
3. Physiological sources of motivation have shown that brain mechanisms are strongly involved in motivational states like hunger and thirst. Electrical stimulation of the brain is also a strong motivator.
4. Cognitive mechanisms of motivation include the processes of cognitive dissonance, defence mechanisms, personal constructs, and cognitive interpretations of approach-avoidance conflicts.
5. Motivating personal action involves psychological mechanisms such as locus of control, self-efficacy beliefs, and attribution styles. Learned helplessness is a state where motivation to take personal action is seriously depleted, as previous experience has suggested that it is not worth trying.
6. People have powerful affiliation motives which motivate them to get on with others. These include a personal need for positive regard, a social need for respect, the tendency to co-operate rather than to confront, and empathy.
7. Social and group motives include the way that people identify with in-groups through social identification, how prejudice can increase through scapegoating, and how shared social representations influence how people are motivated to undertake social action.

Suggestions for further reading

Beal, A. & Sternberg, R. J. 1993 *The Psychology of Gender*. London: Guildford Press

Breakwell, G. 1986 *Coping with Threatened Identities*. London: Methuen

Burn, S. M. 1996 *The Social Psychology of Gender*. London: McGraw Hill

Burr, V. & Butt, T. 1992 *Invitation to Personal Construct Psychology*. London: Whurr

Evans, P. 1989 *Motivation and Emotion*. London: Routledge

Eysenck, H. 1985 *Decline and Fall of the Freudian Empire*. Harmondsworth: Penguin

Fransella, F. 1981 *Personality: Theory, Measurement and Practice*. London: Methuen

Gardner, H. 1985 *Frames of Mind: the Theory of Multiple Intelligences*. London: Paladin

Hayes, N. 1993 *Principles of Social Psychology*. Hove: LEA

Marsella, A., DeVos, G. & Hsu, F. 1985 *Culture and Self: Asian and Western Perspectives*. London: Tavistock

Mischel, W. 1986 *Introduction to Personality: a New Look*. New York: CBS.

Shackleton, V. 1989 *How to Pick People for Jobs*. London: Fontana

Sternberg, R. J. 1985 *Beyond IQ: a Triarchic Theory of Human Intelligence*. Cambridge: Cambridge University Press

?

Self Assessment Questions

1 The evaluative part of the self-concept is known as the:

a) self-image.

b) social identity.

c) self-efficacy.

d) self-esteem.

2 Butler and Haigh showed that the relationship between self-concept and ideal-self concept could be improved by:

a) psychometric testing.

b) client-centred therapy.

c) positive self-efficacy beliefs.

d) cultural contexts.

3 Mbiti described the development of the self-concept in:

a) Britain.

b) Africa.

c) Asia.

d) America.

4 The influences which produce gender identity are mainly:

a) biological.

b) genetic.

c) social.

d) hormonal.

5 Sex typing involves bringing a child up:

a) in accordance with its biological sex.

b) in accordance with its sexual appearance at birth.

c) as the other sex.

d) in accordance with its hormonal development.

6 Psychoanalytic explanations for gender identity in boys centre around:

a) resolution of the Oedipus complex.

b) resolution of the Electra complex.

c) the question of androgeny.

d) defence mechanisms.

7 The New Guinea tribe studied by Margaret Mead who appeared to show opposite sex-role behaviour were the:

a) Arapesh.

b) Mundugumor.

c) Samoans.

d) Tchambuli.

8 Kohlberg's second stage of gender identity is:

a) gender stability.

b) gender constancy.

c) basic gender identity.

d) gender awareness.

9 Bem found that it was most psychologically healthy to engage in behaviour which:

a) was typical of your own sex.

b) was typical of the other sex.

c) was characteristic of neither sex.

d) included characteristics from both sexes.

10 Williams found that the introduction of television made children's sex-role behaviour:

a) more stereotyped.

b) more variable.

c) more like other family members.

d) more emotionally oriented.

11 The idiographic approach looks at:

a) small groups of people.

b) each individual.

c) large groups of people.

d) animals.

12 The ego works on the:

a) pleasure principle.

b) unconscious principle.

c) reality principle.

d) oedipus complex.

13 Eysenck was a:

a) trait theorist.

b) type theorist.

c) humanist.

d) behaviourist.

14 Projection is a:

a) form of learning.

b) type of dream.

c) defence mechanism.

d) stage of development.

15 Libido is a:

a) death wish.

b) life force.

c) defence mechanism.

d) stage of development.

16 Eysenck argued that the basic features of personality were:

a) inherited.

b) learned.

c) a combination of genetic inheritance and learning.

d) developed throughout life.

17 Eysenck identified aspects of personality using:

a) psychoanalysis.

b) factor analysis.

c) imprinting.

d) EEG traces.

18 Cattell identified:

a) 8 major source traits.

b) 3 major source traits.

c) 16 major source traits.

d) 32 major source traits.

19 Carl Rogers is considered to be:

a) a humanistic theorist.

b) a trait theorist.

c) a psychoanalyst.

d) a behaviourist.

20 A phenomenological approach:

a) looks at how each individual makes sense of their world.

b) looks for characteristics which groups of people have in common.

c) looks at the influences of childhood.

d) concentrates on personality traits.

21 Tests that measure mental characteristics are known as:

a) psychological tests.

b) phenomenological tests.

c) psychoanalytical tests.

d) psychometric tests.

22 Rogers's Q-sort technique assesses:

a) the relationship between the self concept and the ideal self.

b) levels of IQ.

c) creative thinking.

d) behavioural problems.

23 A test that measures what it is supposed to measure is said to be:

a) invalid.

b) reliable.

c) valid.

d) predictive.

24 Kelly developed the:

a) personal construct theory.

b) psychoanalytic theory.

c) behaviourist theory.

d) frustration-aggression hypothesis.

25 The normal distribution curve was first identified by:

a) Binet.

b) Galton.

c) Freud.

d) Kelly.

26 The occupational personality questionnaire is designed for:

a) army recruitment.

b) airforce recruitment.

c) schools assessment.

d) job selection.

27 Terman's calculation for intelligence is:

a) $IQ = \frac{\text{chronological age}}{\text{mental age}} \times 100$

b) $IQ = \frac{\text{mental age}}{\text{chronological age}} \times 100$

c) $IQ = \frac{75}{50} \times 100$

d) $IQ = \frac{50}{75} \times 100$

28 One criticism of the army beta tests was that they were:

a) culturally biased.

b) inaccurate.

c) unable to be used on other sections of the population.

d) difficult to administer.

29 Which of the following tests are used in occupational testing?

a) sociability tests.

b) job aptitude and ability tests.

c) personality tests.

d) (b) and (c) above.

30 Idiographic tests assess:

a) the distinctive characteristics of one person.

b) the mental abilities of a group.

c) animal intelligence.

d) levels of motivation.

31 Which of the following areas of the brain is thought to be responsible for homeostasis?

a) the pons.

b) corpus callosum.

c) cerebrum.

d) hypothalamus.

32 Approach-avoidance conflict occurs when we are:

a) afraid.

b) given attractive goals.

c) given both attractive and negative goals.

d) given negative goals.

33 Internal locus of control means:

a) seeing events as being outside of ones control.

b) seeing oneself as being responsible for making events happen.

c) being a dominant personality.

d) being anxious.

34 Self-efficacy is a term used to describe:

a) the amount of belief you have in your own competence.

b) over-eating.

c) levels of motivation.

d) a lack of self-confidence.

35 Learned helplessness occurs when an individual:

a) learns to be active.

b) learns to be aggressive.

c) learns to be passive and powerless.

d) learns to be dominant.

36 Cognitive therapy aims to get people to:

a) change the way they interpret events.

b) look back to their childhood.

c) relearn certain behaviours through operant conditioning.

d) eliminate phobias.

37 Scapegoating occurs when we:

a) blame someone else for our own frustrations and aggression.

b) blame ourselves when something goes wrong.

c) copy prejudiced behaviour.

d) dislike certain social groups.

38 Affiliative needs are:

a) biological needs.

b) needs for relationships with other people.

c) monetary needs.

d) economic needs.

39 Stratton and Swaffer found that mothers who physically abused their children:

a) saw their children's' behaviour as normal.

b) saw their children's' behaviour as being uncontrollable.

c) had naughty children.

d) generally had children who were better behaved than other children.

40 The ventro-medial nucleus is located in the:

a) angular gyrus.

b) pons.

c) brain stem.

d) hypothalamus.

Section 5 - Social Psychology

In this section, we will look at the different ways that we can come to understand other people, and how they in their turn can influence how we act. Throughout our lives we encounter other people, and we develop ideas about what they are like, whether we like them or not, what they think of us, and how they expect us to behave. Social psychology involves the study of all of these areas.

We will begin this section by looking at interpersonal perception: how we see the other people around us, and the way that we develop certain types of attitudes rather than others. Next, we will examine the processes by which we communicate with other people.

We will then go on to look at social influences and how we can affect each others' behaviour, before finally looking at how social groups and social beliefs affect our experience.

Chapter 17 - Interpersonal perception

In this chapter, we will look at some of the ways that we perceive other people. When we meet someone for the first time, we don't have a completely open mind about what they are like. Instead, we use our previous experience and personal constructs to interpret their behaviour, and to compare them with other people that we have known.

Psychology in Action

Interpersonal perception is usually an important factor in job interviews, and may determine the outcome of the situation. For most of us, our first experience is as an interviewee. Besides finding out what the company has to offer, and presenting our formal skills, we also take part in a two-way interpersonal dialogue. On the one hand, we are trying to show, in our dress, speech and manner, that we are the right person for the job, while on the other hand, the interviewer, by the way she presents herself, is displaying an image of the company for our appraisal.

Given the general economic climate, our perception of the interviewer is only likely to be important if it deviates in a negative way from the image we expect. Our own presentation is more important. We cannot do much to alter our height or attractiveness but we can, and consciously or unconsciously often do, alter our accent and form of speech, what we wear and how we move or sit. This can lead to us sitting stiffly upright (especially if we normally slump about) and talking in a stilted manner, which will doubtless increase our nervousness.

It is fine to argue that we should not need to adopt mannerisms and dress that may be alien to us, but from the point of view of the employer it does at least show that we are willing and she will want to employ people who can fit into the prevailing work environment and maybe deal with clients or the public. The interviewer needs to perceive that we have the level of social competence that the job requires.

Implicit personality theory

A considerable amount of research in social psychology has been concerned with the pre-set assumptions that people hold about each other. These are often known as **implicit personality theories**. They are implicit, because we are rarely aware of them, while they still maintain an influence over our behaviour; and they are personality theories because they amount to a complete view of what people are like, not perhaps formed in the same way as those personality theories which we looked at in the last chapter, but just as influential in our thinking and attitudes.

We often find that we will tend to group together sets of characteristics: for instance, if a man was described as being 'miserly', we wouldn't just take from that the idea that he was reluctant to part with his money. We would also tend to think that he had other personality traits as well, such as being bad-tempered and unsociable. Someone, on the other hand, who was described as 'kind' would very likely be judged as friendly and generous as well. These characteristics group together to form whole theories about what personalities are like.

Forming impressions of others

In 1946, Solomon Asch discovered that some descriptions of people seem to influence our judgements about them more than others. He gave a group of research participants two lists of words to study, each list describing a different person. Person A was described as being intelligent, warm, skilful, industrious, determined, practical and cautious. Person B was described as being determined, cold, cautious, skilful, practical, industrious and intelligent. Participants were then asked to rate person A and person B on a number of personality characteristics, like generosity, kindness and humour. How would you have rated them? What impression have you formed of these two people?

You may have noticed that the two lists contain exactly the same words except for 'warm' in the first list and 'cold' in the second. So you might expect that the two lists would produce roughly the same results, but Asch, discovered that they had made a remarkable effect on a participant's impressions. A was described as being generous by 90% of participants and humorous by over 75%. Person B, however, was only thought to be generous and humorous by 10% of participants.

Kelley's study

A similar experiment was performed by Harold Kelley (1950) when he told a class of students that they would be receiving a new instructor for their class discussion and that they would be expected to assess this instructor at the end of the session. Before the class began, a biographical sketch of the instructor was passed around to students, giving details of his teaching experience and character. However, unknown to the students, two sketches were passed around. Half of the students received a passage with a description of the instructor as a 'rather cold person', whilst the other half received an identical passage which described him as a 'rather warm person'. The results were conclusive. The students who had been informed that he was a 'warm' person rated him as being more sociable, considerate and good-natured. 56% of this group, took part in the class discussion, whereas only 32% of the other group did. This single pair of traits had completely altered the research participants' impression of the instructor.

Central traits

This led Asch to conclude that some traits were much more influential than others. He called these traits **central traits**. Asch used several different pairs of traits in similar studies, so that he could find out which were the most powerful in affecting our judgements of others. For instance, he inserted the words 'polite' and 'blunt' in the list mentioned above, in the same positions as 'warm' and 'cold', and found that they didn't alter the research participants' perception much at all. Those two traits, then, were not central.

It may be, though, that those traits didn't alter the participants' perception because they weren't important in that particular **context**. In Kelley's experiment, it was important to the students that the visiting instructor be warm towards them, so they probably took more notice of that characteristic than they would of 'polite'. If a lecturer is cold towards her students, it can make a great deal of difference to how much they take in, but whether or not she is polite may make very little difference to their learning.

Kelley's experiment is important in two respects. Firstly, it used a much more realistic set-up than that used by Asch and, secondly, the outcome reveals that people's impressions of others may affect the way they behave towards them.

The halo effect

Asch wasn't the first person to discover that descriptive words can alter one's impression of a person. In 1920, Thorndike found that, if research participants were given a description of a fictitious person containing one or two positive traits, like kindness and generosity, they tended to see this person as having many more positive characteristics as well. In other words, they saw the person as being on the whole a 'good' person. Thorndike called this the **halo effect**. The reverse is true when negative traits, like cruelty, are presented to the participant. Then, the participant tends to see the person as being generally 'bad'. Symonds found in 1925 that the halo effect seems to be at its strongest when the person making the judgement knows relatively little about the person being judged, or when they are trying to evaluate the person in terms of moral standards (e.g. to say how good or bad they are as people).

The importance of first impressions

It seems that, not only are the number of positive and negative traits important, but the time at which they are presented to us is also important. Asch pioneered some very interesting research along these lines when he investigated what happens when people are given contradictory information about someone else. Imagine being told that a casual acquaintance is lazy, fickle and careless by one of your friends and then being told that the same person is studious and thoughtful, by another friend. How would you come to terms with this contradictory information?

First impressions

Asch discovered that, for most people, this situation creates a problem which they resolve by judging the person on the first information they receive, and ignoring what comes later. This is the **primacy effect**.

It seems to hold true unless there is a time lag between the first piece of information and the second. If this is the case, we are likely to remember the most recent description. This is known as the **recency effect**. From this research we can see that first impressions can be very important in creating the right image, especially if we are not likely to get a second chance to put forward a favourable image.

Stereotyping

We have mentioned that implicit personality theories are concerned with the unconscious predetermined ideas about people's characters that we hold. These ideas can also be extended to cover whole groups of people. When they are extended in this way they are called **stereotypes**. A stereotype occurs when we see all people who belong to a particular group as having the same characteristics. Although we may not be aware of stereotyping people, we do stereotype frequently. A person who says, 'Oh, so you're a feminist then' or, 'I didn't know that you were a student', is implying that knowing what group you belong to tells them quite a lot about you. This person must think she knows what characteristics a feminist is likely to possess and so she will tend to pre-judge the 'feminist' according to her own ideas. The most common pre-judgements, or stereotypes, of groups in our society occur in relation to males and females, different racial groups, and sexual orientations of groups, such as homosexuals or lesbians. Other groups may be stereotyped according to age, or religion, or any other defining characteristic.

Stereotypes probably arise out of a need to make sense of the vast amount of information about people that we have to cope with. As we can't possibly get to know every member of a particular political group, for example, we tend to 'lump them all together'. But although, on the surface it may seem as though stereotyping is a practical way of condensing lots of information, it can have serious effects, especially when a group of people are seen in a negative way. Women's search for career work in our society, for example is hindered by the popular stereotypes of women being 'soft', 'sensitive' and 'fickle'. As, of course, the black person's search for work is hindered by the negative images sometimes applied to black people as a group.

Sex stereotyping

Sex stereotyping is the process of judging people by characteristics which are seen to be common to all males or to all females. Lloyd *et al.* (1980) took four 6 month old babies, two boys and two girls, and dressed them all half the time in boy's clothes and half the time in girl's. When they were dressed as 'girls' they wore frilly pink dresses and were called Jane, and when they were 'boys' they wore blue suits and were called John. Eight mothers, who all had first born babies of around the same age, were then asked individually to play with the children for approximately ten minutes. The results were quite startling; when the baby was thought to be a boy it was offered a hammer-shaped rattle as its first toy and was encouraged to be adventurous and active; when the baby was thought to be a girl, it was given a soft, pink doll to play with, was encouraged to stay quiet and was frequently told how pretty it was. A similar report was made by Rubin *et al.* (1974), when they interviewed the parents of 0-24 hour old babies, fifteen of which were girls and fifteen boys. They were asked to rate their babies on a number of things and even though there was no noticeable difference in the height and weight, etc. of the babies, the girls were seen as being softer, smaller, having finer features and being less attentive than the boys.

These differences between the sexes are often reinforced in the books which children receive at school. On April 6th 1982, an article by J. Penrose appeared in the *Guardian* in which she claimed that the Ladybird Key Words Reading scheme was guilty of reproducing traditional sexual stereotypes. Of the two major characters in the book, Peter and Jane, Peter made all the important decisions, while Jane looked on; Peter took charge more often and spoke more frequently than Jane. He was also described as being very active and adventurous, while Jane was portrayed as totally passive. Perhaps it isn't surprising, therefore, that we find such rigid stereotyping amongst adult populations! When Goldberg *et al.* (1968) asked female students to rate several articles written by people in professional fields, they found that if the students thought the article had been written by a woman, they gave it a lower grade than if they thought a man had produced it. This may have been typical of that particular time, though, and more recent attitudes may be different, because a similar study performed by Mischel in 1974 found that both men and women rated articles written by women for a female-dominated occupation as being more competent than the same article written by a male and vice versa.

Racial stereotyping

Ideas about characteristics which can be attributed to different ethnic or racial groups seem to be equally abundant. In 1933, Katz and Braly took 100 American students and gave them a list of racial groups and a list of words describing personality. Their task was to state the five characteristics which they most commonly associated with each group. The results revealed that many of the students agreed on the characteristics to be associated with each group, even though many of them hadn't had any direct experience of those people. For instance, 48 students thought that Americans were more industrious and altogether nicer than Turks, who were seen as cruel. The stereotype of black people was of a happy-go-lucky group, who were also superstitious and musical. These studies were repeated twenty years later by Gilbert *et al.* (1951) and forty years later by Karling *et al.* (1969), using similar groups of students and, although these students seemed less willing to make snap judgements, stereotyping was still evident. One reason for the slight change in the results may be a greater reluctance on the part of students to take part in stereotyping because of an increased awareness of the social problems this can cause.

Attribution

As we saw in the previous chapter, psychologists like Kelly believe that we are continually trying to make sense of the world around us. In particular, we try to understand and predict people's behaviour. **Attribution theory** is concerned with the rules we follow in trying to explain people's behaviour and everyday events. The basic idea behind attribution theory is that we continually try to discover what has *caused* a person to behave as they have and how this is linked with events that follow.

It seems that people even try to explain the activity of inanimate objects, like squares and triangles, by attributing causality in the movement of one object to another (e.g. saying that one object has caused the other object to move). Heider and Simmel (1944) showed research participants cartoons of shapes moving around. Typically a large triangle, a small triangle and a circle were used. At the end of the film, participants had to relate the events in the film back to the experimenter. Research participants commonly interpreted the events in terms of human experiences, seeing the larger triangle as a bully who chased the smaller, weaker, defenceless triangle. Some even imagined elaborate scenes where the shapes were people (e.g. mother, father, child) trying to communicate with each other. It follows that, if people readily attribute such attitudes and characteristics to *shapes*, then the tendency to do this with other people must be even greater.

Dispositional and situational attributions

Heider was one of the major proponents of attribution theory and he felt that, in making our decisions about the likely causes of an action or event, we take two things into account. Firstly, we try to decide whether a person has acted the way they have because of their personality characteristics (this is called **dispositional attribution** because it refers to a person's internal dispositions or characteristics); or whether the situation they are in at the time has caused this action (this is called **situational attribution**). He claimed that we take these two things into consideration because they have important consequences for our relations with people. If we thought that an air crash had occurred because of bad weather (situational attribution), we would view the pilot in a more favourable light than if we thought his or her negligence had caused the accident (dispositional attribution). Similarly, on a day to day level, we might wonder whether a person is criticising our work because it is really bad, or whether it is just because they are jealous.

Covariance

According to Kelley (1967), when we are making these decisions, we follow a definite set of rules. Firstly, we try to decide whether a person or actor is responsible for their own actions, whether someone else is responsible, or whether the situation itself is the cause. Imagine the following scene: you are sitting on a beach on holiday and you notice a boy that you have seen around often, waving furiously from a dinghy, at people on the beach. You immediately wonder why he is waving. Is he just enjoying himself or is he is danger? The decision you make here may mean the difference between life and death for this boy. In everyday life, too, we often need to make decisions. You may find yourself having to decide whether your next door neighbour's crying has been set off by someone attacking her, or whether it is another fit of depression; or whether someone at work is being nice to you because they genuinely like you or just because the situation calls for polite behaviour. No matter what the situation, Kelley believes that we will try to work out what is happening and in order to do this, we need to have more information.

Behavioural consensus

This information falls into three categories. Firstly we need to know if other people are behaving in the same manner as the person in question. In the case of the boy in the dinghy, we might ask ourselves if other people are waving in the same manner and if they are, we may then conclude that his behaviour is due to the particular situation and not his own disposition. If someone seems to be behaving in the same way as lots of other people, we say that their behaviour has high **consensus**. If their behaviour has high consensus then we are likely to infer that their behaviour has been caused by the situation. If their behaviour has low consensus, i.e. they seem to be the only ones behaving in this way then we are more likely to see their behaviour being the result of their own character.

But, if we decided that the boy in the dinghy was the only one waving at the shore, it could still be possible that he was in danger and that the situation was the cause of his behaviour.

Behavioural consistency

So secondly, we need to know how **consistent** his behaviour is. In other words, does he usually behave like this? If his behaviour is consistent, in other words, if he often waves to people on the shore, then we might infer that he has caused his own actions and is fooling around. If however, it's the first time (low consistency) that he has waved then we might think he's in danger - the situation has caused him to act in this way.

Distinctive behaviour

Finally, we need to know how a person behaves towards different people. Does he behave in this way only in the company of his friend who is with him in the dinghy (in which case we say his behaviour is highly **distinctive**) or does he behave in this way with everyone (low distinctiveness)? If we decide on the first possibility, then his behaviour may well be due to the presence of his friend.

Sometimes, though, we may not have access to all three sources of information, and our judgements of the reasons for other people's behaviour may be wrong. This difficulty has to be faced by judges in courts, when deciding whether a person is responsible for their actions or whether the actions were due to circumstances beyond their control. Consider this example: Steve got into a fight at a disco. Only one other boy was involved (low consensus). Steve already has a record for fighting (high consistency) and he threatened several boys before he turned on Paul (low distinctiveness). If you were a judge in court, what decision would you reach? Now suppose that you discover that everyone reacts to Paul in the same way (high consensus), Steve rarely provokes people (low consistency) and he has never hit anyone before (high distinctiveness), how would this alter your decision?

The discounting rule

Although there is some evidence that we do work out the causes of events like this, we sometimes follow another rule: the **discounting rule**. According to Kelley (1972), this states that if enough evidence suggests that the situation is primarily responsible for a particular action, then we will tend to discount any dispositional evidence which we may encounter. If we discover that a plane has crashed in bad weather, we are more likely to see this as being the cause of the crash and so will tend to ignore information which may suggest that the pilot was to blame. If, however, we feel that a person's actions have occurred *despite* situational pressures, as in the case of someone who speaks out against a particular group despite pressures from the group to keep quiet, then we infer that their action is due to their internal disposition. If, as we are suggesting here, we sometimes ignore some information because other information appears to be more valuable, we may in fact be making biased judgements.

Attributional bias

The two principles of Kelley's, covariance and discounting, which we have looked at, show us what decisions we reach if we follow the information we possess logically. Unfortunately, it seems that we are not always so logical, even when we have access to such information. For one thing, when judging other people's behaviour, we are much more likely to see it as being the result of their own character rather than the situation they are in. In other words, we tend to see others as being responsible for their own behaviour. This type of bias is known as the **fundamental attribution error**. When it comes to our own behaviour, however, we are much more likely to notice how we are influenced by the situation at the time.

Examples of bias

An experiment by Jones and Harris (1967) demonstrated this bias. Research participants were given a talk on racial segregation by someone who had been told to argue either that it was a 'good' thing or that it was a 'bad' thing by the experimenters. Despite the fact that the participants were aware that the person was only arguing what they had been instructed to, they were still convinced that he believed his arguments.

There are obviously some occasions when we are more prone to bias in our judgements than others. One of these occasions is when we are dealing with people whose actions have important consequences for us. Jones and Davis (1965) say that if a person's actions are **hedonically relevant** to us, in other words, if they are likely to affect us in some way, then we are more likely to see that person as being responsible for their actions. If his or her actions seem to be aimed specifically at us, then the tendency to attribute the cause of their behaviour to dispositions is even stronger.

We said earlier that knowing whether a person is alone in his or her actions can provide us with a valuable source of information but it appears that, even when we have access to this information, we don't always take notice of it. Nisbett and Borgida (1975) told some people that they had been unsuccessful in getting research participants who would be willing to take part in an experiment on 'helping behaviour'. They then told these people that they hoped to enlist the help of a particular person for this same experiment and asked them how successful they thought they would be. Despite the discouraging information they'd been given earlier, they nearly all predicted that this person would take part.

Finally, according to Jones and Davis (1965), if people behave as we expect them to behave then we are likely to think that their actions are the result of the situation and so do not really tell us very much about their character. However, if people behave in an unexpected manner, we are more likely to see this as being an indication of their real character. Someone who turned up late for a meal, keeping everybody waiting, but didn't bother to apologise would seem to be giving us more of a clue about their character than someone who turned up on time as expected.

17.1 Experimenter effects and stereotyping

Experimenter effects occur when an experimenter influences the outcome of an experiment, without meaning to. This can happen in several ways: because the experimenter knows what to expect and so unconsciously encourages the research participants to come out with the right answer, or just because the participants react differently to different experimenters.

From among the members of your class, divide yourselves into pairs, with each member of the pair being as different from the other as possible, for instance, in height, sex, skin colour, or dress. Draw up a very simple set of five or six questions that you can ask people - perhaps about recent TV programmes or something else which seems very ordinary. Make sure, though, that the questions include at least one which asks about the participant's attitude to one of the characteristics of one of the partners (but not the other). For instance, if one of you is a 'punk', one of the questions could be about 'punks', and what the person thinks of them.

Go along to a shopping centre, or some other busy place, and ask your questions to as many people as possible. Make sure that each partner gets to ask the same number of people.

When you have finished, compare the answers that you have each obtained on the 'sensitive' question. Did people tailor their answers to the person asking the question?

How could you investigate experimenter effects more deeply?

What does this tell us about the need for controls in social psychology experiments?

Interpersonal attraction

There are several different factors involved in the ways that we come to like or dislike others. Some of the main ones are: **familiarity**, **similarity of attitudes**, **physical attraction**, and **reciprocal liking**.

Familiarity

Zajonc (1968) performed several studies, in which he found that people readily formed very negative attitudes towards a totally imaginary group of people, the 'Wallonians'. Even though the research participants had no direct experience of 'Wallonians', they were prepared to attribute unpleasant qualities to them simply on the basis that they were unfamiliar. Zajonc also found that people would come to like even quite neutral things like nonsense syllables just because they were familiar to them.

Zajonc argued that familiarity forms an important basis for interpersonal attraction: we tend to like people that we see often, perhaps because it means that we see a more complete picture of that individual and their behaviour. Bramel (1969) suggested that we tend to like those people whom we can trust and whose behaviour we can predict, and it is likely that we will be less able to predict the behaviour of relative strangers than of people who are familiar to us.

Similarity of attitudes

As you have probably noticed, we tend to like people who hold similar attitudes and beliefs to ourselves, perhaps because we find it rewarding to find other people who agree with us. There have been several studies which have supported this idea, showing that people generally prefer to make their friends from others like themselves.

There seems to be little doubt that if we approve of someone else's attitudes or opinions, we are more likely to become friendly with that person. Newcomb (1961) performed a study of university students, in which they were provided with rent-free accommodation in return for helping with the research. Newcomb collected information about their likes, dislikes and attitudes, and then placed some of the research participants in rooms with others who shared their beliefs, and some with those who had opposing views. Of the first group, 58% developed good friendships with their partners, while only 25% of the second group did.

Newcomb repeated the study the following year, with another set of students, but this time it was found that the most important factor which affected whether a friendship had developed by the end of the college year wasn't their similarity of attitudes but how close they lived to each other! This research supports both the idea that we like those whom we consider to be similar to ourselves *and* the idea that we tend to like those who live in close proximity.

In 1951, Schachter showed that people who seem to agree with everyone else in a group are often seen to be more likeable than those who go against the group's beliefs. One study involved members of a student group making their attitudes towards a juvenile delinquent known and offering ideas for possible treatment. Most of the group saw the juvenile 'sympathetically' but Schachter arranged for a 'stooge' to express a strong unsympathetic attitude towards the delinquent's behaviour. This stooge was clearly disliked by the rest of the group. In 1959 Schachter offered an explanation as to why we are attracted to those who are like us. He suggested that we feel more at ease and less anxious in such company. Research participants who were asked with whom they would like to wait whilst they awaited an unpleasant experience of some kind, preferred to wait with others in a similar position to themselves, who were also awaiting the unpleasant event.

Physical attraction

Although many of us would say that appearance doesn't matter when you are choosing friends and partners, research indicates that we are mistaken. Walster (1966) arranged a computer-dance for students, placing couples together at random. Each person was rated by a group of judges for their attractiveness and, after two and a half hours, was asked to complete a questionnaire giving their opinions of their partner. Six months later the students were contacted again, and asked if they'd seen their partner since. Of those that had, physical attraction had been the most important reason for remaining in contact, and not whether they'd held similar attitudes and opinions. The judgements of their attractiveness had been pretty accurate in predicting which students would go on another date!

Do couples match each other?

According to a study by Murstein (1972), people tend to choose a partner of similar levels of attractiveness. He asked a group of people to judge the attractiveness of 99 engaged or courting couples. Another 99 photos of men were placed at random with 99 photos of women. Each photo was rated on their level of attractiveness. The results were clear the couples who were going out together were rated as more similar in levels of attractiveness than were the couples matched at random. You may sometimes see illustrations of these findings in the 'just married' columns of your local newspaper, where couples often look very alike.

Although the idea of what is 'attractive' is different in different cultures, physical attractiveness seems to be a highly-valued quality in most cultures. In Western society people who are thought to be attractive are also considered to have other endearing qualities. Dion *et al.* (1972) showed college students photographs of children who had been naughty. She found that the student readily accepted that unattractive children had committed the crimes but were less prepared to accept that good looking children had committed them. Attractive people are also more likely to get jobs, and other people are more likely to think highly of their work. Clifford and Walster (1973) asked teachers from 400 schools to read a report relating to a particular child (the child wasn't known to them). All the cards that the teacher received were identical except for the fact that some had a picture of an attractive boy or girl attached and others had a picture of an unattractive boy or girl attached. The results were very disturbing, because the teachers judged the attractive children, of either sex, to be potentially brighter and have higher intelligence scores than the unattractive children. This has important implications for how children are assessed in schools.

There are several other factors which seem to affect how much we like other people. We tend to like people who appear competent or those who benefit us in some way, and there is another factor which we are going to look at in this section called reciprocal liking.

Reciprocal liking

This occurs when we like other people because we know that they like us. You may have experienced this yourself. Two interesting findings have emerged from research in this area. Firstly, how much we like someone who shows us affection depends very much on how we feel about ourselves. Secondly, the picture of mutual attraction is a little more complex than we probably realise!

Let's look at the first point. Walster (1965) carried out a study in which a female research participant was made to wait in a room and whilst she was waiting, an attractive male student (planted by the experimenter) chatted to her and eventually asked her for a date. The female research participant was then called in to complete two tests as part of the experiment, the results of which were relayed to her. Half of the participants were made to feel that they had performed quite badly and so felt dejected, whilst the other half were given positive feedback about their performance. At this point, the participants were requested to rate five people for their attractiveness, one of whom was the student from the waiting room. The results were conclusive: those participants who felt dejected rated their admirer as being more attractive than those who saw themselves more positively.

Ethical discussion

Walster's (1965) study of attraction involved deliberately manipulating research participants' levels of self-esteem in order to find out if that made a stooge participant more attractive.

Was this an ethically acceptable thing to do?

The second point was made by Aronson and Linder (1965) when they had conducted a study in which a research participant was made to overhear someone talking about her on several different occasions. The person talking about her had been instructed by the experimenter to follow one of four patterns of conversation. They had to make continually nice remarks about her; to start off making nice remarks but become increasingly critical; to start off making unpleasant remarks but gradually make more favourable ones; or to make continually unfavourable remarks. We might expect that the person continually making nice remarks would be seen to be the most likeable and the person making unfavourable remarks, the most unlikable. But, in fact, it was those who had begun unfavourably and then changed their minds, who were rated as being the nicest. Those who had started off liking her but became more critical were viewed in the most unfavourable light. There is perhaps a lesson to be learned from this. People who begin a relationship by being extremely nice to their partners but gradually stop making an effort may be less likely to have a lasting relationship, compared to those who become increasingly more considerate!

Attitudes and prejudice

An attitude can be defined as 'a relatively permanent disposition towards another person or event in our lives'. In other words, it's a specific way of looking at someone or something. On a simple level, an attitude may be a liking or disliking for something. On a more complex level it can include a whole variety of beliefs and feelings for a particular issue. Knowing the attitudes that someone holds can be an important factor in whether we come to like or dislike that person.

17.2 Attitude questionnaire

It is often an interesting exercise to try to develop an attitude questionnaire - but it isn't always as easy as it looks! (For a good book on this, try *Questionnaire design and Attitude Measurement*, by Oppenheim).

The first thing that you need to do is to decide what you are trying to find out. You need to be very clear about this before you start. Then you need to decide what format your answers will take. Will they be 'yes/no', open-ended (where anyone can write what they want), or on a scale (like a five-point scale)? What are the advantages and disadvantages of each technique?

Now, you need to decide which questions you will ask. Is it a good idea for the purpose of your questionnaire to be obvious to your research participants? If not, how are you going to disguise it? What problems might this cause?

When you have written the questions, test them out on a group of people who don't know what your questionnaire is about. Did they give the answers that you expected? What difficulties did they find in understanding the questions? Did you have to change your questions at all? Why?

Now think about the research participants that you are going to use. Who should they be? How are you going to get the best possible sample? What kind of sample did you get in the end? What do you consider the main kinds of problems with sampling are?

Once you have administered your questionnaire, how will you analyse the results? Can you present the results in a simple graph or bar-chart? What problems did you find in sorting out the data that you have obtained?

Will the results that you have obtained really let you know what attitudes people hold? What other things could have influenced the answers that you received? How could you have improved the questionnaire?

Components of an attitude

Psychologists consider that there are three components, or parts, to any attitude: the cognitive, the affective, and the behavioural (or cognitive). The **cognitive component** of an attitude involves our beliefs: the reasons that we can put forward to justify why we feel the way that we do. The **affective component** is the part of an attitude which has to do with feelings, such as whether we like or dislike something, or whether it makes us feel angry. And the **behavioural component** is how the attitude is likely to affect what we do: whether we are likely to take action in accordance with a particular attitude or not.

Attitudes are not always consistent. A study by LaPiere, in 1934, involved travelling around the USA with a Chinese couple at a time when there was a strong prejudice against the Chinese. They visited over two hundred hotels and restaurants, but only encountered one case of prejudice. However, when he returned home, LaPiere wrote to all of these establishments asking whether or not they would take Chinese guests, and 92% of those that replied to the letter (that is, 47% of the 'sample') indicated that they would not! In this case, it seems that the cognitive component of the attitude was not consistent with the behavioural component.

Cognitive dissonance

Even though we may sometimes act in an inconsistent manner, we seem to find it important that the cognitive parts of our attitudes are consistent with each other. In 1957, Festinger put forward his theory of **cognitive dissonance**, in which he argued that if we come to recognise that two or more of our attitudes contradict each other, it puts us in an uncomfortable state of tension, and we will need to change one or other of the attitudes so that the dissonance disappears. (In many ways, this is similar to the way that we adjust our memories and perceptions to fit in with our existing schemata, which we looked at in Chapter 11.)

A study by Festinger and Carlsmith, in 1959, investigated this. They gave research participants a really boring task to do which consisted of filling and refilling a tray of 12 spools with one hand. After half an hour, the same research participants were given a board with 48 square pegs. They had to turn each peg a quarter of the way round for a further half hour. Once they had finished, one set of participants was given one dollar each to go and tell the participants in the waiting room that the task was really interesting. Another set of participants were given twenty dollars to do the same, and a control group didn't receive any money at all, and wasn't asked to speak to the others in the waiting room.

When the research participants were asked later how they had found the experiment, Festinger found that those who had had one dollar had actually come to believe that the task was interesting! But, those paid twenty dollars still thought it was as boring as ever, as did the control group. Festinger concluded that this was because the one dollar reward had not been enough to justify lying about the task, and so the participants were faced with cognitive dissonance. The only way that they could reduce it was to convince themselves that the task had been more interesting than it really was, as that would justify their lying to the waiting participants. Those who had been paid twenty dollars didn't have to justify their lying, because they could always tell themselves that they had done it for the money.

Another study showed how we sometimes modify our attitudes depending on circumstances. Brehm (1956) asked research participants to rate a set of products on an eight-point scale of attractiveness. He claimed to be carrying out market research, and the participants were told that they would be given one of the products as a gift, in return for participating. The gifts which the participants were offered had been selected so that half of the participants had to choose between one attractive and one unattractive product, while the other half were offered a choice between two which had been rated as equally desirable.

After they had chosen, the research participants were asked to read an advertising report on the products and rate them again. He found no change in the ratings from the group who had had to choose between an attractive and an unattractive product; but the group who had had to choose between two attractive choices had changed their ratings. Now, the one which they had chosen was rated as more attractive than the previous one. It seemed that they needed to find some way of justifying their choice, and so they came to regard the one that they had chosen as more attractive.

Prejudice

A prejudice is an attitude which we have developed on the basis of a pre-judgement of a person or situation. We can have positive prejudices or negative ones: we may, for instance, be prejudiced towards a particular group of people and inclined to see everything that they do as good. Mostly, though, when we refer to prejudice we mean a negative set of attitudes towards a particular person or group of people, in which we judge them more harshly than we would other people showing the same behaviour.

Group pressures

One explanation of how prejudices develop was put forward by Pettigrew, in 1958. He argued that group pressures, such as ideas about what is acceptable in a particular sub-culture or social group, play an important part in both the production and the maintenance of prejudice. He carried out a study in the USA, in which he visited four towns in the North and four in the South, telling the research participants that he was investigating the effects of the media on attitudes. Instead, he was collecting notes on racial prejudices.

In addition, he gave each research participant a personality test. The results revealed that the Southerners were far more prejudiced than the Northerners, even though there were no personality differences between the two groups. At the time prejudice was accepted and condoned much more in the South than it was in the North.

The scapegoat theory

Another psychological explanation assumes that frustration is the basis for our prejudice. In complex societies many situations occur which leave us feeling frustrated and the theory is that this frustration can easily turn to anger. We may direct this anger at people or objects less powerful than ourselves, instead of seeing either ourselves or the situation as the cause of our frustration. In other words, we use different groups in our society as scapegoats to take the blame for our failures and frustrations.

A number of studies have supported this idea. Weatherley (1961) lowered research participants' self-esteem by insulting them while they were completing a questionnaire. He then asked them to look at a series of pictures, some being of Jewish people, and tell a story about each of them. He had previously given them another questionnaire designed to measure the extent of their anti-Jewish feelings and he discovered that those with highly anti-Jewish attitudes revealed more aggression when telling stories about the Jewish pictures than they did of the other photos. Not all studies support this **scapegoat theory** though. Ashmore (1970) reviewed many studies in this area and found that while some supported the notion of scapegoating, others did not.

The prejudiced personality

A second set of psychological studies of prejudice suggests that prejudice occurs in some people more than others because those people have personality deficiencies. They may be extremely weak characters or highly neurotic, for example. Research on the prejudiced personality has been influenced by the work of Adorno and Frenkel-Brunswick (1950) in a book called **The Authoritarian Personality**. They began their research into prejudice because of the atrocious treatment of Jews in Nazi Germany, and came up with a questionnaire designed to measure a person's potential for prejudice, which came to be known as the F-scale.

The following statements are examples from the questionnaire. A person in agreement with each statement would receive a high score on a scale of fascism:

- Obedience and respect for authority are the most important virtues children should learn.
- Nobody ever learns anything really important except through suffering.
- What the youth needs is strict discipline, rugged determination and the will to win and fight for family and country.

Through interviewing and giving personality tests to those with a high score on the F-scale, these researchers were eventually able to describe a prejudiced personality.

Such a person was very authoritarian, in favour of strict law and order, supportive of traditional morals and customs, lacked independence of thought, saw issues as being very clear-cut, only valid from their own point of view, and was highly critical of others but not of themselves. Above all, those with this personality syndrome 'bow down' to people in power above them and try to control and manipulate those below them. An interesting point to note is that this type of personality often develops as a result of overly strict disciplinary techniques by parents. Adorno's research participants had parents who punished them severely at the slightest sign of disobedience, yet demanded unquestioning loyalty and were totally insensitive to and intolerant of the child's needs or wishes.

How can prejudice be reduced?

In modern societies people often seem to distrust strangers. Part of this may be due to lack of contact, which prevents us from getting to know them. It seems plausible then, that getting racial groups to mix together should reduce prejudice. Deutsch and Collins (1951) compared a housing estate in New York City where residents were allocated houses irrespective of race, with another estate in New jersey where black residents lived in different buildings to white. Their study supports the above idea because, of the white housewives interviewed on both estates, those on the mixed estate revealed that they had become less racially prejudiced. The white housewives who lived on the segregated estate claimed to have maintained, and in some cases increased, their level of prejudice.

Co-operation

The situation is almost certainly more complicated than this, however. Secord and Beckman (1974) argued that increased contact of black and white workers, for instance, reduces prejudice in areas relating to their work, but not in other areas. It may also reduce prejudice against some individuals but not against the group as a whole.

If people have to unite and pull together in the face of a common enemy or to solve a common problem, then prejudice is greatly reduced. Sherif *et al.* (1961) performed a study using two groups of twelve year old boy scouts attending a scout camp. The boys were randomly divided into two groups; one team was called the 'Bulldogs' and the other team was called the 'Red Devils'. Each group was given a series of tasks to solve together, such as building a bridge or making a fire. Once the boys within each group were working well together and a good team spirit had developed, the experimenters created a series of competitive tasks between the two groups. In order to increase the level of competitiveness, the winning teams were awarded prizes.

One event staged by the experimenters was a camp party. They planned it so that the Red Devils would arrive long before the Bulldogs and would have first choice of the food and drink. Some of the food was extremely nice and some of it was most unappetising. According to plan, the Red Devils ate all the best food before the Bulldogs arrived and a fight later broke out between the two groups. When it was obvious to the experimenters that intergroup competition had reached a high level, they tried to reduce tension by stopping the competitions. They found, however, that the trust which had previously existed between the two groups did not return. They continued to be suspicious of each other, even though they were not in direct competition. Prejudice was eventually reduced when the two groups were made to pull together on tasks which were seen to be necessary for the good of everyone. On one occasion, for example, the camp truck was made to break down and everyone had to help to get it going. Eventually boys from both groups made friends and hostility was reduced.

Other factors

As the need to pull together may arise infrequently, other conditions are important for the reduction of everyday prejudice. To meet people from other groups on a personal level is important, as it is also to see members of discriminated groups in high-status occupations. To receive information (particularly from the media) which breaks down the traditional stereotypes of these groups also helps, as does living in a society in which prejudice is actively discouraged. According to Cook (1978), if all these conditions exist then prejudice may be effectively reduced or even eradicated.

Meeting as equals breaks down prejudices

Summary

1 Implicit personality theories are used to form judgements about other people. These involve the grouping together of several characteristics.

2 Implicit personality theories may also lead to stereotyping of groups of people, on the basis of just one or two attributes.

3 Attribution is the process by which we provide reasons for other people's behaviour by ascribing particular causes to them. This can involve error or bias.

4 Some of the main factors in liking and attraction are familiarity, similarity, physical attraction, and reciprocal liking.

5 Any attitude has three components, which can vary in strength: a cognitive part, an affective part, and a behavioural part.

6 Cognitive dissonance occurs when two or more attitudes that we hold contradict each other. We tend to adjust our attitudes to remove the dissonance.

7 Prejudices are set pre-judgements of particular people or situations. They can be reduced by high social contact and by co-operation.

Chapter 18 - Communication

Throughout our lives, right from the moment that an infant cries to express hunger we are engaging in social interaction of one form or another. Virtually every time that we encounter another human being, some kind of social interaction will take place, whether it's getting on a bus and paying the fare for the journey, or socialising with friends. Interaction of any kind depends on our ability to **communicate** with other people. Without some method of transmitting intentions or signalling to other people, we wouldn't be able to interact socially at all.

Communication is passing information from one person to another. The information can be anything, from a grimace to a friend signalling that you are bored with listening to your teacher, to an elaborately-bound thesis presented by a postgraduate student which presents the outcome of several years research in a formal painstaking document which may only ever be read by a couple of other people, or anything in between.

Verbal communication

Human communication is different from that used by other animals, because of our highly developed languages. These allow us to communicate sophisticated or abstract ideas, and also to talk or write about people or objects which are not immediately present. We can discuss past events, we can develop ideas and theories about possible future happenings, and we can even develop ideas about things which don't exist and couldn't ever exist.

Without language, none of this would be possible. Try telling a friend that you lost a five pound note at the weekend and were worried that you wouldn't be able to pay your bus fares during the week, without using either words or signs which stand for words!

Communication which uses words is known as **verbal communication**, and it allows us to control social interaction in a very sophisticated manner. For instance, we can choose emotive words to describe something and so influence the attitude which our listener develops. You can see this very clearly if you look at the same news item in two papers with different political views, and look for differences in the words that they use (such as whether they refer to the ruling body of a particular country as a 'regime' or a 'government').

It isn't just the choice of words which is important in verbal communication. The types of sentences that we form and the ways that we construct them also make a difference. In Chapter 10 we looked at Bernstein's ideas on elaborated and restricted codes of language, and how these can affect how the individual is seen. We often find, too, that people react differently to different ways of using words. Your favourite writer, for instance, may be your favourite because he or she writes in a style that you particularly like. Although the overall meaning is the same, there is a world of difference between the two sentences: 'Goest thou to tonight's dance?', and 'Are you going to the dance tonight?'. The first sentence conjures up all sorts of ideas and impressions which are completely missing from the second one! So the *form* of the language, and the words used, are important parts of verbal communication.

Symbolic communication

The fact that verbal communication is **symbolic**, as we mentioned before, means that we can use words to talk about things which are not present, or which may not even actually exist. But there is more to it than that; words are flexible, in that we can combine them in all sorts of different ways to produce subtle, or not-so-subtle variations in meaning. We can generate new statements that haven't been said before, or we can organise information into different categories easily because we have a word that will summarise for us what that category is. We can't do any of these things with the kinds of communication which animals use.

One thing which is particularly interesting is the way that the few animals which have been taught to use language, like the apes which have learned to communicate using sign language for the deaf and dumb, have shown that they, too, are able to communicate with each other about things which are not actually present. If their trainer hides some attractive object with one of the chimpanzees watching, and then that chimpanzee is put in with another who was not able to see the hiding of the object, very often the first will communicate the hiding place to the second using sign language. When the second chimpanzee is let out, it goes straight to the hiding place and finds the object. Although this doesn't happen all the time, it seems to happen often enough for us to be fairly sure that the chimpanzees are using the language that they have learned symbolically, as humans do.

Using language to categorise

The fact that we can use language to develop categories, or to classify things into groups, allows us to store a great deal of information, and to identify how things relate to each other. If we were only able to deal with objects which are present, then we couldn't compare things very well, so we would find it very difficult to make broad generalisations about the world and things in it. But by using words as symbols, to stand either for objects, or for some quality which objects have (like warmth), we are able to compare, say, one source of warmth with another one, and to learn from this. So our ability to use language to represent the world seems to be the origin of our ability to understand and manipulate the world.

Language, though, is by no means the only method that we have for communicating. Animals communicate with one another frequently, and yet they do not have language at all. Humans communicate with one another on all sorts of levels, many of which are nothing to do with words: when you can tell that a friend is angry, for instance, it is often from a form of communication which doesn't require your friend to tell you in actual words. This we call **non-verbal communication** - communication without the use of words.

Non-verbal communication

Non-verbal communication is any method of communication which doesn't involve words, or symbols which stand for words. We use non-verbal communication quite unconsciously as we interact with other people. In doing so, we tend to use a wide variety of different signals known as cues. These can be grouped into roughly eight kinds: paralanguage, eye contact, facial expressions, posture, gestures, touch, proxemics, and dress. We will look at each of these types in turn.

Paralanguage

When we talk, we don't just produce words at the same rate and intonation all the time. Instead, we vary how we say things, using tone of voice or timing of questions, to convey information. The additional information that comes to us through speech is known as **paralanguage**, and it can be just as important as the actual words when we are trying to communicate with someone else.

Emotion

Davitz and Davitz (1961) asked research participants to listen to tape recordings, and to assess the emotion being experienced by the speaker, from their paralanguage cues. They found that there was a very high level of accuracy (70%) in distinguishing between such emotions as affection, amusement, admiration, disgust and fear. They also found that there were certain characteristics which different emotions had; and that the manner of speaking associated with each of these could be classified according to speech factors such as loudness, pitch, rate of speaking, rhythm, inflection, and so on. Because each kind of emotion had its characteristic pattern, research participants were able to judge emotions accurately even when they were listening to the speech of people they didn't know.

These patterns can also show up on a speech spectrograph, which is a machine which will record and analyse patterns of speech. Most people use the full range of inflections but in some people who are suffering from some kind of mental illness or from depression, these speech patterns become unusual. Ostwald (1965) found that these people tend to show unusually flattened speech patterns, which show on the spectrograph as being different from normal people's speech. In fact, the more serious the person's disturbance, the more their speech would be different from normal when it was analysed.

Other aspects of paralanguage

These are other aspects of paralanguage, as well as the **tone of voice** that we use. Kasl and Mahl, in 1965, showed that when we are in a highly emotional state, like when we are angry or anxious, we tend to produce a far higher rate of slips of the tongue, stuttering, or repetition of what we are saying. And when we are not sure of what we are saying, or if we are uncertain as to how the listener is likely to receive it, we make far more 'er' and 'um' noises than usual. The person listening to us will, quite unconsciously, pick up these signals and gain an impression of our emotional state from them. Also, Kasl and Mahl found that the actual **timbre** of the voice - how soft or harsh it is - is different in different emotional states. It may, for example, be soft and resonant if we are being affectionate, or it may be loud and blaring if we are angry.

Verbal Vs non-verbal communication

In 1972, Argyle, Alkema and Gilmour performed a study which showed just how important paralanguage is. They used it, together with facial expression, to deliver a message to a research participant in three different styles: one neutral, one hostile, and one friendly. The verbal message that was actually delivered also varied. In some, the words carried a hostile kind of message, in some it was a neutral statement, and in some it was a friendly message. By varying which non-verbal style went with the verbal message, and by asking participants about the message they had received, Argyle, Alkema and Gilmour showed that, in fact, people were five times as likely to react to the non-verbal cues, as they were to the verbal ones. If the non-verbal message seemed to contradict the verbal one - such as a hostile message delivered in a friendly manner - participants tended to ignore the actual words, and only believe the non-verbal message. This shows us just how powerful these signals can be - yet most of the time we are simply not conscious of them!

Psychology in Action

One of the most entertaining sources of non-verbal and verbal communication is the behaviour of politicians. Politicians need to be particularly good at communication, since their livelihood depends on convincing the general public that they are credible and honest. Some of the most important cues that they use are gestures, tones of voice, and posture; and these have often been carefully rehearsed by the politicians concerned, sometimes after carefully training by media consultants. Occasionally, though, an unexpected or particularly unwelcome event produces a non-verbal response which is a bit different from their usual image. It's worth looking out for these occasions.

The verbal communication which politicians use is also interesting to observe. Most people are familiar with the way that politicians deal with awkward questions by giving the answer to an entirely different one, and this is one example of how they manipulate the verbal content of the communication. Some politicians are also particularly good at manipulating the natural pauses and rhythms of conversation to make sure that anyone else who wants to speak has to interrupt them, and appear rude. They also use rhetoric ways of presenting verbal arguments in a deliberately appealing manner. One device which is very common here is the 'rule of three', which is when examples are given three at a time, for example: 'We will improve education, housing, and the environment' or 'We aim for fairness, equality, and prosperity'. These verbal strategies are specially designed to sound good, and to stay in people's minds.

The timing of speech

The **timing** of speech is another way that we can communicate information, often quite unconsciously. Someone who speaks very slowly, may be thought of as very uncertain of what they are saying, as already mentioned, while speaking fast may indicate that the person is anxious or excited. During an ordinary conversation, there are pauses, which tend to be of a standard length, and which signal different things: a short pause may mean that the person has finished explaining or describing one idea, and is about to go on to the next one (like a comma in written words), while a longer pause may be a signal that it is the other person's turn to talk. Rochester (1973) observed and analysed speech patterns in conversations, and showed that sometimes we unconsciously control other people's behaviour by using these signals. To keep someone listening when they want to go, you simply increase the volume and rate of your speaking, and to cut down on the number of pauses. This leaves the other person unable to 'cut in', and feel obliged to stay, or to walk out in the middle of a sentence! It is a strategy often used by politicians in TV interviews!

We can see how useful paralanguage is, when we listen to someone who is good at talking on the telephone. In that situation, there isn't any opportunity to use any of the other non-verbal signals, which rely on touch or sight, so the non-verbal cues given by pauses, tone of voice, and so on, become very important. Someone who is skilled at talking on the telephone will tend to exaggerate these, to compensate for the lack of other cues, while people who don't find telephone conversations easy often have problems because they continue to talk in their normal manner, which makes it very much harder to communicate effectively. If they learn to provide extra paralinguistic cues, they find that telephone conversations become easier and more satisfying.

Eye-contact

Perhaps the thing which we miss above all when we are talking on the telephone, is **eye-contact** with the person that we are talking to. Eye-contact is probably the single most powerful non-verbal cue that we have. Many of our unconscious judgements about other people are based on the amount and type of eye-contact that we have with them. Stass and Willis (1967) set up an experiment in which research participants were introduced to pairs of people and told that they would have to choose one of them as a partner later on in the experiment. One of the people that they were introduced to had been secretly instructed to look directly at the research participant, while they were being introduced, and the other had been instructed to look away from them most of the time. As you might expect, the partner the research participants chose was the one who had looked directly at them during the introduction.

Eye-contact and emotion

Eye contact is a powerful indicator of emotion. We recognise this, when we speak about two people in love 'gazing into each other's eyes'. The more eye-contact we have with someone, the closer we tend to feel to them. Often, we will avoid eye-contact with someone we don't like - and if we do make it, we will adopt an unemotional stare, rather than a friendly gaze. (The difference between the two comes from how widely the eyes are opened, and how much movement the muscles around the eyes are allowed to make.)

A study by Kleinke (1973) investigated how people thought about eye contact. The research participants were asked to chat with each other for ten minutes, in male and female pairs. At the end of the ten minute period, the participants were either told that their partner had looked at them for less than the normal average number of times or for more, while the conversation was taking place. (This was in addition to the times the couple were both looking at each other at the same time.) They were then asked to rate their partners on various characteristics. Those participants who had been told that their partners had looked at them fewer than the average number of times, rated their partner as being less attentive to what was being said. When the partner had looked at them more than the average number of times, though, an interesting difference appeared. The female participants who were told this did not particularly change their opinion of their partners, but the male participants rated their partners as more attractive!

According to Argyle (1975) eye-contact has four important functions in communication: regulating the flow of conversation; giving feedback to the speaker about what they have communicated; expressing emotions; and informing both participants about the nature of the relationship that they are in. We will look at each of these functions in turn.

Regulating the flow of conversation

When it is used to regulate the flow of conversation, eye-contact is one of the most important signals of all. If we want to start a conversation with somebody, we usually do it by looking at them to 'catch their eye'. Or if we want to say something, we will wait until there is a pause and the person speaking looks at us, before we speak. Often, too, if we want to end an utterance (a contribution to a conversation), we signal it by looking at our listener, to say 'it's your turn now'.

From observational studies, Carey (1978) showed that two people are likely to strike up a conversation when they look at each other. Kendon (1967) observed conversations between pairs of students asked to 'get acquainted', and found some very noticeable and reliable patterns. When a person (A) was speaking, they would avoid eye-contact at the beginning of their utterance, look up briefly at the end of sentences or phrases and give the second person (B) a prolonged gaze at the end of their speech. The listener, B, would give longer looks watching A most of the time while they were talking. When A looked up, B would give other signals, such as head nods, as well as making eye-contact. The long look at the end of the speech seemed to be important: Kendon also found that if A doesn't look up at the end of the speech, then B either doesn't answer at all, or takes very much longer before answering. So it seems that we use these signals for regulating conversations quite a lot more than we realise.

Providing feedback

When eye contact is used to convey feedback to others, we can find it quite disturbing if it is interrupted. Argyle, Lalljee and Cook

(1968) showed that if two research participants were in a conversation but one was wearing dark glasses, so that the other couldn't receive eye-contact, the conversation tended to be much more hesitant and to have more pauses and interruptions. In addition, when they asked participants to deliver monologues rather than to have conversations, the speakers made far less eye-contact than normal suggesting that they didn't need the feedback or response from the other person as much.

Lefebré, in 1975, suggested that eye-contact reflects a need for approval from others, and that people who have strong emotional needs for approval make more eye-contact than others. This would tie in with Kleinke's study, showing that research participants who thought their listener hadn't been looking at them also thought they hadn't been attending. The teacher who insists that members of the class should 'look at me', is also demanding the non-verbal signal of attention from them.

Signalling the nature of relationships

Argyle and Dean (1965) showed that the amount of eye-contact which people make in a conversation relates very strongly to the amount of distance that there is between them. When research participants stood 3 m apart, they spent most of their conversation making eye-contact, making it 65% of the time. But when they only stood 0.6 m apart, eye contact was far less – only 45% of the time. It seems as if the eye-contact is in some way compensating for lack of physical closeness, or allowing us to say 'you may be standing very close to me, but I am still not intimate with you'.

Staring at people can often make them feel uncomfortable as well. Ellsworth *et al.* (1972) performed a study in which drivers stopping at a traffic junction would be stared at by a person standing on the corner. They would pull away from the junction far more quickly than drivers did when no-one stared at them!

Expressing emotions

There are two different ways that eye-contact can express our emotions. One is the actual way that we make eye contact. As we mentioned before, we adopt a different kind of gaze if we are staring at people we dislike - holding the muscles around our eyes taut, and the eyes fairly wide open. If we are staring at someone that we like, our eye-muscles are very much more relaxed, so that the eyes are not held open as wide. Other signals may also indicate our feelings, such as the amount that we blink or the position of our eyebrows.

The main way that eye-contact demonstrates emotion, however, is a completely unconscious one. The pupil of the eye tends to dilate when we are looking at something or someone we like; and this can be an unconscious form of communication – we may unconsciously be signalling to someone that we like them, while they may in turn be unconsciously reacting to this! In the middle ages, Italian women used to put a drug into their eyes which had the effect of dilating the pupils, making them more attractive to other people. In fact, the name of the plant from which the drug is extracted, Belladonna, reflects this because it means 'beautiful woman' in Italian.

Hess (1963) performed a series of experiments to see if and how this worked. One of his first studies was on a male assistant, before he investigated the phenomenon on larger numbers of people. He took a series of landscape photographs and one of a nude woman. He arranged the pictures in a random order, and held them up one at a time in front of his assistant, in such a way that Hess could not see the pictures but could see his assistant's pupils. When they came to the seventh photo, the assistant's pupils suddenly dilated: sure enough, that was the one that turned out to be the nude!

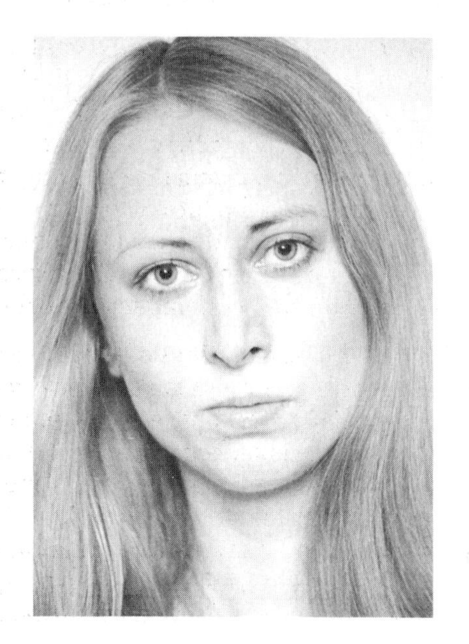

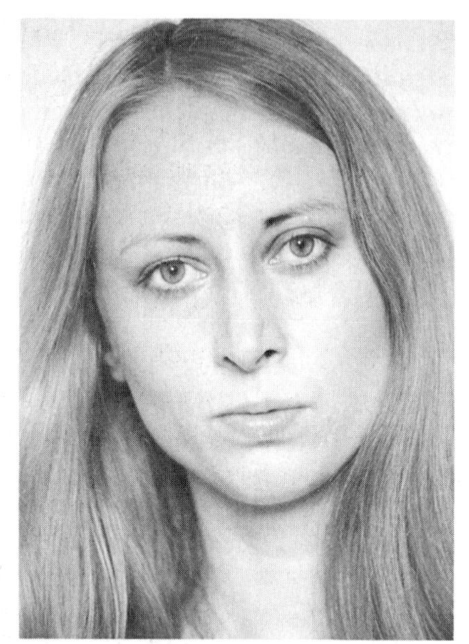

Pupil dilation

In a larger, more controlled study, Hess took pictures of women and had two copies made of each. In one of the copies he had the pupils retouched so that they seemed enlarged. In all other respects the photograph was identical to the matching copy. A series of research participants were asked to rate these, and other photographs for attractiveness, and Hess found that they always rated the one with the dilated pupils as being more attractive than its pair. Strangely enough, they were unable to say why they thought this, when they were asked. Quite a few of the participants thought it must be because she was smiling more, or something similar. So it shows us just what an unconscious, but powerful cue this is. In this context, it's interesting to notice how many of the places where intimate relationships develop have very low lighting. Your pupils also dilate in dim light, and so having low light in nightclubs and restaurants means that you and your partner are more likely to find each other attractive!)

Facial expression

The face and eyes are the parts of the body that we seem to notice most, but they are very complex to understand. We have more muscles for moving our faces than any other kind of animal, which tells us just how important it is for human beings to be able to move our faces subtly. In addition, our facial expressions can change very rapidly: some expressions may only last for 0.2 of a second, and yet still communicate meaning to another person!

Although people have been studying facial expressions for years, there is so much information available to us through the face that we are still only able to make generalisations. We know, for instance, that there are at least eight different positions of the eyebrows and forehead - each with its own meaning; eight more of the eyes and eyelids, and at least ten for the lower part of the face. In different combinations, this adds up to a tremendous number of possible expressions, which allow close friends or family to recognise subtle messages which strangers might miss.

Common facial expressions

Eibl-Eiblesfeldt (1974) analysed several films of people engaging in everyday social encounters, and came to the conclusion that there are some facial expressions which have the same meaning all over the world. When we are first greeting someone, we make a rapid 'eyebrow flash' in which we raise our eyebrows and lower them very quickly. Not only is this found throughout human societies, but it has also been observed among the great apes - so it may be something which we have inherited as a 'recognition signal'. Other eyebrow positions seem to have different meanings; some typical ones are:

fully raised - disbelief

half-raised - surprise

normal - no comment or reaction

half-lowered - puzzled

fully lowered - angry

18.1 Facial expression in communication

Cross-cultural studies

Eibl-Eiblesfeldt also noticed that some more complex patterns of expressions seemed to occur in all human cultures, such as the pattern of eye contact and lowered eyes which seem to demonstrate shyness or coyness, or the basic facial signals of smiling or glowering with anger. But, other non-verbal signals seem to develop as a result of experience and these tend to be different in different human societies. Ekman and Friesen (1969) performed several cross-cultural studies, and showed that many of the basic emotional expressions seemed to be inherited. But because some cultures discourage the showing of certain emotions, the people who have grown up in those cultures do not show that facial expression as strongly as someone who has grown up in a society which allows them to express it.

18.1 Investigating facial expressions

Facial expression is one of the most useful of all our non-verbal signals, and one which we all understand.

One amusing class activity that you can do, is each to write down the name of an emotion or feeling on a slip of paper, and to put all the slips into a hat, or a box.

Each member of the class should take a slip from the hat, without letting anyone else know what it says. Then everyone in turn should mime their emotion while the others guess, from his or her facial expression, what emotion it is.

Are some emotions easier to recognise than others?
Did different people mime the same emotions in the same way?
Were any of the emotions mistaken for some other feeling?

Osgood's categories of facial expressions

Osgood (1966) found that we have roughly seven major groups of facial expressions, although each group has many variations. These are: happiness, surprise, fear, sadness, anger, interest, and disgust/contempt. These groups of expressions seem to be signals which are recognised in virtually all human societies, so it is thought that they may be inherited. However, some variations of facial expressions may come to be culturally developed: like imitations of well-known characters, such as, someone playfully adopting a 'grinning idiot' face, or a 'Kevin' face when joking with friends.

So it seems that we do have quite a lot of scope for expressing emotions and other ideas, through facial expressions. Also, of course, adopting the appropriate facial expression when someone is talking to you is an important signal that you are paying attention. You wouldn't grin when being told about something sad, or look mournful when someone is describing some very happy news that they have just received! Facial expressions can also provide **feedback** in conversation, telling the speaker that you are listening to them.

One way of studying facial expressions is through the technique of **facial electromyography**, using electrical sensors which detect slight changes in the muscles of the face. From this, researchers have started to build up a picture of the way that facial expressions change; and this information is sometimes used to teach how facial communication happens, to people who have problems in social interaction (and often psychological problems as a result).

The facial affect program

Ekman *et al.* provided a detailed analysis of the facial expressions linked to each emotion. This was called the Facial Affect Program, and is sometimes used for social-skills training. After all, if someone continually shows the 'wrong' facial expressions, or doesn't change their expression at all, we tend to think that that person is not really 'normal', so often such people are treated as odd, and so don't form ordinary friendships or have normal interactions with other people. Teaching individuals new social skills, like the appropriate use of facial expressions, is all that they need to break the cycle. When this has been done, they often find that a lot of their other problems just sort themselves out automatically. There are several social skills training centres which do this.

Facial expressions and hemispheres of the brain

Sackeim *et al*. (1978) found that the left side of the face seems to be far more expressive of emotion than the right side. When they divided photographs of people who were showing extreme emotions down the middle and made two pictures fitting two left halves and two right mirror-image halves together, they found that the composite picture which was made up of the two left halves of the face showed a much stronger expression than the composite picture from the right halves of the face. Sackeim suggested that the reason for this is that the left half of the face is controlled by the right side of the brain, which is thought to deal with artistic, emotional and intuitive skills; while the left side of the brain is thought by many psychologists to deal with logical reasoning and language. So if the right side of the brain is dealing with the emotional parts of the self, then it may play a greater part in expressing emotion than the other side.

What is being communicated by each of these figures?

18.2 Posture as communication

Posture

The way that we stand or sit can be a very good indicator of how we are feeling - and it can also be used as a deliberate method of communication. (How would you signal to someone that you were feeling fed up and rebellious?) More often, though, it is unconscious: I remember noticing a very funny sight a few years ago, when a friend pointed to a man sat on a seat, with his elbows on his knees and his hands propping up his chin. He was slumped forward in his seat, and his face wore a very bored look. Above the seat was a huge poster, saying in large letters: 'Bored Silly?' It couldn't have been more appropriate if the man had deliberately chosen to illustrate the poster!

Ekman (1972) asked a group of research participants to make judgements on how other people felt on the basis of looking at photographs. The two areas they were asked to judge was how pleasant or unpleasant the individual was feeling; and also how relaxed or tense. Ekman found that the participants used different non-verbal signals to judge the two characteristics. For the pleasant/unpleasant judgements, participants used pictures of the face, but for judging how tense or relaxed the individual was, they made judgements on the basis of **body posture**. In fact, it is often some aspect of the body which 'gives us away', either our posture or small unconscious gestures which we make that indicates nervousness or anxiety. People who teach self-defence classes often emphasise that one of the things which makes someone look like a possible victim is if they walk in a timid or frightened manner, and they encourage people to learn to walk in a self-confident and upright way which makes them less likely to be attacked.

Gestures

The **gestures** which we make are also a method for communicating additional information to other people. Most of the time, we use gestures fairly deliberately, in order to support and emphasise what we are saying. But sometimes the gestures that we use are unconscious; made without any deliberate intention on our part, and we do not realise that they are giving away information to other people. Signals like nervously tapping the foot or fidgeting with objects in our hands communicate information to the person we are talking to about how we are feeling, often without our realising that we are doing it.

'Postural echo' - an aid to communication

Postural echo

Many gestures are ones which are learned as part of a culture - they seem, more or less, to go with the language and social interaction of the society that we grow up in. Kendon (1967) showed that both posture and gesture are used in conversation, to 'mirror' what the other person is saying to us: the listener will tend to make smaller gestures than the speaker, but nonetheless will make them. This, together with the **postural echo** that many people show, imitating the position of the person who they are communicating with, seems to amount to a signal of attentiveness and empathy to the person who is speaking. If you look around on a summer's day, you can often see postural echo happening when pairs of friends are sitting and talking. Also, if you observe closely, you may easily see gestures being used to indicate understanding on the part of the listener.

Culture specific gestures

Gestures like head-nodding are very widely known, but even they are culture-specific. In some societies, nodding the head for 'yes' isn't used at all - they have other symbols instead, and you can imagine how that can lead to confusion! Similarly, gestures which are used in our society, like the one that hitch-hikers use to get lifts, are also cultural signals, and in other countries these can be misunderstood. If you jerk your thumb at someone in some Mediterranean countries that gesture is considered to be quite an insult! Most of the gestures that we have are *symbols*, standing for a particular idea, and these are almost always learned and vary from one human society to another.

Touch

This is another signal which varies from one human society to another. The amount of **touch** that we permit others to have with us is set by cultural 'norms', and we often feel very uncomfortable if people break those 'norms' in an unconventional way. Jourard (1966) showed that, in Western society, we have certain areas which we consider to be acceptable for touching, but only in certain situations and by certain people. The parts of the body which are considered acceptable for touching vary according to the relationship which the other person has to us. We allow mothers, for instance, to touch us in far more parts of the body than we would allow friends. Touch is a very powerful signal, and it also seems to produce unconscious emotional reactions in us, which may be why many societies consider it to be so important. Western society, and British in particular, seems to be more restricted in its use of touch than many other societies, although Japanese people also do not communicate much using physical contact. Interestingly, though, those people in our society who do use touch a great deal, in greetings and social encounters, are often very popular. So it seems that we do appreciate being touched, even though there may not be frequent occasions when we do it.

Sex differences

A study by Nguyen *et al.* (1975) investigated people's attitudes to touch, and found that there seem to be differences between the sexes in how they saw contact. Women made a clear distinction between forms of touching that showed warmth and friendliness, and forms of touching that showed sexual desire - but men didn't seem to notice any difference. This is something that sex counsellors have found contributing to marital problems. Sometimes one or other of the partners usually the woman - will become afraid to make any contact at all because of the fear that it will be seen as a sexual approach. Some therapies concentrate on getting the couple who are having problems to enjoy touch for its own sake, rather than simply as a route to intercourse. Once they can do that, they often find that the rest of their relationship improves, because touch is such a powerful signal of trust and affection.

Status

If you watch speeded-up film of people walking down a busy street, you can see that they will manoeuvre in quite complicated ways to avoid touching other people as they walk along. We avoid touching strangers, as it is such an intimate sort of signal. But some researchers have also found that, in addition to touch signalling intimacy or closeness, touch as part of communication can signal status. Henley (1977) observed high and low-status individuals as they interacted, and found that there are quite definite status rules about who may touch whom. People of high status are far more likely to start off some kind of contact, such as putting an arm across someone's shoulders, than lower status people. According to Henley, lower-status people will stand and allow themselves to be touched, but do not initiate touching themselves. So it seems that using touch can convey quite complicated messages, unconsciously.

Proxemics

How close we allow ourselves to get to other people is another form of communication. Each society has its own idea of **personal space**, as the distance which is considered comfortable for a conversation or for other forms of social interaction, and members of that society tend to recognise the appropriate distances and to keep to them. But when people from different societies meet, it can sometimes present problems: in Western Europe, the normal conversational distance is about 1-1.5 m; but in some Arab countries it is so much closer than that. When an English person and an Arab have a conversation, if they are not aware of their different conventions, each can end up feeling very uncomfortable. The English person will feel uncomfortable because the other seems to be being far too intimate and standing far too close, while the Arab person will feel uncomfortable because the other doesn't seem to want to have a conversation at all, but keeps moving off into the distance! Being aware of this sort of thing, though, means that it doesn't have to be as confusing when it does happen.

Factors influencing personal space

Within a society, too, there are differences in how close people will stand to one another. Willis (1966) studied 775 research participants in different situations, and found that age seems to make a difference. We tend to stand closer to people of our own age, than to people who are very much older or younger than ourselves. Also, there seems to be a tendency for people to stand closer to women than they do to men - it seems that the 'male role' in society involves keeping a larger distance between yourself and others than the 'female role' does.

In 1959, Hall noted that the degree of friendship seems to affect interpersonal distance - intimate friends stand anywhere between 0 and 0.5 m apart, casual friends stand between 1-1.5m apart, people in purely social encounters stand anything between 1.5-4 m apart, while those in public encounters would sometimes stand as much as 4 m apart to conduct their conversation. These distances were observed by getting a sample of businessmen and other professional adults to engage in conversations, so there is always the possibility that they are slightly exaggerated because of the study procedure - but nonetheless, we do tend to carry round our own little 'personal space', and often we feel aggrieved if anyone intrudes on it.

Russo's investigation into personal space

A study by Russo (1967) illustrated this: in a college library, a colleague of the experimenter would deliberately invade the 'personal space' of other users in the library. Sometimes she would sit directly opposite the student, when there were plenty of other places to sit, and sometimes she would sit very close to them. Russo found that when the researcher sat next to the student and moved her chair to within about 1 ft of theirs, 70% would move within half an hour. Others would change their posture and lean away from the 'intruder', and others would react with hostile glances. Interestingly, only one student out of 80 actually asked the intruder to move away, although it was clear that the others would have liked her to do so!

Very often in normal social situations, we will tend to 'protect' our personal space as much as possible - for instance by piling shopping bags onto the seat on the bus next to us, or by 'claiming' a particular chair at home by sitting in it often enough to establish some idea of a right to it. If someone intrudes into our space when we do not feel that it is necessary, we may wonder whether that person is 'normal': such rules are so thoroughly accepted in society that we expect everyone to observe them. Yet many visitors from other countries regard the British habit of protecting space and avoiding contact with strangers as being very odd and characteristic of this country, so it clearly isn't something which all human beings do.

18.2 Investigating proximity during conversation

Eye contact and proximity are two of the non-verbal cues which signal intimacy. It seems that the more eye contact we display and the closer we stand to someone when having a conversation with them the more likely it is that we are indicating an intimate relationship. But what happens when one of the signals for intimacy, such as eye contact, is removed? Will individuals stand closer to people with their eyes closed, perhaps because they are less worried about unconsciously signalling intimacy?

This activity is designed to investigate this question.

For this activity you will need two partners, some paper, a piece of chalk, a ruler or tape measure and a stop watch or watch with a second hand.

Firstly, you should think of a couple of topics for conversation, because you are going to ask your research participants to talk to each other so it will be a good idea if you can suggest some topics that they can talk about.

Mark a small chalk line on the floor and ask one of your participants to stand on it and not to move off it. This will be your 'stationary' research participant. The other participant can stand anywhere in the room. This is your 'mobile' participant.

Ask your research participants to have two one-minute conversations.

For one of the conversations the stationary participant should have their eyes closed but the mobile participant must keep their eyes open.

In between the two conversations, ask the mobile participant to walk across the room, before going back to the conversation.

At the end of each conversation, measure the distance between the two participants with the ruler or tape measure. (It is a good idea to have this already placed in position on the floor.)

Did you find any difference in the conversational distance, between the 'eyes closed' and 'eyes open' conversation?

Did your participants realise what the study was about? How could you design the study in such a way that they didn't realise?

What other controls would you need to include if you were doing a formal study of this?

Dress

Another way that we communicate with one another, without the use of words, is through dress. We are all familiar with the various uniforms which are used to signal that someone is occupying a particular role in society: a policeman, nurse, or traffic warden for example. But other forms of dress may also communicate information about the person - someone in a professional job for instance, like a solicitor, will tend to dress neatly and in a particular kind of style, while someone who has a more physical job is unlikely to be seen wearing a suit except on very special occasions. So by 'reading' the ways that people dress, we make judgements about them, which give us a rough guide as to how to interact.

18.3 The use of dress as communication

Of course, these judgements can rapidly become stereotypes, in which we treat all people the same way just because their styles of dress are similar. Young people who adhere to a particular style of fashion often complain that older people don't see them as individuals but judge them entirely by their dress, while the older people argue that they shouldn't dress like that if they don't want people to stereotype them! Although it's undoubtedly better to treat people as individuals, and not to stereotype, you can see why the older people sometimes react like that, as in most situations clothes are transmitting messages. They are simply treating the style of dress as a deliberate choice of communication. And, of course, the younger people are doing the same thing, when they stereotype older people who dress 'conventionally'!

Ethical discussion

A sophisticated knowledge of non-verbal communication allows people to become skilled at manipulating others for personal benefit. Sometimes, this is packaged and marketed as psychological skills, like neuro-linguistic programming. Some psychologists regard this as being an unacceptable intrusion into people's personal privacy. Others argue that the packages simply train people to observe reactions in close detail, and this is only what we all do every day anyway, only in a slightly more systematic form.

What do you think?

Classifying non-verbal cues

As you can see, there are quite a varied number of **non-verbal cues** which we can use to transmit information. Non-verbal communication is an enormous part of how we communicate with other people. Although it is mostly unconscious, we can, and do, use it for what is often the most important part of interaction with others. Through all sorts of cues, like tone of voice, dress, eye contact, posture, proximity, gestures, facial expressions and pauses in conversations, we extend and refine our communication to a level of detail and understanding that would be almost completely impossible if all we had going for us was words.

Ekman and Friesen (1969) developed a system for classifying the various non-verbal cues in day-to-day interaction. They argued that non-verbal signals could be roughly categorised into five groups: emblems, illustrators, affect displays, regulators, and adapters.

Ekman and Friesen's system of classification

Emblems

Emblems are non-verbal acts or gestures which have a direct meaning, which can be put in verbal terms as well. For example, during the Second World War in this country, the 'V' sign was used to represent peace and victory. Ekman and Friesen found some emblems which seem to be used in all or most human societies - such as tilting the head on to the hands to represent sleeping - but in general, emblems will tend to vary from one culture to another. Most societies that Ekman and Friesen studied seemed to have emblems for insults, for emotions, and for departures (like waving goodbye).

Illustrators

Illustrators are non-verbal acts which accompany speech, demonstrating what is being said in a different form. For instance, stretching the hands apart to represent 'large' means that the gesture is providing an extra emphasis to the words. Illustrators seem to be used more when what is being explained is difficult to put into words, and, as we know, there are considerable individual differences in how much people use illustrators.

Affect displays

Affect displays are non-verbal cues which reveal our emotional states. They may be facial expressions, gestures, tones of voice, or anything which indicates to an observer that we are experiencing an emotion: such as glaring at someone who has annoyed you, or tapping the feet nervously while waiting for an interview.

Regulators

Regulators are the non-verbal acts which 'regulate' conversations and other interactions. In other words, they make sure that things flow smoothly, and that actions have their proper sequencing. The use of eye-contact to signal someone's turn to speak, is a good example of a regulator. Without eye contact, as we find if talking to a telephone answering machine, it becomes difficult to know how to pace a conversation. Other examples of regulators are the use of facial expressions to indicate continuing interest in the topic which is being discussed - or the opposite, like looking away and assuming an inappropriate facial expression when one is bored and does not want to continue the conversation.

Adaptors

Adaptors are the individual characteristics which people develop, which allow the person to cope in certain situations. For example, when some people get nervous, they will scratch themselves or twiddle a ring or a pencil. We have all got our own idiosyncratic gestures and facial expressions. One of the things which makes a good impersonation successful, is the fact that the mimic will have often caught on to these adaptors, and reproduced them accurately. Sometimes, this means that the impersonation of the individual can be totally convincing, even though they may not actually look like the person! Ekman suggests that we learn most of our idiosyncratic behaviours while we are infants, and carry them on into adulthood, even though they are no longer really appropriate. One reaction to extreme grief, for instance, is to rock oneself backwards and forwards, which may be a regression to the infant experience of being rocked for comfort.

Argyle's system of classification

Ekman and Friesen's classification provides us with one way of sorting out the enormous number and range of cues available in our non-verbal repertoire. However, other researchers, in trying to sort out the mass of information which can be acquired by studying non-verbal communication, have developed other ways of thinking about it. Argyle (1975) identified four major functions of non-verbal communication, and discussed the different cues in terms of how each cue can be used for these four functions. You may find it interesting to try this classification for yourself: go back over the non-verbal cues that have been described earlier on in this chapter, and see how each one might fit into either Ekman and Friesen's classification or Argyle's four functions. The four functions are:

1. that non-verbal communication (NVC) may form an aid to speech, to support what we are saying and to give feedback to the other person;
2. that NVC may be used to replace speech entirely, in the form of gestures which render words unnecessary;
3. that NVC may be used to signal attitudes, such as the dilation of the pupils signalling liking;
4. that NVC may be used to signal emotional states, such as tension of the muscles during anger.

Methods of studying NVC

The studying of non-verbal communication has been undertaken in many different ways by different researchers. Some researchers have concentrated on **ethological**, or naturalistic, observations of non-verbal communication, and have attempted to draw conclusions from these as to the nature and functions of the different cues. For example, Eibl-Eiblesfeldt, an ethologist, performed a study in 1960 which involved filming blind and deaf children in their natural settings to see if their facial expressions were the same as those shown by normally sighted children. He found that, for many of the basic emotions, the children showed exactly the same expressions, although their expressions would fade faster than with normal children. From these observations, Eibl-Eiblesfeldt concluded that basic emotional expressions don't have to be learnt by imitation, so they must be inherited, although they would be developed further by experience in normal children later. Further ethological studies allowed him to observe other kinds of non-verbal cues, such as the 'eye-brow flash' which people make to signal recognition. So ethological observations are one way that researchers can discover more about NVC.

Cross-cultural studies

Cross-cultural studies are another method of studying non-verbal communication. Watson and Graves observed conversational distances between Arab and American students, and were able to assess the precise differences in the usual conversational distances between the two groups of people from these different societies. Other studies have investigated, for instance, the amount of touching that happens in public in different European and Mediterranean countries, or the way in which expressions of emotion are not considered acceptable in some societies, such as Japan. In Ekman's 1972 study of Japanese interaction, he found that expressions of strain and anger during conversation were rigidly suppressed, but that when Japanese businessmen thought that they were not being observed they would let such expressions show on their faces. In that case, it was clear that the cultural expectations of the proper way to behave were inhibiting expression through non-verbal signals, and in another country such inhibition might not be the case at all.

Laboratory studies

Laboratory studies have been another popular way of studying non-verbal communication. Often people will show their ideas about non-verbal communication by acting out a role or a piece of behaviour in the psychological laboratory. For instance, Mehrabian, in 1972, reported a study in which people had been asked to talk to a hat-stand, which represented in turn several different people. He found that when people were talking to the hat-stand as if it were a high-status individual, they addressed their looks and words to a higher point on the hat-stand than when they were supposed to be addressing a low-status person! In a study, Little (1968) asked research participants from different countries to arrange a set of dolls into conversational groups - such as a family, strangers talking, etc. The idea was that these should represent social situations in their country and he found that Greek research participants placed the dolls closest together, while Scottish and Swedish participants placed them farther apart. So this is one way that the ideas people from different countries have about comfortable conversational distances - 'personal space' - could be investigated in the laboratory.

Comparative studies

Yet another method of studying non-verbal communication is by studying the behaviour of animals, and drawing comparisons between these and human behaviour. These are known as **comparative studies**, and may be a bit risky because, although evolution does suggest that we probably have quite a lot of things in common with animals, we don't share characteristics with *all* animals. Some researchers, for instance, have drawn parallels between what birds do and what humans do, which really doesn't seem to be sensible. The differences in brain size and capacity between birds and humans are vast, and humans learn a very large variety of alternative ways of behaving, while birds frequently show inherited behaviour which can't be altered.

But some animal studies can be extremely useful, mostly those studies of animals which are closest to us like apes and monkeys. A study by Andrew (1966) for instance, showed that many emotional expressions are very similar in humans and in other primates. Expressions such as the 'play-grin', or the baring of the teeth in moments of fear (which many of us do as a reflex) seem to be expressions we share with our animal relatives. Also, the pilomotor response of hair standing on end when we are frightened, is also one which we share with other mammals. In humans this mostly shows itself as 'goose-pimples' because our individual hairs are so short. It is a response to fear which you can observe in many animals, even animals as different from humans such as cats and dogs. So, as long as we are careful about which animals we choose to study, we might be able to learn quite a lot about basic non-verbal signals from animal studies.

Summary

1 All social interaction involves some form of communication, which may be verbal or non-verbal.

2 Verbal communication involves the use of language. It allows us to communicate symbolically, and to refer to events or objects which are not present.

3 Non-verbal communication involves the use of a variety of cues to communicate information. Social interaction tends to involve a great deal of unconscious non-verbal communication.

4 There are eight main groups of non-verbal cues: paralanguage, eye contact, facial expression, posture, gesture, touch, proxemics, and dress.

5 Non-verbal cues can signal emotions, attitudes and subtle aspects of relationships.

6 Ekman and Friesen classified non-verbal signals into five kinds: emblems, adapters, illustrators, affect displays and regulators. Each of these represents a different set of uses for the cues.

7 Non-verbal communication has been investigated through ethological or cross-cultural studies, laboratory studies and comparative studies.

Chapter 19 - Social influences

In this chapter, we will be looking at how other people can influence how we act. We will begin by looking at some of the studies of coaction and conformity, where psychologists have investigated the effects of other people's presence and opinions on our own behaviour. Then we will go on to look at some psychological studies of obedience and compliance, where people deliberately try to make other people act in certain ways. Finally, we will look at psychological research into the influence of strangers: at how people react when they see other people in need of assistance, and how people behave in crowds.

Coaction and conformity

A large part of psychology is devoted to the study of how people influence one another's behaviour. It has been established for quite a long time that people can have an effect on each other just by being there. Some people feel that they can truly be 'themselves' only when they are alone, while other people feel happier if they are among others in a crowd or with a group of friends. Triplett (1898) set up one of the first experimental studies of social influence. He asked children to turn a fishing reel as fast as they possibly could, and measured how quickly they could do it. Then he arranged things so that they would either be doing it alone or with a friend or another child. When the children were working in coaction (together), he found that they worked much faster – even just the presence of another person seemed to have a stimulating effect on their behaviour.

Sherif

The presence of other people doesn't just affect how hard we work. It also has a direct effect on how we respond to other people, and sometimes even on the way that we think. One of the first psychologists to demonstrate this was Sherif, back in 1936. Sherif asked people to sit in a dark room and look at a point of light. An interesting perceptual effect happens when we do this, which is that the point of light seems to dance around. It's a visual illusion known as the **autokinetic effect** and it is produced by the continuous slight movements that our eye muscles make. Sherif began by testing the research participants alone, and asking them to estimate how much the light moved. The research participants' guesses ranged widely – some said just a couple of inches, while others said 12 inches or more. People were, however, generally consistent: if someone had said that the movement was just a couple of inches on one occasion, then they would make a guess of a similar size at other times when they were tested.

When the participants were tested in groups, though, so that they could hear each others' estimates, the picture was rather different. Sherif found that the answers people gave began to converge until, eventually, the whole group would agree on a single measurement for the effect. What's more, they would stick to that measurement from then on. Even when the research participants were tested on their own, the measurement that they gave would be like the group estimate and it was often quite unlike the estimate that they had given at first, working alone. The group had developed a **group norm** for the task and this norm was so powerful that it affected the group members' judgements from then on.

Sherif's studies revealed a number of interesting findings about group norms. The first was that having the agreement of a majority was extremely influential in forming the norm: in a group of three, if two people agreed on a measurement but the third person's view was different, the final norm would be like that of the two people and the third person would shift her or his estimate until it was similar to those of the other two. Also, people who were unfamiliar with the task conformed quicker than people who had previous experience of it, which suggested that being uncertain about the correct answer encourages conforming to other people's views.

The Asch paradigm studies

Sherif's work on conformity was the first of a series of research projects which looked at how we conform to others. Perhaps one of the most famous of these studies was the one performed by Asch in 1951. Sherif had chosen an ambiguous task for his studies – a task where there was no clear, correct answer and it was all really a matter of guesswork. By contrast, Asch set up a situation in which there was an obviously correct answer but the research participant would have to go against the majority view in order to stick to it.

The research participants were told that they were participating in a perception study. They were asked to judge the correct length of a given line by identifying which of three sample lines was identical to it. Asch arranged that they would be tested as members of a group, all of whom would report their judgements openly. Unknown to the research participants, however, the rest of the group consisted of 'stooges' who, from time to time, deliberately gave prearranged but obviously wrong answers. The participants clearly found it uncomfortable when they were in a position of disagreeing with the majority and at one time or another during the study many of them gave answers which they knew to be wrong but which conformed with the majority judgements. In total, 74% of Asch's research participants conformed at least once, and 32% of them conformed all the time. Asch reported that the anxieties being experienced by the participants as they heard others giving the wrong judgements and as their turn increased, were clearly visible, even in those who persisted in reporting their answers correctly.

A more recent study by Perrin and Spencer (1980) involved replicating Asch's experiments with a different set of research participants. They found that, despite the clear existence of anxiety on the part of the participants, people did not conform as they did in Asch's study, and suggested from this that the Asch effect might be 'a child of its time' rather than a general effect. However, Doms and Avermaet (1981) questioned this conclusion, reporting that in other modern-day replications of Asch's work the conformity effect was still showing just as strongly. They argued that a possible reason why Perrin and Spencer had not obtained any conformity at all was because of their effort to obtain research participants who had not heard of the original Asch experiments. In doing so, they had used students from disciplines such as engineering, chemistry and medicine. Doms and Avermaet suggested that students from scientific disciplines were likely to believe strongly in the need for accurate measurements and so would feel obliged to give the right answer even though they disliked going against the majority. A precise replication of Asch's study by Vine (1981), using research participants who were closer to Asch's originals, showed conformity results that were very similar to Asch's original findings.

Factors influencing conformity

Asch performed many variations of his study, with the intention of identifying whether the number of people mattered. It emerged that three stooges were enough to create maximum conformity if the 'real' research participant was alone. Having more than three stooges would produce the same level of conformity, even if there were as many as 15. It seems that if we are able to hold our own opinions in defiance of three other people, then we can manage to do it against any number of people!

However, a study by Moscovici, in 1976, suggested that it isn't just the number of people holding a certain view that matters – their consistency matters too. In Moscovici's studies, research participants were asked to make judgements about the colour of a light on a screen, which was blue but sometimes described as green (or the other way round). There were several real research participants in each group, unlike in Asch's work where there had only been one, and two stooges who gave the wrong answers but held to them consistently throughout the experiment. Although the stooges were in the minority, they did have some influence on the judgements made by the research participants. So it seems that we don't automatically just believe the majority: sometimes we can be influenced by someone who holds an opinion consistently.

Types of conformity

People don't always conform for exactly the same reasons. In 1958, Kelman identified three main forms of conformity, each of which could produce conforming behaviour but in different ways. The first of these, and the most superficial, is **compliance**: going along with the majority in order to avoid rejection or in order to gain rewards such as social acceptance or approval. The distinguishing feature of compliance is that the conforming behaviour lasts only as long as the situation. Once the influencing 'agents' are no longer present, the person stops conforming.

Kelman's second form of conformity is that of **identification**. The person conforms to others at particular times and in particular ways because these times are part of a general pattern of relationships which he or she is trying to maintain. In this type of conformity, the conforming behaviour is not an important thing in itself, but it is important because it establishes or maintains some kind of relationship. So, for instance, a shop assistant, who wants to establish a positive working relationship with a supervisor, will conform to the behaviour expected of a 'good' assistant – being pleasant with customers, accurate and fast when serving, polite and attentive to other employees, and so on. Although the person will probably believe each of these acts of conformity to be a 'right' way to behave, none of the individual acts are very important in themselves. They are all part of the person identifying with the role of the assistant and conforming to the identification.

The third form of conformity which Kelman identified was that of **internalisation**. This form of conformity comes from the person's own value system, their way of understanding the world and morality in both small and large matters. It is about doing what we believe in. With this type of conformity, someone may accept another person's influence and conform to their demands or expectations, not because that person is anyone special, but because they wholeheartedly agree with the principles involved.

With this kind of conformity, the conforming behaviour is likely to last for very much longer than the actual situation requires because the person has 'adopted' it for their own and it has become part of their internal value system. An example of this might be when someone discovers that other people (or another person) of their acquaintance are performing some kind of charitable act, such as sponsoring a child in a developing country. The person who discovers this fact may well decide to conform to this behaviour themselves but their reasons for doing so wouldn't be for acceptance or to avoid rejection – they may not even let other people know that they are doing it! They would be conforming because the act is consistent with their own value system and they consider it to be right.

We can see from these forms of conformity that people can act in accordance with others for many different reasons, and also that conformity isn't necessarily a bad thing! However, our likelihood of conforming to others is partly dependent on our own opinions of ourselves, as well on other people's demands on us. Those of Asch's research participants who didn't conform tended to see themselves as 'responsible experimental research participants' who were anxious not to 'mess up' the results of the study by giving an answer which they knew to be wrong. Because of the way they saw themselves, their conformity was lower than others (although if you look again through Kelman's classifications, you can see that, in fact, they were simply conforming in a different way!).

19.1 Investigating conformity

People prefer to get on well with one another, for the most part, rather than disagreeing openly. This can often lead to conformity. You can investigate this by setting up a situation in which it is clear what your own views are, and seeing whether other people agree with you.

For example, you could see whether conformity affects what people say about music. First, get some sheets of paper and write down five different CDs that your friends are likely to know. Then, ask your friends to rate each CD, using a scale of 1 to 10, with a rating of 1 meaning: 'I can't bear this CD', and 10 meaning: 'This is one of my favourite CDs of all time'.

Give half of the people that you are asking a new sheet so that they can see only the names of the CDs and not what other people said. The rest of the time, give people a sheet that already has some ratings on it. They can be your own ratings if you want, and you could tell the person that.

Do the people who know about your own ratings make ones that are similar to yours?

If you were doing this as a proper experiment, what precautions and controls would you need to include?

Obedience and compliance

We often don't notice how much of an influence other people have on our behaviour, but sometimes other people may require us to do things which, as independent individuals, we would regard as morally wrong. One classic example, is the case of someone who joins the armed forces and thereby becomes liable to kill other human beings simply because they have been ordered to do so. If this behaviour were shown in civilian life, it would be regarded as inexcusable and yet, because it forms part of a role which society demands, a soldier is expected to carry it through.

Milgram's research

One impressive study of the power which other people can have over our behaviour was the famous one carried out by Milgram in 1963. He set up an experiment in which volunteer research participants were required to give increasingly severe electric shocks to another person as part of an experiment which they thought was about learning. The participants were aware that they were administering extremely high levels of shock and that these could prove fatal. They could hear the other person, who they had seen strapped into a chair, giving increasingly loud cries of pain at first and then becoming silent as if that person had passed out or died. That person was really an accomplice of the experimenter and the cries of pain had been pre-recorded, but the research participants didn't know that. They were extremely disturbed by what they were being asked to do and frequently argued with the experimenter. None the less, 65% of them gave electric shocks up to the maximum possible level. All of Milgram's research participants found it very difficult to disobey the experimenter by refusing to participate at all, and most found themselves unable to disobey at all.

Factors affecting obedience

Milgram attributed his findings directly to the power of **social roles**. By entering into the experiment and adopting that role, the research participants felt as though they had entered into a social contract which involved them in behaving obediently. Their view of the contract was that it also involved the experimenter behaving responsibly and many research participants said afterwards that they had gone along with it because it took place at a high-status university, Yale, where they assumed the experimenter would be a responsible scientist. When Milgram repeated the experiments in an ordinary office block in town, he found a slightly lower level of obedience, with 50% of the research participants giving the full range of shocks. However, that figure is still pretty high, so, clearly, the prestige of the scientist wasn't the whole reason.

Other factors which were built into the experimental situation also showed how research participants felt trapped into the situation. One was the fact that, when the study first started, the participant and the stooge had drawn lots to see who would take which role. This allowed the participant to think: 'Well, it could just as easily have been me on the receiving end.' (The lots were rigged, of course, but the participant didn't know that.) Another aspect of the experimental situation was the use of verbal 'prods' from the experimenter, saying things like: 'You have no choice, you must continue.' Although this wasn't strictly true, as the participant did have a choice really, it made it much more difficult to refuse to carry on because refusing needed an act of direct disobedience to an authority figure.

Ethical discussion

The publication of Milgram's experiment, with its dramatic implications, caused quite a stir in the psychological community. Baumrind (1964), in a discussion of Milgram's report, outlined some of the possible psychological consequences to subjects from participating in an experiment of this kind and discovering such unpleasant truths about themselves. Although Baumrind talked about possible nervous breakdowns and other outcomes, Milgram himself asserted that these claims had been overstated and that the subjects had not experienced such traumatic consequences. In 1977, he reported how all subjects had been sent a follow-up questionnaire, in response to which less than 1% had said that they had any regrets about participating in the study.

There are, then, two sides to this argument. The fact remains that the subjects could have been at risk and it was not possible to tell beforehand what the outcomes of the study would be. On the other hand, Milgram's study was crucial in revealing some very important truths about human nature.

If you were faced with a similar situation now, would you decide to run such an experiment or not? What would be your reasons for your decision?

Another feature of Milgram's study was the way that the experimenter accepted responsibility for what might happen if the research participants said they did not want to be responsible for harming someone else. So the research participants felt that they were no longer to blame for their actions. Although they knew that what they were being asked to do was morally wrong, they saw their actions as being under the control of the person in charge, rather than under their own control. This made it harder for them to refuse outright to co-operate any more, although they did argue with the experimenter and were clearly agitated and upset. The fact that the experimenter had an official position, and wore a lab coat which symbolised this, also emphasised the expected role behaviour of the research participant. Many other small factors of this sort were built into this study and, together, they all created a strong sense of obligation to continue, which affected most of the research participants. Milgram's study shows us just how powerful these social factors can be.

Obedience in a real-life situation

Another study which shows the power of social roles and expected behaviour, but this time in a real-life setting, was performed by Hofling (1966). It was conducted in a hospital and the aim of the study was to see if nurses would comply with a doctor's instructions even if they went against the hospital regulations. While on duty, a nurse would receive a phone call from a doctor who claimed to be 'Dr Smith from psychiatry', about a particular patient. The nurse would be asked to give the patient a dose of a drug called Astroten. First, they would be asked to go to the drug cabinet, check that the drug was there and to report back. This gave the nurse a chance to see the bottle which was clearly labelled 'maximum dosage 10 mg'. 'Dr Smith' would then ask the nurse to administer 20 mg to the patient.

This request required the nurse concerned to contravene hospital regulations in two ways. The first was by administering a dose of a drug which was above the maximum amount considered safe. The second was by taking instructions over the telephone, which was also forbidden. Despite this, 21 out of 22 nurses involved in the study poured out the medication and were preparing to administer it to the patient when a hidden observer stopped them.

When we read about this study, it is easy to say that the correct behaviour for the nurses was to refuse. But we have to remember that nurses are expected to take instructions from doctors and that they are not expected to disobey them. Also, in the normal course of busy hospital life, regulations are often seen as cumbersome and interfering with medical practices, so being asked to sidestep a hospital regulation was not such an exceptional request. For the nurse to question the doctor's authority, she would have to go against all the unspoken lessons of her training and her day-to-day work. This study shows us very clearly just how powerful these types of social pressure can be.

Other studies of compliance

The Milgram and Hofling studies deal with rather extreme forms of social compliance. In day-to-day life, however, we often comply with things that we think are unreasonable but which don't seem very important. Langer et al. (1978) set up a series of studies where people were asked to comply with requests which were made with little or no justification. In one of them, individuals who were using a photocopying machine were interrupted by an experimenter who asked if he could go first. Sometimes an explanation was given – that he was in a hurry – but at other times no reason at all was stated. They found that a surprisingly high proportion of people would comply with the request with no explanation. In a similar set of studies by Milgram (1963) in the New York subway system, he found that 50% of the people asked to give up their seat to another person with no explanation would comply. Many of us find it extremely difficult to refuse a direct request.

Anxiety and compliance

Whenever he was discussing his work, Milgram emphasised the very strong anxieties which people experience when they are about to challenge expected social behaviour. When he himself tried to take part in the subway experiment, he reported that he felt as if some kind of 'force' was holding him back, and he couldn't bring himself to make such an unreasonable request. His research participants in the obedience experiment also showed a high level of anxiety while they contemplated disobeying the experimenter. Strangely enough, though, once they had actually done it, and 'nerved themselves up' to disobey, all their tension seemed to disappear and they became quite calm. It is emotional reactions like this which show us how deeply we have internalised social norms and role behaviours.

Milgram suggested a 'mini-experiment' which we can use to find out about these feelings in ourselves. He suggested identifying someone you know and respect, who you usually address by their title or surname, for example, a doctor, a lecturer or your boss. Make a decision that, next time you talk to them, you will deliberately address them by their first name. Most people experience increasing anxiety about breaking this little social convention as the time gets closer and will often find all sorts of excuses not to do it ('It's a silly idea anyway, why bother?...').

Self-perception and compliance

How we see ourselves – our self-perception – has been an important area of study in social psychology for many years. According to Cooley (1922), we develop our view of ourselves on the basis of other people's attitudes towards us. Indeed, Cooley felt that how others react towards us may be the most important of all the factors influencing our self-perception. For instance, if you are regarded by your friends as being a highly principled sort of person, then you will tend to hesitate about doing anything which might contradict this idea. Or if you are seen by others to be extremely interested in music, more so than others of your acquaintance, then you will find it much harder to refuse to go along to see a new group playing locally when you are invited, even if it's on a night when you weren't particularly feeling like going out. Although you still can refuse, and you will if it matters enough to you, the attitudes that other people have affect your own views of yourself and your behaviour as well.

This self-definition can sometimes lead us to feel obliged to do things that we might not have done otherwise. A study by Freedman and Fraser (1966) showed how getting people to do one small thing would make them more likely to comply with a much bigger request. This, they argued, was because if someone agrees to perform a particular kind of action, then they will be more likely to see themselves as the kind of person who does that kind of thing. Their self-perception changes, and this makes them readier to comply with the next request.

The study involved American housewives who were visited by the experimenters and asked if they would sign a petition about safe driving. Most of the women agreed. A few weeks later, a different experimenter called on each of the women and asked if they would agree to have a large, ugly sign placed on their lawns, saying 'Drive Carefully'. Of the women who had signed the petition, 55% agreed to posting the sign, while a control group of housewives, who were also asked about this but who hadn't been approached with the petition, were much less willing: only 17% of them agreed. It seemed that when the women had agreed to sign the petition, they had begun to see themselves as the kind of people who were concerned about safe driving. This way of looking at themselves had made them much more likely to conform to the larger request.

Refusing to obey

Sometimes, however, we don't obey other people. Sometimes we become obstinate and stick to our beliefs or actions regardless of how much social pressure we are under. Even in Milgram's studies there were people who refused to obey. Gretchen Brandt had grown up in Nazi Germany and Jan Rensaleer had lived in Holland before and during World War II. Both of them were well aware of the consequences of unthinking obedience and both of them simply refused to obey Milgram's experimenter. Their refusal was quite calm but quite definite. Indeed, Jan Rensaleer only became angry when he was told that he had 'no choice' but to continue with the shocks. He pointed out, heatedly, that a choice was exactly what he did have. When he was told that it was the experimenter's responsibility and not his own, he said that was cowardly and that he himself was responsible for his own actions.

Gamson, Fireman and Rytina (1982) decided to investigate some of the factors which will cause people to rebel. They set up an experiment in which groups of people were asked to videotape a series of discussions. The discussions were about a petrol station manager whose company had sacked him for living with someone to whom he wasn't married. At first, the study seemed perfectly ordinary but, as discussions progressed, it gradually became clear that the whole thing was a set-up and that the researchers were faking evidence to support the petrol company in court. For example, sometimes during the discussions a researcher would come into the room, switch off the tape and ask a particular person to argue as if they were deeply offended by the man's conduct. They would then switch the tape back on and go out of the room again. At the end, the participants were asked to sign an affidavit which gave their permission for the research company to edit the videotapes as they liked and use them as evidence in court.

The researcher ran 33 discussion groups in the experiment, each group consisting of nine people. In all of the groups except one, people refused to sign the affidavit, despite being asked to do so by the experimenters. Groups whose members had highly anti-authority attitudes – these had been measured by a questionnaire beforehand – rebelled more quickly. Even in fairly authoritarian groups, where people were inclined to support authority, there was still some rebellion, although, often, those groups were divided and some individuals did sign. Overall, though, the researchers showed that people will disobey authority when they can see clearly that to obey would be personally wrong. Only a few people, who defined themselves as being supportive of authority in all circumstances, were prepared to go along with what they were asked to do regardless of whether it was morally acceptable or not.

Crowds and bystanders

In most situations, the behaviour that is expected of us is reasonably clear, either because we are playing clear social roles, or because we act in accordance with our self-concept. However, there are some situations that are ambiguous, when we are unsure of how to act. One of these kinds of situations is when we feel that we ought to help a total stranger, either because they have had an accident or because they are being attacked. Although most people know what they 'ought' to do in such situations, there have been several cases in which crimes or even murders have been committed in full view of the public but no one intervened. This non-intervention became known as **bystander apathy**.

Bystander intervention

The more psychologists studied the behaviour of bystanders, however, the more they became sure that 'bystander apathy' was the wrong term to use for what was happening. Sometimes, people will help a stranger and sometimes they won't. So this area of research changed its name. Instead of being called bystander apathy, it is now known as **bystander intervention**. Studies of bystander intervention have shown that there seem to be three main factors in whether bystanders will intervene to help someone else or not – the influence of other people's presence, the way that people comprehend what is going on, and the effects of other people's example. We will look at each of these in turn.

Diffusion of responsibility

The presence of other people seems to matter because everyone expects someone else to do something, or assumes that they have already done it. In the case of the murder of Kitty Genovese, reported by Rosenthal (1964), which was committed in front of 40 or so witnesses in a block of flats and went on for a considerable time, each witness assumed that someone else had called the police. So in the end, nobody did.

Latane and Rodin (1969) performed a study to investigate this. Research participants waited in a room with only a curtain separating them from another room in which a 'secretary' was working. They heard her climb on a chair to reach the bookcase shelf, fall and cry for help, saying that her foot was trapped and that she was in pain. Of the people who were waiting alone 70% came to her rescue, whereas only 40% of those who were waiting in pairs came to help. When they were waiting with other people, it seemed, the research participants considered the other person equally responsible for helping, so if the other person didn't help then they didn't either. This factor is called **diffusion of responsibility**: the more people who are considered able to help, the less any one person feels responsible.

Defining the situation

The way that we understand a situation also affects how we react to it. People define situations for themselves, mentally. If it is defined as an emergency, they are far more ready to help than if they have defined it as a non-emergency. This factor is also influenced by other people's responses. If someone seems to be very calm in a particular situation, we sometimes assume that they have defined the situation as a non-emergency and so we ourselves believe that it is not so serious.

Latane and Darley (1968) asked research participants to sit in a waiting room, waiting for an interview. As they sat there, a wall vent began to pour smoke into the room. The participants were observed through a one-way mirror to see how long it would be before they reported the smoke to someone else outside the room. Of the people who were tested on their own 75% reported the smoke within two minutes. But only 13% of people who were tested in groups reported the smoke at all, despite the fact that during the six minutes of the study the room filled up completely! Those people said afterwards that they thought that the smoke indicated a harmless phenomenon, such as steam or smog, and not fire. Apparently, the presence of other people who were not reacting meant that the research participants defined the situation as a non-emergency and acted accordingly. Of course, the fact that there were several of them implies that diffusion of responsibility may have been an influencing factor as well.

Following the example of others

Other people often set an example for us to follow. Bryan and Test investigated this in 1967. They set up a motorway study in which a 'model' scenario was acted out by the side of a motorway, followed by an opportunity for drivers to imitate the 'model' further on. The 'model' was a broken-down car with a man repairing it by the roadside while a woman stood watching. (The gender roles in this study reflect the date when it was carried out!) Further down the road was a 'test' car, which had a flat tyre, and a woman apparently unable to change it. In one condition of the study – the control group – drivers saw the 'test' situation but not the 'model' beforehand, but in the main study they saw both. Bryan and Test found that 93 out of 4000 passing drivers who had seen the 'model' stopped to help, but only 58 of 4000 in the 'control' group stopped. Although this might not seem like much of a difference, it was statistically significant (in other words, it wasn't likely to have happened just by chance). It implies that seeing another person helping does affect whether we are likely to offer to help other people ourselves.

But are people really so unhelpful? Although we often hear people say that we have become selfish and unwilling to help others, psychological research implies that this isn't the case at all. When we remove factors like diffusion of responsibility and ambiguity in the situation (leading to different definitions), people turn out to be quite helpful after all. Piliavin, Rodin and Piliavin (1969) showed this in the New York subway system – supposedly one of the worst places in the world for bystander apathy. They set up a situation in which a supposed passenger got on to a train and then suddenly collapsed onto the floor. The experimenters recorded whether the person was helped and if so, how long it took and who did it.

They varied the apparent reasons for the collapse. The passenger either carried a cane, implying that it was a physical infirmity which had caused his collapse, or smelled of alcohol, implying that he was drunk. If the man carried a cane, he was likely to be helped 95% of the time – an extremely high percentage. Even when the man appeared to be drunk, he was helped 50% of the time, usually within two minutes. So it seems that if there is no ambiguity and when people's responsibilities are clear (they could see that nobody else was helping), even modern city dwellers can be helpful and co-operative.

Crowds and bystanders

Large masses of people are an everyday part of modern living. We become part of crowds at music concerts, at sports events, when we are shopping and in many other contexts. Most of the time the crowd behaves in the ways that are expected of it and nobody thinks twice about the event. Just occasionally, though, a crowd may behave differently. Something happens which brings people together and the crowd seems to take on a life of its own.

Traditionally, psychologists (and, more important, governments) have rather distrusted crowds. Psychological theories of crowd behaviour emphasised the dangers of crowds and the risks of riot and disorder which could happen if a crowd became 'out of control'. LeBon, for example, writing in 1895, described crowds as dangerous mobs which had reverted to a primitive and vicious state in which people had lost their personal consciences and reverted to a state of barbaric savagery.

Psychology in Action

The theories that people hold about crowd behaviour can make a tremendous difference to the way they respond to crowds. A crowd with a deeply felt grievance can reach a 'flashpoint', at which its behaviour is no longer peaceable but involves aggressive activity and rioting. Traditionally, police and other authorities have held theories of deindividuation and regression – they believe that such crowds become mindless and dangerous mobs, with the individuals in them losing all sense of conscience or personal control.

The problem is that this type of theory can actually make things worse because it tends to lead to aggressive and violent attempts to control the crowd. Benewick and Holton studied why 'flashpoints' happen and found that they occur when the crowd is being treated in a way that it considers to be unfair, or when events occur which appear to the crowd to be typical of the grievances that they already feel. Other researchers, notably Reicher (1984) studying the St Paul's riot in Bristol, have found the same.

Benewick and Holton compared two demonstrations which took place during the miners' strike in Britain in the early 1980s. In one of them, the authorities had expressed the 'mob' theory of crowds and acted extremely repressively. That had turned into a riot. In the second, the authorities had discussed the organisation of the demonstration with the crowd leaders, had given people an opportunity to air their grievances publicly, and had refrained from confrontation. There was no riot.

Deindividuation

Although LeBon's **mob psychology** has become a little dated, a similar idea emerged in the work of a modern psychologist, Philip Zimbardo. In 1969, Zimbardo suggested that people in crowds lose their personal individuality and merge anonymously into the mob. This process of **deindividuation** suppresses personal conscience and rationality, Zimbardo argued, and people who are in this state act in far more cruel or impulsive ways than they would do in their normal individual state.

To investigate deindividuation, Zimbardo (1969) asked groups of college women to give another woman electric shocks. Half of the time the women giving the shocks were dressed in their own clothes, with name-tags, so their personal identities were very apparent. The other half of the time they were dressed in bulky lab coats and hoods which hid their faces and were never referred to by name. Zimbardo found that when the women were deindividuated by being made anonymous, they gave shocks which were twice as strong. Or at least they thought they did – the shocks were faked, of course.

Zimbardo's study seemed to support the idea that deindividuation produced cruel or impulsive behaviour, but it was criticised by Johnson and Downing (1979) who suggested that the reason the deindividuated women behaved more cruelly was because the uniform itself suggested violence. Their hoods and lab coats were reminiscent of the American Ku Klux Klan, an extremely violent racist group. When Jones and Downing repeated the study with one group of women wearing Ku Klux Klan-type costume, one group wearing their own clothes, and another group wearing nurses uniforms, they found that those wearing nurses' uniforms gave fewer and less severe shocks than all the others, even those operating as individuals. So it appears that the extreme outcomes were produced by the costumes which suggested socially appropriate behaviour, rather than by deindividuation as such.

Deindividuation may not inevitably produce cruel and destructive behaviour, as early research seemed to suggest, but it may still take place to some extent. At least, there does seem to be a reduction in self-awareness when people participate wholeheartedly in crowds. Diener (1979) suggested that this lessening of self-awareness is what deindividuation is all about. If someone is in a focused crowd – like a football crowd or a crowd at a rock concert – they don't think about themselves and how they are coming over to other people. Instead, their attention, like everyone else's, is on the main event. As a result, they aren't inhibited by thoughts of what other people will think and are able to act more impulsively.

Social contagion and social norms

Another explanation for the way that people behave in crowds is **social contagion**. This is the idea that people who participate in crowds 'catch' anti-social behaviour from one another. The social contagion approach argues that anti-social crowd behaviour happens as one person begins to act in an anti-social way, and then others join in and imitate it. As more and more people imitate the behaviour, acting in anti-social ways becomes a social norm and most of the crowd members conform to it.

One problem with this type of explanation for crowd behaviour is that it always tends to assume that crowds are disorderly and dangerous and that this needs explanation. In fact, as Benewick and Holton (1987) pointed out, most crowds are peaceful, not disorderly, and consist of shared experiences which people value a great deal. They interviewed people who had attended the open-air mass at Wembley Stadium during the Pope's visit to Britain in 1982, and found that this formed a very special, intensely personal experience for those people, one which was quite different from a suppression of individual personality and conscience. The fact that it was shared by so many others added to its intensity but didn't take away its personal nature.

19.2 Investigating crowd behaviour

We become part of crowds quite often – when we are shopping or playing, or when we are attending music concerts or sporting events – even when we go to the cinema. Sometimes, these crowds are sort of random in their activities, as they are when we are shopping or at the swimming pool, for example. At other times, the crowd is all focused around the same thing, for example, when watching a football match or at a rock concert. Crowds like this can create tremendous excitement for people, and often produce a sense of a kind of deindividuation as people join in cheering or sharing the experience.

It is interesting to see how people experience particularly exciting events. You could find this out by conducting some interviews.

Begin by choosing the event that you want to investigate – it will make it easier if all of the people that you interview have attended the same one. If there has been a big music event nearby, that a lot of your friends went to, choose that. Or you might choose a big sports event or something similar. Whatever it is, find some people – maybe five or six, more if you like – who attended the event, and ask them if you can interview them about it.

Before you start interviewing, you will need to draw up an interview schedule. See Chapter 26 for more detail about this. Essentially, an interview schedule is a list of questions which you want to ask the person concerned and which will, you hope, lead them to give you a description of what being in that crowd was like.

Collect all of the descriptions of being in the crowd that people give you. Look to see if they have anything in common and, if they have, write down what it is.

How would you summarise your findings?

Do your findings fit with the theories of crowd behaviour that you have looked at?

Did you find it easy to keep people to the point, or did they want to talk about other parts of the experience that you weren't interested in?

If you were doing this as a formal psychological study, how would you adjust it?

Even apparently disorderly crowds have their own structures. As Reicher (1984) showed, crowds that seem to be 'out of control' none the less act according to their members' analysis of the social situation. Even if a crowd is rioting and damaging buildings, it doesn't do so randomly: it is the buildings which appear to represent the crowd's sense of injustice and social unfairness which become damaged. In the early 1980s, Reicher gathered a number of personal accounts from the St Paul's riots in Bristol, and showed that the behaviour of the crowd followed a clear pattern which made sense when the feelings of people in that community were understood. The media had portrayed it as a 'mindless riot' but, in fact, the actions of the rioters were far from mindless.

Both deindividuation and social contagion, then, have some weaknesses as explanations of crowd behaviour. Moscovici and Doise (1996) discussed how part of the problem is that psychological theories of crowd behaviour have almost always tried to explain it in terms of people slipping into an inferior and less rational state of mind. Yet as they and Reicher showed, participating in crowds may be nothing of the sort. If the full social context is taken into account, what seems to be irrational behaviour often makes a great deal of sense.

In this chapter, we have seen that other people can influence us to quite a high degree. Just having other people present influences our behaviour: our psychological tendency to comply with the other people and to obey authority can sometimes result in each of us being more easily influenced than we realise. What these studies also tell us, however, is that what really counts is how we see ourselves and how we interpret the situation that we are in. People always try to make sense of what is around them and it is the way that they define the situation which affects how they respond. As we shall see in the next chapter, this is just as true when we are working in groups as it is when we are operating as individuals.

Summary

1 Our behaviour is affected by the presence of other people in a number of different ways. Sherif showed that the presence of other people can exert an influence even when there is no pressure to conform.

2 Asch demonstrated that people will sometimes go along with the majority even when they know that the majority judgement was inaccurate.

3 Studies of obedience performed by Milgram and Hofling showed that people will sometimes obey authority figures even when they know their actions are wrong.

4 Gamson et al. showed that people can resist authority when they are clear about taking personal responsibility for their actions.

5 Self-perception is an important factor in compliance. People who see themselves as co-operative are more likely to comply with others than those who don't.

6 Studies of bystander intervention have shown that diffusion of responsibility and defining the situation are important factors. If these do not apply, then people are usually very helpful.

7 Theories of crowd behaviour have emphasised deindividuation or social contagion as explanations for irrational behaviour. However, more recent approaches suggest that these theories fail to take the social context into account.

Chapter 20 - Social groups and social beliefs

In this chapter, we will be looking at the way that belonging to society shapes our social interaction. People don't just act as individuals. We are all influenced by the social groups that we belong to, the roles that we play in society, and the social beliefs that we adopt. We will begin by looking at how social expectations can affect how we behave: in terms of the social roles that we play and also by producing the powerful phenomenon known as groupthink. From there, we will go on to look at European social psychology and its core theories of social identity and social representation theory; both of which are concerned with the way that belonging to society and social groups directly affects our thinking.

Roles and expectations

In everyday life, we don't expect people to behave randomly. Instead, we expect to behave in ways that fit the particular situation we are in. For instance, if you were sitting in a dentist's waiting room and another person suddenly broke into a song-and-dance routine, you would wonder what was going on. If you couldn't find a reason for this behaviour, you would probably conclude that the person had something 'wrong' with them. Every social situation that we are in carries its own set of **expectations** about the 'proper' way to behave, and fitting in with these is important if we are to be accepted by other people.

Fitting in isn't just a matter of learning one set of rules, though. People who travel a lot, or who mix with different sectors of their own society, learn very quickly that social expectations can vary a lot from one social group to another. What is normal in one area of society may be seen as odd, or even disturbing, by people from a different social sector. These social norms, or expectations, become apparent when we look at the roles that people play in society. Social norms set the kind of behaviour that is acceptable for someone playing a particular role. Most of our day-to-day interactions with other people involve established social roles which carry with them established norms of behaviour.

Society has many roles and any one person will take on a myriad different roles during their lives. For instance, we may find someone beginning the day in, say, the role of 'daughter' to her mother and also of 'sister' to her siblings. On her way to school she may play the role of 'passenger' on the bus and, later, 'pedestrian';

at school she will be 'friend' and also 'pupil' at different times, as well as 'customer' in the school canteen and so on.

Each of these roles carries with it its own set of behaviours relevant to that particular situation. From our earliest childhood, we learn the 'correct' behaviour for the particular situation that we are in. Someone who looked carefully to the left and right before accepting a meal from the canteen staff would be regarded as decidedly peculiar! Yet such behaviour would be normal if they were crossing the road. Someone who behaved towards her teacher in the same way as she behaved towards her younger sister wouldn't just be thought as of odd, she would also meet extreme social disapproval from the school authorities and would almost certainly be punished. There are **social sanctions** for making sure that people act in ways which fit the role expectations for the role that they are playing. These can range from actual punishment, such as getting a school detention or being arrested, to informal sanctions like being laughed at or being avoided because you are thought 'strange'. Sometimes, the informal sanctions are much more powerful than formal ones.

Types of roles

Role expectations are the way that we make sense out of society. They bring order into social life: if everybody acted completely individualistically all of the time, we would never be able to take our interactions for granted. More important, we wouldn't be able to predict how people are likely to act. But the fact that playing a social role involves acting according to social expectations means that we can be much more confident about how other people are likely to behave. Fig 20.1 identifies five different sets of social roles. If you think about these types of roles, you can see that each set involves quite a different type of role behaviour. In fact, each individual role involves a different type of behaviour too. When you try to write them down, it becomes very complicated. Yet, in everyday life, we manage to deal with our different roles quite easily.

Age and sex groupings	e.g. infant, old man, boy, woman
Family groupings	e.g. father, aunt, grandmother
Status groupings	e.g. chairman, manager, foreman, shop steward
Occupational groupings	e.g. teacher, lawyer, mechanic, secretary
Common interest groupings	e.g. sports club member, pub local, video-game enthusiast

Adapted from: Linton, 1945

20.1 Sets of social roles

Internalisation

We begin adopting social roles almost from the moment that we become able to interact consciously with other people. The mother-infant role is the first of many, in the sense that it involves patterned interactions, with expectations on the part of both the mother and the infant about how the other person should act. As we grow older, we take on more and more roles. Goffman (1961) argued that acquiring a new social role is a two-stage process. At first, the individual feels as though the new role, and the role behaviour associated with it, are in some way false or unreal. They feel as if they are simply 'acting a part', like playing a role in a play. Gradually, though, the 'acting' becomes easier and easier to do, and the person comes to adopt that role more or less automatically. This process is known as **internalisation**.

For most of us, the different roles that we play during our everyday lives are so thoroughly internalised that we don't notice that they are different ways of behaving. We switch naturally from one set of role behaviours to another without thinking about it; and we don't feel that we have changed very much. However, to other people the difference may be much bigger. If someone who knows you from home comes to see you at work or college, they may find the difference quite striking. Some psychologists have argued that the best way to understand a human being's behaviour is to know where they were and what role they were playing at the time personality can be virtually unimportant, by comparison.

One of the most dramatic examples of the way that we internalise roles was shown in a study by Haney, Banks and Zimbardo in 1973. They took 21 emotionally stable young men, who had volunteered to participate in a fairly lengthy study, and set up a mock 'prison' in the basement at Stanford University. The volunteers were assigned randomly to act as either 'prisoner' or 'guard'. Nobody told either the prisoners or the guards how they should act: they were free to define their own role-behaviour, but the 'guards' wore uniforms and mirror sunglasses, and the 'prisoners' wore prisoner uniforms. The researchers recorded what happened.

They had originally planned to run the study for a fortnight, but decided to stop it after only six days. The 'guards'' understanding of their social role, and the way that they acted it out, was so extreme that the young men playing the part of 'prisoners' were at risk of being psychologically damaged by the experience. Although physical violence was prohibited, the 'guards' carried out a range of alienating and humiliating practices, such as making it a 'privilege' to go to the toilet. None of the young men concerned were particularly authoritarian or violent personalities, but their understanding of the social roles of prison guards was very powerful and much more extreme than in real life. Once the study was over, many of those who had acted as 'guards' were deeply shocked at how they had behaved and how they had been carried away by the role-behaviour they thought was expected of them.

Ethical discussion

The prison study by Haney, Banks and Zimbardo raises some questions about the whole process of taking part in a psychological study. The study fitted modern ethical criteria well. For example, there was no deception – the participants were told exactly what was involved and what the study was about. There were no instructions to do anything unethical – in fact, nobody told the participants how to act at all. They were left to their own devices. Yet the researchers had to terminate the study early because they were afraid of the harm which might have come to the participants. At the beginning, the researchers had no idea what it would develop into.

Exactly which ethical problems does this study raise?

Self-fulfilling prophecies

Social expectations don't just tell us how to act. They also predict what we should expect to find. And this means that they can also set up self-fulfilling prophecies. We came across self-fulfilling prophecies in Chapter 10, when we were looking at language development, but they can affect every aspect of our social lives. A **self-fulfilling prophecy** is a statement, or an expectation, which comes true simply because it has been made. By describing what the situation is, it causes that situation to be like the description.

This may seem clearer with an example. Suppose you were out with some friends and happened to make a particularly funny remark which they remember. This sets up a social expectation of you as a humorous sort of person. They begin to describe you to other people as 'the joker'. What would you do? Odds are, you would try very hard to think up amusing things to say, in order to keep this reputation. Also, because your friends were expecting you to be funny, they would notice everything amusing you said even if they probably wouldn't have noticed it before. In this case, being called a joker has become a self-fulfilling prophecy. Once the statement, or belief, has been made, it has influenced that particular set of social interactions and has made itself come true. Self-fulfilling prophecies are an important way in which social expectations become internalised.

Psychology in Action

There are plenty of examples of self-fulfilling prophecies around us all the time. They can work at the personal or group level and can have an immediate or later effect. Techniques such as 'psyching-up' a football team before an important match are used consciously by football managers, as is the 'psyching-out' of a boxing opponent to try to convince him he cannot win. In his body-building days, Arnold Schwarzenegger used this technique on his fellow competitors before competitions. His supreme self-belief played an enormous part in convincing other competitors of his ability to win and no doubt communicated itself to the judges as well.

We can also see examples of self-fulfilling prophecies at work on a wider level. Politicians and leaders of commerce and industry often try to convince each other that a recession is over and a recovery is underway, even when economic indicators are mixed. By instilling confidence in each other, it was hoped that investment will increase, interest rates will fall and the economy will pull itself around.

Self-fulfilling prophecies are very common in social interactions: one example might be the sex-stereotyping of babies which we looked at in Chapter 16, or ideas about what old people are like, which mean that we regard any act of independence shown by old people as being stubbornness, and any showing of dependence as being feebleness. Heads I win, tails you lose! Eventually the person has no choice but to conform to these social expectations, and so the prophecy becomes self-fulfilling.

Groupthink

One of the more interesting effects of internalising social expectations is known as **groupthink**. In 1972, Janis described how, sometimes, high-level committees or groups, consisting of people who are supposed to be extremely well informed, end up making absolutely disastrous decisions. The reason for this is that the group has become caught up in, and completely satisfied with, its own internalised way of looking at situations, and this complacency means that it doesn't analyse the situation realistically.

Janis identified a number of historical decisions resulting from groupthink, including the American Government's decision to invade the Bay of Pigs in Cuba, which resulted in a humiliating defeat for them; the decision to market the drug Thalidomide despite warnings that it could be damaging to unborn children; and the decision by the Ford motor company to market the Edsel in the face of information which, if they had taken notice of it, would have told them that they were facing a marketing disaster.

Typically, groups engaging in groupthink don't explore alternatives to the proposal that they are dealing with, and they don't explore the risks involved in their chosen way either. Because the group has already decided on the option that it wants to explore, its members only seek out information in a very patchy way and they are very selective about which information they notice – ignoring uncomfortable facts or deciding that they are not relevant.

In 1983, Janis identified eight major symptoms of groupthink:

1. an **illusion of invulnerability**, in that the group doesn't really entertain the possibility that it might make a wrong decision
2. **rationalisation** of the group's beliefs
3. preserving an **illusion of morality** by assuming that its actions and decisions are always ethical and correct

4 **stereotyping** and dismissing people with opposing views

5 **pressurising** dissenters to make them conform

6 **self-censorship**, in that members of the group will not say that they disagree for fear of being pressurised and attracting hostility

7 an **illusion of unanimity** which is taken as support of the group's views. This illusion happens, of course, because of the other symptoms suppressing awareness of alternative views, but it means that those favouring the group's viewpoint are able to convince themselves that all are agreed

8 **mind-guarding** among group members – that is, not revealing challenging information.

Janis's research into groupthink alerted a great many managers and high-level decision-makers to the dangers of having a highly cohesive group which believes that its decisions are always right. Unfortunately, however, our knowledge of the process doesn't stop it from happening – there were many examples of groupthink during the Thatcher years in Britain, including the decision to try to introduce a poll tax which was a spectacular failure. Such decision-making problems still continue, mainly because it is generally more comfortable for leaders to avoid dealing with people who challenge their ideas.

Groupthink is fostered when decisions are made in a closed group which restricts and selects what information is voiced. Members of the group develop explicit expectations about the roles that others will play, and use those role expectations to dismiss warnings or negative information. For example, when technical staff were warning that the space shuttle *Challenger* should not be launched, their warnings were dismissed by the Committee as being the sort of thing that technical people would be likely to say – with the result that the shuttle exploded and the whole NASA space programme was thrown into jeopardy (Moorhead, Ference and Neck, 1991).

Closed groups easily become isolated from outside influences, and also become extremely cohesive. Groupthink is even more extreme when there is a strong leader who has a personal agenda or a personal bias towards one particular course of action. As Janis showed, one of the main ways of dealing with groupthink is to encourage people to disagree and come up with alternatives. However, it takes an intelligent leader to achieve this, and many people are simply unaware of how dangerous groupthink can be.

European social psychology

Until relatively recently, most social psychology was concerned only with people's individual attitudes, beliefs or habits. There wasn't much social psychology which looked at how groups influence how people act. Janis is one of the exceptions because Janis's work on groupthink shows us how the group can produce results which are qualitatively different from the results those individuals would achieve if working alone. Another, much larger exception occurs with the area of psychological research known as **European social psychology**.

Events in Europe before, during and after World War II showed very clearly that individualistic explanations of social behaviour were simply inadequate to explain what had actually happened. As Arendt (1963) pointed out, most of the Nazis, including well-known ones like Eichmann, were not particularly evil people – although the outcomes of their actions were undoubtedly evil. Eichmann, for example, was directly responsible for transporting millions of Jews, Gypsies and Poles to their deaths in the concentration camps. Yet in his private life he was friendly with, and even tried to save, one or two Jewish people.

Even when they were working in America, European psychologists felt that individualistic explanations were insufficient to explain how whole societies had become caught up in these overwhelming social forces. They were very aware that society and social groups are very powerful influences on social behaviour, and they began to investigate how this influence happens. In 1972, one of these psychologists, Henri Tajfel, founded the *European Journal of Social Psychology* which dealt with psychological research and theories about how people act in their social contexts. European social psychology involves three major theories which form the framework for empirical research: social identity theory, social representation theory, and some aspects of attribution theory.

Sherif and social identification

Social identity theory was developed by Tajfel but it can probably be said to have its origins in the work of Sherif who showed how group mechanisms and, in particular, group identification can make a great deal of difference to the way that we think and act. In 1961, Sherif et al. reported the 'Robber's Cave' study which involved two competing teams among a group of 22 boys attending a summer camp. The boys were encouraged to form friendships in their own group and, at first, they did not know that another group existed. They were friendly enough towards one another but didn't have a particularly strong attitude about their group.

After a few days, the organisers arranged a major competition between the two groups. Almost immediately, the boys began to identify with their own group and to emphasise how their group was different to the other. For example, each group described their own team members as 'brave' and 'tough', while the other team were described as 'unpleasant' and 'underhanded'. This intergroup rivalry continued to develop as the teams competed against one another and the competition often became quite bitter.

After a few more days, the organisers arranged an 'emergency', which meant that the two teams needed to co-operate with one another. Both teams needed to pull together to get out a lorry that was stuck in the mud. The researchers noticed that this event seemed to reduce the hostility between the groups. They followed it up with a number of events which required co-operation, and encouraged the two groups to become friendly again: showing that intergroup hostility could be significantly reduced by friendly co-operation between the groups.

Sherif's study was criticised because the ill-feeling between the two groups was largely generated by the researchers – the boys had known each other and been friends beforehand, and were friends again at the end of the study. Tyerman and Spencer (1983) argued that this meant that it could not be used as evidence that all forms of intergroup conflict could be resolved in that way. None the less, the study raised the whole question of group identification and the way that social identification of this type can produce either hostility or co-operation.

Social identity theory

Tajfel and Turner (1979) drew on Sherif's research, and that of many others, to argue that the human self-concept isn't just an individual matter. We have, of course, our own concept of self as individual, but we also identify with the social groups that we belong to and that group membership is a significant part of how we see ourselves. For example, I might see myself as a psychologist, as a writer of textbooks, as English, as a researcher, as a science fiction fan, or as an amateur skater, since I belong to each of these social categories. They are part of my identity, in the same way that my own individual self is. Sometimes these identities are irrelevant to what I am doing at the time; at other times they can be crucially important.

For example, if I am in a discussion with other people about social knowledge, then my social identity as a researcher will become salient. (Being salient means that it becomes important in that context.) It will influence what I say and how I go about saying it. Later, in another context, a different social identity might become salient: I might, for instance, get into a discussion with some sociologist friends, and at such a time my social identity as a psychologist might come to the fore. It all depends on what is happening at the time, but when a social identity becomes **salient**, it has a direct influence on how we think and how we see ourselves.

20.1 Incompatible role-behaviour

You can play quite an amusing game by acting out different sets of role-behaviour, putting together roles which don't really belong.

First, you need to develop a list of pairs of social roles, for instance, bus-conductor and passenger, doctor and patient, teacher and student. Write each role on a slip of paper and put all the slips together in a box. Working in pairs, each member of a pair should take a slip from the box but not let anyone else know what is on it. Then, the two of them should each act out the appropriate role-behaviour, in interaction with each other.

The other members of the class or group have to guess which role each of them is playing. Which pair did you find the most amusing?

Classification

Social identification rests on two fundamental aspects of human psychology. The first is our tendency to classify things and people into groups or categories. Tajfel (1969) described this as a fundamental mechanism of human perception. The process of **classification** also means, almost inevitably, that differences between categories become exaggerated. For example, Tajfel and Wilkes (1963) asked research participants to judge lengths of lines. Sometimes the lines were unlabelled but at other times they were labelled as either A or B. They found that research participants judged lines which were labelled the same as one another to be more similar than those that were labelled as different, even though this was often completely inaccurate.

The finding is even stronger for social judgements. Doise, Deschamps and Meyer (1978) asked research participants to rate people whom they were interviewing. The people belonged to two different social categories: white Canadian or Canadian Indian. The researchers found that their research participants accentuated those aspects of the interviewees' behaviour that fitted their stereotypes of Canadians or Indians. This process of accentuating differences between groups can also explain the finding that highly prejudiced individuals (for whom categories are very important) tend to make more extreme judgements.

People are also inclined to act to support their own group. Billig and Tajfel (1973) divided research participants into two groups simply by tossing a coin. There was very little similarity between the different members of the group and everyone knew how random the process was. But, when the research participants were asked to perform a task that involved awarding points to other people, they still favoured members of their own group. Just labelling people as belonging to the same group seemed to be enough. If people didn't think in terms of 'groups' , but just referred to one another using code numbers, they did not show such preferences, even though they knew that there were some similarities between themselves and some of the others.

Social comparison and self-esteem

The second fundamental psychological process that underlies social identification is the search for **positive self-esteem**. Belonging to social groups also means that we compare ourselves with members of other social groups. There are lots of different types of social groups. Some are very large, like gender, or ethnic categories; others are smaller, like having a particular trade or profession, or being a member of a community group or club. However, all social groups are located in a real social context – they are part of our society. As society has so many levels and subcultures, that also means that some social groups have more prestige or power than others. Tafjel and Turner argued that identifying with our social groups also involves **social comparison**, and these social comparisons affect how we regard ourselves and how we react to people who belong to other social groups.

Social comparison means that we weigh up groups in terms of their relative social status. So, for example, in a study comparing students' perceptions of universities, Spears and Manstead (1989) found that students from Manchester and Exeter Universities were more inclined to compare themselves with Oxford students than with students from Manchester Polytechnic, and this comparison led them to exaggerate the differences between themselves and the polytechnic students.

Social comparison also affects how strongly we identify with our group because people like to have positive sources of self-esteem. So, if you find yourself part of a group that seems to be inferior by comparison with others, you are likely to do one of three things. You may try to leave the group – for instance, if you were unhappy about being one of the social group known as 'the unemployed', you might try studying part-time so that you could go to college. You might try to distance yourself from it – if you were white and living in a mixed community, and you found that most of the other white people thereabouts were racist, you would probably want to make sure that people knew you were not like them. Another strategy is to try to change the perceived status of your group. For example, the 'Black is Beautiful' movement in America in the late 1960s produced changes in how American society saw black people, and these, in turn, were reflected in how black people saw themselves. Disabled people are currently engaging in the same sort of social battle.

Intergroup mechanisms

Social identity theory, then, can tell us a great deal about how and when people identify with their social groups. It can also tell us when contact between social groups is likely to produce conflicts. Early research into social identity suggested that simply knowing that people belonged to a different group was enough to produce intergroup rivalry and hostility. However, Mummendey and Schreiber (1983) showed that it wasn't anything like that simple. If they are given the opportunity, people are happy to describe other groups as 'equally good', but most of the early studies hadn't allowed that. They had simply required people to choose which group was the best, so, naturally, the participants had chosen their own group. Similarly, Mummendey and Schreiber found that bias towards the in-group disappeared if research participants were allowed to choose how they assessed other groups, instead of being told what criteria to use by the experimenter. In other words, allowing groups to make their own judgements doesn't automatically produce intergroup hostility.

This is quite an important finding. It helps us to understand why racists are always trying to make it appear that their disliked group is in direct competition ('taking our jobs' etc.), even when nothing of the kind is really happening. It shows that making groups compete for necessary resources is likely to produce intergroup hostility, which is a message for managers everywhere. It also shows us why knowing more about other groups can reduce social prejudice – because we then become aware of different criteria that we can use for evaluating that group, and don't see them in simplistic or competitive terms.

20.2 Exploring social identifications

Each of us belongs to quite a number of social groups, ranging from our own families to our national and ethnic groups. We don't identify personally with every group that we belong to, though. So it can be quite interesting to look at which groups people do identify with.

How can you tell whether someone just belongs to a group or whether they really identify with it? One way is to see whether belonging to that group is one of the things that comes up when people are asked to describe their own selves. If it does, then it's a pretty sure bet that they really do identify with that group, to some extent at least. You can investigate this for yourself.

Begin by preparing some sheets of paper, with the beginnings of sentences and lots of space for people to write in. Each sentence should begin in the same way, with the words 'I am'. So what you are really asking people to do is to complete the sentence 'I am ...' ten times, in different ways.

Ask half a dozen people to complete these sheets. Then look through each one and count up how many of the answers relate to a social group. For example, you wouldn't count things like 'I am tall' because that is about personal identity and acts as a description of that individual person. But you would count something like 'I am a college student' because college students count as a social group. Make a list of all of the different social groups that have been mentioned.

Did more of the answers relate to social identifications or to personal identifications?

Were the social identifications that people mentioned of large-scale groups, like gender or nationality, or about smaller-scale groups? Or did they include both?

Were some people more inclined to describe themselves in terms of social identifications than others?

You might also find it interesting to compare older and younger people using this method. Do you think it would be the older or the younger people who would include most social identifications? Why?

If you were doing this as a formal psychological study, what precautions would you need to take?

Social identification affects a very wide part of our everyday life. It also helps us to make sense of a lot of things about human behaviour which are hard to explain using purely individual mechanisms. Hogg and Abrams (1988) showed how social identity theory can be used to explain a large number of other findings in social psychology, including prejudice and conformity. By addressing the whole business of 'us and them', it helps us to understand much more about everyday living. For this reason, social identity theory is one of the fundamental theories of European social psychology.

Social representation theory

The other fundamental theory of European social psychology is **social representation** theory. This was first developed by the French psychologist Serge Moscovici who argued that it is the social representations, or shared beliefs and explanations held by a group or society, that allow people to communicate effectively with one another (Moscovici, 1984). Every culture and every society has its own set of social representations and these are used by the members of that society to make sense out of social living.

Social representations are passed from person to person through conversation and through the media. They don't always stay exactly the same – we don't just swallow everything we are told without thinking about it. Instead, we negotiate our social representations through conversation and adjust them to fit with our own personal constructs (see Chapter 14) and schemas. So, some parts of a social representation do change as they circulate around society, but the central core of the representation remains the same, mainly because it usually serves a deep function or purpose for the people who hold it.

This ideological aspect of social representations means that people in some societies are readier to accept certain explanations than others. In Britain, for example, maternal deprivation theory has survived for over 40 years, despite the huge amount of psychological research which has shown that the child's important relationships can be with people other than the mother, without psychological damage. The idea of maternal deprivation has become more than an academic theory: it has become a social representation, and psychological evidence alone is not enough to shift it.

Social representations also guide social action. Different groups of people sometimes adopt different social representations and this can sometimes produce a breakdown in communication between different groups. Di Giacomo (1980) studied the social representations in a student protest movement at a university in Belgium. It turned out that there were considerable differences between the social representations held by the leaders of the protest movement and those held by the majority of students. The student leaders used concepts like 'student-worker solidarity', and believed that there were parallels between what they were doing and industrial action. The social representations shared by the ordinary students, however, were quite different: they didn't see what students and workers had in common at all. So the attempts of the student leaders to encourage the ordinary students to strike met with complete failure. The different social representations of the two groups, Di Giacomo reported, meant that they weren't communicating with one another at all.

As we have seen, social representations are not static. They change with time, and in ways that are directly influenced by other forces in society. Fischler (1980) showed how social representations of what constitutes an acceptable diet have changed with time, and how those changes reflect the social and economic changes which have taken place over the same period. Some of them have been concerned with the production, distribution and consumption of food, meaning that fresher types of food are available or that foods can be brought from greater distances. Other changes have happened because of new, consumer-based lifestyles which involve different modes of eating, like the increased demand for fast food and snacks rather than meals.

According to Moscovici, everyday conversation is the main source of change in social representations. During conversation, people talk about events that have happened and, as part of that talking, they offer explanations to one another and agree on probable reasons for why the events took place. The media and other forces are important too. In 1984, for example, Jodelet described a study of changes in social representations of the body and showed how these could be linked with other factors, like the influence of youth movements, women's liberation and advertising images.

Anchoring and objectification

The strength of social representations, and the reason why they are so powerful in social life, is that they are able to make new ideas or events seem conventional and familiar. This reduces anxiety and helps people to think that they understand what is happening and can deal with it in familiar ways. Social representations are made to seem familiar through two processes: anchoring and objectification.

Anchoring involves setting the ideas in a familiar context, so that people can grasp them more easily. For example, you might draw on a commonly understood phrase such as 'mid-life crisis' or 'teenage angst' to explain what is going on with a family member, and to anchor it in a familiar context. Alternatively, anchoring might happen by classification, such as describing protesters against a new motorway as 'eco-freaks' or 'rent-a-mob'. This type of classification anchors what is happening in a negative way and makes the protest less likely to be taken seriously. So a social representation of this type would be held and passed on by people opposing the protest they would have accepted it because it served a useful function for their group. However, those who support the protest – will anchor what is going on in a different way. Social representations aren't swallowed wholesale.

Objectification is about making an idea more concrete and tangible and so making it easier to grasp. One way of doing this is by linking the idea with a particular person; for instance, referring to Newtonian physics or Thatcherite policies. In these cases, a scientific theory and an economic theory have both become easier to talk about as a result of objectification. Using the name of the person acts as a kind of shorthand which 'sums up' their theoretical ideas. This type of objectification is known as **personification**. Another type involves using metaphors or images, like describing ideas which relate to ecological awareness as 'green', or using symbols to express what an organisation's culture is like. This type of objectification is known as **figuration** and, again, it makes complex ideas easier to sum up and to refer to in conversation.

Social representations and ideology

The study of social representations also shows how the sociological concept of **ideology** can manifest itself in our thinking. Ideology is about how ideas in society are used to maintain the status quo – to keep society as it is. In one of the first studies of social representations, Moscovici (1961) showed how psychoanalytic theory came to be adopted in France as an ideological force, rather than an expert theory. He identified three phases to this process. The first was the scientific phase, in which psychoanalysis was seen largely as a scientific theory, restricted to professional scientists and medical specialists. This was followed by a second phase in which the image and concepts of psychoanalysis began to become better known in society, particularly among the middle classes. During the process, however, they were changed and modified in such a way as to fit better with socially accepted assumptions. The third phase was the ideological phase, in which the transformed version of psychoanalysis became widespread and generally accepted, and was then used to explain or justify why society is like it is.

Social representation theory is a core theory of European social psychology, and it is well developed in many European countries, although, until recently, it was less well known in Britain. However, that is changing as psychologists become increasingly interested in the way that shared social beliefs affect how people interact and what they consider to be important.

Social attributions

The third major theory within the European social psychology framework is **attribution theory**. Attribution theory itself has been around a long time and we looked at it in Chapter 17. However, within the European context attribution theory has undergone a change of emphasis and is now much more concerned with analysing attributions in groups, and also with why everyday explanations are as they are.

Traditional attribution theories, such as Kelley's covariance theory (see Chapter 17), were criticised by Lalljee (1981) on the grounds that they don't take enough account of prior knowledge and assumptions. Lalljee argued that the attributions that we make incorporate a high degree of social knowledge, including social representations and social identifications – they don't just happen in a context-free manner. For example, if teachers were having a discussion in the staffroom about a low-achieving student, their social beliefs about the nature of intelligence and achievement and their social identification as a particular type of teacher would be directly linked with the type of attribution that they would make. Someone who had different beliefs, or different identifications, could easily make entirely different attributions about why that student wasn't doing too well.

As a result of this, there has been a growing interest in how attribution and explanation are used by different social groups. Taylor and Jaggi (1974) compared the attributions made by Hindu and Muslim groups in southern India about themselves and each other. They found that their research participants tended to make internal attributions for socially desirable behaviour from their own group – believing that the desirable behaviour happened because they were nice people, whereas they made external attributions about socially desirable behaviour from members of the other group believing that it came from the situation that the people were in. If they were being asked to explain socially undesirable behaviour, they saw it as being the other way round.

Attributions and social representations

This type of attribution theory is often strongly linked with social representations. For example, in one study, Moscovici and Hewstone (1983) showed how the split-brain research which we looked at in Chapter 8 became transformed into a folk-scientific belief that the two halves of the brain are two different, independent minds with opposing skills, and that these differences explain social differences because society favours those with the kind of skills found in the left hemisphere.

What happened in this case, as Moscovici and Hewstone showed, was that the findings of scientific research, which showed simply that there are some differences between the two cerebral hemispheres, were gradually changed into something quite different. The difference in functions of the two hemispheres was exaggerated until they were seen as opposites. Then they continued to be exaggerated until, eventually, in popular literature, all sorts of different social phenomena and experiences were attributed to hemisphere differences. This study shows how closely attributions and social representations are linked – the beliefs about hemisphere differences had become social representations which were then used to make certain kinds of attributions rather than others.

European social psychology is different to traditional social psychology mainly because it also deals with the way that society and social groups influence how we live our lives. As an approach, it has allowed many psychologists to re-evaluate a great deal of existing research in social psychology, and it is becoming increasingly popular as a framework among British social psychologists. European social psychology does not simply adopt the reductionist approach of trying to explain social behaviour as being solely the product of individual psychological factors. Instead, it aims to show how wider social and group factors work together with individual factors to produce social outcomes.

Summary

1. Social roles are parts that we play in society. People have expectations about the behaviour that is appropriate for a particular role and often impose sanctions on those who do not conform.
2. People are expected to play a variety of different roles in their everyday lives. Roles become internalised, and social expectations can also become self-fulfilling prophecies.
3. Groupthink is a particular powerful effect of social expectation. It can result in groups of people making disastrous decisions having failed to take into account opposing points of view.
4. European social psychology is the name given to a group of theories which emphasise the importance of the wider social factors in society. It includes social identity theory, social representation theory and social attribution theory.
5. Social identity theory is concerned with the 'us' and 'them' distinctions that are common in society. It explores how membership of social groups influences the way that we see social events.
6. Social representations are the shared beliefs and assumptions that are commonplace in society and which are used to explain why things are as they are. They have links with ideology and are often expressed through images and metaphors.
7. Social attribution theory is concerned with using attributions to explore the social representations of large groups, in order to see how different social groups may make different attributions about everyday events.

Suggestions for further reading

Ajzen, I. 1988 *Attitudes, Personality and Behaviour*. Milton Keynes: Open University Press

Argyle, M. 1978 *Bodily Communication*. London: Methuen

Augoustinos, M. & Walker, I. 1995 *Social Cognition: an Integrated Introduction*. London: Sage

Bethlehem, D. 1985 *A Social Psychology of Prejudice*. London: Croom Helm

Feldman, R. S. 1992 *Applications of Nonverbal Behavioural Theories and Research*. Hillsdale, N. J: Lawrence Erlbaum Associates

Hayes, N. 1993 *Principles of Social Psychology*. London: Erlbaum

Hewstone, M. et al. 1988 *Introduction to Social Psychology*. Oxford: Blackwell

Hogg, M. A. & Abrams, D. 1988 *Social Identifications: a Social Psychology of Intergroup Relations and Group Processes*. London: Routledge

Hogg, M. A. & Vaughan, G. M. 1995 *Social Psychology: an Introduction*. London: Harvester Wheatsheaf

Kelly, C. & Breinlinger, S. 1996 *The Social Psychology of Collective Action*. London: Taylor & Francis

Zebrowitz, L. A. 1990 *Social Perception*. Milton Keynes: Open University Press

? Self Assessment Questions

1 According to Asch, some traits affect our judgements of other people more than others. These traits are called:

a) peripheral traits.
b) powerful traits.
c) central traits.
d) personality traits.

2 Thorndike said that if we know a person has one or two positive traits we tend to see them as having many more. This is called:

a) the Thorndike effect.
b) the trait effect.
c) the halo effect.
d) the self-fulfilling prophecy.

3 Stereotyping means:

a) seeing all Italians as being the same.
b) seeing all members of a group as having the same characteristics.
c) seeing everyone in a specific group as having negative characteristics.
d) seeing the individual differences within a group.

4 Which of the following appear to be important in deciding how likeable or attractive somebody is?

a) proximity.
b) physical attractiveness.
c) competence.
d) similarity of attitudes.
e) all of the above.

5 Walster found that physical attraction:

a) was not an important consideration for people choosing partners.
b) was not more important than any other factor in the choice of partner.
c) was the most important factor in choosing a partner.
d) was only important to teenagers.

6 According to Murstein, couples tend to chose partners who:

a) are of different levels of attraction to each other.
b) are of similar levels of attraction to each other.
c) look like one of their parents.
d) look nothing like themselves.

7 Reciprocal liking means that we:

a) like those who are similar to us.
b) like those who like us.
c) like those who contradict us.
d) like those who are attractive.

8 According to Kelley, if a person's behaviour is of high consensus:

a) no one else is behaving in the same manner.
b) lots of people are behaving in the same manner.
c) one small group of people are behaving in the same manner.
d) if most people agree with it.

9 When two important attitudes appear to contradict each other, this leads to a state of:

a) consonance.

b) cognition.

c) cognitive dissonance.

d) argument.

10 Prejudice means:

a) holding negative attitudes towards a person or group of people.

b) pre-judging people either positively or negatively.

c) holding positive attitudes towards a person or group of people.

d) having no pre-conceptions about members of a group.

11 Paralanguage is:

a) a term for the non-verbal cues we use when talking.

b) the timing of speech.

c) the skill of talking on the telephone.

d) public speaking.

12 Probably the single most powerful non-verbal cue we have is:

a) posture.

b) eye-contact.

c) gesture.

d) dress.

13 Another term for proxemics is:

a) gestures.

b) stereotypes.

c) personal space.

d) eye-contact.

14 Ekman and Friesen argued that non-verbal cues could be categorised into five groups. Which of the following does not belong in that group?

a) emblems.

b) illustrators.

c) proxemics.

d) affect displays.

e) regulators.

f) adapters.

15 Non-verbal communication is any form of communication that:

a) uses words.

b) does not use words.

c) uses categories.

d) involves speech.

16 Ostwald found that people suffering from mental illness sometimes had:

a) normal speech patterns.

b) unusually 'flattened' speech patterns.

c) unusually rapid speech patterns.

d) unusual NVC gestures.

17 Argyle, Alkemaa and Gilmour found that:

a) people are five times as likely to react to non-verbal cues as they are to verbal cues.

b) people are five times as likely to react to verbal cues as they are to non-verbal cues.

c) people ignore non-verbal cues.

d) people ignore verbal cues.

18 Ekman and Friesen carried out several cross-cultural studies of facial expressions and found that:

a) there are no cross-cultural similarities in facial expressions.

b) many basic emotional expressions seem to be inherited.

c) Japanese people use more facial expressions than English people.

d) verbal communication is more important than non-verbal communication in many societies.

19 Facial expressions are sometimes studied through the use of:

a) paralanguage.

b) a galvanic skin response meter.

c) electromyography.

d) bio-feedback.

20 Comparative studies:

a) investigate only human behaviour.

b) compare human behaviour with that of other animals.

c) are concerned with language development in animals.

d) investigate behaviour in different cultures.

21 Triplett found that when children worked in co-action they worked:

a) much faster.

b) much slower.

c) the same as they did when they were on their own.

d) faster with children of the same sex.

22 Which of the following are not included in Kelman's three types of conformity?

a) imitation.

b) identification.

c) compliance.

d) internalisation.

23 In a variation of his experiment Asch found that:

a) if even one confederate breaks with the majority, conformity drops sharply.

b) participants always conformed to four or more people if they were unanimous.

c) the minimum number of stooges needed for one research participant to conform was three.

d) people ignore minority opinions.

24 Milgram showed that:

a) people enjoy giving one another electric shocks.

b) people always refuse to obey orders if they disagree with their instructions.

c) people can 'kill' others in an experimental situation without remorse.

d) people usually obey orders even if they object to what they are supposed to do.

25 In Hofling's study:

a) 50% of nurses obeyed inappropriate instructions.

b) 65% of nurses obeyed inappropriate instructions.

c) 21 out of 22 nurses obeyed inappropriate instructions.

d) 17 out of 55 nurses obeyed inappropriate instructions.

26 Compliance means:

a) outwardly conforming with the majority in order to avoid rejection or to seek approval.

b) really believing the opinions of the majority.

c) temporarily agreeing with the majority because you can identify with their views.

d) accepting the opinions of the majority.

27 Gamson et al. studied rebellion using:

a) door-to-door canvassers.

b) nurses on night duty.

c) videotaped discussion groups.

d) people who had experience of Nazi Germany.

28 Which of the following has not been found by researchers into bystander intervention?

a) that the presence of other people diminishes the responsibility for action.

b) that people do not care about other people and are essentially selfish.

c) that if others around us fail to react we become convinced that it is not an emergency.

d) that how we define the situation affects whether we help out or not.

29 'Diffusion of responsibility' means:

a) the more people who are available to help, the more we feel a responsibility to act.

b) the more people who are available to help, the less we feel a responsibility to act.

c) we do not like making decisions.

d) other people do not affect our tendency to act.

30 Deindividuation is:

a) losing a sense of personal responsibility when in a crowd.

b) fragmentation of the personality.

c) maintaining one's personal conscience in a crowd.

d) catching excitement from other people in the crowd.

31 European social psychology is concerned with:

a) the influence of society on behaviour.

b) racial prejudice.

c) the biological basis of behaviour.

d) the study of animals.

32 Social identity theory argues that:

a) we identify and compare ourselves with other members of our social group.

b) we identify and compare ourselves with members of other social groups.

c) both (a) and (b) above.

d) none of the above.

33 Which of the following is not a symptom of groupthink?

a) exploration of alternatives.

b) an illusion of invulnerability.

c) self-censorship.

d) mind-guarding.

34 Billig and Tajfel (1973) found that:

a) people tend to support members of their own group.
b) people tend to support members of other groups before their own.
c) people always act as individuals.
d) people do not like being part of a social group.

35 Social representations are:

a) dissimilar beliefs within a group.
b) cultural differences in perception.
c) visual illusions.
d) shared beliefs which occur throughout everyday life.

36 Di Giacomo found that communication problems arise when:

a) different groups of people use different social representations.
b) different cultures use different NVC skills.
c) an interpreter is used to interpret a conversation.
d) people are prejudiced.

37 Which part of a social representation is most likely to change?

a) its anchoring.
b) its central nucleus.
c) its peripheral elements.
d) its objectifications.

38 Taylor and Jaggi (1974) found that groups tend to make:

a) more internal attributions for socially desirable behaviour amongst their own group.
b) more external attributions for socially desirable behaviour amongst their own group.
c) few judgements of the behaviour of their own group.
d) unfavourable judgements of other groups.

39 Sherif's study of group identification involved:

a) students from Manchester and Exeter Universities.
b) competing teams at a boys' summer camp.
c) a student protest at a university in Belgium.
d) white Canadians and Canadian Indians.

40 Mummendey and Schreiber showed that:

a) intergroup conflicts happen automatically.
b) competing for resources increases intergroup conflict.
c) competing for resources reduces intergroup conflict.
d) competing for resources produces intergroup conflict.

Section 6 - Developmental psychology

In this section, we will look at the different ways that psychologists have investigated child development. In doing so, we will examine several different sorts of influences on children, starting with the first interactions which take place between parents and their children, and moving on to look at some of the many different ways that children in different cultures are brought up.

From there, we will go on to look at child development from four main perspectives. The first one is the social learning approach to child development, in which the contacts which the child has with other people are examined, to see how they might affect the ways in which children develop. After that, we will look at the psychoanalytic approach to child development: in particular seeing how the work of Freud has demonstrated different influences and aspects of development. The third perspective we will take is that of the structuralist approach within the study of child development, which emphasises the child's biological maturation and the way that its cognition develops in an orderly, sequential manner. Finally, we will look at some of the socio-cognitive approaches to child development, including the study of play, family interactions and Vygotsky's theory of child development.

Chapter 21 - The social-learning approach to child development

In Chapter 2 we dealt with the traditional theories of learning: classical and operant conditioning. The social learning approach to child development has its origins in those theories, but doesn't consider that everything can be explained in terms of conditioning processes alone. Instead, social learning theorists take the view that the child's personality or behaviour develops as a result of social interaction - through rewards and punishments, imitation, identifying with particular role-models, and conforming to expectations. All the social processes which we looked at in the Social Psychology section will come into play during the course of a child's development: social perception and the child's understanding of what people are like; social roles and the expected role-behaviours which go with them; and communication, both verbal and non-verbal.

In this chapter, we will look first at the way that the infant's first relationship develops, through interaction with its parent, because we can see from this how social interaction is one of the very first capabilities that an infant develops. From there, we will go on to look at the work of some of the main social learning theorists, and in particular, the studies which have been done on the processes of imitation and modelling. And then we will look at some of the different ways that children grow up in other cultures throughout the world. It is often by looking at the different social expectations and practices of other cultures that we can come to understand the social learning process most clearly.

Parent-infant interaction

Attachments between infants and parents seem to appear fully when the infant is about 7 months old. Before then, the infant doesn't seem to be particularly disturbed if it is separated from its parents; but after then it will cry, and show other symptoms of being distressed. This attachment, though, doesn't just appear suddenly. Rather, it is built up over the whole 7 months of the child's life by the process of interacting with its parents in different ways. The child is born ready to respond in particular ways to the parents, and parents also behave in particular ways with the child. As this interaction develops, the child and the parents adapt to each other, and gradually an **attachment bond** is formed between them.

The infant's first contact with, and exposure to, the outside world consists very largely of whatever its 'caretaker' (the person who looks after it) does with her or his face, body, hands and voice. Although this doesn't sound much, it can provide quite a varied experience for the infant: being picked up and cuddled is quite different from being talked to; and being smiled at is a totally different kind of stimulation for the infant from being tickled. From this range of behaviour which the parent shows (it doesn't *have* to be the parent who is the baby's main caretaker at all, of course, but it's easier to keep to one word throughout this description!) the baby begins to build up its knowledge of the world.

Infant sociability

As many researchers have shown, in particular Schaffer (1971), the human infant has a tendency to react to other people far more strongly than to other stimuli in its environment such as lights flashing or noises (although they still do react to those, as every parent knows). There seems to be a very strong and very well established tendency towards **sociability** in the human infant. Since human beings, by comparison with many other kinds of animals, are highly social, and don't often live their lives entirely alone (hermits are quite rare, really!), we would expect this. What we are interested in here, are the *ways* in which this tendency towards sociability develops in children.

21.1 Investigating parent-child interaction

One investigation that you can do is to look at parent-child interaction in a natural setting. You should work with a friend, and you will each need a note-pad and pen, a watch, and possibly a portable cassette recorder if you can get hold of one.

Ask someone that you know who has a small child if you can observe them together for a short period of time. Explain that it is part of a psychology project and that you will try not to be in the way.

Arrange yourself in the room as unobtrusively as possible. Decide in advance how long you will carry on observing: fifteen minutes is probably long enough at first. Write down everything that happens between the parent and the child during the time. When you have finished, make a careful note of the situation (e.g. a description of the room and the time of day) and the approximate age and sex of the people participating in the interaction.

Later, look at what you have found and count up the different types of interaction that you have observed. Ask yourself:

How long did each interaction last?

Who began the interaction?

What different kinds of interactions did you observe?

What problems did you encounter in doing the observation?

How much did your presence affect the behaviour of the others?

When you have done this, compare your report with that of your partner and see just how they are different. What explanations can you find for these differences?

Smiling

As long ago as 1954, Ahrens did a study in which she showed that infants seem to have an inherited tendency to smile at something that resembles a human face. When the infant is very young, this tendency shows as a response to a very simple stimulus, such as an oval piece of card with two dots on it, to resemble eyes. As the child grows older, however and its experience develops, it does not respond to such a crude image and needs more detail in the 'face' that is presented to it. By the time that the infant is five months old, it will only respond to an image that is highly realistic, such as a photograph. (Of course, these are just substitutes for the 'real thing' while the researchers try to find out the particular features of the stimulus which a baby responds to. They would always react to real human faces coming close to them.)

What is interesting, as well as the way that the child starts with a basic tendency and learns to make it more sophisticated as it develops, is the actual way that the child responds. This is by **smiling** at the face, and if you think about it, this is a very good way that a baby can ensure that it has a good relationship with its parent, because it means that what the parent gets out of it is also satisfying! It is interaction that the child is prepared for, and mechanisms like this, which mean that the child is likely to have more opportunity to interact with other human beings, are strongly advantageous to the child.

Stratton (1982) points out that the child has a number of independent mechanisms which help in the forming of attachments. Although these usually start off with some form of biological 'pre-programming', they are continually developed and adjusted by the child's experience of interactions. So, for instance, the infant may start off ready to smile at human face shapes, by having some of its visual cortex in the brain particularly ready to respond to the kind of image presented by two dots in an oval shape; but as the child's visual experience develops and its understanding of what it is seeing grows, this becomes more sophisticated, and simple images are no longer enough. The child has experienced satisfying interactions with the more complex stimuli presented by real human faces, and through learning has now added to the simple 'pre-programmed' tendency.

'Baby-talk'

Adults also interact differently with infants than with older children or other adults, in an interesting kind of way. Most of the ways that adults change their behaviour when they are dealing with small children, are ways that make it more easy for the child and the parent to interact. By observing parents with their infants, Stern (1977) showed that this different behaviour was very widespread, and affected such things as the language that the parents used, the ways that they moved their heads and positioned themselves, and the facial expressions they used. Compared to most normal social interactions between adults and older children, a parent's actions towards its infant are quite unusual – try comparing baby talk with ordinary talk!

Psychology in Action

Psychologists are gradually building a picture of the complexity of skills with which the newborn child enters the world. Far from the "blank slate" (*tabula rasa*) the infant was once perceived to be, it seems that they come well equipped in the art of communication.

Early parent-infant interaction plays a crucial role in the child's ability to communicate effectively. But how do hearing-impaired children, who are deprived of early verbal communication, cope? Although children who are introduced to sign language early in life appear to develop language along the same lines as hearing children, many parents and professionals are concerned that children should be exposed to verbal language to develop skills that are akin to more common patterns of communication. Hearing-impaired children are encouraged to lip-read, develop normal speech patterns and improve hearing skills.

In recent years, however, special systems of sign language have been developed. These systems translate words and grammar used in the English language into signs and gestures. The idea is that the child will be exposed to a richer, more varied language and improved parent/infant interaction.

Ferguson (1964) made tape recordings of the ways that mothers talked to their infants, and analysed them later. He found that they all spoke versions of baby talk, even though the mothers concerned were taken from six different language-speaking backgrounds. Each human language, apparently, has its own versions, and all of them alter the way that adults speak to infants consistently: slowing down what they say, changing the vocabulary that they use so that it is easier to understand, and often talking in a higher voice than usual. Stern (1977) commented that it seemed that mothers all round the world performed their language's counterpart of transforming 'pretty rabbit' to pwitty wabbit'! If you get the chance, try listening to the way in which people talk to babies - maybe even yourself as well - and see just how these changes are made. It seems that infants respond very positively to them, and as a behaviour in human beings it is very common. Snow (1972) found that even non-parents and children alter their speech when talking to infants.

Imitation

Another important way that adults and infants interact is through **imitation**. Even very young children have been shown to imitate their mothers' expressions, and mothers (or parents) often use very exaggerated facial expressions when they are talking with infants. Stern (1977) showed how infants as young as a couple of weeks old were engaging in interactive sequences with their mothers, where they would imitate the mother's expressions as she made them. Metzoff and Moore (1977) found that the main kinds of imitation which very young infants (12-21 days old) could manage were mouth opening and sticking out their tongues, but as they grew older they would develop more sophisticated skills. Again, you may have observed how mothers often play these kinds of games with their small babies, often derided as 'making faces and cooing at them'. However these games are very valuable to the baby's growing understanding of social interactions and are a beginning of the non-verbal communication which, as we have seen, is so important to people.

Parent-infant interaction

Turn-taking

It also seems as if these sorts of interactions set the fundamentals of human interaction by establishing 'turn taking' behaviour in the child. There seems to be a very strong tendency for infants to enjoy repetitive games, such as 'peek-a-boo' or 'throw-your-teddy-out-of-the-cot' and, as any parent will tell you, they seem happy to carry on with them for hours! This pattern is of course the same as the pattern for any interaction; baby acts, then parent acts, then baby acts again; and these games seem to be very basic ones. It seems likely that the infant is biologically 'pre-programmed' for them. But, of course, they also depend on other people, so it is very important that the infant does have periods of interaction with others who are sensitive to their needs.

A study by Jaffe (1973), involved filming mothers and infants while they were engaging in baby talk and face-pulling interactions. Jaffe found that the **timing** of these interactions (how long the mother's turn lasted, and how long the baby took for its turn) mirrored exactly the patterns of timing that adults have in their conversations! Although this could be just a coincidence, it seems more likely that the children are learning for future social interaction in this way.

Crying

We all know, I think, that infants have ways of communicating with their parents at a distance - through **crying**. For a creature which is helpless in terms of moving itself around, this is probably a strategy which helps survival a great deal, and we often find that infant vocalisation in a species is tied in with the kind of other abilities which the young animal has. Precocial animals which can follow their parents around, like foals, don't really need to vocalise much while they are very young; whereas kittens which are blind and which are unable to crawl around at first, mew when they are not with their mothers for a period of time in order to attract their mother's attention.

Human mothers often have an 'automatic' kind of understanding of their baby's crying and whether it means that the infant is hungry, in pain, or just plain angry! Wolff (1969) showed that there were actual differences in the sounds of these different types of crying by analysing the sounds and timing intervals of them. It seems that it is these differences that mothers respond to when they 'just know' when something is wrong with the child. (This again, of course, is not something magical to mothers, as other people who know an infant may also develop it, and many mothers take some time to distinguish their infant's messages.) But here, too, is a highly adaptive form of non-verbal communication that allows the child and parent to communicate efficiently.

Eye-contact

One of the most important areas of communication between mother and infant and one on which a lot of research has concentrated, is **eye-contact**. Fitzgerald (1968) found that the dilation of the pupils which, as we have seen is one way that we unconsciously signal liking to other people, is also a signal which babies show, to their parents in particular, by about four months old. Earlier than that they will show it to any face. This would seem to suggest two things: firstly, that people who interact with the infant will receive other messages apart from the smiling which will tell them that the infant is also enjoying the interaction; and secondly, that the child develops preferences in terms of the individuals around it by about 4 months of age. These preferences are likely to form the basis for the child's later attachments. A famous ethological study by Shaffer and Emerson in 1964 showed that children, in addition to being able to develop several attachments simultaneously, were most likely to form attachments to the person who showed most 'sensitive responsiveness' when dealing with them and not necessarily to the person who was looking after them all day. If the most sensitive person was also the person who was the baby's main 'caretaker', then all well and good. However, in some cases, the person who looked after the child seemed to be insensitive to its signals, not recognising them at all. In those cases, Shaffer and Emerson found, the child would often have formed its main attachment to another person, sometimes someone that it only saw for a short period each day, but always someone who was responsive to its signals and interacted with it.

The eye contact which parents and infants make is extremely important for them, as it is in all face-to-face human interactions. Bennett (1971) performed a study investigating which of the infant's signals affected parents' views of their babies most, and found that eye contact was by far the most important. Babies who made a lot of eye contact tended to be judged as being more intelligent or as more sociable than babies who didn't engage in eye contact much.

Lack of eye contact

Lack of eye contact with an infant can be quite devastating for its mother if she is not aware that this is what is the matter. (Don't forget that most non-verbal communication is quite unconscious - we respond to the signals appropriately, but often we are not sure exactly what we are reacting to.) In the case of blind babies, for instance, the eye contact is missing for obvious reasons. In fact, a blind baby will often tend to turn its head away, in order to hear better. A study by Fraiberg (1974) showed that mothers tend to interpret this as a sign of rejection, and feel unhappy about the infant as a result. Knowing about this, though, means that parents of blind babies can recognise that the child is actually attempting interaction with them, and so they can come to find it rewarding instead of frustrating.

A study by Klaus (1970) showed that the experience of eye contact with their baby was quite an important one in giving mothers a sense that their infant was a real person who was having a relationship with them. Parents tend to respond to this and make it easier for the baby as well. Sacetzau and Papousek (1977) observed parent-infant interaction, and found that parents usually try to stand or sit in such a way as to be central in the infant's visual field, to make eye contact easier for the baby. Also, each time they do have eye contact with the infant, parents tend to make a 'greeting response', involving raising the eyebrows, smiling and talking, and opening their eyes widely. This encourages the infant to develop social interactions with others, as its own behaviour (in making eye contact) is having an effect on the behaviour of its parent - something which the infant seems to find highly rewarding. As the infant slowly accumulates control over its environment, including the ability to engage in interactions with others, it also gains the confidence to explore, and to practice new skills. At the same time, the parents are becoming adjusted to their baby and are learning to recognise the signals that it is making; such as how to recognise slight differences in expressions, and what they mean. In this way, non-verbal communication sets the basis for the development of attachments between the infant and the parents, and also provides very early experience which will be useful in later social interactions with a wider circle of people.

Infant reflexes

We can see, then, that the infant is born equipped with a set of behaviours which will encourage the development of interactions. Many of their reflexes, too, are ones which really only make sense when the baby is seen with its mother. One famous **infant reflex** is the Moro reflex in which, if someone bangs on the table that the infant is lying on, it flings its arms outwards and then brings them together on its chest, often crying and opening its eyes wide. Reflexes like this are found in new born babies, although they often disappear entirely after about five days. The Moro reflex is one which is often used to test whether a new born infant's brain and body are functioning normally, and used in this way it just seems like a curiosity. However, Prechtl (1965) observed the Moro reflex operating in babies who were clinging to their mothers, and it became obvious that this was actually a valuable adaptive response to something startling, resulting in the infant clinging more closely to the mother. We can see also, I think, that this would be a stimulus which would mean that the mother, in turn, would feel more protective towards the baby.

In all this, though, it is important to recognise that there are lots of **individual differences**. Not all parents are responsive to their children in the same ways, and the infant rapidly learns to adapt its behaviour to that of its parents. There are also from birth many individual differences between babies. Some of them may cry more than others, some don't like to be cuddled and held or wrapped up tightly, and some have other kinds of differences. This also means, since the relationship is an interaction and not an automatic process, that the parents will react in different ways, and this may be an origin for long-term differences in relationships. You can often hear mothers of several children describe how each one has been different from the moment they were born. This means that the parent is going to treat them differently as a result, so the differences will continue, and according to Stratton (1982) may possibly develop into long-term character traits. However, as he points out, seeing a straight-line link between what an infant is like and the mature person it becomes is clearly unrealistic as parents change their behaviour with their children, and children develop new ways of interacting with their parents. Nonetheless, individual differences in infants often set up expectations and judgements about character on the part of their parents, which can result in their encouraging the infant (and later on the child) to act in certain ways.

The social learning process

When we look at the longer-term process of child development, we can see that it involves a process of **socialisation**, in which the child learns to conform to the norms of its society and to act in ways that are considered acceptable. Although this process may involve different expectations from one society to the next, it seems that the highly sociable nature of children means that they are very prepared to learn and to respond to social influences.

Broadly speaking, there seem to be three main ways that socialisation is encouraged in the child: through the processes of **imitation and identification**, through direct training involving **punishments and rewards**, and through the transmission of **social expectations**. Many social learning theorists consider that it is the process of imitation and identification which is the most important of these three.

Imitation

From the beginning a child will observe and imitate the people around it: small toddlers often take great delight in being allowed to do 'grown-up' things like helping with the washing-up. Also, small children often play games which involve their adopting particular social roles and imitating the adults that they have seen in those roles. All this is part of a process by which the child learns a range of behaviours which it can put to use in later life.

Imitation is often described as 'a short-cut to learning'. It involves the copying of a specific act or set of actions and allows the child to learn a range of physical skills very quickly and efficiently. Some learning theorists see the child's readiness to learn through imitation as a very generalised kind of **learning set** (see Chapters 2 and 9), in which the child has a general state of preparedness to learn by copying other people's actions. Through imitation, the child is able to learn far more than it could possibly pick up if it had to be directly taught all the time.

Identification

There is a second-stage process that is also involved in observational learning. Often, a child will learn a more general style of behaviour by taking on a whole role, or by modelling itself on another person. Although this may start off with the process of imitation - the learning quickly becomes internalised, so that the child comes to identify with that person or that role. **Identification** takes place over a much longer period of time than imitation, and it is thought that much of our learning of social roles, such as our sex role learning, occurs through the process of identification.

Imitation and identification

Because of this, social learning theorists consider that the presence of appropriate **role-models** for the child is very important in development. They argue that the child needs to have people around who it can copy, so that it can develop an idea of just how a real person might carry out a particular social role. Such role models provide a general set of guidelines for the child, so that it can behave appropriately in later life.

Bandura's studies

Bandura et al. (1963) carried out a series of experiments investigating imitation in children. They took 96 children aged between 3 and 6 years old, and divided them into four groups (24 children in each group). The groups were then shown different scenes. The first group watched an adult behaving aggressively towards a large rubber 'bobo' doll. This included the adult punching the doll, shouting at it, and hitting it with a hammer. The second group watched the same adult behaving in exactly the same way, but this time instead of seeing it in real life, they saw it on film. The third group saw the same sequence of actions towards the doll, but they were shown it as a cartoon set in a fantasy land. And the fourth group was a control group, who were not shown any violent behaviour at all.

21.1 A 'bobo' doll

After they had seen the scenes, the children were put into a room to play with some toys, including a 'bobo' doll like the one that they had seen. The experimenters then deliberately frustrated the children by taking the toys away from them just as they were enjoying their play. They were then allowed to carry on playing, and observed through a one-way mirror. Each child's behaviour was rated by the hidden observers, and the number of aggressive actions which they performed during a 20 minute period was counted. The results were as follows:

average number of aggressive acts	
real-life model	83
filmed model	92
cartoon model	99
no model	54

We can see from this that the children who had seen an aggressive model performed far more aggressive actions than those who had not. Bandura also noted which aggressive acts were specific copies of the model's actions, and which were more general aggressive behaviour. He found that the children who had observed the real life model had reproduced more of the specific actions, while those who had seen either the film or the cartoon produced more general actions.

Bandura also found that the children did not imitate all models equally. They were far more likely to imitate models who they saw as similar to themselves, such as those of the same sex. He also showed that the consequences which the child saw could in some cases affect how likely it was that the behaviour would be imitated - a process known as **vicarious** learning. A study which he performed in 1965 involved showing groups of nursery school children a film of an adult behaving aggressively towards a 'bobo' doll 'because the doll was being disobedient'. One group just saw that, while the other group of children saw a later part as well, where another adult came in and told the first one off. When they were tested, the children who had seen the adult punished didn't imitate the behaviour as much as the first group. However, when Bandura offered rewards to the children for imitating the model, he found that there was no difference between the two groups. Even though they had not shown the behaviour immediately, they had still learned it - which showed that there can be a difference between what children have learned, and what immediately shows in their behaviour.

Ethical discussion

Bandura's study of children's reactions to the modelling of aggressive behaviour inevitably resulted in some children learning to act in a more aggressive manner.

Do you think this was ethically acceptable?

Effects of reinforcement

Other researchers investigated how **positive reinforcers**, like praise or encouragement, can affect learning through imitation. Patterson, Littman and Bricher (1967) performed a ten week observational study of nursery school children, and found that what followed an aggressive act seemed to be important in determining whether or not the child would perform that aggressive act again. If the aggressive action was ignored or punished (for instance, by the other child fighting back), then it was less likely to be repeated. But aggressive acts which had satisfying consequences for the aggressor, such as the other child bursting into tears or the aggressor being praised by friends, were more likely to be repeated.

Patterson et al. also found that if a child who was usually a victim began to fight back and was successful, the child often became aggressive itself, but if the attempt to fight back was unsuccessful then the child tended to remain passive. It seems that both kinds of consequences may affect how ready the child is to learn: consequences for the model, and consequences for the child itself.

Mussen and Rutherford (1963) investigated warmth and closeness in relationships, and the effects that this can have on the process of identification. They found that boys who had warm, affectionate relationships with their fathers tended to score higher on tests of masculinity than boys whose relationship with their fathers were more reserved. The same applied to girls: the closer their relationship with their mothers, the more strongly the girls in the study tended to identify as feminine.

We can see from these studies that imitation and identification can be important mechanisms in how children learn. Other kinds of studies have investigated different aspects of social learning, such as the effects of different types of punishments on the child. Although children learn a great deal by imitation and identification, there are also some things which are taught by means of direct reactions from adults, and often this is an important way that children are trained to act in the ways that society expects.

21.2 Studying the effects of violent TV

This is an exercise which you can do in class, or with several other people.

Imagine that you are a member of a team of research psychologists, who have been given a sizeable (though not unlimited) research budget, to enable you to investigate one particular question.

Your task is to design a study which will allow you, once and for all, to find out whether violence on television causes violence in children and young people.

Either on your own, or in a small group of not more than four people, work out exactly how you would carry out such a study. When you are doing it, pay particular attention to these questions:

1 How are you going to measure levels of violence?

2 How are you going to obtain the research participants for your study and how many of them will you need?

3 How will you make sure that the violence you study is caused by the television and nothing else?

Remember also that a psychological study must be ethical and not cause distress or damage to any research participants (see Chapter 21).

When you have designed your study, or the best one that you think you can manage, compare it with that of your friends, or of the other groups in your class.

Did you all suggest the same type of study?

How were your measurements of violence different?

What did each group mean by violence?

Finally, write down what you have learned from this about the problems of collecting psychological evidence. How far do the problems that you have encountered apply to the psychological studies that you have learned about?

Punishment

Although each society 'shapes' its children's behaviour by rewards and praise (or by amusement or attention on the part of the adults, which children also seem to find rewarding) there is another side to training which each society also uses: **punishment** of 'bad', or socially inappropriate, behaviour. In some societies, the 'punishment' may be very little. One of the New Guinea tribes studied by Margaret Mead, the Samoans, had a belief that children would naturally mature into sociable and appropriate behaviour. Inappropriate behaviour was very rarely directly punished as it was assumed that they would grow out of it when they were older. At the same time, they were not allowed to become a nuisance to other people, so if they cried or were difficult, the children were removed from their elder's company. Although this may not sound very much, it is in a way a mild sort of punishment as the child's behaviour produced consequences for the child which were not particularly pleasant. (Incidentally, Mead also reported that the Samoan adults were stable, friendly and well-balanced individuals, and it may be that the lack of serious punishment in childhood contributed to that. But we cannot be sure, as there could also have been other influences.)

In Western society, at any rate, the type of punishments which parents use seems to correlate quite strongly with the development of a strong sense of conscience in the child. A study by Mackinnon in 1938 showed that those of a set of students who had demonstrated that they had strong consciences (by not cheating in a test when they had had the opportunity) had also had psychological punishments from their parents when they were younger; while those who had cheated - and so presumably did not have strong consciences - had had physical punishment. This distinction seems to be quite an important one, which needs a bit of explaining.

When we are talking of physical punishments, we don't just mean actually hitting or beating children. Mackinnon's study included as physical punishment such penalties as being kept in, losing pocket money, etc. The important thing is that there is an actual *penalty* which the child pays. In psychological punishment, on the other hand, there isn't necessarily any sort of penalty but the child is reprimanded on the basis of the hurt he or she has caused the parent or other person involved, or is in some way made to feel guilty and responsible for their actions. It is the *social* relationships involved which are the important aspect of this type of punishment. The child may feel that it has let its parents down, or that it has caused unnecessary suffering to someone else, but apart from apologising there isn't necessarily anything that it has to do in atonement.

Hill (1964) argues that the reasons why psychological punishments seem to be so effective in producing strong consciences in children, is because of the act of apology. Gradually, this becomes internalised, so that rather than just saying 'sorry' the child comes to feel 'sorry', and later guilty or responsible. With physical punishment, on the other hand, the child can see things as much more external a penalty to be paid for the behaviour but that is all. So all physical punishment would produce, would be a fear of being 'found out' and not necessarily a strong conscience at all.

Some psychologists consider punishment to be a highly inefficient and time-wasting way of socialising children. B. F. Skinner (1971) argues strongly that the use of positive and negative reinforcement is much more effective in training children than the use of punishment is. As he points out, punishing a child for doing the wrong thing, may stop it (temporarily) from doing that thing – but that doesn't stop it from going off and doing something equally bad, or even worse! Whereas rewarding a child for the 'correct' behaviour means that the child is aware of what it should be doing and is more likely to carry on doing it. By doing that it is not doing anything wrong.

The importance of explanation

The importance of **explanations** for children, in terms of what is expected of them and why rules exist, is another aspect of socialisation that can differ from one part of society to another. In a longitudinal study of child-rearing patterns in Nottingham, in 1963, Newson and Newson found that working-class parents tended to give their children more direct commands and orders without explanations, whereas middle-class parents would tend to explain to their children the reasons behind rules and regulations. This seems to encourage a child to behave sociably. In many non-technological societies, too, the reasons for particular customs and rules are systematically explained to the child as it grows older, so that by the time the child is an adult it is not only aware of *how* it is expected to behave but also of *why* this is. So the **cognitive** side of training is also important. How the child understands what is happening, and the sense that it makes of the rules and behaviour around it, is another very important factor in child development.

Cross-cultural child-rearing patterns

America and Russia

Different societies have very different ways of socialising their children, and these can affect the kinds of social interactions which take place with those children, quite dramatically. Bronfenbrenner (1970) published a study which was a comparison of child-rearing practices in the United States of America and in Russia. Although in some respects the needs of the two societies were fairly similar (they were both extremely large, highly industrialised nations, for instance) their child-rearing practices were very different.

Individualism vs co-operation

American children tend to be encouraged in **individualism** from a very early age. Each child's experiences will tend to be different from those of its compatriots, and although they are encouraged to behave sociably towards other children, many parents and educators in America tend to regard it as 'natural' that the child should be at times aggressive, or selfish in its relationships with other children. By contrast, in Russia a strong effort is made to ensure that children deal with each other **co-operatively**, and aggression or selfishness are not seen as inevitable at all. Rather, those in charge of children actively discouraged signs of it from the time of the child's first encounters with other children.

Rather than being cared for individually, as many American children are in their pre-school years, children from the USSR were mostly cared for in kindergartens, with trained personnel all of whom were well aware of the goals of the society, which was to produce adults who would work co-operatively for the good of the society. These goals remained clear throughout schooling as well and it meant that many other influences on the child, apart from those of the child's family, were taken very seriously. Youth organisations helped the child to develop out of school pursuits which worked towards the 'community spirit' and class 'teams' encouraged the child to think of working hard at school as being for the general good rather than simply the individual's own good. Also much children's literature and television was directed towards social goals.

By contrast, the influences on the American child may be far more diverse, and often contradictory. Teachers and parents, for instance, may condemn violence and aggression, yet the child sees 'heroes', both in realistic and cartoon form, who win in the end through using violence. The child may be told to value unselfishness, and yet find that the people who command considerable respect are those who have made large amounts of money without giving it away at all.

In Bronfenbrenner's study, he was particularly struck by the influence of the child's peer group, especially during the teenage years. In America, the peer group tended to hold values which in many cases could be directly opposite to those of the wider society, such as encouraging 'drop-outs' or theft. In Russia on the other hand, the peer group influence tended to work on children in exactly the way that society would want it to - to encourage hard work, and community spirit. Bronfenbrenner believed this to be a direct result of the deliberate encouragement of co-operation, and the network of social influence surrounding the children throughout their childhood. Many of the conditions of life in Bronfenbrenner's study have changed now, of course; and there is much more alienation than before. But the main schooling and child-rearing practices are still much the same.

China

Kessen (1975) reported on child-rearing practices in the People's Republic of China. Like the USSR, China had adopted a very deliberate policy of socialising its young people in the direction that the society values. Children in China were quite directly taught to value co-operation above individualism, and that one should not wish to 'show off' one's own achievements but rather to 'serve the people'. Nurseries existed even for very young children and most work places had a nursery where mothers with young infants had regular breaks for feeding the children. Although some children are looked after at home by grandparents, it seems that the majority of children attended a nursery until the age of about three, and then a kindergarten, before going to school proper.

The importance of the community

One thing which was very striking in China was the way that the whole community seemed very clear about what was expected of the child. Kessen reported that any sort of act of aggression even like pushing for a toy, was very rare indeed. The message the child receives from its parents, grandparents (who could often remember the pre-revolution days, and so valued the current system), teachers, or educational writers, was of a single, consistent aim of mutual co-operation and support. The child was encouraged to think of itself far more as a member of society than as an individual, and was expected to put society's needs before its own wishes. Unlike Russia, even children's entertainment and art usually had some kind of revolutionary message. It was rare to find children drawing something with no 'virtue', like a flower – rather, they would be encouraged to draw scenes representing socially desirable activities such as ploughing fields, or building canals. Kessen reported that the children showed astoundingly high levels of proficiency in such skills as representational art, dancing, memorisation and presenting short plays.

Although both were communist societies, the Russian and Chinese systems of child-rearing were quite different: the Russians valuing individual excellence far more than the Chinese, who encouraged their children to help others along instead of pursuing individual goals. Both societies, though, were characterised by extremely high amounts of affection and interaction with the children by all adults, not just those who had immediate care of them. In both societies, unlike some Western ones, the children mostly grew up to be keen to contribute to society and to promote its ideals and goals.

Israel

The kibbutz system in Israel is another society where children are reared 'communally' rather than individually by their parents. In order to allow both parents to work, there are extensive child-care arrangements. The children of a kibbutz are looked after by a special nurse/foster mother, called a **metapelet**, from just a few days old, and the parents will visit, or the child will visit the parents, from time to time. For different kibbutzim the arrangements vary, in some the children return to their parents' house to sleep every night, while in others they live in the children's house, and only visit their parents' house once a week, and in others there are in-between arrangements. Again, the children are encouraged in mutual co-operation, but Sidell (1972) indicated that there are higher levels of aggressive behaviour seen between children on Israeli kibbutzim than ever seen among, for instance, Chinese children.

Adapting to multiple caretakers

However, in terms of their emotional needs, it seems to be very clear that the communal systems of child-rearing do not present the child with the kind of difficulties that many Westerners would expect. The children concerned seem to adapt well to multiple caretakers (having several people looking after them), and often seem to thrive on the increased amounts of stimulation and affection which they receive as a result. They also develop strong relationships with their parents. Bettelheim (1970), in connection with kibbutz children, argued that their adjustment to multiple mothering seemed to be made very much easier by the fact that all their mother-figures held the same central value system and ideas concerning child-rearing. If this is an important factor, we can see how it would apply to Chinese and Russian child-rearing practices, too.

Zimbabwe

Gelfand (1979) studied the upbringing of children in Shona society, a traditional people in Zimbabwe. He found that the pattern of child-rearing which the Shona used represented a complete social and educational system for the child, but without having separate 'institutions', like schools, to teach any single part of the information that the children have to learn. As they grow older, children are encouraged to develop their intellectual skills through riddles, games and puzzles. They learn about social roles in society through observing their elders, and through playing particular games which prepare them, such as the imitating-marriage game known as 'mahumbwe'. As the child grows older, more and more is expected of it, and all the adults encourage the child in these games and activities, until it is considered to be 'grown up'.

Involving the grand-parents

Shona society has some interesting aspects to its child rearing practices. From birth, the child is constantly with its mother, who attends to its needs and looks after it until it is a toddler. The infant will even sleep next to its mother, in between her and her husband. But after it has been weaned and is starting to explore, the child is traditionally sent to its grandparents' house to live for a few years. For some children, the stay with the grandparent lasts for the rest of their childhood, but others will return to their parents when they are seven or eight years old. So, rather than being the parents' prime responsibility, it is the grandparents who teach the growing child social discipline, correct behaviour, and see to its development in other ways. For a boy, the grandfather takes the main responsibility, while for a girl it is the grandmother who teaches her what she needs to know and be able to do in Shona society.

Cross-cultural child transport

Gelfand found that this practice continued among Shona people even when they had adapted to an urban way of life and the grandparents too were living in the towns; the child would be sent to stay with its grandparents for a period, either to the town or to the country. So, in some ways, the most difficult period of child-rearing, while the toddler adapts to its new independence but also needs to be trained in social skills and co-ordination, is undertaken by the more experienced members of the family, which must take quite a burden away from the parents! It is stressed, though, that the amount of time the child spends with its grandparents will always vary, and that for some it is only a couple of years.

The western approach

This sharing of responsibility for child-rearing, among several members of the family, is not uncommon, although the particular Shona practice doesn't seem to be followed by many other peoples. Nonetheless, the Western approach where the responsibility for the whole upbringing of the child until it is five years old rests on just two (or less) people, seems to be uncommon rather than the usual practice in human societies. In most human societies, too, the emphasis is on the child as a member of society rather than as an individual, as children are taught to recognise their social obligations and duties and become aware of the part that they will play in the whole scheme of things, very early on. The Western child, by contrast, tends to be kept separate from the whole society (perhaps because Western society is simply too complex) until a much later age. Children are not allowed into adult work-places (although in Russia attempts have been made to increase this) and the world of childhood has a whole set of pastimes and activities which bear little relationship to the adult behaviour which is expected of the person in later life.

We also tend to stress the individual side of personality. Rather than seeing ourselves as being members of society first, we tend to notice and look for differences in ourselves, and to highlight areas of individual talents or inclinations. In a lot of ways, this seems to be the main difference between Western upbringing and that of children in other human societies: where many put the society before the individual, we tend to put the individual before the society.

Multi-cultural Britain

Although we have spoken of Western patterns of child rearing as if they were all the same, it is important to realise that this isn't really the case at all. In Britain today we have a strongly **multi-cultural** society, with many different practices and influences on children. The ways in which many Indian, Pakistani, or West Indian children are brought up in this society can be very different from those of white children. Also, the ways in which working-class children are brought up are often vastly different from the kinds of upbringings that middle-class children have.

For many teachers and social workers in multi-cultural areas, the problem is to find ways of interacting with children and parents who have very different practices without losing respect for their ways of living, but also without avoiding changes which may be necessary for the children. It is only recently that such professionals have become aware of the great differences that there are between different people in British society, and the problems that these can present. Schools, for example, emphasise individual development, and the right of the child to make its own decisions about the future - but for many Asian families, such decisions are not considered to be individual decisions, but to do with the whole family and, as in China, individualism may seem egotistical and selfish. So we can see that the influences which go towards socialising a child in a society as complex as ours may be very varied, and may at times produce a kind of conflict for the individual that does not really exist in some other parts of the world.

Summary

1 Attachments between parents and infants develop through a process of interaction between the infant and its caretaker, from the very first weeks of life.

2 Infants and parents interact using a variety of non-verbal signals, which are thought to set the basis for future social contacts.

3 Imitation is a major method of learning for children, allowing them to pick up sequences of behaviour quickly and efficiently.

4 Identification is a longer-term process, by which a child may come to internalise the values and role-behaviour of a role-model.

5 The types of punishments used by parents may affect the likelihood of a child developing a strong conscience in later life.

6 Different societies have different ideas on child-rearing. Social influences on children in Russia are more consistent than in America.

7 Many cultures emphasise the child as a member of society primarily, and direct their child-rearing practices accordingly.

Chapter 22 - The psychoanalytic approach to child development

Freud

In Chapter 14, we looked at the theory of personality that was put forward by Freud in 1901. In that chapter, we saw how Freud considered that there was a deeply-buried part of the mind, called the **unconscious**, which was not usually open to conscious examination but which nonetheless affected the ways that the person acted and felt.

Freud's idea was that the unconscious mind contained repressed memories of early childhood experiences and, in particular, of early childhood conflicts and emotions. These were contained in one of the two mainly unconscious parts of the personality, the **id** and **superego**. However, they were prevented from breaking through to consciousness because the **ego**, the part of the personality which was in contact with reality, developed defence mechanisms to protect itself. However, Freud found that the unconscious mind could show in cases when the ego was off-guard, such as in a disguised form in the person's dreams or in slips of the tongue or the way that the person interpreted ambiguous pictures.

Catharsis

Freud developed a method of investigating and bringing to the surface these highly emotional memories, or **traumas**. He used free-association and dream analysis to discover what these early memories were, and through the process of **catharsis** - the re-living of the emotions associated with them - his patients were able to learn new ways of coping with their conflicts, such that their psychosomatic symptoms of illness would disappear.

22.1 Exploring free association

Freud believed that many of our unconscious desires and fears could be brought to the consciousness through the use of the technique of free association. This involved his patients in responding to selected words by saying any words which sprung to mind when they heard them.

You can have fun investigating this technique for yourselves.

Firstly, find yourself a partner to work with. Before you start, each of you should produce a set of words on a sheet of paper (about twenty in all).

When you have each compiled a list, take it in turns to read your list to your partner and write down their responses.

Now look at your list of words and your partners responses. Try to work out a possible reason why you or your partner might have associated certain words together. Be imaginative.

What are the main problems in using such a technique to look at how people think?

What alternative explanations can you find for your responses?

Psychosexual stages

The more Freud investigated these early traumas, the more he became convinced that the first five years of life had a permanent effect on the development of the personality. He concluded that the child passed through five stages of development, known as the **psychosexual stages** because of Freud's emphasis on sexuality as the basic drive in development. These stages are: the **oral stage**, the **anal stage**, the **phallic stage**, the **latency period**, and finally the **genital stage**. It was the first three stages which took place in the first five years of life.

The oral stage

The first stage is in the first year of life, in which the child's main source of pleasure is the mouth. It gains considerable pleasure from oral activities such as sucking and biting and this is important, Freud thought, in the type of personality that it develops. At first, the infant's main pleasure is in sucking and swallowing, known as the **oral optimism** phase. Later on in this stage the main pleasure is obtained from biting and chewing - the **oral sadistic** phase. If it found the former more satisfying, Freud thought the child would grow up to become dependent, passive, and also extremely gullible (likely to swallow any story!). Whereas if the infant's main pleasure came from biting and chewing, it would grow up to become highly aggressive, verbally or physically.

The child could become **fixated** on the mouth as a source of pleasure, if it was weaned either too early or too late. If that were the case, then it would grow up to be the kind of person who was always putting things in their mouth: cigarettes, ends of pencils, and the like, Freud also considered that highly independent people were showing a reaction-formation against the dependency of the oral phase. In other words, they were over-compensating for that dependency by becoming the opposite of dependent!

The anal stage

The second of Freud's psycho sexual stages is from one to three years of life. During this phase the **libido** - the sexual drive and energy of the individual - now becomes focused on the anus, and the child derives great pleasure from the act of defecating. This is the age at which the child will be toilet-trained, and Freud considered that the toilet-training itself could affect the later personality. If the child's parents were too strict, the child might become **anal-retentive**, and enjoy holding on to its faeces rather than using the potty readily. In that case, Freud thought, it would become a mean, grasping, stubborn kind of personality in later life. On the other hand, if the child found using the potty too pleasurable, it could become **anal-expulsive**, and in later life it would be over-generous and giving.

In addition, if the potty-training took place too early or too late, the child could become **anally fixated**, which would also affect its character. The anal personality, according to Freud, was characterised by obsessive neatness and orderliness, and little spontaneity - the ideal bureaucrat, in fact!

The phallic stage

The phallic stage, from three to five years old, was the stage where the child's sexual identification was established. During this stage, Freud hypothesised that a young boy would experience what he called the **Oedipus complex**. This would provide the child with highly disturbing conflicts, which had to be resolved by the child identifying with the same-sexed parent.

The oedipus complex

Oedipus was a legendary Greek king who unwittingly killed his father and married his mother. Freud thought that, during the phallic stage, the young boy develops an intense sexual love for his mother. Because of this, he sees his father as a rival, and wants to get rid of him. The father, however, is far bigger and more powerful than the young boy, and so the child develops a fear that, seeing him as a rival, his father will castrate him. (This stems from the little boy noticing that little girls don't have a penis, and thinking that they have been castrated.)

Because it is impossible to live with the continual castration-threat anxiety provided by this conflict, the young boy develops a mechanism for coping with it, using a defence mechanism known as 'identification with the aggressor'. He stresses all the ways that he is similar to his father, adopting his father's attitudes, mannerisms and actions, feeling that if his father sees him as similar, he will not feel hostile towards him. It was this process of identification, Freud thought, that established the young boy's sexual identification, and if this process could not take place, Freud considered that the young child would be likely to grow up homosexual.

Criticisms of the Oedipus complex

There have been several criticisms of Freudian ideas on the Oedipus complex and the necessity for its successful resolution. One of them is the way that many male children growing up in one-parent families, with no father present, do not seem to suffer any crisis of male identity at all. A study by Malinowski in 1927, of the Trobriand Islanders, showed that in a whole society where resolution of the Oedipus complex was impossible there was no weakening of male identification. In that society, it is the mother's brother who is the head of the household, and therefore the powerful figure in the child's life. So there is no perceived rivalry between him and the young child, making the Oedipus complex and its resolution irrelevant to that culture.

Girls, according to Freud, develop penis envy, which later becomes converted into a desire to bear children as the young child begins to recognise that it is impossible for her to develop a penis of her own. Some have suggested that Freud's view of **penis** envy was symbolic of the relative powerlessness of women in society at the time that he was developing his theory, and that it symbolises the girl's struggle to reject the inferior position that society was forcing on her. However, other students of Freud consider that he meant it literally, although it is interesting to speculate how he thought children learned about the presence or absence of penises in a time when children even had baths wearing cotton shifts for fear that they would catch sight of their bodies!

Although, as we have seen, Freud developed an elaborate theory of child development, his data was almost entirely obtained from his adult patients and their buried memories. Freud wanted to explain why so many of his female patients seemed to have deeply-traumatic memories of sexual encounters with their fathers. Initially, he thought that it must be real incest, but he was eventually persuaded that this was not so. (Although, interestingly, recent research seems to be demonstrating that child sexual abuse is very much more common than people have previously thought, so perhaps Freud was on the right track there after all.)

Unconscious wish fulfilment

Freud came to the conclusion that these memories must represent some form of unconscious wish-fulfilment on the part of his female patients, and that they were actually remembering the deepest desires of their childhood. Accordingly, he developed his theories of the Oedipus and Electra complexes to explain how these desires had happened.

There are other explanations for these memories. Middle-class women in Victorian society tended to be brought up extremely uninformed about the basic facts of life, including sexuality. For instance, the reason why lesbianism wasn't made illegal in England while male homosexuality was, was because Queen Victoria said that women didn't know about things like that, and that making a law against it would inform them! Middle-class women were brought up to believe that their husband would take the place of their father, by protecting and providing for them. For many women, their first sexual encounter on their wedding night came as a totally unexpected experience, and to their unconscious minds, could easily have been seen as being raped by their fathers.

Ethical discussion

Recent evidence has shown that sexual abuse of children may be much more widespread than people previously believed. Freud himself began by believing that the very distressing memories held by his patients about having been sexually abused by their fathers were true. However, when he began to make his ideas public, he was persuaded that this was not the case. Instead, he argued that the women he was treating had fantasized these episodes, and that they were examples of subconscious wish-fulfilment.

Some feminist writers cite psychoanalytic theory as one of the main reasons why society has not taken either rape or child sexual abuse seriously in the past.

Do you agree with this view?

The latency and central stages

The fourth of Freud's psychosexual stages is known as the latency period, from age five to puberty. Once the Oedipus complex has been successfully resolved, Freud thought the libido became diffused throughout the whole body, rather than concentrated in any particular area. Only when the child hit puberty did it again become focused on the genitals, and the young adult's attentions now became focused on the opposite sex. This was the genital stage, which lasted throughout adulthood.

Little Hans

Although most of Freud's work was done with adults, he did at one stage have an opportunity to study a particular child known as 'Little Hans'. Freud didn't actually work directly with little Hans, but instead worked through correspondence with Hans' father, who was familiar with Freud's theories, and wrote to him when he first suspected that Hans had become a case that Freud might be interested in. Freud suggested possible lines of questioning which the father could try with Hans, and the father tried them and reported to Freud what had taken place.

Hans was a small boy of four years old, who had developed a phobia of horses. Since the family lived opposite a busy coaching inn, that meant that Hans was unhappy about leaving the house, because he saw many horses as soon as he went out of the door. When he was first asked about his fear Hans said that he was frightened that the horses would fall down and make a noise with their feet. He was most frightened of horses which were drawing heavily laden carts and, in fact, had seen a horse collapse and die in the street one time when he was out with his nurse. It was pulling a horse-drawn bus carrying many passengers and when the horse collapsed Hans had been frightened by the sound of its hooves clattering against the cobbles of the road.

Freud interpreted Hans' phobia as symptomatic of his Oedipus complex. He saw the fact that Hans was reluctant to leave the house as indicating that he would rather stay at home with his mother and he considered that the horses, being large and powerful, symbolised his father. When the father, instructed by Freud, suggested to Hans that he was actually frightened that the horse would bite him, Hans insisted at first that it was because he was frightened about it making a noise with its feet but later accepted his father's suggestion. Freud considered that this represented a disguised form of castration threat anxiety.

When Hans was three and a half, his mother had given birth to a girl baby, called Hannah. Because of the established custom at the time, nobody had mentioned the pregnancy to Hans; his mother had simply gone away and returned with the baby. Although Hans had been told that the stork had brought the baby, as most children of his time were, Freud thought that he had probably noticed his mother's changed shape and that that was what was symbolised by heavily-loaded carts. His anxiety about them represented the anxiety that he felt about this new rival for his mother's affection.

22.2 Alternative explanations for 'Little Hans'

This is an activity which you can do as a class exercise.

You should divide yourselves into two teams: one team being the 'behaviourists', and the other team being the 'psychoanalysts'. The two teams are going to debate the Case of Little Hans.

Each team has half an hour to prepare its arguments. During that time, you should go through the case of Little Hans, and write down as many different reasons as you can why this case supports either the Freudian approach to child development, or the behaviourist approach. (The behaviourist argument is based on Hans having acquired his phobia through classical conditioning; and the psychoanalytic argument is based on Hans having acquired it as an expression of his Oedipus complex.)

Then the two teams face each other, and toss a coin to see which team will go first. Each team has five minutes to present its case, and then the other side are allowed to ask up to five questions. After that, the two teams each argue for their side, until finally there is a vote on the issue, to see which explanation the class will accept.

Anna Freud's work

Although Freud only had the opportunity to study this one child, his work in this area was taken up later by his daughter, Anna Freud. Her approach concentrated more on the ways that the child developed ego-defence mechanisms. She considered that the ego worked towards balance and harmony, so that it would try to compensate for any extreme aspects of personality, such as by fostering a love of gentleness in a highly aggressive person. This meant that the defence mechanisms which the ego used would tend to work towards these goals.

Anna Freud identified five main ego-defence mechanisms:

- **Denial in fantasy** - for example, a child might cope with its fear of a powerful father by inventing an imaginary lion as a friend - making the child just as powerful as its father in its imagination!

- **Denial in word and act** - a child might simply refuse to acknowledge a threat, or source of threat. For instance a small boy might insist that he is just as big and powerful as his father.
- **Restriction of the ego** - the process of deliberately not allowing a part of the personality to develop, but cultivating other parts instead, e.g. a child told off for telling lies who refuses to play imagination games.
- **Identification with the aggressor** - for example, a child who has just been to the dentist's might play at being the dentist himself.
- **Excessive altruism** - an exaggerated concern that the child's friends should achieve success instead of the self.

Although Anna Freud was mainly concerned with children, these defence mechanisms can also be observed among adults, and they were designed to clarify and add to those defence mechanisms outlined by Freud rather than to replace them.

Psychology in Action

Psychotherapy is a practical application of Freudian theory. The basic premise to this therapy is that once people are made to realise some of the unconscious processes that are causing anxiety, the symptoms will be alleviated. Commonly, such therapies centre around childhood experiences and their effects on later personality development.

You may remember the much-publicised story of Sybil who, having been severely abused by her mother, developed multiple personalities. Each personality was unique and the relationship between the personalities was complex. One personality spoke French for example, while the others displayed no knowledge of French. Some personalities were aware of each other, while others were not.

Through intensive psychotherapy Sybil was encouraged to remember her early relationship with her mother, which had been severely repressed, and she was thus able to let go of her other personalities. She was eventually able to lead a reasonably normal life.

Psychoanalytic theory after Freud

The interest in Freud's theory continued after his death, although many psychologists who still accept his basic approach modified his ideas in several ways. Many, for instance, challenge his ideas that emotional development is dependent on the resolution of conflicts between the biological urges and the demands of society. Instead, they see the social relationships which a child develops with those around him playing a greater part in his development. These psychoanalysts are known as the 'neo-Freudians', and one of the most well-known of them is Erik Erikson.

Erikson

In the main, the neo-Freudians have concentrated on the development of the **ego**, which they feel was an area largely neglected by Freud. An example of this is provided by the theory of **psychosocial development** proposed by Erikson in 1959. Like Freud, Erikson believed that the individual encounters a series of conflicts which need to be resolved for healthy personality development; but the conflicts in Erikson's theory are not centred around parts of the body. Instead they are concerned with the individual's relationships with others in society. Psychological problems occur when the individual is insufficiently prepared to cope with society's changing demands.

Erikson's stages of development

Erikson outlined eight stages in his theory, each of which faces the individual with a different conflict. However, the successful resolution of earlier conflicts is needed to ensure that the individual is able to deal with later ones, so it can be seen as a step-by-step progression.

The first stage in Erikson's theory involves the conflict of **trust/mistrust**: the infant must establish its basic attitude to the world about it. If it meets with satisfaction and comfort at this stage, this will help it to develop a more trusting attitude. As the infant becomes a toddler, it encounters the second conflict of **autonomy/doubt**. The new physical challenges which it faces may feed its confidence, or alternatively may simply make the young child feel inadequate. Again the overall attitude with which the child will go forward needs to be established.

The third stage comes as the child continues to develop socially and physically, and is faced with the conflict between **initiative and guilt**. As the child is being asked to take more and more responsibility for its life, it may come to develop a strong sense of capability and initiative; or alternatively it may simply end up feeling guilty at not having carried out its responsibilities properly. From there, the older child encounters the conflict of **industry/inferiority** as it finds itself meeting more and more new challenges. The child may work hard to overcome them, or alternatively it may simply develop a characteristic feeling of inadequacy.

The fifth stage in Erikson's theory is encountered by the adolescent, who has the **identity/role-confusion** conflict to resolve. Playing so many new social roles and becoming a member of different social groups means that the child needs to develop an integrated sense of self-identity, or it will become overwhelmed by the profusion of parts that it has to play. As a young adult, the sixth conflict is encountered, which is that of **intimacy** in relationships (or a relationship) with others vs. **isolation**.

In maturity, the individual faces a conflict of **generativity/stagnation**: is their life to be a fulfilling, productive one, or simply a passive, unchanging one? And the final stage which Erikson outlined is encountered in old age, when the individual must come to terms with the reality of approaching death, and has a conflict of facing it with either **integrity or despair**.

We can see from Erikson's theory that the idea of ego development continues throughout life, and that each age presents its own set of problems and conflicts. This is a rather different approach to that of Freud, particularly in its emphasis on continuous life development. Many of the more orthodox psychoanalytic theorists, though, still consider that the first five years of life are crucial in determining later personality.

Bowlby's theory of maternal deprivation

A theory which stemmed directly from the psychoanalytic emphasis on the first few years of life as all-important in development was put forward by Bowlby, in 1951. Bowlby considered that relationships between infants and their mothers developed as a result of a process known as **imprinting**. This was a special kind of learning, which occurred in the first stage of infancy, and which established a deep attachment on the part of a young animal towards its parent. (We looked at the process of imprinting in more detail in Chapter 1.) Imprinting had been studied extensively in animals, and Bowlby considered that a similar process was responsible for the development of attachments between human infants and their mothers, at the age of about seven months.

Monotropy

Because of this, Bowlby developed the idea of **monotropy**: the idea that a human infant would develop only one special attachment to its mother, which was completely different from the other relationships which it developed, and that it would cause the child great distress and lasting damage if it was broken. It was essential, he thought, that the infant remained in almost continual contact with its mother during the first five years of life.

Bowlby performed a retrospective study of 44 juvenile delinquents, and found that 17 of them had been separated from their mothers for a period of time before the age of five years. He concluded that their juvenile delinquency was evidence of the lasting damage which the period of maternal deprivation had produced, and that separating young children from their mothers, even temporarily, could have this kind of effect. Other studies claimed to have demonstrated similar damaging effects of maternal deprivation, such as maternally deprived children being less intelligent, or suffering from 'affectionless psychopathy' (i.e. a complete lack of social conscience or social relationships).

Rutter (1979) showed that most of these studies were in fact demonstrating the effects of factors other than maternal deprivation, such as the effects of institutional care, or of privation of relationships (i.e. not having the opportunity to form any relationships at all). In an ethological study of infant relationships, Shaffer and Emerson (1964) found that infants often seemed to develop **multiple attachments** (that is, they formed equally important relationships with more than one person), and also that they formed their relationships with the people who interacted with them most sensitively, rather than simply with the person who looked after them all the time. (This study signalled the beginning of the research on **parent-infant interaction** which we looked at in the last chapter.)

Development in later years

Clarke and Clarke (1976) questioned the idea that the first few years of life were as crucial as psychoanalytic theory claimed. They pointed to several cases where children had recovered from extremely damaging experiences during those years, and said that it seemed as though the influence of the psychoanalytic approach to child development had meant that researchers had neglected the processes of development in the later years of childhood. It certainly seems as though there is only a limited amount of evidence supporting the importance of early experience, but not very much research has yet been undertaken on the alternative approaches.

Summary

1 Freud considered that people were often influenced by unconscious wishes, and by emotional traumas laid down in childhood.

2 He considered that the child passed through five psycho-sexual stages: oral, anal, phallic, latency, and genital. The first three stages were important in determining later personality.

3 In the third stage the child was faced with the resolution of the Oedipus or the penis envy complex, which would determine sex-role identification.

4 Freud's study of Little Hans illustrated his ideas on how the Oedipus complex could provide traumas and how it could be resolved.

5 Anna Freud continued Freud's ideas, investigating the use of ego-defence mechanisms in children.

6 Erikson, a post-Freudian, developed a theory of eight psycho-social conflicts, which needed resolution at stages throughout the whole of an individual's life.

7 Bowlby's theory of maternal deprivation arose from the psychoanalytic idea of the early years being all-important in development.

Chapter 23 - The structuralist approach to child development

Piaget's theory of cognitive development

Some psychologists have concentrated on the ways that children **organise** what they are learning. They see development as a systematic, structured process. One of the most valuable of these structuralist theories was put forward by a Swiss psychologist, Jean Piaget, in 1953.

The origins of Piaget's ideas

As a young boy, Piaget was very interested in animals and how each species was specially equipped to adapt to its environment. All animals have special features, bodily structures, like hard shells or the ability to change colour, which ensure that they have a decent chance of survival. Piaget became fascinated by the process of evolution, not only by the kinds of physical evolution peculiar to each species but also by the evolution of their mental structures. All animals, he hypothesised, have to learn about the special features of their environment. They have to learn what to do when faced by potential threat such as a predator, where to find food and how to build shelters and care for their young. Piaget's background was primarily in zoology (the scientific study of animals) but it progressed into the realms of **epistemology** (the study of knowledge), when he became interested in the ways that animals learn about their environment.

In 1920 Piaget went to work in Paris under Dr T. Simon, one of the first inventors of the intelligence test (along with Alfred Binet). Piaget was given the task of producing a standardised French version of some English intelligence tests. This meant that he had to make sure that all the tests were worded in the same way and the questions placed in exactly the same order so that all children had the same chance of success in the test from the outset. Piaget was not wholly enthusiastic about the prospect of carrying out this task but as the development of the tests progressed he noticed some very interesting factors. Many children were making mistakes on the tests. This in itself may not seem surprising but Piaget realised that the mistakes were not made randomly: children of the same age were making very similar mistakes. It became apparent to him that children of different ages were not simply 'brighter' or less 'bright' than children of other ages, but that their thinking was different or distinctive at each particular age.

This discovery set Piaget on the road to finding out what views of the world were held by children of different ages, and how their thinking changed from the time they were babies to the time they reached adulthood. With this aim in mind, Piaget used what is now known as the **clinical interview** method, where he asked children lots of questions and noted their replies. If a child gave an unusual answer then he tried to ascertain how it had come to have that view - how its understanding of the world could lead to that error.

This method of interviewing is meant to put the child at ease and to encourage it to talk to the interviewer without the interviewer interfering in the child's natural thought processes. Although the interviewer has a set idea of the things he or she wishes to find out, he or she tailors the questions to fit the child they are talking to at the time. Using this method, Piaget put questions to hundreds of children between the ages of three and twelve, on such topics as God, the moon, the sun, and their ideas about justice.

Qualitative changes in cognition

From these interviews, Piaget came to the conclusion that it wasn't just the amount of knowledge which distinguishes a young child from an older child. There was actually a qualitative difference in their thoughts. To him, changes in the way a child thought about the world signified a change in cognitive, or intellectual, development. As the child's intellect develops, it becomes increasingly capable of carrying out actions upon its environment which will ensure its survival. As soon as it can talk for instance, it can tell people how it feels and what it needs, unlike the infant who is at the mercy of its caretakers. This forms the beginning of a progression of development which eventually ends with the acquisition of abstract logic.

Piaget saw intelligence as being the ability of an animal to adapt to its environment and to changes within the environment. This intelligence was not acquired all at once by the child, but developed in set stages. These stages, Piaget believed, were the same for each individual. At each stage the child learns new forms of behaviour and develops its capacity for logical thought. Each stage was characterised by different cognitive abilities in the child. Although some children may be better equipped by their environment to pass on from one stage to another more quickly than other children, Piaget considered that all children needed to pass through the stages in the same sequence. Each stage added to the abilities learned in the previous stage.

The formation of schemata

Piaget saw intelligence as developing through interaction with the environment. The child, being active, continually operates on its environment, by doing things and seeing the effect that the action has. When it is thinking about things it is performing mental operations. An **operation** is any set of actions which produce an effect on the environment. As the child masters new skills, these are represented in its thought processes in the form of cognitive structures known as **schemata**.

A schema contains all the ideas, memories, skills, and associations to do with a particular set of operations on the environment. Piaget considered that cognitive development occurred through the process of building up and developing new schemata, and extending existing ones so that they applied to a wider range of experience. As we grow and interact with our environment, we are continually developing and changing our schemata.

A schema is the cognitive structure which we use to guide and direct our behaviour. We do not encounter each new thing in our lives afresh every day. Instead, we draw on our previous experiences and skills to let us know what to do. To use an example from Chapter 9, if you go out to catch a bus in a strange town you don't assume that you don't know anything about catching buses just because you are in a different place. Instead, you put your previous knowledge about catching buses to use; that is, you use the schemata which you have already developed through your previous experience to guide your behaviour.

We mentioned in Chapter 9 that Piaget considered that thinking only arose as a result of unexpected events. What he meant was that when we are able to use our existing schemata easily with no problems then we are not likely to give the event another thought. If you want to catch a bus, and things were exactly the same as you had always found in the past, then it wouldn't be likely to bother your thinking. But if you suddenly found that the customs of bus-catching were very different - for instance, that you had to go and buy your ticket from a local shop rather than on the bus itself - then you would be very likely to think about it. The new practice would be outside what Piaget called the **range of convenience** of your existing schemata, and so both your usual behaviour and your schema about catching buses would need to be changed.

Equilibration

Piaget considered that an event like this, which meant that existing schemata couldn't be applied in the normal way, caused a mental state of imbalance: **disequilibrium**. We would try to adjust that lack of balance, he thought, through the mental process of **equilibration**: of adjusting our schemata through the two processes of assimilation and accommodation until we could cope with the new situation.

Assimilation

Assimilation is the process of extending the range of convenience of the schema, simply by extending it so that it can now be used to cope with the new information. In other words, assimilation is when new information is absorbed into the schema, but without the schema itself changing particularly. If you found that catching buses in the new town was exactly the same as in your previous town, then you would simply assimilate that information - your schema about bus-catching would now apply to a wider range of buses, and it wouldn't have had to change.

Accommodation

If, on the other hand, you found that most aspects of bus-catching were the same, but there were some differences - such as the new town always having one-man-operated buses whereas buses in your previous town had always had a driver and a conductor - then you would need to adjust your schema to cope with this new variation. The new schema would have to alter its 'shape' to fit the new information: a process which Piaget called **accommodation**. In cases where the new information was very different indeed, the process of accommodation might even result in a new schema being formed, by the existing schema splitting into two.

The body-schema

Piaget considered that assimilation and accommodation happened together as part of the process of equilibration, and formed the basis of cognitive development. The very first schema of all which the child developed was the **body-schema**, as the young infant gradually grasped the idea that some things were 'me' and always present, whereas some were 'not me' and only present sometimes. Once that schema had been formed, the child's growing experience would mean that it would gradually come to extend and sub-divide the schema, through assimilation and accommodation. In this way it would learn about different parts of its body, and it would also develop an increasing awareness of the way that the outside world contained many different things.

The reduction of egocentricity

This brings us on to another important central concept in Piaget's theory, and one which is now regarded as quite controversial because it doesn't fit with the evidence on infant sociability that we looked at in Chapter 21 (among other reasons). This is Piaget's idea that cognition develops in the early years through the gradual reduction of **egocentricity**, and that the main reason why children's thinking is so different from adults is because they are still egocentric.

From the moment that it is first born, Piaget thought, the child is totally egocentric. This means that it is unable to comprehend a world outside of itself, seeing the whole universe as simply an extension of its own being. Through its developing experience, this view comes to be gradually whittled down. For instance, the formation of the body schema which we have just described is one of the first reductions of egocentricity.

The object concept

Later in infancy, the child comes to the realisation that objects do have a continuing existence even if it is not paying attention to them, in other words, the child develops **object constancy**. Piaget demonstrated how this is missing in young infants of less than 9 or 10 months old, by hiding a small toy that they were playing with, under a cloth or an upside-down cup right in front of their eyes. The infants made no attempt to reach the toy and Piaget thought that this was because it was, quite literally, 'out of sight, out of mind'! Because the child had no concept of objects as things with a continuing existence, it was not aware that the toy continued to exist even though it couldn't be seen. The development of the object concept, Piaget thought, represented another step in the reduction of egocentricity.

The ability to 'decentre'

A third step in the reduction of egocentricity came when the child was about 5 or 6 years old, in what Piaget termed the pre-operational stage. According to Piaget, it was only at this time that the child became able to **decentre**; to imagine what things must be like from someone else's point of view. He demonstrated this by an experiment using three papier-mâché mountains on a table-top and a small doll.

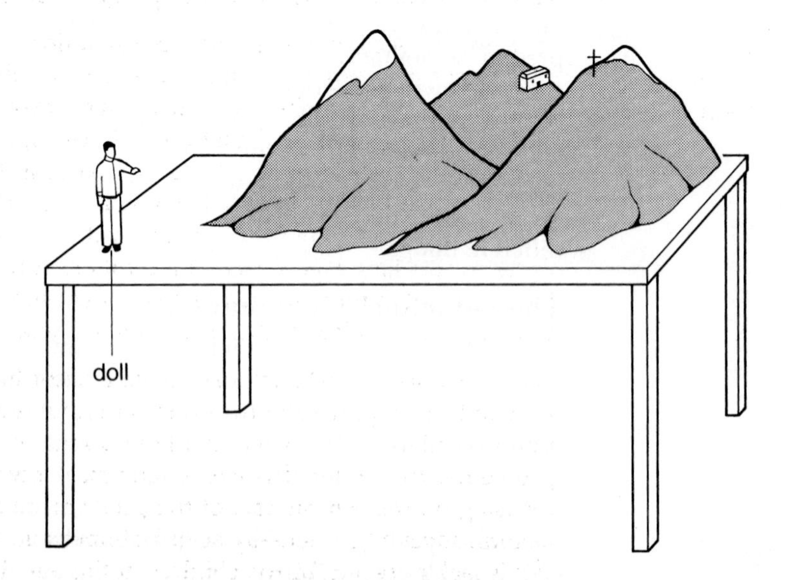

23.1 Piaget's 'three mountains' task

The child was seated, looking at the mountains, and the doll was placed by the side of them. The child was then asked to pick out, from a series of photographs, just which view of the mountains the doll would be able to see. Children near the beginning of the pre operational stage were unable to do this. Instead, they would pick out what they themselves could see, and Piaget took this as another sign of their egocentricity. By the time they were about 7 years old, Piaget considered that egocentricity was no longer affecting their thinking; but he thought that the reduction of egocentricity was the key to a great many of the ways in which a young child's thinking was different from an adult's.

Stages of cognitive development

Piaget believed that all children pass through a series of stages in their cognitive development. These are:

1 0-2yrs (approx) the sensori-motor stage

2 2-7yrs (approx) the pre-operational stage

3 7-11 yrs (approx) the concrete operational stage

4 11 yrs-adulthood the formal operational stage.

The sensori-motor stage

The **sensori-motor stage** is the very first period of cognitive development, in which the child's main task is to organise and to interpret the information that it is receiving through its sensory organs, and to develop motor co-ordination, in other words, to learn to co-ordinate its muscles. During this time, as we mentioned previously, it begins by developing the body-schema, and this is also when it will develop object constancy.

The pre-operational stage

It is in the second stage, the pre-operational stage, that the differences between children's and adults' thinking can be seen most clearly. This is the stage during which language develops, and again, Piaget thought that the child's use of language showed a gradual reduction of egocentricity. At first, the young child demonstrates totally **egocentric speech**, with little awareness of the needs of the listener; but gradually it becomes aware that in order to use language for communication, it needs to tailor its language rather more to an interaction than simply to express its thinking. (We looked at this point in more detail in Chapter 10.)

As we mentioned earlier, it is at this time, according to Piaget, that the child develops the ability to 'decentre', to take another person's point of view. But when thinking about different kinds of problems, the child also has a tendency towards **centration**: focusing on the central part of the problem, and ignoring other factors which might actually be quite important. One example of this is lack of **reversibility**: children at this age find it difficult to see operations as reversible. A child might learn, for instance, that

4 x 4 = 16, but would not be able to go from there to the conclusion that 16 ÷ 4 = 4. Or it may admit that it has a father, but not be able to admit that its father also has a child. Although one operation is just the reverse of the other, the child tends to focus on one side of the problem and has difficulty swapping it round.

Conservation

Another example of centration appears in the preoperational child's inability to grasp the principles of **conservation**. This is perhaps the most famous of all the different parts of Piaget's theory. By 'conservation', Piaget meant the idea that an object might change in shape or appearance, but still retain the same mass or quantity. He performed several conservation studies, such as placing two equal rows of counters in front of a child and asking if the two rows were the same. When the child agreed that they were, Piaget would spread out one row, so that it was much longer than other the other, and ask the child again. Typically, the pre-operational child would say that there were more counters in the longer row. There were several variations on the conservation studies: rolling pieces of clay from round balls to long sausage-shapes; or pouring coloured water from a short, fat glass to a long, thin one. Each time, the child would concentrate on the most obvious aspect of the change, and ignore the associated ones which meant that volume or quantity remained the same.

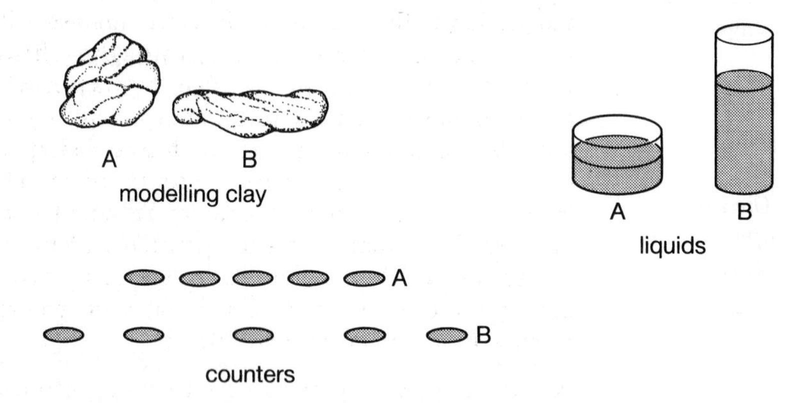

23.2 Examples of Piaget's conservation tasks

The main task of the pre-operational stage was to prepare the child for the later stages; and to this end, the child was learning more about the world all the time. One characteristic of this stage which Piaget noticed, was the tendency to **over-generalise** rules that it had learned, only by applying the rule in practice did the child learn the different ways that it could be used. For instance, a child in the early part of this stage might call all small animals 'doggy', but the more it did so, the more it would realise that there are different kinds of small animals and that they each have different names. Through the processes of assimilation and accommodation, it would extend its schemata by applying them to the world, until they formed a workable set of structures for dealing with the world. By the end of the pre-operational stage the child would be reasonably well-equipped with appropriate schemata to deal with the main kinds of challenges in its environment.

The concrete operational stage

Piaget's third stage was the **concrete operational stage**. At this time, a child's thinking was very like that of an adult, but it would have difficulty in dealing with purely abstract concepts, as it needed to relate things to the real world in order to understand them. Children in this stage are characterised by a fondness for collecting information about the world: they often collect lists of facts, or extensive data about a particular topic of interest.

The formal operational stage

By the fourth stage, **the formal operational stage**, the child's thinking is like that of an adult. It can now handle abstract logic, develop hypotheses (theories) about the world and test them out as a scientist might, and use abstract concepts in its thinking. Piaget considered this the highest form of thought, and argued that from this point on the child could extend its knowledge, and was no longer tied down by egocentricity or other such limitations.

By looking at these stages, we can see how the process of **adaptation to the environment** which interested Piaget so much, happened gradually throughout the child's cognitive development. He considered that the way in which the child's thinking developed mirrored the process by which rational thought had come to evolve in the human being. That the child's early stages represented earlier forms of thinking which had evolved, and which helped the animal to adapt to its environment. He considered that it was the gradual widening of awareness, represented by the reduction of egocentricity, which allowed the development of increasing control over the environment and of rational thought and forward planning.

Although Piaget considered that cognitive development happened through interaction with the environment, he nonetheless thought that it was an inherited process as a certain form of thinking could not develop until the child was genetically ready for it. However, the state of readiness could happen earlier if the environment was extremely stimulating, or later if the child did not have much opportunity to explore different problems. One of the criticisms which has been put forward of the Piagetian approach has been that it has been unable to explain the way that physically handicapped children are able to develop intellectually, often to a high level, despite their inability to perform operations on the environment.

Ethical discussion

Despite the fact that Piaget himself regarded it as the least important part of his theory, the four Piagetian stages were widely taught to teachers working in state schools for many years, as providing reasons why children should only be asked to undertake tasks that were appropriate for the developmental stages.

These ideas, however, were very much less common among teachers working in the private sector, who continued to teach young children measurement and calculations from very early on. The result was an increasing differentiation in expectations of children's abilities, between state and private schools.

Piaget's theory was well-established in psychology for many years, but recent evidence suggests that children's thinking may be a great deal more sophisticated than he proposed.

What are the ethical implications of this change of view?

Do researchers have a duty to make their findings available to the public? If so, how should they cope with changes of direction and theory?

Criticisms of the Piagetian approach

Some of the more general criticisms of Piaget's theory concentrate on the fact that Piaget sees children as being totally active in their quest to understand their environment. His theory has had important implications for many educators, who, taking his theory literally, believe that children should be left to 'discover' and learn about their environment through doing things themselves and with a minimum of adult supervision and intervention. The child should not be made to watch the teacher plan or build things but should be encouraged to do things for itself. Another implication to be derived from his theory is that each child goes through the stages at its own pace and so cannot be 'pushed' through by teachers. Jerome Kagan (1971) criticises Piaget for his failure to recognise the important role played by a child's home background and the society in which it lives, in fostering intellectual development. In his view the child *can* learn from outside influences, in the same way that it can learn from its own actions.

The clinical interview

There are several criticisms of Piaget's methods. Firstly, his use of the clinical interview method casts doubt upon the value of the material gleaned from such interviews. During the interviews, he had no set questions to follow. This may be seen as an advantage in that children were allowed to express themselves in their own language and questions could be pitched at their level of understanding. However, there is no way of telling how Piaget might have influenced the children by either the questions he put to them or in the interpretation of their answers.

More recent evidence from researchers like Margaret Donaldson, suggests very strongly that children are able to reason logically well before the age cited by Piaget. Barke (1975) for instance, found that by the time they were four, many children could choose the view that a *Sesame Street* character could see, even from different positions. Martin Hughes (1975) set up a similar investigation to that provided by Piaget's mountain experiment. Children sat in front of a table containing four walls set at right angles to one another to form a cross, and were given two dolls, one a policeman and the other a boy doll. The policeman was placed so that it could see into two of the sections divided by the 'walls', and the child was asked to hide the doll behind a section of the wall where the policeman would not be able to see it.

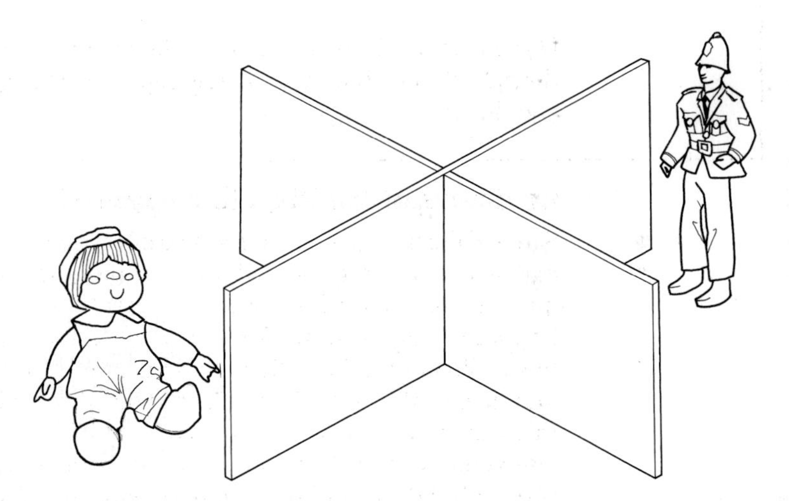

The child has to 'hide' the boy doll from the policeman.

23.3 Hughes' 'policeman doll' study

Although this was a similar experiment to that set up by Piaget, it was different in two very important respects. Firstly, Hughes gave the children a chance to ask questions and if they went wrong in the early stages, he would explain how they had erred (although this was rarely the case). Secondly, the children really enjoyed the task because they could relate to it. His results were startling, in that most three and four year olds could perform the task accurately, even when more walls and policemen were introduced. Hughes believed that this demonstrated that children of this age were not as egocentric as Piaget had implied.

Naughty teddy

McGarrigle (1974) carried out the conservation studies which Piaget had developed, but with a vital difference. In the conservation tasks such as the one concerning the two rows of counters, a **naughty teddy** would swoop in and stretch out one row of counters. Under these circumstances, children of between four and seven were not persuaded into thinking that the longer row contained more counters, because they realised that naughty teddy had rearranged the row. It has been suggested that when an adult experimenter commits a similar act, the child says that something must have been changed, because of the difference in status between the child and the adult.

Recent research by people like Donaldson (1978) suggests that children are more logical in their thoughts and actions than Piaget gave them credit for. When experiments are set up in such a way that the children are given the best chance of understanding the situation, (i.e. so that they are related to the children's experiences), and when the experimenter is aware that children might be easily persuaded into giving an incorrect answer by the way the questions are phrased, then children are much more likely to show that they have thought in a logical manner.

23.1 Investigating concept formation

This is a study which you will probably need to do as a class exercise, unless you happen to know quite a lot of children!

To do this, you will first need to collect a set of pictures which children can easily sort out into sets. Try to get about 16-20 pictures, of several different kinds. For instance, you might have some pictures of animals, some of plants, some of transport, and some of household objects.

Mount all of your pictures onto postcard-sized pieces of card. (You can cover them with clear sticky-backed plastic if you like).

Discuss with your friends the details of how you are going to carry out the study. The main thing is that you should try to get hold of children of varying ages, and ask them to sort the cards out into sets. When they have done this, you should ask them why they sorted them out like that and note down what they said.

Code each of the explanations that the child gives into the following four categories.

a. No particular explanation (e.g. 'don't know')

b. Simple statements about what each picture is like but without any attempt to relate them to each other (e.g. 'the apple is green')

c. Descriptions of how the objects are related (e.g. 'The apple and the tree go together because apples grow on trees')

d. Category or class names (e.g. 'fruit', 'furniture')

Compare the answers that you obtain from older and younger children. Are there differences in the types of explanations that they give?

What explanation can you suggest for this?

What controls would you need to introduce if you were doing this as a formal experiment?

Alternative approaches to cognitive development

Many researchers consider that Piaget's idea of cognitive development happening through the reduction of egocentricity is not really supported by modern evidence. In recent years, a considerable amount of work has been done on the social influences on children's cognitive processes. In Chapter 21 we saw how the child has mechanisms of sociability from a very early age, and how attachments develop in the first few months through social interaction. If the child were as egocentric as Piaget suggested, such attachments would not be possible as the child would not recognise the other person as an independent object until many months later.

The social context

We have already mentioned some of the variations of Piaget's experiments which show that children can, in fact, solve types of problems which Piaget considered to be impossible, but only if those problems are set in a social context which they can understand. Hughes' study of the boy doll and the policeman doll, for instance, still requires the child to 'decentre', but this time places the task in a social context, that of the boy hiding from the policeman. This is something which the child can identify with, and therefore the child has little difficulty with the task. Similarly, McGarrigle's study of 'naughty teddy' places the alterations to the materials in the Piagetian task in a social context, which the child can relate to, and the child demonstrates the cognitive skill in question.

Other studies have shown that the child is often acting in quite a socially sophisticated way in the Piagetian experiments. Rose and

Blank (1974) tried the same studies, but this time they only asked the child 'are they the same?' once - after the change had been made. When they did that, most of the children appreciated that the amounts were in fact the same. In the standard Piagetian task, the children had concluded that their being asked the same question twice meant that they had got the answer wrong the first time, and so they had changed it. This type of thinking draws on considerable knowledge on the part of the child, of the ways that adults behave and conventions about asking questions and implicit meanings. Rather than showing the limitations of children's thinking, it shows how socially subtle they can be!

Disembedded thinking

Donaldson (1978) argued that the real problem with the Piagetian tasks is that they are testing **disembedded thinking** on the part of the child: they are asking the child to solve problems unrelated to the child's own knowledge and experience. This, she argues, is the reason why children perform so poorly on these tasks, but perform far better on ones which are placed solidly in the realms of what children already know, by embedding them in an appropriate context.

Many modern researchers of cognitive development consider that the study of **social cognition** is a more fruitful field than Piaget's structuralist approach, and an increasing amount of research has been conducted into this. Bearison (1982) argued that it is not possible to explain children's cognitive development purely in terms of their individual encounters with the environment. He has demonstrated how children learn far more readily and efficiently when they are working together than when they are working alone. Although as yet Piaget's theory is still the most influential of the cognitive development theories, it seems distinctly possible that it will become superseded by the socio-cognitive approach in future years.

Moral development

Piaget's theory of moral development

One important aspect of Piaget's theory of cognitive development is that which links a child's level of reasoning to its morality. Morality concerns the ways in which a child thinks about what is right and wrong, and this is an important part of its socialisation. Every society has its own ideas about acceptable kinds of behaviour, and children are brought up to observe the rules of their own society, as we have seen in Chapter 21.

Piaget's major contribution to the theory of children's social development was provided in a book called *The Moral Judgement of a Child* (1932) in which he examined children's attitudes towards rules, their judgements on certain crimes, and their ideas about justice.

Understanding rules

In an attempt to explore their understanding of rules, Piaget chose to play games of marbles with children of various ages. He chose this game because, more often than not, it is developed by children themselves and is rarely taught by adults. The children under observation were asked to show him how to play the game, and in doing so, to teach him the rules. From his observations, Piaget discovered that a child's view of rules and what is right and wrong develops in much the same way as their intellect develops. For instance, children of three years and under seemed to follow some kind of order in their play, but did not deem it necessary to stick to this order; in fact, they frequently changed the rules.

Between the ages of three and six, most of the children would simply copy some of the rules that they saw the older children using, but they were not really capable of playing a proper game with other children. They often appeared to be playing their own version of the game even when playing with others. Piaget linked this finding to his earlier discovery that pre-operational children were very egocentric. (By this we mean that such children tend to see things from their own point of view all the time and lack the cognitive structure to take account of the views of others.)

There are differences, too, in whether children saw rules as flexible. Although they are not really capable of following the rules as older children do, pre-operational children seem to have a view of rules as having been invented by some authority above them, as being fixed and unchangeable. By the time they reach the concrete operational stage though, most children realise that they can devise their own rules and that rules are not devised by some arbitrary authority.

Children's definitions of justice

A similar change in reasoning can be found in the way children think about justice. Piaget questioned many children of various ages as to what they thought about different crimes, telling them stories about people lying, cheating and stealing. He concluded that pre-operational children can be characterised by their **moral realism**. By this he meant that their assessment of how bad an act or lie was depended very much on the consequences of the act or lie. For example a child who accidentally knocks over a whole row of plates is thought to be more naughty than a child who deliberately breaks one. These children then, did not take the intention of the crime into account. Lies were seen as naughty words, not because the children had any notion of why they were wrong, but because the consequence was to be punished by parents.

When they are around eight years old, children lose this moral realism and they begin to take the **intention** of the person into account. Now a person who intentionally knocks over a plate is regarded as acting in a way that is worse than one who accidentally breaks many.

Psychology in action

Piaget thought that there was a link between a child's level of cognitive reasoning and its sense of right and wrong. Part of the process of learning right from wrong involves understanding rules and when and why they are imposed. According to Piaget, pre-operational children rarely understand that rules are developed by a group for the good of a group as a whole. They see rules as being imposed upon them by someone in authority.

Pre-operational children also seem to base their judgement of an act on the consequences which it produces and not the act itself. For instance, a child who deliberately knocks over a bottle of milk which results in little mess would be seen as less naughty than a child who accidentally knocks over a bottle of milk but causes more mess. It isn't until the child is around eight years old that it begins to take the intention of the act into account and work out an appropriate punishment to fit the crime.

Very briefly then, with regard to justice, pre-operational children take a very dogmatic view. On the whole, Piaget thought they were also unable to relate the nature of the punishment to the crime. They thought simply that the more severe the punishment for any crime, so much the better. Interestingly, they also had a notion of 'imminent justice', which was that any accidents which occur after a crime, occur *because* of the crime. For example, a person who trips up as they run away from the scene of a crime is being punished for their crime. This same sense of imminent justice can also be seen in adults, in the concept of 'poetic justice'. Piaget describes this level of moral development as one of 'adult restraint' because children think that whatever an adult may say, goes; and that adults are always right and appropriate in the punishments that they give out. Older children, though, are increasingly capable of finding punishments which 'fit the crime', known as reciprocal justice.

As Piaget sees it, then, there is a gradual progression in a child's sense of morality. The young child is at a **heteronomous** stage, where discipline is imposed by people above it and the child accepts their rules. The older child is at an **autonomous** stage, where it can think for itself, and its morality is a product of its own reasoning, rather than being imposed by other people.

Kohlberg's theory of moral development

Another structuralist account of moral development was put forward by Kohlberg, in 1963. He was interested in investigating the ways that people came to resolve moral dilemmas, and investigated moral development by presenting children and adults with a series of moral problems. Each of these offered a dilemma of doing good for someone or obeying society's rules. For instance, one of his dilemmas was the case of a man who broke into a chemist's shop to steal medicine for his dying wife. The research participant was asked to judge what was right and wrong in this sort of case, and how wrong-doing should be punished.

23.2 Investigating moral development

Both Kohlberg and Piaget investigated moral development by telling children of different ages stories which presented some kind of moral dilemma. They found that children of different ages tended to give different kinds of answers to the problems.

You can investigate moral development using the same technique. Firstly, you will need to develop a set of four moral dilemma problems. (An example of this kind of problem is the story of the man who broke into a chemist's shop to steal medicine for his dying wife. Research participants had to judge whether the man was right or wrong to do what he did and to explain the reasons for their answers.)

Working in pairs or small groups draw up a set of four moral dilemma problems.

Present your problems to as many different people as possible - try to get people of as many different ages as you can. For each participant, note down their age and the judgements that they made.

Arrange all your answers in order of age of the participants. Can you see any developments in the types of judgements being made?

What explanation can you give for these results?

How do your findings compare with those of Piaget and Kohlberg?

From analysing the results on the basis of the arguments that people used when they were trying to reach a decision, Kohlberg developed a theory of three main stages in moral development, each of which had two distinct levels.

The first stage was the **pre-moral stage**, where the person holds certain ideas purely for their instrumental value to that person. In level one, the person holds certain moral ideas purely in order to avoid punishment, while in level two the ideas are held because that means that other people will be nice to that person.

The second stage was the **stage of conventional morality**, and in this stage the individual is mainly concerned with following social rules. In level one of this stage, the individual seeks general social approval and conforms to the morals of others in order to achieve this. In level two, the individual develops a strong support for 'law and order' as it is considered morally right in itself to obey the laws and rules of society.

The third stage is known as the **stage of autonomous morality**. In this stage the individual is developing a personal moral code, rather than automatically accepting the codes laid down by other people. In level one of this stage, the individual accepts the laws of society because she or he feels that they are democratically enforced for the good of all. In level two, people have established their moral codes and principles by personally reflecting on issues and developing their own ideas, and may come to disagree with some of society's rules if they feel them to be morally wrong.

Links with Piaget's theory

You may be able to see the links between this theory and that highlighted by Piaget, in that the first stages of morality exist in individuals when their morals are shaped by those above them, as they seek to gain approval and avoid punishment from others. The later stages are revealed in people whose morals are the result of careful reflection, and there is a general increase in the level of autonomy which the individual shows as it progresses through the stages.

The studies of Kohlberg and Elfenbein (1975) showed that many ten year olds were still at the first level of moral development, and that a great many adults never reached the final levels. Kohlberg argued that the development of cognitive (mental) structures, greatly affects not only our level of thinking but also the way we behave in the world. He felt that a good way to help people develop their moral thinking is for them to hear points of view from people who are at a higher stage of moral development than themselves. This is important for parents who wish to help develop their children's moral development, as simply telling the children what is right and wrong without explaining the reasons behind it may only encourage the child to stay at the level of development it has already reached.

Summary

1 Piaget suggested that cognitive development happened through the formation of schemata. These are formed by the assimilation of new information and the accommodation of existing schemata to new data.

2 Egocentricity is reduced through the development of the body-schema, the object-concept, and the ability to 'decentre'.

3 Piaget identified four stages of cognitive development: the sensori-motor stage; the pre-operational stage; the concrete operational stage; and the formal operational stage.

4 Critics of Piaget have argued that his tasks were too artificial to test children's real cognitive abilities, and have also criticised the way that he carried out his studies.

5 Many modern researchers consider that social cognition is a more relevant approach to intellectual development than Piaget's theory.

6 Piaget's theory of moral development was that children progressed from a 'heteronomous' stage to an 'autonomous' stage as they matured.

7 Kohlberg identified three stages of moral development: the pre-moral stage and the stages of conventional morality and autonomous morality.

Chapter 24 - The socio-cognitive approach to child development

In this chapter, we will look at the child's growing understanding of its social world. We have already looked at social learning how children learn appropriate behaviour from other people and also at cognitive development – how the child develops an understanding of the world and how to do things. However, children don't just learn what to do: they also learn to predict how other people are likely to react. They learn about their own bodies and what they can and can't do – both physically and in terms of what is socially acceptable. Some of that knowledge comes from social-learning or direct teaching, but a great deal of it comes through play and interaction with other people especially family members. That is what we will be looking at in this chapter.

Play

There are, of course, many different types of play. Children play with toys; they play with household or natural objects; they play with one another; they play with language; they engage in physical play; and they make up pretence games. We will look briefly at each of these before we look at the various theories and functions of play which have been described by psychologists.

Playing with objects

Producing toys for children is a major industry in modern society. Children enjoy playing with objects and they use them for a wide variety of purposes. Not surprisingly, as a child grows older, the way that it plays with objects becomes more sophisticated. Lowe (1975) observed how children between nine months and three years play with objects, and found that there seems to be a pattern to their development, with different activities happening at different ages. That pattern is described in Fig 24.1.

As anyone who has dealt with several children knows, every child is different. Babies are born with different temperaments, they respond differently to stimuli and they develop their own unique patterns of activity. Gradually, throughout childhood and adolescence, these differences in temperament become shaped and structured by the child's social experiences and the things which it learns about the world. Eventually, this interaction produces what we refer to as **personality**.

Age	Activity
9 months	Grasps things, brings them to the mouth, waves them about, looks at them.
12 months	Looks carefully at things, waves them, puts in mouth or bangs them about; may practise familiar actions.
15 months	Inspects objects closely; rehearses activities with familiar objects, e.g. pretends to drink from a cup.
21 months	Uses two or more objects together, e.g. using a toy as a passenger in a toy train.
24 months	Play with objects becomes increasingly realistic; the child acts out its own experiences and those of close family members.
30-36 months	Pretend play develops further; the child gets toys to 'act' for themselves.

Adapted from: Lowe, 1975

Fig 24.1 Changes in children's play

Corinne Hutt (1966) explored some of those differences in temperament by looking at the way that children explored an entirely new object. The object was referred to as a 'supertoy', and it consisted of a wooden box which had wheels, buzzers, bells, counters, pedals and levers. Playing with the levers and the pedals produced various results: the bell, the buzzer, or both, could sound, and the counters might become covered up. The 'supertoy' could be set up so that anything a child did produced a major effect, with everything going off at once.

Most children found the supertoy extremely attractive: when the toy was set up like this, they would play for much longer than when it was set up in such a way that only one or two things happened at the same time. A few children, though, were nervous about the supertoy and didn't play with it at all. When these children were studied again four years later, Hutt and Bhavrani (1972) found that they were developing personalities that were different from most of the others. The boys were unadventurous and lacking in curiosity, while the girls were socially withdrawn and shy.

This is one of the very few studies which seems to draw a link between childhood behaviour and later personality – although, of course, it doesn't tell us just how that link has come about. It may have been straightforward, with both temperament and personality being signs of an inherited introversion or something similar. Alternatively, those children might have had childhood experiences which taught them to be cautious about new things, and those experiences could have produced shyness as the child grew older. A third possibility is that both findings could have resulted from some other, external cause, such as child abuse which often produces withdrawal, and which the researchers were not in a position to investigate.

Playing with others

There have been a number of studies of how children go about playing with other children. As children develop through their pre-school years, they become more sociable and more capable of sharing and co-operating with other children. Parten (1933) performed one of the first systematic studies of pre-school children playing together, looking at 42 nursery school children. From these observations, Parten identified five different stages which happen between the ages of two and four and a half. These stages are given in Fig 24.2.

1	Solitary play	The child plays alone, apparently unaware of others.
2	Onlooker play	The child still plays alone, but watches other children and sometimes reacts to them.
3	Parallel play	Two children play the same type of games, often side-by-side, without appearing to interact directly.
4	Associative play	Two or more children interact through conversation or sharing, but don't play the same game.
5	Co-operative play	Children play directly with others at the same game or task.

Adapted from: Parten, 1933

24.2 Stages of play in pre-school children

Cohen (1987) criticised many of the studies of how children play with one another, including these stages, on the grounds that they didn't really reflect the child's main experience of play. Because the observations were carried out in nurseries and playschools, they involved children playing with others of the same age. However, most of the time children play with people of different ages: they play with brothers and sisters, with their parents and with other adults in the family. So the type of play which they engage in is quite different from the type of play which researchers see in the nursery.

For example, Ross and Goldman (1977) observed children playing socially in nurseries and found that two-thirds of the two year olds that they watched were unable to play 'turn-taking' games properly. They concluded that the children weren't old enough to do this yet. However, other psychologists argued that they only got those findings because the other children were relative strangers. If the same children were observed in their own homes, playing with family members whom they knew well, they were perfectly able to engage in 'turn-taking' games, and often did.

Playing with words

Another type of play is playing with language. Young children enjoy learning new words, and many words used by very young children have distinctive, repeated sounds, such as 'baa-baa' or 'doggy-woggy'. Many psychologists believe that this type of 'baby-talk' helps the very young child to acquire language.

Once language has been learned, children play with it often. Rhymes are particularly popular with pre-school children, and nursery rhymes or their equivalent occur in almost all human cultures. Children enjoy the sound of rhymes but they also serve a valuable learning purpose because they help children to become more sensitive to the subtle differences between words. Bradley and Bryant (1983) showed that children who had experience with rhyming and rhyming games in young childhood learned to read more easily than children who had only a limited experience of rhymes. The rhyming had helped them to become more sensitive to slight differences between words.

Language games continue as the child grows older. Often, children play with language among themselves and develop their own language games and puns. Some children even develop private languages, which they use between one another. When the child goes to school, it learns other language games and puzzles from other children. Iona and Peter Opie (1959) travelled round Britain asking children about their games, and found that many of them were very old and that some even went back hundreds of years. They had been passed on from child to child but were not taught by adults. Instead, these language games were part of a childhood cultural tradition which had its own continuity, entirely separate from adult culture.

Physical play

Physical play ranges from simple running about or rough-and-tumble play, to games requiring peak physical fitness and finely tuned co-ordination. For adolescents and adults, physical play tends to take the form of playing music or doing sport, but with younger children it is often all about activity for its own sake. Young children, as any parent knows, are very inclined to be active and some of their activities, such as running, climbing – whether on trees or furniture – and jumping, seem to be innate – perhaps a relic from our evolutionary past. Children do them spontaneously and without being taught.

But children also benefit from physical play. Some of these benefits are obvious: active physical play helps children to develop their muscles and their cardio-vascular system and, if accompanied by a good diet, sets the foundations for physical fitness in adult life. These activities also help the child's cognitive development. The body-schema (see Chapter 23) becomes clearer as the child develops an awareness of its own abilities and of its growing competence in dealing with the world. Because physical play is so important, there is some concern about children growing up in urban environments which do not provide open spaces for physical activity. Children who grow up without physical play often become listless and passive, with little or no appetite, and doctors have recently found that they can even begin to develop heart disease.

Pretend play

Garvey (1977) showed how pre-school children are particularly likely to engage in dramatic play – acting out familiar scenes or stories, or sometimes fantasies and fairy stories. Younger children usually act out stories about family roles and domestic activities, but older children are more likely to adopt wider social roles, like doctors and nurses. These acting games are an important part of how the child develops its understanding of the world. As the child acts out the roles, it practises applying its social knowledge – a process that is often a source of considerable amusement for eavesdropping adults!

Pretend play often involves objects which are used as 'props' for imaginary activities. The child transforms these objects, mentally, as it plays so a handkerchief might become transformed into a sheet for a doll's bed or a tablecloth for a picnic. Golumb (1977) studied these **transformations**, and found that the object needs to be appropriate, or at least to fit with the child's existing world-knowledge. If an inappropriate transformation is suggested by an adult, the child rejects it. In one case, for example, a child objected to being asked to 'feed' a doll with a pencil because she knew that pencils were poisonous. So even though this type of play involves the use of the imagination, it is still linked closely to the child's existing world-knowledge and it has to fit that context.

Stages of play

In Chapter 23, we looked at Piaget's theory of cognitive development and found that Piaget believed that development occurs in distinct stages. This was also true of the way that he regarded play. The first of Piaget's stages of play is **mastery play**, which happens during the first two years of life, and in which the child is learning how objects and people respond to physical activity and particular words or commands. Effectively, the child's play at this time is all about learning to control its environment.

The second stage is **symbolic play**, during which the child explores how objects or items can be used to represent other things. Language games reflect the way that words and numbers can be used as symbols, while pretend play allows the child to gain some idea of what life is like for other people or in different contexts. This stage, according to Piaget, occurs between the ages of two and seven, corresponding to the pre-operational period of cognitive development.

The third stage of play, according to Piaget, is **play with rules**. When they reach about seven years of age, children begin to play co-operative, structured games which have very definite rules and structures. As the child grows older, this type of play becomes increasingly important, which reflects the child's development through the concrete and formal operational stages. Eventually it becomes formalised into sport or other kinds of adult leisure activity.

Sylva, Roy and Painter (1980) performed a series of observations of children in playgroups. From their observations, they developed a complex coding system for observing children playing. Some of the categories that they used are listed in Fig 24.3. They also distinguished between **complex play**, and **simple play**. Sometimes, a child would do something in a challenging way, with a high level of complexity, while at other times the child would do the same activity but without the challenges. Playing in a sandpit, for example, might just involve building simple structures, or it might involve setting out and constructing something much more ambitious. Sylva et al. concluded that activities with a clear goal structure were particularly good for children because they fostered a sense of achievement and helped the child to become self-motivated in its learning.

Coding category	Example
Large muscle movement	*running, climbing*
Manipulation	*water or sand play, sewing, arranging objects*
Three Rs	*reading, writing, sums, looking attentively at books*
Large-scale construction	*building dens, trains, etc.*
Small-scale construction	*using Lego, Meccano, etc.*
Pretend	*transforming objects using imagination*
Scale-version toys	*arranging miniature objects, e.g. dolls house, farm, toy soldiers*
Informal games	*spontaneous shared activities between two or more children*
Games with rules	*skittles, snakes and ladders*
Music	*listening, playing, singing or dancing*
Social interaction	*talking to others, or being with them, but not playing*
Cruise	*active movement, looking around for something to do*
Purposeful movement	*going deliberately towards an object, person or place, or searching for something or someone*
Watching	*watching other people or events*

Adapted from Sylva, Roy & Painter, 1980

Fig 24.3 Some categories for coding play

Sylva's observations showed, too, that involvement from adults or older children was important. Adults help a child to progress by making things more difficult or providing extra challenges. Children progressed far more quickly with this type of encouragement than children who were allowed to explore without guidance. This finding contradicted Piaget's ideas but fits with Vygotsky's theory of child development which we shall be looking at later in this chapter.

Relationships in childhood

Children don't just learn through play. They also learn through their relationships with other people. In Chapter 21, we saw how the young infant has a powerful tendency to respond to other people. The infant's interactions with other people influence its attachments, and this does not stop when infancy is over. Throughout our lives we develop relationships with other people. They begin with our immediate family but also extend into friendships with other people.

Children's friendships

Selman (1980) looked at how children develop friendships with their peers, by interviewing children and asking them to respond to questions about friendship. The questions each posed some kind of dilemma and the children had to say how they would act. Their answers showed that there seemed to be a series of steps in the way that children perceive what friendship is all about. While Selman didn't want to make the mistake of attaching precise ages to each stage – every child is different, after all – he did give approximate developmental times when each stage was likely to be reached.

Selman's stages of children's friendships

For most pre-school children, the concept of friendship hasn't really developed. Selman referred to this as stage zero. In this stage, children just consider their 'close friends' to be whoever is around at the time. The first stage in actually developing friendships comes in early primary school as the child begins to see other children as someone they can play with or who helps them. However, this is simply a matter of whoever serves the child's needs at the time.

In later primary school, children become more aware of **reciprocity**: the fact that a friendship should benefit both partners, not just one. For children in stage two, friendship involves co-operation and mutual satisfaction. In this stage, your friend is the person who pleases you, and so you also try to please them. But these friendships aren't lasting if the satisfaction stops, the friendship stops too. So friendship in the second stage is entirely dependent on reward and pleasure: it has little to do with any deeper or more lasting attachment.

Gradually, the child's concept of friendship develops into the third stage, in which friendship is seen as very important, involving personal **trust** and **intimacy**. According to Selman, children in this stage become more aware of how their friendship is seen by outsiders – they begin to focus on the relationship itself, as well as on the person concerned. Friends are seen as people to share secrets with. Also, the friendship can survive small conflicts – it is only really challenged by major conflicts which involve breaking the trust or intimacy of the relationship.

The final stage in Selman's model, stage four, occurs in adolescence and adulthood. During this stage, people become aware that there are different types of relationship, and that they can offer different types of satisfactions. Moreover, people have different needs which may require different relationships for their satisfaction. So friendships are seen as being of different kinds, and as open to change or growth. Some are maintained constantly, some are abandoned, and others change their character as the people concerned develop.

Youniss's model of friendship

Another psychologist who studied how children's friendships develop was Youniss, in 1980. This study involved interviewing large numbers of children, of various ages. In the interviews, each child was asked to tell a short story, of about one or two sentences, about how they might let another child know that they liked them or that they were friends. They also wrote down what would be involved in being unkind to someone. Youniss found that children of different ages told different kinds of stories, but that there were definite themes which related to different ages. These themes are described in Fig 24.4.

Age	**Themes**
6-8 years	Friendship is seen as all about sharing and giving: toys, sweets etc. Also about socially acceptable behaviour, as defined by adults ('playing nicely').
9-11 years	Friendship is seen as all about fairness, and reducing inequality through sharing with others.
12-14 years	Friendship is seen as supporting friends psychologically, e.g. by not laughing at them, or helping them when they are upset.

Adapted from: Youniss, 1980

Fig 24.4Themes in children's friendships

Youniss's research shows a shift from physical factors to psychological ones as the child gets older. Children become much more aware of individual needs, and their views of friendship change. One of those changes is that friendship is seen as reciprocal which means that each member of the partnership has a responsibility to the other. Also, and very important, children become more interested in psychological factors like intimacy or similarity than in physical factors, like sharing toys or living nearby. Whether you can trust your friend becomes much more important than where your friend lives.

The studies by Youniss and Selman mainly involved interviewing children, so there is always the chance that the researchers were simply told what the child thought an adult wanted to hear. Corsaro (1985) studied children's friendships by observing three to five year olds secretly as they played at nursery school, and also sometimes by joining in with their activities as they played. The children were videotaped and their conversations and actions were carefully analysed.

24.1 Concepts of friendship

The study by Selman, which we looked at in the chapter, involved dilemma-stories being told to children of different ages. Here is a story which is typical of the ones that Selman used.

'Holly is eight. She likes to climb trees and she is better at it than any of her friends. One day, she falls off a low branch of a big tree. She doesn't hurt herself but her father sees it and makes her promise not to climb trees any more.

Later on, the same day, Holly meets her friend Shaun who is very upset. His kitten is stuck up a tree and can't get down. It might fall. Nobody except Holly can climb trees well enough to reach the kitten. But she has promised her father than she won't climb trees any more.'

Selman asked children questions about the story and, in particular, whether they thought that Holly should help her friend out or obey her father. Selman's study showed that children of different ages gave different answers. In any study, though, there are lots of individual differences. That means that even people of the same age will often give different answers.

Try developing a set of these dilemmas for yourself. If you and your friends don't climb trees very much, then think of situations which are more like the kinds of things that you do. When you have a set of three or four dilemmas, try giving them to your friends and members of your family, and asking for their opinions.

Did they all give the same answers?

Were there differences between older and younger people?

If you were doing this as a formal study, what controls would you need to include and what precautions would you need to take?

Corsaro found that social context was a particularly important factor in the way that children saw their friendships. Indeed, they would often use claims of friendship as a way of preventing other children from joining in their games, or as a way of joining in with other children. When they discussed friendship as they played, it seemed to be as a way of strengthening their bonds and defining why they were important to one another. In other words, the children were not just seeing friendship as something which existed and which they learned about – they were actively constructing an idea of friendship and using it in their social interactions for their own ends.

Family interaction and social awareness

The realisation that children are actively involved in their own social development and that they can use social knowledge for their own ends, is one which challenges many of the earlier ideas about child development. What it suggests is that childhood isn't just a matter of passive unfolding of development, or of a gradual understanding of the outside world. Instead, it is an active process in which the child is busy constructing its understanding of the world and using its knowledge as it does so.

The idea of the child as an active agent in its social and cognitive development is supported by studies of how young children interact in their families. Dunn (1988) argued that earlier theories of child development had underestimated children because they had asked them to react to abstract, hypothetical situations. Children aren't very good at that. However, real life observation shows that children become aware of the complexities of social living very early on. They learn to use, adjust and even negotiate rules of social behaviour long before they are old enough for school.

Dunn's conclusions came from a set of **ethological** observations, in which researchers visited families with pre-school children on several occasions and for quite long periods of time. The children became accustomed to the observers so they acted naturally even though they were being observed. It quickly became apparent from the observations that the children had a far more sophisticated knowledge of social interaction than researchers had previously realised.

Understanding other people

Dunn identified four main areas in which children showed a remarkably high degree of awareness. The first was understanding other people's **feelings**. Even children who were less than two years old indicated that they were aware, and sympathetic, when someone was distressed or upset. As they grew older, that understanding was often applied in a rather less positive way, by deliberately upsetting their siblings (their brothers or sisters). They knew how their siblings would react to particularly annoying acts and often took great delight in teasing them. It may have been irritating for their parents but the fact that they were able to tease their siblings in this way showed that, actually, they had quite a high level of understanding of other people's feelings.

The second area which Dunn identified was that of understanding other people's goals or **intentions**. Children can co-operate with their older brothers or sisters in pretend play while they are still less than two years old, and co-operation always requires some understanding of what the activity is about. Dunn's observations showed that children as young as 14 months old can understand intentions and goals as they play with their older siblings, and that they deliberately act to help the game along. It became more common, however, when the child was between 18 months and two years old.

Dunn's third area was to do with the understanding of **social rules**. Again, the research showed that children are capable of understanding social rules much sooner than traditional child psychologists believed. Between one and three years of age, children learn a great deal about what is and is not allowed. However, they don't just learn these rules rigidly, as Piaget suggested. They learn about them in practice, through interaction with their mothers, their siblings and other people around them. While they are learning, they manipulate the rules and test them out. By doing this, pre-school children gain a very clear idea of which rules are absolute and must always be kept, and which rules are only general ones which can be broken occasionally. When they are asked to talk about rules, they show the kind of limited understanding that Piaget and other researchers found, but when their behaviour is observed in its real-life contexts, the researchers could see that their understanding of rules was much more complex. It was practical knowledge, not theoretical.

Of course, understanding rules isn't the same thing as obeying them! The children in Dunn's study often broke rules deliberately – they knew perfectly well what it was to be naughty, and they used that knowledge often. They also developed very strong ideas about their own rights, which frequently produced tantrums and angry 'scenes'. Dunn found a very strong connection between what children had tantrums about when they were 18 months old, and what they argued most about when they were three. The two reactions tended to be about the same issues, and Dunn suggested that perhaps the anger that the children felt when they were younger became channelled into verbal arguments as they grew older. Emotion might be an important feature in cognitive development but it is not one which researchers have really thought about much before.

Psychology in Action

In recent years there has been a great deal of concern about young people growing up without a social conscience. Cases of child killers, or of children who appear to feel no empathy for their victims when they inflict pain, have disturbed society. The media reflex is to blame the parents. But parents need to know what type of thing to look out for in their children, and this is where psychology can help.

Judy Dunn's research, and also research into the child's theory of mind, show us that empathy, and the ability to understand that other people have different experiences and thoughts, seem to develop around the age of three and a half. Paul Harris (1989) showed that this ability is very closely linked to the child's understanding of emotion. Children mature at different rates, of course, so some children would be four rather than three when they developed the ability to empathise with others.

Knowing that this ability should appear at round about this time may tell us what we should look out for. If a child reaches five years old and shows no sign of being able to empathise with others, then perhaps parents and teachers need to look carefully at how they can teach social values to that child; perhaps that child will need special attention given to that area of its upbringing. Ignoring this problem may mean that the child never develops empathic abilities in later life. That doesn't mean that it would turn into a killer, of course – there are several other social factors involved in that, not just this one. However, it does mean that it would lack one of the psychological safeguards which makes it impossible for most people to go in that direction.

The fourth area in which Dunn found children to be more sophisticated than researchers had believed them to be was in understanding other people's minds. The children in the study often showed a considerable awareness of other people's understanding. As they grew older, and particularly when they reached about three and a half, they showed an increased awareness of what people were likely to be thinking. Even when they were smaller, they could predict what sort of things would make Mummy angry – indeed, they often used this knowledge in exploring their understanding of rules and goals.

The child's theory of mind

Other researchers, too, have investigated children's understanding of other minds. Cole (1986) performed a study in which children were given a present which they either liked or didn't like. The researchers knew which was which because the children had been asked to rate the items in order of attractiveness first – and also because, once the experiment was over, they were allowed to swap the presents for ones they wanted more! During the study, one group of children received their presents alone, while the other group had other people with them.

The children who were alone showed their disappointment openly, but those who had other people with them hid their disappointment and smiled and said 'thank you'. They knew that it was proper to pretend that they were not disappointed, in order to spare the feelings of the person who had given them the present. So, Cole argued, they used their understanding of other people's minds to make sure that they acted in a socially appropriate way. But, of course, they might just have been acting as they had been told to act by the parents..

Understanding false beliefs

Wimmer and Perner, in 1983, performed a study which showed very clearly that children do develop an understanding of other people's minds. The study involved acting out a story, using dolls and toys. The story went like this: *'Sally goes into a room and places a marble in a basket. Then she goes out again. Anne comes in, sees the marble, takes it, and hides it in a box. Then she goes out of the room. Then Sally comes back to look for her marble.'*

The children in Wimmer and Perner's study were asked to predict where Sally would look for her marble. Children aged four and over gave the right answer easily: Sally would look for her marble in the place where she had left it because she did not know that Anne had hidden it. But children aged three said that Sally would look for her marble in the box: they did not appear to realise that Sally's knowledge would be different from their own. Wimmer and Perner performed a large number of other studies like this and found that an awareness of other people's minds seems to develop when a child is about three and a half years old. Before that, children don't seem to be able to predict what people are likely to think, but after that they can. Of course, it goes on developing and becoming more complex all through childhood – and adulthood too.

What these findings tell us is that children are a great deal more socially competent than earlier researchers believed. They are active agents in their own development, controlling what happens to them and practising what they have learned. Moreover, even pre-school children use their knowledge deliberately to influence the people around them. What the child learns is real-world, practical knowledge, about rules, intentions and other people's minds. Other people are the most important thing in the child's life, so a child learns about other people very quickly. However, it is a long time before the child can describe the abstract principles relating to that knowledge, which is why many earlier researchers underestimated the young child's understanding.

Ethical discussion

Many of the earlier theories about child development have resulted in children's social understanding being systematically underestimated. As a result, attempts to teach young children right and wrong, and more complicated issues about values and morals, have sometimes been considered pointless. Nowadays, we know that even very young children are capable of grasping these concepts, at least in how they relate to people that they know well, and that, therefore, they can be taught much earlier.

What are the ethical and social implications of all this?

Vygotsky's theory of child development

As we've seen, children learn best from other people. We may have an inherited tendency to attempt to understand our world and to try to make sense out of the sensory stimuli that we received, but we don't develop our understanding of the world that we live in without interacting with others. As we saw in Chapter 21, children are particularly sensitive to other people: they are very ready to learn from others, and having another person's attention is a more interesting stimulus, both to infants and to children, than just about anything else.

Children learn a great deal about their social and physical worlds by observing other people and picking up information informally. However, once they are learning about more than simple everyday survival, children learn more effectively if they are taught. Every human society develops ways of structuring its children's experiences so that they are able to learn from older people in their communities. In industrial and many other societies, that happens mainly through formal schooling.

The great Russian psychologist, Lev Vygotsky, was particularly interested in the relationship between being taught by adults and the child's cognitive development. Vygotsky developed his theory in the 1920s, although it was only translated into English in the

1960s. However, many modern psychologists are finding the theory extremely useful because it helps to draw together and make sense our of our recent research findings. For example, Vygotsky was aware of Piaget's work but, unlike Piaget, he believed that the social environment was just as important in the child's cognitive development as biological maturation. As we saw in Chapter 23, modern research shows that Piaget seems to have seriously underestimated social influences in this area.

Vygotsky's view of language development

In Chapter 10, we looked at Vygotsky's approach to language but that was only part of a larger theory. The approach to language emphasised that the social functions which language serves are a vital part of language development – language is not purely a cognitive process, but a means for engaging in social action. There is a cognitive basis for language development, but its social basis is just as important.

Vygotsky's theory expresses the importance which he gave to social influences and to the child's tendency to seek out and be motivated by social interaction. Vygotsky regarded the child's culture as a vitally important part of its development because of the interaction between social interaction and cognitive development. The young child experiences its culture by interacting with other people, and also through the language which it learns. It is this experience which motivates the child to learn more about the world.

Much of the child's exposure to culture comes through teaching, and in Vygotsky's model teaching is essentially a social activity. Teaching machines have been in existence for many years but, despite the predictions of behaviourist psychologists such as Skinner, they have never really caught on. The reason for this is that children learn best through human interaction – not just through the teaching which they experience in school, but also the everyday teaching which parents and older siblings give to children. It is this interaction, according to Vygotsky, which directs the child's learning and brings the child on so that it learns far more than it would have learned by itself.

The zone of proximal development

Vygotsky proposed that each child has a wide area of cognitive potential. This is the potential knowledge and expertise that the child could reach if it experienced the right kind of teaching and guidance from other people. He called this the **zone of proximal development** and it is sometimes referred to as the ZPD for short. The ZPD is the cognitive development which the child wouldn't manage on its own but will manage with help from other people.

Studies of isolated children have shown that a child will not achieve much in the way of psychological development without contact with others. With the appropriate guidance though, children learn much more. Even isolated children have shown startling recovery once they began to receive social contact and the right kind of teaching.

Teaching provides the child with a structure, so that it can fit new experiences into a framework that makes sense, and use that as a basis to develop its own understanding. The teacher – whether formal or informal – provides exercises which, like physical exercises, allow the child to rehearse and practise its new knowledge. Sometimes these exercises are informal, like a mother checking that a small child can remember an animal's name. Sometimes they are structured and formal, such as homework exercises set by a school teacher. They all help the child's cognitive development by stretching it that little bit further. This is what the zone of proximal development is all about.

24.2 Types of play and leisure activities

It isn't only small children who play. Adults and teenagers play, too. We play sport, and lots of times that is for the fun of it as much as for the competitive edge. We go swimming or skating, we play games like darts or pool, and we have hobbies, such as fixing the car, DIY or model-making. In fact, most people have something that they play at, which they enjoy doing and may take quite seriously, but which doesn't have any serious purpose.

Piaget distinguished three different types of play, and concluded that they appeared in a particular order as the child developed. The first is mastery play, in which the child aims to develop and perfect physical skills. The second is symbolic play, in which the child uses symbols, problem-solving and imagination in its playing. The third is play with rules, where there are external, agreed rules which determine what can and can't be done. You might like to see whether the play that adults and teenagers do can also be fitted into these categories.

Begin by asking your friends or family members to describe what they do in their leisure time. Make a list. Remember to ask them about hobbies and interests, as well as sports. Ask them, too, what games they enjoy playing – sometimes people are very fond of board games or card games but wouldn't describe them as a hobby or interest. Try to get as full a list as you can.

When you have your list, divide a sheet of paper into three columns and write one of the three types of play at the top of each column. Then take the leisure activities on your list one at a time and decide which column each one should go in.

Sometimes the same activity may fit more than one column. That's OK, write it down twice. Or you may find an activity which doesn't seem to fit any of the columns. If you do, think about it very carefully and decide whether you need another column or not.

When you have finished your chart of types of play and leisure activities, take a look at it and see what you have found.

Do adults or teenagers go in for some types of play more than others?

What conclusions can you draw from your findings?

Is children's play completely different to that of adults or teenagers or are there some similarities?

Scaffolding

Bruner proposed that the guidance and teaching provided by adults and older siblings acts as a kind of **scaffold** which supports the child while it is trying out new knowledge, and provides a safe context for putting new bits of knowledge in place. Because this type of learning is structured and guided by older people, the child is able to go much further than it would have been able to go alone. However, providing that scaffolding isn't always a conscious act on the part of older people. We are often entirely unaware of what, or just how much, small children are learning from us as we talk to them. Judy Dunn's studies, as well as the studies of infant sociability which we looked at in Chapter 21, show just how ready the child is to pick up practical knowledge about social interaction. As the child learns from the teachings of others, that practical knowledge, as well as other bits of information, becomes more sophisticated and also becomes organised into the forms of knowledge that the child's culture considers to be appropriate.

In this chapter, we have looked at some of the ways that the child develops its social understanding and awareness. Play, of various forms, allows the child to practise its knowledge and to develop skills and expertise which it will use in later life. Children's friendships, their awareness of other people's feelings and intentions and their understanding of other people's minds, develop as they grow older but even very young children can sometimes show a remarkable degree of sensitivity to the feelings of people in their own families. Much of this research can be understood in the context of Vygotsky's theory of child development which emphasises the importance of teaching and guidance from others in the child's developing social awareness.

Summary

1. Children play with objects, each other, language, physically and with their imaginations.
2. Piaget identified three stages of play: mastery play, symbolic play and play with rules.
3. Children's concepts of friendship develop and become more sophisticated as they grow older. These changes appear to follow a regular pattern.
4. Dunn showed that even quite young children revealed awareness of other people's intentions and feelings if they were studied in their own family environment.
5. Researchers have shown that the child develops a theory of mind at about three and a half, at which point it begins to be able to predict how other people are likely to think.
6. Vygotsky's theory of child development emphasises the importance of the social environment in allowing the child to develop its full potential.
7. Following Vygotsky's model, Bruner proposed that teaching from adults and others acts as a kind of 'mental scaffolding', providing support for the child to develop its cognitive abilities.

Suggestions for further reading

Berger, K. S. 1983 *The Developing Person Through the Lifespan*. New York: Worth.

Birch, A. & Malim, T. 1988 *Developmental Psychology: from Infancy to Adulthood*. Bristol: Intertext

Bremner, G. 1988 *Infancy*. Oxford: Blackwell

Butterworth, G. 1993 *Principles of Developmental Psychology*. London: Erlbaum

Cohen, D. 1993 *The Development of Play*. 2nd edn. London: Routledge

Coleman, J. C. & Henry, L. 1990 *The Nature of Adolescence*. 2nd edn. London: Routledge

Donaldson, M. 1978 *Children's Minds*. London: Fontana

Dunn, J. 1988 *The Beginnings of Social Understanding*. Oxford: Blackwell

Harris, P. 1989 *Children and Emotion: the Development of Psychological Understanding*. Oxford: Blackwell

Hayes, N. 1998 *Foundations of Psychology* 2nd edn. London: Nelson

Hinde, R. A. & Groebel, J. 1991 *Co-operation and Prosocial Behaviour*. Cambridge: Cambridge University Press

Mussen, P., Conger, J., Kagan, J. & Huston, A. 1990 *Child Development and Personality* 7th edn. London: Harper & Row

? Self Assessment Questions

1 Attachments between human infants and parents seem to appear fully when the infant is about:

a) 10 minutes old.

b) 4 weeks old.

c) 7 months old.

d) 1 year old.

2 Ahrens showed that infants have an inherited tendency to:

a) cry when they see an oval piece of card with two dots on it.

b) turn away from a human face.

c) smile at something that resembles a human face.

d) smile at animals.

3 Schaffer and Emerson performed a study which showed that infants were able to develop attachments to several people. It was:

a) an ethological study.

b) an ecological study.

c) an animalistic study.

d) a humanistic study.

4 An ethologist studies:

a) children.

b) behaviour in the natural environment.

c) the mind.

d) behaviour in the laboratory.

5 Social learning theorists emphasise:

a) punishments and rewards.

b) the transmission of social expectations.

c) the processes of imitation and identification.

d) the first five years of a child's life.

6 Bandura discovered that children observing aggressive models, by comparison with those who had not observed such models, were:

a) more likely to show aggression.

b) just as likely to show aggression.

c) less likely to show aggression.

d) more likely to co-operate with one another.

7 Which one of the following statements is true?

a) children display learning in their behaviour immediately.

b) children take in and learn more than they actually show in their behaviour.

c) children learn aggressive acts quicker than other behaviour.

d) children learn co-operation before learning other types of behaviour.

8 A strong conscience is usually associated with:

a) negative reinforcement.

b) psychological punishment.

c) physical punishment.

d) positive reinforcement.

9 In the kibbutz system children are reared:

a) communally.

b) by grandparents.

c) by parents.

d) by siblings.

10 Britain is a:

a) cross-cultural society.

b) cross-sectional society.

c) multi-cultural society.

d) none of the above.

11 Which three stages of psycho-sexual development are supposed to take place in the first five years of life?

a) the anal stage, the phallic stage, the latency period.

b) the oral stage, the anal stage, the latency period.

c) the oral stage, the anal stage, the phallic stage.

d) the oral stage, the phallic stage, the latency period.

12 The second phase of the oral stage is known as:

a) the oral sadistic phase.

b) the oral masochistic phase.

c) the oral optimism phase.

d) the oral fixation stage.

13 According to Freud, the anal personality is characterised by:

a) excessive aggression.

b) dependency.

c) obsessive neatness and orderliness.

d) anxiety.

14 Oedipus was a character in Greek mythology who:

a) unwittingly killed his father and married his mother.

b) fell in love with his own reflection.

c) killed his mother and married his sister.

d) spent ten years trying to get home after the Trojan wars.

15 Freudian theory lays stress on:

a) the first five years of life.

b) the first ten years of life.

c) conflicts arising throughout a person's lifetime.

d) the first two years of life.

16 The only child studied by Freud was:

a) Little Albert.

b) Little Hans.

c) Naughty Teddy.

d) Oedipus.

17 Neo-Freudians:

a) disagree with Freud.

b) accept Freud's basic approach but modify his ideas in some ways.

c) are followers of Anna Freud.

d) accept Freud's theories.

18 Erikson's model of psycho-social development focuses on:

a) the conflict between the id and superego.

b) the resolution of the Oedipus complex.

c) the relationships that an individual has with others in society.

d) cross-cultural studies of behaviour

19 According to Erikson, psychological problems occur:

a) when an individual is insufficiently prepared to cope with society's changing demands.

b) when a person's id is very strong.

c) only when we reach adolescence.

d) when a person has a strong conscience.

20 Monotropy refers to the idea that an infant develops:

a) an equal attachment to both parents.

b) at a faster rate with multiple caretakers.

c) a special attachment to its main caretaker only.

d) a special attachment to its mother.

21 Jean Piaget was:

a) a behaviourist.

b) a psychoanalyst.

c) a structuralist.

d) a feminist.

22 Epistemology is:

a) the study of children.

b) the study of animals in their natural habitat.

c) the study of knowledge.

d) the study of the brain.

23 Which of the following methods did Piaget frequently use?

a) dream analysis.

b) clinical interviews.

c) laboratory experiments.

d) classical conditioning.

24 Piaget saw intelligence as being:

a) measurable by a person's score on an IQ test.

b) measurable by a person's score on a conservation task.

c) the ability of an animal to adapt successfully to its changing environment.

d) none of the above.

25 An 'operation' in Piaget's theory is:

a) an action that a child only performs in the sensori-motor stage.

b) any set of actions that produce an effect on the environment.

c) a cognitive structure that we use to guide our behaviour.

d) a stage of development.

26 The second stage in Piaget's theory of cognitive development is:

a) the sensori-motor stage.

b) the pre-operational stage.

c) the formal operational stage.

d) the oral stage.

27 A child who has developed the ability to 'conserve' can:

a) solve problems logically.

b) 'decentre'.

c) realise that certain properties of an object do not change simply because its appearance has changed.

d) do calculations.

28 A pre-operational child has not yet acquired:

a) conservation.

b) object permanence.

c) body schema.

d) a conscience.

29 Piaget believed that children learn best through:

a) association.

b) guidance.

c) discovery learning.

d) conditioning.

30 The second of Kohlberg's stages of moral development is:

a) post-conventional morality.

b) conventional morality.

c) concrete-operational morality.

d) pre-moral stage.

31 According to Parten, the third stage in the development of play is:

a) onlooker play.

b) associative play.

c) co-operative play.

d) parallel play.

32 Cohen criticised studies of play on the grounds that:

a) they included children from widely different ages.

b) they didn't include playgroups and nurseries.

c) most play takes place within the family.

d) children prefer to play with children of their own age.

33 Bradley and Bryant's study of rhyming showed that rhymes:

a) can help children in learning to read.

b) only take place in the playground.

c) can teach children to ignore spelling.

d) sometimes date back hundreds of years.

34 According to Piaget, symbolic play develops during the:

a) concrete operational stage.

b) pre-operational stage.

c) formal operational stage.

d) stage of moral realism.

35 Selman believed that in the second stage of friendship, children see friends mainly as:

a) someone to play with.

b) someone you can trust and be close to.

c) people who can offer many different types of satisfactions.

d) someone who provides reward and pleasure.

36 Which of the following is <u>not</u> something that two-year-olds can do:

a) be sympathetic when someone is upset.

b) plan out activities with others.

c) understand social rules.

d) understand what other people are thinking.

37 Studies suggest that children become aware of what others are thinking:

a) at 14-18 months.

b) while they are two years old.

c) while they are three years old.

d) between 18 and 24 months.

38 Having a theory of mind means:

a) understanding that other people think differently from yourself.

b) understanding that other people can think.

c) understanding that people tell lies sometimes.

d) never having to say you're sorry.

39 ZPD stands for:

a) zone of psychological development.

b) zone of personal difference.

c) zone of proximal development.

d) zone of proximity and distance.

40 According to Bruner, scaffolding occurs through:

a) guidance and support by adults.

b) developing ideas which will act as a framework.

c) linking one personal schema with another.

d) rearranging existing ideas.

Section 7 - Methodology

In this final section, we will look at how psychologists obtain the evidence which they use to form the basis of their theories. In most psychology courses, practical work is an important part of the assessment because psychologists believe that it is essential for students of psychology to have the experience of trying to collect their own data, and to find out all of the pitfalls and problems that are involved. We will look at some of those pitfalls and problems here, and at some of the different ways that psychological evidence may be obtained. We will also look at the accepted method for writing up psychological reports as this, too, is an important part of the practical course. In the second chapter, we will look in more detail at psychological research methods and some of the issues that they raise.

As you read through the next two chapters, try thinking back over the psychology that you have learned, and applying the points that you are reading about to it. As well as being useful revision for your exam, this will help you to get used to the way that psychologists think about their work, and to understand why many psychological debates take place.

Chapter 25 - About psychological research

If you've got this far through this book, you will have realised by now that psychology depends a great deal on research – on obtaining practical evidence for its theories or ideas. Psychology develops because psychologists conduct research, and because they draw conclusions about the way that the human mind works from looking at what that research reveals. There's nothing particularly special about that – all scientists work in the same way. However, there are some things about psychology which give it special requirements when it comes to conducting research.

One of these comes from the fact that psychologists are primarily interested in human beings, and human beings are immensely complicated creatures. Also, psychologists are human beings themselves (yes, really!), which means that their own personal experiences can easily influence the way that they think about psychological events. Research into human decision-making has shown that we are far too ready to generalise from our own experiences – in the normal run of things, we tend to assume that our own experience is typical of everyone else's. But that is a very dangerous assumption because human beings live in so many different ways and have so many different kinds of experiences.

Another of psychology's distinctive features is that, as psychologists, we are interested in human behaviour and experience, which means, almost by definition, that most psychological research is carried out on human beings. Some psychologists also conduct research on animals – studying animal behaviour partly because it is interesting in its own right, and partly because it can sometimes tell us something about human beings too. Studying people or animals is very different from studying the properties of matter, or the nature of light or motion, and it means we have to take great care in the way that we carry out our research.

Ethical issues in psychological research

The psychology in this book describes the findings of research psychologists throughout the twentieth century. During that time, ideas about science and scientific research have changed quite a bit. For example, it was only really towards the end of the twentieth century that scientists began to develop an attitude of respect for the people who took part in their experiments. Some of the medical studies which took place in the middle and early parts of the century showed a shocking disregard for the long-term well-being of their 'subjects', and thought nothing of causing considerable distress. Research psychologists – or some of them, at least – took a similar approach, regarding the people who participated in their research simply as 'subjects' who were there to be manipulated at the experimenter's whim.

This situation began to change after Milgram published his studies of obedience in 1963. Another researcher, Baumrind, published a paper the next year, which discussed the potential psychological damage that Milgram's research participants might have experienced. In fact, Milgram was very careful about the follow-ups to the studies and all except one of the research participants reported that they were glad they had taken part. However, Baumrind was concerned with what might have happened, rather than with what actually did happen, and her paper sparked off a debate about the ethical responsibilities of psychologists. This resulted in the development of strict ethical codes for psychologists and psychology students conducting research. A summary of the main points in the ethical code of the British Psychological Society is given in Table 25.1.

1 Investigators must always consider ethical implications and psychological consequences for research participants.

2 Investigators should inform participants of the objectives of the research and gain their informed consent.

3 Withholding information or misleading participants is unacceptable. Intentional deception should be avoided.

4 Participants must be fully debriefed so that they can complete their understanding of the nature of the research.

5 Investigators must emphasise the participant's right to withdraw from the experiment at any time.

6 All data obtained must be treated as confidential unless otherwise agreed in advance.

7 Investigators must protect participants from physical and mental harm during or arising from investigations.

8 Studies based on observation must respect the privacy and psychological well-being of the people studied.

9 Investigators must exercise care in giving advice on psychological problems.

10 Investigators share responsibility for ethical treatment, and should encourage others to rethink their ideas if necessary.

Adapted from: British Psychological Society, 1990

Fig 25.1 Ethical standards for psychological researchers

Ethical principles for researchers

The codes of conduct which psychologists have to follow when they are carrying out psychological research are mainly concerned with making sure that the experimenter shows a proper **respect** for the people participating in the research. For example, modern researchers must take great care to protect the rights of the participants taking part in the study. The participant is entitled to withdraw from the study whenever they want, and they must know that they are free to do so. You may have noticed, too, that we have begun referring to them as 'research participants' rather than as 'subjects'. This, too, is a recognition that they are people who have voluntarily chosen to participate in the research, and not simply experimental material to be manipulated at the experimenter's whim.

Psychologists conducting research have the responsibility to protect research participants from harm caused as a result of the study. This means taking steps to make sure that the person doesn't experience any pain or distress, or any possible long-term damage. If a psychologist wishes to investigate something where there is a potential risk to their research participants, such as investigating a particular drug, they must have a special licence to investigate that area, and they also need to apply to their professional organisation for permission to carry out the study.

This ruling applies to psychological distress as well as to physical harm. One outcome of Milgram's studies, for example, was that most of the participants were deeply disturbed to find themselves capable of carrying out orders to the extent of putting another human life at risk. Some of these people had difficulty in coming to terms with this and experienced psychological distress as a result, although, as we said before, when they were contacted a year later they said that, none the less, they were glad they had taken part in the research.

Another aspect of the ethical considerations which psychologists must consider is that they must make sure, wherever possible, that research participants are not placed in a position where they are being deliberately deceived. If it is necessary for some temporary deception to be used, the researcher needs to apply to the ethics committee of their department or professional organisation for permission. The committee then weighs up whether the deception is acceptable and whether, in their judgement, psychological damage could result from the experimental procedure. They may or may not give the researcher permission to continue. Even when deception is considered acceptable in the short term, the researcher is always obliged to explain the deception to the research participants once their part in the study has been completed. This is known as **debriefing**.

Psychology in Action

Like other scientists, psychologists often have to talk with the media about their research and what it means and this sometimes presents problems. One problem is to do with being able to explain things in simple everyday language. Psychologists don't just invent jargon for the sake of it. They use it because it allows them to express what they want to say very precisely. However, the ordinary public often don't understand the jargon – or even misunderstand it, like the way that 'schizophrenia' is often taken to refer to multiple personality, where, really, it refers to a split between the person and reality.

Another problem is that the media expect experts to give definite conclusions. But science doesn't really work like that. It deals with probability and influences. Psychologists don't like saying that one thing is definitely caused by something else because they always bear in mind that some other factor might be involved – and where it concerns people, it usually will. To the media, however, this sounds as though they are unsure or don't know because, in everyday talk, people are definite about their opinions, and being tentative means that you don't know. As a result, scientists and the media often misunderstand one another.

A third problem is to do with the quest for easy answers. When something happens, the media like psychologists to pinpoint one straightforward cause. But modern psychologists realise that things are interrelated, and that human actions have multiple causes. Even the most basic psychological processes can be studied from several levels: they are influenced by culture, by social groups, by cognitions, by personal values, by habits and environmental experience, by physiology, by biochemistry, by neurones and by genes all at once. So a psychologist often has to respond to a suggestion about the cause of a problem by saying that things aren't that simple. This can sound as if they are avoiding the point, when, really, they are telling the truth. Sometimes, the media over-simplify what psychologists are saying in order to focus on one cause, when what the psychologist actually said identified several influences, not just one.

Ethical principles for students

Most psychology students conduct some kind of psychological research as part of their course and ethical considerations are just as important for those studies as they are for professional psychological research. In Britain, the Association for the Teaching of Psychology has developed a set of guidelines for students undertaking psychological research. The ATP guidelines are focused around a number of questions which any student who is about to design or carry out a study for their coursework should address. The questions you should be asking yourself about your coursework studies are:

- Should I be conducting this kind of study at all?
- What is the most ethical way of carrying out this study?
- Am I sufficiently competent to carry it out?
- Have I informed the participants of all that they need and would expect to know before taking part?
- Have the participants willingly agreed to take part?
- How do I ensure that all research records are confidential and anonymous and will remain so?
- How do I ensure that my research is carried out professionally and in a way that protects the rights of those involved?

These ethical questions are a fundamental part of planning a psychological study, so they need to be addressed at a very early stage in the proceedings. It might seem to be making a lot of fuss about nothing, but any research which deals with human beings needs to be able to show a proper respect for the people who have agreed to help the researcher by taking part in the study.

What all this means, of course, is that anyone who plans to conduct psychological research needs to think very carefully about the methods that they will be using and how they will go about it. There are lots of different ways of conducting psychological research, and some of them pose more ethical problems than others. In the next chapter, we will be looking at the different ways of conducting psychological research in more detail. But whatever kind of research you choose to undertake, there is one more thing you will need to do: you will have to write a report about it!

25.1 Ethical implications of psychological studies

As we have seen, ethical implications are extremely important for psychologists and psychology students. Look at the ethical principles given in Fig 25.1 and make a list of the different topics that they cover – 'informed consent', 'deception', and so on.

Taking each topic on your list in turn, look through the psychology that you have covered and find a study which raises questions about the topic. It might be an example of a study which breaks the ethical guidelines (or would have done if they had existed at the time). Or it might be an example of a study which has explicitly kept to them.

When you have found your study, practise describing it and the way that it raises questions in ethical issues, in just four or five sentences. This will be good practice for your exam!

If you can, try to spread your examples over the whole range of psychology. Take the six main sections of this book as your guide so that you include some cognitive studies, some physiological ones, some individual ones, and so on.

Reporting psychological research

Both psychologists and psychology students need to write reports about research that they have conducted. Research reports have two purposes. First, they tell people what you have found. Second, they tell people what you have done – clearly enough so that they could do the same if they wanted to.

Why do reports?

Published reports in journals are one of the most important ways that psychologists inform each other about their research. These reports describe the findings of the study but they also describe the methods that the psychologist used to conduct the study and what problems they encountered. There are two reasons for this. The first is that, sometimes, the research method which a researcher has used isn't really a very good way of looking at that topic. However, if we don't know how the researcher went about doing the study, we can't tell how appropriate their methods were, so we can't tell how useful or informative the study actually was. So reporting the method used in the study is important for **evaluation**.

The second reason why reports have to state exactly how the psychologist did the research is to do with **replication**. In psychological research, it is always possible that the results only happened because of an experimenter's persuasive personality, or some other factor which was overlooked. Sometimes, replication isn't important – there are some types of psychological research which are concerned with distinctive and unique experiences and we wouldn't expect those to be the same on every occasion. Even in those circumstances, however, it is helpful to know exactly how the information was obtained. A great deal of psychological research looks for general information which would apply to other people in the same circumstances.

When research is being reported, it is very important that the person reporting it explains clearly what the underlying principles of the research are. They need to consider research criteria and to explain what type of research it is because that helps to explain why they have adopted the particular research method that was used. They also need to look at the way that the research participants were chosen because that can be important as well. Reporting psychological research involves addressing a number of these general aspects about the research, as well as simply stating what the researcher actually did.

Research criteria

As we have seen, the aims of a psychological researcher can vary. Some researchers are interested in finding out general psychological mechanisms which will operate in much the same way for most people. Some researchers are interested in studying unique individual experiences which only happen under very special circumstances, but which can still tell us something about what it is to be a human being. Some researchers are interested in studying and interpreting the meanings of social interactions. Each of these types of psychological research addresses different research issues and adopts different research criteria.

Overall, there are three main research issues which psychologists and psychology students need to take into account if they are designing their own psychological studies or if they are evaluating other people's research. These are the questions of reliability, validity and generalisability. **Reliability** is the matter of whether the same research procedure would produce the same outcomes on another occasion and with different people. **Validity** is the question of whether the thing that we are measuring, or looking at in the study, is really what we intended to look at. **Generalisability** is the question of whether our research findings will apply to others as well, or whether they only apply to the people that we were studying.

Types of research

As we've seen, these research criteria don't apply equally to all forms of research. Sometimes, psychologists choose to do what we call **nomothetic** research which is all about trying to find out general laws or principles. This type of research involves studying groups of people rather than single individuals so that we can gain general information. It also involves making sure that the measures that we use in the research are reliable. Most psychological experiments fall into this category and so do questionnaire-based surveys. In these cases, research findings often take the form of numbers – what we call **quantitative data**. These are analysed using statistical tests which give information about probability and how likely it is that these particular results could have happened simply by chance.

On another occasion, a psychologist might choose to undertake **idiographic** research. This type of research isn't concerned with finding out general laws, but with studying a particular individual or just a few individuals – in detail. It is useful because it allows a psychologist to investigate in much more depth than they could do if they were studying large groups, and it tends to have a high level of validity but not much generalisability. Case studies also mean that the psychologist can collect different types of data and get a fuller picture that way. Case studies are the main forms of research which fall into this category. The data which the psychologist gathers from a case study can be analysed in a lot of different ways, but it doesn't usually involve statistical tests and probability. Instead, researchers conducting case studies are more likely to use descriptive statistics, such as graphs or pie-charts, and also **qualitative analysis.**

Some psychologists, particular if they are working in health psychology or social psychology, choose to undertake **hermeneutic** research. This type of research is concerned with the meanings which people find in everyday living. Like idiographic research, it is often high in validity, but it isn't likely to be reliable as human experiences vary so much. Psychologists doing hermeneutic research aren't particularly interested in people's behaviour or objective reality. Instead, their interest is in how people experience their lives, and what they mean when they interact with one another. As a result, this type of research often involves open-ended interviews so that the psychologist can gather **accounts** of human experiences. A psychologist conducting hermeneutic research will also often use qualitative analysis. This is a way of analysing data which usually uses words to describe the findings and to identify the main themes and issues which are raised in the material, instead of using numbers.

Sampling

In any psychological study which involves groups of people, whether it is an observational study, an experiment or a survey, it is important to be careful how the research participants are chosen. We call a group of research participants a **sample** because, obviously, it isn't possible for us to test everybody in the whole world when we want to find out something about human beings. Even if our interest is more limited, such as only being interested in English college students, it still wouldn't be possible to test all of them. So, instead, we take a sample, which is a number of people who we hope will be representative (or typical) of the population that we are interested in.

There are several ways in which we can try to make sure that our sample is truly representative of the population. One of them is **random sampling** – in other words, setting up a situation in which anyone in the population has an equal chance of being selected. For instance, if we were interested in students in a particular technical college – our population we might collect together the names of every student registered with that college, give each one a number and select our sample by throwing dice or picking numbers from a hat. That would mean that any member of the population had an equal chance of being chosen, so it would be a truly random sample.

Another method of obtaining a representative sample is by **quota sampling**. If we know that there are different types of people in the population, and we can say what all of those types are, then we could obtain our sample by choosing a set number from each type. So, for instance, we might select a number of full-time students, day-release students, evening-class students, and so on. This would make sure that our sample was typical of the population.

Unfortunately, in many psychological studies we don't have much chance of obtaining a truly representative sample and, instead, we have to take an opportunity sample which is just whoever we can get. Although this isn't the best possible method of sampling, it is the one which most students have to use for their psychology practical work. This is because obtaining a sample by either quota or random methods can turn out to be very lengthy and often also quite expensive.

Sampling is one of several types of detail about psychological research which someone who is writing up a research report needs to describe. It's important because trying to generalise from an un-representative sample might mean that we come to entirely the wrong conclusions about what our research shows. That means that when other psychologists come to examine our research, they may conclude that it isn't adequate evidence for the phenomenon that we are investigating. We have met a few examples of that type of problem earlier in this book, particularly in Chapter 3.

Ethical discussion

You will probably have noticed by now that all of the ethical discussions in this book have ended with questions. The reason for this is because ethical issues in psychology are complicated; and sometimes it is necessary to do research which might involve breaking one ethical principle, carefully. Psychologists need to balance their judgements and to make choices and decisions about ethical issues. This is why we have ethics committees, rather than single individuals. Training psychologists and psychology students in ethical principles involves training them to think about these things and to apply their judgement.

Are any of the ethical principles for psychologists absolute rules, with no exceptions that you could possibly think of?

Writing a research report

Psychological reports are a vitally important way for psychologists to exchange information. Because of this, there are certain basic conventions which a psychological report must keep to, and which students also have to follow when they are reporting their practical work. Psychology practical reports have several different sections, each of which contains different information. There is a reason for each of the sections, so it is worth looking at them individually. There are also some differences in the ways that various types of research are reported, so we will look at those too. We will begin by looking at experimental research reports because those are the most common type, and because several other types of psychological research follow that pattern. Then we will look at how a very different type of study might be reported: an interview study involving qualitative analysis. These have similar sections but they have some differences too.

Reporting a psychological experiment

1 The abstract

A practical report usually starts off with a section called an 'abstract'. This is a brief summary of the whole study, which allows someone who is just glancing through a whole lot of reports to see if this one is likely to interest them. The abstract summarises the purpose of the study, the method that was used to investigate things, the outcome of those methods, the results of the statistical analysis, and the general conclusions which can be drawn. It doesn't go into much detail because that is in the main report, but it gives enough information for somebody to see rapidly what has been done and what has been found.

2 The introduction

The next section is the 'introduction'. The purpose of this section is to introduce the **hypothesis** which is being investigated. A hypothesis is a prediction which is made from a particular theory, or explanation, and which forms the basis of a study. A theory is based on several previous observations or studies. This means that this section needs to outline the previous research in the area, showing how the theory has been formed. Then it needs to go on to show how this theory can also lead to the specific prediction which is being investigated in this study. In this way it introduces the hypothesis by giving the full theoretical background.

3 The method

The third section of a report is the 'method' section. In this, you need to give enough detail for someone else to replicate exactly what was done. So you need to describe the sample of subjects by describing how it was obtained, how many there were, what they were like, etc. You also need to describe any equipment and materials that were used, and to outline the procedure that the subjects and experimenters followed very clearly. This section should also include descriptions of all the different controls which were built in to the study, and also a brief description of the statistical methods which were used to analyse the results including why those particular methods were chosen.

4 The results

The next section is the 'results' section. This needs to summarise the findings in such a way that people can read what you have found at a glance. Usually, people expect you to put all the calculations and lists of raw data in an appendix at the back of your report, but to include here anything which will show the total results clearly, such as diagrams, bar-charts, scattergrams, and so on. It must also, of course, give the final results of any statistical tests which you have performed on the data.

5 The discussion

Next is the 'discussion' section. This is in many ways the most important of all, because it's in this section that you consider all the problems and implications of the study which has been conducted. Your 'discussion' should include a description of each of the things that was wrong with the study, including suggestions for ways that they could be improved in an ideal version of it. It also needs to look at any additional findings which emerged as you were carrying out the study, and which you think would be interesting to consider at in more detail. Also, some space should be given over to the theoretical conclusions which can be drawn from your findings (although some people prefer this to go into a separate section). The theoretical conclusions are important whether you have found what you expected to or not. If you have supported your hypothesis, then you need to state very clearly what this implies. If you haven't, then you need to look for an alternative theory that could explain your findings.

6 The appendix

At the end of your report you should have an 'appendix'. This should contain any calculations that you have done to get your results. It should also contain samples of questionnaires or any other bits of materials that were used. It must also have a bibliography: a list of the books that you used while you were doing the study or writing up the report.

Reporting a qualitative interview study

1 The abstract, or summary

This section is much the same as for an experimental report. It is a brief summary of the whole study. It describes, briefly, the purpose of the study, the method that was used, the main themes and ideas which have emerged from the interview material and the general conclusions which can be drawn. It doesn't go into much detail because that is in the report, but it gives enough information for somebody to see rapidly what has been done and what has been found.

2 The introduction

The 'introduction' is also very similar to that of an experimental report, except that it is not about introducing a hypothesis – qualitative research doesn't usually involve hypothesis-testing. What this section does is to describe the context of the research, some of the psychological theories or ideas which are relevant to it, and the overall aim of the study. So this section needs to describe other psychological work in the area, and to show the thinking behind the investigation. Sometimes, an introduction of this kind will also give a theoretical background to the use of the particular research method.

3 The method

The third section of a report is the 'method' section. In a qualitative interview study, this will usually focus on the people who are being interviewed, giving a brief description of them in terms of why their experiences are relevant for this study. It will describe how many interviews were conducted, how long they lasted, the time period during which they took place, and any other information which might be useful in making it clear just how the information was obtained.

4 Results and discussion

One of the main ways that a qualitative research report is different from an experimental one is that there usually isn't a separate 'results' section. Instead, the results and the discussion are combined, because it is in this section that the researcher discusses what has come out of the interviews, and what it all means. In most studies of this kind, the researcher will have listened to tapes of the interviews over and over again, and identified a number of themes – topics which people talk about quite a bit. So, in the discussion, the researcher will describe these themes, bringing in quotations from the interview which seem to sum up what people have said, and discussing what the quotations actually mean. Typically, a report of this kind would be likely to deal with five or six main themes, bringing in at least a couple of quotations for each one. If you are reporting this type of research as part of some coursework, it is also a good idea to include some discussion on how the study itself was carried out and whether it could have been done better. It is usual to end the discussion with some overall conclusions about the findings.

5 The appendix

A qualitative research report will need to have an 'appendix' too. Although it won't contain calculations, it may contain extra information which supplements the information in the discussion, such as additional quotations or even whole interview transcripts. Sometimes appendices for these types of reports give factual information which can help to throw light on why the person being interviewed was concerned about a particular topic. Most important of all, this section should include a bibliography: a list of the books that you have used while you were doing the study or writing up the report.

25.2 Research criteria: a revision exercise

In this chapter, we have looked at several different types of research criteria. One set concerns the questions of reliability, validity and generalisability. Another set concerns nomothetic, idiographic and hermeneutic research.

Begin by taking the first set, that of reliability, validity and generalisability. Taking each chapter of this book in turn, look at one study and see what you can say about its validity, its reliability and its generalisability. Try to write at least one sentence on each of these, as they relate to the study you are looking at. Then choose a study from the next chapter and do the same thing.

Carry on doing this until you have described a study from each of the chapters in the book, except this one and Chapter 26. That will give you 24 studies in all and, by the end of it, you will understand much more about those studies and also quite a lot about reliability, validity and generalisability.

You can see from this that each section of a research report has its own purpose: the **abstract** to summarise it; the **introduction** to give the background to the research and to explain how this particular project came about; the **method** to say exactly what was done; the **results** (in an experimental report) to say what was found; and the **discussion** to look at what it all means, and to evaluate the study as a whole. You'll also find that learning to write reports like this helps you to think more clearly about what you have done and to understand it better. Once they have got used to them, many students find the practical part of their psychology course to be the most interesting of all. We hope you will, too.

Summary

1 The fact that psychology uses human beings as its research material means that psychologists have to take particular care when conducting psychological research.

2 Ethical issues for psychologists emphasise respect for research participants and the responsibility of the researcher not to deceive or cause harm them.

3 Students conducting psychological research should answer a series of ethical questions about each project, in order to ensure that it is being conducted in an ethical manner.

4 Psychological research reports are important because they provide other psychologists with the information they need to evaluate the study, and also to replicate it.

5 Reliability, validity and generalisability are all criteria which are important in assessing the value of psychological research. However, all of them do not always apply to every type of psychological study.

6 Nomothetic studies are concerned with finding out general principles and mechanisms; idiographic studies are detailed studies of individuals; hermeneutic studies look at the social meanings in everyday living. Sampling is particularly important in nomothetic studies.

7 Research reports follow a set pattern, with different sections appearing in a particular order. This enables other researchers to get to the relevant information clearly and quickly. Qualitative research reports often follow a slightly different pattern to experimental reports.

Chapter 26 - Psychological research methods

In this chapter, we will be looking at some of the practical aspects of conducting psychological research and, in particular, at the different ways that psychologists gather data. We will begin by looking at some of the issues which arise because psychology is a scientific discipline: the fact that our material under study changes, thinks and has opinions of its own gives us some rather special problems by comparison with some of the other sciences. Then we will go on to look in detail at the major research methods used by psychologists, and at some of the issues which are involved if we want to use them.

Psychology and scientific methods

The study of psychology shows us that we need to be very careful if we are trying to gather systematic knowledge about human beings. This is partly because, as human beings, we have some deep biases in the way that we think. One of these is the tendency to generalise from our own experience – to think that because we personally are used to something, it is therefore something which happens quite often, or is quite likely to happen. In fact, our experience might be quite untypical. Another source of bias is the way that what we see is so strongly influenced by what we expect to see, as we learn from the study of memory and perception. In some cases, as we have seen, our expectations can become self-fulfilling prophecies, so that we make things come true simply because we expect them to be true.

There are several other sources of bias in our thinking – they are part of what makes studying psychology so fascinating, and this book is full of them. Perhaps the most important factor of all is the way that we are totally unaware that any of these biases are happening. We feel, consciously, as though we are being objective and analytical when really, we aren't being anything of the kind. These mechanisms are not always bad – they help us to survive in a complex world and they are part of what makes a human being one of the most adaptable animals that has ever lived on this planet. But, they do raise a number of problems when it comes to understanding human psychology.

Throughout the centuries, people have described human actions and speculated about human psychology. Literature, philosophy, and history are full of speculations. Sometimes these descriptions can give us valuable insights into events. However, the problem is that they can't give us systematic, dependable knowledge about human psychology because our unconscious biases, and the way that they affect how we see the world, are so powerful. What seems like an invariable rule of human behaviour often turns out to be quite culture-specific; not happening at all in other societies or other cultures.

Because of this, psychologists have always been very careful to adopt a scientific approach to their data. Indeed, it is the fact that psychology approaches its subject matter so carefully, and gathers its data in a systematic and scientific form, which makes it special. Psychology as a science first began in the second half of the nineteenth century, and from the very beginning researchers knew that they needed to be very careful about the information they collected and the conclusions that they drew.

Ethical discussion

Several modern psychologists have criticised traditional psychological methodology as being manipulative and unrealistic. Research participants are regarded as passive instruments, there to be tricked, deceived and used. Psychological controls are designed to ensure that subjects are prevented from acting as autonomous human beings during the experiment.

Increasingly, these psychologists are turning to new paradigm research which emphasises open methods of enquiry, like interviewing and collaboration with research participants. They regard traditional methodology as ethically dubious because it is so manipulative.

What do you think?

Scientific approaches

There are two main approaches to scientific research. One of these is known as the **hypothetico-deductive** approach, in which the scientist begins with a theory, and then investigates whether it seems true by generating hypotheses and testing them. This is the type of approach that an analytical chemist might use, experimenting with various substances in order to test out a hypothesis about what is likely to happen in certain circumstances. The other type is the **inductive** approach, in which the scientist draws out general principles or ideas from the data that they have collected. This is the type of approach that a palaeontologist might use to make sense out of the fossils and geological strata in a particular location.

Psychology uses both of these approaches. The early psychologists tended to use inductive methods a great deal, often using **introspection**, or self-analysis, as a research technique. In the first half of this century, psychology went through a dramatic revolution under the influence of behaviourism. During this time, psychologists were not expected to study the mind, or anything except human or animal behaviour, and they were only expected to use the hypothetico-deductive approach. The behaviourists believed that inductive approaches, at least in psychology, were unscientific. (They didn't say anything about their use in biology, astronomy, or any of the other sciences, though.) More recently, as psychology emerged from the behaviourist domination, psychologists went back to studying the mind and other aspects of human experience, and the inductive approach also began to reappear in contexts where it seems to be useful.

The hypothetico-deductive approach

The hypothetico-deductive approach begins with a theory which is an explanation for why something happens. The theory itself will have been based on some previous observations. These can be either informal ones, drawn from experience, or ones which have been carefully developed from the results of other studies, or maybe from inductive research. We then have to put the theory to the test, to see if it will hold true in real life. We do this by carrying out research.

Scientists use a special term for ideas which are put to the test in this way: they call them **hypotheses**. A hypothesis is a prediction about what will happen in a particular situation. It is always based on a theory, and expresses what the experimenter thinks will happen if the theory is true. So the forming of hypotheses is a vital part of this type of scientific method. Once the hypothesis has been formed, the researcher sets up a systematic study in order to test the hypothesis and see if it holds up. The results of that study allow the researcher either to reject the hypothesis or to accept it. If it is accepted, it is used to support the theory. If it is rejected, it suggests that the theory may not be appropriate and a new theory may be needed. (See Fig 26.1.)

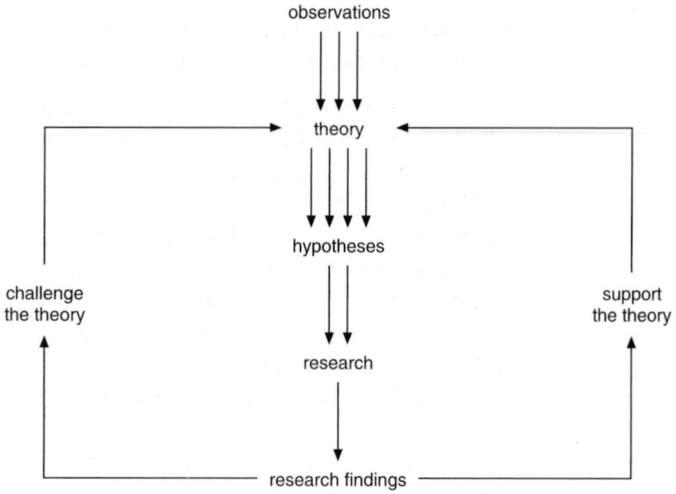

26.1 The research cycle

The inductive approach

The inductive approach doesn't begin with a theory. It begins with the collection of data. But, this data collection has to be from an original source because if the psychologist were to use reports, or other people's descriptions, they would have the types of bias that we looked at just now. Some types of inductive research are reasonably straightforward – for example, Penfield's investigations of areas of the cerebral cortex involved stimulating different areas and asking the patient how they felt. That enabled the researcher to develop theories about the nature of the cerebral cortex. Other psychologists use interview data to learn about people's experiences. Once the data has been collected, the psychologist analyses it, looking for common themes and principles which it might reveal. This type of analysis is a lengthy and demanding process because it goes through several stages: it is sometimes harder to do good-quality, rigorous inductive research than it is to do a hypothetico-deductive study.

Inductive research is generally used when psychologists are exploring a completely new area, and particularly if that area is concerned with human experience. For example, Smith (1997) was interested in how women's experiences of pregnancy changed as the pregnancy wore on. Instead of beginning with a theory, Smith began by collecting data from the women – looking at what they said in interviews, their personal constructs, and a range of other information. By identifying themes which came up often, and looking at how they changed at different stages of the pregnancy, Smith was able to produce a description of some of the ways that the women felt their identities had changed during the process.

Although the behaviourists saw them in opposition, these two approaches to scientific research don't really come into conflict. They are simply used for different purposes. Often, a theory is developed using an inductive approach and then tested out using the hypothetico-deductive approach. For many years, psychology ignored the inductive approach, even though a lot of clinical and developmental researchers (even Piaget) used it. Modern psychologists are much happier to use whichever approach seems to be more appropriate for the problem that they are trying to explore.

Most psychology coursework is based on the hypothetico-deductive method – as we have said, it is difficult to do inductive research really well, so that approach is generally only used by professional researchers who have been trained in the standards of rigour and detail that are needed. Badly done inductive research can be full of bias and distortions, without the researcher realising that this has happened. So it is generally more practical for psychology students to stick to hypothetico-deductive methods where there are clearer ways of making sure that the research is being carried out properly.

Psychology in Action

Police and psychologists are currently developing a special interviewing technique to increase the accuracy of eyewitness accounts. This technique is known as the cognitive interview. Police trainees are used in trials to assess the effectiveness of the technique. They are asked to watch a video of a crime and then take part in an interview as a witness.

The interviewing procedure is based on current knowledge of memory processes and uses the following outline. Witnesses are asked to reconstruct the event, including the feelings they experienced at the time. This is known to be a powerful aid to memory. They are then asked to recall every detail, no matter how trivial, in the hope that one memory will trigger off another. In addition, they are asked to take a different perspective of the event and view it through the eyes of another person present at the scene of the crime. Finally, they are asked to recall events in a different order.

This interviewing technique has proved highly successful so far. It seems that more information can be accurately recalled using this technique than with other interviewing techniques.

Research methods

Psychological research takes many different forms. Which form of research you choose to do depends on what you want to find out and what sort of resources you have available. Hypotheses can be tested in psychology by experiments, by observational studies, by case studies, by interviews, and by surveys, and each of these methods has its own advantages and disadvantages.

Experiments

The most rigorous method of testing a hypothesis that is available to the scientist is the laboratory experiment. This is where a researcher tests out ideas in a controlled environment, and sets up conditions which will cause particular effects to happen. The advantage that the experimental method has is that we can use it to establish whether or not something is causing something else. Because we can set up the conditions and observe the changes which result, we can be reasonably sure (if everything has been properly controlled) that the conditions have actually caused those changes.

Suppose, for example, that we have been working in a nursery for a few weeks and we notice that whenever we give children feedback about their work (i.e. tell them what they are doing is right or wrong), they seem to do much better at similar tasks in future. We can put this observation to the test by setting up an experiment to investigate it.

Hypothesis formation

First of all, we form a specific hypothesis to be tested, for example that: 'Children who receive feedback about their performance in English will do better in a future English test than children who do not receive feedback.' Notice that we have made the hypothesis very specific as, although our general theory may be that feedback helps most forms of learning, in practice we will only be able to test out a very limited range. So the hypothesis we form reflects this. We can then set up an experiment to test that particular hypothesis. The idea behind this experiment, then, would be to find out whether or not feedback is an important part of children's learning.

Independent and dependent variables

As feedback is the important factor that we are investigating in this experiment – the factor which we think will affect the child's ability to learn – we give it a special name: the **independent variable**. The independent variable is something which we set up to see if it is affecting a person's behaviour or performance in some way.

In this case, the behaviour or performance that we are expecting to be affected is how well the child will do in the English test. We call this factor the dependent variable. It is the **dependent variable** that we measure to see if it changes as a result of our independent variable.

One thing which might cause problems could be that we wouldn't know whether the children had actually done better because of the feedback or because of some other factor because we did not have anything to compare their performance with. We might find that the children we were studying improved but this might be just because they were a little older or more used to doing that kind of thing. We need some way of finding out whether the improvement that we have seen is really because of the feedback that the children received.

Control groups

One way to do this is to select two groups of children and to give one group feedback and the other group none. We would then be able to see how the children would normally do in that situation and compare this with how they would do with the feedback. Then, as long as we had taken care of all the other influences, the only difference between the two groups would be the independent variable, so we could look at the two groups of scores and compare them to see if they were any different. The comparison group is known as the **control group**, and the group which experiences the condition in which we are interested (in this case feedback) is called the experimental group.

Confounding variables

We also need to make sure that the two groups of children are of the same age, education and background because, otherwise, we might accidentally choose a group of children who were already much better at English than the other group. Making sure that the two groups are exactly the same is known as **matching** the groups. If we hadn't matched the groups, and the experimental group did better on the second test, we wouldn't be able to say whether it was really due to the feedback or to their previous skills. Problems like these are known as **confounding variables** because they are things which can vary in an experiment and confound (or upset) our experimental findings. There are many different kinds of confounding variables and in a scientific experiment all of them need to be controlled as much as possible.

Designs

Sometimes, the best way of controlling variables such as age, sex and background is not to have two different groups at all. In the 'feedback' study, we could give each child a period of instruction when they were receiving feedback, then test them and compare that with the results from another period of the same length when they were learning but not receiving feedback. If we were comparing each child's score with another score from the same child, then we would know that all the individual differences had been controlled. This kind of design is known as a

related-measures design. The type of design where we have different people undergoing each condition of the independent variable (feedback or no feedback) is called an **independent-measures design.**

Order effects

Although related-measures designs are usually stronger, because they control more variables, they can present their own problems. In our study, one such problem might be that people would get better at the English test simply because they had had more chances to learn it. That would be a practice effect. Alternatively, in some other kinds of studies people might do worse on the second occasion simply because they were tired. This is called a fatigue effect. Both of these problems arise from the order in which things have been presented to the subjects, and so they are known by the general term of **order effects**.

Counter-balancing

We can control order effects by a procedure known as **counter-balancing**. In this we make sure that half of the research participants do one condition of the independent variable first, and the other half do the other condition first. So, in the case of our feedback study, half of the participants would have feedback first and then do the non-feedback condition later, while the other half would do it the other way round, with the non-feedback condition first. When we finally look at our findings, we will be looking at the whole group's scores, so any order effects will have been cancelled out: they will have affected the two conditions of the independent variable equally.

Environmental variables

As we mentioned earlier, one of the major characteristics of an experiment is control. In the case of our example, we need to make sure that nothing else is likely to be affecting the child's performance in the English test. Therefore, we need to take care that all the different **environmental variables** which might affect the results are either ruled out or else arranged so that they affect both conditions equally. For example, if we found that there was a loud drilling going on in the road outside while we were testing the non-feedback condition, this could be an environmental factor which could affect our results. It might mean that children in the feedback condition would do better because they could concentrate better. If we didn't control the background noise, it might give us a misleading result by making the feedback group seem to do even better, so we would have to organise our conditions so that just as many children in the feedback group as in the non-feedback group experienced the drilling. If it affected both conditions of the independent variable equally, then it wouldn't be a confounding variable.

It is important, then, for the researcher to weigh up what he or she considers to be the main advantages and limitations of using the experimental method for their particular investigation. Will a controlled environment and accurate measurement of behaviour yield more data? Will that compensate for the fact that the laboratory may not reflect a real-life situation? What about the problem that people may not behave 'naturally' in an artificial set-up? All of these are questions that researchers need to tackle.

Observational studies

There are many situations where we can't use the experimental method when we are trying to understand human behaviour. While it might be possible to study the effects of being temporarily separated from their mothers on a group of young children by observing their reactions in a laboratory, we couldn't separate mothers and infants for long periods of time simply for the purposes of an experiment. That kind of investigation is neither practical to perform nor ethically sound.

Instead, in a situation like that we would gather data using **observational studies**. Observational studies can't tell us about causes because there may always be some other factor that we don't know about – we can't control observational studies in the same way that we can control experiments. However, they can tell us about correlations – whether two things go together, or whether one thing happens in certain conditions and not in others.

Laboratory-based observations

Sometimes, psychologists choose to observe behaviour under controlled conditions. For example, there have been studies of children's play where the children were brought into a special playroom and allowed to choose what they wanted to play with. The playroom was equipped with observational equipment, including two-way mirrors, which allowed the observers to watch what the children were doing unobtrusively. (Two-way mirrors are special mirrors which look ordinary from one side but act like a window from the other side. Using these mirrors meant that the children could not see the adults watching them and so were able to act more naturally.)

Ethological observations

Some of the psychological research that we looked at in Chapter 21, on the way that attachments form between mothers and their infants, came from observational studies which involved looking at how mothers and infants acted in their own homes. Observations of behaviour in the natural environment are called **ethological** studies. There are many other examples of them in psychology – a great deal of our knowledge about animal behaviour, for example, comes from ethological studies and not laboratory experiments. Ethological studies have what we often refer to as **ecological validity** – that is, they are true to real life –

and so they are very useful ways of finding out how people behave when they are not trying to act 'properly' for a psychological researcher.

Observational coding

Some kinds of observational studies simply involve reporting or noting down what has happened, but most of them are far more structured than that. As a general rule, a scientific observer will have a number of categories so that they can note down instances of each type of behaviour that they see, as often as they see it. This makes it easier for researchers to gather information that is relevant to their hypothesis. The hypothesis will contain predictions about the different types of behaviour that have been expected, so collecting the data in a systematic way allows the reporter to see whether it has been supported or not.

Establishing coding categories in this way also allows the researcher to make sure that important types of behaviour are all included. However, it can also backfire because it may not include a category for an unexpected but important kind of behaviour. For example, early observational studies of aggressive behaviour often failed to include categories for noting down peacemaking or reconciliation behaviour, and so they gave a distorted picture as a result.

Case studies

Sometimes, researchers are interested in conducting detailed studies on just one or two individuals. The study by Gooch on hemispherectomies, which we looked at in Chapter 8, or Gregory's study of a blind man who was given his sight when he was adult, which was described in Chapter 4, involve studying just one or two people in quite a lot of detail. This method is known as the **case study** approach. It has the disadvantage that we may not know quite how typical the people whom we are studying are. On the other hand, it means that we can look at things far more deeply than we could if we were trying to look at large numbers of people.

Choosing a case to study

A case study might be just a single individual, as it was in Gooch's study, but it can also be a single group – perhaps of a particular group of friends or a sports team. Or it might be a single organisation – a small company or a particular local council. Case studies don't have to be about a single individual, but they do have to be one example of the thing which is being studied. For example, Hayes and Lemon (1990) reported a case study of a small computer company. They had been advising the management about social identification processes and how to help employees to feel that they belonged and were part of a whole team. There were about 24 individuals involved in the study, but only one case: the company concerned. If you are planning to conduct a case study, you need to be very clear about what it is that you are taking as your case or example because it is easy to get confused on this matter.

Triangulation

Psychologists who conduct case studies don't often use one single method. Instead, they use several different methods to find out more about the psychological processes and phenomena that are involved. For example, in a case study of someone whose ability to recognise faces might have been affected by brain damage, the psychologist would be likely to gather data from a range of sources: clinical data from medical staff involved; direct experimental measurements; personal accounts of their experience from the person who was being studied, and so on. Using several different methods to understand what is going on is known as **triangulation**, and it helps psychologists to be more confident about their data, particularly when the individual research methods on their own are inconclusive. If all of the different methods seem to lead towards the same kind of conclusion, then we can be reasonably confident that there really is something there.

26.1 Research methods: a revision activity

In this chapter, we have described five different types of psychological study: experiments, observational studies, case studies, interviews and surveys. As you have read through this book, you will have encountered examples of all of these research methods.

Make a chart with five columns. Head each column with a type of psychological study.

Now read through your notes. Each time you come to a study, work out what type it was. Enter it on your chart.

When you have finished one area of psychology (cognitive psychology, physiological psychology, etc.), take a look at your chart. Are some types of psychological research more common in this area than another?

Draw up another chart for a different area of psychology. Does that area favour the same type of research method as the one you have already done? Or does it seem to use different methods? If it does use different methods, can you explain why?

When you have drawn up charts for each area of psychology, you will find that you have a much keener awareness of the kinds of methods that psychologists have used and also a useful overview of which types of research methods are used in different areas of psychology.

Confidentiality

One of the most important things about a case study, of course, is the matter of **confidentiality.** Maintaining the confidentiality of individuals is an important ethical concern for psychologists doing any kind of research. However, because case studies are so detailed, and can involve deeply personal information, it can be easy to guess who a person reported in a case study is. So disguising personal details is absolutely vital for anyone who is reporting a case study. It's also important that the person has agreed to be the participant in a case study in the first place. Using data from someone without their full consent is unethical.

Interviews

A great many modern psychologists use interviews as part of their research methods. Sometimes, a psychologist will conduct a study which is purely based on interviews. For example, Hayes and Lemon's (1990) case study of social identification in a computer firm involved interviewing all of the employees and also the management. More often, though, psychologists use interview data along with other types of measurement. Interviews can also be analysed in different ways, ranging from **qualitative analysis**, which looks at the themes and ideas that people talk about, to **content coding**, where the researcher develops categories into which to fit the content, and simply counts how often each category comes up.

Clinical interviews

Developmental psychologists and health psychologists often use **clinical interviews** as the basis of their research data. The best known of these are Piaget's studies of cognitive development. Piaget interviewed children and asked them to try to solve puzzles or problems. Then he would ask them why they had given that particular answer. Their explanations gave him information which he could use to deduce how their minds were working and what they could and couldn't do. There were some problems with Piaget's approach, as we saw in Chapter 23, but they came from taking the problems out of context, not from the use of clinical interviews.

Structured interviews

Sometimes a researcher has to conduct a large number of interviews about a very precise topic. In those cases, researchers often use **structured interviews**. These are interviews where all of the questions have been written down in an interview schedule which states exactly which question should come when. In fact, it is a bit like a questionnaire, only the answers are said aloud rather than written down. Interviewers have to be carefully trained to do structured interviews, to make sure that they are able to keep to the script that they have been given because, otherwise, they might accidentally suggest an answer to the interviewee when they didn't mean to.

Structured interviews can be very useful when a researcher needs to compare the answers from different people because the structure makes sure that everyone talks about the same topics. However, they have some problems too, in particular that the researchers may not really find out what people think. It's the same problem that questionnaires have: they often don't allow enough scope for people to explain what they, personally, do and, as a result, they can make human behaviour seem to be simpler than it really is.

Rapport interviews

Structured interviews are used, as we have said, for comparing people with one another, but some interview studies go into much more depth and are more concerned with finding out the personal experience of the individual they are dealing with. **Rapport interviews** are interviews which are designed to encourage the person to talk as freely as possible. The idea is to build up a rapport – a friendly feeling – between the interviewer and the person being interviewed, so that the person feels able to say what they really think. An interview schedule is often involved in rapport interviews, but it tends to be a very general one, perhaps listing half a dozen topics. It is usually shown to the interviewee, so that they can be clear about what the interviewer is interested in.

Surveys

Surveys are a way of collecting large amounts of data in a reasonably efficient manner. They involve using questionnaires to collect information. Sometimes, the questionnaires are administered orally, as a kind of structured interview. At other times, the questionnaire is written down and either handed to people or sent to them through the post. Psychologists have sometimes found surveys to provide useful research material. The study by Evans, which we looked at in Chapter 7, consisted of a large-scale survey asking people about their sleep patterns, and this gave us some valuable information. Sometimes, though, the kind of information that a survey can give is a bit too superficial for psychological interests, so they are often combined with a deeper form of investigation, such as an observational study or rapport interviewing.

Questionnaire design

The questionnaires used in surveys have to be carefully designed. That isn't a simple task, although, superficially, it can often seem so. The main problem lies in making sure that you produce a questionnaire which really does allow you to find out about your subject, given the fact that the people you are asking are all individuals with very different prior experiences, attitudes and understanding. A good questionnaire has to allow for these differences, and also has to make itself crystal clear to every member of its target population.

Questionnaires aim to elicit information from people in a manner which will allow the researcher to make generalisations about the topic. However, people designing a questionnaire often feel that they already know the sort of answer they expect people to come up with and that's a large part of the problem. Learning to design a good questionnaire is partly learning to expect people to respond in unpredictable ways – they almost always do!

Stages of questionnaire design

Producing a good questionnaire involves several distinct stages, each of which is important:

1 working out the aims of the questionnaire
2 selecting appropriate question styles
3 designing the questions
4 piloting the questionnaire
5 revising the questionnaire
6 administering the questionnaire
7 analysing the results

Notice that a questionnaire designer doesn't begin to write the actual questions until the third stage. People who are not used to questionnaire design often try to begin by writing out questions before they have a very clear idea of what they want from the questionnaire. Then they end up with a confused tangle that's almost impossible to analyse. If you are planning to do a questionnaire study, first make sure that you know what you want from each question, exactly why you want it, and how you are going to analyse the information that it gives you. Then, once you know all these things, you will be ready to write the questions.

Piloting a questionnaire

A questionnaire also needs to be **piloted** – that is, tested out on a group of people who are typical of the ones who will be asked to answer the final questionnaire. The reason for this is because, no matter how hard a researcher tries, or how experienced they are, there will always be things that people say which they haven't thought about. When you pilot a questionnaire, you ask people to try it out and to tell you about any difficulties they found with the questions. The feedback which those people give you is the basis for revising and improving the questionnaire.

26.2 Experiments and non-experimental methods: a revision exercise

It is worthwhile comparing some studies with others. Take one topic – perhaps the topic covered in one chapter of this book. Take a piece of paper and draw a line down the middle. Label one side 'Experiments' and the other side 'Non-experimental studies'.

When you have done that, look at each of the studies in that topic and allocate each one to the proper column. See if you can find any pairs of studies where psychologists have been using different methods to look at the same thing. (If you are working with a friend, when you have finished doing this you could compare your two lists to see if they agree.)

Now look at each of the experiments in turn. For each one, write down:

1 the independent variable (the thing that caused the results)
2 the dependent variable (what the psychologists measured)
3 any controls that were included in the study
4 any confounding variables that could have affected the results.

Now look at each of the non-experimental studies. For each one, write down:

1 what kind of a study it is (e.g. case study, ethological observation)
2 what kind of research participants were involved (such as, children, college students)
3 what the findings implied
4 what other explanations could be put forward for these findings.

(Again, if you are working with a friend, you could compare your answers and see if you have come to the same conclusions.)

By doing your revision in this way, you will find that you have revised both the particular topic and the psychological methodology together – two lots of work in one!

We can see, then, that research psychologists have quite a range of tools at their fingertips. Each of the research methods we have looked at here has its relevance in psychology, and there are also some other methods that psychologists use which we don't have space to describe here. The important thing is to choose the research method which is appropriate for the research question that is being investigated – as we've seen, they each have their strengths and weaknesses.

Summary

1 Research psychologists have to be very careful how they conduct their research because, as human beings, they can easily be biased in their observations of other human beings.

2 Scientists use both the hypothetico-deductive approach and the inductive approach, depending on their material. Psychologists use both approaches too, although the hypothetico-deductive approach is more usual.

3 Experiments are ways of discovering causality, by using carefully controlling variables to identify which ones will produce particular effects.

4 Observational studies include naturalistic observations and laboratory ones. The data may be gathered freely, or in a structured way, using coding frames.

5 Case studies allow the detailed exploration of a single person, group or organisation. They often involve several different ways of tackling the data. Confidentially is particularly important in case studies.

6 Interview studies are increasingly used by psychologists. They may take the form of clinical interviews, structured interviews or rapport interviews.

7 Surveys are questionnaire-based studies which allow data to be collected from large numbers of people. Questionnaires need to be carefully designed to ensure that they really serve the purpose for which they are intended.

Suggestions for further reading

Banyard, P. & Grayson, A. 1996 *Introducing Psychological Research.* Basingstoke: Macmillan

Coolican, H. 1995 *Introduction to Research Methods and Statistics* in *Psychology.* London: Hodder & Stoughton

Gross, R. D. 1990 *Key Studies in Psychology.* London: Hodder & Stoughton

Hayes, N. 1995 *Psychology in Perspective.* Basingstoke: Macmillan

Hayes, N. ed. 1997 *Doing Qualitative Research in Psychology.* Hove: Psychology Press

Heyes, S. et al. 1986 *Starting Statistics in Psychology and Education: a Student Handbook.* London: Weidenfeld & Nicholson

Lisney, M. 1989 *Psychology: Experiments, Investigations and Practicals.* Oxford: Blackwell

McNiff, J, & Stanley, M. 1994 *GCSE Psychology Coursework: a Practical Guide.* Bournemouth: Hyde Publications

Stratton, P. & Hayes, N. 1993 *A Student's Dictionary of Psychology* 2nd edn. London: Edward Arnold

Taylor, I. & Hayes, N. 1990 *Investigating Psychology.* London: Longman

Wadeley, A. 1991 *Ethics in Psychological Research and Practice.* BPS Open Learning Units, Leicester: British Psychological Society

? Self Assessment Questions

1 **Which of the following is not one of the ethical principles which should be followed by research psychologists?**

a) participants can withdraw from the study at any time if they want to.

b) participants should not be deliberately deceived.

c) researchers should stick to one clear research method.

d) researchers should be careful if they are giving participants advice.

2 **A psychologist must not:**

a) cause research participants pain or distress.

b) carry out surveys.

c) research into the workings of the brain.

d) study animals.

3 **The main purpose of writing psychological reports is to permit:**

a) replication and evaluation by other psychologists.

b) a full account of the project to be made public.

c) students and researchers to find information about the topic.

d) students to learn about them for exams.

4 **A reliable measure produces:**

a) inconsistent results.

b) abnormal results.

c) temporary results.

d) consistent results.

5 **What do we call psychological research which aims to uncover general rules about human behaviour?**

a) idiographic.

b) nomothetic.

c) humanistic.

d) hermeneutic.

6 **Case studies are typical of which of the following types of research:**

a) idiographic.

b) nomothetic.

c) positivistic.

d) hermeneutic.

7 **A random sample implies that:**

a) each research participant has been specially selected.

b) any member of the population has an equal chance of being selected.

c) research participants are allocated to one of two groups without bias.

d) the same number of males and females have been selected.

8 **When a researcher conducts a study using members of the psychology class as participants, which type of sample is it?**

a) a random sample.

b) a quota sample.

c) a representative sample.

d) an opportunity sample.

9 Apart from the title, which is always the first section in a psychological research report?

a) the method.

b) the introduction.

c) the abstract.

d) the discussion.

10 Which of the following describes the purpose of the 'discussion' in a research report?

a) an evaluation of the study.

b) a description of how the study was carried out.

c) a summary of the study and its findings.

d) a description of the outcomes of the study.

11 The hypothetico-deductive research method always begins with

a) a theory.

b) an experiment.

c) a hypothesis.

d) data collection.

12 Research methods where data-collection comes first, and theory later, are known as:

a) hypothetico-deductive.

b) inductive.

c) hermeneutic.

d) idiographic.

13 A hypothesis is:

a) a variable that is manipulated.

b) a large sample of research participants.

c) a prediction about what will happen in a particular situation.

d) a type of experimental design.

14 In an experiment, one variable is manipulated to see if it has any effect on another variable. The manipulated variable is:

a) the independent variable.

b) the dependent variable.

c) the confounding variable.

d) the manipulative variable.

15 A related-measures design is:

a) when research participants are matched in pairs.

b) when each research participant takes part in both conditions of an experiment.

c) when research participants are randomly allocated to one or the other of the experimental conditions.

d) when twins or siblings are used in the study.

16 Observational studies can inform researchers about:

a) causality but not correlation.

b) correlation but not causality.

c) correlation and causality.

d) neither correlation nor causality.

17 Case studies:

a) always involve just one individual.

b) are only carried out on clinical questions.

c) are always longitudinal.

d) can deal with a group or set of people, rather than a single person.

18 Using several research methods and obtaining similar findings is known as:

a) prediction.

b) triangulation.

c) amelioration.

d) recapitulation.

19 An interview schedule is:

a) a list of questions to be asked in the interview.

b) a timetable for conducting interviews.

c) a summary of the main points made in an interview.

d) a sequence of interviewees.

20 The first stage in questionnaire design is:

a) piloting the questionnaire.

b) designing the questions.

c) selecting the sample.

d) working out the aims of the questionnaire.

Classroom work

This section contains a set of short answer questions and a separate set of essay questions which relate to the material covered in each section. The questions will help to assess the level of understanding attained by a group of students or by an individual and therefore help to identify areas of weakness.

They may be used as part of a classroom exercise or as material for students to work through in their own time.

Short answer questions

Nature and nurture

1 Name the two major schools of thought involved in the nature-nurture debate.

2 Which school of thought did J. B. Watson belong to?

3 Write a brief summary of the ideas put forward by Watson and contrast them with those proposed by Gesell.

4 What special role do our genes perform?

5 What do the terms 'dominant genes' and 'recessive genes' refer to?

6 Write briefly on the subject of 'cloning'.

7 What do you understand by the term 'genetic engineering'?

8 What example did Hebb use to describe the link between genetic and environmental influences on development?

9 State two of the characteristics that were thought by Lorenz and Tinbergen to signify inherited behaviour.

10 Briefly summarise the processes involved in imprinting.

11 Describe 'one trial learning'.

12 Explain how classical conditioning works.

13 What do the terms 'generalisation' and 'discrimination' mean?

14 Write about one study that demonstrates classical conditioning in humans.

15 Briefly describe three ways in which an unconditioned stimulus and a conditioned stimulus may be paired.

16 What does the 'law of effect' refer to?

17 Name one way in which operant conditioning differs from classical.

18 Outline the four main types of reinforcement schedule used in operant conditioning.

19 Explain what is meant by the term 'secondary reinforcer'.

20 State one difference between cognitive theories of learning and behaviourist theories of learning.

21 What three important points did Binet make in connection with his intelligence tests?

22 What do you know about eugenics?

23 To what are biologists referring when they talk about a person's 'genotype' and 'phenotype'?

24 Traditionally there have been three main sources of evidence for the idea that intelligence is inherited. What are they?

25 Give two criticisms of twin studies.

26 In a short paragraph, describe the study made by Skodak and Skeels on adopted children.

27 State two problems associated with studies of schizophrenia.

28 Write about one study which illustrates how our expectations can affect the way we interpret behaviour.

29 R. D. Laing put forward an argument relating environmental factors to the onset of schizophrenia. Describe his views.

30 What does Lorenz say about aggression?

31 Jot down three different types of sensory information.

32 Briefly describe one study which illustrates how human beings can adapt to a new visual world.

33 What have we learned from animal studies about the physiological processes involved in perception?

34 What conclusions did Annis and Frost draw from their studies of Cree Indians?

35 What role does activity play in perception? Illustrate your answer using one study.

36 What do you understand by the term 'size constancy'?

37 Outline Gibson and Walk's study of depth perception in infants.

38 What have we learned about human perception from studying blind people who have had their sight restored?

39 Jot down the different areas that have been explored in connection with the nature-nurture debate in perception.

40 Write about two monocular cues to depth.

Physiological psychology

41 The nervous system can be roughly divided into two parts. What are they?

42 Write a brief passage describing how the somatic nervous system works.

43 What names are given to the three main types of neurones?

44 Describe in detail how a message may be passed from one neurone to another.

45 How are we able to detect differences in the loudness or pitch of sounds?

46 What is a reflex arc?

47 Outline the working of one neurotransmitter.

48 Why is the cerebrum thought to be the most important structure in the human brain?

49 Each cerebral hemisphere can be divided into four lobes. Can you name them?

50 Briefly describe two structures of the brain.

51 What did Walter Cannon mean by the 'fight or flight response'?

52 Describe the bodily changes that occur during the fight or flight response.

53 Explain how polygraphs are used to detect 'lies'.

54 Explain how the sympathetic and parasympathetic divisions of the autonomic nervous system work.

55 Describe one study that investigated the effects of arousal of humans or animals.

56 Briefly explain the Yerkes-Dodson Law.

57 Describe the technique of systematic desensitisation as it is used in the treatment of phobias.

58 Compare the James-Lange theory of emotion with the Cannon-Bard theory.

59 Describe one cognitive theory of emotion.

60 What results did Marañon find when he injected his research participants with adrenaline?

61 What is so special about paradoxical sleep?

62 Describe one study that links the pons to REM sleep.

63 What effects does shift work have on our body clock?

64 Describe one study that has investigated jet lag.

65 Summarise the ideas put forward by Dement and Wolpert with regard to dreaming.

66 Outline Freud's theory of dreaming.

67 Describe an alternative view of dreaming to that proposed by Freud.

68 What is sensory deprivation, and how has it been studied?

69 How can EEG measures help us to understand consciousness?

70 Give a brief description of three types of psychoactive drugs.

71 What is known about the hippocampus with reference to memory? Refer in your answer to Milner's study.

72 Give one criticism of the conclusions drawn by Milner.

73 Define the term 'The nature-nurture debate on perception'.

74 Give a detailed account of the way in which we perceive shapes.

75 What do you know about the language areas of the brain?

76 What do you understand by the term 'localisation' of the brain functions?

77 What have we discovered about the workings of the brain through split-brain studies?

78 Describe one split-brain study in detail.

79 Why have Gooch's studies of hemispherectomy proved interesting?

80 Write a brief passage on sensory projection areas.

Cognitive psychology

81 How does Piaget's view of 'thinking' differ from that proposed by Freud?

82 What does the term 'directed thinking' usually refer to?

83 Outline the three stages of creativity that many eminent artists seem to go through.

84 Describe one experiment that appears to demonstrate insight learning.

85 Highlight the basic differences between convergent and divergent thinking.

86 How may the techniques of brainstorming and lateral thinking be used in the business world?

87 Why does Wason argue that human logic is not always the same thing as formal logic?

88 Outline one criticism of computer models of thinking.

89 Write a brief passage explaining how schemata are formed, giving a specific example.

90 Describe one study that investigated the strategies people use to learn new concepts.

91 What do you know about the linguistic relativity hypothesis?

92 Vygotsky believes that language develops from early social interactions. Explain this point of view in a little more detail.

93 Write a passage describing the class differences in language, as suggested by Bernstein.

94 Give a detailed account of the work of Labov.

95 Describe one study that shows the effect of people's expectations on the achievements of children.

96 What stages of language acquisition did Fry identify?

97 Explain what is meant by the term 'telegraphic speech'.

98 Outline Skinner's theory of language acquisition.

99 Name two criticisms of Skinner's work put forward by Noam Chomsky.

100 Write about one attempt to teach animals language.

101 What does the statement 'memory is an active process' mean?

102 What do you know about the method of serial reproduction?

103 What is 'Korsakoff's syndrome'?

104 According to Freud, why do we forget?

105 What does the term 'state dependent learning' refer to?

106 Give one reason why the context in which we learn seems to be an important factor in that learning.

107 Write down the different modes of storing memory that Bruner suggested we have.

108 Give brief details of each of these modes of representation.

109 Giving experimental evidence, explain how using imagery can aid memory.

110 What is the 'level of processing' model of memory?

111 Give a definition of perception.

112 State briefly why perception is thought to be an active process.

113 What does the Necker cube tell us about perception?

114 What principles of perception were identified by the Gestalt psychologists?

115 Write about one of the principles of perception.

116 Name two factors that seem to influence perception.

117 What do you understand by the term 'perceptual set'?

118 What does the term 'selective attention' refer to?

119 Outline one experiment which deals with selective attention.

120 State one way in which Neisser's theory of attention differs from other theories of attention.

The individual

121 Distinguish between the self-image and the self-esteem.

122 Describe Butler and Haigh's study of self-esteem.

123 Outline Mbiti's distinction between Western and African self-concepts.

124 What were the three parts of the self-concept identified by Lewis and Brooks-Gunn?

125 What is the difference between sex identity and gender identity?

126 What is sex typing, and why does it matter?

127 Give two criticisms of the Freudian explanation for gender differences.

128 Describe one study of social learning and gender differences.

129 What is androgeny, and how is it important in understanding gender differences?

130 What effects do the media appear to have on gender differences?

131 Write a paragraph explaining the nomothetic and idiographic approaches to the study of personality.

132 What techniques did Freud use to study personality?

133 Outline the three parts of the personality as described by Freud.

134 Briefly describe one defence mechanism used by the ego and explain how it works, using an example.

135 Describe one trait of theory of personality in detail.

136 Give one criticism of Cattell's theory of personality.

137 The theories of Rogers and Kelly are often considered to be 'humanistic'. What do you understand by this term?

138 What are 'personal constructs'?

139 Write a brief description of Rogers's Q-Sort technique.

140 What is meant by the 'ideal self'?

141 What is the difference between a nomothetic and an idiographic test? Give an example of each one.

142 What is a normal distribution curve?

143 What is meant by the term 'standard deviation', and why is the concept useful?

144 What are the four types of validity used to evaluate psychometric tests?

145 How are psychometric tests standardised?

146 How is IQ calculated?

147 What is 'g' in intelligence testing?

148 Briefly describe Sternberg's model of intelligence.

149 What is the role of an occupational psychologist?

150 Describe two types of tests used by psychologists in occupational testing.

151 What is meant by the term 'motivation'?

152 Describe Grossman's 1960 study of eating behaviour in rats.

153 Explain what Morgan meant when he referred to 'primary' and 'secondary' drives.

154 What is homeostasis?

155 What is meant by the term 'cognitive dissonance'?

156 Why does 'locus of control' seem to be an important element in mental health?

157 Describe a study that demonstrates the importance of self-efficacy.

158 How does cognitive therapy work?

159 What are affiliative needs?

160 Describe Stratton and Swaffer's study of attribution.

Social psychology

161 How important are first impressions? Explain, using the terms 'primacy effect' and 'recency effect'.

162 Describe one study which illustrates sex stereotyping.

163 What did Katz and Braly find in their study of ethnic stereotyping?

164 Briefly explain how attribution theory is important for our understanding of other people.

165 Explain what is meant by the 'fundamental attribution error'.

166 Outline one study which suggests that similarity of attitudes is an important factor in long-term relationships.

167 In what ways do attractive people seem to benefit in Western society? Refer to experimental evidence.

168 What are the three components of an attitude?

169 Explain how frustration can be a basis for prejudice.

170 Outline two factors which may be effective in reducing prejudice.

171 What is meant by the term 'communication'?

172 Describe three ways that verbal communication is important to us.

173 Write down as many non-verbal cues as you can think of.

174 According to Argyle, what four functions does eye contact serve?

175 Describe two studies that show how non-verbal communication may vary according to culture.

176 Describe a study which investigates the importance of personal space.

177 Name two factors which may affect how closely we approach others.

178 What is 'paralanguage'?

179 Describe in detail one of the methods used in studying non-verbal communication.

180 What are the five groups of non-verbal signals which were used by Ekman and Friesen?

181 What is conformity?

182 Describe Asch's study of conformity. What did Asch find?

183 Briefly describe two of the variables which Milgram said were responsible for obedient behaviour.

184 Outline two features of the requests made to the nurses in Hofling's study which contravened hospital regulations.

185 How have psychologists studied rebellion?

186 Describe a study of self-perception and compliance.

187 What is meant by the term 'bystander intervention'?

188 Give two reasons why people may fail to intervene in an emergency.

189 What is deindividuation?

190 What did Reicher say about the nature of crowds and crowd behaviour?

191 Describe two of the five groupings of social roles identified by Linton.

192 Describe three social roles that you have adopted today. What other people were involved in the playing of these roles?

193 Explain what is meant by the term 'self-fulfilling prophecy'.

194 What is meant by the term 'groupthink'?

195 Outline three symptoms of groupthink.

196 How did European social psychology come about?

197 Describe the two psychological mechanisms underlying social identification

198 How does salience affect social identification?

199 What are social representations and how do people acquire them?

200 Briefly define anchoring and identification in social representation theory.

Child development

201 State one way in which social learning theory differs from traditional learning theory.

202 Describe one study that supports the idea that infants have an inherited tendency towards sociability.

203 In the light of work on mother-infant interaction, what advice would you give to the mother of a blind baby?

204 What is the 'greeting response'?

205 Explain the term 'vicarious learning'.

206 According to social learning theory, children are more likely to copy some models than others. Which models are most likely to be copied?

207 Describe one experiment that demonstrates how children may learn aggression through watching the actions of others.

208 Why does Hill argue that psychological punishment is more effective than physical punishment?

209 Give two differences that Bronfenbrenner found between Russian and American child-rearing patterns.

210 Outline two problems that Western teachers or social workers might encounter in dealing with members of a multi-cultural community.

211 Name two methods that Freud used in order to investigate his patients' unconscious memories.

212 Outline Freud's psychosexual stages of development.

213 Describe the parts played by the Oedipus and penis envy in the development of a child's sex-role.

214 Who was Little Hans?

215 State two criticisms of Freud's theory.

216 Describe two of the five defence mechanisms identified by Anna Freud.

217 Name one neo-Freudian and outline his/her approach

218 State one way in which Erikson's theory differs from that of Freud.

219 Outline the stages of psychosocial development proposed by Erikson.

220 Describe Bowlby's view of the infant-mother relationship.

221 Write a brief explanation of the background to Piaget's theory.

222 Outline Piaget's first stage of cognitive development.

223 What role do schemata play in our cognitive development?

224 Briefly describe the processes of assimilation and accommodation.

225 Who was 'naughty teddy'?

226 What did Piaget mean by the term 'egocentricity'?

227 Give two criticisms of Piaget's theory.

228 Why is the study of social cognition seen to be more fruitful by many modern researchers than Piaget's structuralist approach?

229 How does Piaget's theory of moral development relate to his overall theory of cognitive development?

230 Briefly outline Kohlberg's stages of moral development.

231 Describe Hutt's 'supertoy' study of children's play.

232 Discuss Cohen's criticisms of conventional studies of social play.

233 What have researchers discovered about pretend play?

234 Briefly describe Piaget's three stages of play.

235 What functions do children's friendships serve?

236 How did Dunn go about studying family interaction?

237 Describe the four areas of social knowledge in pre-schoolers studied by Dunn.

238 Describe one study of the child's theory of mind.

239 What did Vygotsky mean by the zone of proximal development?

240 Briefly outline Bruner's concept of scaffolding.

241 What factors make psychological research different from research in other sciences, such as physics?

242 Why are ethical issues so important in psychology?

243 List the ten ethical principles for researchers outlined by the British Psychological Society.

244 Outline and discuss two functions of psychological research reports.

245 What do you understand by the term 'reliability'?

246 What do you understand by the term 'validity'?

247 What are nomothetic, idiographic and hermeneutic research?

248 Describe two methods of sampling used in psychological research.

249 In a research report, what is the purpose of the abstract?

250 Outline the similarities and differences between a qualitative research report and an experimental research report.

251 Outline the two main approaches to scientific research.

252 What is the purpose of experimental control?

253 What do the terms 'independent' and 'dependent' variable mean? Explain their role in an experiment.

254 When would you be likely to use counterbalancing and why?

255 Outline one study with which you are familiar which makes use of the observational method.

256 What are the main differences between ethological and laboratory observations?

257 Describe one psychological case study that you have learned about on your course.

258 What is triangulation, and how is it helpful to researchers?

259 Distinguish between a structured interview and a rapport interview. Give one advantage and one disadvantage of each.

260 List and describe the seven stages of questionnaire design.

Essay questions

Section 1 - Nature and nurture

1 Compare and contrast the two schools of thought involved in the nature-nurture debate in development.

2 What part do genetic inheritance and environmental influences play in our development?

3 Using experimental evidence, discuss the processes involved in imprinting.

4 Compare and contrast the processes and applications of classical and operant conditioning.

5 What role does reinforcement play in operant conditioning?

6 How do cognitive theories of learning differ from the more traditional behaviourist approaches?

7 What evidence is there to suggest that aggression is inherited?

8 What is a 'retreat into madness', and what connection does it have with our understanding of mental illness?

9 'Any consideration of nature and nurture is inherently political'. Discuss this statement with reference to any of the following: intelligence, schizophrenia, aggression.

10 How have psychologists investigated the nature-nurture debate on perception?

11 How much evidence is there for the idea that perceptual abilities are learned?

12 What can visual illusions tell us about perceptual processes?

Section 2 - Physiological psychology

13 What types of neurones make up the nervous system, and what are their functions?

14 What is meant by the term 'synaptic transmission'? Outline the roles that neurotransmitters can play in human psychology.

15 Using research evidence, describe and discuss the functioning of three major structures in the brain.

16 What physiological changes occur during the 'fight or flight' response? How do these changes connect with our experience of emotion?

17 Outline and discuss the main techniques used in the treatment of phobias.

18 What is stress, and what effects does it have?

19 What is sleeping, and why do we do it?

20 What is a 'circadian rhythm'? What evidence is there that circadian rhythms affect human psychology?

21 Outline and critically evaluate the main theories of dreaming.

22 How far can the functions of the cerebral cortex be considered to be localised?

23 What do psychologists know about the way that human beings process language in the brain.

24 Is there evidence that the left and right hemispheres of the brain control different abilities? How extreme are the differences between the two hemispheres?

Section 3 - Cognitive psychology

25 What factors can aid or inhibit problem-solving and reasoning? Illustrate your answer with evidence from psychological research.

26 Outline and discuss the major models of thinking and creativity.

27 Describe and evaluate some studies of concept formation in human thinking.

28 What is the relationship between language and thinking?

29 How does a child learn to talk? What factors can influence language acquisition?

30 Compare and contrast two different theories of language acquisition.

31 How far does psychological evidence support the idea that memory is an active process?

32 What explanations have psychologists put forward for forgetting? How far can these explanations help students who are learning material for examinations?

33 What is the two-process theory of memory, and how has it been challenged?

34 What is perceptual set, and how has it been studied by psychologists?

35 What factors can influence how we perceive things?

36 What is selective attention? What have we learned about selective attention from experimental studies?

Section 4 - The individual

37 What are the main factors that contribute to the development of the self-concept?

38 Outline and critically evaluate the main theories of gender-role development.

39 Is there evidence that the media can influence gender development in children? How can this influence be minimised?

40 Outline and discuss critically Freud's theory of adult personality.

41 Compare and contrast one idiographic and one nomothetic theory of personality.

42 Outline and discuss Rogers's theory of personality.

43 What standards are necessary to ensure that a psychometric test is adequate, and how are these standards applied when developing a psychometric test?

44 Critically evaluate some of the main approaches to intelligence testing.

45 How are psychometric tests used by occupational psychologists?

46 What is the drive theory of motivation? How far does it explain motivation in human beings?

47 Outline and discuss three sources of personal motivation, giving a real-life example of each one.

48 What is self-efficacy, and how can it help us to understand human actions?

Section 5 - Social psychology

49 What is stereotyping, and why does it matter?

50 What psychological evidence is there for why we like some people more than others?

51 What do you understand by the term prejudice? Giving psychological evidence, state how you could reduce prejudice in society.

52 What methods have been used to investigate non-verbal communication? Support your answer by describing specific studies.

53 Compare and contrast verbal and non-verbal communication in social interaction.

54 Giving experimental evidence, discuss the use of three of the following non-verbal cues: paralanguage, eye contact, facial expression, dress, proxemics.

55 How may the presence of other people affect our behaviour?

56 Critically evaluate one study of obedience and one study of either conformity or rebellion. What can we learn from these studies?

57 Outline and discuss critically the main theories of crowd behaviour.

58 What are the main processes involved in groupthink? How may groupthink be minimised?

59 What is European social psychology? How does it differ from traditional social psychology?

60 What have psychologists discovered about social representations?

Section 6 - Developmental psychology

61 'The human infant is an inherently sociable being.' Discuss this statement.

62 Discuss the importance of non-verbal communication between parent and infant.

63 How do studies of cross-cultural child-rearing patterns contribute to our knowledge of developmental psychology. Illustrate your answer by drawing on at least three studies.

64 Outline and discuss critically the Freudian approach to child development.

65 Describe and evaluate any one neo-Freudian theory of child development.

66 What problems are presented by psychoanalytic explanations of child development?

67 Outline and discuss critically Piaget's theory of cognitive development.

68 Why do children fail on pre-operational tasks? What alternatives to the Piagetian explanation can you offer?

69 Compare and contrast the theories of moral development put forward by Piaget and Kohlberg.

70 What have psychologists discovered about the different types of children's play?

71 Children appear to be more psychologically sophisticated than earlier researchers believed. Discuss some of the research evidence for this.

72 Outline Vygotsky's theory of child development, and discuss its implications for teachers and parents.

Section 7 - Methodology

73 What are ethical guidelines, and why are they so important to psychologists?

74 What are the three major types of psychological research? Give examples of each of them from the psychology that you have studied.

75 What features do psychological research reports contain, and why?

76 Critically evaluate the use of the experimental method in psychological research.

77 Discuss, giving specific examples, the use of non-experimental methods in psychology.

78 If you were asked to do some research into a particular aspect of child development, what factors would you take into consideration when choosing your methods of investigation?

Glossary

ability tests	Psychometric tests which are designed to measure what someone is already able to do, as opposed to what they might be able to learn in the future.
abstract	The part of a research report which summarises the whole project, including the outcomes.
accounts	Verbal descriptions of experience, usually given in interviews but sometimes as written reports.
affiliation motives	Motives which direct behaviour towards making sure that the affiliative needs (for family, friendship or 'belonging') can be satisfied.
affiliative needs	Needs which relate to having continuing contact with other human beings, which are concerned with 'belonging' to a set of people in some way, such as through families, social groups or friendships.
alpha rhythms	Patterns of electrical activity of the brain which appear in an electro-encephalogram (EEG) when the subject is in a relaxed state, and/or daydreaming.
alternate-forms method	A system for judging how reliable a psychometric test is, which involves comparing the results produced by two different versions of the same test, if they are given to the same subjects.
androgenital syndrome	A biological condition resulting from female children receiving male hormones while in the womb. As infants they sometimes display male genitalia, usually surgically removed, but there is only very slight evidence for behavioural change as a result.
androgynous	Having the characteristics of both male and female. Bem showed that androgynous personalities were psychologically healthier than conventional 'masculine' or 'feminine' personalities.
approach-avoidance conflict	When a goal is attractive but also has some drawbacks, it often seems more attractive while it is a long way in the future, but less so the nearer it comes. A person may become torn between wanting to achieve the goal and wishing to avoid it.
attenuation	The weakening of a signal, usually one which is being processed in terms of selective attention.
attribution theory	The explanation of social perception by examining how people allocate intention or meaning to the behaviour of others.
autokinetic effect	An optical illusion in which a point of light in a totally dark room appears to move about.
bystander apathy	The refusal of strangers to help someone who is clearly in need of it.

bystander intervention When a stranger helps someone who is clearly in need of it.

cardio-vascular system The heart, lungs and blood circulation systems of the body.

categorical self The part of the self-concept containing factual information, such as height, age or gender.

client-centred therapy Therapy based on Carl Rogers's theory of personality, which aims to provide clients with a secure and positive emotional base so that they can explore their own ideas and find their own solutions to problems.

cloning The process of creating genetically identical animals artificially, by causing the cells of parent animals to reproduce and develop into whole animals based on genetic information in the cell nucleus.

coaction Acting alongside of, or with, another person, but without active co-operation or interaction.

cognitive development The process of developing understanding and memory and acquiring knowledge, which occurs throughout childhood.

cognitive-developmental theory The idea that gender identity arises from a mixture of biologically based stages of development and the person's developing awareness of gender role and its application.

cognitive therapy A form of psychotherapy which is based on changing people's beliefs, attitudes and attributions about their worlds, and so helping them to act more positively and to change things for the better.

complex play Play which presents the child with challenges – opportunities to achieve results through overcoming difficulties or problems.

compliance Acting in the same way as other people while actually having different personal beliefs or inclinations.

componential intelligence The part of Sternberg's triarchic model of intelligence which is concerned with, and consists of, mental processes and abilities.

concrete operational stage The third of Piaget's four stages of cognitive development, characterised by a need to relate problems to real circumstances or events.

concurrent validity A method of assessing whether a psychometric test is valid (i.e. really measures what it is supposed to) by comparing it with some other measure which has been taken at the same time (i.e. which is occurring concurrently).

conditioned response A learned response which is produced to a conditioned stimulus.

conformity Acting in the same way that other people are acting.

construct validity — A method for assessing whether a psychometric test is valid (i.e. really measures what it is supposed to) by seeing how it matches up with theoretical ideas about what it is supposed to be measuring.

contextual intelligence — The part of Sternberg's triarchic model of intelligence which emphasises that intelligent acts always take place in a context – something which is an intelligent thing to do in one context may be stupid in another. Contexts range from being very specific, like an immediate circumstance or situation, to very broad, like an entire culture or society.

controllable attributions — Judgements about why things happened, which contain the idea that they could potentially be directed or controlled – generally by the person who is making the attribution.

correlation — When two variables change, such that when one is large, the other tends to be either large or small; or if one is small the other also tends to be either small or large.

correlation coefficient — A number between -1 and +1 which expresses how strong a correlation is. If this number is close to 0, there is no real connection between the two; if it is close to +1 there is a positive correlation – in other words, if one variable is large the other will also tend to be large; and if it is close to -1, there is a negative correlation – in other words, if one variable is large, the other will tend to be small.

criterion validity — A method for assessing whether a psychometric test is valid (i.e. really measures what it is supposed to) by comparing it with some other measure. If the other measure is assessed at roughly the same time as the original one, then the type of criterion validity being applied is concurrent validity; if it is taken much later, it is predictive validity.

cultural context — The total cultural environment within which a person develops. This includes unspoken assumptions, social values and beliefs, as well as cultural artefacts and lifestyles.

debriefing — Explaining the purpose of an activity and discussing what has happened in it, after the event.

deindividuation — The process of losing one's personal identity and simply becoming part of a crowd.

delta rhythm — Patterns of electrical activity of the brain which appear in an electro-encephalogram (EEG) when the person is concentrating very hard.

dependent variable — The thing which is measured in an experiment, and which changes depending on the independent variable.

depth cue — Something which gives an indication of how far away an object is.

diffusion of responsibility The idea that people feel less obliged to take action when there are other people present who could do so and are therefore just as responsible for what happens.

digit memory span The number of items that a person can repeat accurately from a list of digits (letters or numbers) which is read out to them only once. Most people can remember about seven, but it is normal for digit memory span to be anywhere between five and nine. Digit memory span is thought to correlate with intelligence. Since digit span tests often form a component of intelligence tests, this may not be very surprising.

discrimination The skill of distinguishing one stimulus from another, usually learned through selective conditioning.

discussion The part of a research report in which the researcher explores the possible meanings and implications of the results obtained from the study.

disembedded thought Thinking which is not applied in any meaningful context, but is just treated as a separate, distinct task with no relevance to the real world.

drive theories Theories of human motivation which explain why we do things, using the idea that our behaviour is directed towards reducing some inner need. The need then sets up an internal tension, and the desire to reduce this tension forms a pressure to act (the drive) which is only reduced when the need becomes satisfied.

ecological validity A way of assessing how valid a measure or test is (i.e. whether it really measures what it is supposed to measure), which is concerned with whether the measure or test is really like its counterpart in the real, everyday world. In other words, whether it is truly realistic or not.

egocentricity The assumption that the entire world centres about the self, and that nothing else exists except for that which impinges directly on the person.

empathy Sharing in someone else's feelings.

epistemology The study of how knowledge works: what counts as valid argument or evidence in different fields of expertise or knowledge.

ethical principles Principles which set out what is considered to be honourable, honest and socially acceptable practice.

ethnological observations Observations of animals or human beings, which are carried out in their own natural circumstances.

eugenics The political idea that the human race could be improved by eliminating 'undesirables' from the breeding stock so that they cannot pass on their supposedly inferior genes. Some eugenicists advocate compulsory sterilisation, while others seem to prefer mass murder or genocide.

evaluation Making judgements about the value, or worth, of something.

evoked potential A characteristic pattern of electrical activity in the brain which shows up on EEGs (electro-encephalograms), and is produced in response to a particular stimulus.

existential self The part of our self-concept which is unique and makes us different from other people.

experiential intelligence The part of Sternberg's triarchic theory of intelligence which is concerned with what the individual has learned from their own personal experience.

face validity Whether a test or measure looks on the surface as though it probably measures what it is supposed to.

formal operational stage The fourth of Piaget's four stages of cognitive development, emphasising abstract thinking and logical reasoning.

g The abbreviation for 'general intelligence': a kind of intelligence which is supposed to underpin all different types of mental operations, as opposed to more specific types of talents or aptitudes.

gender-schema theory The idea that gender identification occurs as a result of the child acquiring schema about appropriate behaviour and characteristics for people belonging to a particular gender, and then trying to live in accordance with their schema.

general mental ability tests Another term for intelligence tests, which is preferred in occupational testing circles.

generalisability How far the findings from a piece of research can be applied to other people or to human beings in general.

group norm The unspoken agreement about what is acceptable behaviour for members of a particular social group.

hallucinogens Drugs which can cause people to have hallucinations – to see or experience things which are not actually there.

hermeneutic research Research which is all about exploring social meanings and values.

ideal-self The perfect self that we would each like to be.

identification Feeling that you are almost the same as, or very like, another person, and that this gives you something special in common with them.

ideology A set of overriding political or philosophical beliefs which govern the assumptions of a particular culture or society.

idiographic research — Research which is all about identifying the special or unique characteristics of individuals.

idiots-savants — People who appear mentally retarded with respect to general intellectual abilities, yet show outstanding mental ability in one narrow area – like being able to add up extremely rapidly and accurately, or calculate the days of the week of any specific date in the past few thousand years.

independent variable — The conditions which an experimenter sets up to cause an effect in an experiment. These vary systematically, so that the experimenter can draw conclusions about changes.

instinct theories — The name given to the old-fashioned idea that the reasons why people do things or act in certain ways is because they are driven by some kind of inborn pressure, or 'instinct'.

intergroup rivalry — Competition between different social groups, which can often lead to powerful hostility.

internalisation — Conforming with others because of a personal belief in the rightness of the conforming behaviour.

introduction — The part of a research report which describes why the study was carried out, and what the researchers aimed to discover.

job aptitude tests — Psychometric tests which assess whether someone is likely to be good at a particular job – in other words, whether they have the right type of mental skills or talents so that they should be able to learn the job quickly and easily.

locus of control — Where control of what happens is perceived to come from. An internal locus of control means that the person sees it as coming from within themselves – so they are largely in control of what happens to them, or at least in a position to influence it. An external locus of control means that it is perceived as coming from sources outside of the person, and so is not something which the individual can influence.

looking-glass self — The theory that most of our ideas about ourselves are drawn from how other people react to us, and that, therefore, the self-concept is a kind of 'mirror', reflecting other people's views.

mastery play — Play which is all about learning skills or physical co-ordination.

mean — A measure of central tendency calculated by adding up all the scores in a set and dividing them by the number of scores in that set. Also known as the arithmetic average.

median — A measure of central tendency, which is calculated by ranking all the scores in a set in order, from lowest to highest, and choosing the middlemost one.

method	The procedures which are followed when carrying out a research project, or the section of a research report which describes those procedures.
mob psychology	An early psychological theory of crowds as reverting to a 'primitive' state and becoming unpredictable, impulsive and dangerous.
mode	A measure of central tendency which is calculated by choosing the score in a set which occurs most often.
monotropy	A theory put forward by Bowlby, that infants form only one very strong attachment to their mothers, different from their attachments to other people.
nomothetic research	Research which compares large groups of people in order to uncover general rules and principles of human behaviour.
normal distribution curve	A pattern of scores, distributed on a graph, which appears on that graph as a bell-shaped curve. Also known as the Gaussian distribution, this has mathematical properties which mean that the probability, or likelihood, of a given score can be calculated simply by knowing the value of the mean and the standard deviation.
occupational psychologists	Psychologists who deal with people at work. Some occupational psychologists are concerned with recruitment or selection: fitting people to jobs. Others are concerned with human interactions at work: how organisations and departments are managed.
one-trial learning	A rapid form of learning, which takes only one event to be learned, such as avoiding a food which has made you sick.
opportunity sample	A sample in which the researcher cannot use systematic sampling methods, but has simply used the research participants that are readily available.
paradigm	The framework of assumptions and ideas which a group of scientists or professionals uses as the basis of their judgements and approach.
play with rules	Play which involves structured sequences and exchanges according to pre-determined laws or principles, Most adult games fall into this category.
population norms	Tables of typical results for psychometric tests, which are used to judge whether one single individual's score is typical for their population group or not.
predictive validity	A method of assessing whether a psychometric test is valid (i.e. really measures what it is supposed to) by seeing how well it correlates with some other measure, which is assessed later, after the test has been taken.
pre-operational stage	The second of Piaget's four stages of cognitive development, characterised by an ability to focus on

only one attribute of an object at a time, and an inability to 'decentre'.

pretend play Play which involves the use of the child's imagination.

private self The part of the self-concept which is purely personal and unknown to other people.

psychometric tests Methods of measuring mental characteristics. Psychological tests have been developed to measure a wide range of things, including creativity, job attitudes and skills, brain damage and, of course, 'intelligence'.

quota sampling A form of sampling in which the sample consists of a certain number of cases from different categories, in order that the sample reflects the parent population as much as possible.

random sampling A form of sampling in which any member of the population being studied is equally likely to be selected for the research.

reciprocity A relationship or interaction based on fair exchange or exchanges between the people or animals participating.

reliability Whether a test or experimental measure will give the same results under the same conditions on a different occasion.

replication Copying a piece of research in order to ensure that the results are a reliable finding.

research participants People who agree to take part in a research project.

results The outcome of a research project, or the section of a research report which gives a factual description of that outcome.

role behaviour Acts and activities which are associated with, and considered to be typical of, playing a particular social role.

sample The group of subjects or participants used in a study: the selection of people, animals, plants or objects drawn from a population for the purposes of studying that population.

scaffolding Supporting the child's learning by providing structure and guidance, in the form of planned teaching and providing sequences of appropriate learning experiences.

scapegoating The process of putting the blame for difficult economic circumstances or other sources of frustration on to some disliked but 'inferior' social group, and so increasing prejudice and intergroup hostility.

schema A way of representing knowledge in the mind, whereby the representation of a particular topic includes information, memories, skills and plans for future action.

self-concept The general idea or picture that we have of ourselves, including evaluations and opinions as well as factual information.

self-efficacy beliefs The belief that one is capable of doing something effectively. Self-efficacy beliefs are closely connected with self-esteem, in that having a sense of being capable and potentially in control tends to increase confidence. But the concept is often thought to be more useful than the generalised concept of self-esteem as people may often be confident about some abilities, or in some areas of their lives, but not in others.

self-esteem The amount that we value ourselves and our distinctive abilities or attributes.

self-image Our own internal picture of what we are like, as people, mainly based on factual information rather than evaluation.

self-perception The way that we see ourselves, usually with respect to a particular topic or issue.

sensori-motor stage The first of Piaget's four stages of cognitive development, characterised by receptiveness to sensory information and the development of the very first schemata through explorations of movement in the environment.

sensory deprivation The cutting out of all incoming sensory information, or at least as much of it as possible.

sex typing Assigning a child to a particular gender category, and treating it in ways which fit that category from then on.

sex-appropriate behaviour Behaviour which is considered by society in general to be typical of, and desirable for, those belonging to a particular gender. Ideas of sex-appropriate behaviour vary over time, and between societies, cultures and sub-cultures.

simple play Play which occupies the child without presenting challenges or difficulties.

social comparisons The process of comparing one's own social group with others, in terms of their relative social status and prestige. Social comparison is important, in that people will tend to distance themselves from membership of a group which does not reflect positively on self-esteem by comparing favourably with other groups.

social contagion The idea that crowds become unruly because people 'catch' unruliness from a few role-models and everyone begins to act in the same way.

social context The overall social environment in which a person lives or acts. It includes the person's knowledge about social acceptability and social norms as well as direct interaction with others.

social identification theory A theory which emphasises how membership of social groups forms a significant part of the self-concept, and can determine reactions to other people and events, such that people respond primarily as group members and not as individuals.

social learning Learning which comes from interaction with other people or with society, directly or indirectly.

social representation theory A theory which looks at how shared beliefs develop and are transmitted in social groups and in society as a whole. Such shared beliefs serve an important function in explaining reality and in justifying social action.

split-half method A system for judging how reliable a psychometric test is, which involves splitting the test into two and administering each half of the test to the same people, then comparing the results.

standard deviations A statistical measure which describes how the scores in a normal distribution are spread out on either side of the mean. It expresses the typical amount of diversity which can be expected.

standardisation (a) The process of making sure that the conditions of a psychological study or psychometric test are always identical; (b) the process of establishing how the results of a psychometric test will usually come out in a given population, by drawing up sets of population norms; (c) the process of comparing a new psychometric test with older, more established measures of the same thing.

survey A technique of collecting opinions from large numbers of people, generally involving the use of questionnaires.

symbolic play Play which is all about the use of symbols, such as words, numbers or signs.

testicular feminising syndrome A physical condition in which someone who is genetically male fails to develop male sexual characteristics, and appears female.

test-retest method A system for judging how reliable a psychometric test or measure is which involves administering the same test to the same people on two different occasions, and comparing the results.

transformations Cognitive adjustments made to information or knowledge, in such a way that they become relevant for different uses.

triarchic intelligence A theory of intelligence developed by Sternberg (1985) which argues that intelligence needs to be understood from three distinct viewpoints: (i) the cultural and social context in which an intelligence act occurs; (ii) how the person's own previous experience has shaped their responses; (iii) the mental skills and abilities involved in solving problems.

unconditional positive regard A relationship in which the person is sure of receiving positive regard from the other person, regardless of their past or present actions or decisions.

validity The question of whether a psychometric test or psychological measure is really measuring what it is suppose to.

vocational guidance tests Psychometric tests which are designed to help people to find out what kind of jobs they are suited for.

zone of proximal development (ZPD) The extent of the potential cognitive growth that the child is able to achieve under adult guidance and tuition.

Index

Note: **Bold** page numbers refer to the Glossary, full details of which are on pages 543–53